S0-BUB-871

MATHEMATICS FOR BUSINESS

Mathematics 4 Business

MATHEMATICS FOR BUSINESS WITH CANADIAN APPLICATIONS

Mathematics 4 Business

With Canadian Applications

T. Brian Killip
Camosun College

DRYDEN, CANADA
A Division of Holt, Rinehart and Winston of Canada, Limited
Toronto Montreal Orlando Fort Worth San Diego Philidelphia London Sydney Tokyo

Canadian Cataloguing in Publication Data
Killip, T. Brian (Thomas Brian), 1946-
Mathematics for management and finance with Canadian applications

1st Canadian ed.
Includes index.
ISBN 0-03-922710-3

1. Business mathematics. I. Title.

HF5691.K5 1992 650′.01513 C91-094392-3

Editorial Director: Scott Duncan
Acquisitions Editor: Ron Fitzgerald
Developmental Editor: Cheryl Teelucksingh
Editorial Assistant: Lee Donald
Director of Publishing Services: Steve Lau
Editorial Manager: Liz Radojkovic
Editorial Co-ordinator: Marcel Chiera
Production Manager: Sue-Ann Becker
Production Assistant: Denise Wake
Interior Design: Robert Garbutt Productions
Cover Design: Dave Peters
Typesetting and Assembly: True To Type Inc.
Printing and Binding: John Deyell Company

Cover: The image on the cover is a photograph of the frieze by the Canadian artist Charles Comfort. This frieze, produced for the Toronto Stock Exchange building, depicts the different types of industries found in Canada.

This book was printed in Canada on acid-free paper.

1 2 3 4 5 96 95 94 93 92

Preface

This book is an introductory mathematics and finance text designed for use at the first- or second-year level of a college business program. The text has been written to provide a balance in the presentation of topics, recognizing the difficulty some students have in understanding arithmetic and algebraic operations, while providing sufficiently challenging material for those students who find mathematics relatively straight forward. To accomplish this balance, the presentation of the material is different from a traditional mathematics text.

The approach taken in this text is to provide two methods of presenting mathematical material. The first method uses word explanations about why or how we undertake a particular operation. These explanations will be used by those students who best learn with written explanations. The second approach is by example, and, where possible, a business example. Both approaches, the written and the solved examples, allow students to learn the material in the manner most suited to their learning style.

One element that is emphasized throughout the book is that students should use an approach to solving a problem that they best understand, providing, of course, that it incorporates all the necessary elements to finding the correct solution. That is, since there are different ways to solve a problem, students are encouraged to use the method with which they are most comfortable. In many examples more than one method to solve the problem is presented.

Special Features

Some features of the book that are designed to help the student and assist in the instruction of the material are:

- The text commences with an overview of arithmetic and algebra to allow for students who may need to review their knowledge of basic arithmetic and algebra before turning to the topics on the mathematics of finance.
- Each chapter starts with a statement of student learning objectives. These objectives are designed to provide an overview of the skills and concepts to be learned upon completion of the chapter.
- All topics are presented in an easy-to-read style and are followed by examples to reinforce the understanding of the material. All topics have at least one solved example, with many topics having numerous examples.
- Every effort has been made to incorporate Canadian business examples, whether the topic is in algebra or in the mathematics of finance. Many of the examples are based on actual business situations. All examples use a step-by-step approach to solving the problem.
- Each major section is followed by a problem set that reviews the concepts discussed.
- Students are provided with the *complete solutions* to the odd numbered problems. These are presented in the back of the book. Detailed solutions have been provided to help the student learn and understand the material.
- Each chapter concludes with a glossary of terms and a summary of the formulas, which includes a brief explanation of where each formula is used.
- For the examples in Chapters 7 to 12, solutions using a financial calculator are provided in addition to the algebraic solution which uses a scientific calculator.
- At the end of each chapter there are review problems. Students are not provided with solutions to these review problems since the questions are designed to provide a source from which instructors can select assignment questions.
- The Instructor's Manual provides complete solutions to the problems, including a step-by-step approach where appropriate. Every effort has been taken to ensure the accuracy of the solutions.

The essential elements of arithmetic and algebra are presented in Chapters 1 to 4, with markup and markdown being discussed in Chapter 5. The topics on mathematics of finance are covered in Chapters 6 through 12. In many colleges, the topics in the last six chapters can be covered in a one-semester course. For those teaching on a two-quarter course, Chapters 1 to 6 can be covered in the first quarter, with Chapters 7 to 12 being the focus for the second quarter.

Acknowledgements

The first published version of Chapters 6 through 12 was written for a distant learning situation, where students did not have an instructor. This version was to act as support material, and was designed to supplement a text chosen for the course. At the time of publishing this book, the material was still being used by the Open Learning Agency in British Columbia, with students in British Columbia, Hong Kong, and other parts of the world. The author wishes to acknowledge the support the Open Learning Agency provided for the first version of Chapters 6 to 12, and appreciates its permission to incorporate part of the material into this book. One person who was involved in the first version of the material for the Open Learning Agency was Dianne Dienno. Her suggestions were of great assistance in developing the material for the Open Learning Agency.

Many people have had a role in this text. Students have provided valuable insights that have helped to refine explanations. My colleagues Alex Rosewicz, Doug Murray, Chris Graham, and John Evans at Camosun reviewed various portions of the text and provided helpful suggestions. To Bonnie Killip, I wish to recognize her major contribution in the reviewing of the chapters and making suggestions on how to improve the clarity of explanations and general readability of the material. Bonnie's suggestions have been a major source of helpful changes. Also, I must acknowledge the work of Greg Killip who spent many hours working out the solutions to the text problems.

This text has evolved from many useful suggestions provided by reviewers from across Canada. To each of you, I do appreciate your work, and I am sure the students who use this text will benefit from your suggestions.

Reviewers

V. Neate	Southern Alberta Institute of Technology
G. McFarlane	Humber College
W. Saunders	Algonquin College
A. Bruto	Cambrian College
N. Moore	Northern Alberta Institute of Technology
B. Sheriff	British Columbia Institute of Technology
D. Kirwin	Sheridan College of Applied Arts and Technology
E. Hales	Georgian College of Applied Arts and Technology
F. Cox	Centennial College
S. Martin	John Abbott College
B. Hobson	Georgian College
B. Friesen	Saskatchewan Institute of Applied Science and Technology
W. Wiebe	Saskatchewan Institute of Applied Science and Technology
B. Buchanan	Vancouver Community College

Finally, to all the people at Holt, Rinehart and Winston — Warren Laws, who first talked me into this project, Scott Duncan, Cheryl Teelucksingh, Andrew Livingston, and many others who played a significant role in assisting with the completion of the project, I am indebted.

T. Brian Killip
Victoria, B.C.

Publisher's Note to Students and Instructors

This textbook is a key component of your course. If you are the instructor of this course, you undoubtedly considered a number of texts carefully before choosing this as the one that would work best for your students and you. The authors and publishers spent considerable time and money to ensure its high quality, and we appreciate your recognition of this effort and accomplishment. Please note the copyright statement.

If you are a student, we are confident that this text will help you to meet the objectives of your course. It will also become a valuable addition to your personal library.

Since we want to hear what you think about this book, please be sure to send us the stamped reply card at the end of the text. Your input will help us to continue to publish high-quality books for your courses.

Contents

6. Simple Interest 212

7. Compound Interest 254

8. Annuities 306

CHAPTER 1

Basic Arithmetic Operations

The system that we use for writing numbers and performing basic arithmetic computations has its origin in India and is called the Hindu-Arabic system of numeration. Today, with the technology of electronic calculators, the origin of our number system seems unimportant. In fact, some may argue that the need to undertake simple calculations is not very important since calculators can do it faster and more accurately. Unfortunately, this is not true. In the real world, one does not always have a calculator available and must rely on the knowledge of how to do some mental calculations. Equally important is the need to be able to assess whether the numbers our calculator gives are correct, since it is very easy to push the wrong key and get an erroneous result. Also, it is valuable to understand the rules your calculator uses to find the answer you require.

The need to perform simple computations in business is frequent and requires each of us to have a good understanding of the rules and procedures of arithmetic.

In this chapter, we will review many elementary concepts of arithmetic. If you find that the material is second hand to you, move on to the chapters on decimals, percentages, and the rules of algebra.

OBJECTIVES

The approach taken in this chapter is to use simple business problems to assist in the review of the arithmetic. When you have finished with this chapter, you should be able to do the following:

1. understand and use the arithmetic operations of addition, subtraction, multiplication, and division;
2. understand the operations involving 0 and 1 as well as the rules governing negative numbers. You also must understand the use of brackets in specifying arithmetic operations and be able to use brackets in performing arithmetic operations;
3. understand the concept of fractions and be able to perform the operations of addition, subtraction, multiplication, and division with fractions.

1.1 Basic Rules of Arithmetic

The way we undertake the basic operations of arithmetic (addition, subtraction, multiplication, and division) uses the concept of the place value of numbers. Place value refers to the value each digit of a number has — based on its location in the number (place value).

Our number system — the decimal system — has the place value of digits increasing by tenfold for each place we move from left to right in a number. Consider the number 123,456,789,121,235. In this number the place value of each digit is noted below. The comma is used to separate the number groups. However, another approach used today is to separate number groups with a space rather than a comma, i.e., 123 456 789 121 235.

Place Value	Number Group
1 - hundred trillions 2 - ten trillions 3 - trillions	trillions group
4 - hundred billions 5 - ten billions 6 - billions	billions group
7 - hundred millions 8 - ten millions 9 - millions	millions group
1 - hundred thousands 2 - ten thousands 1 - thousands	thousands group
2 - hundreds	hundreds
3 - tens	tens
5 - units	units

The thing to note is that in each group the digits are increased tenfold over each other. For example, in the thousands group the first is in hundreds of thousands — a tenfold increase over the next digit, the ten thousands, which is a tenfold increase over the last digit in this group — thousands. It is this grouping that gives the place value of numbers. This place value concept is fundamental to all our arithmetic operations.

If we consider the number 32,546 we can analyze it by place value using the appropriate number groups as follows:

3 - represents 3 values of 10,000 (30,000)
2 - represents 2 values of 1,000 (2,000)
5 - represents 5 values of 100 (500)
4 - represents 4 values of 10 (40)
6 - represents 6 values of 1 (6)

A. Addition

We all know that the term addition means to add up or accumulate numbers, dollars, or anything that can be measured in a numeric sense. After we have added the quantities, we end up with one number called the **sum**.

For example, if one was to count all the money in a cash register at a small store, the total amount of money in the register is called the sum of all the paper money (one, two, five, etc., dollar bills), all coins, and any cheques. A step that is important in all addition is the placing or alignment of numbers that are being added — that is, we must make sure that the numbers are lined up according to their place value. The importance of this is shown in the following three examples:

EXAMPLE 1.1

Add the following numbers: 1; 11; 111; 1,111; 11,111.

Solution

```
     1    Note how all the numbers have been lined
    11    up in columns (place value). These
   111    columns are critical to adding since the
 1,111    units of each column correspond to units
11,111    of 1, 10's, 100's, 1,000's, and 10,000's.
------
     5 <---- 1 + 1 + 1 + 1 + 1
    40 <---- 10 + 10 + 10 + 10
   300 <---- 100 + 100 + 100
 2,000 <---- 1,000 + 1,000
10,000 <---- 10,000
------
12,345 <---- The sum of the numbers.
```

To stress how important the units that each column represents are, suppose we were adding dollars and cents in a cash register. The following example attempts to show just how we treat numbers in adding — the key element is that we must always add the same units to the same units — that is, place value.

EXAMPLE 1.2

A cash register had the following amount of money in it at the end of each day for one week: \$57, \$66, \$75, \$254, \$71, \$147, and \$121. What was the total amount of money counted from the cash register for the week?

Solution

```
 $ 57    In this example, we have all the columns
   66    lined up again. The first column on the right
   75    is the dollar units, the next column is the ten
  254    dollar units, and the third column is the hundred
   71    dollar units.
  147
  121
 ----
   31 ←—— 7 + 6 + 5 + 4 + 1 + 7 + 1 [first column]
  360 ←—— 50 + 60 + 70 + 50 + 70 + 40 + 20 [second column]
  400 ←—— 200 + 100 + 100 [third column]
 ----
 $791
```

It may be of interest for you to check the additions above by adding the numbers in the reverse order. For example, if we take the first column from Example 1.2 you would have 1 + 7 + 1 + 4 + 5 + 6 + 7, which is 31. This property is called the **commutative property of addition,** meaning that you can add a column of numbers in any order and get the same result (sum).

EXAMPLE 1.3

Group the following numbers into any pairs of two and add. Then add the numbers separately to show that whether you add the numbers separately or in groups the sum is the same.

4, 5, 6, 6, 8, 9, 5, 2, 3, 4

Solution As you can see, there are a number of possible pairs. One grouping you might have selected may be:

$$(4 + 5) + (6 + 6) + (8 + 9) + (5 + 2) + (3 + 4) = 52$$

$$9 + 12 + 17 + 7 + 7 = 52$$

Which is the same sum as:

$$4 + 5 + 6 + 6 + 8 + 9 + 5 + 2 + 3 + 4 = 52$$

Note: If you selected another grouping of two numbers, good! There are many other possibilities and one choice of grouping is as good as another — however, whatever our grouping of two numbers, the sum must turn out to be the same.

In this last example on addition, the concept that is being demonstrated is called the **associative property of addition**. This is just another way of saying you can group numbers into separate additions and get the same result.

B. Subtraction

The term subtraction refers to the process of finding the difference between two numbers. For example, if you made $500 and your employer deducted $150 for taxes, you would end up with $350. The process that we used to reach the $350 is called subtraction. The $500 is called the **minuend,** the $150 is referred to as the **subtrahend,** and the $350 you get to keep is the **difference,** or **remainder**. In most real world situations, these technical terms are never used and, therefore, we will not use them beyond this section of the book.

Like addition, we need to be careful to recognize the importance of the place values of numbers when performing subtraction. The examples that follow show you the process of subtraction.

EXAMPLE 1.4

Subtract 300 from 1,500.

Solution

	1,500	
Less	– 300 ⟵	The (–) sign is used to show that 300 is being subtracted from 1,500. This sign will be considered in a later section of this chapter.
Difference	1,200	

EXAMPLE 1.5

From $56 subtract $4 and show all work.

Solution

	$56	
Less	– 4 ⟵	Again, note the use of the (–) sign for subtraction.
Difference	$52 ⟵	Remember, this term is also known as the remainder.

C. Multiplication

One way to look at multiplication is to think about it as repetitive addition of the same number. For example, suppose you want to determine the total number of bottles of wine that are in a shipment. If the shipment has 50 cases with 25 bottles in each case, you could simply add up 25 for the number of cases you have. If you had 50 cases, this would imply the addition of 50 numbers — each having a value of 25. Using multiplication permits us to do the same thing as adding 25, 50 times, but with only one calculation, using the two numbers, 25 and 50. To understand multiplication, we should get a handle on some of the basic terms used:

1. Product

The product refers to the result of the multiplication of numbers. In our example, the product of 25 and 50 would be 1,250. The term product is determined by 25×50, where the $\times$ refers to the process of multiplication, just as + referred to addition. One thing to watch for is that sometimes the $\times$ is replaced by "·", e.g., $25 \cdot 50 = 1{,}250$ and, as we will see in the algebra review, the $\times$ is often just understood to be present and is not stated.

2. Factors

Both 25 and 50 are referred to as factors in multiplication. The only reason this is mentioned is that often in algebra we are looking for factors, which as you now know means looking for components that can be multiplied to give a particular product.

Beyond basic definitions, there are some mathematical properties of multiplication. Don't worry, we are not interested in you being able to use the correct term. It is essential, however, that you understand exactly what the property means — this is vital for our later discussion of algebra.

Property 1 **Commutative Property of Multiplication:** This means that two numbers can be multiplied in any order and the resulting product will be the same. For example:

$$5 \times 7 = 35 \text{ and } 7 \times 5 = 35$$
$$\text{Therefore: } 5 \times 7 = 7 \times 5$$

Property 2 **Associative Property of Multiplication:** This means that three, four, or more numbers can be grouped and multiplied in any order and the resulting product will be the same. For example:

$$5 \times 3 \times 6 \times 7 = (5 \times 3) \times (6 \times 7) = 630$$
$$\text{or} \quad 5 \times 3 \times 6 \times 7 = (5 \times 6) \times (3 \times 7) = 630$$
$$\text{or} \quad 5 \times 3 \times 6 \times 7 = (7 \times 6) \times (3 \times 5) = 630$$
$$\text{or} \quad 5 \times (6 \times 7) \times 3 = 630$$

EXAMPLE 1.6

Find the product of 321 and 35.

Solution

$$\begin{array}{r l}
321 & \\
\times\ 35 & \\
\hline
1{,}605 & \longleftarrow 321 \times 5 = 1{,}605 \\
+ & \\
9{,}630 & \longleftarrow 321 \times 30 = 9{,}630 \\
\hline
11{,}235 & \text{Product}
\end{array}$$

What you should do is to try the multiplication of 35 × 321 and confirm that the product is the same.

D. Division

The process of division should be thought of as sharing or breaking the number into equal parts. In Example 1.6, if we divide 11,235 by 35, there are 35 parts each of size 321. As with multiplication, there are some terms that we should know and be able to use.

The symbol ÷ is used to tell one that division is the operation to perform, and can be found on any electronic calculator.

1. Quotient

This refers to the number of parts into which the number has been broken, i.e., divided into parts. For example, 6 divided by 3 yields a quotient of 2. That is, 6 has been divided into 2 parts each of size 3.

2. Dividend

This refers to the number to be divided or broken into parts. In the example of 6 divided by 3, 6 is the dividend and is being broken into equal parts of size 3.

3. Divisor

The divisor refers to the number of groups into which the dividend is being divided. In our simple example of 6 divided by 3, the divisor is 3.

4. Remainder

Often division does not give an even number of parts for the quotient. In our example the quotient was 2. Suppose the division had been 5 divided by 3. In this case, the quotient would have been 1 (1 part, size 3) and 2 remaining. This remaining 2 is a portion of a part left over and very important to the division process. The examples that follow show how we handle a remainder:

EXAMPLE 1.7

Divide 459 by 9.

Solution

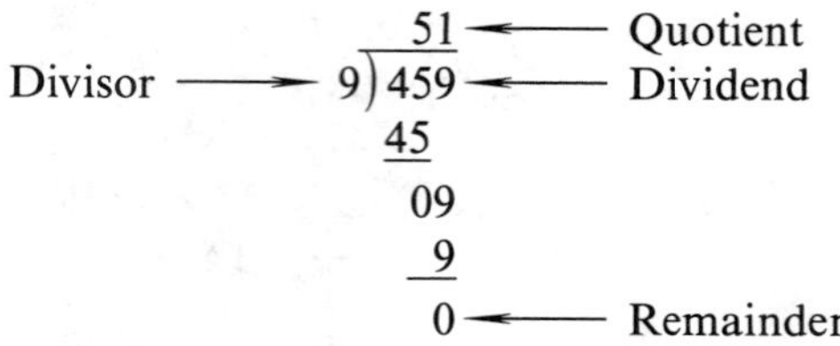

EXAMPLE 1.8

Divide 459 by 8.

Solution

```
                 57 ←— Quotient
Divisor ——→ 8)459 ←— Dividend
             40
              59
              56
               3 ←— Remainder
```

In division, we can check our answers by performing a multiplication of the quotient and the divisor. In our example, this would be 2×3, which is 6, the same as our dividend, confirming that the division is correct.

For Examples 1.7 and 1.8, checking the answers would be done as follows:

Checking Example 1.7

```
 51 ←— Quotient
× 9 ←— Divisor
459 ←— Dividend
```

Checking Example 1.8

```
 57 ←— Quotient
× 8 ←— Divisor
456
+ 3 ←— Remainder
459 ←— Dividend
```

We will return to division once you have been introduced to fractions and decimals.

EXERCISE 1.1

A. Addition: Find the sum for each of the following.

1. 500; 37; 58; 123

2. 15,380; 412; 17; 512

3. 1,543; 2,315; 157; 29; 142

4. 123,456; 8,956; 456; 48,945; 56,458

5. 4,521; 789; 45,872; 15

B. Subtraction: Find the difference for each of the following.

6. 145 from 438

7. 11,234 from 134,345

8. 23 from 4,456

9. 21,300 from 58,379

10. 18,312 from 127,412

C. Multiplication: Find the product for each of the following.

11. 15×14

12. $21 \times 2{,}312$

13. 123×257

14. $1{,}378 \times 2{,}498$

15. 21×124

D. Division: Perform a division for each of the following and specify the remainder.

16. $15 \div 3$

17. $178 \div 14$

18. $2{,}371 \div 128$

19. $10{,}371 \div 151$

20. $65 \div 12$

E. Miscellaneous: Undertake the appropriate arithmetic procedure for each of the following questions.

21. John purchased the following equipment: a computer for $1,500, a printer for $367, and a desk and chair for $650. How much did he spend in total?

22. After three weeks of using the new equipment (from Question 21),

John found that the new printer he had purchased would not do all the things he wanted. If John returned the first printer and bought a more expensive printer for $750 (he got a full refund on the first printer), how much in total did he spend on computer equipment? How much more did the new printer cost?

23. Janet has a small stereo store and is purchasing some new tapes from a supplier. The tapes cost Janet $5.00 each and she is purchasing four cases, (each case has 24 tapes). How much will the order cost?

24. Janet (from Question 23) has been told that if she buys five or more cases of cassettes she can purchase each case for $84. If Janet purchases five cases, how much is she paying for each cassette?

25. If Janet purchases 10 cases of cassettes and each case costs $72, what is the cost per cassette?

1.2 Operations with 0 and 1, Signing of Numbers, and Grouping with Brackets

There are some special properties for calculations involving 0 and 1. The understanding of these properties is essential to performing many arithmetic calculations and algebraic operations.

Not only is the use of 0 and 1 important, but also the use of signed numbers — using negative (–) and positive (+) signs. To provide an understanding of each, we shall work through a series of examples. These examples are designed to highlight how each sign affects the basic arithmetic operations.

In the last part of this section, we shall examine how we can group numbers using brackets (), as well as determine the order in which arithmetic computations must occur when using brackets.

It is important to be able to use these concepts easily since they are significant to our understanding of the later topics that apply arithmetic and algebraic methods to business and finance problems.

A. Operations with 0 and 1

To ensure that you have a clear understanding of how 0 and 1 influence computations, the following examples summarize the major rules that must be understood. The sequence will follow the topics of Section 1.1 — addition, subtraction, multiplication, and division. You will find that the operations of multiplication and division are the only ones where 1 is considered. There are no special properties of 1 in addition or subtraction.

(i) Addition and Subtraction Involving 0

When 0 is added to a number, the resulting sum is not changed. For example, $5 + 0 = 5$. Another way of thinking about this is to remember $0 + 0 = 0$.

In subtraction, a similar result occurs. If you subtract 0 from any number, the difference is the same number. However, if you subtract a number from 0 the result is quite different — this type of problem will be examined when we look at the signing of numbers in the next section.

EXAMPLE 1.9

Find the sum of 35, 46, 13, and 0; from this sum subtract 55 and 0.

Solution

STEP 1 Addition

```
35
46
13
--
94 ←—— Sum without zero.
 0
--
94 ←—— Addition of zero does not change the sum.
```

STEP 2 Subtraction

```
  94 ←—— The sum from above.
– 55
----
  39 ←—— The difference without zero.
–  0
----
  39 ←—— Subtracting zero does not change the difference.
```

(ii) Multiplication and Division with 0 and 1

Multiplication Involving 0 or 1

When multiplying **different** numbers where **one** of the numbers is 0, the resulting product will always be 0. For example, $5 \times 0 = 0$. No matter what the situation, if 0 enters into the multiplication as one of the distinct numbers being multiplied then the product of the numbers will be 0 — there are no exceptions to the rule.

In the multiplication of numbers where one of the numbers is 1, the multiplication with 1 does not change the product. Consider the product of $5 \times 6 \times 1 = 30$, which is the same as 5×6.

Division Involving 0 or 1

Division, on the other hand, offers us a slightly different problem. For example, $5 \div 0$ will give us a very large number, so large that we say it is not defined.

You can see the logic if you think about the following:

$$\frac{4}{4} = 4 \div 4 = 1; \frac{4}{2} = 4 \div 2 = 2; \frac{4}{1} = 4 \div 1 = 4$$

What you should notice is that as the number that is being divided stays constant, and the number being used as the divisor (in our example 4, 2, and 1) gets smaller, the resulting quotient gets larger. At 0 the size of the quotient is so large that we say it is undefined. The symbol for the quotient with 0 is ∞, called infinity — strictly, division with 0 is referred to as an undefined operation.

However, if 0 is divided by a number then the quotient is 0. For example:

$$\frac{0}{4} = 0 \div 4 = 0; \frac{0}{2} = 0 \div 2 = 0; \frac{0}{1} = 0 \div 1 = 0$$

Division with 1 has no consequence to the quotient. For example:

$$\frac{4}{1} = 4 \div 1 = 4; \frac{6}{1} = 6 \div 1 = 6$$

SUMMARY OF THE RULES WITH 0 AND 1

Multiplication by 0:	Number × 0 = 0	e.g., (3 × 0 = 0)
Division by 0:	Number ÷ 0 = undefined	e.g., (3 ÷ 0 = undefined)
0 divided by a number:	0 ÷ Number = 0	e.g., (0 ÷ 3 = 0)
Multiplication by 1:	Number × 1 = Number	e.g., (3 × 1 = 3)
Division by 1:	Number ÷ 1 = Number	e.g., (3 × 1 = 3)

B. Operations with Signed Numbers — Positive (+) and Negative (–) Numbers

Signing of numbers refers to the sign in front of the number. For example, the number 5 is said to have a positive sign in front of it, even though it is not written. Its presence is assumed. Whereas, a negative number will always have the negative sign (–) in front of it.

Visually this can be seen by using a number line with 0 as the centre point.

Exhibit 1.1

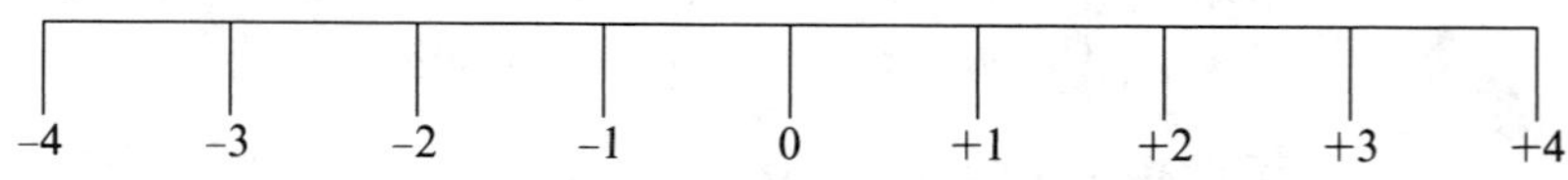

Consider the following examples:

–6 means negative 6; the sign of the number is said to be negative.

+6 means positive 6, and is the same as 6.

(i) Signed Numbers: Addition and Subtraction

The addition and subtraction of signed numbers will require one to do the operation as indicated by the sign. If all the numbers have the same sign, even if they are all negative, then we always add the negative numbers, for example, $-2 + -3 + -5 = -10$. When there are a number of additions involving both negative and positive numbers, it is best to perform the addition of the numbers with the same sign first, then perform the final operation on the two sums. For example, if we had $-2 + -3 + -5 + 4 + 3 + 5$, then the easiest way is to deal with the negative numbers separately from the positive numbers and then bring the two results together to complete the operation. In this example, $-2 + -3 + -5 = -10$ and $4 + 3 + 5 = 12$, bringing the two sums together for the final operation gives us $12 + -10 = 2$. Example 1.10 uses this procedure.

EXAMPLE 1.10

Find the sum of –365, –460, 1,355, and 0.

Solution The sum of the positive numbers is:

$$\begin{array}{r} 1{,}355 \\ \underline{0} \\ 1{,}355 \end{array}$$

The sum of the numbers with the negative sign is:

$$\begin{array}{rr} - & 365 \\ \underline{-} & \underline{460} \\ - & 825 \end{array}$$

Now taking this sum we subtract it from the sum of the positive numbers:

$$\begin{array}{rr} + & 1{,}355 \\ \underline{-} & \underline{825} \\ + & 530 \end{array}$$

Everything could have been done in one step, but by breaking up the process it made the procedure easier to follow.

One other rule that must be understood is where a negative sign is applied to a number that already has a negative sign, for example, –(–5). To handle this situation the rule you must use is that a "negative, negative number" is a positive number.

Consider the following example.

EXAMPLE 1.11

Find the sum of –(–365); –460; 1,355; and 0.

Solution

$$
\begin{array}{rr}
-(-365) = + & 365 \\
 & 0 \\
+ & \underline{1{,}355} \\
 & 1{,}720
\end{array}
\quad \text{Note the change in sign.}
$$

Now taking this sum we subtract the sum of the negative numbers — here there is only one negative number rather than a sum of negative numbers.

$$
\begin{array}{rr}
+ & 1{,}720 \\
\underline{-} & \underline{460} \\
+ & 1{,}260
\end{array}
$$

As can be seen, the negative sign in front of the negative number –(–365) causes the sign of the number to change to a positive sign. This is an important rule and will be used often during later topics in the finance sections.

(ii) Multiplication and Division with Signed Numbers

When we are multiplying with numbers that are signed, the resulting product also will have a sign. The following rules illustrate how the signing of the product works.

Signed Numbers and Multiplication

Rule 1. If both numbers are negative, the resulting product will be a positive number. For example, $-5 \times -6 = +30$.

Rule 2. If one of the numbers is negative and the other is positive, the resulting product will be negative. For example, $-5 \times 6 = -30$.

Rule 3. If both the numbers are positive, the resulting product will be positive. For example, $5 \times 6 = 30$.

Rule 4. When multiplying more than two numbers, all with different signs, the best way to remember how to sign the final product is to group the numbers into pairs and then use rules 1, 2, or 3 when multiplying each pair. This is a little confusing, so consider the following example:

$$\begin{aligned} 5 \times -6 \times -7 \times -8 \times 3 &= -30 \times 56 \times 3 \\ &= -1{,}680 \times 3 \\ &= -5{,}040 \end{aligned}$$

Where:

$5 \times -6 = -30$	The product of the first pair.
$-7 \times -8 = 56$	The product of the second pair (note the positive sign in the product, from rule 1).
3	This is the last term in the original expression.

(iii) Signed Numbers and Division

The process of dividing signed numbers is similar to multiplication. To understand how division is affected by signed numbers, the following rules must be remembered.

Division Rules

Rule 1. When dividing two numbers where either the divisor or the dividend is negative, the resulting quotient is negative. For example, $6 \div -3 = -2$ and $-10 \div 5 = -2$.

Rule 2. When dividing two numbers where both have negative signs, the quotient will always give a positive number. For example, $-10 \div -5 = 2$.

Rule 3. Dividing two positive numbers always yields a positive quotient, in our example, $10 \div 5 = 2$.

C. Order of Operations and Grouping of Numbers Using Brackets

Often calculations in business involve many sets of numbers and it is important that one understands the order of operations to perform. By order of operations, we mean which is done first: addition, subtraction, multiplication, or division. To help us determine which operation to use, we often group operations by using brackets. In fact, there are many instances when there are many groupings that require more than one set of brackets. The general sequence is $\{[()]\}$, where () are used first, [] if a second set of brackets is needed, and finally {} if a third set is used.

When a group of numbers requires more than one operation, the operations are performed in the following order:

ORDER OF OPERATIONS

1. Perform all operations within the brackets. If there are more than one set of brackets, start at the "innermost" set (see Example 1.12).
2. After the operations in brackets are completed and the brackets removed, perform the necessary multiplication and division, moving from left to right.
3. Complete the operations by performing the necessary addition and subtraction, again moving from left to right.

EXAMPLE 1.12

Find the answer to $\{45 + [5 \times (4 + 5)]\} \div 10$.

Solution

STEP 1 First go to the "innermost brackets", the () type, and perform the calculations necessary. In our example we have:

$$(4 + 5) \text{ or } 9$$

Which gives: $\{45 + [5 \times 9]\} \div 10$

STEP 2 Second, perform the operation to be done on the term inside the [] brackets.

$$[5 \times 9]$$

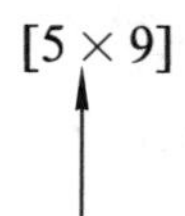

This gives: $\{45 + 45\} \div 10$

STEP 3 Now we can remove the square brackets, [], leaving us with $\{45 + 45\} \div 10$;

STEP 4 Work the final operation inside the last set of brackets, {}, which is to add 45 to 45. This gives 90, and then,

STEP 5 Perform the last operation, 90 divided by 10, or $\{90\} \div 10 = 9$.

Therefore, the final answer is 9.

EXAMPLE 1.13

Find the answer to $25 + [18 + 16 \times (4 + 5)]$.

Solution

STEP 1 Work out the sum inside the () brackets, or $4 + 5 = 9$, which gives us:

$$25 + [18 + 16 \times (9)]$$

STEP 2 Perform the multiplication of $16 \times (9)$, or 144, which gives us:

$$25 + [18 + 144]$$

STEP 3 Perform the addition inside the [] brackets, or $18 + 144$, which gives 162, leaving the expression:

$$25 + [162]$$

STEP 4 Complete the final addition, $25 + 162$, or 187, the final answer.

The last example in this section on brackets is to show how to apply a negative sign when it is outside a group of numbers in brackets, where some numbers inside the brackets are also negative numbers. As you will see, it is critical to make sure the correct sign is applied, since the results change dramatically if the negative sign is incorrectly used.

Another purpose of Example 1.14 is to demonstrate a way of writing multiplication — without using the × sign. For example, $3 \times (4 + 5)$ could be written as $3(4 + 5)$. In the second case, $3(4 + 5)$, the × sign is understood. In each case, the product is the same, 27. Work through Example 1.14 carefully to make sure you understand that we drop the × (multiplication) sign, as well as incorporating the influence of a negative sign for the operations within the brackets.

EXAMPLE 1.14

Find the answer to $-3(-45) + -2(40 - 60)$.

Solution

STEP 1 Work out the computations inside the brackets:

$$-3(-45) = 135 \quad \text{Note the sign change.}$$

and

$$\begin{aligned} -2[40 - 60] &= -2[-20] \\ &= 40 \end{aligned}$$

STEP 2 Add the two numbers: $135 + 40 = 175$.

The final answer is 175.

EXERCISE 1.2

Perform the operations as required.

1. $34 \times 4 \times 0$
2. $23 \times 46 \times 1$
3. $45[34 + 34(56 \times 3)]$
4. $-12(3{,}234 - 4{,}000)$
5. $-3 \times -56(23 - 43)$
6. $-48 \div 12$
7. $45 \div \{[(56 - 30) - 13] + -4\}$
8. $21 \times \{[(30 \times 3) \div 6] \div 5\}$
9. $34 \div [(23 - 6) \times -1]$
10. $[(12 \times 23) + (-13 - 12)] \times 2$

1.3 Fractions

In business, fractions are commonly used. A fraction is a number that represents a portion of another number. Numbers such as 2, 3, and 467 are what we call whole numbers. A fraction refers to part of one of these numbers and always implies a division. When we discussed division earlier, we learned that there are three terms — dividend, divisor, and quotient. In a fraction, the dividend is called the **numerator** and the divisor is known as the **denominator**. For example, $\frac{1}{4}$ is a fraction, read as one-quarter, where 1 is the numerator and 4 is the denominator. Another way this fraction could have been written is $1 \div 4$. The term quotient is not used with fractions since a fraction will always be specified in terms of a numerator and a denominator.

Before we turn to the addition, subtraction, multiplication, and division of fractions, there are some new terms that we must understand. These new terms are: **reduced fractions, proper fractions, improper fractions, complex fractions,** and **mixed fractions (numbers)**.

A. Reduced Fractions — Fractions in Their Lowest Terms

If one had a fraction such as $\frac{4}{12}$, we would say that the fraction is not in its lowest terms — that is, not in a reduced form. A reduced form means that the numerator and denominator cannot be made smaller by dividing each by the same number evenly and still yield the same fractional value. To reduce $\frac{4}{12}$ we could divide both the numerator and denominator by 4. This would give $\frac{1}{3}$, which is the same as $\frac{4}{12}$, and is referred to as the **reduced form of the fraction**. Sometimes the expression "reducing a fraction to its lowest term" is used to describe the reduced form. Let's look at a couple of examples.

EXAMPLE 1.15

Reduce $\frac{3}{9}$ to its lowest terms.

Solution To reduce each term of the fraction we must divide both the numerator and the denominator by the same term. One number that will divide evenly into each is 3. Therefore dividing each by 3 gives:

$$\frac{3}{9} = \frac{3 \div 3}{9 \div 3} = \frac{1}{3}$$

Performing the indicated division gives the fraction:

$\frac{1}{3}$, which is the reduced form of $\frac{3}{9}$.

Another way of referring to the reduction of a fraction is through **cancellation**. Cancellation refers to the process of reducing the numerator and denominator to reach the reduced form of the fraction. In our example, $\frac{3}{3}$ cancels to 1, and $\frac{3}{9}$ cancels to $\frac{1}{3}$.

EXAMPLE 1.16

Reduce $\frac{45}{105}$.

Solution Examining both the numerator and denominator, we can see that 5 can be divided evenly into each term.

$$\frac{45}{105} = \frac{45 \div 5}{105 \div 5}$$

$$= \frac{9}{21}$$

Now can we reduce the fraction further? If we examine both the numerator

(9) and the denominator (21), we see that there is one number that will divide into both — 3.

Consequently, the reduced form is $\frac{3}{7}$.

EXAMPLE 1.17

Reduce $\frac{45}{270}$.

Solution Again, we can see that 5 will divide evenly into the numerator and denominator. Dividing numerator and denominator by 5 yields:

$$\frac{45}{270} = \frac{45 \div 5}{270 \div 5}$$
$$= \frac{9}{54}$$

Is this the reduced form? No! If we look at both the numerator and denominator we see that both can still be divided evenly by 3 and 9. To save calculations, we always choose the largest. If we select 3, we will have to do the same step again since there will still be a term common to both the numerator and denominator. Now dividing each by 9 yields:

$$\frac{9}{54} = \frac{9 \div 9}{54 \div 9} = \frac{1}{6}, \text{ the reduced form of } \frac{45}{270}.$$

> *Note:* One step we might have tried is to see if the numerator and denominator are multiples of each other, i.e., will the numerator divide evenly into the denominator? In this example, if we had divided both the numerator and the denominator by 45 (the value of the numerator) we would have found $\frac{1}{6}$ directly and saved ourselves one calculation. This step is worth trying on fractions that have large numerators and denominators, especially when the common factor in them may not be obvious.

B. Proper, Improper, Complex Fractions, and Mixed Numbers

A **proper fraction** is a fraction where the numerator is less than the denominator. For example, $\frac{2}{3}$ is a proper fraction. On the other hand, when the numerator is greater than or equal to the denominator we say the fraction is an **improper fraction,** for example, $\frac{6}{6}$, $\frac{6}{4}$, and $\frac{16}{5}$ are examples of improper fractions.

Complex fractions are fractions where one or more fractions are found in the numerator or denominator. Examples of complex fractions are $\frac{1/4}{5}$ and $\frac{1/2}{17}$. A complex fraction can be converted to a proper or improper fraction by dividing the numerator by the denominator — we will return to this when we discuss the division with fractions.

Sometimes fractions consist of both whole numbers and fractions, for example, $2\frac{1}{2}$ or $5\frac{1}{4}$. When both a whole number and a fraction are present we say the fraction is a **mixed number**. Mixed numbers can be expressed as an improper fraction by using the following procedure.

> We convert $3\frac{1}{2}$ to an improper fraction by multiplying the denominator (2) by the whole number (3) and adding this product to the numerator as follows:
>
> $$3\frac{1}{2} = \frac{(2 \times 3) + 1}{2}$$
>
> $$= \frac{7}{2}$$

On the other hand, an improper fraction may be expressed as a mixed number. For example, $\frac{19}{5}$ can be written as $3\frac{4}{5}$, a mixed number. This mixed number comes from dividing 19 by 5 (this gives the 3) and placing the remainder of 4 over 5, giving the $\frac{4}{5}$ portion of the mixed number.

C. Addition and Subtraction with Fractions

(i) Addition of Fractions

The addition of fractions requires that the denominator for each fraction be the same. For example, adding $\frac{3}{4}$ and $\frac{2}{4}$ can be handled by adding the numerators and putting this sum over the common denominator, 4, giving us $\frac{5}{4}$, which can be expressed as the mixed number $1\frac{1}{4}$. **The rule you must follow is to make sure the denominators are the same, then add the numerators**

and place this sum over the common denominator. For example, $\frac{2}{3} + \frac{3}{4}$ requires us to find a common denominator (by common denominator we mean finding a denominator that is the same for both fractions). The first number that is common to each denominator, 3 and 4, is 12. Therefore, we change each fraction to a fraction that has 12 as the denominator. For this example, $\frac{2}{3}$ becomes $\frac{8}{12}$ (found by multiplying the numerator and the denominator by 4), and $\frac{3}{4}$ becomes $\frac{9}{12}$ (found by multiplying the numerator and denominator by 3).

Now we have:

$$\frac{8}{12} + \frac{9}{12} = \frac{17}{12}$$

This gives us $1\frac{5}{12}$, a mixed fraction. Let's consider two examples:

EXAMPLE 1.18

Find the sum of $\frac{1}{2}$, $\frac{3}{4}$, and $\frac{1}{8}$.

Solution To do this addition, we must change each fraction so that the fractions have the same denominator — while still keeping the original value of the fraction. To do this, we look at the denominator to see if there is a common term into which each will divide evenly. The first number that all denominators will divide evenly into is 8.

$\frac{1}{2}$ can be rewritten as $\frac{4}{8}$, which is found by multiplying the numerator and denominator by 4.

That is: $\frac{4 \times 1}{4 \times 2} = \frac{4}{8}$

$\frac{3}{4}$ can be rewritten as $\frac{6}{8}$, which is found by multiplying the numerator and denominator by 2 giving us:

$$\frac{2 \times 3}{2 \times 4} = \frac{6}{8}$$

$\frac{1}{8}$ already has a denominator of 8.

Now that all the denominators are the same, we add the numerators and place this sum over the common denominator, 8. Therefore, adding the numerators and placing the sum over the common denominator gives:

$\frac{4+6+1}{8} = \frac{11}{8}$, which is a mixed number and can be written as $1\frac{3}{8}$.

EXAMPLE 1.19

Find the sum of $2\frac{1}{2}$, $5\frac{1}{4}$, and $\frac{1}{12}$.

Solution First we convert the mixed numbers into improper fractions, which gives:

$$2\frac{1}{2} = \frac{(2+2)+1}{2} = \frac{5}{2}$$

$$5\frac{1}{4} = \frac{(4\times 5)+1}{4} = \frac{21}{4}$$

And the other fraction in the sum is $\frac{1}{12}$.

Next, we must find a common denominator for each fraction. Since 12 can be evenly divided by each denominator (2, 4, and 12), we can use it as a common denominator. In fact, 12 is the smallest term that is common to 12, 4, and 2, into which each can divide evenly.

Finally, we must convert all the improper fractions to fractions with 12 as the denominator — the common denominator. Therefore:

$\frac{5}{2} = \frac{30}{12}$ This is done by multiplying the numerator and denominator by 6.

$\frac{21}{4} = \frac{63}{12}$ This is done by multiplying the numerator and denominator by 3.

$\frac{1}{12} = \frac{1}{12}$ This already has a denominator of 12 and therefore nothing needs to be done to this fraction.

Now adding the numerators and placing this sum over the common denominator of 12 yields:

$$\frac{30+63+1}{12} = \frac{94}{12}$$

$\frac{94}{12}$ should be written as $7\frac{10}{12} = 7\frac{5}{6}$.

(ii) Subtraction of Fractions

The process of subtraction uses the same procedure as addition: first find the common denominator and subtract the numerators. Consider the following examples:

EXAMPLE 1.20

Subtract $\frac{7}{32}$ from $\frac{1}{2}$.

Solution As with addition of fractions, we must first find a common denominator. The first number that comes to mind is 32, since 2 divides evenly into 32 — that is, 32 is the lowest common multiple of the two numbers.

$\frac{7}{32}$ Since 32 is already in the denominator there is no need to do anything to this fraction.

$\frac{1}{2} = \frac{16}{32}$ Found by multiplying the numerator and denominator by 16.

The last step is to subtract the values of the numerators and place this difference over the common denominator of 32. This is done as follows:

$$\frac{16 - 7}{32} = \frac{9}{32}$$

EXAMPLE 1.21

Subtract $\frac{5}{16}$ from $\frac{7}{12}$.

Solution As with Example 1.20, the first step is to determine the lowest common denominator. What you must ask yourself is, into what number will both 16 and 12 divide evenly? 32 will not work, since 12 cannot divide evenly into 32. The next number that 16 will divide evenly into is 48. As it turns out, 12 will divide evenly into 48. Now we have our lowest common denominator. Converting the two fractions to their lowest common denominator gives:

$\frac{5}{16} = \frac{15}{48}$ Found by multiplying numerator and denominator by 3.

$\frac{7}{12} = \frac{28}{48}$ Found by multiplying the numerator and denominator by 4.

Subtracting the numerators with the common denominator:

$$\frac{28 - 15}{48} = \frac{13}{48}$$

D. Multiplication and Division of Fractions

(i) Multiplication of Fractions

In business, there are many examples of the use of fractions. If you look in the financial pages of your daily newspaper, you will find the stock price quotations on the Toronto and Vancouver stock markets. You will see the price quotations include fractions. For example, $58\frac{1}{2}$ would suggest the price of the stock is $58.50, where the fraction is used to describe the number of cents.

Multiplication involving fractions is also common in business and government. For example, how often have you heard someone say that almost a third of every tax dollar goes to pay the interest on the debt of the government? If the government receives 100 billion in tax dollars, how much of this goes to pay the interest? If this number is hard to comprehend, refer to the grouping of numbers in Section 1.1. To answer this question, we could use the method of multiplication of fractions.

When multiplying fractions, you will be pleased to know that there is no need to worry about finding a common denominator. In fact, all that we must do is to ensure that the denominator of one fraction is multiplied by the denominator of the other fraction, and that the two numerators are multiplied together.

For example, if you wanted to determine how many tax dollars are used for interest payments, we would take $\frac{1}{3}$ of the 100 billion as follows:

$$\begin{aligned} \frac{1}{3} \times \$100 \text{ billion} &= \frac{1}{3} \times \frac{100}{1} \\ &= \frac{100}{3} \\ &= \$33\frac{1}{3} \text{ billion} \end{aligned}$$

That's right: if the federal government collects $100 billion, and if a third of the tax dollars goes to interest payments, then $\$33\frac{1}{3}$ billion is the interest expenditure.

Let's turn to an example involving the multiplication of fractions.

EXAMPLE 1.22

Multiply the following fractions and express the answer in the reduced form.

(a) $\frac{2}{3} \times \frac{3}{4}$

(b) $\frac{5}{16} \times \frac{3}{10}$

(c) $\frac{15}{23} \times \frac{7}{12}$

Solution (a)

$$\frac{2}{3} \times \frac{3}{4} = \frac{2 \times 3}{3 \times 4} = \frac{6}{12} = \frac{1}{2}$$

(b)

$$\frac{5}{16} \times \frac{3}{10} = \frac{5 \times 3}{16 \times 10} = \frac{15}{160} = \frac{3}{32}$$

(c)

$$\frac{15}{23} \times \frac{7}{12} = \frac{15 \times 7}{23 \times 12} = \frac{105}{276} = \frac{35}{92}$$

When one is multiplying fractions, the order of the fractions is not important. For example, $\frac{1}{2} \times \frac{3}{4}$ is the same as $\frac{3}{4} \times \frac{1}{2}$.

One last thing to note in the multiplication of fractions is to realize that the process may be speeded up if there are common terms in both fractions, thus permitting us to cancel terms before multiplying. Consider Example 1.23, which uses cancellation of terms before multiplying:

EXAMPLE 1.23

Multiply the following fractions using cancellation where possible.

$$\frac{3}{7} \times \frac{2}{3}$$

Solution

$$\frac{3}{7} \times \frac{2}{3} = \frac{\not{3} \times 2}{7 \times \not{3}} = \frac{2}{7}$$

The 3's cancel because they are common to both expressions.

The last three examples show the uses of fractions in three simple business situations:

EXAMPLE 1.24

John and Irene both own a small business worth \$75,000. If John owns $\frac{2}{5}$ of the business and Irene wants to buy him out so that she will own the business, how much would she need to pay John for his interests?

Solution The solution to this problem can be found by using multiplication of fractions. To perform the solution, all that we need do is multiply \$75,000 by $\frac{2}{5}$ to find John's portion, which Irene would need to pay to John if she wishes to be the sole owner.
Therefore we have:

$$\frac{2}{5} \times \$75{,}000 = \frac{2 \times \$75{,}000}{5} = \$30{,}000$$

Irene would need to pay John \$30,000 for his share of the business.

EXAMPLE 1.25

A share (share refers to common stock, a form of ownership in a company) in a company called Arctic Services Ltd. is trading (selling) on the Toronto Stock Exchange at $32\frac{1}{2}$ (\$32.50). If you wanted to purchase 15 shares of Arctic Services Ltd., how much would it cost you?

Solution As you can see, we have a mixed fraction, so the first thing we must do is to convert this fraction to an improper fraction. Therefore:

$$\$32\frac{1}{2} = \frac{\$65}{2}$$

Multiplying this times the number of shares we are purchasing will give us the purchase price — not including any fees to the broker who acts for you in the purchase.

Thus:

$$\begin{aligned}\frac{\$65}{2} \times 15 &= \frac{65 \times 15}{2} \\ &= \frac{975}{2} \\ &= \$487.50 \text{ is the price for the shares.}\end{aligned}$$

Sometimes it will be necessary to multiply mixed fractions. When this is required we simply convert each fraction to an improper fraction and multiply the numerators and denominators of the improper fractions. Example 1.26 shows how to multiply mixed fractions:

EXAMPLE 1.26

Multiply $43\frac{1}{2} \times 31\frac{1}{4}$.

Solution

$$\begin{aligned}43\frac{1}{2} \times 31\frac{1}{4} &= \frac{87 \times 125}{2 \times 4} \\ &= \frac{10{,}875}{8} \\ &= 1{,}359\frac{3}{8}\end{aligned}$$

(ii) Division with Fractions

The rule for division of fractions is quite straight forward. The rule to remember is: **when dividing two fractions, invert the second fraction (the divisor) and multiply.** Consider Example 1.27:

EXAMPLE 1.27

Divide $\frac{1}{2}$ by $\frac{1}{4}$.

Solution The rule is to invert the second fraction ($\frac{1}{4}$) and multiply. Therefore, if we invert and multiply we get:

$$\frac{1}{2} \times \frac{4}{1} = \frac{1 \times 4}{2 \times 1}$$
$$= \frac{4}{2}$$
$$= 2$$

Another way of thinking about this example is to remember that there are two quarters in a half!

Complex fractions (for example, $\frac{½}{5}$) require us to perform a division. However, a much easier way is to undertake a multiplication. For example, $\frac{½}{5}$ can be expressed as a proper fraction by multiplying the denominator and the numerator by 2, which causes the $\frac{1}{2}$ in the numerator to become 1 and the 5 in the denominator to become 10, giving us the fraction $\frac{1}{10}$. If we had $\frac{5}{½}$ we would multiply the numerator and denominator by 2; this would give 2×5 or 10 in the numerator and $2 \times \frac{1}{2}$, or 1, in the denominator. Therefore, the final answer is $\frac{10}{1}$, or 10, a whole number.

EXAMPLE 1.28

Find the answer to the following complex fractions.

(a) $\frac{½}{4}$

(b) $\frac{¼}{8}$

(c) $\frac{15}{½}$

Solution

(a) $\frac{½}{4} = \frac{½ \times 2}{4 \times 2}$

$= \frac{1}{8}$

We multiplied the numerator and the denominator by 2 to remove the fraction in the numerator. To keep the value of the fraction this also must be done to the denominator.

(b) $\dfrac{1/4}{8} = \dfrac{1/4 \times 4}{8 \times 4}$

$= \dfrac{1}{32}$

The numerator and denominator are multiplied by 4 to remove the fraction in the numerator. To keep the value of the fraction this also must be done to the denominator.

(c) $\dfrac{15}{1/2} = \dfrac{15 \times 2}{1/2 \times 2}$

$= 30$

The numerator and the denominator are multiplied by 2 to remove the fraction in the denominator. To keep the value of the fraction this also must be done to the numerator.

EXERCISE 1.3

A. Reducing of fractions — expressing fractions in their lowest terms.

Reduce each of the following fractions to their most reduced form.

1. $\dfrac{34}{204}$ **2.** $\dfrac{25}{625}$ **3.** $\dfrac{15}{45}$

4. $\dfrac{456}{1{,}520}$ **5.** $\dfrac{72}{90}$ **6.** $\dfrac{56}{70}$

7. $\dfrac{123}{492}$ **8.** $\dfrac{245}{735}$

B. Express each of the following improper fractions as a mixed fraction.

9. $\dfrac{5}{4}$ **10.** $\dfrac{15}{4}$ **11.** $\dfrac{7}{2}$

12. $\dfrac{16}{3}$ **13.** $\dfrac{18}{4}$ **14.** $\dfrac{134}{5}$

15. $\dfrac{89}{8}$

C. Perform the operation indicated for the following.

16. $\dfrac{3}{4} + \dfrac{1}{3}$ **17.** $\dfrac{7}{8} - \dfrac{2}{3}$ **18.** $\dfrac{5}{6} + \dfrac{4}{5}$

19. $\frac{16}{17} + \frac{3}{34}$

20. $\frac{13}{14} - \frac{2}{5}$

21. $\frac{34}{40} - \frac{3}{8}$

22. $\frac{12}{23} + \frac{13}{69}$

23. $\frac{14}{15} - \frac{3}{5}$

24. $\frac{13}{15} \times \frac{2}{3}$

25. $\frac{1}{3} \div \frac{1}{2}$

26. $\left[\frac{1}{5} \div \frac{3}{4}\right] \times \frac{5}{6}$

27. $\frac{4}{5}\left[\frac{3}{4} - \frac{2}{5}\right] \times \frac{-3}{8}$

28. $\frac{21}{24}\left[\frac{-3}{5} \times \frac{4}{7}\right] \times \frac{-3}{4}$

29. $\left[\frac{6}{19} \times \frac{1}{2}\right] \div \frac{1}{2}$

REVIEW EXERCISES

Perform the indicated operation. If fractions are involved, reduce all fractions to the reduced form (lowest common denominator).

1. $456 + 345$

2. $124 - 34$

3. $-345 \div -5$

4. $448 \div 8$

5. $500 \div -13$

6. $516 + [34\,(-21 + 12)](-3)$

7. -4×-612

8. $-2[21 \times -4(12 \times -3)]$

9. $\frac{1}{6} + \frac{1}{3}$

10. $(\frac{1}{3} - \frac{1}{4}) \times 0$

11. $\frac{14}{15} + \frac{4}{9}$

12. $\frac{34}{39} - \frac{3}{13}$

13. $[(\frac{1/2}{9}) + \frac{3}{4}]$

14. $2\frac{1}{4} + \frac{3}{8} - \frac{1}{2}$

15. $(64\frac{1}{2} - 54\frac{1}{4}) \times \frac{1}{2}$

16. $14 - \frac{3}{28}$

17. $\frac{1}{2} \div \frac{3}{4}$

18. $\frac{13}{16} \div \frac{1}{8}$

19. $22(\frac{6}{7}) \div 2(\frac{5}{9})$

20. $[3(\frac{3}{8}) + 12(\frac{3}{16})] \div \frac{7}{8}$

GLOSSARY OF TERMS

Associative Property of Addition this property means that numbers can be grouped into separate additions to get the sum of the numbers.

Associative Property of Multiplication this property means that numbers can be grouped into separate multiplications and then multiplied to get the product of all the numbers.

Cancellation of Numbers when numbers are being multiplied and divided, there may be common terms in both the numerator and denominator that allow for cancellation. For example:

$$\frac{12 \times 7}{4 \times 7} = \frac{{}^{3}\cancel{12} \times \cancel{7}}{\cancel{4} \times \cancel{7}} 3$$

In this case, 4 divides evenly into 12, giving 3. 7 cancels with 7. The symbol used to note the cancellation of 7 is $\cancel{7}$.

Commutative Property of Addition this is a property of addition that states that a column of numbers can be added in any order and the resulting sum will be the same.

Commutative Property of Multiplication this is a property of multiplication that states that a series of numbers can be multiplied in any order and the resulting product will be the same.

Complex Fraction see Fraction.

Dividend see Quotient.

Divisor see Quotient.

Fraction a fraction is a way of expressing a portion of a number. Fractions have two parts, a numerator and a denominator. In the proper fraction $\frac{1}{4}$, 1 is the numerator and 4 is the denominator. A fraction may be written as $\frac{5}{2}$, called an improper fraction, which can be written as $2\frac{1}{2}$, a mixed number (mixed because it is a number with both a fraction [$\frac{1}{2}$] and a whole number [2]). Also, fractions can be complex if they look like $\frac{1/2}{3}$. Notice that the numerator is a fraction in a complex fraction.

Grouping the process of bringing numbers together using brackets. The use of brackets gives rise to the order of operations, which is to perform all operations within the brackets first, before performing operations between the different groupings.

Improper Fraction see Fraction.

Lowest Common Denominator the lowest number into which all denominators can be divided evenly. Lowest common denominators are necessary for the addition and subtraction of fractions.

Minuend the number from which one subtracts another number. For example, $5 - 3 = 2$, where 5 is the minuend and 2 is the difference or remainder.

Mixed Number see Fraction.

Place Value in a number that has more than one digit, each digit has a value based on its location (place) in the number. For example, in 345, 3 is hundreds, 4 is tens, and 5 is the units value.

Product this is the result of the multiplication of two or more numbers. For example, $25 \times 50 = 1{,}250$, where 1,250 is the product, 25 and 50 are the factors in the multiplication.

Proper Fraction see Fraction.

Quotient the number of parts a number has been "broken" into as a result of division. For example, $8 \div 2 = 4$, where 4 is the quotient, 8 is the dividend, and 2 is the divisor. Since 2 divides evenly into 8 (i.e., there are exactly 4 twos in 8) the remainder is 0.

Remainder see Quotient.

Sum the result of the addition of two or more numbers.

CHAPTER 2

Ratios, Decimals, and Percentages

In Chapter 1 we reviewed the operations of addition, subtraction, multiplication, and division as well as the rules for fractions. What was not discussed was the relation between fractions, ratios, and percentages, which are all regularly used in business.

Ratios are commonly used in finance and accounting. Decimals, on the other hand, are used in interest rate calculations for determining the cost of borrowing money. Percentages are used frequently in the retail business to set the selling price of a product over cost — called markup. Applications of each of these concepts will occur throughout later chapters and will require a firm foundation of the material in this chapter.

OBJECTIVES

When you have completed this chapter you will:

1. understand **ratios** and be able to interpret ratios for business problems;
2. understand the concept of **decimals** and the relationship between fractions and decimals, referred to as **decimal equivalents**;
3. understand the concept of **percentages** and explain the relationship among percentages, decimals, and fractions, all fundamental to everyday business calculations.

2.1 Ratios

A ratio is a comparison of one number to another. For example, a 5 to 1 ratio — expressed as 5:1 — means that the first number occurs 5 times for every 1 occurrence of the second number.

Carrying our example a little further, if we say that the number of workers in a factory who have grade 12 education is five times more than those who have not completed high school, then the ratio of grade 12 graduates to non-grade 12 graduates is 5 to 1.

In the stock market, if we say that the number of shares being traded in the resource industries on a particular day is 8 times more than any other grouping of industries, then we are saying that for every non-resource stock traded, 8 resource stocks were traded.

Often, ratios are not expressed in the 5 to 1 or 8 to 1 form. In some instances we may see a ratio such as 3 to 2 or 5 to 4. In the last two examples, the interpretation is the same as the 5 to 1 ratio, except when we say 3 to 2, which means that for every 3 of the first item we have 2 of the second item. If you listen to the stock market quotations, you may hear that the number of declines relative to increases were in an 8 to 5 ratio. In plain English this means that for every 8 stock price decreases there were 5 increases — sometimes stated as "declines led advances by an 8 to 5 margin".

In all cases we see that a ratio can be converted to a fraction. Consequently, the rules we apply to ratios are the same as the rules we use in fractions.

Consider the following example:

EXAMPLE 2.1

The provincial government offers a local community organization a grant based on the agreement that for every three dollars the community group can raise the government will give the organization one dollar. If the community organization has held a fund raising drive and raised $39,000, how much money can the group expect from the government?

Solution Since the condition for the government grant matches one dollar for every three raised, the ratio is 1 for every 3 raised. The community organization has raised $39,000, thus the government will provide $13,000. This answer was found by using the ratio of 1 to 3. Given that the community group raised $39,000, the government must provide:

$$\frac{1}{3} \times \$39{,}000 = \$13{,}000$$

EXAMPLE 2.2

A company that wishes to develop a piece of land for rental apartments is advised that in order to get the approval for the project it must allocate 2 square metres of space per 8 square metres of finished area for low cost housing accommodation. The company plans to build a 48,000 square metre building on twelve floors — 4,000 square metres per floor. How much space will be required for low cost accommodation? If the size of each suite is 100 square metres, how many low cost suites will be built?

Solution

STEP 1 The requirement of 2 square metres out of 8 square metres for low cost apartments can be expressed as an equivalent ratio of 1 square metre per 4 square metres of finished space. The manner in which we arrived at this was to divide each of the numbers of the ratio by a common term — 2 — just like we did when we were looking for a common denominator for fractions.

STEP 2 Since there is a requirement to have a ratio of 1 in 4 square metres for the low cost accommodation, we then express the ratio of 1 in 4 as a fraction, or $\frac{1}{4}$, and multiply this by the total size of the building, that is:

$$\frac{1}{4} \times 48{,}000 = 12{,}000$$

Thus, there will be 12,000 square metres for low cost housing suites.

STEP 3 The second part of the question was to determine how many low cost suites would be built. Since each suite has a size of 100 square metres, there would be $\frac{12{,}000}{(100)}$ or 120 low cost suites made available by the project.

Ratios can be simplified just as fractions can be simplified. In business they are often expressed in the most convenient form, which may not necessarily be the reduced form.

Another situation involving ratios occurs when something has to be allocated according to a ratio. For example, if the apartment problem in Example 2.2 had read, the ratio of low cost accommodation to regular housing space must be 2 to 8, then the solution would be quite different. That is, by stating that the ratio must be 2 to 8 it means that out of every 10 square metres, 2 must be for low cost accommodation and 8 for regular housing. In terms of a ratio, this would be a 1 to 5 ratio. What makes this problem so different is the wording of the ratio. Consider the following example, which has a slight change in wording from Example 2.2:

EXAMPLE 2.3

A company that wanted to develop a piece of land for rental apartments is advised that in order to get approval for the project it must allocate the square metres of finished area in a 2 to 8 ratio for low cost housing accommodation, with the low cost accommodation getting the smaller portion of the ratio. The company plans to build a 48,000 square metre building on twelve floors — 4,000 square metres per floor. How much space will be required for low cost accommodation? If the size of each suite is 100 square metres, how many low cost suites will be built?

Solution

STEP 1 The requirement of a ratio of 2 to 8 square metres for low cost apartments can be expressed as an equivalent ratio of 1 metre per 5 square metres of finished space. The manner in which we arrived at this was by adding the numbers of the ratio, giving us 10. This means that for every 10 square metres of space, 2 go to low cost accommodation and 8 to regular housing units. These can be expressed as the fractions $\frac{2}{10}$ and $\frac{8}{10}$, respectively.

STEP 2 Since there is a requirement to have a ratio of 2 to 8 square metres for low cost accommodation, we then express the ratio of 2 to 8 as a fraction, or $\frac{1}{5}$ (which is the reduced form of the fraction $\frac{2}{10}$), and multiply this times the total size of the building, that is:

$$\frac{1}{5} \times 48{,}000 = 9{,}600$$

Thus, there will be 9,600 square metres for low cost housing suites.

STEP 3 The second part of the question was to determine how many low cost suites would be built. Since each suite has a size of 100 square metres, there would be $\frac{9{,}600}{(100)}$ or 96 low cost suites made available by the project.

The important thing to understand is that the difference between Example 2.2 and 2.3 is the wording of the ratio. The underlined portions of Example 2.3 highlight the difference.

A business example of a ratio is what banks and credit unions call high ratio mortgages. Mortgages are long term loans on real estate. A high ratio mortgage means that the amount of the mortgage is very high relative to the value of the real estate being purchased.

For example, if one was purchasing a $200,000 house, and the size of the mortgage was more than $150,000 (the mortgage is more than $\frac{3}{4}$ of the purchase price) it would generally be referred to as a high ratio mortgage. In the mortgage business, a mortgage that is greater than $\frac{3}{4}$ of the purchase price is generally considered a high ratio mortgage.

EXERCISE 2.1

1. General Computers employs 300 technicians and 200 office staff. What is the ratio of office workers to technicians?
2. The production of a special paint requires the use of three chemicals per litre in these amounts: $\frac{1}{5}$ of chemical A, $\frac{1}{6}$ of chemical B, and the remainder of chemical C. If 1,200 litres of paint are produced, how many litres of each chemical are required?
3. John makes $750 per week. From this, $200 in taxes are deducted and other deductions total $100. What is the ratio of taxes to weekly pay? What is the ratio of other deductions to weekly earnings?
4. Upon graduation, three business students start a video business. Sharon has $\frac{1}{3}$ of the shares, Adam has $\frac{1}{4}$ of the shares, and Cheryl has the balance. If the total investment in the business was $6,000, how much did each shareholder invest?
5. Assume the government debt (called the national debt) in Canada is made up of $300 billion of federal government debt, $150 billion of provincial government debt, and $75 billion of local government debt (townships, cities, municipalities, etc.). What is the ratio of the national debt held by each government type?
6. Canada's principal trading partners are the United States (77% of each trade dollar), Japan (5%), the United Kingdom (3%), European countries ([EEC countries] 5%), and the remainder is with other countries. Out of each dollar from trade, what is the ratio that gives the proportion of the trade dollar with other countries?

2.2 Decimals

Like fractions, decimals are a way of expressing parts of whole numbers. The sign used for a decimal is the period, and precedes the number. Decimals represent parts of a whole number and are expressed in tenths, hundredths, thousandths, etc., of the whole number. In everyday life and business, the most common use of decimals is representing cents in monetary quotations, for example, $99.95. In this case we read this as 99 dollars and 95 cents. **The decimal is used to tell us the fraction of a dollar,** in addition to the whole number of dollars — in this case, 99 dollars.

Since the calculations with money are so basic to business, it is important to have a solid understanding of how to use decimals and interpret their meaning.

A. Interpreting Decimals

Before we get into the operations of addition, subtraction, multiplication, and division with decimals, it is important to be able to interpret what a number with a decimal implies. Suppose a small business that purchases steel by the kilogram for a price of $3.50/kg were to purchase 5500.5 kg. How would one read these decimals? First, if we consider the price of $3.50, we would say they are paying 3 and one-half dollars per kilogram, or in the language of decimals, "three point five dollars". The same interpretation applies for the quantity of steel purchased. They have bought five thousand, five hundred point (decimal) five kilograms. **Note the word <u>point</u> being used interchangeably with the word decimal.** Depending on the units of measurement, the statement of what a decimal may measure will be different. To illustrate this, study Example 2.4.

EXAMPLE 2.4

Read each of the following numbers to yourself and write down the meaning of each, using the language of decimals:

(a) 0.50 (b) 0.545 (c) 0.115
(d) 20.135 (e) 0.005 (f) 2.3421

Solution (a) 0.50 = 50 hundredths, or one-half, or point five, or decimal five — all mean the same.

(b) 0.545 = 545 thousandths, or point five four five, or decimal five four five.

(c) 0.115 = 115 thousandths, or point one one five, or decimal one one five.

(d) 20.135 = twenty and 135 thousandths, or twenty point one three five, or twenty decimal one three five.

(e) 0.005 = five thousandths, or point zero zero five, or decimal zero zero five.

(f) 2.3421 = two and three tenths, four hundredths, two thousandths, and one ten-thousandth, or two point three four two one, or two decimal three four two one.

B. Rounding of Decimals

Often decimals are not expressed to the exact number of places. Rather, they are rounded or truncated (cut off) at a convenient point. For example, if a calculation in dollars and cents gave us $99.234, the final answer would be expressed to the nearest cent, or $99.23. The 0.004 would be dropped. However, if the answer that we calculated is $99.236, the answer would be expressed as $99.24. In the first case, we say we are rounding down. In the second case, we are said to be rounding up. The rules for rounding up or down are as follows:

Rounding Rules

If the first number to be dropped is 5 or more, increase the last number to be kept by 1. In the example above, $99.236 is to be rounded to two places, that is, the nearest cent. Since the number to be dropped is 6, we increased the last number to be kept, which was 3, to 4, giving us $99.24.

If the first number to be dropped is less than 5, the last number to be kept is not changed. In the example above, $99.234 is to be rounded to two places, and, since the number to be dropped is 4, we do not change the last number to be kept, which gives us $99.23.

EXAMPLE 2.5

Round the following numbers to the required number of decimal places.

(a) 0.50, round to nearest whole number (no decimal).
(b) 0.545, round to the nearest two decimal places.
(c) 0.115, round to the nearest one decimal place.
(d) 20.135, round to the nearest three decimal places.
(e) 0.005, round to no decimal place.
(f) 2.3421, round to two decimal places.
(g) 0.134568, round to three decimal places.

Solution

(a) 1 Using the rounding rule, the number to be dropped is 5, so we will round <u>up</u> to a whole number. If increasing the last number to be left by 1 when rounding, using the rule above, 0 becomes a 1, and the final answer is 1.
Thus, 0.5 rounded to the nearest whole number is 1.

(b) 0.55 Using the rule of increasing the last digit by one when the number to be dropped is 5 or more.

(c) 0.1 Using the rule of decreasing the last digit by one when the number to be dropped is less than 5.

(d) 20.135 No change is required since this number is already expressed to three decimal places.

(e) 0 0.005 becomes 0.01 when rounded to two decimal places, 0.0 at one decimal place, and 0 with no decimal places.
(f) 2.34 Since the number to be dropped is less than 5.
(g) 0.135 Since the first number to be dropped is 5, we round up the last term from 4 to 5.

C. Addition, Subtraction, Multiplication, and Division of Numbers with Decimals

(i) Addition of Decimal Numbers

When we are adding decimal numbers, it is important that the decimals are all aligned. This will ensure that the tenths, hundredths, thousandths, etc., are in the right order, that is, in the same column. For example, if we had to add the following numbers, note the steps we go through before the addition.

3.146, 4.25, 24.987, 23.56, 108.3457

Step 1 First we align the numbers so that the decimals are in line.

$$\begin{array}{r@{.}l} 3&146 \\ 4&25 \\ 24&987 \\ 23&56 \\ 108&3457 \end{array}$$

Step 2 This step is optional but it helps us in keeping things straight for addition. In this step, we set up the numbers with the same decimal places by adding zeros to each number so that each number has the number of decimal places equal to the number with the most decimal places. In our example it is 108.3457. This gives all numbers the same number of decimal places, without changing the value of each number. *Note*: 4.25 is the same as 4.2500.

$$\begin{array}{r} 3.1460 \\ 4.2500 \\ 24.9870 \\ 23.5600 \\ 108.3457 \end{array}$$

Step 3 Now undertake the addition.

$$\begin{array}{r} 3.1460 \\ 4.2500 \\ 24.9870 \\ 23.5600 \\ \underline{108.3457} \\ 164.2887 \end{array}$$

EXAMPLE 2.6

Add the following numbers and round your answer to the nearest tenth (one decimal place).

$$4.234 + 5.678 + 15.1 + 0.125$$

Solution First we align the numbers so the place values are correct. Then add zeros as appropriate. This gives:

$$\begin{array}{r} 4.234 \\ 5.678 \\ 15.100 \\ \underline{0.125} \end{array}$$

25.137, or 25.1, rounded to the nearest tenth.

(ii) Subtraction of Decimal Numbers

The process of subtraction with decimal numbers is similar to addition. First we align the numbers, fill in the zeros as required, and then perform the subtraction. Consider Example 2.7:

EXAMPLE 2.7

Subtract 34.5678 from 765.345 and round the answer to the nearest hundredth (two decimal places).

Solution First align the numbers and add zeros as necessary.

$$\begin{array}{r} 765.3450 \\ \underline{-\ \ 34.5678} \end{array}$$

730.7772, or 730.78, rounded to the nearest hundredth (two decimal places).

(iii) Multiplication of Decimal Numbers

Multiplication of decimal numbers requires us to perform the multiplication and then place the decimal point based on the following rule:

Multiplication Rule for Decimals

When multiplying numbers with decimals, count the total number of decimal places in both numbers we are multiplying. Then, place the decimal point directly before the number in the product, which is the same number of places as the decimal count, counting from right to left.

EXAMPLE 2.8

Multiply 19.99 × 2.344 and round to the nearest thousandths (three places).

Solution

```
   19.99 ←—— Two decimal places.
   2.344 ←—— Three decimal places.
    7996
   79960
  599700
 3998000
46.85656 ←—— To five decimal places — counting, from the right, five
             numbers, since there are five decimal places in total from
             the original numbers.
```

Note that we counted the number of decimal places in each number being multiplied (2 + 3), and then placed the decimal point in front of the number in our answer (product), which is 5 places to the left of the last number in the product. Rounding our answer to the nearest thousandths, we get the final answer of 46.857.

EXAMPLE 2.9

Multiply 44.345 × 25.1. Round your answer to the nearest tenth (one decimal place).

Solution

```
     44.345  — Three places.
       25.1  — One place.
      44345
    2217250
    886900
 1,113.0595  — Using the multiplication rule for decimals, the decimal is
               placed four places from the right.
```

Rounding to one decimal place gives 1,113.1.

(iv) Division with Decimal Numbers

Division with decimal numbers requires us to move the decimal point in the divisor to the right as far as possible and move the decimal point in the dividend the same number of places. Once the decimal points have been moved in the divisor and dividend we can then perform the division. This is a little more complex than multiplication, so study Example 2.10:

EXAMPLE 2.10

Divide each of the following numbers:

(a) 34.5 ÷ 2.5
(b) 15.3 ÷ 3.0
(c) 45.5 ÷ 0.09

Solution (a) $2.5\overline{)34.5}$ is written as $25\overline{)345.0}$.

Before the division, we move the decimal point in the divisor (2.5) to the right, giving us 25. Then we do the same to the dividend (34.5), which gives us 345. Now we can perform the division.

$$
\begin{array}{r}
13.8 \\
25\overline{)345.0} \\
\underline{25} \\
95 \\
\underline{75} \\
200 \\
\underline{200} \\
0
\end{array}
$$

0 ← Remainder

(b)

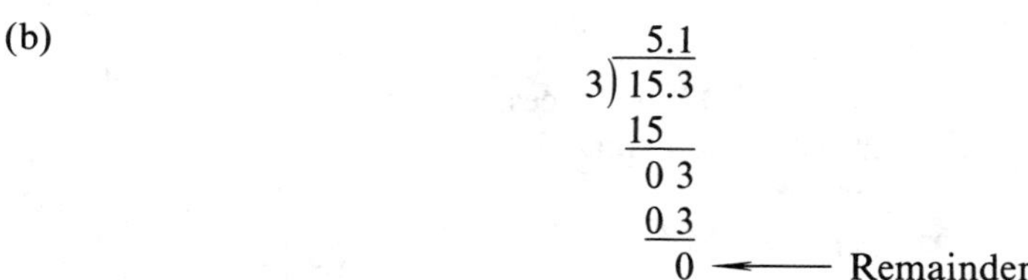

In this example, we did not need to move the decimal point since there was no decimal point in the divisor.

(c) $0.09\overline{)45.5}$ this is rewritten as $9\overline{)4550.0.}$

The difference in this example is that we moved the decimal point in the divisor by two places (from 0.09 to 9). Therefore, we had to do the same to the dividend (from 45.5 to 4,550). This was done by multiplying each number by 100.

Moving the decimal point makes the division a little more direct. Now, performing the division we have:

$$\begin{array}{r} 505.55 \\ 9\overline{)4550.00} \\ \underline{45} \\ 050 \\ \underline{45} \\ 50 \\ \underline{45} \\ 50 \\ \underline{45} \\ 5 \end{array}$$

Note how the decimal point in the answer and the dividend are "lined up".

5 ⟵ Remainder

As you can see, the answer will be a continual number of 5's after the decimal. This is called a **repeating decimal**. If we round the answer to two decimal places, the final answer would be 505.56.

D. Fractions and Mixed Numbers to Decimals

(i) Fractions to Decimals

Decimals are most commonly used in place of mixed numbers. For example, $2\frac{1}{2}$, a mixed number, can be written as 2.5 where the 0.5 is the $\frac{1}{2}$ unit. The problem we must solve is how to find the decimal equivalent for a fraction — that is, how do we convert the fraction into a decimal? The method we use to convert the fraction to a decimal is to perform the division indicated by the fraction. For example, to get the decimal equivalent of $2\frac{1}{2}$, $\frac{1}{2}$ must be converted to a decimal. To accomplish this we divide the numerator by the denominator as shown below:

$$\begin{array}{r} 0.5 \\ 2\overline{)1.0} \\ \underline{1} \\ 0 \end{array}$$

0.5 ⟵ Quotient

Divisor (denominator) ⟶ 2

1.0 ⟵ Dividend (numerator)

0 ⟵ Remainder

Therefore, the decimal equivalent to $2\frac{1}{2}$ is 2.5.

Often the division does not work out to be so simple. In fact, there are many cases where there is no final answer to the division. Consider the following examples of more difficult fractions:

EXAMPLE 2.11

Convert the following two mixed fractions to a number with three decimal places.

$$\text{(a) } 7\frac{2}{7} \qquad \text{(b) } 3\frac{2}{3}$$

Solution (a) $7\frac{2}{7}$ requires us to convert the $\frac{2}{7}$ into a decimal. The procedure is to divide the 2 by the 7 as follows:

```
                    0.28571    <—— Quotient
Divisor ——>   7)2.00000    <—— Dividend
                  14
                   60
                   56
                    40
                    35
                     50
                     49
                      10
                       7
                       3    <—— Remainder
```

In this problem it turns out that there is no solution. Rather, the decimal places will continue without any final answer — at least until we stop the division. This is one form of a repeating division. Each of the numbers repeat themselves in blocks of 6 numbers (0.285714285714, etc.,) whereas, in Example 2.10(c), the 5 repeated indefinitely after the decimal.
The final answer to three decimal places is 7.286.

(b) $3\frac{2}{3}$ requires us to convert the $\frac{2}{3}$ into a decimal. The procedure is to simply divide the 2 by the 3 as follows:

```
                    0.66666    <—— Quotient
Divisor ——>   3)2.00000    <—— Dividend
                  18
                   20
                   18
                    20
                    18
                     20
                     18
                      20
                      18
                       2    <—— Remainder
```

Thus, the mixed fraction $3\frac{2}{3}$ has a decimal equivalent of $3.6666\dot{6}$ — where the $0.6666\dot{6}$ is a repeating decimal (the · above the 6 means repeating decimal). Rounding to three places gives 3.667 as the answer.

(ii) Decimals to Fractions

When dealing with a fraction, the fraction is converted to a decimal equivalent by dividing the numerator by the denominator. The process is similar to that used with the fractional part of a mixed number. If you want to convert a decimal number to a fraction, it must be expressed in terms of a division. For example, if we wanted to express 0.375 as a fraction, we would write it as $\frac{375}{1{,}000}$ and, if possible, simplify it to its reduced form. In this case, $\frac{3}{8}$. The thing to note is that the decimal is expressed as a fraction according to the number of places the decimal is carried, that is, tenths, hundredths, thousandths, etc. Let's consider an example that demonstrates three cases:

EXAMPLE 2.12

Express the following decimals as fractions and reduce to their lowest terms.

(a) 0.32
(b) 0.2456
(c) 0.68794

Solution (a) 0.32 is a decimal to two places, or to the nearest hundredth. Therefore, to express this as a fraction we would rewrite it as $\frac{32}{100}$. Now finding the reduced form we have:

$$\frac{32}{100} = \frac{16}{50}$$

$$= \frac{8}{25}$$

(b) 0.2456 is a decimal to four places or to the nearest ten thousandth. Therefore the corresponding fraction is:

$$\frac{2{,}456}{10{,}000} = \frac{1{,}228}{5{,}000}$$

$$= \frac{614}{2{,}500}$$

$$= \frac{307}{1{,}250}$$

(c) 0.68794 is a decimal to five places or to the nearest hundred thousandth. Thus, the corresponding fraction is:

$$\frac{68{,}794}{100{,}000} = \frac{34{,}397}{50{,}000}$$

EXERCISE 2.2

A. Round the following numbers as indicated.

1. 15.342 — round to one decimal place.

2. 34.465 — round to two decimal places.

3. 0.2345612 — round to the nearest hundredth.

4. 1.298472 — round to the nearest thousandths.

5. 0.0534 — round to one decimal place.

6. $67.13 — round to the nearest dollar.

B. Perform the operation as indicated. Round all answers to two decimals.

7. 0.05 + 23.456 + 0.0358 – 45.23

8. 1.56 + 23.5347 + 632.5123 – 24.185

9. 1.34 × 45.2

10. 0.02 × 45

11. 0.24 ÷ 78

12. 0.5 ÷ 0.7

13. 0.5 × $55.30

14 0.1345 ÷ 1.5234

15. 0.498 × 0.349

16. 2.26 – 13.4537 + 841.5481 –25.787

C. Solve the following problems.

17. If your car travelled 1,000.4 kilometres on 41 litres of gasoline, how many kilometres per litre did you travel?

18. If you make $8.23 per hour, how much would you earn per week for a forty hour week?

19. Jessie was hired to do some garden work and was paid $55.00 for the work. The time worked was 16 hours. What did Jessie earn per hour?

20. Steve Ma imports wicker furniture. His tax on the last shipment was $333.33. The value of the shipment was $66,666.00. What is the decimal equivalent tax paid on the furniture? What is the fraction of the total price paid in taxes?

21. Express the following as required.

(a) $\frac{3}{4}$ as a decimal equivalent.

(b) 0.4 as a fraction.

(c) $\frac{5}{4}$ as a decimal equivalent.

(d) 0.45 as a fraction.

(e) $\frac{7}{3}$ as a decimal equivalent.

(f) 0.34 as a fraction.

2.3 Percentages

As with decimals, percentages are common in business. All you need to do is to turn to a newspaper and there will be advertisements telling you about price reductions, often in percentage terms. Not only will you see percentages used in advertisements but also in articles discussing the percentage of people unemployed, the percentage increase in prices (a measure of inflation), or the interest rate (in percentage terms) being charged on consumer loans.

Percentages are simply another way of expressing fractions, decimal numbers, and, in some cases, mixed numbers. The term percentage refers to a measurement unit of hundredths, and the symbol used to indicate percentage is % — **the percentage sign**. Any number that is followed by the % sign refers to a number measured in hundredths. Since percentages are measured in hundredths we tend to think about the base of percentages as 100% — **a base means something we use as a reference point for comparison.** For example, if you are told that consumer prices have risen by 6.5%, you would interpret this as a relatively small increase. It is a "relatively" small amount because it is relative to the base of 100%. If you were told that prices had increased by 100%, you would say that prices had doubled. The way we arrive at this last statement is to think about the price of a litre of gasoline. If the price last year was $0.55 per litre and this year it is $1.10, we can see that the price has risen by its previous value. That is, the price has increased by $0.55, which is 100% of what it was a year ago. This would mean that the price has doubled over the past year.

Sometimes the word percentage is implied by the term **rate**. The use of the term rate is most common in the banking industry. Often when one discusses the rate of interest, it is quoted or expressed as a percentage.

A. Finding the Percentage

When we want to find the percentage it implies that two numbers are being compared, one relative to the other. Students are aware of percentages, since their grades on most exams and assignments are reported in percentages.

The computation of a percentage is done by division and then multiplication of the quotient (answer) by 100%, the base of percentage. For example, if 45,000 people in a community of 75,000 people want a certain project to occur, then we would say 60% of the people are in favour of the project. The way we arrived at this percentage was:

Step 1 Divide 45,000 by 75,000, which gives:

$$\begin{array}{r} 0.6 \\ 75{,}000\overline{)45{,}000.0} \\ \underline{45{,}000} \\ 0 \end{array}$$

Step 2 Multiply 0.6 by 100%, which gives 60%.

All percentages require these two steps. Work through the following example.

EXAMPLE 2.13

A piece of real estate was purchased for $55,000. Exactly one year later it was sold again for $66,000. What was the percentage increase in price that occurred in the sale of this property?

Solution First we must determine by how much the property increased. This is simply the difference between what was paid for the property and for what it was sold, or $66,000 – $55,000 = $11,000. To determine the percentage increase we compare the $11,000 gain to what was paid for the property.

Original price = $55,000
Gain = $11,000

$$\text{Percentage increase} = \frac{\$11{,}000}{\$55{,}000} \times 100\%$$

$$= 0.2 \times 100\%$$

$$= 20\%$$

Therefore, we would say that the increase is 20% over what was paid for the property.

Percentages do not always work out to be exact, since the decimal equivalent may have many decimal places or a repeating decimal. To show how we handle this, see Example 2.14:

EXAMPLE 2.14

John received a score of 43 out of 70 on his finance exam. (a) What was his percentage score? Round your answer to the nearest tenth of a percentage. (b) What was the decimal equivalent to the nearest tenth?

Solution

STEP 1 Divide 43 by 70, which gives:

```
       0.61428
   70)43.000
      42.0
       1.00
        .70
        .300
        .280
        .0200
        .0140
        .00600
        .00560
        .00040  <—— Remainder
```

STEP 2 Multiply the decimal equivalent by 100%.

$100\% \times 0.61428 = 61.428\%$, or 61.4%, to the nearest tenth of a percentage.

(b) The decimal equivalent score to the nearest tenth is 0.6.

B. Fractions, Decimals, and Percentages

As discussed in the previous section, a fraction can be readily expressed as a percentage by first transforming it to a decimal and then to a percentage. For example, $\frac{4}{5}$ can be expressed as the decimal 0.80, which is expressed as the percentage 80%. What is important to note is that the decimal is dropped and the % sign is inserted. The thing to understand is that the % term refers to hundredths, and if the fraction yields a decimal equivalent that has more than two decimal places, then there will be a decimal place in the percentage equivalent. For example, $\frac{3}{8}$ can be written as 0.375; the corresponding percentage is 37.5%. Note that the decimal comes after the hundredth term. The following example shows how we convert fractions and decimals to percentages.

EXAMPLE 2.15

Express the following fractions as percentages, and, where decimals are required, round to four places.

(a) $\frac{2}{3}$

(b) $\frac{7}{12}$

(c) $\frac{121}{200}$

(d) $\frac{25}{4,535}$

Solution (a) $\frac{2}{3}$ must first be written as a decimal equivalent, that is, 0.6667. Remember, to get the decimal we divided 2 by 3, which gives 0.666666 (a repeating decimal). Rounded to four places gives 0.6667. Now, as a percentage, 0.6667 is written as 66.67% — we moved the decimal two places to the right and added the % sign (i.e., we multiplied 0.6667 by 100%).

(b) $\frac{7}{12}$ as a decimal equivalent is $7 \div 12$, or $0.583\dot{3}$ (repeating), and is rounded to four decimal places. The percentage equivalent is 58.33%.

(c) $\frac{121}{200} = 121 \div 200$

$= 0.605$, or 60.5%

(d) $\frac{25}{4,535} = 25 \div 4,535 = 0.00551268$

$= 0.55\%$ This has been rounded to four places, since 0.55% is 0.0055 rounded to four places in decimal notation.

The next example demonstrates the process of converting percentages to fractions. Follow the steps closely.

EXAMPLE 2.16

Convert the following percentages to fractions and express the fractions in their reduced form.

(a) 51% (b) 34.5% (c) 67.345% (d) 0.315%

Solution (a) $51\% = \frac{51}{100}$

(b) $34.5\% = \frac{345}{1{,}000}$

$= \frac{69}{200}$

(c) $67.345\% = \frac{67{,}345}{100{,}000}$

$= \frac{13{,}469}{20{,}000}$

(d) $0.315\% = \frac{315}{100{,}000}$

$= \frac{63}{20{,}000}$

C. Arithmetic Operations with Percent

(i) Addition and Subtraction of Percentages

In general, the easiest way to add or subtract numbers involving percent is to leave the number in the percentage form. The following examples show each operation and how best to handle the operation required:

EXAMPLE 2.17

(a) Add 15% and 25%.

(b) Subtract 4% from 21%.

Solution (a) $15\% + 25\% = 40\%$

(b) $21\% - 4\% = 17\%$

(ii) Multiplication with Percentages

For multiplication and division with percentages, the most appropriate method to use will depend upon the type of problem you are solving. If you are simply multiplying a number times a percentage, for example, $3 \times 15\%$, the easiest way to find the solution is to leave the percentage as a percentage, giving a product of 45%.

If you are finding the percentage of a number — the most common business situation — then the method to use requires you to convert the percentage to a decimal equivalent and then perform the multiplication. For example, if 15% of 95 is required, then convert the percentage to 0.15 and then perform the multiplication, that is, 0.15×95, or 14.25.

Another example that often arises is multiplying two or more percentages. This is done by converting the percentages to decimal equivalents, then multiplying, and then converting the final answer back to a percentage.

The following examples show different situations involving multiplication of percentages:

EXAMPLE 2.18

Multiply $4 \times 21\%$.

Solution For this problem we simply perform the multiplication without converting the percent to decimals. Therefore, the answer is:

$4 \times 21\% = 84\%$

EXAMPLE 2.19

A newspaper advertisement claims that a car stereo system is on sale at 35% off the regular price of \$399. What is the sale price?

Solution In this type of problem we want to find the percentage of a number — note the wording, percentage of. To find the sale price, we first find 35% of the original price and then subtract the savings from the original price.

Finding 35% of \$399 is done by using the decimal equivalent of 35% and then performing the multiplication, that is:

$$35\% = 0.35$$
$$0.35 \times \$399 = \$139.65 \text{ — the savings off the regular price.}$$

Now finding the sale price requires us to subtract the savings from the regular price, or:

$$\$399 - \$139.65 = \$259.35$$

Another way of doing this problem is to think of the sale price as being 65%

of the regular price. This was arrived at by thinking of the regular price as 100%, then subtracting the discount of 35%. Thus, 100% – 35% = 65%. Now we multiply the regular price of $399 by 0.65, the decimal equivalent of the 65%. This gives:

$$0.65 \times \$399 = \$259.35, \text{ the same as above.}$$

Therefore, the sale price of the stereo is $259.35 using either approach.

EXAMPLE 2.20

John has just purchased a computer for $1,400 and a printer for $395. He has bought these in the province of British Columbia and must pay a sales tax of 6%, applied to the original price, and the GST of 7%, applied to the original price. Find the amount of all taxes paid and the total cost of purchasing the two pieces of equipment.

Solution As with Example 2.19, this problem is best handled by first converting the percentage to a decimal equivalent and then performing the multiplication to find the amount of the sales tax. This is done as follows:

$$\begin{aligned} 6\% &= 0.06 \\ 0.06 \times (\$1{,}400 + \$395) &= 0.06 \times \$1{,}795 \\ &= \$107.70 \end{aligned}$$

Note the use of brackets. This makes the statement of the required calculation a little more straight forward.

Since we know the price of the equipment and we know the GST is 7% of the sales price, the dollar value of the GST will be:

$$(\$1{,}795) \times 0.07 = \$125.65$$

Therefore, the total cost of the purchases is:

$$\$1{,}795 + \$107.70 + \$125.65 = \$2{,}028.35$$

The total amount of tax was $107.70 + $125.65, or $233.35.

The other method that can be used is to add the 6% to 100%, which gives us 106%. That is, the price is 106% of the equipment price when the sales tax is added. The GST applies 7%, thus increasing the original price 107%, therefore, the total tax to be paid on the original price is 6% plus 7%, or 13%. Using a decimal equivalent of 1.13, we can find the final price as:

$$\$1{,}795 \times (1.13) = \$2{,}028.35, \text{ which includes all the taxes.}$$

For the alternative method above, to find the dollar amount of the tax we simply subtract $1,795 from $2,028.35, which gives us $233.35, the value of the tax paid.

EXAMPLE 2.21

Jean has just purchased some printing work from a local printer. When she arrives to pay the bill, she is expecting to pay \$300, which she was quoted a week ago. When she goes to pay the bill she is advised that there is federal and provincial sales tax of 6% and 9%, respectively. The tax is calculated by first calculating the provincial tax. Then the federal tax is applied to the original price plus the provincial tax. What is the dollar amount of the provincial tax, and what will be the total price for the printing?

Solution First, we must calculate the provincial sales tax, which is 9% of the cost of the printing. To do this, we must convert the 9% to a decimal equivalent, which is:

$$9\% = 0.09$$

Therefore, the provincial tax payable is:

$$0.09 \times \$300 = \$27$$

Now, we were told that the federal tax is calculated on the original price plus the provincial tax. To find the federal tax payable, we multiply the federal tax times the original price plus the provincial sales tax, that is:

$6\% = 0.06$ — the decimal equivalent of the federal sales tax.

Original price + provincial sales tax = \$300 + \$27, or \$327. Thus, the federal tax is:

$0.06 \times \$327 = \$19.62$

The total cost of the printing is \$327 + \$19.62, or \$346.62.

The last type of calculation that needs further explanation is finding a percentage of a percentage. Consider Example 2.22:

EXAMPLE 2.22

A builder of new housing tells you that his labour cost for building a \$200,000 house has risen by 10%. If labour costs are approximately 40% of the total cost of building a \$200,000 house, by how much, in dollars, will the cost of this type of house rise because of the increase in labour costs?

Solution Your initial reaction may be simply to multiply \$200,000 by 10%. However, if labour costs are only 40% of the \$200,000, then the actual increase in the cost to build the house will be only 10% of 40%. To make this clear, let's first find out how much the labour costs are for a \$200,000 house. Using our decimal equivalents, we know that 40% is the same as 0.4. Therefore, the labour portion of a $200,000 house is:

$$0.4 \times \$200{,}000 = \$80{,}000$$

Now, if labour costs have risen by 10%, this will apply only to the $80,000, the labour costs to build a new house. Therefore, the increase in labour costs are:

$$0.10 \times \$80{,}000 = \$8{,}000$$

Thus, labour costs have risen by $8,000. We should find that the new cost of building this type of house will be $200,000 + $8,000, or $208,000.

A more direct method for solving this problem is to find 10% of 40% and multiply this amount by $200,000. To determine 10% of 40% we can multiply the two percentages — after they have been converted to decimal equivalents. This would give:

> $0.1 \times 0.4 = 0.04$, that is, a 10% increase in a cost that is 40% of all costs will cause the total to rise by 0.04, or 4%. Thus the increase in total cost caused by increasing labour costs will be:
>
> $0.04 \times \$200{,}000 = \$8{,}000$ — the same as above.

Consequently, the new cost will be $200,000 + $8,000, or $208,000. (Note that labour costs are now more than 40% of total costs.)

Example 2.22 was designed to show how one can find the percentage of a percentage by multiplying the two percentages in their decimal equivalents. This is a useful calculation in business and will be used later in the chapters on financial mathematics.

(iv) Division with Percentages

The process of division with percentages relies on decimal equivalents. The steps involved are first, convert the percentage to a decimal equivalent and, second, perform the required division using the decimal equivalent as the divisor. Example 2.23 highlights the procedure:

EXAMPLE 2.23

Divide 250 by 12.5%.

Solution First, convert the percentage to a decimal equivalent, or 0.125. Using the decimal equivalent, perform the division.

$$250 \div 0.125 = 2{,}000$$

Therefore, when 250 is divided by 12.5% it yields 2,000. Another way of thinking about this is to remember that 12.5% of 2,000 is 250.

The concept of percentage is important in business and finance. Therefore, it will be very useful to attempt a good sampling of the following review exercises before moving on to the next chapter.

EXERCISE 2.3

1. Find 15% of 45.
2. Find 71% of 250.
3. Express 0.3445 as a percentage rounded to one decimal place.
4. Express $\frac{1}{3}$ as a percentage rounded to two places.
5. Express as a percentage: 27 out of 25,500.
6. Find 15% of 20%.
7. General Computers has just increased its work force by 115 people. If this represents a 30% increase in the number of employees, how many employees did they have before this hiring?
8. If a company has $350,000 in exports to China and this represents approximately 78% of their annual sales, what are their annual sales?
9. If the price of a good has risen from $15.00 to $21.00, what is the percentage increase in the price? If the price ($15) had risen by 75%, what would be the new price?
10. A computer is sold to make a profit over cost of 25%. If the computer's selling price is $1,500, what was its cost?
11. A company uses a special electronic part in the production of its telephone systems. This part represents 45% of the price of the telephone system. The system currently sells for $240,000. If the cost of this special part rises by 10%, what will the new price have to be if the company plans to pass all cost increases to purchasers?
12. A bank offers you 11% on your money for one year. If you invest $5,000, how much money will you have at the end of the year?

REVIEW EXERCISES

1. Neon Corporation employs 500 installers and 50 office staff. What is the ratio of office workers to installers?
2. Shares in a small company are allocated to the three shareholders as follows: $\frac{1}{3}$ to shareholder A, $\frac{1}{7}$ to shareholder B, and the remaining shares

to shareholder C. If there are a total of 2,100 shares, how many shares does each shareholder own?

3. Ann makes \$1,000 per week. From this, \$250 in taxes are deducted and other deductions total \$150. What is the ratio of taxes to weekly pay? What is the ratio of other deductions to weekly earnings?

4. Round the following numbers as indicated.
(a) 1315.21 — round to one decimal place.
(b) 134.455 — round to two decimal places.
(c) 1.5612234 — round to the nearest hundredth.
(d) 1,378.298 — round to the nearest thousandth.
(e) 0.10522 — round to one decimal place.
(f) \$2,367.57 — round to the nearest dollar.

5. Perform the operation as indicated. Round all answers to two decimal places.
(a) $1.05 + 23.456 + 0.230358 - 67.67$
(b) $34.6 + 313.347 + 23{,}632.5123 - 89.535$
(c) 3.21×67.7
(d) 0.0402×135
(e) $0.673 \div 54$
(f) $0.555 \div 0.11$
(g) $0.375 \times \$34{,}576.30$
(h) $2{,}574.1345 \div 1.5234$

6. John's cheque for a week's work is \$1,500. What is his hourly pay if he worked 35.75 hours?

7. If 15% of a company's \$15,000,000 investments is in fish farms, how many dollars do they have invested in fish farms?

8. Sales of a company in 1989 were \$3,000,000. If sales in 1990 are expected to rise by 6%, what are the expected sales for 1990?

9. Janet is going to purchase a new car. She is told that she must place a 16.5% down payment and make payments. If the down payment is \$1,500, what is the price of the car? If she is told that her monthly payments will be 3% of the money owing (price less down payment), what would be the monthly payments? Round your answer to the nearest dollar.

10. Jemco increased sales by \$50,000 per month to \$80,000 as a result of a new product line they are selling. What is the percentage increase?

11. Government spending is expected to rise by \$24 billion next year. If this is an 8.5% increase, what was government spending this year in dollars, and what is it expected to be next year?

12. Express the following as required:
(a) $\frac{53}{421}$ as a decimal equivalent.
(b) 0.365 as a fraction.
(c) $\frac{65}{4}$ as a decimal equivalent.

(d) 0.7445 as a fraction.

(e) $\frac{75}{143}$ as a decimal equivalent.

(f) 0.1279 as a fraction.

GLOSSARY OF TERMS

Decimal a way of expressing the parts of a whole number. Decimals are expressed in tenths, hundredths, thousandths, etc.

Percentage another way of expressing parts of a whole number. A number is said to be 100% of itself. The parts that make up the number are expressed as a percentage and will be less than 100%. For example, 100% of 10 is 10; 20% of 10 is 2.

Ratio a comparison of one number to another. For example, 5 to 1 means one number appears five times to one of another number.

CHAPTER 3

Basic Algebraic Concepts

Algebraic methods in business are used to solve problems in accounting, finance, economics, and marketing. Often solutions to business problems take only minutes using algebra, whereas without algebra the solution might be approached by trial and error. This can be costly and inefficient. Moreover, in some instances, without the assistance of algebra, solutions to quantitative business problems would be almost impossible to find.

Many situations arise where algebra may assist business. For instance, a small business needs to figure out the exact number of units of a product it must sell to cover all costs. Another business needs a quick and efficient way to provide quotations for work upon which it has been asked to bid. These are examples where a little algebra may assist a business enormously.

Clearly, algebra does not provide a solution to all quantitative problems of business. However, the fact that it can be used frequently is reason for students of business to have an understanding of the basic concepts and procedures of algebra.

The overall objective of this chapter and the following chapter is to provide information on the algebraic essentials for business. To achieve this objective, business examples are used where possible. Where possible, examples demonstrate a business situation. In some cases, the examples are quite long because they try to provide a realistic perspective on how algebraic methods are used in the "real world".

OBJECTIVES

When you have finished this chapter you should be able to do the following:

1. explain the meaning of an algebraic expression and use it to express relationships that will assist in the solving of business problems;
2. use the following concepts within a business context: algebraic expressions, variables, equations, coefficients, and linear equations;
3. explain the meaning of an exponent and be able to use the rules of exponents in working with algebraic expressions;
4. complete algebraic operations involving the addition, subtraction, multiplication, and division of algebraic expressions;
5. understand the concept of factoring and use factoring to simplify algebraic expressions;
6. understand the meaning of an equation and be able to solve a one-variable equation for an unknown variable.

3.1 Algebraic Expressions

A. Algebraic Expressions — Basic Concepts

Algebra often conjures up ideas of complex formulas. In fact, this is not so for most business applications of algebra. Before we discuss how the basic rules of addition, subtraction, multiplication, and division apply to algebra, let's make sure we understand what the term algebra means.

When we discussed arithmetic in Chapter 1, we used numbers to perform the operations of addition, subtraction, multiplication, and division. With algebra, however, we are not limited to numbers. Algebra expands the use of the rules of arithmetic to letters, numbers, or both to express relationships. These relationships are given a variety of names including expressions and equations. **The relationships in algebra are formed between variables (letters) and numbers, or variables and variables. The term variable in algebra is used to describe something that can change in an algebraic expression. In business the variable might be the number of units of a good produced.**

An example of an algebraic expression is $x + y$, where x and y are called variables. The concept of variables will be explained in detail once we have reviewed how the operations of arithmetic apply to algebraic expressions. The key difference in algebra is that arithmetic operations are now applied to letters as well as numbers.

B. Arithmetic Rules and Algebraic Operations

The arithmetic rules discussed in an earlier chapter also apply to algebraic operations. If x, y, and z stand for three algebraic variables, the arithmetic rules apply to these algebraic variables as they would to numbers. The use of arithmetic rules for algebraic variables is summarized in Tables 3.1 and 3.2.

Table 3.1: Basic Arithmetic Operations Applied to Algebraic Expressions

Arithmetic Rule Applied to Variables	**Examples Using Numbers for the Variables** Let $x = 14$, $y = 12$, and $z = 2$.
ADDITION	
Two variables x and y:	
$x + y = y + x$	$14 + 12 = 12 + 14$ $= 26$
Three variables x, y, and z:	
$(x + y + z) = (y + z) + x$	$(14 + 12 + 2) = (12 + 2) + 14$ $= 28$
MULTIPLICATION	
Two variables x and y:	
$xy = yx$	$14 \times 12 = 12 \times 14$ $= 168$
Three variables x, y, and z:	
$xyz = yzx = zyx$	$14 \times 12 \times 2 = 12 \times 2 \times 14$ $= 2 \times 12 \times 14$ $= 336$
DIVISION	
Two variables x and y:	
$x \div y = \frac{x}{y}$	$14 \div 12 = \frac{14}{12}$ $= \frac{7}{6}$
Three variables x, y, and z:	
$x \div y \div z = (x \div y) \div z$	$14 \div 12 \div 2 = (14 \div 12) \div 2$ $= 0.5833$
$(x \div y) \div z = \frac{x \div y}{z}$	$(14 \div 12) \div 2 = \frac{14 \div 12}{2}$ $= 0.5833$

Table 3.2: Properties of 0 and 1 When Used with Algebraic Variables

Properties of 1	**Examples** Let $x = 14$, $y = 12$, and $z = 2$.
ADDITION A variable x, plus 1: $x + 1 = 1 + x$	$14 + 1 = 1 + 14$
MULTIPLICATION A variable x, multiplied by 1: $x \times 1 = x$ Two variables multiplied by 1: $xy \times 1 = xy$	$14 \times 1 = 14$ $14 \times 12 \times 1 = 14 \times 12$
Properties of 0	**Examples** Let $x = 14$, $y = 12$, and $z = 2$
ADDITION A variable x, plus 0: $x + 0 = x$	$14 + 0 = 14$
SUBTRACTION When x is subtracted from zero, the result is: $0 - x = -x$	$0 - 14 = -14$
MULTIPLICATION A variable x, multiplied by 0: $x \times 0 = 0$ Two variables multiplied by 0: $xy \times 0 = 0$	$14 \times 0 = 0$ $14 \times 12 \times 0 = 0$
DIVISION Dividing a variable by 0: $x \div 0 =$ Undefined $= \infty$	$14 \div 0 =$ Undefined $= \infty$

The properties of 0 and 1 introduced in Chapter 1 have the same properties for algebraic terms as was found for numerical values. In Table 3.2, where x and y represent variables, a review of the properties of 0 and 1 is provided.

C. Basic Terminology in Algebra

The best way to understand the meaning of the terms used in algebra, such as variables, equations, and expressions, is with an example. Suppose you are going to go into business for yourself and decide that business cards are necessary to leave with possible clients. A small printing company advises you that what you want in a business card will cost \$500 as a set-up charge for the printing plate and, in addition, it will cost \$0.05 per card for each card printed. Without algebra, if you had decided that you wanted 1,000 cards, you would find the cost for the 1,000 cards by using the following arithmetic method:

$$\$500 + \$0.05(1{,}000) = \$550$$

With algebra, it is possible to express the printing cost with an expression that can be used for any number of cards. This is done by introducing a variable. The introduction of a variable makes the expression an algebraic expression. To formulate an algebraic expression, we would introduce a letter for the variable, say y, and let y stand for the number of business cards to be printed. Using y in place of the number of cards, we can write an expression for the cost of y business cards as:

$$\$500 + \$0.05y$$

To make this expression into an equation we introduce the equal sign and make the expression equal to the total cost of y business cards.

$$\$500 + \$0.05y = \text{total cost of } y \text{ business cards}$$

This equation will give the total cost for any number of business cards you want to order. In the example above, y could be 1,000, 2,000, or any other number of cards. Because the value of y can change, it is called a variable.

From this simple example there are some terms that we should understand:

Variable

If y is a variable, then the value of y will <u>change</u> depending upon the number of business cards you want printed. Note that y is a letter that stands for the number of cards you purchase. This letter could have been any letter. The fact that there is now a letter in our cost formulation, as opposed to the number (1,000), makes the expression an algebraic expression.

Expression

An expression refers to a statement that defines a relation between variables. For example, the expression that describes the cost of business cards is $\$500 + 0.05y$.

Equation

An equation defines a relation between numbers and variables, or variables and variables. An algebraic expression becomes an equation if an equal sign (=) is used to express the specific relationship. For example:

$$\$500 + 0.05y = \text{Total Cost}$$

is an equation because of the equal sign. It equates the number of cards and set-up costs to the total cost. Once the equal sign is applied we have an equation. Equations are sometimes called formulas if they are used to find an unknown when given a value for a variable.

Coefficient

This refers to the number in front of the variable and means that this number multiplies the value of the variable. In our example, 500 + \$0.05y, 0.05 is the numerical coefficient and multiplies the variable y. In algebra, any number in front of a variable is called a coefficient and can be a fraction, a decimal number, or a whole number. The y in $0.05y$ is called a literal coefficient. If the expression has a letter in front of another letter, say $3ax$, where a and x are variables, then ax is called a **literal coefficient** and 3 is the **numerical coefficient**. If a term is simply x or another variable, the numerical coefficient is 1 although it is never stated, e.g., $1x = x$.

Term

A term refers to the parts of the expression. In the example, Total Cost = \$500 + \$0.05y, \$500 and $0.05y$ are the terms of the cost equation.

Factor

If two or more numbers are multiplied, each number, or the product of the numbers, is called a factor. Consider $0.05y$: 0.05, $0.05y$, and y are each called a factor.

Substitution

Substitution means assigning a number or another algebraic term in place of a variable. For example, in \$500 + \$0.05y, if we want y = 1,000, then we substitute 1,000 for y in the expression to get \$500 + \$0.05(1,000).

The examples that follow are designed to show how the information from a business problem can be stated in algebraic terms, and then produce a result that has a business application. Generally, the most difficult part of the problem is translating the written information into a concise algebraic statement.

EXAMPLE 3.1

Sharon has a window washing business and often has to provide quotations to people for doing their windows. Sharon has found that a price of \$8.00 per window will cover her costs and provide a small profit. The price of \$8.00 is for each window of a house with a basement and a main floor. If the house has two floors (main floor and upstairs) plus a basement, the average price to clean each window for the second story is \$15.00, which covers costs and makes a small profit. Sharon will not do homes with more than two floors and a basement.

Make up an equation that would allow Sharon to count the number of windows on any house and work out a price for a potential customer. Let the variable w stand for the number of windows for the basement and the first floor. Let u be variable for the number of windows on the second floor.

Solution The first thing Sharon would do is to set up an expression for the number of windows in the basement and on the main floor. This would be \$8w.

Where applicable, houses with a second floor will have a cost of \$15 per window. Using u as the term for the number of windows on the second floor would give an expression of \$15u.

Thus, if a house had a basement and a main floor and had ten windows ($w = 10$) the quotation for window cleaning would be \$8(10), or \$80. Similarly, if a house had a second floor with 15 windows on the second floor ($u = 15$), the quotation for the second floor would be \$15(15), or \$225.

Bringing the two expressions together, the **equation** Sharon could use for quoting would be:

$$\$8w + \$15u = \text{quoted price to do the windows on all jobs.}$$

In this case, the equation could be called a **formula,** since Sharon will use it repeatedly, just substituting different values for w and u.

EXAMPLE 3.2

Sharon has been asked to give a quotation for washing the windows for an old house that has two floors and a basement. The number of windows in the basement and on the main floor is 12. On the second floor there are 16 windows. Using the expression you set up in Example 3.1, \$8w + \$15u, find the price Sharon should quote for this window washing job.

Solution The formula we will use is

$$\$8w + \$15u = \text{Quotation},$$

where the values for w and u will be 12 and 16, respectively. Substituting the numbers for w and u gives:

$$\$8(12) + \$15(16) = \$336, \text{ the price she should quote using the formula.}$$

EXERCISE 3.1

A. For each of the following expressions identify the numerical coefficients.

1. $3x$

2. $(-23x)$

3. $23x + 43xy$

4. $15a + 30ax - 12xy$

5. $546xy - (-23xy)$

6. $0.25o + 0.33p + 0.5r - 1.5y$

7. $(2.3L + 0.26N + 121N)$

8. $3ay + (-5ay)$

B. Identify the literal coefficients in the following expressions.

9. $4s - 12r$

10. $-31d - 3x - 12b$

11. $t + 3s - 15s$

12. $3.54x + 8.5ya$

13. $24xd - 0.13sx$

14. $2x - 0.15xy$

15. $0.25jk - am$

16. $\frac{hl}{8}$

C. Perform the necessary addition or subtraction of the following algebraic expressions. Evaluate each expression by substitution as far as possible if $x = 1$, $y = 3$, $a = 4$, $d = 3$, $t = 7$, $s = 9$, and w, u, r, and b are not known.

17. $34x + 3x$

18. $4x - (-23x)$

19. $132x + 3xy + (-4x) + 15xy$

20. $4xa + 3ax - 12xy$

21. $14axy - (-23axy) - 56axy - (-24axy)$

22. $34w + 15y + 0.5w - 1.5y$

23. $(3y + 13x + 12u) - (-12y + 2x - 13u)$

24. $32a + 3ay + (-4a) - 5ay$

25. $4s + 5r + 5.5s - 11.5r$

26. $(-31d - 3x - 12b) - (-2d + 22b - 13x)$

27. $2t + 3s + (-5t) - 5s$

28. $2.534x + 3.340x$

29. $2.4x - (-0.13x)$

30. $0.2x + (-4.2x) + 3xy - 0.15xy$

31. $(1.4a + 1.43x) - (-1.2a - 0.25x)$

D. For the following questions, develop the required algebraic expressions and answer the questions as requested.

32. An electrician estimates that it costs \$20 per square metre to wire a new single story house with no basement. This includes all labour and material costs. If the house has a second story the cost per square metre on the second story is \$25. If the house has a basement the cost per square metre is \$5.

(a) Develop an expression to estimate the cost to wire a new house. Let M, S, and B stand for main floor, second story, and basement.

(b) A house has 200 square metres on the main floor and a basement of 200 square metres. What is the cost of wiring using the cost expression from (a)?

(c) A house has 150 square metres on the main floor, a basement of 100 square metres, and an upstairs of 175 square metres. What is the cost of wiring using the cost expression from (a)?

33. It is estimated that a land developer can get four lots per acre of raw land. Based on experience, the average development cost per lot is \$65,000, which includes all services and new roads. On average, a serviced lot sells for \$145,000. Let A stand for the number of acres, L for the number of lots from a development, and P for the price of the acreage before development.

(a) Set up an expression that will give the profit from a land development project. (*Hint*: your expression will be a profit expression, which includes costs and revenues.)

(b) A developer has purchased 40 acres for \$10,000,000. According to the expression set up in (a), what is the expected profit?

(c) A developer purchases 0.5 acres for \$100,000. What is the expected profit?

(d) A developer purchases 2.5 acres for \$400,000. What is the expected profit?

3.2 Rules of Exponents

Most often the algebraic expressions we use are more complex than the ones discussed so far. For example, we often work with expressions that have different exponents and look like:

$$4x^3y + 5x^2$$

The numbers 3 and 2, which appear "raised" above x, are called exponents of x. The term exponent is sometimes referred to as the power of a number. **A positive integer exponent or power refers to how many times a number, variable, or algebraic expression is multiplied by itself.** For example, $4 \times 4 \times 4$ can be written as 4^3. The 3 is referred to as an exponent or power and tells us how often the number is to be multiplied by itself.

In business and economics, there is a need to use **exponents or powers** in many problems where algebraic expressions are used. The use of exponents or powers is of particular importance in finance, since the formulas used for compound interest on money, mortgages, loans, and retirement plans require the use of exponents.

In algebra we often write what is called the general form of an exponent as:

x^n: where x is the variable and n is the exponent. For example, with x^3 the 3 would be the value of n in the general form. (Although x is a variable, when exponents are involved some refer to x as a base.)

In order to understand exponents and the laws that govern the use of exponents, there are some basic definitions that must be understood. These are summarized in Table 3.3.

Table 3.3: Definitions for Exponents

Definitions of x^n for x greater than 0	Example
1. If n is a positive integer: $x^n = x \times x \times x \times x \ldots$	If $x = 3$, and $n = 4$, then $3^4 = 3 \times 3 \times 3 \times 3 = 81$
2. If n is equal to zero, then $x^0 = 1$	If $x = 3$, and $n = 0$, then $3^0 = 1$
3. If n is equal to one, then $x^1 = x$	If $x = 3$, and $n = 1$, then $3^1 = 3$
4. If n is positive, then $x^{-n} = \frac{1}{x^n}$	If $x = 3$, and $n = 2$, then $3^{-2} = \frac{1}{3^2} = \frac{1}{9}$
FRACTIONAL EXPONENTS	
5. If n is a positive integer, then $x^{\frac{1}{n}} = \sqrt[n]{x}$ (called a radical). $\sqrt[n]{x}$ is also referred to as the nth root of x.	If $x = 4$ and $n = 2$, then $4^{\frac{1}{2}} = \sqrt[2]{4} = 2$
6. If m and n are positive integers, then $x^{\frac{m}{n}} = (\sqrt[n]{x}\ )^m$	If $x = 8$, $m = 2$, and $n = 3$, $8^{\frac{2}{3}} = (\sqrt[3]{8}\ )^2 = 4$
7. If m and n are positive integers, then $x^{\frac{-m}{n}} = \frac{1}{x^{\frac{m}{n}}}$	If $x = 8$, $m = 2$, and $n = 3$, $8^{\frac{-2}{3}} = \frac{1}{8^{\frac{2}{3}}} = \frac{1}{4}$

When an exponent is negative it implies division. More complicated forms of exponents are fractional exponents, such as $x^{\frac{1}{n}}$ or $x^{\frac{m}{n}}$, which means finding the nth root of a number, before the number has been raised to the mth power. These types of exponents are defined in Sections 5 to 7 in Table 3.3. The root of a number is the opposite of raising a number to an exponent. For example, $4^{1/2}$ is referred to as taking the root of a number or in this case, finding the second root of 4 (also called the square root). The concept of finding a root can best be shown by the following examples:

$8^{\frac{1}{3}} = 2$ The third root of 8. Finding the third root means finding a number that, when raised to the third power, gives 8. If we raise 2 to the third power, $2 \times 2 \times 2 = 8$.

$16^{\frac{1}{4}} = 2$ When 2 is raised to the fourth power it gives 16. Thus, 2 is called the fourth root of 16, since $2 \times 2 \times 2 \times 2 = 16$, and therefore $16^{\frac{1}{4}} = 2$.

The symbol $\sqrt[n]{x}$ is called a radical and refers to the nth root of x, where $\sqrt[n]{x} = x^{\frac{1}{n}}$ and $\sqrt[\frac{n}{m}]{x} = (x^{\frac{1}{n}})^m$, where m and n represent positive numbers.

The laws that govern how exponents are to be applied to numbers are summarized in Table 3.4. Work through the examples in the table to make sure each law is understood. The examples that follow show how each of the laws and definitions can be used.

Table 3.4: Laws of Exponents

Law	Examples: $n = 3$, $m = 4$
1. $x^n \times x^m = x^{n+m}$	$x^3 \times x^4 = x^{3+4} = x^7$
2. $(x \times y)^n = x^n y^n$	$(x \times y)^3 = x^3 y^3$
3. $(x^n)^m = x^{n \times m}$	$(x^3)^4 = x^{3 \times 4} = x^{12}$
4. $\frac{x^n}{x^m} = x^n \times x^{-m} = x^{n-m}$	$\frac{x^3}{x^4} = x^3 \times x^{-4} = x^{-1} = \frac{1}{x}$
5. $\frac{x^n}{y^n} = \left[\frac{x}{y}\right]^n$	$\frac{x^3}{y^3} = \left[\frac{x}{y}\right]^3$

The examples that follow use the definitions and laws of exponents in Tables 3.3 and 3.4. Read the examples carefully to ensure you understand the operations of exponents.

EXAMPLE 3.3

Complete the computations for the following exponent questions.

(a) $4^2 \times 4^3$
(b) $(5 \times 2)^4$
(c) $(12^2)^3$
(d) Using Law 4, show that $3^0 = 1$.

Solution (a) $4^2 \times 4^3$ This is an example of Law 1.

$$4^2 4^3 = 4^{2+3}$$
$$= 4^5$$
$$4 \times 4 \times 4 \times 4 \times 4 = 1{,}024$$

(b) $(5 \times 2)^4$ This example uses Law 2.

$$(5 \times 2)^4 = 5^4 2^4$$

or

$$(5 \times 2)^4 = 10^4$$
$$(10)^4 = 10 \times 10 \times 10 \times 10 = 10{,}000$$

(c) $(12^2)^3$ This is Law 3.

$$(12^2)^3 = 12^{2 \times 3}$$
$$= 12^6$$
$$= 2{,}985{,}984$$

(d) The final example, showing that $3^0 = 1$, requires the use of Law 4:

$$\frac{3}{3} = \frac{3^1}{3^1}$$
$$= 3^{1-1}$$
$$= 3^0$$
$$= 1$$

EXAMPLE 3.4

Complete the computations for the following exponent questions.

(a) $x^4 \times x^6$ (b) $(y \times x)^8$ (c) $(a^2)^7$

Solution (a) This is an example of Law 1. Therefore:

$$x^4 \times x^6 = x^{4+6}$$
$$= x^{10}$$

(b) $(y \times x)^8 = y^8x^8$ Applying Law 2.

(c) This example uses Law 3, and can be solved as follows:

$$(a^2)^7 = a^{2\times 7}$$
$$= a^{14}$$

EXAMPLE 3.5

Perform the following divisions.

(a) $4^3 \div 4^2$
(b) $4^4 \div 4^4$
(c) $6^3 \div 2^2$
(d) $x^4 \div x^2$
(e) $x^4 \div x^6$

Solution (a) $4^3 \div 4^2 = \frac{4^3}{4^2}$

$$= \frac{4 \times 4 \times 4}{4 \times 4}$$
$$= 4^{3-2}$$
$$= 4^1$$
$$= 4$$

(b) $4^4 \div 4^4 = \frac{4^4}{4^4}$

$$= \frac{4 \times 4 \times 4 \times 4}{4 \times 4 \times 4 \times 4}$$
$$= 4^{4-4}$$
$$= 4^0$$
$$= 1$$

(c) $6^3 \div 2^2 = \frac{6^3}{2^2}$

$$= \frac{6 \times 6 \times 6}{2 \times 2}$$
$$= \frac{216}{4}$$
$$= 54$$

(d) $x^4 \div x^2 = \dfrac{x^4}{x^2}$

$= \dfrac{x \times x \times x \times x}{x \times x}$

$= x^2$

(e) $x^4 \div x^6 = \dfrac{x^4}{x^6}$

$= \dfrac{x \times x \times x \times x}{x \times x \times x \times x \times x \times x}$

$= \dfrac{1}{x^2}$

$= x^{-2}$

In part (e), above, it should be noted that the final answer uses a negative exponent. Remember, a negative exponent implies division, which in this case is $\dfrac{1}{x^2}$, or x^{-2}.

EXAMPLE 3.6

Using Law 5, find $12^4 \div 3^4$.

Solution $12^4 \div 3^4 = \dfrac{12^4}{3^4}$

$= \dfrac{12 \times 12 \times 12 \times 12}{3 \times 3 \times 3 \times 3}$

$= \left[\dfrac{12}{3}\right]^4$

and

$\left[\dfrac{12}{3}\right]^4 = [4]^4$

$= 4 \times 4 \times 4 \times 4$

$= 256$

EXAMPLE 3.7

The following radicals can be expressed using both fractional exponents and decimal equivalent forms. Study each example.

(a) $\sqrt[4]{6^2} = 6^{\frac{2}{4}}$

$= 6^{\frac{1}{2}}$

$= 6^{0.5}$

(b) $\sqrt[4]{x^2} = x^{\frac{2}{4}}$

$= x^{\frac{1}{2}}$

$= x^{0.5}$

(c) $\sqrt[8]{y^5} = y^{\frac{5}{8}}$

$= y^{0.625}$

(d) $\sqrt[3]{3^2} = 3^{\frac{2}{3}}$

$= 3^{0.66667}$ Rounded to 5 places.

(e) $\dfrac{1}{\sqrt[3]{3^2}} = \dfrac{1}{3^{\frac{2}{3}}}$

$= 3^{-0.66667}$

(f) $\dfrac{1}{\sqrt[3]{x^2}} = \dfrac{1}{x^{\frac{2}{3}}}$

$= x^{-\frac{2}{3}}$

$= x^{-0.66667}$

In the next example, the results have been found by using the power or exponent function on an electronic calculator. All numbers have been rounded to three decimal places.

EXAMPLE 3.8

Using an electronic calculator, confirm the following answers.

(a) $\sqrt[4]{8^3} = 8^{\frac{3}{4}}$

$= 8^{0.75}$

$= 4.757$

(b) $\sqrt[4]{7^2} = 7^{\frac{1}{2}}$

$= 7^{0.5}$

$= 2.646$

(c) $\sqrt[8]{12^5} = 12^{\frac{5}{8}}$

$= 12^{0.625}$

$= 4.726$

(d) $\sqrt[3]{9^2} = 9^{\frac{2}{3}}$

$= 9^{0.667}$

$= 4.330$ If $\frac{2}{3}$ is used on the calculator, the answer is 4.327.

(e) $\dfrac{1}{\sqrt[3]{8^2}} = \dfrac{1}{8^{\frac{2}{3}}}$

$= 8^{-0.667}$

$= 0.25$

(f) $\dfrac{1}{\sqrt[3]{16^2}} = \dfrac{1}{16^{\frac{2}{3}}}$

$= 16^{-0.667}$

$= 0.157$

The root of an expression using the radical sign, $\sqrt{\ }$, is understood to be a positive root. If a negative root is required, then the negative sign would precede the $\sqrt{\ }$ term, e.g., $-\sqrt{\ }$).

EXERCISE 3.2

A. Where possible, write the following expressions in their simplest form, for example, $2^2 \times 2^2 = 2^4$. Then evaluate the expression using an electronic calculator where appropriate. Answers in the text are based on rounding exponents to three decimal places.

1. $3^3 \times 3^2$ **2.** $x^0 x^n$ **3.** $4^2 \times 5^2$

4. $(8^2 \times 8)^0$ **5.** $7^0 \times 2^5$ **6.** $(x^2)^3$

7. $(1.4)^1(1.8)^0$ **8.** $x^3y^2x^2$ **9.** x^2x^3

10. $(2^3)^2$ **11.** $(r^2r)^2$ **12.** $x^2y^2b^2$

13. $(1 + 0.08)^2$ **14.** $(1 + 0.01)^{12} - 1$ **15.** $(1 + 0.005)^4$

16. $\dfrac{(1 + 0.0125)^3 - 1}{0.0125}$ **17.** $(x^2\, y^3)x$ **18.** $\dfrac{(1 + 0.15)^{24} - 1}{0.15}$

19. $(y^2y^3y^2)^2$ **20.** x^2y^0

B. Express the following radicals as fractional exponents and then evaluate the expression using an electronic calculator. Answers are based on rounding to three decimal places.

21. $\sqrt[3]{12}$ **22.** $\sqrt{4}$ **23.** $(\sqrt[4]{5^2}\,)^2$

24. $\sqrt[3]{324^5}$ **25.** $\sqrt[2]{1.5}$ **26.** $\sqrt[3]{23^2}$

C. Express the following radicals as decimal equivalents and evaluate, where possible, using an electronic calculator.

27. $\sqrt[2]{4^3}$ **28.** $\sqrt[8]{x^5}$ **29.** $\sqrt[5]{a^2}$

30. $\sqrt[6]{4^4}$ **31.** $\dfrac{1}{\sqrt[2]{2^4}}$ **32.** $\dfrac{3}{\sqrt[4]{y^3}}$

3.3 Types of Algebraic Expressions

Algebraic expressions can be classified as either **monomials** or **polynomials**. **Monomials** are expressions that have only one term. An example of a monomial is:

Monomial $4x$ or $4z$

Polynomials are expressions that have two or more terms in the expression, for example:

Polynomials A: $3x + 5$
B: $3xy + 3x + 4$

The name **binomial** means the expression has two terms — e.g., A above. **Trinomial**, B above, refers to an expression with three terms. It is common to use the term polynomial to describe expressions that have two or more terms.

EXAMPLE 3.9

Identify whether each of the following is a monomial or a polynomial. If there are any polynomials, where appropriate, identify whether the expression is a binomial or trinomial.

(a) $5x$
(b) $4x - 6y + 7$
(c) $12c + 0.5y$
(d) $13a + 14c + (56t + 23)$

Solution

(a) $5x$ ← This is a monomial since there is only one term.

(b) $4x - 6y + 7$ ← This is a polynomial, and, since it has three terms, it is a trinomial.

(c) $12c + 0.5y$ ← This is a polynomial, and, because there are only two terms, it is a binomial.

(d) $13a + 14c + 56t + 23$ ← This expression is a polynomial. Because there are four different terms, it is neither a trinomial nor a binomial.

EXERCISE 3.3

For each of the following, identify whether the expression is a polynomial or monomial. Also, if the expression is a polynomial, specify whether the term is a binomial or trinomial.

1. $34x + 3x$
2. $-12r$
3. $-22p - 5x$
4. $x + 2y - 15y$
5. $3.5x + 8.5y + 10r$
6. $15r - 0.13$
7. $155xy$
8. $0.78fg - 4$
9. $\frac{ax}{2}$

3.4 Algebraic Operations

A. Addition and Subtraction of Monomials and Polynomials

(i) Monomials: Addition and Subtraction

In Table 3.1 we demonstrated how the arithmetic operations could be applied to algebraic expressions. Now we need to understand how these operations apply to more complex expressions.

When adding or subtracting algebraic expressions, the operation can only be done if the literal terms are the same, that is, if they have the same letters with the same exponents. This is called adding and subtracting **like terms**. The procedure of finding like and unlike terms is called **collecting terms**. Thus, the sum or difference will be done by adding or subtracting the numerical coefficients after the terms have been collected. The following examples show the use of like terms:

EXAMPLE 3.10

Add the following monomials: $6xy$, $3xy$, and xy.

Solution Each term has the same literal terms (xy). Therefore, the sum of these three terms is simply the sum of their numerical coefficients. Namely:

$$6 + 3 + 1 = 10. \text{ Therefore: } 6xy + 3xy + xy = 10xy$$

The addition could have been written as:

$$(6 + 3 + 1)xy = 10xy$$ Remember, the term xy has a coefficient 1.

If any of the terms have unlike terms, for example, $6y$ and $3x$, these terms cannot be combined since they are unlike terms.

EXAMPLE 3.11

Add the following monomials: $2bx^2$, $(-3bx^2)$, $5x$, and $(-6x)$.

Solution Collecting like terms and adding gives:

$$2bx^2 + (-3bx^2) + 5x + (-6x) = -bx^2 - x$$

The procedure of subtraction of monomials requires that the numerical coefficients of the like terms be subtracted.

EXAMPLE 3.12

Subtract the following monomials: $15bx$ from $26bx$.

Solution $26bx - 15bx = (26 - 15)bx$

$26bx - 15bx = 11bx$

EXAMPLE 3.13

Subtract the following monomials: $(-3ax^2)$ from $15ax^2$.

Solution

$$15ax^2 - (-3ax^2) = ax^2 (15 + 3)$$
$$= 18ax^2$$

Note sign change from $-(-)$ to $+$.

(ii) Polynomials: Addition and Subtraction

When polynomials are added together, the basic principle of adding and subtracting like terms is applied. In doing this we group the like terms and do the addition or subtraction and then bring the terms together.

EXAMPLE 3.14

Add the following polynomials:
$(12xy + 2ax + 8)$ and $(15xy + ax + 5)$.

Solution Set the expression up as an addition, with columns of like terms:

$$\begin{array}{r} 12xy + 2ax + 8 \\ \underline{15xy + ax + 5} \\ 27xy + 3ax + 13 \end{array}$$

$\longleftarrow$ Final sum of the polynomials.

EXAMPLE 3.15

Subtract the following polynomials:

$(2y^2 - 4a + 3c)$, from $(5y^2 -2a - 6c)$.

Solution Set the expression up as a subtraction with columns of like terms:

$$\begin{array}{r} 5y^2 - 2a - 6c \\ \underline{-(2y^2 - 4a + 3c)} \\ 3y^2 + 2a - 9c \end{array}$$

Change the signs of the terms inside the brackets.

EXERCISE 3.4

Perform the necessary addition/subtraction as required for the following algebraic terms.

1. $6x + (-3x)$
2. $12xy - (-xy)$
3. $(3x + 2x - 3) + (x + 15)$
4. $(3t + 7t) - (t + 2t)$
5. $40x - 6x$
6. $(4ay + 2x + 3) - (3ay + 4x)$
7. $(-45xy) - (5xy)$
8. $(13s + 4g - 2a) + (g + s + a)$
9. $(3xy + 5b - 7s) + (5b - 7s)$
10. $(3c + 5m) - (7c - 8m + 4)$
11. $16x - (-4x) + (2x)$
12. $24r + 3r - (-r)$
13. $(2ax + 4ax) - (-3ax + 5ax)$
14. $2x - (3x + 6x - x)$
15. $(13x + 3x) - (2x - 3x)$
16. $(4x + 3y - 3d) - (3x + 6y)$
17. $(-12cs) - 9cs$
18. $4x - (3a + 5a - x)$
19. $34x + (-15x) + a$
20. $12n - 3mn - (n + mn)$

B. Multiplication and Division of Monomials and Polynomials

(i) Multiplication: Monomials and Polynomials

Multiplication of monomials and polynomials is undertaken by multiplying the numerical coefficients and multiplying the literal coefficients. If there are similar literal coefficients in both the monomial and polynomial, we can use exponents to summarize these like terms. The use of exponents is very common in the multiplication and addition of polynomials.

EXAMPLE 3.16

Multiply the two monomials $3xy$ and $4a$.

Solution

$$\begin{aligned} (3xy)(4a) &= (3)(4)(xya) \\ &= 12xya \end{aligned}$$

EXAMPLE 3.17

Using the laws of exponents in Table 3.4, multiply the four monomials $4a$, $4ax$, $6a^2$, and $2x^2$.

Solution

$$\begin{aligned}(4a)(4ax)(6a^2)(2x^2) &= (4 \times 4 \times 6 \times 2)(a^{1+1+2})(x^{1+2}) \\ &= 192a^4x^3\end{aligned}$$

Multiplying a polynomial by a monomial requires that each term of the polynomial be multiplied by the monomial. The final answer for the multiplication will be the sum of the separate products for each term. Read Example 3.18, which demonstrates this point.

EXAMPLE 3.18

Using the laws of exponents in Table 3.4, multiply $(3x + 2y - 3a)$ by $3x$.

Solution

$$\begin{aligned}(3x + 2y - 3a)(3x) &= (3x3x + 3x2y - 3x3a) \\ &= 9x^{1+1} + 6xy - 9xa \\ &= 9x^2 + 6xy - 9xa\end{aligned}$$

Sometimes the problem is more complex and may involve the multiplication of several algebraic expressions involving terms with different exponents. When we have many terms, each must be handled separately and then brought together for a solution. The procedure used when we have multiple terms is shown in Examples 3.19 and 3.20.

EXAMPLE 3.19

Multiply $(4x^2a^3 + 6x^2y)$ by $5x$.

Solution

STEP 1

$$\begin{aligned}(4x^2a^3 + 6x^2y)(5x) &= (5x4x^2a^3 + 5x6x^2y) \\ &= 20x^{2+1}a^3 + 30x^{2+1}y \\ &= 20a^3x^3 + 30x^3y\end{aligned}$$

It is important to note that we generally express the answer to a problem, such as Example 3.19, in a more simplified form using the process of factoring. Factoring will be reviewed a little later in this chapter.

The last type of multiplication for algebraic expressions is the multiplication of a polynomial by a polynomial. The method used to perform the operation requires the multiplication of **each term of one polynomial by each term of the other polynomial**. Then, the separate multiplications are brought together by addition.

EXAMPLE 3.20

Multiply the two polynomials $(3x^2 + 4xy)$ and $(5x + 3y^4)$.

Solution

STEP 1	$(3x^2 + 4xy)(5x) = 15x^3 + 20x^2y$	Multiply each term of the first polynomial by the first term of the second polynomial.
STEP 2	$(3x^2 + 4xy)(3y^4) = 9x^2y^4 + 12xy^5$	Multiply each term of the first polynomial by the second term of the second polynomial.
STEP 3	$15x^3 + 20x^2y + 9x^2y^4 + 12xy^5$	Bring the terms together by addition.

The order in which the multiplication of terms is done is not critical. Another approach that could have been used is to take the first and second terms and multiply these by the second expression; the resulting product is the same.

(ii) Division: Monomials and Polynomials

When we divide algebraic expressions, the process is to divide the numerical and literal coefficients to find the quotient.

EXAMPLE 3.21

Divide $40x$ by $2x$.

Solution

$$\frac{40x}{2x} = \frac{20\cancel{x}}{\cancel{x}}$$

$$= 20$$

If there had been two different variables, the division could have been undertaken on only the numerical coefficients. Example 3.22 demonstrates this point.

EXAMPLE 3.22

Divide $40x$ by $5y$.

Solution $\frac{40x}{5y} = \frac{8x}{y}$

The division of a monomial by a monomial can be dealt with by using Law 4 of exponents.

EXAMPLE 3.23

Perform the division of $65x^4 \div 13x$.

Solution

$$\begin{aligned} 65x^4 \div 13x &= \frac{65x^4}{13x} \\ &= \frac{5x^4}{x} \\ &= (5x^4)(x^{-1}) \\ &= 5x^{4-1} \\ &= 5x^3 \end{aligned}$$

Dividing a polynomial by a monomial is a similar type of problem, but here <u>each</u> term of the polynomial must be divided by the monomial. The next example shows two possibilities. In each case, note how the process requires each term of the polynomial to be handled separately:

EXAMPLE 3.24

Perform a division on each of the following:

(a) Divide $6ax^4 + 9a^2x^6$ by $3ax$.
(b) Divide $12a^3x^2 - 16a^2x^3$ by $4a^2x$.

Solution (a) $6ax^4 + 9a^2x^6 \div 3ax$

$$\frac{(6ax^4 + 9a^2x^6)}{3ax} = \frac{6ax^4}{3ax} + \frac{9a^2x^6}{3ax}$$

Performing a division on each term of the expression is done as follows:

$$\begin{aligned} \frac{6ax^4}{3ax} &= \left(\frac{6}{3}\right)\left(\frac{a}{a}\right)\left(\frac{x^4}{x}\right) \\ &= 2x^3 \end{aligned}$$

First term

$$\frac{9a^2x^6}{3ax} = \left(\frac{9}{3}\right)\left(\frac{a^2}{a}\right)\left(\frac{x^6}{x}\right)$$

$$= 3ax^5 \qquad \text{Second term}$$

Bringing the two terms together, the final answer to the division is:

$2x^3 + 3ax^5$

(b) $(12a^3x^2 - 16a^2x^3) \div 4a^2x$

$$= \frac{12a^3x^2}{4a^2x} - \frac{16a^2x^3}{4a^2x}$$

Now, performing the division on each term we have:

$$\frac{12a^3x^2}{4a^2x} = \left(\frac{12}{4}\right)\left(\frac{a^3}{a^2}\right)\left(\frac{x^2}{x}\right)$$

$$= 3ax \qquad \text{First term}$$

$$\frac{-16a^2x^3}{4a^2x} = \left(\frac{-16}{4}\right)\left(\frac{a^2}{a^2}\right)\left(\frac{x^3}{x}\right)$$

$$= -4x^2 \qquad \text{Second term}$$

Bringing the terms together, the quotient of the division is:

$3ax - 4x^2$

Another division that may arise is the division of a polynomial by a polynomial. This is a slightly more difficult division, but uses the same principle of dividing each term of one polynomial by the other polynomial. Since this type of division is not required for the later topics for the mathematics of finance, it will not be discussed in this book.

EXERCISE 3.5

Perform the necessary multiplication/division as required for the following algebraic expressions.

1. $4x(-3x)$

2. $40xy(-xy)$

3. $(3a + 4x - 20x)(x + 4)$

4. $\frac{(3t + 7t)}{(t)}$

5. $\frac{36x}{6x}$

6. $(3xy + 4x + 6y)(8xy + 4x)$

7. $\dfrac{(-90xy + 15x^2y^{-1})}{(5xy)}$

8. $\dfrac{(24g^4s + 4gs)}{(4g^{-3}s^2)}$

9. $(15vx - 3xv^2)(vx + v^2)$

10. $(0.5c^2z)(4z^{-3})(15c^{-3}z)$

11. $(-16x)(-4x)$

12. $(24r)(3r)$

13. $(2ax + 4ax)(-3ax)$

14. $\dfrac{(4x + 8x - 4x)}{2x}$

15. $\dfrac{x^2y^2(3x)}{(xy)}$

16. $(4x^4 + 3y^2)(3y^2 - 3x)$

17. $\dfrac{(-18x^4y^2)}{2x^{-2}y}$

18. $\dfrac{(4x)\,(5a^3)}{(3a^2xy)}$

19. $34x^2(-15x)12ax$

20. $(6x^5 - 4s^2)(6bs - 7s^{-2})$

3.5 Factoring of Algebraic Expressions

Factoring of expressions is a process designed to make the computations with algebraic expressions more manageable and less complex. The process of factoring requires one to look for what is called a **common factor** to each term of the expression.

A. Finding a Monomial Factor

Factoring an expression requires one to scan an expression and look for a factor that is common to each term.

For example, $xy + xz$ can be rewritten using the process of factoring by identifying the common factor, in this case x. The key to factoring is the use of brackets: (), [], and {}, discussed in Chapter 1. Thus, $xy + xz$ can be written as:

$$xy + xz = x(y + z)$$

We can see by the expression that we have a multiplication of a polynomial by a monomial as a result of factoring x from each term of the expression. The method by which the factor $(y + z)$ is obtained is to divide $xy + xz$ by x. This would yield $(y + z)$.

The expression $xy + xz$ is called the expanded form of the factored form, $x(y + z)$.

Factoring can be applied to both numerical and literal factors. Consider the following examples, which take single polynomial expressions and turn the factored form of the expression into a product of a more simple polynomial and monomial:

EXAMPLE 3.25

Factor $3x + 9y$.

Solution $3x + 9y = 3(x + 3y)$

If the final expression of Example 3.25, $3(x + 3y)$, is examined, it shows that if the terms inside the brackets are multiplied by 3, the original expression will be obtained, i.e., $3x + 9y$. In the next example, study how the division is made to arrive at the factored expression.

EXAMPLE 3.26

Factor the following.

(a) $3x + 4x^2$
(b) $2x^2 + 3x^2 + 4x^3y^2$
(c) $P + Prt$
(d) $A + 500A^2$

Solution (a) Find the common term. In this example it is x. Factoring out the x from both expressions by dividing the original expression by x yields:

$$3x + 4x^2 = x(3 + 4x)$$

A check can be made by multiplying the terms inside the brackets by x to arrive at the original expression.

(b) In this problem, there are three terms that have x^2, so factoring out this common term yields:

$$\begin{aligned} 2x^2 + 3x^2 + 4x^3y^2 &= x^2(2 + 3 + 4xy^2) \\ &= x^2(5 + 4xy^2) \end{aligned}$$

A check can be made by multiplying the terms inside the brackets by x^2 to arrive at the original expression.

(c) Factoring out the common term, P, gives:

$$P + Prt = P(1 + rt)$$

(d) Factoring the common term, A, yields:

$$A + 500A^2 = A(1 + 500A)$$

B. Binomial Factors

Often the terms that are factored are more complex than those considered so far. The most common example occurs when there are a series of algebraic terms, and the term that is factored is a binomial, not simply a monomial. To illustrate this point, consider the following example:

$$(1 + x) + (1 + x)^2 + (1 + x)^3 + (1 + x)^4$$

Fortunately, the logic involved in factoring the above expression is the same used in the earlier examples. What must be found is a term or terms common to each term or collection of terms in the expression.

In this example, the common term is $(1 + x)$, which is a binomial. Factoring this term from the expression gives:

$$(1 + x)[1 + (1 + x) + (1 + x)^2 + (1 + x)^3]$$

It is important to note the use of the [] besides the () brackets. The use of brackets is of particular importance in this type of factoring. Make sure you understand how they have been used to separate the expressions.

EXAMPLE 3.27

Factor $6yz - 2xz + 12ay - 4ax$.

Solution The easiest way is to factor the obvious terms:

$6yz - 2xz + 12ay - 4ax = 2z(3y - x) + 4a(3y - x)$

Looking to see if there are any other factors, it can be seen that $(3y -x)$ is common to both terms of the factored expression. Factoring this expression gives:

$$2z(3y -x) + 4a(3y -x) = (2z + 4a)(3y -x)$$

EXERCISE 3.6

Factor the following expressions.

1. $4x + 16$
2. $3x^2 - x$
3. $36 + 6x^2$
4. $15x + 3x^2 - 45$
5. $3y^3 + y^2 + y - y^3$
6. $3xy - 4y + 3y^2$
7. $P + Prt$
8. $(1 + a)^2 + 3(1 + a)^3 - 4(1 + a)^4$
9. $S - Sdt$
10. $ay + ay^2 + a^2y$
11. $12x^3 - 4x$
12. $3ay + 4ax - 8cx - 2cy$
13. $400sw - 100sx - sw + 12wx$
14. $3x^2 + 4x + 1$

3.6 Finding a Solution to an Algebraic Equation

The term equation was used earlier when the concept of an algebraic expression was introduced. In earlier examples, the procedures for operations on algebraic expressions were reviewed. In this section, you will be shown how to formulate an algebraic expression and then solve the expression for an unknown term.

Before proceeding, the concept of an equation must be clearly understood. From our earlier discussion, remember that an equation is a statement of equality between two algebraic expressions or between an algebraic expression and a number. Two examples are:

$$3x + 5x = x + 4 \quad \text{Two algebraic expressions.}$$
$$3x + 5x = 4 \quad \text{Algebraic expression and a number.}$$

Our objective is to find a method to determine a numerical value for x that allows the equality sign to be satisfied. This value of x is called **the solution to the equation**. The next section focuses on the methods one can use to find a value for an unknown variable, and consequently a solution to the equation.

A. Solving Equations with One Variable

Solving equations with only one variable means finding a numerical value for the variable that will satisfy the equality sign of the equation. For example:

$$3x + 4 = 5x$$

If $x = 2$, the equation is satisfied since the left and right sides are 10. That is:

$$3(2) + 4 = 5(2)$$

and:

$$10 = 10$$

Although the expression $3x + 4 = 5x$ has x on both sides of the equation, it still is a one-variable equation. If an equation has an x and y term then it is referred to as a two-variable equation (e.g., $3x + 4y = 17$). **If all the variables have an exponent of 1, the equation is said to be a linear equation.**

The terms that must be understood in working with equations are:

Members of the Equation

The expressions on each side of the equal sign (=) are called members of the equation. Often people refer to the members as the right and left hand sides of the equation. For instance,

$$3x + 18 = 6x - 9$$

$3x + 18$ is the left member, or left side, of the equation.
$6x - 9$ is the right member, or right side, of the equation.

Solving the Equation

Solving an equation means finding a number that, when used in place of the variable, satisfies the equation. In the example, $3x + 18 = 6x - 9$, the solution would be $x = 9$. What was done to find the solution was to replace x with numbers until we found a number for x that made both sides of the equation equal. In our case:

$$3(9) + 18 = 45 \text{ and } 6(9) - 9 = 45$$

We can say that a solution of $x = 9$ satisfies the equation. The technical term for 9 is the **root of the equation.**

(i) Solving Equations Using Addition and Subtraction Rules

When finding a solution to a linear equation, the objective is to find a numerical value for the variable that satisfies the equation. To illustrate this point, a solution to $x - 7 = 5$ can be found by adding 7 to each side of the equation. If this is done, we would have:

$$x - 7 + 7 = 5 + 7, \text{ or } x = 12$$

The 7 was selected because when it is added to the left side of the equation it has the effect of eliminating the -7. However, to satisfy the equality sign the addition of 7 must occur to both sides of the equation. **This principle — adding the same term to both sides of the equation — is fundamental and must be clearly understood.** Consider the following example:

EXAMPLE 3.28

Find the solution to the following equations using the addition principle.

(a) $x - 9 = 15$

(b) $3x - 5 = 2x + 20$

(c) $4 + x = 16$

Solution (a) $x - 9 = 15$

To find a value for x, isolate x on the left side of the equation. Adding 9 to the left hand side leaves only x. To maintain the balance of the equal sign, also add 9 to the right hand side. This would give:

$$x - 9 + 9 = 15 + 9$$
$$x - \not{9} + \not{9} = 15 + 9$$
$$x + 0 = 24$$

Therefore, $x = 24$ is the value of x that satisfies the equation.

(b) $3x - 5 = 2x + 20$

This expression requires two additions to be done to isolate x. First, add 5 to both sides of the equation:

$$3x - 5 + 5 = 2x + 20 + 5$$

$$3x = 2x + 25$$

Now, isolate x by adding $-2x$ to both sides of the equation. *Note*: this operation involves adding a negative number to both sides of the equation.

$$3x + (-2x) = 2x + 25 + (-2x)$$

$$x = 25$$

(c) $4 + x = 16$

As with part (b), add (–4) to both sides of the equation, giving us:

$$4 + (-4) + x = 16 + (-4)$$

$$x = 12$$

The use of subtraction is a procedure similar to the addition process. In fact, for parts (b) and (c) of Example 3.6 we could have simply subtracted $2x$ and 4 from both sides of the equation, instead of adding $(-2x)$ and (–4), since subtraction and adding a negative number to a positive number are equivalent operations.

(ii) Solving Equations Using Multiplication and Division

Often we find that algebraic expressions cannot be solved with only the addition or subtraction of terms. Many solutions to algebraic expressions require multiplication and division, as well as addition and subtraction. Consider the following expression:

$$3x = 15$$

It is obvious that the value of x must be 5 if the equality is to be satisfied. However, to find the solution for x we can either multiply both sides of the equation by $\frac{1}{3}$ or divide each side by 3, since these are equivalent operations. If we multiply each side by $\frac{1}{3}$ we have:

$$\left(\frac{1}{3}\right)\left(3x\right) = \left(\frac{1}{3}\right)\left(15\right)$$

This permits us to cancel the 3's.

$$\left(\frac{1}{\cancel{3}}\right)\left(\cancel{3}x\right) = \frac{15}{3}$$

$$x = 5$$

The principle of using multiplication and division is most helpful in more complicated linear equations. An example of a more complicated situation is:

$$3(x + 4) + 2x = 4(x + 6) - 5x$$

In this type of problem the most direct way to solve for x is to treat each part of the expression separately: do the indicated operation, and then solve for x. For this example, the steps one might take are:

STEP 1 Left side:

$$3(x + 4) + 2x = 3x + 12 + 2x$$

Eliminate the brackets on both sides of the equation by performing the necessary operations.

Right side:

$$4(x + 6) - 5x = 4x + 24 - 5x$$

STEP 2

$$3x + 12 + 2x = 4x + 24 - 5x$$

Place the completed operations from Step 1 into the original equation.

STEP 3

$$5x + 12 = 24 - x$$

Reduce the number of terms by adding the similar terms giving $5x + 12$ on the left hand side of the expression, and $24 - x$ on the right hand side.

STEP 4

$$5x + 12 - 12 + x = 24 - 12 - x + x$$

Subtract 12 from both sides of the equation, and add x to both sides, giving us:

$$6x = 12$$

STEP 5

$$\frac{6x}{6} = \frac{12}{6}$$

The final step is to divide each side by 6, which will give us our solution for equation.

$$x = 2$$

After we have found a solution to an equation, we often check the solution by substituting the solution value of the variable back into the original equation. This assures us that our solution does satisfy the equation. In the last example, the checking would be done by substituting $x = 2$ into the original equation, that is:

$$3(x + 4) + 2x = 4(x + 6) - 5x$$

Now substituting 2 for each x gives:

$$\begin{aligned} 3(2+4)+2(2) &= 4(2+6)-5(2) \\ 3(6)+2(2) &= 4(8)-5(2) \\ 18+4 &= 32-10 \\ 22 &= 22 \end{aligned}$$

Thus, the solution $x = 2$ is correct and satisfies the equation.

EXAMPLE 3.29

Find a solution for the following equations and check the answer.

(a) $4x + 3(x + 3) = 15 + 2(x + 4)$
(b) $3x - 7(0.5x + 13) = -37 + 7(x - 2x)$
(c) $3x + 2x + x - 15 = 27$

Solution (a) $4x + 3(x + 3) = 15 + 2(x + 4)$

STEP 1 Left side: $4x + 3(x + 3) = 4x + 3x + 9$

Remove the brackets on both sides of the equation by performing the necessary operations.

Right side: $15 + 2(x + 4) = 15 + 2x + 8$

STEP 2 $4x + 3x + 9 = 15 + 2x + 8$

Set the right hand side equal to the left hand side.

STEP 3 $7x + 9 = 2x + 23$

Reduce the number of terms by adding the similar terms.

STEP 4 $7x + 9 - 9 - 2x = 2x + 23 - 9 - 2x$

Subtract 9 and $2x$ from both sides of the equation, giving us:

$5x = 14$

STEP 5 $\dfrac{5x}{5} = \dfrac{14}{5}$

The final step is to divide each side by 5, which will give us our solution for x.

$$x = \frac{14}{5}$$

$$= 2.8$$

STEP 6

$$4(2.8) + 3(2.8 + 3) = 15 + 2(2.8 + 4)$$

Checking the answer by substituting $x = 2.8$ into the original expression:

$$4(2.8) + 3(5.8) = 15 + 2(6.8)$$

$$11.2 + 17.4 = 15 + 13.6$$

$$28.6 = 28.6$$

(b) $$3x - 7(0.5x + 13) = -37 + 7(x - 2x)$$

$$3x - 3.5x - 91 = -37 + 7x - 14x$$

Working out the terms with brackets and rewriting the equation gives:

$$-0.5x - 91 = -37 - 7x$$

$$-0.5x + 7x = -37 + 91$$

Bringing the terms together we add 91 and $7x$ to both sides, which gives:

$$6.5x = 54$$

Dividing both sides by 6.5:

$$x = \frac{54}{6.5}$$

$$x = 8.30769$$

$$3x - 7(0.5x + 13) = -37 + 7(x -2x)$$

Checking the solution, remove the brackets by multiplying.

$$-0.5x - 91 = -37 - 7x$$

After combining terms, we substitute 8.30769 for x.

$$-0.5(8.30769) - 91 = -37 - 7(8.30769)$$

$$-95.153846 = -95.153846$$

The solution works!

(c) $$3x + 2x + x - 15 = 27$$

$$6x - 15 = 27$$

Adding the similar terms.

$$6x = 42$$

Adding 15 to each side of the expression.

$$\frac{6x}{6} = \frac{42}{6}$$

Dividing each side of the expression by 6.

$$x = 7$$

$x = 7$ is the solution for x.

$$3(7) + 2(7) + 7 - 15 = 27$$

Checking the solution by substituting 7 for x.

$$27 = 27$$

Our solution for x is verified.

(iii) The Solution of an Equation with Two Variables

Equations also may involve a solution for a variable that has as its solution an unknown variable. For example:

$$4x + 3y = 10$$

$$4x + 3y - 3y = 10 - 3y$$

To solve for x, we would first subtract $3y$ from each side of the expression.

$$4x = 10 - 3y$$

$$x = \frac{10 - 3y}{4}$$

Solving for x, we divide each side of the equation by 4.

What makes the difference in this solution is that there is not a unique solution for x, at least in a numerical sense, since the value of x will change for different values substituted for y.

Finding a solution for a two-variable equation is a common application in business and should be well understood. Consider Example 3.30, which shows the solution of equations with more than one variable.

EXAMPLE 3.30

Solve the following equations for x.

(a) $2x - y = 15$

(b) $0.5x - 2y + s = 10$

(c) $x(1 + i) = 3s$

Solution (a)

$$2x - y = 15$$

Add y to each side of the equation.

$$2x - y + y = 15 + y$$

$$2x = 15 + y$$

Dividing each side by 2 to find a solution for x yields:

$$x = \frac{15 + y}{2}$$

(b) $$0.5x - 2y + s = 10$$

In this expression there are three variables. The procedure for finding x is the same as in part (a), that is, isolate x on one side of the equation. To do this, add $2y$ and subtract s from both sides of the equation which gives:

$$0.5 - 2y + s + 2y - s = 10 + 2y - s$$

$$0.5x = 10 + 2y - s$$

$$x = \frac{10 + 2y - s}{0.5}$$

Dividing each term by 0.5.

$$x = \frac{10}{0.5} + \frac{2y}{0.5} - \frac{s}{0.5}$$

$$x = 20 + 4y - 2s$$

Solving for x.

(c) $$x(1 + i) = 3s$$

$$\frac{x(1 + i)}{(1 + i)} = \frac{3s}{(1 + i)}$$

Dividing each side of the equation by $(1 + i)$ yields the solution for x as:

$$x = \frac{3s}{(1 + i)}$$

EXERCISE 3.7

A. For each of the following expressions, find a solution for the unknown variable. Use an electronic calculator to assist you where necessary.

1. $2t - 14 = 0$

2. $24x + 12 = 44$

3. $5x - 15 = 10$

4. $35x + 10 = 90 + 15x$

5. $x(1.01) = 500$

6. $x = 10{,}000\left[\frac{1 - (1 + 0.01)}{0.01}\right]$

7. $3x + 15 = 2x + 45$

8. $23r - 17 = 3r + 77$

B. For each of the following expressions find a solution for x.

9. $3x + 4r = 10$

10. $x(1 + it) = P$

11. $x(1 + i) + x(1 + i) + x(1 + i) = 500$

12. $2t + 14x = 100$

13. $24x + 12y = 44y$

14. $25y - 15 = 10x$

15. $15y + 15 = 15y + 15x$

16. $x(1.10) = 500y$

17. $x - 20{,}000 = \dfrac{[1 + (1 + 0.11)]}{0.11}$

18. $13y + 10x = 2x + 45y$

B. Algebraic Equations Involving Fractions and Decimals

Algebraic expressions that have fractional or decimal equivalent numerical coefficients require us to use the rules of fractions or the rules of decimal equivalents discussed in Chapter 1.

At one time, it was the practice to look for common denominators in an algebraic expression with fractions and then solve the equation for the unknown variable. However, this is not the most common method any more — at least in a business context. With the wide use of the electronic calculator and the computer, expressions with fractions generally have the fractions converted to decimal equivalents. After the conversion, the solution to the algebraic expression is found — this is particularly true in business. The only problem is that sometimes there may be a difference in the solution for a variable, depending upon whether one uses fractions or decimal equivalents in one's method of solution.

Example 3.31 shows a situation where a difference occurs in the solution because of rounding of the number of decimal places. As will be seen in Example 3.31, the two methods — one using fractions and one using decimal equivalents — produce solutions that are marginally different because of the rounding error. This rounding error sometimes occurs with decimal equivalents.

EXAMPLE 3.31

Find the solution to $\frac{1}{6}x - 10 = 5$

Solution 1 Using fractions.

$$6\left[\frac{1}{6}x\right] - 6(10) = 6(5)$$

Multiplying both sides of the equation by 6, the lowest common denominator.

$$x - 60 = 30$$

Add 60 to both sides to find x.

$$x = 90$$

Solution 2 Using decimals.

Rewrite the equation using decimal equivalents

$$0.1667x - 10 = 5$$

Rewrite the equation using decimal equivalents in place of the fraction $\frac{1}{6}$.

$$0.1667x = 15$$

Isolate x by adding 10 to each side of the equation.

$$\frac{0.1667x}{0.1667} = \frac{15}{0.1667}$$

Divide each side by 0.1667.

$$x = 89.9820$$

As shown in Example 3.31, the solution obtained when using fractions produced a result that was marginally different from the solution with the decimal equivalents. If the number of decimal places had been carried further, the answers would have been the same. Sometimes the solution for the variable will be the same regardless of the method used. Example 3.32 demonstrates such an example:

EXAMPLE 3.32

Find a solution for x in the following equation using the rules of fractions and then solve the problem using decimal equivalents in place of the fractions.

$$\frac{1}{3}x + 15 = -\frac{2}{3}x + 45$$

Solution 1 Using fractions.

$$\frac{1}{3}x + 15 = -\frac{2}{3}x + 45$$

$$3\left[\frac{1}{3}x\right] + 3(15) = 3\left[-\frac{2}{3}x\right] + 3(45)$$

First, multiply both sides by the lowest common denominator, 3. Note that each term is multiplied by 3.

$$x + 45 = -2x + 135$$

Add $2x$ and subtract -45 from both sides of the equation.

$$3x = 90$$

$$x = 30$$

Solution 2 Using decimal equivalents.

$$\frac{1}{3}x + 15 = -\frac{2}{3}x + 45$$ Convert the fractional coefficients to decimal equivalents.

$$0.3333x + 15 = -0.6667x + 45$$ Add $0.6667x$ and subtract 15 from both sides of the equation; then add similar terms.

$$0.3333x + 15 + 0.6667x - 15 = -0.6667x + 45 + 0.6667x - 15$$

$$x = 30$$

The question that may come to mind is, which method should be used? The answer is, it depends on the problem. Very complex expressions with fractions are more easily solved for the variable using decimal equivalents with the assistance of an electronic calculator. Other problems, like Example 3.32, are better handled using the rules of fractions. As a consequence, it will be up to the person solving the problem to decide whether decimals or fractions are used. The only thing that must be recognized is that the two methods may produce slightly different answers. Using a calculator with six or more decimal places will produce answers that are very close to each other.

The following exercises require a solution for an unknown variable. Fractions and decimal equivalent methods should be used for each so that the size of differences can be observed.

EXERCISE 3.8

Solve for the unknown variable in each question.

1. $\frac{1}{2}x + 5x = 165$

2. $\frac{1}{3}x - \frac{2}{3}x = -30$

3. $\frac{2}{7} + 3x = 0.55$

4. $\frac{1}{6}(1 + x) - 30 = 45$

5. $\frac{3}{8}(1 + 4x) - 10 = 2x + \frac{1}{8}x$

6. $\frac{1}{6}(1 - x) - 10 + 45 = \frac{5}{6}x + 4$

7. $\frac{3}{4}(16 + 4x) + 100 = 150 + \frac{1}{4}x$

8. $1{,}500 = 1{,}300\left(1 + \frac{250}{365}r\right)$

9. $1{,}680 = 1{,}500(1 + 0.12t)$

10. $1{,}000(1 + 0.05)^2 = \frac{1}{2}x - 100$

3.7 Break-even Analysis: A Business Application of an Algebraic Solution

In business, algebraic equations can be used to determine how much of a product or service must be sold to cover all the costs as well as make a profit. Finding the point where sales revenue is exactly equal to costs is called the **break-even point**. This point, **where costs and revenue are identical,** can be found by using an algebraic solution to an equation.

Another example of where algebra can be used in business is in the establishment of a formula to help a business in preparing cost estimates for contracts. The business card example in the first section of this chapter was a simple example of how a formula could be developed and used to provide a measure of cost.

In this section, you will learn how to develop expressions from the information given in a word problem. This is often the most difficult part, translating words and numerical information into equations or algebraic expressions.

For example, suppose that you were the owner of a small furniture manufacturing shop. How much would your sales need to be in order to cover paying the rent, wages to yourself and employees, utilities, insurance, and any equipment that you have leased or purchased? The answer to this question would be to find the break-even point. That is, the point where total dollar sales or total business revenue is sufficient to generate enough money to cover all your direct costs. The term direct cost is used because these are costs that can be recorded and are also acceptable to your accountant or bookkeeper. There are other indirect costs such as the interest forgone on any money that you have invested in the business, or all the time you spend organizing the operations of the business, which is not reflected in your wages. Indirect costs will not be considered in our discussion of break-even analysis because they require us to make certain assumptions. However, in the real world of business they must be recognized since they represent a cost of "doing" business and are sometimes forgotten in cost analysis by business people.

To see how we can use algebra for business problems, let us continue with our furniture business to define the terms **cost** and **revenue**. Once these are clear then we can apply the rules of algebra to help us solve a business problem.

Definition of Costs and Revenue

Total Variable Cost

Total variable costs are those costs that occur as a result of producing a good or service. For example, if you produce maple or oak furniture, your variable costs would be the materials and labour. If you produce nothing, your variable cost is zero. As soon as you start to produce, you incur a variable cost.

Total Fixed Cost

Fixed costs are costs that must be paid regardless of whether you are producing anything or not. Continuing with the furniture operation, examples of fixed costs would be the rent on your shop, insurance, tools, and any other costs you must incur whether you produce a piece of furniture or not.

Total Cost

Total cost refers to all costs, variable and fixed. Therefore, if you want to find total cost you must add variable and fixed costs together.

Total Revenue

Total revenue is the total amount of money brought in by the operation of a business. Often it is found by multiplying price per unit (sometimes called revenue per unit or average revenue) by the number of units sold.

It is important to understand that when variable and fixed costs are considered there are two ways they can be viewed: in total or so much per unit. In the furniture example, if the furniture shop produces 100 fine oak tables, there is a total variable cost for 100 tables, but there is a variable cost per table. That is, a variable cost per unit produced. As for fixed cost per unit, we tend to think about dividing the total fixed cost over all the units produced, which would give us a fixed cost per unit. That is, divide the fixed cost by the number of furniture units produced.

The most difficult part of using algebra to solve a break-even problem is translating the information into an algebraic statement. Example 3.33 demonstrates how the information in a business situation can be translated into an algebraic problem and then, using the rules of algebra, produce the desired information.

EXAMPLE 3.33

Nancy and Sharon are planning to open a small furniture shop where they will make fine oak reproductions of turn-of-the-century chairs and tables. After working out all their expected costs, they have estimated that a chair will take 4 board feet of oak that costs $10 per board foot, plus another $25 for finishing materials, including varnish, sand paper, and miscellaneous items. The labour time per chair is estimated to be 9 hours for construction and finishing work. Nancy and Sharon plan to pay themselves $25 per hour for their time.

Tables are expected to take 30 board feet of oak. The finishing materials are estimated at $75 per table and the construction time is expected to take 30 labour hours. Each table is sold with four chairs.

The fixed costs for the operation are rent for a work shop at $28,000 per year, which includes utilities. Other required costs are insurance at $2,500 per year and the purchase of $3,000 worth of tools.

Nancy and Sharon plan to sell their table and chairs at the same price other firms in the business charge: $3,500 for a table and four chairs. What is the number of chairs and table sets that must be sold to break even?

Solution The reading of the problem is the difficult part of the question. First let's define the costs:

Variable Costs

Chairs:		Variable cost per chair.
Oak cost per chair:	$40	$10 per board foot times 4 board feet per chair ($4 \times \$10 = \$40$).
Material cost per chair:	$25	Given in the problem.
Labour cost per chair:	$225	$25 per hour times 9 hours per chair ($9 \times \$25 = \$225$).
Variable cost per chair:	$290	The sum of the above, i.e., $40 + $25 + $225.

Tables:		Variable cost per table.
Oak cost per table:	$300	$10 per board foot times 30 board feet per table ($30 \times \$10 = \$300$).
Material cost per table:	$75	Given in the problem.
Labour cost per table:	$750	$25 per hour times 30 hours per table ($30 \times \$25 = \$750$).
Variable cost per table:	$1,125	The sum of the above, i.e., $300 + $75 + $750.

Bringing the variable costs for chairs and tables together, the variable cost of four chairs and one table (a set) will be:

4 chairs at $290 per chair:	$1,160
1 table at $1,150:	1,125
Variable Cost per set	**$2,285**

Fixed Costs

In the problem, the costs that are fixed are rent, equipment, and insurance. These costs will be the same whether any chairs and tables are made. That is, once the money is spent on the fixed costs these costs will not change with the number of chairs and tables produced. The fixed costs are:

1. Rent and utilities:	$28,000
2. Insurance:	2,500
3. Tools:	3,000
Total Fixed Costs	**$33,500**

Finding the Break-even Point

If we let x stand for the number of units (1 table and 4 chairs), then the equation that will describe our total cost is:

Total Cost = Total Fixed Cost + Total Variable Costs

Total Cost = $33,500 + $2,285$x$

The term $2,285$x$ says that whatever number of sets they sell, this number when multiplied by $2,285 will tell us the total variable costs. For example, if two sets are sold, the total cost is $33,500 + $2,285(2), or $38,070.

Total Revenue:

The other side to this problem is the revenue from the sale of the table and chair sets. Since x stands for the number of units sold, and we know from the problem that the price is going to be $3,500 per set, then we know that the expression for total revenue will be $3,500$x$. Therefore, the revenue expression is stated as:

Total Revenue = $3,500$x$

For example, if only two sets are sold, the revenue is $3,500(2), or $7,000.

Bringing revenue and cost together, we know that at the break-even point, the firm is just covering their costs and making no profit. Thus, if we set the revenue equation equal to the cost equation, we can look for a value of x that makes the revenue and cost equations the same. Therefore:

TOTAL REVENUE		TOTAL COSTS
$3,500$x$	=	$33,500 + $2,285$x$

The above expression is now a one-variable equation, just like the ones we solved earlier. To find the solution for x, we first subtract \$2,285x from both sides of the equation:

$$\$3{,}500x - \$2{,}285x = \$33{,}500 + \$2{,}285x - \$2{,}285x$$

$$\$1{,}215x = \$33{,}500$$

$$\frac{\$1{,}215x}{\$1{,}215} = \frac{\$33{,}500}{\$1{,}215}$$

Dividing both sides of the equation by \$1,215 to find x.

$$x = 27.572$$

This tells us that they must sell approximately 28 sets to break even. The reason the answer is rounded up to 28 is that at 27 units they would be just "short" of breaking even.

Checking our solution: using the exact value of x we substitute 27.572 into our cost and revenue equation. If our break-even solution is correct, the revenue and the cost should be the same. Checking this by substitution gives:

Total Cost of 27.572 units:

$$\$33{,}500 + \$2{,}285\,(27.572) = \$96{,}502.02$$

$$\text{Total Cost} = \$96{,}502.02$$

Total Revenue at 27.572 units:

$$\$3{,}500(27.572) = \$96{,}502.00$$

$$\text{Total Revenue} = \$96{,}502.00$$

Note: The number of decimal places used for x was to reduce the size of the rounding error (\$0.02 in this case). If the value $x = 28$ had been used there would have been a difference in the dollar value for cost and revenue.

EXAMPLE 3.34

The High Tech computer shop assembles and sells computers. After reviewing their accounting data, the following was determined:

Fixed costs: \$100,000 per year
Variable costs: \$1,450 per computer
Sales capacity per year: 1,000 computers
Selling price per computer: \$2,450

(a) What is the break-even point?
(b) What number of computers would need to be sold to make a \$25,000

profit? Profit refers to how much money is remaining from revenue after all costs (fixed and variable) have been covered.

(c) At what percent of capacity is the break-even point?

Solution Let the number of computers sold be x. Then the expression that describes costs will be:

Total Costs = \$100,000 + \$1,450x

The revenue is calculated as:

Total Revenue = \$2,450x

(a) The break-even point will be where costs and revenue are the same, or:

$$\$2{,}450x = \$100{,}000 + \$1{,}450x$$

Solving for x, first subtract \$1,450x from both sides of the expression.

$$\$2{,}450x - \$1{,}450x = \$100{,}000 + \$1{,}450x - \$1{,}450x$$

$$\$1{,}000x = \$100{,}000$$

Dividing each side by \$1,000 gives:

$$\frac{\$1{,}000x}{\$1{,}000} = \frac{\$100{,}000}{\$1{,}000}$$

$$x = 100$$

This means High Tech must sell 100 computers to break even.

Checking, substitute $x = 100$ into our revenue and cost expressions to ensure that the solution is correct. This yields:

Total Costs:	\$100,000 + \$1,450(100) = \$245,000
Total Revenue:	\$2,450(100) = \$245,000

Therefore, if High Tech sells 100 computers it will break even, just covering all costs.

(b) To find out how many computers High Tech would need to sell to make a profit of \$25,000, simply take the expression for cost and add \$25,000. This would now read:

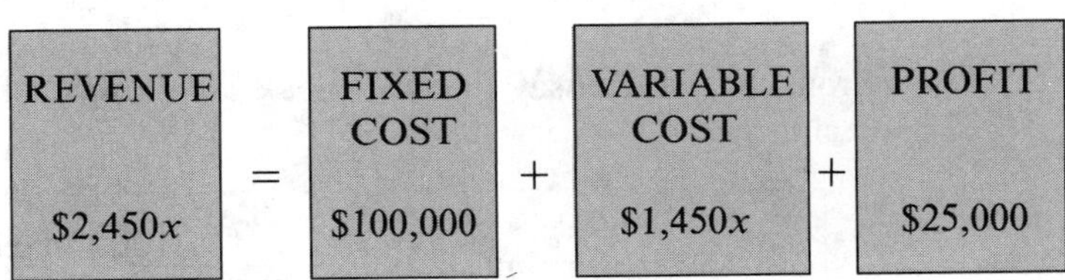

Isolating x, we subtract \$1,450 from both sides of the expression and add the common terms:

$$\$2,450 - \$1,450 = \$125,000 + \$1,450 - \$1,450$$

$$\frac{\$1,000x}{\$1,000} = \frac{\$125,000}{\$1,000}$$ Dividing each side by \$1,000 gives:

$$x = 125$$

Therefore, if High Tech sells 125 computers it will cover all costs and make a profit of \$25,000.

(c) Determining the percent of capacity at the break-even point:

Capacity = 1,000 computers per year
Break-even point = 100

Therefore, the break-even point is 10% of capacity. This was found as follows:

$$\frac{100}{1,000} = 0.1, \text{ or } 10\% \text{ of capacity.}$$

It is worth noting that the last two examples could be solved through other approaches. One such approach is to use the concept of **contribution**. Contribution refers to the difference between price and variable cost per unit. For example, if a company has a fixed cost of \$10,000, a variable cost per unit of \$6, and sells its product for \$10, then the contribution would be \$10 – \$6 or \$4 per unit.

The notion of contribution is that the price (revenue per unit) goes toward covering variable and fixed cost per unit. Thus, the amount left over, after the variable cost has been covered, contributes toward covering fixed cost. If one knows the contribution per unit, one can determine how much in total must be sold so that the total contribution covers total fixed costs. Moreover, contribution is also the source of profit. That is, once the total fixed costs are covered, the contribution per unit begins to add to profit. In our example, the break-even point using contribution would be:

$$\frac{\$10,000}{\$4/\text{unit}} = 2,500 \text{ units would need to be sold to break-even.}$$

From this we can say that the break-even point using the contribution approach is:

$$\text{Break-even point(in units)} = \frac{\text{Total Fixed Costs}}{\text{Price/unit} - \text{Variable Cost/unit}}$$

To find the level of output to generate a particular level of profit, one would simply add this profit to the fixed costs. Then, determine what level of sales (in units) is necessary to generate the profit, using the contribution approach. That is:

$$\frac{\text{Fixed Costs} + \text{Required profit}}{\text{Price/unit} - \text{variable cost/unit}} = \text{Required unit sales}$$

In our example, if the company was seeking a profit of \$22,000, then the required level of sales (in units) would be:

$$\frac{\$10{,}000 + \$22{,}000}{\$10 - \$6} = 8{,}000 \text{ units}$$

Another procedure for solving break-even problems is to use a graphic approach. This will be shown in Chapter 4 after the concept of a graph has been explained.

EXERCISE 3.9

A. Given the information below, for each situation, find the cost and revenue expressions, and then, find the break-even point.

	Variable Cost per Unit	Total Fixed Costs	Selling Price per Unit
1.	\$15.00	\$45,000	\$20.00
2.	\$1.50	\$2,500	\$2.50
3.	\$1,500.00	\$140,000	\$2,450.00
4.	\$0.35	\$500	\$0.50
5.	\$500.00	\$250,000	\$1,750.00
6.	\$705.00	\$2,500	\$800.00

B. Formulate the following business problems into an algebraic statement and find the value of the unknown variable.

7. A firm manufactures computer software that sells for \$450. If it costs \$150 in variable costs for each package sold and the firm has fixed costs of \$250,000, what is the break-even point?
8. Assume the computer firm in Exercise 7 wanted to make a profit of \$50,000. What would be the number of software packages they would have to sell to make this level of profit?
9. Dianne has just opened a home inspection service for people who are purchasing a house and want to have the structure inspected. She has leased office space including utilities for \$6,000 per year. To get

started, she also had to purchase a secondhand truck and tools for \$12,500. Each inspection costs her about \$125, which includes her wages. If Dianne plans to charge \$175 per inspection, how many inspections must she do to break even? How many inspections must she do if she wishes to make a profit of \$15,000?

10. A small publishing company currently sends all its material out to a printing company that charges \$6.50 per page on average. The manager of this publishing company thinks it would be worthwhile to acquire the necessary equipment and do their printing in-house. If the printing is done in-house, the estimate of the costs per page is \$6.00. To do the printing within the publishing company, the printing equipment required would cost \$1,500,000. At what number of pages printed will the outside cost (using the printer outside the publishing company) and the cost inside be the same? If the annual number of pages printed last year was 4 million, what would you recommend the publishing company do?

11. A company that manufactures natural gas converters for automobiles is considering using a new installation method that requires new equipment. Currently the cost per converter installed on a car or truck is \$1,250. The new system being considered is expected to reduce the installation cost to \$900 per unit. If the new equipment will cost \$50,000, how many installations must they do with the new equipment to break even?

REVIEW EXERCISES

A. For each of the following expressions identify the numerical coefficients.

1. a

2. $14(-23x)$

3. $2x + xy$

4. $a + 0.5ax$

5. $x + y - z$

B. Identify the literal coefficients in the following expressions.

6. $4a$

7. $4x + 3c$

8. $4s - 2a$

9. $85ay$

10. $2x - 0.13s$

C. Perform the necessary addition or subtraction of the following algebraic expressions and evaluate each expression if $a = 2$, $t = 4$, $s = -4$, $x = 0$, and $y = 1$.

11. $3x - 4y$

12. $4a + 3x$

13. $2a + 4t - (7s) + 25xy$

14. $0.4ax + 0.3ax + 100xy$

15. $24ay + 3ay + 5a - (24as)$

D. For each of the following, identify whether the expression is a polynomial or monomial. If the expression is a polynomial, identify whether it can be called a binomial, trinomial, or neither.

16. $tx + 8y$

17. $2a$

18. $a + 2s - 4by$

19. $5x - 8sy - 50a$

20. $r - 0.13$

E. Factor the following expressions.

21. $8x + 16x^2$

22. $4x^3 - x^2$

23. $6x + 6x - 2$

24. $45a + 15a^2 - 45$

25. $12x^3 + x^4 + x^2 - x^3$

26. $9xy - 8y + 3y^2$

27. $S + Srt$

28. $(1 + x)^4 + 3(1 + x)^6 - 4(1 + x)^3$

F. For each of the following expressions, find a solution for the unknown variable. Use an electronic calculator to assist you where necessary.

29. $45y - 450 = 0$

30. $-2x + 6 = -44$

31. $0.5a - 14 = 124$

32. $100 = 120 - 15x$

33. $0.01a = 500 + 100.01a$

34. $x - 50{,}000 = \dfrac{[1 - (1 + 0.01)^{-2}]}{0.01}$

35. $S + 15{,}000 = \dfrac{(1 + 0.10)^{-12}}{0.01} + 25S + 100{,}000$

G. For each of the following expressions find a solution for x.

36. $0.5x + 2e = 24$

37. $p(1 + tx) = s$

38. $3x(1 + i) - 2x(1 + i) + 400(1 + i) = 500$

39. $20asz + 14xy = 100s$

40. $124as + 14y - 4x = 44y$

H. Solve each of the following expressions for x by converting the fractional numerical coefficients to decimal equivalents. Carry all calculations to four decimal places.

41. $\dfrac{1}{3}x + 6x = 250$

42. $\dfrac{1}{2}x + \dfrac{2}{4}x = -30$

43. $\dfrac{2}{9} + 6x = 1.40$

44. $\dfrac{1}{3}(1 + x) - 10 = 50$

45. $\dfrac{3}{7}(1 - 4x) - 2 = 2x - \dfrac{1}{9}x$

I. Formulate the following problems into an algebraic form and solve for the unknown variable as required.

46. Ace manufacturing produces windows that come in a frame. Ace has found that the cost per square foot of window, including labour and materials, is $45. The price they charge for a finished window is $60 per square foot. If their fixed costs are $110,000, what is the break-even level of sales. What is the break-even point in terms of square footage of windows manufactured?

47. A company is contemplating changing the method it uses to produce fireplace inserts. The choice of methods has been narrowed down to two methods. Method A will have an annual fixed cost of $50,000 and will have an estimated variable cost of $500 per unit. Method B has an estimated annual fixed cost of $75,000 and is estimated to have a variable cost of $300 per unit. At what level of sales would the firm be indifferent between the two methods? Assume the insert sells for $800 per unit. (Indifference means that the costs for each method would be the same.) If sales are expected to be 1,000 inserts, what method would generate the largest profit?

48. A company sells a product for $25 per unit. Using q for quantity, TC for total cost, TFC for total fixed cost, TVC for total variable cost, and TR for total revenue, answer the following questions.

(a) What is the total revenue if the company sells 1,200 units? What is the total revenue equation? (Remember, use q for quantity and TR for total revenue.)

(b) The variable cost per unit is estimated to be 40% of the revenue per unit and the fixed costs are $8,000. Determine the total cost, fixed cost, and variable cost equations.

(c) What is the break-even point for this firm?

(d) If fixed costs were to rise by 25%, find the new break-even point.

(e) If the company wanted to make a profit of $37,000, what would the level of sales in units need to be? Compute the break-even point for the orginal fixed costs and the new fixed costs given in part (d).

GLOSSARY OF TERMS

Binomial an expression with two terms.

Break-even Point the point at which a business's revenue is exactly the same as its costs. The break-even point is the output or service level necessary to make revenue and costs the same.

Coefficient there are two types of coefficients: numerical and literal. Numerical coefficients are numbers in front of a variable, e.g., $4x$, 4 is a numerical coefficient and x is the literal coefficient.

Contribution the difference between revenue and variable costs. Contribution per unit is found by subtracting variable cost per unit from the price per unit. Contribution goes toward covering the fixed cost and once these are covered contribution adds to profit.

Equation a relation between variables and numbers that use an equality sign to express the relation.

Exponent refers to the number of times a number or variable is multiplied by itself. The term power is also used to describe an exponent.

Expression an expression defines a relationship between variables or numbers.

Factoring the procedure of simplifying an expression by collecting like terms in the expression.

Fixed Costs costs that do not change with the volume of output. Fixed costs are costs that are incurred even if no product is produced. Examples are taxes, insurance, and depreciation on equipment.

Monomial an expression with only one term.

Polynomial an expression with two or more terms.

Term a term is one of the parts of an expression or equation. For example, in $3x + 5y = k$, $3x$ and $5y$ are terms.

Variable a term or part of a term in an algebraic expression that may take on different values. A variable is normally represented by a letter.

Variable Costs costs that change with the volume of output.

CHAPTER 4

Additional Topics in Algebra

Algebra is used to help solve many business problems. For example, a manufacturing problem may require the solution of equations with more than one variable. On other occasions, a business may need to present information in a graphic form. Information is translated from an algebraic expression into the visual form of a graph. In finance we may need to determine precisely the value of money at different points in time, or, determine how long it will take for a sum of money to accumulate to a desired amount. These are all important applications of algebra to business problems. These examples are useful applications for the topics of this chapter.

OBJECTIVES

When you complete this chapter, you will be able to do the following:

1. understand the meaning of linear systems of equations and be able to find the solution for unknown variables in simultaneous systems of equations;
2. understand a rectangular coordinate system, construct a graph of a linear equation, and interpret the meaning of a slope and intercept for a linear equation;
3. apply graphic procedures to break-even analysis and use graphic procedures to solve simultaneous equations;
4. understand the meaning of a mathematical series and be able to find a specific term or sum for both geometric and arithmetic progressions;
5. understand the concept of a logarithm and be able to use logarithms to solve for an unknown exponent.

4.1 Systems of Linear Equations

The term **system of linear equations** means working with two or more linear equations at the same time. The importance of a system of linear equations in business is that we occasionally need to express a series of statements (e.g., costs, revenue, production, etc.), each by an equation. In most circumstances, we not only have to express the equations, but also we want to find a value for each variable in the system that **simultaneously will satisfy all the equations.** An example of a system of equations with two equations and two variables would be:

$$3x + 7y = 15$$

$$4x + 15y = 10$$

These two equations are called independent simultaneous equations (or just independent equations). They are called independent because each equation is not another form of the other. To understand this point consider the following two equations:

$$2x + 5y = 10 \quad ①$$

$$4x + 10y = 20 \quad ②$$

If both sides of equation ① were multiplied by 2, equation ① would be:

$$2(2x) + 2(5y) = 2(10)$$

$$4x + 10y = 20$$

As can be seen, $4x + 10y = 20$ is the same as equation ②, above. When this happens we say the equations of the system are dependent equations. When this dependence occurs it is not possible to find a *unique* value for x and y that satisfies both equations simultaneously.

In Chapter 3, we found that when an equation had one variable, a unique solution for the variable could be found; that is, the value of x was equal to a specific number that satisfied the equation. However, a single linear equation with two variables has an unlimited number of possible solutions that can satisfy the equation. For example:

$$x + y = 8$$

This equation can be satisfied with $x = 0$, $y = 8$; $x = 1$, $y = 7$; $x = 2$, $y = 6$; as well as an infinite number of other combinations of values of x and y, which sum to 8. However, if we have two independent equations with x and y it may be possible to find unique values for x and y that satisfy the two equations simultaneously (assuming there is such a solution, since sometimes there are none). This is what we want to learn: how to solve a linear system of equations to find a specific value of x and a specific value of y that will satisfy the equation system.

In the previous chapter, break-even analysis had two equations: one for cost and one for revenue. In each of these equations, there was only one variable — the output x. The difference with linear systems is that we may have two or more equations, each of which will have at least one variable. If there are two equations, then there must be one independent variable per equation to find a solution (and sometimes there may be no solution). In general, the conditions that must be satisfied in a linear system of equations if we are to find a solution for the variables are: **the number of equations and the number of variables must be the same and that the equations are independent.**

In this book we will only deal with the solution for systems that have two equations. However, the methods we use for two equations can be extended to a linear system of equations with n equations and n variables.

There are three methods that can be used to solve systems of equations with two variables. The first is the method of elimination using the rules of subtraction and/or addition. The second method uses elimination by substitution. The third procedure, the graphic approach, will be discussed in a later section of this chapter, once the topic of graphs has been fully explained.

A. Solving of a Linear System of Equations Using Elimination Through Subtraction and/or Addition

The most direct way to solve a system of two linear independent equations is to eliminate one of the variables (unknowns), and solve the resulting equation for the remaining variable. The first method we will use to find a solution for the variables in the system of equations is **by eliminating a term** and applying addition or subtraction to the equations. Consider Example 4.1, which finds a simultaneous solution for a linear system of equations with 2 equations. Remember, the word **simultaneous solution** means finding a value for each variable that satisfies both equations at the same time.

EXAMPLE 4.1 Solution of a linear system of equations by elimination using the addition/subtraction method

Find the solution to the following system equations by using the addition/subtraction method of elimination.

$$4x + 3y = 8 \quad ①$$

$$2x + 9y = 4 \quad ②$$

Solution

STEP 1 First, we must be able to eliminate either the x or y variable. The most direct way is to select one variable, say y, and decide what numbers we would need to multiply each equation by to get the numerical coefficients for y to be the same in each equation. Looking at equation ①, we see that if $3y$ was multiplied by 3 we would get $9y$, which is the same as the y term in equation ②. We cannot simply multiply one term of an equation by another term without doing the same to the entire equation. Why? Because to maintain the equality, what is done to one side of an equation must be done to the other side. Thus, we must multiply both sides of equation ① by 3.

$$3(4x + 3y) = 3(8)$$

$$12x + 9y = 24$$

The system of equations now looks like:

$12x + 9y = 24$ ① — After multiplication by 3.

$2x + 9y = 4$ ②

STEP 2 Next eliminate the y term by subtracting one equation from the other. Subtracting equation ② from equation ① gives:

$$\begin{array}{r} 12x + 9y = 24 \\ \underline{-(2x + 9y = \;\; 4)} \\ 10x + 0y = 20 \\ 10x = 20 \end{array}$$

Subtracting equation ② from equation ①, to eliminate the y variable.

STEP 3 Find a solution for x by dividing each side by 10:

$$\frac{10x}{10} = \frac{20}{10}$$

$$x = 2$$

STEP 4 To find a value for y, substitute $x = 2$ into either of the equations. This yields a value of y that will satisfy both of the equations *when* $x = 2$. Substituting $x = 2$ for x in equation ② (we could have selected equation ①):

$$\begin{aligned} 2x + 9y &= 4 \\ 2(2) + 9y &= 4 \\ 4 + 9y &= 4 \\ 9y &= 0 \\ y &= 0 \end{aligned}$$

Therefore, the values of x and y that simultaneously satisfy both equations are $x = 2$ and $y = 0$.

To check if the values of x and y satisfy both equations, substitute $x = 2$ and $y = 0$ into both equations:

$$\begin{aligned} 4x + 3y &= 8 \quad ① \\ 4(2) + 3(0) &= 8 \\ 8 &= 8 \end{aligned}$$

$$\begin{aligned} 2x + 9y &= 4 \quad ② \\ 2(2) + 9(0) &= 4 \\ 4 &= 4 \end{aligned}$$

As we can see, both equations are satisfied and thus the simultaneous solution for this system is $x = 2$ and $y = 0$.

In Example 4.1 we decided to multiply equation ① by 3, and subtract equation ② from equation ①. Another method, which is equivalent, is to multiply equation ① by –3 and then add the two equations. This alternate method would also permit us to eliminate the y term.

B. Solving of a Linear System of Equations Using Elimination Through Substitution

The second method that will eliminate one of the terms in a system of linear equations is called the **substitution method**. This method requires us to substitute one equation for one of the variables of the other equation. The key to this method is that we must find a solution for either x or y in one equation and then use this solution in the other equation. You should study Example 4.2 carefully before proceeding.

EXAMPLE 4.2 **Solution of a linear system of equations using the substitution method**

Find a value of z and c that satisfies the following two equations simultaneously.

$$5z - 3c = 3 \quad ①$$

$$z + 4c = 4 \quad ②$$

Solution

STEP 1 Select the equation that can most readily be solved in terms of one of the variables. Equation ② can be directly solved for z by subtracting $4c$ from each side of the equation, which would give:

$$z + 4c - 4c = 4 - 4c \quad ②$$

$$z = 4 - 4c$$

STEP 2 Substitute equation ②'s solution for z into z in equation ①:

$$5z - 3c = 3 \quad ①$$

$$5(4 - 4c) - 3c = 3 \quad \text{Substitute } z = 4 - 4c.$$

$$20 - 20c - 3c = 3$$

$$20 - 23c = 3 \quad \text{Subtract 20 from both sides of the equation.}$$

$$-23c = -17 \quad \text{Divide each side by –23 to find } c.$$

$$c = \frac{17}{23}$$

$$c = 0.73913$$

STEP 3 Substitute $c = 0.73913$ into one of the equations and solve for z. Using equation ② we have:

$$z + 4c = 4 \quad ②$$

$$z + 4(0.73913) = 4 \quad \text{Substituting } c = 0.73913.$$

$$z = 4 - 4(0.73913) \quad \text{Solving for } z.$$

$$z = 1.04348$$

Therefore, the simultaneous solution for the system is $z = 1.04348$ and $c = 0.73913$.

Checking this, we substitute the values for z and c into our original equations and get:

Substituting $z = 1.04348$ and $c = 0.73913$.

$$5z - 3c = 3 \quad ①$$

$$5(1.04348) - 3(0.73913) = 3$$

$$5.21740 - 2.21739 = 3$$

$$3.00001 = 3 \quad \text{(It's close enough!)}$$

$$3 = 3$$

$$z + 4c = 4 \quad ②$$

$$1(1.04348) + 4(0.73913) = 4$$

$$1.04348 + 2.95652 = 4$$

$$4 = 4$$

A business example that requires the solution of simultaneous equations is shown in Example 4.3. As with our earlier problems, the most difficult part of the problem is translating the information into an equation form to solve for the variables.

EXAMPLE 4.3

A small computer company has two types of computers (Computer A and Computer B), each performing a very specific operation. In checking its accounting records, the company finds that it has sold $27,500 worth of computer time, which amounts to 150 hours. The computer company charges $200 per hour for Computer A and $150 per hour for Computer B. How many hours of computer time has been sold for each computer?

Solution Let the variables be A and B, where A stands for the number of hours sold on Computer A, and B the number of hours sold on Computer B. In the problem, we have two pieces of information. First, we know that between the two computers 150 hours of time has been sold. This can be expressed as:

$$A + B = 150 \quad ①$$

Second, and on the revenue side, we know that each hour on Computer A generates \$200 in revenue, while each hour on Computer B produces \$150 in revenue. We also know that the total time sold for Computers A and B is worth \$27,500. This can be expressed by the following relationship:

$$\$200A + \$150B = \$27{,}500 \quad ②$$

From the above, we can formulate the system of equations:

$$A + B = 150 \quad ①$$
$$\$200A + \$150B = \$27{,}500 \quad ②$$

Remember, A and B represent the number of hours sold on each computer.

Using the method of substitution, solve for A in equation ①, and substitute this expression for A in equation ②.

$$A + B = 150 \quad ①$$
$$\text{A} = 150 - B \quad \text{Solved for } A.$$

Substituting $A = 150 - B$ into equation ② gives:

$$\$200A + \$150B = \$27{,}500 \quad ②$$
$$\$200(150 - B) + \$150B = \$27{,}500 \quad \text{Substituting for } A.$$
$$\$30{,}000 - \$200B + \$150B = \$27{,}500$$
$$-\$50B = -\$2{,}500 \quad \text{Divide both sides by } -\$50.$$
$$B = 50$$

To find a value for the number of hours for Computer A, substitute $B = 50$ into either equation and solve for A. Use equation ① since it is easier to solve for A when $B = 50$. This gives:

$$A + B = 150 \quad ①$$
$$A + 50 = 150 \quad \text{Substituting } B = 50$$
$$A = 100$$

Therefore, the number of hours sold on each computer that produces exactly \$27,500 and uses 150 hours of computer time is 100 hours on Computer A and 50 hours on Computer B.

Checking:

$$A + B = 150 \qquad ①$$

$$100 + 50 = 150 \qquad \text{It checks.}$$

$$\$200A + \$150B = \$27{,}500 \qquad ②$$

$$\$200(100) + \$150(50) = \$27{,}500 \qquad \text{It also checks.}$$

EXERCISE 4.1

Find the simultaneous solution for the following system of equations.

A. Use the elimination-by-subtraction/addition method and check your answer.

1. $4x - 3y = -3$
$5x - y = 10$

2. $x - y = 5$
$x + y = 1$

3. $2x + 7y = 5$
$3x + 2y = 6$

4. $x - 2y = 7$
$2x + y = 4$

5. $x + y = 25$
$x - y = 1$

6. $10x + 4y = 18$
$2x + 4y = 2$

B. Use the elimination-by-substitution method and check your answer.

7. $x - y = -3$
$5x - y = 10$

8. $x - y = 3$
$x + y = 1$

9. $x + 2y = 5$
$-x + y = 6$

10. $x + 2y = 7$
$x - y = 3$

11. $x + y = 25$
$x - y = 1$

12. $5x + 2y = 4$
$2x - 4y = 2$

4.2 Constructing Graphs of Algebraic Equations

Graphic analysis is very common in business. If you pick up a copy of a business newspaper you will find graphs used throughout the paper. Some examples are graphs of stock prices, graphs of interest rates over time, or graphs of the value of the Canadian dollar with respect to the U.S. dollar. Another common use of graphs is in economics, where they are used to portray supply and demand equations. One reason graphs are used so frequently is because they portray information in a visual form that is easy to read and understand. However, behind most graphs are equations and, therefore, we must understand how to translate equations to a graphical form.

A. Terminology of Graphs

Graphs are constructed on a system that is called the **Rectangular Coordinate System**. This system uses the principle of referencing everything to two perpendicular lines that intersect at right angles. Two such lines are shown in Figure 4.1. The vertical line, the y line, is called the ***y*-axis**. The horizontal line, the x line, is called the ***x*-axis**. The point where the two lines intersect is called the **origin** and is the reference point for both the y- and x-axis.

Figure 4.1

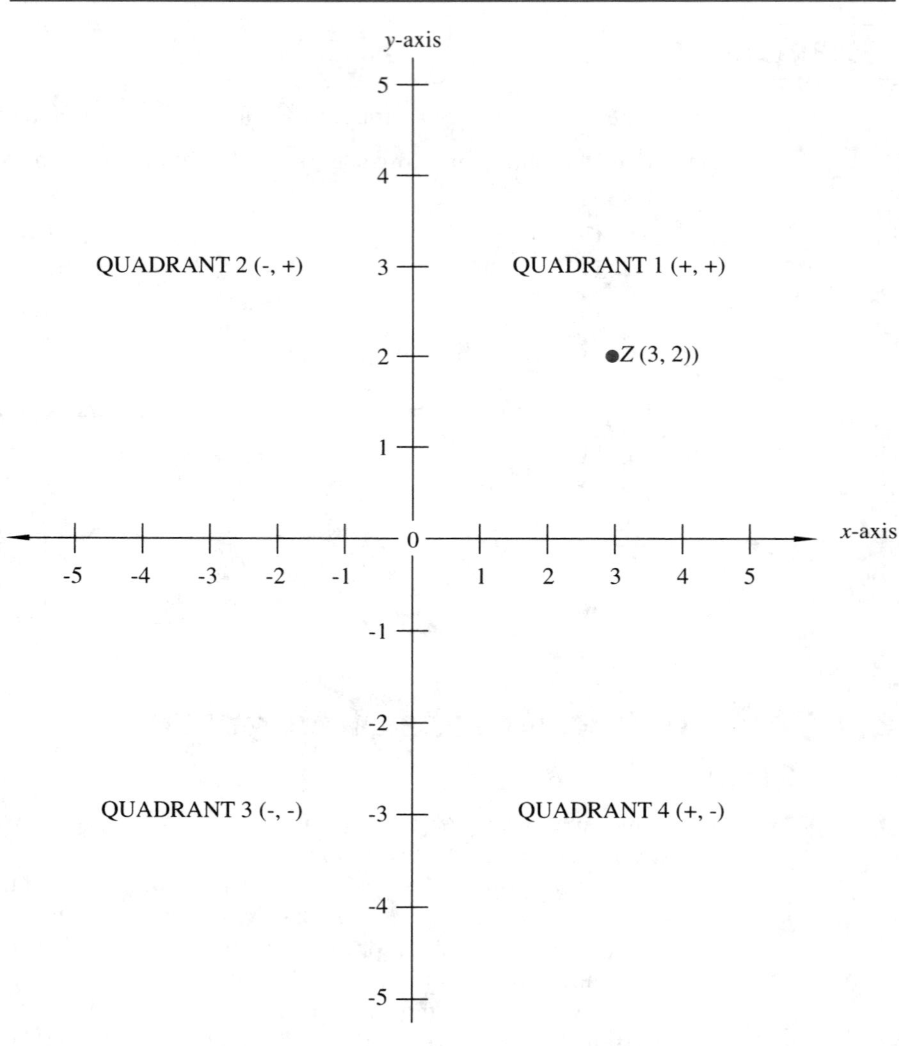

The numbers on each axis in Figure 4.1 represent a position relative to the origin, point 0. By convention, the numbers on the x-axis and to the right of the origin, 0, are positive numbers, and numbers to the left of the origin on the x-axis are negative. Similarly, for the vertical scale, numbers above the origin are positive and numbers below the origin are negative. The key element to the axes is that it is possible to find the precise location of any point by using the number scale on each axis. The values for a point on each of the axes are called the **coordinates of the point**.

A rectangular coordinate system has four **quadrants**, each numbered in a counterclockwise manner. Quadrant 1 (see Figure 4.1) is the region where values of x and y will be 0 or positive. Coordinates that have negative values of x and y have very limited use in business. In most business and economic problems Quadrant 1 is the portion of the coordinate system that is used.

Graphs include units of measurement on the axis. In business, the unit of measurement on the vertical and horizontal axes will depend upon the problem being considered. A common unit on the vertical axis is dollars. The horizontal scale has a variety of possible units. The most common measurements are quantity (produced, demanded, or supplied) and time. The choice of the units for each axis will depend upon the variables being analyzed.

B. Location of a Point

To describe the location of point Z (see Figure 4.1) relative to the x- and y-axis, we would define the position of Z by using the units of the horizontal and vertical scales. In Figure 4.1, we can see that Z is located at the point where $x = 3$ and $y = 2$. This point, $(x = 3, y = 2)$, is referred to as the coordinates of point Z. By convention, when specifying each coordinate, the first value in the brackets refers to the location of the point on the x-axis and is called the x coordinate. The second value in the brackets refers to the location of the point on the y-axis and is called the y coordinate.

The notation for the coordinates of a point, (x, y), gives us the precise location of the point — relative to each axis.

The first step in constructing a graph is to identify the position of points on the coordinate system; the second step is to plot these points on the graph. Study how the positioning of coordinates is done in Example 4.4:

EXAMPLE 4.4

On the following graph, find the coordinates (ordered pairs) of the points A, B, C, D, E, and F.

Figure 4.2

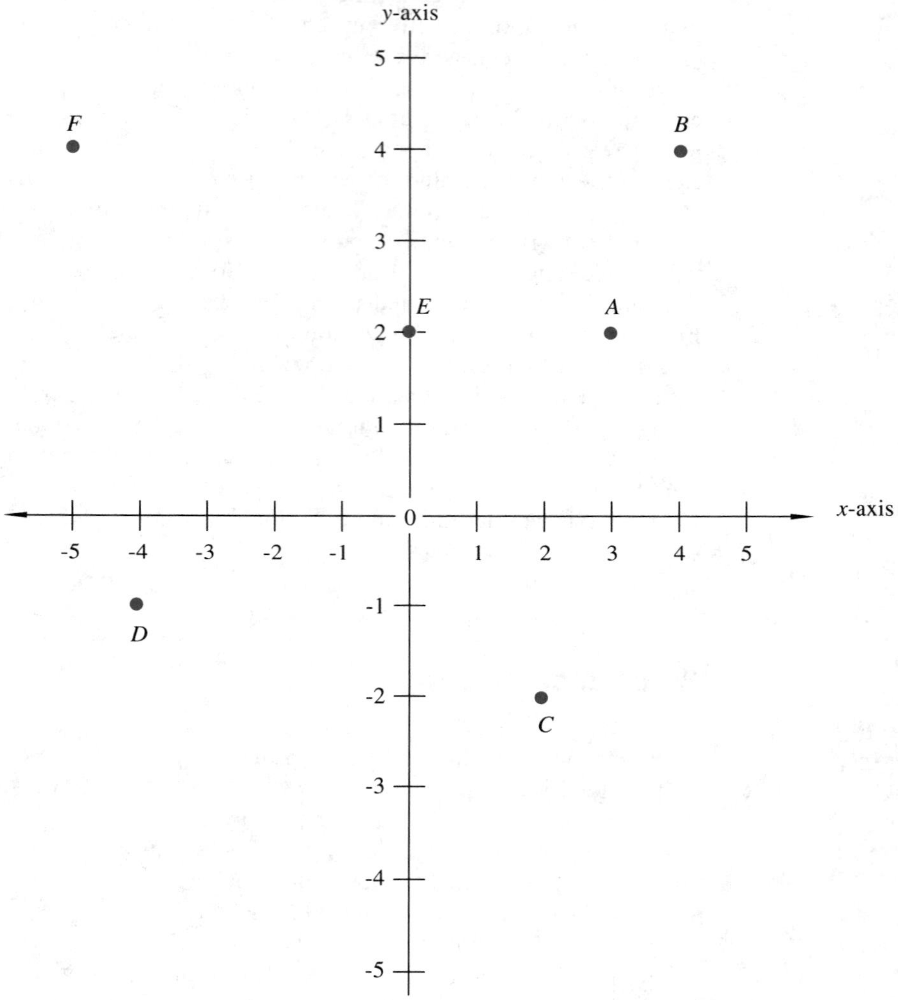

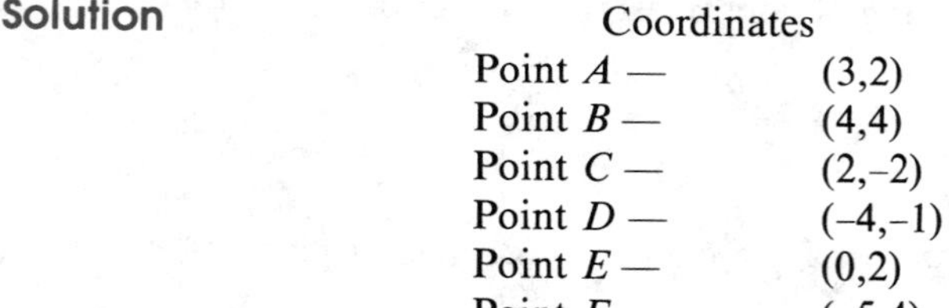

Solution

	Coordinates
Point *A* —	(3,2)
Point *B* —	(4,4)
Point *C* —	(2,–2)
Point *D* —	(–4,–1)
Point *E* —	(0,2)
Point *F* —	(–5,4)

If we draw a straight line — at right angles to each axis — to a specific point you will note that a rectangular box is formed. This is true for any two lines drawn at right angles to each axis and intersecting at a specific point. If you can imagine drawing many vertical lines through each value of x on the x-axis and many horizontal lines through each value of y on the y-axis, you will see a series of little boxes develop. Consider Figure 4.3 and observe the boxes that develop at the points A (3,3), B(–4,2), C(2,1), and D(4,–4) when the points are connected with perpendicular lines from each axis. These little boxes are the basis for the name rectangular coordinate system.

Figure 4.3

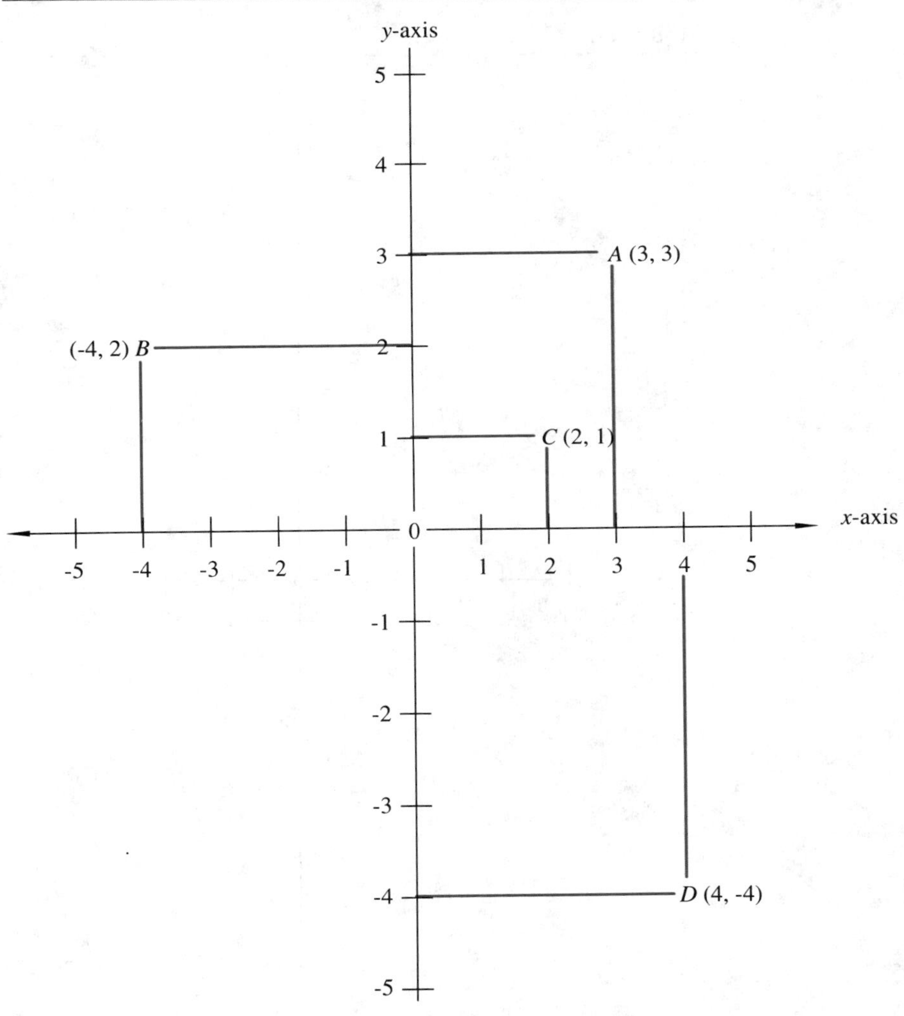

C. Graphs of a Linear Equation

A linear equation when plotted on a graph will be a straight line — the term linear means just that, a straight line. To graph a linear equation, just identify

EXAMPLE 4.5

Plot the following coordinates on the graph.

$$A\,(5, 5)\ [\text{i.e., } (x = 5, y = 5)]$$
$$B\,(1, 1)$$
$$C\,(4, 4)$$

Solution **Figure 4.4**

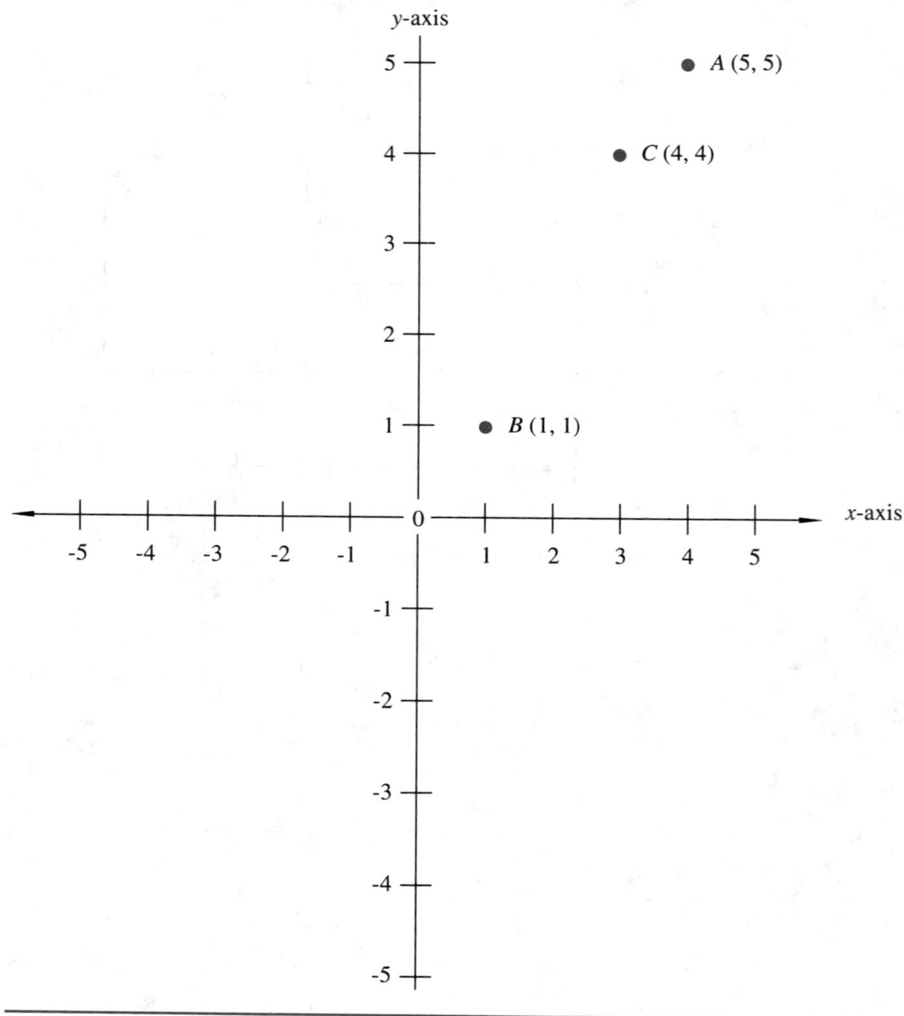

sets of coordinates that satisfy the equation, locate these on the graph, and then join the coordinates with a line. To understand this approach study Example 4.5, which requires you to plot a series of coordinates and connect them with a line.

Although drawing a line graph requires one to identify only two points, it is recommended that a third point be identified to ensure that the points do form a straight line. For example, if we were drawing the graph of the equation $y = 3 + 5x$, it would be necessary to find a set of coordinates, which could then be joined by a line. Since any point on a straight line will have coordinates that satisfy the linear equation, we need to plot at least three points to construct the graph of a straight line. To demonstrate this principle, consider Example 4.6. In this example, we will determine a set of coordinates that satisfy the equation and then place these coordinates on the graph. What is evident is that the points can be connected with a continuous line.

EXAMPLE 4.6

Find four sets of coordinates for the linear equation:

$$y = 1 + 2x$$

Locate these coordinates on the graph and then join them with a continuous line.

Solution The most direct way to find four sets of coordinates is to assign values to x and determine the corresponding values for y. The values that were selected for x (0, 1, 2, 3) were chosen only because they were convenient to use. Other values could have been selected.

x values	y values for each x $y = 1 + 2x$	Coordinates (x, y)
0	$y = 1 + 2(0) = 1$	(0, 1)
1	$y = 1 + 2(1) = 3$	(1, 3)
2	$y = 1 + 2(2) = 5$	(2, 5)
3	$y = 1 + 2(3) = 7$	(3, 7)

Plotting the points on the graph in Quadrant 1, the upper right hand portion of our rectangular coordinate system, we have:

Figure 4.5

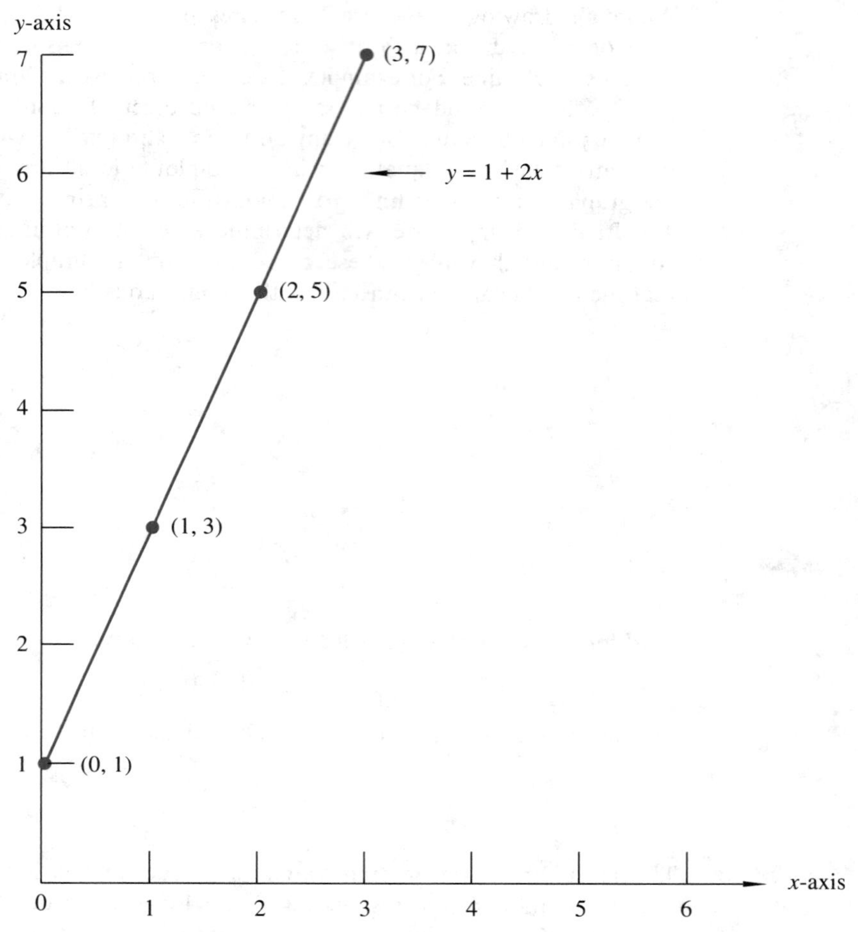

From Example 4.6 we can summarize the steps to plotting a linear equation (a straight line). These steps are:

1. Construct a table of coordinates by substituting values of x and determining the corresponding values of y. (*Note:* one could have an equation like $x = 3y + 2$. Here you would substitute y values and determine the x values to find the coordinates.)

2. Plot the coordinates from the table on the graph.

3. Join the coordinates with a straight line.

It is worth noting that the plotting of a linear equation requires only three coordinates. This is most helpful since it reduces the need to compute many coordinates. You should choose two coordinates that are sufficiently far apart so that the line drawn will accurately represent the equation. The third coordinate is often found just to check the accuracy of the line.

D. Intercepts and Linear Equations

One approach to selecting two coordinates is to select the two coordinates where the line crosses the x- and y-axis. **A point where the line crosses an axis is called an intercept**. Where the line crosses the y-axis is called the y-intercept; it is found by replacing x in the equation with 0 and determining the corresponding value of y. To determine the x-intercept we find the value of x when y is replaced by 0, i.e., set $y = 0$. Example 4.7 shows how one might plot a linear equation using the intercepts:

EXAMPLE 4.7

Graph the following equations using the x- and y-intercepts as the coordinates.

(a) $x - y = 3$
(b) $2x + y = 6$

Solution (a) First we find the x- and y-intercepts.

For $x - y = 3$

when $y = 0$ $\quad x = 3$

and

when $x = 0$ $\quad y = -3$

Therefore, the two coordinates for the x- and y-intercepts are:

x-intercept — (3, 0)
y-intercept — (0, −3)

Figure 4.6

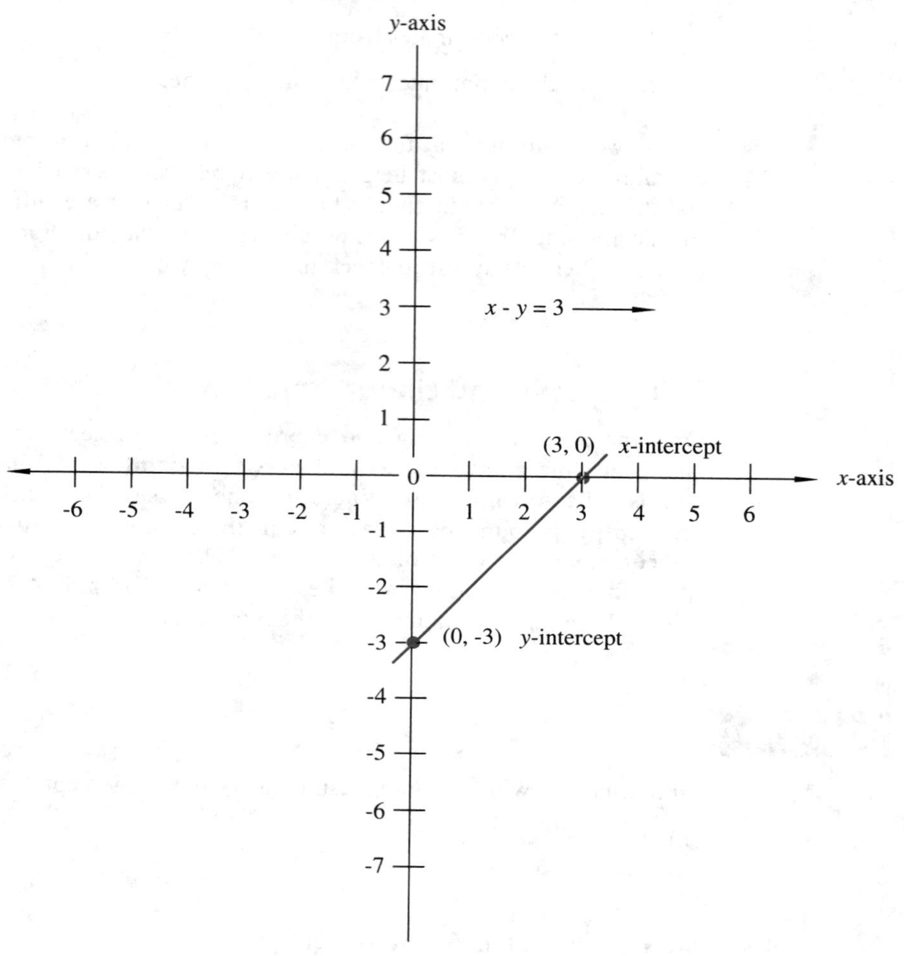

(b) Using the same approach as in (a), we find the x- and y-intercepts. These are:

For $2x + y = 6$

when $y = 0$ $\qquad x = 3$

and

when $x = 0$ $\qquad y = 6$

Therefore the intercepts are:

x-intercept — (3, 0)
y-intercept — (0, 6)

Plotting the intercept coordinates and drawing the line gives:

Figure 4.7

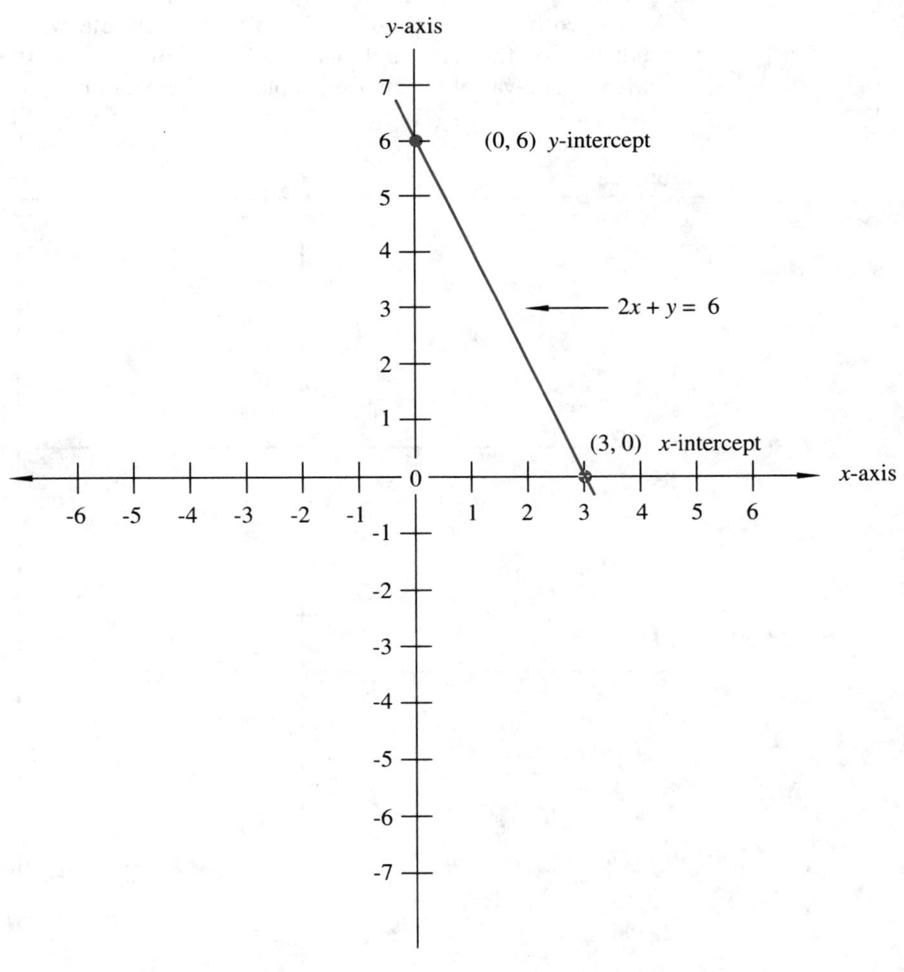

There is one last situation that may arise in plotting the graph of an equation: the graph of a constant, an equation with only one variable. This would occur if one of the numerical coefficients is zero. For example:

$$y = 4 \quad ①$$
$$2x = 10 \quad ②$$

In each of these cases, the line of the equation will be parallel to one of the axes. In particular, equation ① will be a horizontal line, parallel to the x-axis and 4 units above it; it crosses the y-axis at $y = 4$. In the second equation, the line will be a vertical line through $x = 5$, parallel to the y-axis.

Consequently, any equation with only one variable will be a straight line through one of the axes and parallel to the other axis. It should be noted that when a one-variable equation is plotted there can be only one intercept.

Figure 4.8

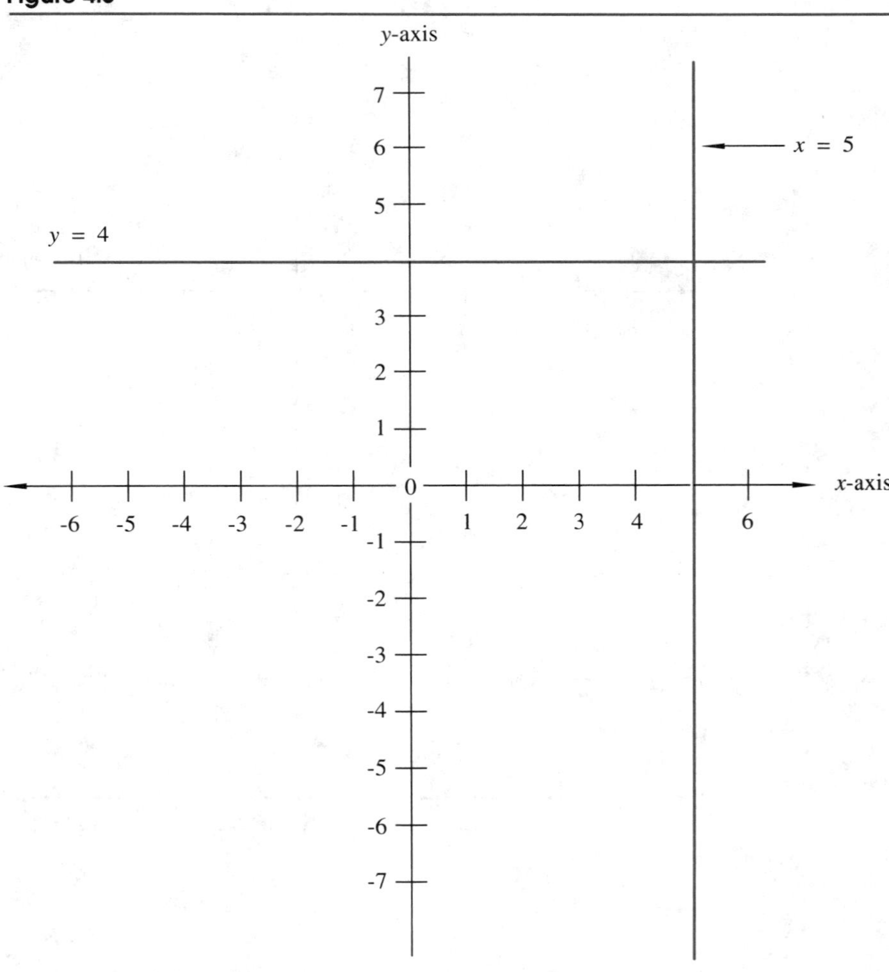

The two equations below are plotted in Figure 4.8 and show the graph of a one-variable equation.

$$y = 4 \quad ①$$
$$x = 5 \quad ②$$

EXAMPLE 4.8

Construct a graph of the following equations.

(a) $3x = 12$

(b) $2y = 6$

Solution (a) Solving for x gives:

$$3x = 12$$
$$x = 4$$

(b) Solving for y gives:

$$2y = 6$$
$$y = 3$$

Figure 4.9

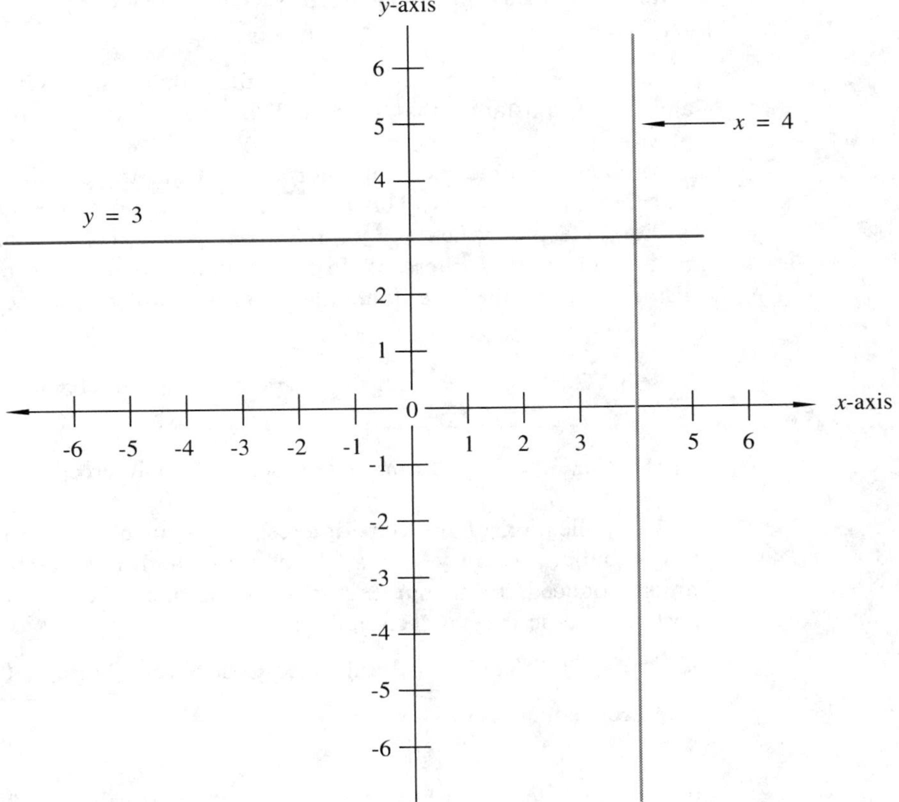

E. Slope of a Linear Equation

In the graph of a line, the steepness, or the angle of inclination of the line relative to the x-axis, is referred to as the **slope**. What the slope tells us is how a change in x will change y. For example, for the linear equation:

$$y = 4 + 5x$$

it can be seen that as x changes, y changes by 5 times the change in x. In this equation, the coefficient of x, namely 5, tells us that if x changes by 1, then y will change by $5x$. This coefficient, 5, is called the slope of the line. Consider the value of y if $x = 1$ and if $x = 2$. This would give:

$x = 1$:	$y = 4 + 5(1) = 9$	The difference
$x = 2$:	$y = 4 + 5(2) = 14$	or change in y is 5.

In the above equation, we can see that for the one unit change in x, from 1 to 2, y changes by 5. This change in y for each unit change in x is what the slope measures.

The slope describes the exact nature of the relationship between the y variable and the x variable. In mathematics, the term **dependent variable** is often used to describe the y variable, since its value depends upon the x variable. The x variable is called the **independent variable**. For the equation:

$$y = 4 + 5x$$

it can be seen that y depends upon the value assigned to x, since both 4 and 5 are constants, that is, 4 and 5 remain fixed regardless of the value of x.

Another valuable piece of information from the equation $y = 4 + 5x$, is that the y-intercept is 4. This follows from our knowledge that the y-intercept is the value of y when $x = 0$. In this equation we see that when $x = 0$, $y = 4$, which is the y-intercept. In mathematics, there is a general equation for a straight line, called the **slope-intercept form,** which is written as:

$$\boxed{y = b + mx} \longleftarrow \text{Slope-Intercept Form}$$

In the slope-intercept form, b represents the y-intercept and m is the slope of the line.

An application of the slope-intercept form in business would be the total cost equation, where y stands for total cost and x represents the number of units produced. From our examples in Chapter 3, you will recall that total costs were described by the relation:

$$\text{Total Cost} = \text{Total Fixed Cost} + \text{Total Variable Cost}$$

If the cost equation was:

$$y = \$5{,}000 + \$10x$$

it is possible to give a business interpretation to values \$5,000 and \$10. The \$5,000 does not change with x; if $x = 0$, the point of no output, then the total costs, y, are \$5,000. This value would be the fixed costs. As output is increased by one unit, the total cost, y, goes up by \$10. Thus \$10, the slope of the line, would be the variable cost per unit.

The importance of knowing the slope is that it gives us an idea of the direction of the line. If a line has a positive slope — a positive coefficient for x — then the line is said to slope upward to the right. If the slope is negative — a negative coefficient for x — then we know the line slopes downward to the right. To show both cases consider the equations:

$y = 3 + 2x$	The slope is + 2 and thus the line slopes upward to the right.
$y = 4 - 4x$	The slope is –4 and thus the line slopes downward to the right.

The graph of these two equations is shown in Figure 4.10.

Figure 4.10

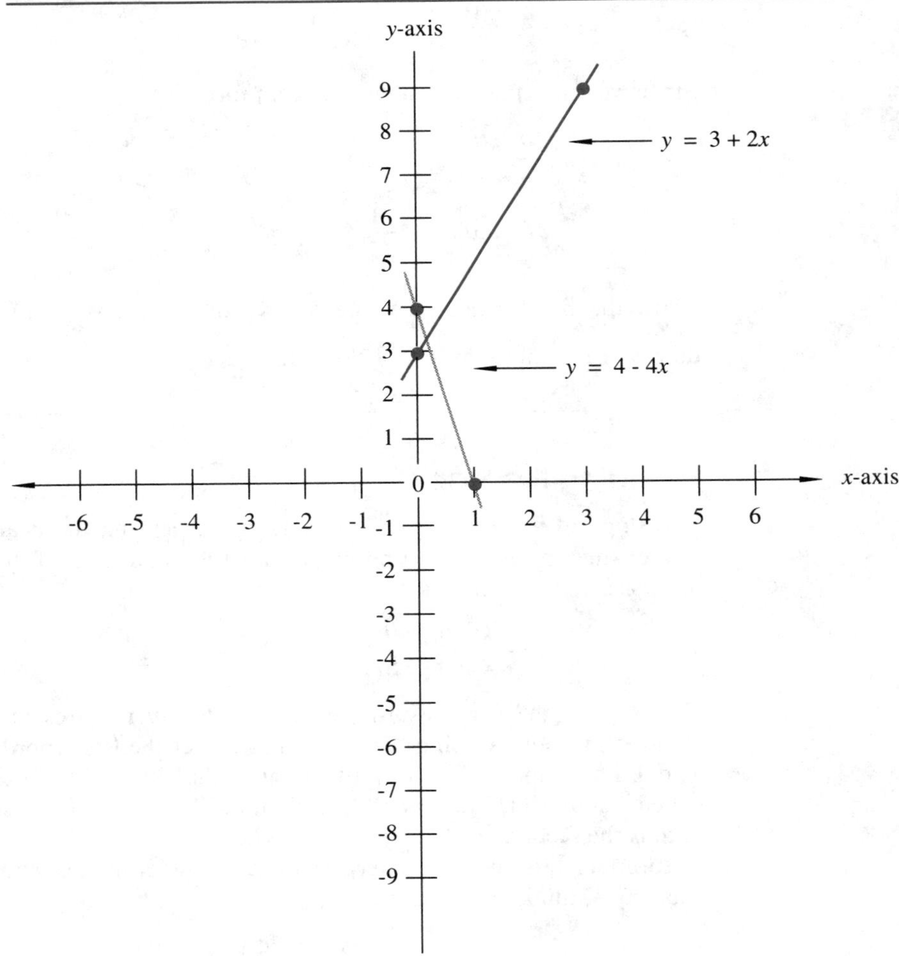

To see the importance of the slope-intercept form in understanding the relation between x and y, study Example 4.9:

EXAMPLE 4.9

Express $3y + x = 12$ in the slope-intercept form and find the value of the slope and the intercept. What direction does the line slope?

Solution

$3y + x = 12$ Rearrange the equation to isolate y on the left side.

$3y = 12 - x$ Divide each side by 3.

$$y = \frac{12}{3} - \frac{x}{3}$$

$$y = 4 - \frac{1}{3}x$$

Since we know from the slope-intercept form,

$y = b + mx,$ where b is the intercept and m is the slope, for our example we can say:

$$b = 4, \text{ and } m = -\frac{1}{3}$$

Thus, the point where the line crosses the y-axis is 4, and the line slopes downward to the right with a slope of $-\frac{1}{3}$.

F. Finding the Slope

The slope of a line, m, can be found by measuring the change in y relative to a change in x. We can find m by constructing a ratio of the relative change in y for a given change in x as:

$$m = \frac{\text{Change in } y}{\text{Change in } x}$$

To compute the slope using the relation for m requires us to measure the changes in y and x using two coordinates. Let the first coordinate be (x_1, y_1). The 1 for x and y is a way of defining the first value of x and y — it is called a subscript. The second coordinate will be defined by using the subscript 2; thus the second coordinate would be (x_2, y_2).

To understand how we interpret these two coordinates with their respective subscripts, think about each as:

when $x = x_1$, $y = y_1$, and
when $x = x_2$, $y = y_2$.

Therefore, by measuring the relative change in y, from y_1 to y_2, as a result of changing x from x_1 to x_2, a ratio of the changes would be constructed. This ratio would be:

$$m = \frac{\text{Change in } y}{\text{Change in } x} = \frac{y_2 - y_1}{x_2 - x_1} \qquad \textbf{Formula 4.1}$$

Thus, if you know two coordinates of a line, then the slope of the line can be found by comparing the coordinates in the slope formula. In terms of a business example, consider Example 4.10:

EXAMPLE 4.10

An accountant of a small manufacturing company is checking the production and cost records. She discovers that when production was at 1,000 units, total cost was \$6,000. She also found that when production was 1,500 units, the total cost was \$7,500. If she knows that total cost and production are related in a linear manner, using y for total cost and x for the number of units, help her do the following:

(a) Find the slope of the total cost equation.
(b) Using the slope-intercept form, find the total cost equation from the information provided.
(c) Interpret the business meaning of the slope and intercept for this problem.

Solution (a) The information in the problem gives two coordinates, (1,000, \$6,000) and (1,500, \$7,500). In addition, we are told to let y represent total cost and x the number of units. Defining the coordinates in terms of x and y for Formula 4.1 gives:

$x_1 = 1{,}000$, $y_1 = \$6{,}000$ and
$x_2 = 1{,}500$, $y_2 = \$7{,}500$

Substituting these coordinates into Formula 4.1 gives:

$$\frac{y_2 - y_1}{x_2 - x_1} = \frac{\$7{,}500 - \$6{,}000}{1{,}500 - 1{,}000}$$

$$\frac{y_2 - y_1}{x_2 - x_1} = \frac{\$1{,}500}{500}$$

$$\frac{y_2 - y_1}{x_2 - x_1} = \$3$$

$$m = \$3$$

Therefore, \$3 is the slope of the line.

(b) To find the cost equation we turn to the slope-intercept form, $y = b + mx$. Since we know m = \$3, we can solve for b by substituting values for x and y, from either one of the coordinates given. That is, we can substitute a pair of values for x and y that satisfies the equation. Therefore:

$y = b + mx$	Substituting m = \$3
$y = b + \$3x$	Select one of the given coordinates, say (1,000, \$6,000). Substitute (1,000, \$6,000) for x and y.
$\$6{,}000 = b + \$3(1{,}000)$	
$\$6{,}000 - \$3{,}000 = b$	
$\$3{,}000 = b$	Rearrange.
$b = \$3{,}000$	

Now we substitute $m = 3$ and b = \$3,000 into the slope-intercept form:

$y = b + mx$ Substitute m = \$3 and b = \$3,000.
$y = \$3{,}000 + \$3x$

This is the total cost equation and tells us that for every unit produced the cost goes up by \$3. In addition, it tells us that if output is zero, cost will be \$3,000. *Note*: the coordinate for y_2 and x_2 (\$7,500, 1,500) could have been used to determine b.

(c) The interpretation is that for every unit of output costs rise by \$3. Thus, we would say that, in this example, \$3 must be the variable cost per unit. Since the term \$3,000 remains constant for all values of x, then this must be the fixed cost portion of total costs.
A check of the solution for the equation could be found by substituting values for x and determining whether the values for y are as expected.

G. The Slope of Horizontal and Vertical Lines

The slope of horizontal and vertical lines are special cases. First, let's consider a horizontal line.

When one places a horizontal line on a graph it means that y is constant for all values of x. That is, no matter what the value of x, the value of y remains constant. In terms of the slope-intercept form of the line, $y = b + mx$, this would mean that $m = 0$, since x values have no influence on y. If $m = 0$, then,

$$y = b$$

In terms of the slope-intercept form, the expression would be:

$$y = b + 0x$$
$$y = b$$

Example 4.11 shows the situation where the slope is zero:

EXAMPLE 4.11

Graph the equation $y = 5$, and find the values of the slope and y-intercept.

Solution Using our slope-intercept equation $y = b + mx$, it can be seen that:

$$y = 5 + 0x$$
$$y = 5$$

In terms of the slope formula, the change in y is 0 for any change in x, or:

$$\frac{\text{Change in } y}{\text{Change in } x} = \frac{0}{\text{Change in } x}$$
$$= 0$$

Thus, b must be 5 and $m = 0$.

The graph of the equation $y = 5$ is:

Figure 4.11

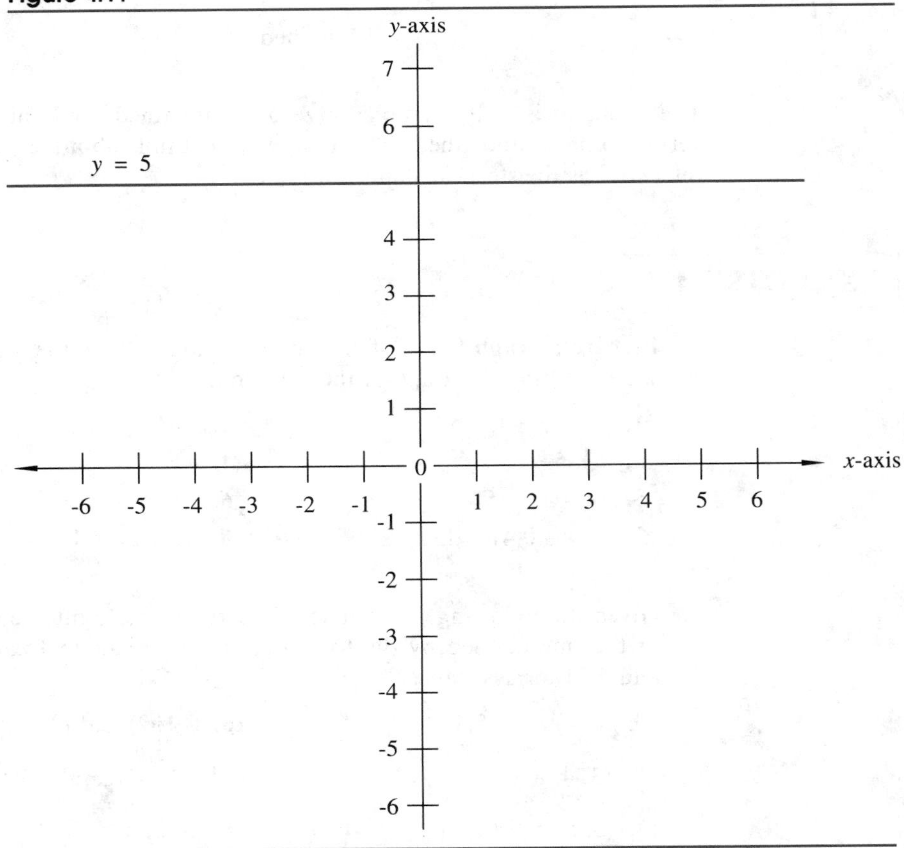

It is important to remember that the slope of a horizontal line is zero. This tells us that there is no change in y as a result of a change in x. In terms of a business example, if you were to plot fixed costs on a graph, where the horizontal scale was units of output and the vertical scale was dollars, then the fixed cost line would be horizontal, telling us that fixed costs are constant for all levels of output, x.

A vertical line is another special case and is more difficult to comprehend. What a vertical line implies is that the value of x remains constant for all values of y. In terms of the slope-intercept form of the linear equation, the value of b will be zero, since the line never intersects the y axis. In fact, x is constant for all values of y — that's right, all values. In terms of the slope formula, because x is constant for all values of y, this means that the change in x is zero. This would give:

$$\frac{\text{Change in } y}{\text{Change in } x} = \frac{y_2 - y_1}{x_2 - x_1}$$

$$= \frac{y_2 - y_1}{0}$$

$$= \text{Undefined}$$

The problem is that division by zero is undefined, and thus the slope of a vertical line is undefined. The best way to think about a vertical line is to refer to it as the steepest slope of all lines.

EXERCISE 4.2

A. Prepare a graph for the following equations. Show the x- and y-intercept when plotting the graph of the equation.

1. $2x + y = 10$

2. $x - y = 10$

3. $x = 5$

4. $y = 4$

5. $4y = 3x + 5$

6. $y = 2x - 1$

7. $0.5x - 0.4y = 1$

8. $3y = 2x + 1$

B. Given the following coordinates, find the slope, y-intercept, and equation of the line defined by the two coordinates. Refer to Examples 4.9, 4.10, and 4.11 for assistance.

9. (0, 4) and (5, 0)

10. (−1, 2) and (3, −14)

11. (3, 4) and $(1, 2\frac{1}{2})$

12. (−1, −2) and (4, 1)

13. (3, 5) and (4, 5)

14. (5, 2) and (8, 2)

4.3 Graphic Solution to a Linear System of Equations

In our discussion of linear systems of equations, it was stressed that our objective was to find values for x and y that simultaneously satisfied a system of two linear equations. Another way of looking at a simultaneous solution is to think of the rectangular coordinate system, and look for a coordinate that is common to both equations. This coordinate can be found by plotting the two equations on a graph. At the point where the lines of the equations intersect will be a coordinate where the value of x and y is the same for both equations. This common coordinate is the simultaneous solution to the system of equations. Consider Example 4.12:

EXAMPLE 4.12

Find the simultaneous solution to the following equation system using a graphic approach.

$$2x + y = 100 \quad ①$$
$$x - 2y = -50 \quad ②$$

Solution

STEP 1 Find the intercepts for each equation:

Intercepts for equation ①:

Setting $x = 0$,

$$\begin{aligned} 2x + y &= 100 \quad ① \\ 2(0) + y &= 100 \\ y &= 100 \end{aligned}$$

Setting $y = 0$,

$$\begin{aligned} 2x + y &= 100 \\ 2x + (0) &= 100 \\ x &= 50 \end{aligned}$$

Thus, for equation ① we have (0, 100) and (50, 0) as the y- and x-intercept coordinates.

Finding the intercepts for equation ②:

Setting $x = 0$,

$$\begin{aligned} x - 2y &= -50 \quad ② \\ (0) - 2y &= -50 \\ y &= 25 \end{aligned}$$

Setting $y = 0$,

$$\begin{aligned} x - 2y &= -50 \quad ② \\ x - 2(0) &= -50 \\ x &= -50 \end{aligned}$$

For equation ② we have (0, 25) and (–50, 0) as the y- and x-intercept coordinates.

STEP 2 Plotting these points on our graph and drawing the lines gives:

Figure 4.12

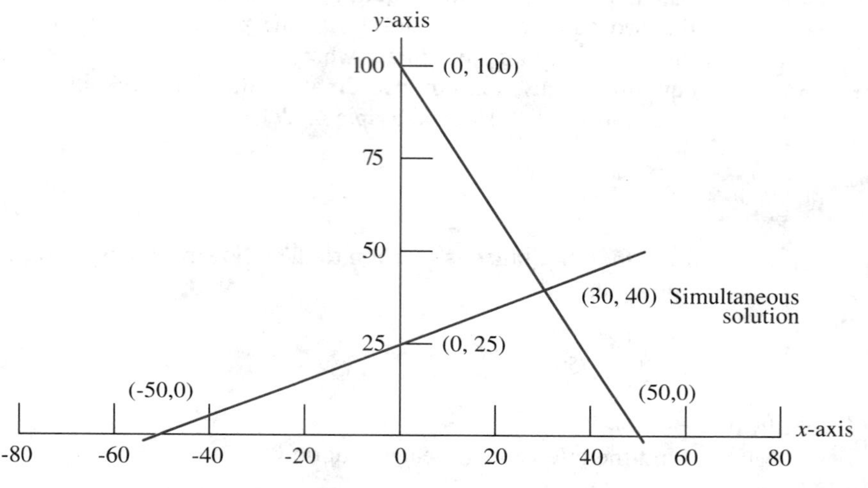

From the graph it is possible to determine that the lines of the two equations intersect at the point when $x = 30$ and $y = 40$.

To check the intersection, we can solve the two equations using the substitution approach. From equation ①, we solve for y:

$$2x + y = 100 \qquad ①$$
$$y = 100 - 2x \qquad ① \qquad \text{Solve for } y.$$

Substituting $y = 100 - 2x$ into equation ② gives:

$$x - 2y = -50 \qquad ②$$
$$x - 2(100 - 2x) = -50$$
$$x - 200 + 4x = -50$$
$$5x = 150$$
$$x = 30$$

To get y we substitute $x = 30$ into equation ①:

$$2(30) + y = 100$$
$$60 + y = 100$$
$$y = 40$$

Thus, we see that the graphic solution to the system of equations and the algebraic method give identical simultaneous solutions: $x = 30$ and $y = 40$.

EXERCISE 4.3

Using a graphical approach find the solution for the following linear systems of equations. Check your answers using substitution.

1. $4x - 3y = -3$
$5x - y = 10$

2. $x = 5$
$x + y = 1$

3. $2x + y = 5$
$3x + 2y = 2$

4. $x - 2y = 6$
$x + y = 4$

5. $x + y = 9$
$x - y = 1$

6. $x + 2y = 9$
$2x + y = 2$

4.4 Graphical Approach to Break-even Analysis

The use of graphs in break-even analysis allows one to observe how costs and revenue change with changes in output. In general, the vertical axis (y-axis) is defined in terms of dollars, with costs or revenues placed on this axis. The volume of output, in units, is usually placed on the x-axis. To see how the axes are set up, consider the following example:

EXAMPLE 4.13

A company produces plastic coffee filters and has the following costs:

Variable cost per unit: \$0.50
Total Fixed Costs: \$6,000
Selling price per filter: \$4.50

What is the break-even point? Graph the total cost equation, the total revenue equation, the fixed cost equation, and show the break-even point on the graph.

Solution The most direct way to solve the problem is to define a cost and a revenue equation. Letting x represent output in units, and using the information from the problem in addition to the cost relationship:

$$\text{Total Costs} = \text{Total Fixed Costs} + \text{Total Variable Costs}$$

Substituting we get:

$$\text{Total Cost} = \$6{,}000 + \$0.50x$$
$$\text{Total Revenue} = \$4.5x$$
$$\text{Fixed Cost} = \$6{,}000$$

At the break-even point cost and revenue are equal, therefore:

Total Revenue	=	Total Fixed Cost	+	Total Variable Cost
$\$4.5x$	=	$\$6{,}000$	+	$\$0.50x$

$$\$4x = \$6{,}000$$
$$x = 1{,}500 \text{ units}$$

Therefore, the break-even point is at 1,500 units.

To show the revenue and cost equations on the graph, we first must find coordinates for each equation. Choosing easy-to-use values of x and y, we use $x = 1{,}000$ and $x = 2{,}000$ (*Note:* any other values could have been used). Now, find the value of y for the assumed x-values. The coordinates are listed below for each equation.

Find total cost for $x = 1{,}000$ and $x = 2{,}000$.

$$\text{Total Cost } y = \$6{,}000 + \$0.50x$$

	Coordinates
Substituting $x = 1{,}000$	
Total Cost = \$6,000 + \$0.50 (1,000)	
Total Cost = \$6,500	(1,000, \$6,500)
Substituting $x = 2{,}000$	
Total Cost = \$6,000 + \$0.50 (2,000)	
Total Cost = \$7,000	(2,000, \$7,000)
Find total revenue for $x = 1{,}000$ and $x = 2{,}000$.	
Total Revenue = \$4.5x	
Substituting $x = 1{,}000$	
Total Revenue = \$4.5 (1,000)	
Total Revenue = \$4,500	(1,000, \$4,500)
Substituting $x = 2{,}000$	
Total Revenue = \$4.5 (2,000)	
Total Revenue = \$9,000	(2,000, \$9,000)

Total Fixed Cost = \$6,000 constant for all x.

Plotting the cost and revenue equations gives:

Figure 4.13

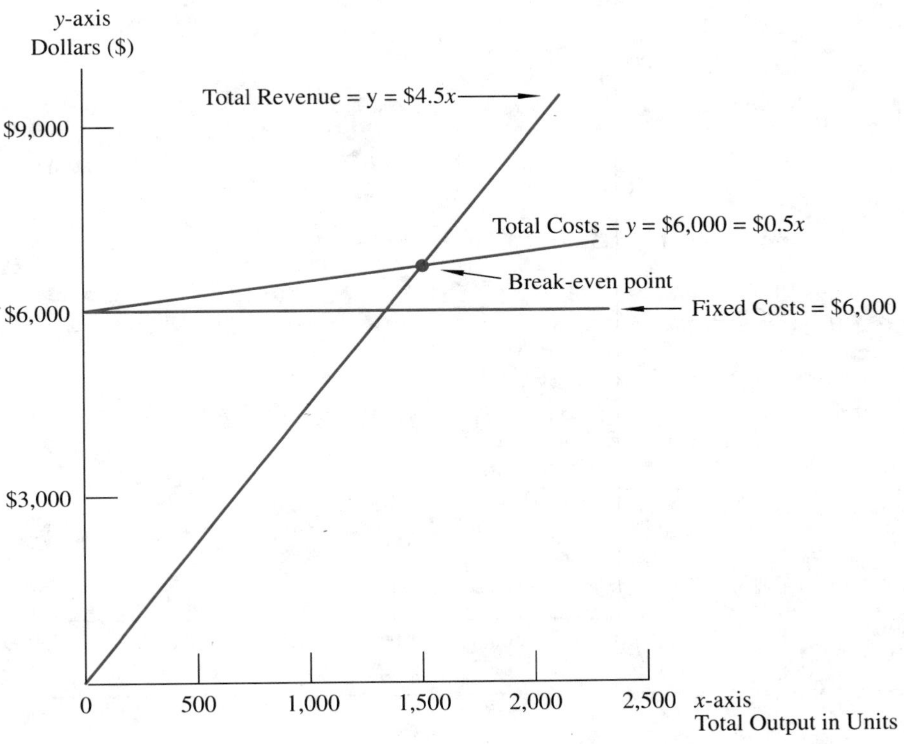

In Example 4.13, output larger than the break-even point allows the firm to make a profit. This profit can be measured by the vertical distance between the total cost and revenue equations, to the right of the break-even point; a loss would be the vertical distance to the left of the break-even point. The graph below shows the profit and loss areas.

Figure 4.14

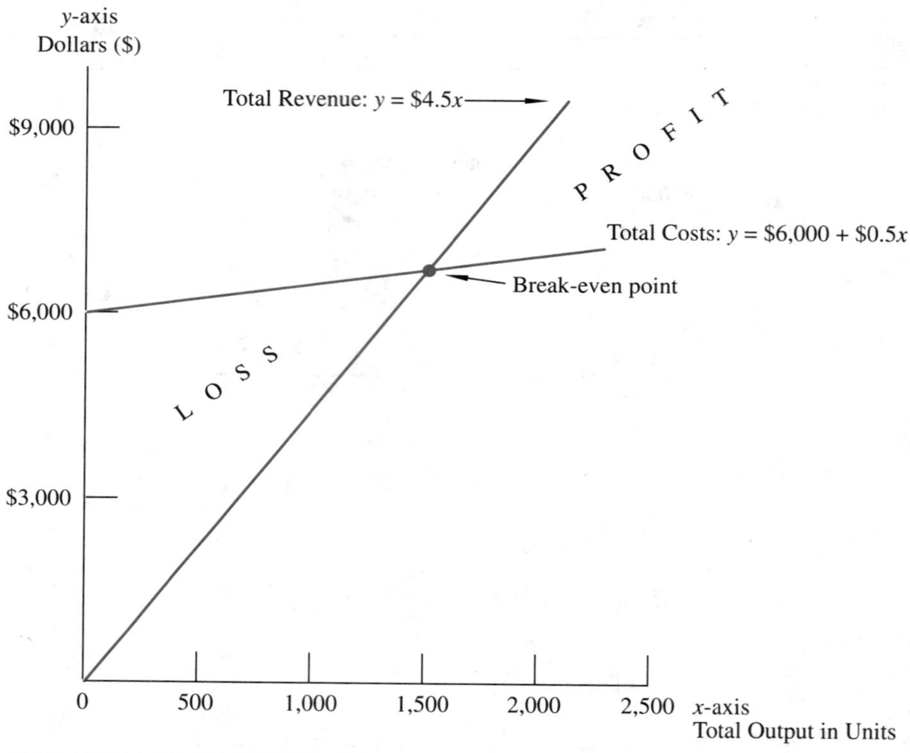

EXERCISE 4.4

Approximate the break-even point for the following business problems using a graph. Find the exact break-even point by using the algebraic approach. For each graph, sketch the profit and loss areas.

1. A company has fixed costs of \$30,000. Variable costs per unit are constant. At 10,000 units of output, the total variable costs are \$50,000. If the product sells for \$10, what is the break-even point? What is the dollar value of sales at the break-even point?

2. A small company has a product that costs \$0.30 per unit to manufacture. The company has fixed costs of \$15,000. If the product sells for \$0.69, what is the break-even level of output? What would be the level of output necessary to make a profit of \$20,000? What are the sales in dollars at the point where a profit of \$20,000 is made? Use a graph to show the break-even output and the output point necessary for the profit of \$20,000.

3. The Telstar Company is considering an advertising program that will add \$70,000 to fixed costs this year (once committed to the advertising program it is obliged to make the expenditures). The product it sells is a television converter that currently sells for \$50. The unit production cost is \$30 per unit. The current fixed costs are \$150,000, excluding the advertising costs. How many additional units must be sold to justify the advertising expenditure? What is the new break-even point?

4.5 Mathematical Progressions

In later sections of this book, it will be necessary to find the sum of values of money over time. The formulas that we will be using will give us the sum of money over time, where this sum is based on the addition of a series of terms (different numbers).

The addition of these terms can be quickly determined by knowing the type of pattern that has been used to generate the numbers — that is, the mathematical relationship between each term. There are two common types of sequences used to generate numbers in a particular pattern. These two types of sequences are called arithmetic and geometric progressions. Each generate numbers in a precise order. However, the choice of which progression — arithmetic or geometric — will depend upon how the differences between successive values of the terms in the series are related.

Our objective in learning about arithmetic and geometric progressions (also called series) is to be able to find one or more terms of the sequence without having to work out all the terms in the sequence. The value of finding the terms of the sequence will be of great assistance when it is necessary to find the value of money at different points in time.

For example, if you have a loan and the loan is charged interest, you may want to determine how much you will owe in two years. If you do not make any payments toward the loan, then you would only be interested in finding the value of the original amount borrowed plus all the accumulated interest. The amount you would owe at the end of the loan is the sum of a sequence of numbers — the interest over time and the amount you borrowed. The most important part of this example is our need to find only the dollar value at the end of the two years. The exact amount you owe in six months would not be of particular importance if the loan is not to be repaid for two years.

To avoid having to work out all the intermediate terms or numbers in the series, we use the properties of a series to help us. One of these properties allows us to compute the value for any term in the sequence, without having to evaluate other terms in the sequence.

A. Arithmetic Progressions

(i) Finding the Value of the *n*th Term of an Arithmetic Progression

An arithmetic progression is a sequence of numbers that are in a definite order or pattern. Each number in the sequence is dependent upon the previous number in the sequence, in a precise manner. The manner in which the terms of the sequence are determined results from the **addition of a constant to the previous term in the series**. For example:

1, 5, 9, ___, ___, ___

What are the next three terms? As can be seen, the second and third terms, 5 and 9, result from adding 4 to the first term and 4 to the second term in the sequence. Each new term is the result of adding 4 to the preceding term of the sequence. Thus the blanks for the next three terms should be 13, 17, and 21. For each term, we see there is a **common difference of 4. The common difference can be found by subtracting the first term from the second term.**

EXAMPLE 4.14

Find the common difference and the missing terms in the following sequences.

(a) 3, 5, 7, ___, ___, ___, ___
(b) –3, 0, 3, ___, ___, ___, ___
(c) –4, –2, 0, ___, ___, ___, ___
(d) 7, 15, 23, ___, ___, ___, ___

Solution (a) 3, 5, 7, ___, ___, ___, ___

First we find the common difference:

$5 - 3 = 2$, and $7 - 5 = 2$. Therefore, the missing terms must be:

9 $(7 + 2)$, 11 $(9 + 2)$, 13 $(11 + 2)$, and 15 $(13 + 2)$

or

3, 5, 7, <u>9</u>, <u>11</u>, <u>13</u>, <u>15</u>

(b) –3, 0, 3, ___, ___, ___, ___

Find the common difference by subtracting the terms $0 - (-3) = 3$, and $3 - 0 = 3$. Therefore, adding this common difference to the last term in the sequence gives us:

–3, 0, 3, <u>6</u>, <u>9</u>, <u>12</u>, <u>15</u>

(c) −4, −2, 0,____, ____, ____, ____

Finding the common difference we have:

−2 − (−4) = 2. Thus, the remaining terms must be:

−4, −2, 0, <u>2</u>, <u>4</u>, <u>6</u>, <u>8</u>

(d) 7, 15, 23, ____, ____, ____, ____

The common difference is 15 − 7 = 8. Thus, the missing terms are:

7, 15, 23, <u>31</u>, <u>39</u>, <u>47</u>, <u>55</u>

What we must do is find an expression for an arithmetic progression so that we can find the *n*th term of the sequence, without having to work out all the terms of the sequence. For example, in part (d) above, how could we determine the 100th term of the sequence? To be able to do this directly, without having to find each term of the sequence, requires us to find a formula that will permit us to find the term directly. To derive a formula we must define the terms of an arithmetic progression using letters, then we will assign numbers to the letters when we know which term of the progression we are seeking. The definitions we require are:

a— the value of the first term in the sequence;

d— the common difference between each term of the sequence;

n— the number of terms in the sequence;

t_n— the *n*th term in the sequence;

S_n— S is the sum of the terms in the sequence, and in the general case, the sum of n terms.

Now using the symbols we have defined it is possible to say:

$t_1 = a$ = first term of the sequence;

$t_2 = a + d$ = the second term in the sequence;

$t_3 = a + 2d$ = the third term in the sequence, which is simply $a + d + d$;

$t_4 = a + 3d$ = the fourth term in the sequence and is found by adding $a + d + d + d$.

The thing to note is that the coefficient for d is always one less than the term being found. Therefore, $a + 3d$ would be the fourth term of an arithmetic sequence. Suppose the first term in the sequence was 100 ($a = 100$) and the difference between each term was 50 ($d = 50$), then the fourth term in the sequence would be 100 + 3(50), or 250. From this, we can say that the value of the nth term in the sequence is:

$$t_n = a + (n - 1)d$$ **Formula 4.2**

To see how this expression works, consider Example 4.15, which uses the examples worked out in Example 4.14:

EXAMPLE 4.15

Find the last term (the last blank) for the four sequences in Example 4.14, by using Formula 4.2:

$t_n = a + (n - 1)d$

Solution (a) From Example 4.14, (a): 3, 5, 7, ___, ___, ___, ___

$a = 3$ The first term in the sequence.

$d = 2$ The common difference.

$n = 7$ The last blank is the 7th term in the sequence.

Substituting all the numbers for the letters in the expression for t_n, the 7th term of the sequence is:

$t_n = a + (n - 1)d$

$t_7 = 3 + (7 - 1)2$

$t_7 = 15$ The same as we found in Example 4.14 (a).

(b) From Example 4.14, (b): –3, 0, 3, ___, ___, ___, ___

$a = -3$ The first term in the sequence.

$d = 3$ The common difference.

$n = 7$ The last blank is the 7th term in the sequence.

Substituting all the numbers for the letters in the expression for t_n, the 7th term of the sequence is:

$t_n = a + (n -1)d$

$t_7 = -3 + (7 - 1)3$

$t_7 = 15$ The same as we found in Example 4.14 (b).

(c) From Example 4.14, (c): –4, –2, 0, ___, ___, ___, ___

$a = -4$ The first term in the sequence.

$d = 2$ The common difference.

$n = 7$ The last blank is the 7th term in the sequence.

Substituting numbers for the letters in the expression for t_n, the 7th term of the sequence is:

$t_n = a + (n - 1)d$

$t_7 = -4 + (7 - 1)2$

$t_7 = 8$ The same as we found in Example 4.14 (c).

(d) From Example 4.14 (d): 7, 15, 23, ____, ____, ____, ____

$a = 7$ The first term in the sequence.

$d = 8$ The common difference.

$n = 7$ The last blank is the 7th term in the sequence.

Substituting the numbers for letters in the expression for t_n yields:

$t_n = a + (n - 1)d$

$t_7 = 7 + (7 - 1)8$

$t_7 = 55$ The same as we found in Example 4.14 (d).

(ii) The Sum of an Arithmetic Progression

The most often used property of arithmetic progressions in business is finding the sum of a specific number of terms where each term represents a period of time.

To illustrate how to find the sum of an arithmetic progression, the following example is presented. Find the sum of the arithmetic series:

5, 7, 9, 11, 13

There are two ways we can find the sum. One way is:

$45 = 5 + 7 + 9 + 11 + 13$ ⟵ Adding from the first term to the last term and;

$45 = 13 + 11 + 9 + 7 + 5$ ⟵ Adding from the last term to the first term.

Now, if you add each term, that is, first term + last term, second term + second last term, etc., you see the sum of the two terms is constant at 18. That is,

45 =	5 +	7 +	9 +	11 +	13	Sum from first term to last term.
45 =	13 +	11 +	9 +	7 +	5	Sum from last term to first term.
90	18	18	18	18	18	Sum of terms.

To find the sum of the series of these 5 numbers:

$$\frac{18 \times 5}{2} = \frac{90}{2} = 45$$

We divide by 2 since the series has been added twice — once from each end of the series.

However, if you look closely you will see that the sum could have been found by doing the following:

$$\frac{[\text{first term} + \text{last term}]\ [\text{number of terms}]}{2} = \frac{[5 + 13]\ 5}{2}$$

$$= 45$$

Finding an expression for the sum of an arithmetic progression can be formulated by using the earlier definitions:

a— the value of the first term in the sequence;
d— the common difference;
n— the number of terms in the sequence;
t_n— the nth term in the sequence;
S_n— the sum of the terms in the sequence.

Therefore, since we know the sum of an arithmetic series can be found by:

$$\frac{[\text{first term} + \text{last term}]\ [\text{number of terms}]}{2} = \frac{[a + t_n]\ n}{2}$$

$$= S_n$$

we can say that the sum of an arithmetic series can be found by the following formula:

$$S_n = \frac{n}{2}(a + t_n)$$ **Formula 4.3**

To see how Formula 4.3 works, let us return to Example 4.14. In part (a), the problem was to find the last four terms. Instead of finding four separate terms, suppose we had wanted to find the sum of all seven terms, that is, the sum of 3, 5, 7, 9, 11, 13, and 15. Using our formula for S_n, we have:

$a = 3$, the first term in the sequence;
$t_n = 15$, the 7th or last term of the sequence;
$n = 7$, the number of terms.

Placing these values in our formula for S_n gives:

$$S_n = \frac{n}{2}(a + t_n)$$

$$S_n = \frac{7}{2}(3 + 15)$$

$$S_n = 63$$

Checking to see if this sum is correct, add each term of the original sequence:

$$3 + 5 + 7 + 9 + 11 + 13 + 15 = 63$$

EXAMPLE 4.16

Find the sum of the terms for parts b, c, and d from Example 4.14. Check your answer.

Solution (b) –3, 0, 3, 6, 9, 12, 15

$a = -3$ The first term in the sequence.
$t_7 = 15$ The 7th or last term of the sequence.
$n = 7$ The number of terms.

Placing these values in Formula 4.3 to find S_n gives:

$$S_n = \frac{n}{2}(a + t_n)$$

$$S_n = \frac{7}{2}(-3 + 15)$$

$$S_n = 42$$

Checking this sum:

$$-3 + 0 + 3 + 6 + 9 + 12 + 15 = 42$$

(c) –4, –2, 0, 2, 4, 6, 8

$a = -4$ The first term in the sequence.
$t_7 = 8$ The 7th or last term of the sequence.
$n = 7$ The number of terms.

Placing these values in Formula 4.3 for S_n:

$$S_n = \frac{n}{2}(a + t_n)$$

$$S_n = \frac{7}{2}(-4 + 8)$$

$$S_n = 14$$

Checking this sum:

$$-4 + -2 + 0 + 2 + 4 + 6 + 8 = 14$$

(d) 7, 15, 23, 31, 39, 47, 55

$a = 7$ The first term in the sequence.
$t_7 = 55$ The 7th or last term of the sequence.
$n = 7$ The number of terms.

Placing these values into Formula 4.3 gives:

$$S_n = \frac{n}{2}(a + t_n)$$

$$S_n = \frac{7}{2}(7 + 55)$$

$$S_n = 217$$

Checking this sum:

$$7 + 15 + 23 + 31 + 39 + 47 + 55 = 217$$

EXAMPLE 4.17

Given an arithmetic progression, 34, 40, 46, . . . find the:

(a) sum of the first 10 terms;
(b) 15th term and the sum of the first 15 terms;
(c) 8th term and the sum of the first 8 terms.

Solution (a) Use Formula 4.2 [$t_n = a + (n - 1)d$] to find the last term t_n, then use Formula 4.3 to find the sum.

$$S_n = \frac{n}{2}(a + t_n)$$

First, defining the terms:

$d = 6$ Common difference.
$a = 34$ The first term in the sequence.
$n = 10$ The number of terms.

Applying Formula 4.2 to find t_n:

$$t_n = a + (n - 1)d$$
$$t_{10} = 34 + (10 - 1)6$$
$$t_{10} = 88$$

Now that we have t_{10} we can find the sum using Formula 4.3 and find S_n as follows:

$$S_n = \frac{n}{2}(a + t_n)$$

$$S_n = \frac{10}{2}(34 + 88)$$

$$S_n = 610$$

(b) As with part (a), we use Formula 4.2 to find the 15th term, t_{15}, then use Formula 4.3 to find the sum of the first 15 terms. First, defining the terms for the formula:

$d = 6$	Common difference.
$a = 34$	The first term in the sequence.
$n = 15$	The number of terms.

Applying Formula 4.2 to find t_n:

$$t_n = a + (n - 1)d$$
$$t_{15} = 34 + (15 - 1)6$$
$$t_{15} = 118$$

S_n can now be found by using Formula 4.3:

$$S_n = \frac{n}{2}(a + t_n) \qquad \text{Substituting } n, a, \text{ and } t_{15}.$$
$$S_n = \frac{15}{2}(34 + 118)$$
$$S_n = 1{,}140$$

(c) As with part (b), we use Formula 4.2 to find the 8th term, t_8, then use Formula 4.3 to find the sum of the first 8 terms. First, defining the terms for the formula:

$d = 6$	Common difference.
$a = 34$	The first term in the sequence.
$n = 8$	The number of terms.

$$t_n = a + (n - 1)d$$
$$t_8 = 34 + (8 - 1)6$$
$$t_8 = 76$$

The sum can now be found by using Formula 4.3 as follows:

$$S_n = \frac{n}{2}(a + t_n)$$
$$S_n = \frac{8}{2}(34 + 76)$$
$$S_n = 440$$

EXERCISE 4.5

A. Find the last term and the sum for the following arithmetic progressions.

1. 2, 5, 8, . . . to 6 terms

2. 4, 8, 12, . . . to 8 terms

3. 0.1, 0.5, 0.9, . . . to 6 terms

4. 2, 8, 14, . . . to 15 terms
5. 0.1, 0.9, 1.7, . . . to 6 terms
6. 10, 5, 0, . . . to 20 terms
7. 9, 6, 3, . . . to 10 terms
8. $\frac{1}{12}, \frac{1}{4}, \frac{5}{12}, \ldots$ to 7 terms
9. –2, –6, –10, . . . to 12 terms
10. 2.5, 5.5, 8.5, . . . to 7 terms
11. 2, 16, 30, . . . to 6 terms
12. 2.5, 5.5, 8.5, . . . to 25 terms

B. You have learned how to find a, S_n, t_n, d, and n for an arithmetic series. For the following find a value for the remaining parts of the series.
13. $t_5 = 10$, $d = 2$, $n = 5$; find S_n and a.
14. $t_5 = 34$, $a = 4$, $n = 5$; find S_n and d.
15. $S_n = 48$, $a = 3$, $n = 6$; find t_6 and d.
16. $S_n = 42$, $a = 2$, $n = 6$; find t_6 and d.
17. $a = 3$, $n = 4$, $S_n = 30$; find t_4 and d.
18. $n = 5$, $a = 5$, $d = 4$; find t_5 and S_n.
19. $a = -16$, $n = 10$, $S_n = 20$; find t_{10} and d.
20. $a = 1.5$, $n = 7$, $t_7 = 16.5$; find S_n and d.

B. Geometric Progressions

(i) Finding the nth Term of a Geometric Progression

A geometric progression is a sequence of numbers in which each term is found by multiplying the preceding term by a constant. For example, 2, 4, 8, 16, . . . is a geometric progression since each term is a result of multiplying the previous term by a constant. In this situation, 2 is the constant. This constant is called the **common ratio** and can be either a positive or negative number. For example, if the first term of a geometric progression is 4 and the common ratio (the constant in the multiplication) is 3, the first four terms of the progression would be:

$$\begin{aligned} \text{First Term} &= 4 \\ \text{Second Term} &= 4(3) &&= 12 \\ \text{Third Term} &= 4(3)(3) &&= 4(3^2) = 36 \\ \text{Fourth Term} &= 4(3)(3)(3) &&= 4(3^3) = 108 \end{aligned}$$

If you examine one of the terms, say the third term, 36, you can see that it is found by multiplying the first term, 4, by the constant ratio, 3, squared. Further, the fourth term is found by multiplying the first term by the constant ratio raised to the third power. Consequently, we can say that the *n*th term of the series will be the first term multiplied by the constant ratio raised to the power $n - 1$. This would be stated as:

Given a first term of 4, with a common ratio of 3, the nth term of the series is:

$$t_n = 4(3^{n-1})$$

For example, if we wanted to find the 6th term of the series it would be found as:

$$\begin{aligned} t_6 &= 4(3^{6-1}) \\ &= 4(3^5) \\ &= 972 \end{aligned}$$

Defining the parts of a geometric series as:

a = the value of the first term;
r = the value of the common ratio;
t_n = the value of the last term of the sequence;
n = the number of terms in the sequence;

the value of the nth term, t_n, can be found by using the formula:

$t_n = ar^{n-1}$ = the value of the nth term of a geometric progression. **Formula 4.4**

EXAMPLE 4.18

Find the value of the term required for the following geometric sequences.

(a) 2, 6, 18; find the 6th term of the sequence.
(b) 1, 4, 16; find the 7th term of the sequence.
(c) 1.12, 3.36, 10.08; find the 9th term of the sequence.
(d) 0.96, 0.528, 0.2904; find the 5th term of the sequence.

Solution (a) 2, 6, 18; finding the value of the 6th term of the sequence:

Define the values for a, n, and r:

$a = 2$ First term of the series.
$n = 6$ The number of terms.
$r = \left(\frac{6}{2}\right)$ Common ratio.
$= 3$

Substitute these values into Formula 4.4:

$$\begin{aligned} t_n &= ar^{n-1} \\ t_6 &= 2(3^{6-1}) \\ t_6 &= 486 \end{aligned}$$

(b) 1, 4, 16; finding the value of the 7th term of the sequence:

Define the values for a, n, and r:

$a = 1$ First term of the series.

$n = 7$ The number of terms.

$r = (\frac{4}{1})$ Common ratio.

$= 4$

Substitute these values into Formula 4.4:

$$t_n = ar^{n-1}$$
$$t_7 = 1(4^{7-1})$$
$$t_7 = 4{,}096$$

(c) 1.12, 3.36, 10.08; finding the value of the 9th term of the sequence:

Define the values for a, n, and r:

$a = 1.12$ First term of the series.

$n = 9$ The number of terms.

$r = \frac{3.36}{1.12}$ Common ratio.

$= 3$

Substitute these values into Formula 4.4:

$$t_n = ar^{n-1}$$
$$t_9 = 1.12(3^{9-1})$$
$$t_9 = 7{,}348.32$$

(d) 0.96, 0.528, 0.2904; finding the value of the 5th term of the sequence:

Define the values for a, n, and r:

$a = 0.96$ First term of the series.

$n = 5$ The number of terms.

$r = \left(\frac{0.528}{0.96}\right)$ Common ratio.

$= 0.55$

Substitute these values into Formula 4.4:

$$t_n = ar^{n-1}$$
$$t_5 = 0.96[(0.55)^{5-1}]$$
$$t_5 = 0.087846$$

Note that in the formula for t_n, the nth term can be used to find any term of a sequence simply by treating the term you are seeking as the last term. This concept is used later when we want to find the future value of money (the original amount plus interest).

(ii) Finding the Sum of a Geometric Progression

As with finding the sum of an arithmetic progression, the sum of the terms of a geometric progression will be denoted by S_n. To find a formula for the sum of a geometric progression, we use a procedure similar to that used when we developed an expression for the sum of an arithmetic progression.

First we define the sum as:

$$S_n = a + ar + ar^2 + ar^3 + ar^4 + \dots + ar^{n-1} \quad ①$$

If we multiply both sides of the expression for S_n by r we get:

$$rS_n = ar + ar^2 + ar^3 + ar^4 + ar^5 + \dots + ar^n \quad ②$$

If we subtract expression ② (rS_n) from expression ① (S_n) we get:

$$S_n - rS_n = [a + ar + ar^2 + \dots + ar^{n-1}] - [ar + ar^2 + \dots + ar^{n-1} + a^n]$$

$$S_n - rS_n = a - ar^n$$

In the last expression, $a - ar^n$ comes from the subtraction of rS_n from S_n. In each expression, the terms are the same except for the first term in S_n, namely a, and the last term in rS_n, namely ar^n.

Factoring out common terms and solving for S_n yields:

$$S_n - rS_n = a - ar^n$$

$$S_n(1 - r) = a(1 - r^n)$$

Rearranging to find S_n, the sum of a geometric progression, gives:

$$S_n = \frac{a(1 - r^n)}{(1 - r)} \quad \dots \qquad \textbf{Formula 4.5}$$

To see how Formula 4.5 works, try Example 4.19, which uses the series from Example 4.18:

EXAMPLE 4.19

Find the sum of the following sequences.

(a) Find the sum of the first 6 terms of the sequence 2, 6, 18.
(b) Find the sum of the first 7 terms of the sequence 1, 4, 16.
(c) Find the sum of the first 9 terms of the sequence 1.12, 3.36, 10.08.
(d) Find the sum of the first 5 terms of the sequence 0.96, 0.528, 0.2904.

Solution (a) The sum of 2, 6, 18, up to the 6th term of the sequence.

Define the values for a, n, and r:

$a = 2$ First term of the series.

$n = 6$ The number of terms.

$r = \left(\frac{6}{2}\right)$ Common ratio.

$= 3$

Substituting these values into Formula 4.5 gives:

$$S_n = \frac{a(1 - r^n)}{(1 - r)}$$

$$S_n = \frac{2(1 - 3^6)}{(1 - 3)}$$

$$S_n = \frac{2(1 - 729)}{(1 - 3)}$$

$$S_n = 728$$

(b) The sum of 1, 4, 16, up to the 7th term of the sequence:

Define the values for a, n, and r:

$a = 1$ First term of the series.

$n = 7$ The number of terms.

$r = \left(\frac{4}{1}\right)$ Common ratio.

$= 4$

Substitute these values into Formula 4.5:

$$S_n = \frac{a(1 - r^n)}{(1 - r)}$$

$$S_n = \frac{1(1 - 4^7)}{(1 - 4)}$$

$$S_n = \frac{1(1 - 16{,}384)}{(1 - 4)}$$

$$S_n = 5{,}461$$

(c) The sum of the sequence 1.12, 3.36, 10.08, up to the 9th term of the sequence can be found as follows:

Define the values for a, n, and r:

$a = 1.12$ First term of the series.

$n = 9$ The number of terms.

$r = \left(\frac{3.36}{1.12}\right)$ Common ratio.

$= 3$

Substitute these values into Formula 4.5:

$$S_n = \frac{a(1 - r^n)}{(1 - r)}$$

$$S_n = \frac{1.12(1 - 3^9)}{(1 - 3)}$$

$$S_n = \frac{1.12(1 - 19{,}683)}{(1 - 3)}$$

$$S_n = 11{,}021.92$$

(d) The sum of 0.96, 0.528, 0.2904, up to the 5th term of the sequence:

Define the values for a, n, and r:

$a = 0.96$ First term of the series.

$n = 5$ Number of terms.

$r = \left(\frac{0.528}{0.96}\right)$ Common ratio.

$= 0.55$

Substitute these values into Formula 4.5:

$$S_n = \frac{a(1 - r^n)}{(1 - r)}$$

$$S_n = \frac{0.96(1 - 0.55^5)}{(1 - 0.55)}$$

$$S_n = \frac{0.96(1 - 0.050328437)}{(1 - 0.55)}$$

$$S_n = 2.025966$$

EXERCISE 4.6

A. Find the *n*th term, t_n, and the sum, S_n, of the following geometric progressions.

1. 2, 6, 18, . . . to 6 terms

2. 1, 5, 25, . . . to 10 terms

3. 0.1, 0.3, 0.9, . . . to 6 terms

4. 2, 5, 12.5, . . . to 15 terms

5. 1, 0.5, 0.25, . . . to 9 terms

6. 3, 12, 48, . . . to 8 terms

7. 3, 9, 27, . . . to 12 terms

8. $\frac{1}{12}, \frac{1}{6}, \frac{1}{3}$, . . . to 5 terms

9. −2, 6, −18, . . . to 12 terms

10. 2.5, 5.0, 10, . . . to 6 terms

11. −1, 8, −64, . . . to 12 terms

12. 2.5, 7.5, 22.5, . . . to 25 terms

B. You have learned how to find a, S_n, t_n, r, and n for a geometric series. For each of the following, find the value for the specified terms.

13. $t_2 = 10, r = 2, n = 2$; find S_n and a.

14. $t_4 = 81, r = 3, n = 4$; find S_n and a.

15. $t_5 = 32, a = 2, n = 5$; find r and S_n.

16. $r = 4, a = 2, n = 6$; find t_6 and S_n.

17. $t_{10} = 512, a = 1, n = 10$; find r and S_n (use exponent laws for r).

18. $n = 5, a = 5, r = 4$; find t_5 and S_n.

19. $a = 12, n = 5, r = 4$; find S_n and t_5.

20. $a = 1.25, n = 20, t_{20} = 260.2085$; find S_n and r using the exponent laws for r.

4.6 Logarithms

Before 1970, one of the basic tools used in the physical sciences and business for evaluating complex multiplications, operations with exponents, and certain divisions was the logarithm. Logarithms were used extensively in finance, engineering, and navigation before the introduction of the electronic calculator and the personal computer. Now with the new electronic technology, the need to use logarithms has been reduced significantly, or so it seems. In reality, many computations the computer and calculator perform use logarithms, though it is not apparent to the user.

Logarithms are still used as a tool in business, especially in statistics and finance. Our interest in logarithms is with their application to finance problems where it is often necessary to find an unknown exponent. It is the application of logarithms that permits us to find an unknown exponent. Before using logarithms, it is helpful to gain an understanding of exactly what is meant by a logarithm.

A. What Is a Logarithm?

To understand the concept of a logarithm, consider the following expressions:

$$2^4 = 16$$
$$3^6 = 729$$
$$5^3 = 125$$
$$10^2 = 100$$

Using the notation of exponents, called **exponential form**, the equivalent statement for logarithms can be stated as:

$b^x = N$ ⟵ The exponential form, and using the language of logarithms, x is the logarithm of N.

Taking our previous examples, we can now write each exponential expression using logarithms as:

Exponential Form	Logarithmic Form
$b^x = N$	$\log_b N = x$
$2^4 = 16$	$\log_2 16 = 4$
$3^6 = 729$	$\log_3 729 = 6$
$5^3 = 125$	$\log_5 125 = 3$
$10^2 = 100$	$\log_{10} 100 = 2$

In each example, a number has been raised to an exponent to produce another number. Thus **we see that a logarithm is an exponent**. For example, in the first expression, 2 has been raised to the power of 4 to produce 16. In the language of logarithms, 4 is a logarithm of 16 when the base is 2. To state this in another way, if N is a positive number (in our case 16), and if x is an exponent (in this case 4) of a number b, called a base (2 in this example), then x is the logarithm of N. The logarithm of a number is expressed using the following notation:

$\log_b N = x$ ⟵ Read as: the logarithm of N to the base b, is x.

Using some more examples, we can see the relationship among b, x, and N:

Exponential Form	Logarithmic Form	Base b	Number N	(Logarithm) Exponent x
$3^4 = 81$	$\log_3 81 = 4$	3	81	4
$5^2 = 25$	$\log_5 25 = 2$	5	25	2
$10^4 = 10{,}000$	$\log_{10} 10{,}000 = 4$	10	10,000	4

In each case we see the logarithm is simply the exponent to which the base must be raised to give the original number N.

EXAMPLE 4.20

Write the following expressions in logarithmic notation. For each, specify the exponential form, the logarithmic form, the base, and the logarithm.

(a) $2^5 = 32$ (b) $25^{\frac{1}{2}} = 5$ (c) $13^3 = 2{,}197$

Solution Using the general form, $\log_b N = x$, we have:

	Exponential Form	Logarithmic Form	Base b	Number N	Logarithm x
(a)	$2^5 = 32$	$\log_2 32 = 5$	2	32	5
(b)	$25^{1/2} = 5$	$\log_{25} 5 = \frac{1}{2}$	25	5	$\frac{1}{2}$
(c)	$13^3 = 2{,}197$	$\log_{13} 2{,}197 = 3$	13	2,197	3

In business and the physical sciences there are two logarithms that are used with considerable frequency. The first is called a **common logarithm**, and has a base of 10. The second is called a **natural logarithm** and has as its base e, where $e = 2.718282\ldots$; there is no end to the number of decimal places.

(i) Common Logarithms

Common logarithms always have a base of 10 and are written as $\log y = x$, where the base 10 is understood. For example:

$\log 100 = 2$ ← Here the base 10 is understood. If this expression was to be written in exponential form it would be 10^2 or 100.

Remember, when you see the expression $\mathbf{\log y = x}$, without a subscript, the base of the logarithm is 10. Base 10 logarithms are often used because

10 is the basis of our number system. To see the usefulness of base 10 logarithms read the following:

Logarithmic Form	**Exponential Form**
$\log 1 = 0$	$10^0 = 1$
$\log 10 = 1$	$10^1 = 10$
$\log 100 = 2$	$10^2 = 100$
$\log 1{,}000 = 3$	$10^3 = 1{,}000$
$\log 10{,}000 = 4$	$10^4 = 10{,}000$
$\log 100{,}000 = 5$	$10^5 = 100{,}000$
$\log 1{,}000{,}000 = 6$	$10^6 = 1{,}000{,}000$

From the above we should take note of two things. First, it is possible to estimate a common logarithm before using the calculator to find the logarithm of a number. For example, if one was looking for the log of 50, it must be a number greater than 1 but less than 2. Further, for a number like 15,000, we know the logarithm of the number must be between 4 and 5, and in particular, it will be closer to 4 than 5.

The second thing that can be seen is that although logarithms (or logs) increase by unit values (1, 2, 3, etc.), the numbers for which we are finding the logarithm increase in magnitude of 10 times the previous number (10, 100, 1,000, etc.). It is this last property that made logarithms so useful in computations involving large numbers.

(ii) Natural Logarithms

As mentioned, natural logarithms refer to logarithms with a base of e, where $e = 2.718282\ldots$. The value of e results from the expression:

$$\left[1 + \frac{1}{n}\right]^n$$

In this expression, we find that as n becomes a very large number the value of this expression "tends" toward the value e.

The last point can be shown by evaluating $\left[1 + \frac{1}{n}\right]^n$ for $n = 100$, $n = 1{,}000$, and $n = 1{,}000{,}000$. Using an electronic calculator:

for $n = 100$:

$$\left[1 + \frac{1}{n}\right]^n = \left[1 + \frac{1}{100}\right]^{100} = 2.704814$$

for $n = 1{,}000$:

$$\left[1 + \frac{1}{n}\right]^n = \left[1 + \frac{1}{1{,}000}\right]^{1{,}000} = 2.716924$$

for $n = 1{,}000{,}000$:

$$\left[1 + \frac{1}{n}\right]^n = \left[1 + \frac{1}{1{,}000{,}000}\right]^{1{,}000{,}000} = 2.718281$$

As can be seen, as n gets larger the value of the expression tends toward 2.718282.

Natural logarithms tend to be the most common logarithm, on the electronic calculators used in business and can be computed by depressing the **ln** key. If you take your calculator and depress the ln key for the following numbers you should get these results:

Logarithmic Form	Exponential Form
$\ln 1 = 0$	$e^0 = 1$
$\ln e = 1$	$e^1 = 2.718282$
$\ln 10 \doteq 2.302585$	$e^{2.302585} \doteq 10$
$\ln 100 \doteq 4.605170$	$e^{4.605170} \doteq 100$
$\ln 1{,}000 \doteq 6.907755$	$e^{6.907755} \doteq 1{,}000$

If you look at each value, you will note that ln 100 is twice ln 10, ln 1,000 is three times ln 10, and so forth. This relationship can be used to approximate natural logarithms as a check when using a calculator, since it is easy to input the wrong number.

EXAMPLE 4.21

Specify the following logarithms in exponential form and then evaluate the logarithm using an electronic calculator (round to four decimal places).

(a) ln 30 (b) ln 50 (c) ln 450 (d) ln 2.718

Solution:

	Logarithmic Form	Logarithm	Exponential Form
(a)	$\ln 30 =$	3.4012	$e^{3.4012} = 30$
(b)	$\ln 50 =$	3.9120	$e^{3.9120} = 50$
(c)	$\ln 450 =$	6.1092	$e^{6.1092} = 450$
(d)	$\ln 2.718 =$	0.9999	$e^{0.9999} = 2.718$

EXERCISE 4.7

A. Write the following expressions in the logarithmic form.

1. $2^7 = 128$

2. $13^2 = 169$

3. $144^{0.5} = 12$

4. $256^{0.25} = 4$

5. $9^{\frac{1}{3}} = 2.080084$

6. $15^0 = 1$

B. Write the following logarithms in exponential form.

7. $\log_3 243 = 5$

8. $\log_{15} 58.09475 = 1.5$

9. $\log_5 625 = 4$

10. $\log_{32} 0.5 = -0.2$

11. $\log_9 6{,}561 = 4$

12. $\log_5 15{,}625 = 6$

B. Rules of Logarithms

Now that we have the basic understanding of logarithms for base 10 and base e, it is important to understand how some basic arithmetic calculations are done using logarithms.

If we let A and B be two positive numbers, then we can state the basic rules of logarithms as follows:

Table 4.1

Rules for Logarithms	**Examples** Let $A = 10$, $B = 1{,}000$, and $n = 3$.
RULE 1	($A = 10$ and $B = 1{,}000$)
Base 10 $\log (AB) = \log A + \log B$	$\log (10 \times 1{,}000) = \log 10 + \log 1{,}000$ $\log (10 \times 1{,}000) = 1 + 3$ $\log (10 \times 1{,}000) = 4$ $10^4 = 10{,}000$
Base e $\ln (AB) = \ln A + \ln B$	$\ln (10 \times 1{,}000) = \ln 10 + \ln 1{,}000$ $\ln (10 \times 1{,}000) = 2.302585093 + 6.907755279$ $\ln (10 \times 1{,}000) = 9.210340372$ $e^{9.210340372} = 10{,}000$
RULE 2	($A = 10$ and $B = 1{,}000$)
Base 10 $\log \left[\frac{A}{B}\right] = \log A + \log B$	$\log (\frac{10}{1{,}000}) = \log 10 - \log 1{,}000$ $\log (\frac{10}{1{,}000}) = 1 - 3$ $\log (\frac{10}{1{,}000}) = -2$ $10^{-2} = 0.01$
Base e $\ln \left[\frac{A}{B}\right] = \ln A - \ln B$	$\ln (\frac{10}{1{,}000}) = \ln 10 - \ln 1{,}000$ $\ln (\frac{10}{1{,}000}) = 2.302585093 - 6.907755279$ $\ln (\frac{10}{1{,}000}) = -4.605170186$ $e^{-4.605170186} = 0.01$
RULE 3	($n = 3$ and $A = 10$)
Base 10 $\log (A^n) = n(\log A)$	$\log 10^3 = 3\log 10$ $3\log 10 = (3)(1)$ $3\log 10 = 3$ $\log 10^3 = 1{,}000$
Base e $\ln (A)^n = n(\ln A)$	$\ln 10^3 = 3\ln 10$ $3\ln 10 = 3\ (2.302585093)$ $3\ln 10 = 6.907755279$ $e^{6.907755279} = 1{,}000$

The rules in Table 4.1 should be understood. Rule 3 is very important to the financial computations that follow in later chapters. The solutions for the following examples require the use of an electronic calculator. If you only have a [log] key on your calculator, use it in the exact steps noted. But remember, your intermediate answers will be different. However, your final answer will be the same — regardless of the base you select for logarithms.

It is important to understand that numerical differences may arise from rounding of decimal places. Also, differences also may arise if two people are working side-by-side with the same numbers, but using different calculators. Because the electronics in each calculator can differ, each calculator may give slightly different numbers in rounding of decimals when there are many decimal places. This is not a serious problem. The differences normally arise after five decimal places.

The following example uses Rule 3 throughout since it is the operation you must be able to perform in the finance sections of later chapters. The use of logarithms for multiplication and division is not often required because of the availability of electronic calculators.

EXAMPLE 4.22

Use logarithms to evaluate the following expressions:

(a) $(50)(75)^n = 500$

(b) $5{,}000 = 1{,}000(1 + 0.01)^n$

(c) $10{,}000 = 500\left[\dfrac{1 - (1 + 0.005)^{-n}}{0.005}\right]$

(d) $18{,}000 = 600\left[\dfrac{(1 + 0.125)^n - 1}{0.125}\right]$

Solution (a) $(50)(75)^n = 500$

STEP 1 Divide both sides by 50:

$$(75)^n = \frac{500}{50}$$

$$(75)^n = 10$$

STEP 2 Taking logarithms of both sides:

$$\ln 75^n = \ln 10$$
$$n(\ln 75) = \ln 10$$

STEP 3 Solve for n:

$$n = \left[\frac{\ln 10}{\ln 75}\right]$$

$$n = 0.533315907$$

Solution (b) $5{,}000 = 1{,}000(1 + 0.01)^n$

STEP 1 Rearrange the expression and divide each side by 1,000:

$$(1 + 0.01)^n = \frac{5{,}000}{1{,}000}$$

$$(1.01)^n = 5$$

STEP 2 Take logarithms of both sides:

$$\ln(1.01)^n = \ln 5$$
$$n\ln(1.01) = \ln 5$$

STEP 3 Solving for n:

$$n = \left[\frac{\ln 5}{\ln (1.01)}\right]$$

$$n = \frac{1.609437912}{0.00995033}$$

$$n = 161.7471757$$

Solution (c) $10{,}000 = 500\left[\frac{1 - (1 + 0.005)^{-n}}{0.005}\right]$

STEP 1 Divide both sides by 500:

$$\frac{10{,}000}{500} = \left[\frac{1 - (1.005)^{-n}}{0.005}\right]$$

$$20 = \left[\frac{1 - (1.005)^{-n}}{0.005}\right]$$

STEP 2 Multiply both sides by 0.005:

$$(20)(0.005) = 1 - (1.005)^{-n}$$

STEP 3 Remove brackets and subtract 1 from both sides:

$$\begin{aligned} 0.1 &= 1 - (1.005)^{-n} \\ 0.1 - 1 &= -1.005^{-n} \\ -0.9 &= -\ 1.005^{-n} \end{aligned}$$

STEP 4 Rearranging the sides of the equation:

$$-\ (1.005)^{-n} = -0.9$$

STEP 5 Multiply both sides by –1 to eliminate the negative sign:

$$(1.005)^{-n} = 0.9$$

STEP 6 Taking logarithms of both sides:

$$-n\ln 1.005 = \ln 0.9$$

STEP 7 Solving for n:

$$-n = \left[\frac{\ln 0.9}{\ln[1.005]}\right]$$

$$-n = -21.1247396$$

$n = 21.1247396$ After multiplying each side by –1.

Solution (d) $18{,}000 = 600\left[\frac{(1 + 0.125)^n - 1}{0.125}\right]$

STEP 1 Divide each side by 600:

$$\frac{18{,}000}{600} = \left[\frac{(1.125)^n - 1}{0.125}\right]$$

$$30 = \left[\frac{(1.125)^n - 1}{0.125}\right]$$

STEP 2 Multiply each side by 0.125:

$$\begin{aligned} (30)(0.125) &= (1.125)^n - 1 \\ 3.75 &= (1.125)^n - 1 \end{aligned}$$

STEP 3 Rearranging and adding 1 to both sides:

$$(1.125)^n = 4.75$$

STEP 4 Taking logarithms gives:

$$n\ln(1.125) = \ln 4.75$$

STEP 5 Solving for n:

$$n = \left[\frac{\ln 4.75}{\ln(1.125)}\right]$$

$$n = 13.2289392$$

EXERCISE 4.8

A. Express the following in a logarithmic form.

1. $3^5 = 243$

2. $5^5 = 3{,}125$

3. $6^7 = 279{,}936$

4. $3^4 = 81$

5. $2^{-9} = 0.001953125$

6. $18^{½} = 4.2426407$

7. $144^{-2} = 0.000048225$

8. $144^{½} = 12$

9. $3^x = 27$

10. $4^{2x} = 256$

B. Using an electronic calculator, evaluate the following expressions, and, where appropriate, evaluate the unknown term.

11. $\ln 15$

12. $\ln 8{,}103.084$

13. $4^{2x} = 65{,}536$

14. $5{,}000 = 277.08 \left[\frac{1 - (1 + 0.01)^{-n}}{0.01}\right]$

15. $5^x = 15{,}625$

16. $10{,}000 = 500 \left[\frac{1 - (1 + 0.015)^{-n}}{0.015}\right]$

17. $\ln 65$

18. $10{,}000 = 500 \left[\frac{(1 + 0.02)^n - 1}{0.02}\right]$

REVIEW EXERCISES

A. Solve the following using the methods of either elimination by addition/subtraction or substitution.

1. $2x - 4y = -9$
$x - 5y = 15$

2. $y = 10$
$2x + 3y = 1$

3. $x + 0.5y = 10$
$3x - y = 15$

4. $0.25x - 0.2y = 9$
$0.5x + y = 20$

5. $3x + y = 4$
$x - y = 1$

6. $3x + y = 12$
$x + y = 2$

B. Construct a graph of the following equations. Show the x- and y-intercept when graphing the equation.

7. $4x + y = 16$

8. $x - y = 20$

9. $x = 15$

10. $y = 2$

11. $y = x + 8$

12. $2y = 10x - 2$

13. $1.5x - 2y = 9$

14. $2y = 4x + 1$

C. Given the following coordinates, find the slope, y-intercept, and equation of the line defined by the two coordinates.

15. (0, 5) and (1, 11)

16. (0, 3) and (2, –1)

17. (10, 16) and (0, 10)

18. (4, –11) and (0, 5)

19. (0, 7) and (2, 1)

20. (5, 75) and (2, 90)

D. Using a graphical approach find the solution for the following linear equation systems.

21. $4x + y = 10$
$3x + 2y = 5$

22. $x = -5$
$x + y = 2$

23. $2x + y = 30$
$x + 2y = 24$

24. $x + y = 4$
$x - 2y = 6$

E. Business applications of algebraic and graphic techniques.

25. Ace Manufacturing produces windows that come in a frame. After many windows, Ace has found that the cost per square foot of window, including labour and materials cost, is \$45. The price it charges for a finished window is \$60 per square foot. If its fixed costs are \$110,000, what is the break-even point in sales and in square footage of windows manufactured?

26. A company is contemplating changing the method it uses to produce microcomputer chips. The choice of methods has been narrowed down to two methods. Method A will have an annual fixed cost of \$100,000 and will have an estimated variable cost of \$750 per unit. Method B has an estimated annual fixed cost of \$125,000 and is estimated to have a variable cost of \$600 per unit. Using a graph, show at what level of sales the firm will be indifferent between the two methods? Assume the computer chip sells for \$800 per unit. If sales are expected to be 1,500 computer chips, what method would generate the largest profit?

27. In economics, the equation that describes the demand for a good or service is plotted with price on the vertical scale (y-axis) and quantity of the good purchased on the horizontal axis (x-axis). Also, according to economics, as the price of a good rises the quantity demanded will fall. The supply equation shows that the quantity supplied of a product will increase with price. At some point the demand and supply equation will have the same coordinates — this gives us the market equilibrium price and quantity. For the following equations, where q stands for quantity and p for price, identify if the equation is a demand equation or a supply equation.

(a) $2q - p = 0$

(b) $p - 4 = q$

(c) $2p + q + 2 = 0$

(d) $3q + 4p = 10$

(e) $3q - 2p + 4 = 0$

(f) $q - 10 = \frac{p}{4}$

28. A company sells a special type of television converter for $500 per unit. Using q for quantity, TC for total cost, TFC for total fixed cost, TVC for total variable cost, and TR for total revenue, undertake the following:

(a) What is the total revenue if the company sells 1,000 units? What is the total revenue equation? (Remember, use q for quantity and TR for total revenue.) Graph the total revenue equation.

(b) The variable cost per unit is estimated to be 30% of the revenue per unit and the fixed costs are $45,000. Determine the total cost, fixed cost, and variable cost equations. Graph each equation on the same graph.

(c) What is the break-even point for this firm? Show the break-even point on the graph.

(d) If fixed costs were to rise by 20%, show the new fixed cost curve on the graph constructed in part (b).

F. Find the nth term, t_n, and the sum, S_n, for the following arithmetic progressions.

29. 1, 3, 5, . . . to 10 terms

30. 8, 6, 4, . . . to 6 terms

31. 10, 7, 4, . . . to 8 terms

32. 0.2, 0.6, 1, . . . to 5 terms

33. 0.1, 0.5, 0.9, . . . to 5 terms

34. –1, –5, –9, . . . to 12 terms

G. Find the *n*th term, t_n, and the sum, S_n, of the following geometric progressions.

35. 1, 4, 16, . . . to 6 terms

36. 3, 9, 27, . . . to 12 terms

37. 2, 5, 12.5, . . . to 10 terms

38. $\frac{1}{8}, \frac{1}{4}, \frac{1}{2}$, . . . to 5 terms

39. 0.2, 0.8, 3.2, . . . to 6 terms

40. −1, 5, −25, . . . to 12 terms

H. Using an electronic calculator, evaluate the following expressions, and, where appropriate, evaluate the unknown term.

41. ln 45

42. ln 148.4132

43. $4^{2x} = 65{,}536$

44. $50{,}000 = 419.60 \left[\frac{1 - (1 + 0.0075)^{-n}}{0.0075}\right]$

45. $3^x = 81$

46. $100{,}000 = 1{,}434.71 \left[\frac{1 - (1 + 0.01)^{-n}}{0.01}\right]$

SUMMARY OF FORMULAS

Formula 4.1	$m = \frac{\text{Change in } y}{\text{Change in } x} = \frac{y_2 - y_1}{x_2 - x_1}$	The formula to find the slope for a straight line.
Formula 4.2	$t_n = a + (n - 1)d$	The formula to find the nth term of an arithmetic series.
Formula 4.3	$S_n = \frac{n}{2}(a + t_n)$	The formula to find the sum of an arithmetic series with n terms.
Formula 4.4	$t_n = ar^{n-1}$	The formula to find the value of the nth term of a geometric progression.
Formula 4.5	$S_n = \frac{a(1 - r^n)}{(1 - r)}$	This formula finds the sum for a geometric series with n terms.

GLOSSARY OF TERMS

Arithmetic Progression a series of numbers that are in a pattern where each number in the pattern is based on the previous number. The difference between each number is the common difference, d. This difference is constant for the series.

Geometric Series a series of numbers such that each term is found by multiplying the preceding term by a constant. This constant is the common ratio, r.

Intercept the point at which a line crosses one of the axes. The point where a line crosses the y-axis is called the y-intercept. The point at which the line crosses the x-axis is called the x-intercept.

Logarithm a logarithm is the exponent to which a base must be raised to achieve a particular number. Two logarithms commonly used are those with a base of 10 (called common logarithms); the other type uses a base of e (called natural logarithms).

Quadrant The rectangular coordinate system is made up of four quadrants. In business, the quadrant that is most relevant is quadrant 1, which has positive values for both x and y.

Rectangular Coordinate System the name given to the system used to graphically depict equations.

Slope the measure of how steep a line is. The slope tells us how much y will change for a given change in x.

Slope Intercept Form $y = b + mx$, where b is the intercept and m is the slope. If m is positive, the line slopes upward to the right. If m is negative, the line is downward sloping.

Solution for a Simultaneous System of Equations a value for each variable in the equation system that satisfies all the equations simultaneously.

CHAPTER 5

Invoicing and Commercial Discounts: Merchandise Pricing — Markup and Markdown

The use of simple arithmetic computations in business goes on every working day, in every business, regardless of size. The topics of this chapter — invoicing, trade discounts, cash discounts, markup, and markdown — are normally considered part of the merchandising function: things that are not visible to the consumer.

Each of these aspects of merchandising requires the use of the basic tools of arithmetic and algebra discussed in the previous chapters.

OBJECTIVES

When you have completed this chapter you will be able to:

1. understand the business form called an invoice, make the appropriate entries on an invoice, determine the invoice amount, and explain the purpose of each section of the invoice;
2. understand the concept of a trade discount, and use single and multiple trade discounts to determine the net price of a good;
3. use the terms of payment to decide whether a cash discount is applicable on a particular invoice, and, when a partial payment is made, figure out the size of the cash discount that is applicable;
4. use the concepts of markup and markdown to find the selling price of a good.

5.1 Invoicing Goods

When a buyer purchases goods, there is a need to have a record of the transaction. This record will show the goods purchased, the quantity of each good purchased, the price per unit, the terms of payment, and other important information. Such a record is called an **invoice**. Sometimes the invoice acts as a record of a sale and is referred to as a sales invoice. The best way to understand an invoice is to examine a typical invoice. Figure 5.1, below, is a sample of what an invoice might look like.

All the numbers in the circles correspond to the components of the invoice

Figure 5.1 Sample Invoice

	① **Invoice Number** **C 435689**
② **Venture Sporting Supplies** 145 Bay Street Toronto, Ontario M3X 3Y9	④ **Date of Purchase** 09-07-92 ③ **Customer Number** HS-4356
Sold to Hightest Sports 3775 Duke Road Victoria, B.C. V8X 3W9	**Shipped to** Hightest Sports 3775 Duke Road Victoria, B.C. V8X 3W9

Salesperson	Shipped Via	⑭ Terms
⑮ Judy Copps	⑤ Loomis Courier Service	3/10, 1/20, n/30

⑥ Quantity Ordered	⑦ Quantity Shipped	⑧ Unit Type	⑨ Item Number	⑩ Product Description	⑪ Unit Price	⑫ EXTENSION TOTAL
50	50	pr.	12695	Track Shoes — Lts.	55.50	2,775.00
12	10[1]	ea.	R-342T	Tennis Racq. — Md.4	89.46	894.60
12	11[1]	ea.	J-12tl	Ski Jackets — Md.13	159.23	1,751.53
20	20	doz.	B-34J1	Tennis Balls — Md.9	22.49	449.80

	⑬ Invoice Total	$5,870.93
	Less Trade Discount (35%)	-2,054.82
1. Items on back order, will be shipped when available.	Net Price	3,816.11
	Sales Tax	NA
	GST @ 7% (7% of Net Price)	NA
	Shipping Charges	125.25
	Invoice Amount	$3,941.36

and are explained below. In examining Figure 5.1, you must keep in mind that this invoice is only a sample. Since each business has unique needs, there are many different types of invoices used to record the sale of merchandise.

1. **Invoice number:** This is a reference for the seller and used for accounting references.
2. **Name of the Seller and Buyer:** Venture Sporting Supplies is the seller and Hightest Sports is the buyer.
3. **Customer Number:** This refers to the number the seller has given to the purchaser for the accounting and billing records. Within this number, there may be a code that identifies the size of discount offered to the buyer.
4. **Date of Purchase:** The invoice date is 09-07-92. This is the date the invoice was prepared.
5. **Shipped Via:** This refers to the company that is the carrier. In this example, the carrier is Loomis.
6. **Quantity Ordered:** The actual amount ordered by the customer.
7. **Quantity Shipped:** This is the amount shipped. What is actually shipped may be different than the amount ordered, since occasionally a supplier may be out of a product. The supplier will ship later once they have received or produced the item. When an item is out of stock and to be shipped later it is referred to as a **back order**.
8. **Unit Type:** The unit type refers to how the good is sold. In the example, we see the goods are sold by pairs (pr.), single units (ea.), and by the dozen (doz.).
9. **Item Number:** This is an identification code for the goods for inventory and warehousing needs.
10. **Product Description:** This is a clear statement of the type of good sold, i.e., shoes, gloves, etc.
11. **Unit Price:** The unit price is the price per unit of the good sold. In this example, the unit prices are quoted per pair, per unit, or per dozen.
12. **Extension Total:** The extension total is the unit price multiplied by the quantity shipped. This multiplication gives the total cost for each type of product. The extension column determines the basis for the invoice amount.
13. **Trade Discounts:** These refer to the discount that is applicable to the buyer. Trade discounts vary depending upon the volume of business the buyer does with the seller and the type of good. A trade discount is a method used to find the wholesale price of a product. Trade discounts will be discussed in detail in the next section of this chapter.
14. **Terms of Payment:** Terms of payment refer to how soon the invoice must be paid. Often, to encourage early payment, a supplier will allow a cash discount for early payment. In our example, the 3/10, 1/20, n/30 in the "Terms of Payment" section of the invoice mean that if the invoice is paid within 10 days of the invoice date, the buyer may deduct 3% of the **net price** of the invoice. This discount does not apply to taxes or to transportation costs, since they are costs external

to the supplier of the good. If the invoice is paid after 10 days, but within 20 days of the invoice date, there is a 1% cash discount; and, if the invoice is paid after 20 days, the total balance is due 30 days from the invoice date (that is, net in 30 days, n/30).

15. **Salesperson:** This is a record of the person who made the sale or contacted the buyer. This information is important if any inquiries result after delivery. In addition, if the salesperson is paid a commission, this may be the only record of the salesperson who made the sale.

EXAMPLE 5.1

The invoice below was issued by Ronic Mills for an order of floor covering for a new housing project. The quoted price for Ansel IV was $\$75.50/m^2$ and the price for Armstrong Kitchen flooring was $\$36.46/m^2$. The carpet is sold to Unitex Carpets. Based on the invoice below, find the invoice entries for the boxes with the question marks.

Figure 5.2 Sample Invoice

Invoice Number **B 138921**

Ronic Mills
1345 William Head
Metchosin, B.C.

Date of Purchase 10-15-92
Customer Number UCL-189

Sold to
Unitex Carpets
1553 1st Avenue
Winnipeg, Manitoba

Shipped to
Unitex Carpets
1553 1st Avenue
Winnipeg, Manitoba

Salesperson	Shipped Via	Terms
J. Anderson	Volke Transport Services	1/20, n/30

Quantity Ordered	Quantity Shipped	Unit Type	Product Type	Product Description	Unit Price	EXTENSION TOTAL
150	150	Sq.m.	12-957	Ansel IV carpet	?	?
300	300	Sq.m.	12-345	Armstrong Kit. Floor	?	?

Invoice Total	$	?
Less Trade Discount (25% of invoice total)		?
Net Price		?
Shipping Charges		152.50
Tax (7% GST on net price)		?
Sales Tax (provincial tax 6% of sub-total)		?
Invoice Amount	$	

Solution The unit prices for each floor covering are:

Ansel IV carpet:
— The unit price is $75.50/m^2$.
Armstrong Kitchen Floor:
— The unit price is $36.46/m^2$.

The appropriate entries for the extension column are:

Ansel IV:
— Extension total: $75.50 × 150, or $11,325
Armstrong Kitchen Floor:
— Extension total: $36.46 × 300, or $10,938

The invoice total is the total before any trade discounts, taxes, or transportation costs are applied. This total would be the addition of the extension entries in the extension column. These were found above. Therefore, the invoice total and the remaining entries will be:

Invoice Total = $11,325 + $10,938, or $22,263	
Invoice Total	$22,263.00
Trade Discount = 0.25 × 22,263	
Less Trade Discount (25% of invoice total)	5,565.75
Net Price = $22,263 – $5,565.75	
Net Price	16,697.25
Shipping is given	
Shipping Charges	152.50
GST = 0.07(16,697.25 + 152.50)	
Tax (7% GST; applied to net price)	1,168.81
Sales Tax = 0.06(16,697.25)	
Sales Tax (provincial tax 6% applied to net price)	1,001.84
Invoice Amount	$19,020.40

5.2 Trade Discounts

A. Single Trade Discounts

When a retail business (retail means where the final sale to the consumer occurs, e.g., Eaton's), or wholesale business (wholesalers are sometimes called distributors, e.g., Acklands) purchases its goods from a supplier (a manufacturer) there is a discount offered. This discount is called a **trade discount**. In general, trade discounts are applied to a catalogue price or a list price. The list prices often appear in a published price list to businesses — sometimes a catalogue, sometimes a computer print-out of products and prices. Frequently the list price or the catalogue price is also the suggested retail price when the good is sold to a retail consumer. An example is a tradesman, such as a plumber, who must purchase necessary materials for each job. Usually, the plumber purchases the materials from a wholesaler. The wholesaler sells the materials to the plumber at a "list price" (from a catalogue or published list price), less a trade discount on the list price. In the end, the plumber charges his/her customer the list price. By charging the list price the plumber earns a revenue to cover profit plus the time taken to pick up the materials.

The size of a trade discount will vary from firm to firm. Normally, the larger the buyer and/or the larger the order, the larger the trade discount provided. Since trade discounts are applied as a percentage of the list price, a wholesaler can adjust for price increases by changing the size of the trade discount without having to change the list price. That is, dropping the size of the trade discount raises the price of the goods, and the supplier does not have to republish its catalogue or price list.

When the trade discount is subtracted from the list or catalogue price, what remains is called the **net price**. The net price is what must be paid for the goods. Thus we can say:

Net Price = List Price (Catalogue Price) – Trade Discount **Formula 5.1**

EXAMPLE 5.2

A plumber is plumbing a new house with materials having a list price of \$3,550.60. A trade discount of 25% is offered to the plumber. How much would the net amount of the invoice be? (Forget taxes and transportation.)

Solution To find the trade discount, we multiply the list price (catalogue price) by the discount rate (25%), thus:

Since 25% = 0.25, the trade discount is

$$0.25 \times \$3{,}550.60 = \$887.65$$

Applying Formula 5.1:

Net Price = List Price (Catalogue Price) – Trade Discount
Net Price = \$3,550.60 – \$887.65
Net Price = \$2,662.95

When a retailer purchases goods for resale they are purchased from a wholesaler or wholesale agent. The wholesaler purchases the goods from the manufacturer. Sometimes, if the retailer is extremely large, the retailer may be able to purchase directly from the manufacturer. Consequently, there is no strict rule about where a retailer might purchase goods for resale.

In Example 5.2, it was shown that a trade discount is a percentage discount that is applied to the list or catalogue price. The size of the trade discount will depend largely on the volume of business done by the buyer with the supplier. In general, the larger the amount purchased — on a regular basis — the larger the trade discount offered. To find the **dollar amount of the trade discount** we simply apply the relation:

Dollar Amount of Trade Discount = Rate of Trade Discount × List Price

EXAMPLE 5.3

Ace Printing Services purchases coloured stencils from a wholesaler at a list price of $135.00 per box. If Ace gets a 30% trade discount find:

(a) the amount of the discount;
(b) the net price of the good.

Solution (a)

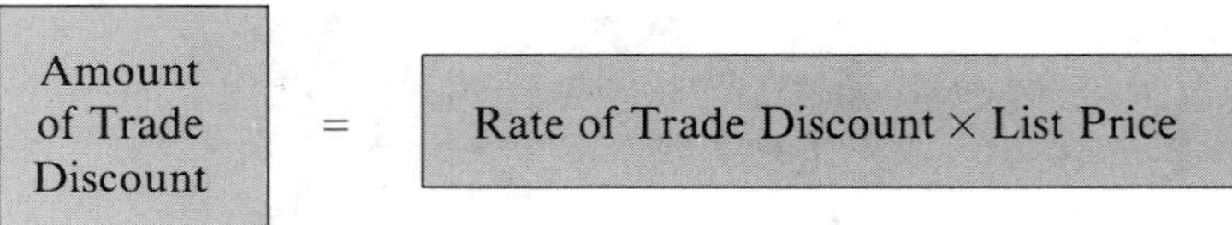

Rate of Trade Discount = 30%, or 0.30

List Price = $135.00

Amount of Trade Discount = 0.30 × $135.00
= $40.50

(b) The net price of the stencils is:

Net Price = List Price – Trade Discount

Net Price = $135.00 – $40.50
= $94.50

Another way of finding the net price is to use what is called the **Net Cost Factor** approach, or simply the ***NCF*** approach. The net cost factor allows one to calculate the net price directly by determining what percent of the list price is to be paid by a buyer. In Example 5.3, since the trade discount was 30%, we can conclude that the net price must be 70% of the list price. To see if this works, take the list price and multiply it by 70%. This gives:

$135.00 × 0.7 = $94.50 The same net price as determined in Example 5.3.

From the above there are two relations we can state. The first defines the net cost factor as:

Net Cost Factor (NCF) = 100% – % Discount

We can also state the net price as:

Net Price = $NCF \times$ List Price

To make things a little more simple, the previous expressions can be rewritten using the following definitions:

LP = List Price

NP = Net Price

d = Trade Discount Rate   Converted to a decimal equivalent.

NCF = Net Cost Factor

= $(1 - d)$

Thus, bringing all the terms together, the expression for the amount of a trade discount and the net price (NP) paid can be written as:

Amount of Trade Discount = $d(LP)$	**Formula 5.2**

$NP = LP(1 - d)$	**Formula 5.3**

EXAMPLE 5.4

Auto Van Repairs buys parts from AB Supplies. Using the trade discounts applicable, compute the net price for the following parts.

(a) One fuel injector, list price $54.00, less trade discount of 35%;
(b) One electronic ignition system, list price $269.40, less trade discount of 40%;
(c) One box of spark plugs, list price $60.00, less trade discount of 25.5%;
(d) Three cases of lubricants, list price $29.09 per case, less trade discount of 20%.

Solution (a) List price, LP = \$54.00, trade discount, $d = 0.35$ (decimal equivalent of 35%); applying Formula 5.3, Net Price, $NP = LP(1 - d)$. Substituting each value gives:

$NP = \$54(1 - 0.35)$

$NP = \$54(0.65)$

$NP = \$35.10$, the net price of the injector;

(b) $LP = \$269.40$, $d = 0.40$ (decimal equivalent of 40%); applying Formula 5.3:

$NP = LP(1 - d)$

$NP = \$269.40(1 - 0.40)$

$NP = \$269.40(0.60)$

$NP = \$161.64$, the net price of the ignition system;

(c) $LP = \$60.00$, $d = 0.255$ (decimal equivalent of 25.5%); applying Formula 5.3:

$NP = LP(1 - d)$

$NP = \$60.00(1 - 0.255)$

$NP = \$60.00(0.745)$

$NP = \$44.70$, the net price of a box of spark plugs;

(d) $LP = \$29.09$, $d = 0.20$ (decimal equivalent of 20%); applying Formula 5.3:

$NP = LP(1 - d)$

$NP = \$29.09(1 - 0.20)$

$NP = \$29.09(0.80)$

$NP = \$23.27$, the net price of one case of lubricants

NP of three cases $= \$23.27 \times 3$

$= \$69.81$.

On occasion a supplier may specify the trade discount in dollar terms rather than as a percentage. If this occurs, a buyer may wish to compute the percent or decimal equivalent of the trade discount. Such a calculation would permit a comparison between different suppliers. This comparison is important when quotations are in dollars by one supplier and percentages by another supplier. The method we would use to compute the trade discount rate, d, would be:

$$\text{Trade Discount Rate, } d = \frac{\text{Dollar Amount of Discount}}{\text{List Price}} \qquad \textbf{Formula 5.4}$$

EXAMPLE 5.5

Marathon Books has just received an invoice for an order of books it recently received. The list price of the books was \$1,234.50 and the trade discount offered was \$411.67. Compute the trade discount rate that has been applied by the supplier.

Solution Using Formula 5.4, we first define the terms we know:

Dollar Amount of Discount = \$411.67

List Price = \$1,234.50

Applying Formula 5.4, the trade discount rate, *d*, is:

$$d = \frac{\$411.67}{\$1,234.50}$$

$$= 0.3335, \text{ or } 33.35\%$$

B. Multiple or Chain Discounts

It is not uncommon for more than one trade discount to be offered by a wholesaler or manufacturer to a buyer. The reason multiple discounts are offered by a supplier are varied. Some usual reasons are overstock of a product, a special manufacturer's promotion on a new or discontinued good, or the size of the order (and sometimes the size of the buyer). When the order is large or the customer is large, in general, the greater the discount. One way to handle an additional discount is to offer buyers multiple discounts.

The term **chain discount** is used to describe multiple discounts. A chain discount is a more descriptive term for applying multiple discounts since they are applied in sequence, or in a chain of calculations. Study Example 5.6, which shows how a buyer computes the net price after applying multiple trade discounts:

EXAMPLE 5.6

Acme Software offers trade discounts of 25% and 20% to Heller Computer Sales. If Heller has just purchased a selection of software that has a list price of \$7,500, find the net price of the purchase.

Solution In finding the net price, we must understand how the trade discounts are applied in sequence.

Applying the first discount gives the first net price (NP_1):

$$NP_1 = LP(1 - d_1) \qquad d_1 \text{ is the first trade discount.}$$
$$NP_1 = \$7{,}500(1 - 0.25)$$
$$NP_1 = \$5{,}625$$

Applying the second discount gives the final net price (NP_2):

$$NP_2 = NP_1(1 - d_2) \qquad d_2 \text{ is the second trade discount.}$$
$$NP_2 = \$5{,}625(1 - 0.20)$$
$$NP_2 = \$4{,}500$$

The final net price that Heller Computer Systems would pay for software that has a list price of \$7,500, given trade discounts of 25% and 20%, is \$4,500.

In the solution of Example 5.6, we cannot simply add the trade discounts, (i.e., 25% + 20%), since this would not yield the correct list price. However, we can combine the discounts if we use the following method:

LP = list or catalogue price
d_1 = the first trade discount
d_2 = the second trade discount
d_3 = the third trade discount
d_n = the nth trade discount

Now for each trade discount we can formulate an expression for the Net Cost Factor for each trade discount as:

$$NCF_1 = (1 - d_1)$$
$$NCF_2 = (1 - d_2)$$
$$NCF_3 = (1 - d_3)$$
$$\ldots$$
$$NCF_n = (1 - d_n)$$

Bringing the discounts and NCF's together we can find a single *NCF* that incorporates all the trade discounts. This is done by multiplying the individual *NCF*'s as:

Net Cost Factor For Multiple Discounts $= (1 - d_1)(1 - d_2)(1 - d_3) \ldots (1 - d_n)$ **Formula 5.5**

From Formula 5.5 it is possible to specify the Net Price when multiple or chain discounts are available as:

$$\text{Net Price} = LP(1 - d_1)(1 - d_2)(1 - d_3)\ldots(1 - d_n)$$ **Formula 5.6**

Applying Formula 5.6 to the list price in Example 5.6, the net price can be found directly by applying the *NCF* based on all the discounts. This is done as:

$$\begin{aligned}\text{Net Price} &= \$7{,}500(1 - 0.25)(1 - 0.20)\\ &= \$4{,}500\end{aligned}$$

EXAMPLE 5.7

Venture Sporting Goods has just placed an order with its primary supplier. Since Venture is a major buyer of sporting goods, it receives multiple trade discounts. For each of the following purchases compute the net price directly by using Formula 5.6.

(a) Three dozen pairs of ski boots, listed at \$350.95 per pair, less trade discounts of 20%, 25%, and 30%;
(b) Thirty-two sets of ski poles, listed at \$75.45 per pair, less trade discounts of 30%, 15%, and 10%;
(c) Twenty sets of harnesses, listed at \$186.95 per set, less trade discounts of 25% and 10%;
(d) One hundred pairs of ski gloves, listed at \$50.95 per pair, less trade discounts of 10%, 15%, and 20%.

Solution (a) Find the net price of the ski boots:

$$\begin{aligned}\text{Total List Price: } LP &= 36 \times \$350.95\\ &= \$12{,}634.20\end{aligned}$$

$d_1 = 0.20$, $d_2 = 0.25$, $d_3 = 0.30$

Applying Formula 5.6:

$$\begin{aligned}\text{Net Price} &= \$12{,}634.20(1 - 0.20)(1 - 0.25)(1 - 0.30)\\ &= \$12{,}634.20(0.80)(0.75)(0.70)\\ &= \$12{,}634.20(0.42)\\ \text{Net Price} &= \$5{,}306.36\end{aligned}$$

(b) Finding the net price of the ski poles:

Total List Price: 32 × $75.45 = $2,414.40

$d_1 = 0.30$, $d_2 = 0.15$, $d_3 = 0.10$

Now, applying Formula 5.6:

Net Price = $2,414.40(1 – 0.30)(1 – 0.15)(1 – 0.10)
Net Price = $1,292.91

(c) Finding the net price of the ski harnesses:

Total List Price: 20 × $186.95 = $3,739.00

$d_1 = 0.25$, $d_2 = 0.10$

Applying Formula 5.6:

Net Price = $3,739.00(1 – 0.25)(1 – 0.10)
Net Price = $2,523.83

(d) The net price of the ski gloves:

Total List Price: 100 × $50.95 = $5,095.00

$d_1 = 0.10$, $d_2 = 0.15$, $d_3 = 0.20$

Applying Formula 5.6:

Net Price = $5,095.00(1 – 0.10)(1 – 0.15)(1 – 0.20)
Net Price = $3,118.14

EXERCISE 5.1

1. A computer store just purchased 21 computers. The list price for a computer is $3,500 per unit and is subject to a 25% trade discount. What would the extension total column entry on the invoice be? What is the dollar value of the trade discount?
2. What is the net price the computer store would pay for the computers purchased in problem 1?
3. Complete the following invoice by filling in the sections with a question mark (?).

Quantity Ordered	Quantity Shipped	Product Description	Unit Price	Extension Total
10 Boxes	6 Boxes	Computer Diskettes	27.50	?
10 @ 80MB	10 @ 80MB	Computer Hard Drive	456.95	?
4	4	GLS Printer	350.65	?
		List Price		?
		Trade Discount (33%)		?
		Net Price		?
		Freight Charges		150.00
		Invoice Total		?

4. The Green Leaf garden store has just received an order for the following:

> 25 Douglas fir trees @ $23.95 per tree;
> 10 bags of grass seed @ $12.50 per bag;
> 45 planting pots @ $1.25 per pot.
> Transportation costs for this order are $35.00.

If the Green Leaf store is selling these to Audrey's Garden Shop, make up an invoice that would show the purchase of these items. The trade discount offered by Green Leaf to Audrey's is 20%.

For problems 5 to 14 find the answer to the entries with a question mark (?).

	Trade Discount %	List Price	Net Price	Net Cost Factor (*NCF*)
5.	15%	$ 450	?	?
6.	14%, 13%, 8%	$ 600	?	?
7.	?	$1,200	$ 850	?
8.	?	$2,500	$1,800	?
9.	14%, 12%, 6%	$4,600	?	?
10.	?	?	$3,340	0.5
11.	10%, 8%, 15%	?	$6,860	?
12.	30%, 15%	?	$7,540	?
13.	?	?	$3,230	0.75
14.	?	$ 650	?	0.65

15. A computer store has ordered four different computers for resale. The price of each computer is $6,500. The store is eligible for a trade discount of 40%. What is the amount of the trade discount?

16. A new stereo is listed at $1,800 and sold to a retailer with trade discounts of 20%, 15%, and 5%. What is the net cost to the retailer?

5.3 Terms of Payment: Cash Discounts

If cash discounts are offered they will be specified on the invoice. In the invoice presented in Section 5.1, there was a box on the invoice with the label "**Terms**". The **Terms** section of the invoice outlines the terms of payment that are offered to the buyer. To encourage early payment, suppliers sometimes offer a **cash discount**. In the Terms section of the invoice (see Figure 5.1), the expression "3/10, 1/20, n/30" appeared. The meaning of the first term is that if the invoice is paid within 10 days of the invoice date, the buyer is entitled to a 3% cash discount from the net price (i.e., 3/10). Further, if the buyer pays after 10 days of the invoice date, but on or before 20 days after the invoice date, the buyer is entitled to a 1% cash discount off the net price (i.e., 1/20). After 20 days, the total of the invoice is due, with the full payment expected 30 days after the invoice date (i.e., n/30 — the n stands for the net amount of the invoice).

As mentioned, one reason a cash discount is offered by suppliers is to encourage early payment. This early payment greatly helps a supplier since it increases its cash flow and minimizes the need for the supplier to borrow monies for its day-to-day operations.

There are different ways that the terms of payment may be offered by a supplier. These differences depend upon the type of invoice dating that is used for the terms. The three most common methods of dating are:

1. Ordinary Dating
2. End of Month Dating
3. Receipt of Goods Dating

A. Ordinary Dating

The terms 3/10, n/30 are examples of ordinary dating. The first number, 3, represents the percentage discount and the second number, 10, indicates how long after the date of the invoice the discount will be permitted. The term, n/30, simply means that the net amount of the invoice is due in 30 days.

EXAMPLE 5.8

Volk Transport in British Columbia orders parts for its trucks from Acme Parts in Ontario. On the last invoice from Acme, the net price was $2,345.60. The terms of payment were 2/10, n/30. Answer the following questions.

(a) If the invoice is paid within 10 days of the invoice date, what will be the cash discount? What will be the amount paid to Acme Parts?
(b) If the invoice is paid 15 days after the date of the invoice, what will be the cash discount?

Solution (a) If payment is made in 10 days the size of the cash discount is 2% of the net price of \$2,345.60, therefore:

$$\text{Cash Discount} = 2\% \times \$2{,}345.60$$
$$= 0.02 \times \$2{,}345.60$$
$$= \$46.91$$
$$\text{Amount Paid} = \text{Net Price} - \text{Cash Discount}$$
$$= \$2{,}345.60 - \$46.91$$
$$= \$2{,}298.69$$

(b) If the payment is made after 10 days of the invoice date the cash discount is zero. Since the payment is 15 days after the invoice date there is no cash discount.

EXAMPLE 5.9

An invoice with a net price of \$1,225.50 was dated September 30, 1992. The terms of payment are 3/10, 1/20, n/30. Calculate the amount paid and the cash discount if:

(a) the invoice is paid October 6, 1992;
(b) the invoice is paid October 15, 1992;
(c) the invoice is paid October 21, 1992.

Solution (a) October 6: The payment is within 10 days of the invoice date. Therefore, the cash discount is 3% (3/10) of the net price:

$$\text{Cash Discount} = 0.03 \times \$1{,}225.50$$
$$= \$36.77$$
$$\text{Amount Paid} = \$1{,}225.50 - \$36.77$$
$$= \$1{,}188.74$$

(b) October 15: The payment is made after 10 days but within 20 days of the invoice date. Therefore, the cash discount is 2% (2/10) of the net price:

$$\text{Cash Discount} = 0.02 \times \$1{,}225.50$$
$$= \$24.51$$
$$\text{Amount Paid} = \$1{,}225.50 - \$24.51$$
$$= \$1{,}200.99$$

(c) October 21: The payment is made after the periods where cash discounts are available. The amount due will be \$1,225.50, the full amount of the invoice.

B. End of Month Dating

End of month dating (E.O.M.) implies that the terms of the payment are extended and are available from the end of the month shown on the invoice. For example, if an invoice is dated September 5 and has the terms 2/10, n/30 E.O.M., the discount of 2/10 is available from the end of the month plus 10 days, or October 10. In effect, end of month dating means that the invoice is treated as if it were dated at the end of the month, and is due for payment in the month or months following.

Another way a supplier may specify E.O.M. dating is to use the word **prox** in the terms of payment, such as 2/10/prox. The word prox is an abbreviation for the Latin word **proximo** meaning next or following month. For example, an invoice dated March 16 with terms 3/10/prox is eligible for the cash discount until April 10.

There is an important exception to E.O.M. if the invoice is dated after the 26th day of a month. When this occurs some firms will permit the discount to apply for an additional month. For example, if an invoice was dated August 27, the discount period would commence on October 1. This practice is more common in the United States than in Canada.

The use of the E.O.M. method is usually found in industries where the buyer may not be able to sell the goods for some period after receipt of the goods. This could arise if there are assembly or processing requirements before the goods can be sold.

EXAMPLE 5.10

An invoice with a net price of $225.50 was dated October 4. The terms of payment are 2/10, 1/20, n/30 E.O.M. Calculate the amount paid and the cash discount if:

(a) the invoice is paid October 16;
(b) the invoice is paid November 8;
(c) the invoice is paid November 15.

Solution Since the invoice terms are E.O.M., the discount period for the cash discount 2/10 will apply to November 10 and the terms 1/20 will apply to November 20.

(a) October 16: If the invoice is paid on or before this date the cash discount is 2% of the net price.
Therefore:

$$\text{Cash Discount} = 0.02 \times \$225.50$$
$$= \$4.51$$
$$\text{Amount Paid} = \$225.50 - \$4.51$$
$$= \$220.99$$

(b) November 8: If the invoice is paid on this date, the cash discount is also 2% of the net price, as in part (a).
Therefore:

$$\text{Cash Discount} = 0.02 \times \$225.50$$
$$= \$4.51$$
$$\text{Amount Paid} = \$225.50 - \$4.51$$
$$= \$220.99$$

(c) November 15: If the invoice is paid on this date, the cash discount is 1% of the net price.
Therefore:

$$\text{Cash Discount} = 0.01 \times \$225.50$$
$$= \$2.26$$
$$\text{Amount Paid} = \$225.50 - \$2.26$$
$$= \$223.24$$

C. Receipt of Goods Dating

Another method that is sometimes applied to cash discounts is referred to as receipt of goods dating, abbreviated as R.O.G. If the terms provide for R.O.G., this means that the cash discount period begins when the goods are received. For example, 2/10, n/30 R.O.G. means that a 2% discount is available up to and including 10 days after receipt of the goods. Otherwise, the net price on the invoice is due 30 days after receipt of the goods.

Often the R.O.G. method of dating is used where delivery time is substantial — usually involving rail, water, or truck transport.

EXAMPLE 5.11

An invoice with a net price of $125.00 is dated June 10 and the goods are received on July 2. The terms of payment are 3/10, n/30 R.O.G. Calculate the amount paid and the cash discount if the invoice is paid July 12.

Solution The discount period will commence from the date of receipt of the goods. Here, 10 days from the receipt is 10 days from July 2. Since the invoice is paid on July 12, it is the last day of the discount period. Therefore the cash discount the amount paid is:

$$\text{Cash Discount} = 0.03 \times \$125.00$$
$$= \$3.75$$
$$\text{Amount Paid} = \$125.00 - \$3.25$$
$$= \$121.25$$

D. Partial Payments

The terms of payment are important since the cash discounts do represent substantial savings to the buyer. Sometimes, even when the terms are very favourable, the buyer may not be able to raise the full amount of the payment within the cash discount period. Yet, the buyer may be able to provide a partial payment within the cash discount period. When a partial payment is made, the buyer should be able to take advantage of a cash discount on the portion of the invoice paid.

Before turning to an example, one thing that should be noted is that some suppliers may not permit a cash discount on partial payments. If this is the case, the invoice will generally make it clear that the terms of the cash discount apply to only a full payment. The following example shows how the cash discount is accounted for when partial payments are made:

EXAMPLE 5.12

An invoice for the purchase of a computer for $2,500 was dated August 1 with the terms 2/10, n/30. If a partial payment of $1,000 is made on August 10, what amount is owing on the due date?

Solution To find the value of the partial payment, it is important to remember that a payment of $1,000 within the cash discount period has a value of more than $1,000. Since there is a cash discount of 2%, the amount of $1,000 is 98% of its cash value when paid within the cash discount period (i.e., $1,000 is "98% of the value of a $1,000 payment in the discount period"). Thus the value of the $1,000 payment must be:

$$\frac{\$1{,}000}{0.98} = \$1{,}020.41$$

Therefore, a payment of $1,000, within the cash discount period, has the equivalent value of $1,020.41.

Therefore, the amount owing after 30 days is:

Invoice Amount – Equivalent Cash Payment

or

$$\$2{,}500 - \$1{,}020.41 = \$1{,}479.59$$

Thus, $1,479.59 will be the amount owing at the end of 30 days.

EXERCISE 5.2

For problems 1 to 5 find the full payment required to pay the invoice.

	Payment Terms	Date of the Invoice	Date Goods Received	Invoice Amount	Date of Payment
1.	1/10, n/30	Oct 12	Oct 12	$5,230	Oct 22
2.	3/5, n/30	Sept 15	Sept 15	$2,350	Sept 17
3.	4/10, 2/30, n/60	Nov 12	Nov 12	$1,200	Dec 13
4.	2/10, n/30 E.O.M.	Dec 5	Dec 15	$2,400	Jan 15
5.	2/10, n/30 R.O.G.	June 18	July 3	$3,900	Aug 1

For problems 6 to 10, find the missing entries noted with a question mark (?). Where a partial payment is made, assume the partial payment is made on the last day eligible for cash discounts.

	Payment Terms	Amount of Invoice	Amount of Payment	Value of Payment	Balance Due
6.	1/10, n/30	$4,350.00	$2,000.00	?	?
7.	3/5, n/30	$3,509.12	$1,345.00	?	?
8.	4/10, 2/30, n/60	$2,549.13	$1,230.00	?	?
9.	2/10, n/30 E.O.M.	$3,546.00	?	$3,000.00	?
10.	2/10, n/30 R.O.G.	$235.34	?	$125.00	?

11. What amount would be owing on two invoices, one dated September 20 for $1,237.76 and the other for $3,567.00, dated October 1? Assume the terms are 2/15 on the first invoice and 1/10 on the second invoice, and assume that both invoices are paid on October 11.

12. Volk Transport ordered a large number of truck parts, which arrived on October 15. The invoice was 3/15 and the full amount of the invoice was $6,500. If a payment of $3,000 was made on October 30 (a partial payment will be credited with the discount) find:

a. What is the equivalent cash value of the payment toward the invoice balance?

b. What does Volk Transport still owe after the payment?

5.4 Retail Pricing — Markup and Markdown

Each firm has a method it uses to arrive at a selling price. The method used to determine a selling price will vary depending upon the demand for the product, the competition, as well as the cost of the good or service being sold.

Although these factors have a role in the pricing decision, the emphasis in the following discussion will be on cost and profit.

Costs and revenue are the basis for another important aspect of operating a business — profit. Thus, we can say that the price a business establishes for a good or service it sells must reflect:

- the cost for the good or service;
- the operating cost of the business — these include wages, storage, cost of borrowed money, and other things necessary to carry on the business operation;
- the profit necessary to make it worthwhile to stay in business.

The terms markup and markdown are used to describe the process used to set the price of goods and services offered by businesses.

A. Markup

Markup is the difference between the selling price of the good and the cost of the good to the retailer. Markup can be based on either the cost of the good or the selling price of the good.

Despite the method used, each has one thing in common: pricing goods must consider the cost of the good, the business overhead, and the profit that the business expects to earn. This relationship can be stated as:

Selling Price = Cost of the Good + Overhead + Profit

If we use the following definitions:

SP = Selling Price
C = Cost of the good
O = Overhead
P = Profit
M = Markup

The statement for selling price can then be expressed by the formula:

$$SP = C + O + P$$ **Formula 5.7**

Now, if we think about overhead and profit as the components that are used to determine the markup, we can further express the above as:

$$M = O + P$$ **Formula 5.8**

The selling price will be determined by the cost of the good and the markup or:

Selling Price = Cost of the Good + Markup

In general, we think about markup as being overhead and profit combined. Thus, the selling price is normally expressed as:

$$SP = C + M$$ **Formula 5.9**

It is also common to see the terms **margin** or **gross profit** used instead of markup. So, if you see a question asking you to determine the gross profit or gross margin on a good or service, the question is asking you to find the markup.

EXAMPLE 5.13

A computer costs the computer store $1,250. If the overhead costs per computer sold is $125 and the profit expected on each computer is $200, find:

(a) the selling price;
(b) the markup.

Solution (a) To find the selling price of the computer we first define the terms:

$C = \$1{,}250$, $O = \$125$, and $P = \$200$

Applying Formula 5.7 to find the selling price, SP:

$SP = C + O + P$

$SP = \$1{,}250 + \$125 + \$200$

$SP = \$1{,}575$

(b) To find the markup we use Formula 5.8:

$M = O + P$

$M = \$125 + \$200$

$M = \$325$

Normally markup is expressed as a percentage or rate, rather than in dollars and cents. When percentages or rates are used to determine the markup, the percentages are either based on the cost of the good or the selling price of the good. Let's examine each method.

(i) Markup Rate Based on Cost

To find the markup rate, or percentage based on cost, requires us to set up a ratio of markup to cost. We will use the terms:

M for markup
C for cost of the good
R_{mc} for the rate of markup

The rate of markup based on cost would be:

$$R_{mc} = \frac{M}{C} \qquad \textbf{Formula 5.10}$$

From Formula 5.10 we also can see that markup can be expressed in terms of the rate of markup and the cost. This would give us:

$$M = R_{mc}C \qquad \textbf{Formula 5.11}$$

To use Formula 5.11 to find the selling price of a good, SP, apply the markup rate to the cost to find M, and add this to the cost C. Example 5.14 shows how to use the rate of markup based on cost:

EXAMPLE 5.14

What is the selling price of a compact disk player costing $250 to a store if the store uses a 25% markup based on cost?

Solution We know from Formula 5.10 that selling price SP is found as:

$$SP = C + M$$

From Formula 5.11 we know that $M = R_{mc}C$. Therefore, substituting this for M in Formula 5.10 gives:

$$SP = C + M \qquad \text{Substitute } M = R_{mc}C$$
$$SP = C + R_{mc}C$$

And, we know $C = \$250$ and $R_{mc} = 25\%$, or 0.25. Therefore, substituting these values we have:

$$SP = \$250 + 0.25(\$250)$$
$$SP = \$312.50$$

Therefore, the selling price of a compact disk player that costs $250 and has a 25% rate of markup applied to the cost is $312.50.

EXAMPLE 5.15

Find the selling price of a good that costs the retailer $450 if it is marked up by $33\frac{1}{2}\%$ over cost.

Solution We know $C = \$450$ and $R_{mc} = 0.335$.
Now using $SP = C + R_{mc} \cdot C$, and substituting the values we have:

$$SP = \$450 + 0.335(\$450)$$
$$SP = \$600.75$$

Therefore, the selling price is $600.75.

EXAMPLE 5.16

A product was purchased by a retailer for $6,000 and sold for $8,500. What was the rate of markup, based on the cost of the good?

Solution This problem can be solved by directly applying Formula 5.10, or:

$$R_{mc} = \frac{M}{C}$$

Where:

$$M = \$8{,}500 - \$6{,}000, \text{ or } \$2{,}500, \text{ and } C = \$6{,}000$$

Thus, the rate of markup is:

$$R_{mc} = \frac{\$2{,}500}{\$6{,}000}$$
$$= 0.4166\dot{6}, \text{ or } 41.67\% \qquad \text{To two decimal places.}$$

Often the markup rates produce prices that are different from the price the retailer decides to charge. For example, suppose a good costs $14.10 and a markup rate of 50% over cost is applied. Thus, the price charged would be 150% of cost (cost = 100%, markup = 50% over cost), or 1.5 × $14.10, or $21.15. What a retailer may do to try to make the good more appealing to the consumer is to set the price at $20.99. Consequently, markup based on cost may only provide an estimate of actual price charged.

Sales or reductions in selling price also may be anticipated by a retailer. Consequently, in this circumstance the initial price set for a good may be higher than given by applying a markup over cost. The reason for this is that when the item is placed on sale, it appears as if the savings at the sale price are greater and thus is a better deal for the consumer.

In the first part of the chapter, it was noted that invoices offer trade discounts. Sometimes, a business will use the trade discount as the basis for the markup. That is, if a good has a list price of \$100 and a trade discount of 30%, the net price would be \$70. Sometimes retailers will use the list price as the retail price. Thus, a good purchased for a net price of \$70 (after the 30% trade discount) would be sold at a retail price of \$100. In fact, it is common for retailers to receive a computer print-out from a supplier that specifies the retailer cost as well as a suggested retail price — the list price.

Another approach to pricing products by retailers is to reduce the markup on certain high demand items to attract consumers to their store. This practice is common in the retail grocery business. Although we have set up the formula to determine a selling price based on a markup over cost, this may only be an approximate price since many other factors must be considered by a business in setting the price of a particular good.

(ii) Markup Rate Based on Selling Price

In the previous section, the selling price of a good was based on the cost of the good, plus a fixed percentage of cost (markup). However, often businesses offer a large range of products called a product line. What businesses often do is set a markup rate for a product line, where the markup rate is based on the **selling price**.

Consider a stereo store that handles a large range of products. In this circumstance, assume the markup on stereo receivers is 35%, 30% on compact disk (CD) players, 40% on receivers, and 35% on tape decks. To find the selling price for the stereo equipment, using a markup based on selling price, requires us to find a selling price for which the markup is 30% of the selling price, 35% of the selling price, and so on, for each product line the stereo store sells. Work through Example 5.17, which outlines how the selling price can be found when the markup is based on a percentage of the selling price.

EXAMPLE 5.17

A and B Stereo purchased a Panasonic receiver for resale at a cost of \$310.50. A and B apply a markup rate of 35% of the **selling price** on all receivers. Find the selling price of the stereo receiver.

Solution Since the markup percentage is 35% of the selling price, the cost will be the remaining percentage, or 65%. Put another way, the cost will be 65% of the selling price. We know:

$$C = \$310.50$$

$$SP = \text{Selling Price}$$

Since 65% of the selling price is cost, we can say:

65% of $SP = \$310.50$

$0.65SP = \$310.50$ Convert to decimal equivalents.

$SP = \dfrac{\$310.50}{0.65}$ Divide each side by 0.65 to find SP.

$SP = \$477.69$ Round to the nearest cent.

Therefore, we can say that if the stereo receiver is sold at a price of \$477.69, the percentage markup is 35%, based on the selling price.

To check this, find M, the markup, using the relation:

$$M = SP - C$$
$$M = \$477.69 - \$310.50$$
$$M = \$167.19$$

Now find the percent that the markup, M, represents of the selling price, SP. Therefore:

$$\frac{M}{SP} = \frac{\$167.19}{\$477.69}$$

$\doteq 0.35$, or 35% The sign $\doteq$ means approximately equal to.

From Example 5.17 we can formulate an expression to find the selling price, SP, when the markup percentage is based on the selling price. If we define R_{mp} as the markup rate based on the selling price we have:

R_{mp} = the markup percentage based on selling price

$100\% - R_{mp}$ = the percentage of the price that the product cost represents

$(100\% - R_{mp})SP = C$ the dollar cost of the good

Now solving for SP we have:

$$SP = \frac{C}{(100\% - R_{mp})}$$

If decimal equivalents are used, then the selling price would be found by:

$$SP = \frac{C}{(1 - R_{mp})}$$ **Formula 5.12**

And since $SP = C + M$ thus, $C = SP - M$.

$$R_{mp} = \frac{M}{SP}$$ **Formula 5.13**

In Formula 5.12, R_{mp} is expressed as a decimal equivalent. To see how this formula works, let's take the information from Example 5.17.

In Example 5.17 we found the selling price (SP) of the stereo receiver when the cost was \$310.50 (C), under the condition that the product line was marked up at a rate of 35% of the selling price. Using Formula 5.12, the selling price can be found directly as follows:

$$C = \$310.50$$

$$R_{mp} = 35\%, \text{ or } 0.35$$

Now substituting these values into Formula 5.12, we have:

$$SP = \frac{C}{(1 - R_{mp})}$$

$$SP = \frac{\$310.50}{(1 - 0.35)}$$

$$SP = \frac{\$310.50}{(0.65)}$$

$$SP = \$477.69$$

The use of Formula 5.12 makes finding the selling price straight forward when markup is based on selling price. Also, if the selling price and the markup rate, based on selling price, are known, it is possible to find the cost, C. Similarly, if SP and C are known we can find R_{mp}. Example 5.18 shows where we can use Formula 5.12:

EXAMPLE 5.18

Given the following information about stereo products offered by A and B Stereo, find the required information.

(a) If a stereo receiver costs \$275 and the markup is 35% based on selling price, find the selling price.

(b) A compact disk player retails at a selling price of \$250.95 and the markup is 30% based on selling price. Find the cost to the store of the compact disk player.

(c) A compact disk sells for \$24.95. The store's cost to purchase the compact disk is \$18.95. What is the markup rate if markup is based on price? What would the markup rate be if the markup was based on cost?

Solution (a) Defining the terms we have:

$$C = \$275$$

$$R_{mp} = 35\%, \text{ or } 0.35$$

We are looking to find SP given C and R_{mp}. Applying Formula 5.12 we have:

$$SP = \frac{C}{(1 - R_{mp})}$$

$$SP = \frac{\$275}{(1 - 0.35)}$$

$$SP = \$423.08$$

Thus, the selling price of the stereo receiver is \$423.08.

(b) Defining the terms we have:

$$SP = \$250.95$$

$$R_{mp} = 30\%, \text{ or } 0.30$$

We are looking to find C given SP and R_{mp}. Applying Formula 5.12 we must rearrange the formula to find C. This would be done as:

$SP = \frac{C}{(1 - R_{mp})}$	Rearrange by multiplying both sides of the equation by $(1 - R_{mp})$.
$SP(1 - R_{mp}) = C$	Rearranging gives C.
$C = SP(1 - R_{mp})$	Now substitute the values.
$C = \$250.95(1 - 0.30)$	
$C = \$175.67$	

The cost of the compact disk player must have been \$175.67.

(c) Defining the terms we have:

$$SP = \$24.95$$

$$C = \$18.95$$

First we find M by using Formula 5.9, and then use Formula 5.13 to find R_{mp}, which gives:

$SP = C + M$	Rearranging to find M.
$M = SP - C$	Substituting for $SP = \$24.95$ and $C = \$18.95$.
$M = \$24.95 - \$18.95$	
$M = \$6.00$	
$R_{mp} = \frac{M}{SP}$	Using Formula 5.13 and substituting for M and SP:
$R_{mp} = \frac{6.00}{24.95}$	
$R_{mp} = 0.2405$	

The markup rate is 24.05% of the selling price.

This question also asks us to compute the markup rate using the markup based on cost approach. To find this markup rate we turn to the earlier Formula, 5.10, which allows us to find R_{mc}, the markup rate based on cost. Therefore:

$$R_{mc} = \frac{M}{C} \qquad \text{Formula 5.10.}$$

Finding M, the markup, we have:

$$SP = M + C \qquad \text{Rearranging to find } M.$$

$$M = SP - C$$

$$M = \$24.95 - \$18.95$$

$$M = \$6.00$$

Substituting the values we have:

$$R_{mc} = \frac{\$6.00}{\$18.95}$$

$R_{mc} = 0.3166$, or 31.66% Markup based on cost.

In Example 5.18, part (c), note that markup rate based on selling price is less than markup rate based on cost. For any good this will be true since the base for the calculation of the percentage is larger when price is used than when cost is used. That is, selling price is generally higher than the cost of the good. Thus, any dollar markup will always be a lower percentage of selling price than if the same dollar markup is expressed as a percentage of cost.

EXERCISE 5.3

For each of the following find the unknowns.

	Product Cost	Price	Markup	R_{mp}
1.	$1,200.00	$1,795.00	?	?
2.	$3,500.00	?	$1,800.00	?
3.	?	$1,250.00	?	0.3
4.	?	$3,750.00	$1,200.00	0.32
5.	?	$1,200.00	$ 850.00	?
6.	$1,249.35	$2,500.00	?	0.25
7.	$ 500.00	?	$ 75.00	?
8.	?	$3,250.00	?	0.3
9.	?	?	$1,200.00	0.4
10.	?	$2,200.00	$ 750.00	?

Given the following information, find the unknowns.

	Product Cost	Price	Markup	R_{mc}
11.	$200.00	$ 395.00	?	?
12.	$500.00	?	$ 200.00	?
13.	?	$ 250.00	?	0.3
14.	?	$3,740.00	$1,500.00	?
15.	?	$3,200.00	$ 850.00	?
16.	$249.35	$ 500.00	?	0.25
17.	$400.00	?	?	0.41
18.	?	$1,150.00	?	0.3
19.	?	?	$7,200.00	0.4

20. A new television was sold by a store for $1,112.95 and a markup rate of 37.5% was applied to cost. What was the cost of the television to the store?

21. A local camera store sells automatic 35 mm cameras for 30% over the camera cost. If the dollar markup on a camera is $120.00, what is the cost of the camera to the dealer? What is the rate of markup if price had been the basis of the markup?

22. A pair of hiking boots, purchased at a list price of $68.00, less trade discounts of 20%, 15%, and 5%. The rate of markup applied is 30%, based on selling price. What is the selling price of the hiking boots?

B. Markdown

Often you will open your local newspaper and find retailers offering a variety of products and services on sale at a "reduced price" — a SALE. Many reasons are given for special prices offered by merchants. These range from inventory clearances, going out of business (and you can never understand how they have been going out of business for as long as you recall), making room for a new product line or the current year's products, as well as a variety of other reasons. In all cases, where a merchant reduces the normal selling price, the reduction in price is called a **markdown**. A markdown is the dollar amount the normal price has been reduced. A markdown rate is the percentage the price has been reduced. In practice, retailers simply talk about markdown and use dollars and percentages interchangeably, since the consumer knows what is meant by the sale.

Firms have different pricing practices. For example, some retailers bring in special merchandise for a sale and say that it is being offered at a special price, such as 50% off the normal price. The problem is that there never has been a normal price, since this merchandise has not been sold before. Whether this is a markdown or not is debatable. One example of where this practice occasionally occurs is with apparel products (both men and women's apparel). Here, special clothing is brought in for a sale, and the consumer is advised of the large discounts which are being made off the "regular price".

Before turning to an example, one thing to remember is that markdown implies a reduction in the selling price. If the markdown is in dollars, it is subtracted from the normal selling price to find the new price. If a percentage markdown is being applied, the percentage is applied to the normal selling price to determine the new price.

EXAMPLE 5.19

An art store advertises that a particular artist's prints have been selling for $500. However, a special offer is being made and the prints have been marked down to $425 per print. What is the dollar amount and the rate of the markdown?

Solution Dollar Amount of Markdown = $500 – $425

= $75

Rate of the markdown is found by the ratio:

$$\frac{\text{Dollar Amount of Markdown}}{\text{Normal Selling Price}}$$

In this example we have:

$$\text{Rate of Markdown} = \frac{\text{Dollar Amount of Markdown}}{\text{Normal Selling Price}}$$

$$= \frac{\$75}{\$500}$$

$$\text{Rate of Markdown} = 0.15, \text{ or } 15\%$$

EXAMPLE 5.20

A Panasonic Laser Partner printer was purchased by a computer store for $1,500.50 and then marked up 30% based on selling price. The store has just been notified that this printer will be discontinued and replaced by a new printer, the Laser Plus. The computer store decides to discount the Laser Partner by a 25% markdown. What is the markdown price of the printer? Also, find the dollar amount of the markdown.

Solution First find the selling price using Formula 5.12:

$$SP = \frac{C}{(1 - R_{mp})}$$

$$SP = \frac{\$1{,}500.50}{(1 - 0.30)}$$

$$SP = \$2{,}143.57$$

Therefore, if the selling price is \$2,143.57, and the markdown rate is 25%, the dollar amount of the markdown is:

$$\text{Markdown} = \$2{,}143.57(0.25)$$
$$= \$535.89$$
$$\text{Markdown Price} = \$2{,}143.57 - \$535.89$$
$$= \$1{,}607.68$$

EXERCISE 5.4

	Product Cost	Selling Price	Markup	Markdown	Markdown Price
1.	\$1,200.00	\$1,795.00	$R_{mp} = ?$	25%	?
2.	\$2,500.00	?	\$1,800.00	30%	?
3.	?	\$1,250.00	\$ 500.00	12%	?
4.	?	\$3,740.00	\$1,200.00	?	\$3,000.00
5.	?	\$1,100.00	\$ 875.00	10%	?
6.	\$1,235.35	\$2,450.00	$R_{mc} = ?$	?	\$2,000.00
7.	\$ 500.00	?	$R_{mp} = ?$	25%	\$1,000.00

8. A new television was sold by a store for \$1,112.95 and a markup rate of 37.5% was applied to cost. What was the cost of the television to the store? If the television was put on sale at 20% off the regular price, what is the markdown price?

9. Tom Terrific Deal Appliances bought self-cleaning ovens for a list price of \$700, less 10% and 15%. If the stoves are first offered for sale at a markup of 30% of price, what was the selling price? If the stoves are offered at a sale price of 15% off the regular price, what is the sale price? How much does Tom make on each oven sold?

10. If Tom, in problem 9, has markup policy such that all his products can be offered for sale at a continuous sale price of 10% off the regular price, what must the markup rate be so that the markup received (even after the 10% off) is 30% of the cost?

11. A television that costs the dealer $2,349.35 is priced at $3,195.95. If the dealer uses a markup based on selling price, what is the markup rate? If the product is offered for sale at $250 off the regular price, what is the rate of markdown?

REVIEW EXERCISES

1. A book store purchased 230 copies of a new book. The list price for each book is $35.00 per unit and subject to trade discounts of 15% and 5%. What would the extension total column have as an entry on the invoice? What is the dollar value of the trade discount?
2. Complete the following invoice where a (?) appears:

Quantity Ordered	Quantity Shipped	Product Description	Unit Price	Extension Total
15 doz.	15 doz.	Tennis Balls	17.50 doz.	?
12	12	Tennis Racket	213.64	?
14 pairs	14 pairs	Golf Gloves	9.65 pr.	?
		List Price		?
		Trade Dis. (22%, 8%)		?
		Net Price		?
		Freight Charges		15.00
		Invoice Total		?

3. What is the net price the book store would pay for the books purchased in problem 1?
4. Find the *NCF* for a computer listed at $14,500 if the selling distributor offers trade discounts of 15%, 10%, and 5%. What is the net price of the computer? The selling firm also offers terms of 3/10. What is the potential dollar discount offered on the computer if all discounts are taken?
5. A dishwasher is listed for $950 and is sold to a dealer for $700. What is the single trade discount that is being offered to the buyer?
6. A new energy efficient stove was sold to a dealer for $900. If the trade discount offered was 30%, what is the list price of the stove?
7. For each of the following multiple discounts find the *NCF*:

   a. 15%, 7.5%, 5%

b. 30%, 15%, 10%
c. 24%, 12.3%
d. 5%, 1%, 0.5%
e. 20%
f. 12%, 3%
g. 4%, 7%, 2%

8. Anne's framing shop is a major buyer of a special type of framing material. Anne has been shopping around and has found three suppliers who supply a product that is of similar quality. One firm, Tiex, offers the material at $20 per metre less 10%, 5%, and 3%. Another firm, Beons Ltd., offers the same quality of product at $30 per metre, less $33\frac{1}{2}$%, 14%, and 4%. The third firm, Andre's, offers the product for $8 per metre and offers no trade discounts. Where should Anne purchase her framing material if all claim they will deliver the product when requested?

9. The net price of a calculator is $75.80. What is the list price if the trade discount was 15%?

10. What is the list price of a product that was sold at a net price of $150.45, if discounts of $33\frac{1}{2}$% and 20% are offered?

11. A product is sold at list price by a retailer to its customers. The list price is the basis for trade discounts of 30%, 20%, and 10% that resulted in a net price of $274.30. What is the list price?

12. The Insta Print Shoppe decides to pay four invoices simultaneously on October 3. The terms for each invoice are 2/10, 1/20, and n/30. If the invoices were dated September 25 and were in the amounts of $450.69, $980.55, $1,223.35, and $13.39, what is the total amount of the payment that would be required to pay all the invoices?

13. Abercombe Ltd. is planning to reduce an outstanding invoice by $850. The invoice is for $3,340.32 and dated September 13 with terms 3/10 and n/30. The payment is remitted on September 22. What is the size of the payment to get an $850 credit on the invoice? (The firm with which Abercombe deals allows cash discounts on partial payments.)

14. The products below are offered for sale by a company. Each is subject to trade discounts of 30%, 20%, and 10%. Find the net amount of the invoice payment required for each product. Terms are 2/10, n/30, and all payments are made within the required time to take advantage of the cash discount.

a. 12 pairs of ski boots listed at $349.90 per pair.
b. 16 dozen tennis balls at $49.95 per dozen.
c. 120 boxes of golf balls listed at $39.90 per box.

15. Complete the following table where question marks appear.

	Markup Based on Selling Price	Cost	Selling Price	Dollar Markup	Markup Based on Selling Price
a.	20%	$123.45	?	?	?
b.	?	$367.95	$499.99	?	?
c.	10%	$ 67.99	?	?	?
d.	?	$893.23	?	?	30%
e.	?	$765.89	$967.99	?	?
f.	30%	$541.25	?	?	?
g.	?	$ 15.45	?	$2.44	?

16. General Damico Ltd. is offering a special product that reduces the hydrocarbon emissions from automobiles. The product is offered at 30% off the regular price of $129.99. What is the selling price? If the trade discount the supplier of the product offered General Damico had been 40% off the list price of $120, what is the markup rate, based on cost, after the product has been marked down 30% from $129.99?

17. A pet store has just stocked up on a special order of health food for dogs. The food is sold by the 20-kg bag. The food is purchased for $34.00 from the dealer and the price paid incorporates a 30% trade discount. If the product is placed on sale at 20% off the list price, what will be the sale price? What is the dollar discount being offered at the sale price?

18. R.J. Appliances sells appliances at a 35% markup. Currently R.J. is negotiating on a large shipment of dishwashers that it is planning to purchase at a list price of $580, with trade discounts of 30% and 20%. Because of the special deal, R.J. plans to mark-up the product 35% over cost and then apply a 10% markdown. What will be the sale price of each dishwasher? If R.J. estimates that overhead costs are 18% of every dishwasher sold, how much profit will R.J. make on each unit sold?

19. A store has ordered three different dishwashers for resale. The list price of each dishwasher is $650, $425, and $568. The store is eligible for a trade discount of 40% and 20%, as well as terms of 2/10, n/30. What is the purchase price of each dishwasher to the store if it takes advantage of all discounts? If the store uses a markup rate of 30% based on price, what is the selling price of each? What would this markup rate be if it was based on cost? Finally, if the store decides to mark down the price of each dishwasher by $50, what is the sale price of each dishwasher?

20. A new auto transmission is listed at $1,800 and sold to an automotive retailer with trade discounts of 20%, 15%, and 5%. What is the net cost to the retailer? If the product markup is 20% on cost, what is the selling price? Suppose that the retailer discovers that there is no market for the transmission, since a new and improved version has just been released. If a customer offers to pay $1,250, should the retailer take it?

SUMMARY OF FORMULAS

Formula 5.1 Net Price = List Price (Catalogue Price) – Trade Discount

Formula 5.2 Amount of Discount = $d(LP)$

Used to find the dollar amount of a trade discount. *LP* is the list price and the *d* is a single, decimal equivalent, trade discount.

Formula 5.3 $NP = LP(1 - d)$

The net price, *NP*, given the list price, *LP*, and a single trade discount *d*. (*d* is a decimal equivalent.)

Formula 5.4 Trade Discount Rate

$$d = \frac{\text{Dollar Amount of Discount}}{\text{List Price}}$$

The value of the trade discount, *d*, given the dollar amount of the discount and the list price.

Formula 5.5

$$NCF \text{ For Multiple Discounts} = (1 - d_1)(1 - d_2)(1 - d_3) \ldots (1 - d_n)$$

Used to find the *NCF*, (net cost factor), given the different trade discounts $d_1, d_2 \ldots d_n$. The *NCF* is a single discount factor to be applied to the list price.

Formula 5.6

$$\text{Net Price} = LP(1 - d_1)(1 - d_2)(1 - d_3) \ldots (1 - d_n)$$

Used to find the net price by applying the *NCF* to the list price, *LP*, of a good.

Formula 5.7 $SP = C + O + P$

Used to find the selling price when cost per unit, *C*, overhead per unit, *O*, and profit, *P*, per unit are known.

Formula 5.8	$M = O + P$	Markup, M, in dollars is found by adding the overhead per unit, O, and profit per unit, P.
Formula 5.9	$SP = C + M$	Selling price, SP, is found by adding the cost per unit, C, plus the markup per unit, M. Each term in this formula is in dollars.
Formula 5.10	$R_{mc} = \dfrac{M}{C}$	The rate of markup, R_{mc}, based on cost, is found by dividing the ratio of dollar markup, M, by the cost per unit, C. This formula applies when the markup is based on the cost.
Formula 5.11	$M = R_{mc}C$	Used to find the markup, M, in dollars, when the rate of markup, R_{mc}, and the cost per unit, C, are known.
Formula 5.12	$SP = \dfrac{C}{(1 - R_{mp})}$	Used to find the selling price, SP, when the markup rate is applied to the selling price. R_{mp} is the markup rate based on selling price.
Formula 5.13	$R_{mp} = \dfrac{M}{SP}$	Used to find the rate of markup based on selling price.

GLOSSARY OF TERMS

Cash Discount a discount based on early payment of an invoice. This discount is shown in the terms of payment section of the invoice.

Catalogue Price the price quoted by a supplier for a product, exclusive of any trade discounts. The catalogue price is adjusted by the trade discount to determine the price paid by a buyer — this adjusted catalogue price is sometimes referred to as the wholesale price.

Chain Discounts when a series of trade discounts are provided by a supplier to a buyer. Normally chain discounts are applied as one discount, called the net cost factor.

End of Month Dating (E.O.M.) when the period for the cash discount does not commence until the end of the month of the date of the invoice. In some circumstances, the term proximo dating is used for E.O.M.

Invoice the record of sale of goods that includes unit price, quantities ordered, buyer and seller names, trade discount applicable, shipping charges, and taxes.

List Price see catalogue price.

Markup is the difference between the selling price of a good and the costs associated with the sale of the good.

Markup Rate the percentage applied to either the cost or the percentage of selling price to find the dollar value of the markup. When price is used as the basis it will always produce a lower markup rate than when cost of the good is used to find the markup rate.

Markdown the amount the price of a good has been reduced for sale purposes. The rate of markdown is the dollar amount of the markdown divided by the normal selling price.

Multiple Discounts see chain discounts.

Net Cost Factor the percentage of list price the buyer will pay for a good. The net factor cost is a single percentage that incorporates all the trade discounts offered to a buyer.

Net Price the net price is the price paid by a buyer once the trade discount has been subtracted from the list or catalogue price.

Ordinary Dating when the basis of a cash discount is from the date on the invoice for the number of days specified.

Partial Payment when only a part payment for an invoiced amount is paid, but paid within the period in which the cash discount applies.

Receipt of Goods Dating when the time period for the cash discount is based upon the date the goods are received.

Terms of Payment the section of an invoice that tells the buyer what type of cash discount is offered for early payment of an invoice.

Trade Discount the discount provided to a buyer who is purchasing goods from a wholesaler or supplier for resale. Trade discounts are percentages applied to the list or catalogue price.

CHAPTER 6

Simple Interest

This chapter introduces you to some commonly used terms in business and finance. These concepts, principal, maturity value, present value, and equivalent value, are the most common applications of simple interest in business and in your personal finances.

The ideas presented in this chapter form the basis of most topics in later chapters. A thorough understanding of how interest works is an important prerequisite for carrying out many financial transactions in the business world.

It is common for each of us to need to borrow money for purchases such as a car, a house, major appliances, and other goods that require large expenditures from the average person's income. Businesses, from small one-person operations to huge conglomerates, also borrow money to finance various stages of growth. When one uses someone else's money there is always an associated cost called **interest**. The cost of borrowing, interest, depends on such things as:

- interest rate,
- length of time the money is borrowed,
- method used to calculate the interest, and
- amount borrowed.

The type of loan an individual negotiates with a bank, credit union, or finance company also is important since different loan arrangements, such as promissory notes and demand loans, have different conditions for repayment.

It is important to understand the ideas presented in this chapter, since they form the building blocks for the financial topics in the remaining chapters of the text.

OBJECTIVES

When you have completed this chapter you should be able to solve simple interest problems and understand the terms used in the application of simple interest. Specifically, you should be able to:

1. explain the meaning of the terms simple interest, amount, maturity value, present value, interest rate, discounting, and equivalent values;
3. use simple interest formula to find future value (maturity value), principal (present value), time, simple interest, proceeds, and simple discount;
4. differentiate between interest bearing and non-interest bearing notes;
5. discount a note and find the maturity value for promissory notes, demand notes, and demand loans.

6.1 Simple Interest

In this first section we'll look at the three components that are needed to calculate simple interest: **principal, interest rate,** and **time**. During our discussion of time, we'll examine two different kinds of time, **exact time** and **approximate time,** and how the measure of time affects the calculation of interest.

A. Basic Simple Interest

The borrowing of money is something that each of us will do over our lifetime — some more than others! Borrowing funds as a means of purchasing a car, a boat, paying for an education, or for other major expenditures, is done regularly by all Canadians and Canadian businesses. **When we borrow money we are expected to pay for the use of the money — this is called interest.**

One way of thinking about interest is to compare it to the rent paid for an apartment, or, in the case of a business, the rent paid for an office or building space. In each case, the payment of a rent compensates the owner for the use of an asset. The same principle applies when you are paid interest on your savings account or Canada Savings Bond — the interest you are paid is a rent for the use of your money by the bank or government, respectively.

When we borrow money, the amount we borrow is called the principal.

For example, if we borrow $20,000 for a new car, $20,000 would be the principal. To determine how much interest must be paid for money borrowed, the interest rate must be known. **The interest rate refers to the percentage that will be used to calculate the cost of borrowing.** The interest rate is quoted on an annual basis. For example, if the car loan of $20,000 has a cost of 15% per year, then we would pay $3,000 ($20,000 × 0.15) interest for one year's use of the money.

Often payments are made toward the repayment of a loan; generally, payments are monthly. In these cases, the principal of the loan will not be $20,000 for a full year since the payments generally reduce some of the outstanding principal each month. Thus, there must be a measure that accounts for how long a principal has been outstanding — **this measure is called time.**

The time a principal may be outstanding can be expressed in days, months, or years. However, in all cases, the interest rate and the time will always be measured in the same terms. For example, a loan that has been outstanding for 35 days would have to be measured in terms of a year, that is, 35/365, where the 365 days is equivalent to one year. Note that the interest rate is expressed annually and the time is also expressed as a fraction of a year.

To calculate simple interest, the following formula is used:

$$I = Prt$$ **Formula 6.1**

Where:

I = interest
P = principal
r = interest rate (per year)
t = time (in years or fraction of a year)

EXAMPLE 6.1

Brian Robson went to his bank and borrowed $10,000 to purchase a used car. Brian agreed to pay the full amount of the loan in seven months, plus interest, at an interest rate of 15% per annum (year).

(a) If Brian repays the full amount of the loan in seven months, what is the cost of the loan? (i.e., what is the interest paid?)
(b) If Brian had arranged to repay the loan in fifteen months, what would be the cost of the loan? (Cost of the loan is the simple interest.)

Solution (a) In this example:

$P = \$10{,}000$

$r = 0.15$ (15% per year)

$t = \frac{7}{12}$ Note that $\frac{7}{12}$ is a fraction of a year.

Thus, the calculation for interest is:

$$I = \$10{,}000(0.15)\left(\frac{7}{12}\right)$$

$$= \$875$$

(b) For fifteen months, the only change is with time.

$$t = \frac{15}{12}$$

Thus, the calculation for interest is:

$$I = \$10{,}000(0.15)\left(\frac{15}{12}\right)$$

$$= \$1{,}875$$

B. Calculating the Number of Days

Since time is often expressed in days rather than in months, the number of days in the year must be determined prior to any interest calculations. For example, a loan made on July 10 for 60 days can be interpreted two ways:

- Does one assume that 60 days is equivalent to two months? In that case, the loan would be due on September 10.
- Does one take the exact number of days and calculate that the loan is due on September 8?

The answer to these two questions depends upon whether **exact time** or **approximate time** is being used. In Canada, the practice is to use exact time, that is, the exact number of days for time (for either a loan or an investment). If the calculations use the exact number of days for interest calculations, the interest is referred to as **exact interest**. However, if one uses the rule that each month has 30 days, and a year has 360 days, then the **approximate time** is being used. If one has a problem where only the number of months is specified, without any dates, then the approximate time must be used to find the interest.

(i) Exact Time

Exact time, as the name implies, uses the precise number of days for time of the loan or investment. Thus a period of 180 days, for example, will be less than six months. The easiest way to calculate exact time is to use a table (see Table 6.1) that numerically identifies each day of the year from 1 to 365. This table permits the easy measurement of the exact number of days for interest computations.

Table 6.1 Number of Days in the Year

Day of month	Jan.	Feb.	Mar.	April	May	June	July	Aug.	Sept.	Oct.	Nov.	Dec.	Day of month
1	1	32	60	91	121	152	182	213	244	274	305	335	1
2	2	33	61	92	122	153	183	214	245	275	306	336	2
3	3	34	62	93	123	154	184	215	246	276	307	337	3
4	4	35	63	94	124	155	185	216	247	277	308	338	4
5	5	36	64	95	125	156	186	217	248	278	309	339	5
6	6	37	65	96	126	157	187	218	249	279	310	340	6
7	7	38	66	97	127	158	188	219	250	280	311	341	7
8	8	39	67	98	128	159	189	220	251	281	312	342	8
9	9	40	68	99	129	160	190	221	252	282	313	343	9
10	10	41	69	100	130	161	191	222	253	283	314	344	10
11	11	42	70	101	131	162	192	223	254	284	315	345	11
12	12	43	71	102	132	163	193	224	255	285	316	346	12
13	13	44	72	103	133	164	194	225	256	286	317	347	13
14	14	45	73	104	134	165	195	226	257	287	318	348	14
15	15	46	74	105	135	166	196	227	258	288	319	349	15
16	16	47	75	106	136	167	197	228	259	289	320	350	16
17	17	48	76	107	137	168	198	229	260	290	321	351	17
18	18	49	77	108	138	169	199	230	261	291	322	352	18
19	19	50	78	109	139	170	200	231	262	292	323	353	19
20	20	51	79	110	140	171	201	232	263	293	324	354	20
21	21	52	80	111	141	172	202	233	264	294	325	355	21
22	22	53	81	112	142	173	203	234	265	295	326	356	22
23	23	54	82	113	143	174	204	235	266	296	327	357	23
24	24	55	83	114	144	175	205	236	267	297	328	358	24
25	25	56	84	115	145	176	206	237	268	298	329	359	25
26	26	57	85	116	146	177	207	238	269	299	330	360	26
27	27	58	86	117	147	178	208	239	270	300	331	361	27
28	28	59	87	118	148	179	209	240	271	301	332	362	28
29	29		88	119	149	180	210	241	272	302	333	363	29
30	30		89	120	150	181	211	242	273	303	334	364	30
31	31		90		151		212	243		304		365	31

Note: For leap year add 1 to the tabulated number after February 28.

EXAMPLE 6.2

Colwood Paints takes out a business loan to purchase new inventory. Using exact time, find the number of days the loan is outstanding if the loan period is from September 20, 1991, to December 25, 1991.

Solution There are two methods one can use to find the exact number of days. Using the first method, take a calendar and identify the number of days for each month. (*Note:* Remember, you include the first or the last day of the loan, but not both.)

	Number of Days	
September	10	September 21–30 inclusive. (September 20, is not included.)
October	31	
November	30	
December	25	December 25 is included.
Total	96 days	

The second and easier method is to use Table 6.1. First we find the number in the table (day of the year) for September 20 — 263. Then, we find the number for December 25 — 359. Subtract the two:

	Day of the Year
December 25	359
September 20	263
Difference	96 days

It is important to recognize that when 263 is subtracted from 359 it excludes the start date (or end date) as part of the calculation.

(ii) Approximate Time

The second procedure for calculating time uses approximate time, where each year is assumed to have 360 days and each month is considered to have 30 days. This basis is used to determine how long money has been borrowed or invested. This measurement is called **approximate time**. Example 6.3 demonstrates this situation:

EXAMPLE 6.3

Alec Lindsay took out a loan on March 20 for five months. Find the number of days Alec had the loan outstanding using approximate time.

Solution From March 20 to August 20 is five months. Now, treating each month as 30 days, the approximate time is 30×5, or 150 days.

EXAMPLE 6.4

A small store took out a loan of $1,500 on March 10, 1991, and agreed to repay the loan in full in four months. If the interest rate being charged is 12%, determine the interest using (a) exact time and (b) approximate time.

Solution (a) To calculate interest using exact time, we must find the number of days, using Table 6.1:

July 10 (four months later)	191
March 10	69
Difference	122 days

Applying the formula, $I = Prt$, where

$$P = \$1{,}500$$

$$r = 0.12$$

$$t = \frac{122}{365}$$

Now calculating simple interest:

$$I = \$1{,}500(0.12)\left(\frac{122}{365}\right)$$

$$I = \$60.16$$

(b) Using approximate time, $t = \frac{4}{12}$, or $\frac{120}{360}$.

With approximate time each month is treated as having 30 days. Therefore, the interest is calculated as follows:

$$I = Prt$$

$$I = \$1{,}500(0.12)\left(\frac{4}{12}\right)$$

$$I = \$60.00$$

Although there is only a difference of \$0.16 in this example, a larger principal will cause the difference to be larger.

If you have ever borrowed money in the United States you may have found that the number of days for the year was 360 rather than 365 days. When the exact number of days a loan or investment is computed, one may end up with two interest calculations. If the exact time money is borrowed is measured as a fraction of 365 days, the calculations give **exact time and exact interest.** When the exact time money is borrowed is measured as a fraction of 360 days per year, then we have **exact time with ordinary interest**. Note how the term exact time is being used; it refers to the exact number of days money is borrowed (or invested). When the approximate time is used the interest can be either ordinary or exact interest, depending on how the number of days money has been outstanding is measured. As a consequence, when the two measures of interest (ordinary and exact) and the two measures of time (approximate and exact) are combined, it actually produces a combination of four possible ways to compute interest. These are:

Exact interest using exact time;
Exact interest using approximate time;
Ordinary interest using exact time; and
Ordinary interest using approximate time.

EXAMPLE 6.5

A loan of \$8,000 is taken out on August 31 and repaid on December 15. Find the interest due under each of the methods noted above, if the interest rate on the loan is 15% per annum.

Solution First, let's find the two measures of time:

Exact Time

December 15	349	From Table 6.1.
August 31	243	
Number of days (exact)	106	

Approximate Time

Number of days in December	15
Number of days for Sept.–Nov. (3×30)	90
Number of days (approximate)	105

Using the formula $I = Prt$ to calculate the interest, we have:

Exact interest, using exact time:

$$I = \$8{,}000(0.15)\left(\frac{106}{365}\right)$$

$$I = \$348.49$$

Exact interest, using approximate time:

$$I = \$8{,}000(0.15)\left(\frac{105}{365}\right)$$

$$I = \$345.21$$

Ordinary interest, using exact time:

$$I = \$8{,}000(0.15)\left(\frac{106}{360}\right)$$

$$I = \$353.33$$

Ordinary interest, using approximate time:

$$I = \$8{,}000(0.15)\left(\frac{105}{360}\right)$$

$$I = \$350.00$$

As can be seen from the above example, the method used to calculate the interest makes a substantial difference in how much interest is paid (charged to a borrower). The combination of ordinary interest and exact time produces the largest interest payment and, as you might guess, is known as the **Banker's Rule**. The Banker's Rule is more common in the United States. **In Canada, the rule applied is exact time and exact interest, providing the actual number of days can be determined.** If the time is specified in months then ordinary interest with approximate time is used. When the dates are given, we will use the Canadian approach to calculate interest, that is, using the exact time.

When calculating the number of days, there are two things that must be kept in mind. First, when determining the number of days between two dates, count either the beginning date or the end date, but not both. The subtraction of numbers in the day of the year in Table 6.1 takes this into account.

Second, when using Table 6.1 to calculate the exact time, the table must be adjusted for **leap years**. Leap years are years divisible by 4, such as 1992 and 1996. In leap years, February has an extra day. Therefore, you must add 1 to each value in Table 6.1, starting with February 28, to adjust for the leap year.

EXERCISE 6.1

To make sure that you have a firm grasp of the concepts presented in this section, try the following practice exercises on interest and time calculations.

1. Find the interest for the following:
 a. \$1,000 at 10% for one year
 b. \$1,000 at 10% for six months
 c. \$1,500 at $11\frac{1}{2}\%$ for five months
 d. \$725 at $18\frac{1}{2}\%$ for eight months

2. Find the exact time for the following periods:
 a. February 20 to September 1, 1991
 b. June 15 to October 20, 1992
 c. January 5, 1990, to May 15, 1991

3. Determine the due date using approximate time for the following:
 a. 30 days after May 20
 b. 90 days after August 10
 c. 3 months after August 30

4. Using the exact time, find the ordinary and exact interest for the following:
 a. \$1,550 for 180 days at 16%
 b. \$1,400 for 62 days at 15%

5. If \$730 is borrowed on July 4, 1991, for three months, find the interest that would be due using the four combinations of time and interest. Assume the interest rate is 18% per annum.

6. A three month loan of $1,540 is negotiated at an interest rate of 10% and is taken out on September 12, 1991. Compute the exact interest due on the loan using (a) exact time and (b) approximate time.

For the remaining sections of this chapter, unless otherwise directed, use exact time and exact interest *when dates are given.*

6.2 Determining the Maturity Value (Amount, Future Value), Rate, and Time

In this section we will determine the future value of money, called the **maturity value or amount**, as well as explain the formulas for determining time and the interest rate, and in particular, how these formulas can be used in simple business problems.

A. Maturity Value (Amount)

The maturity value or amount of money refers to the sum of interest and principal. What is important to understand is that money has different values at different points in time. The difference in value comes about through the accumulation of interest. The expression **time value of money** is used to recognize that money has a different value at different points in time. The term maturity value comes from the idea of growth over time, where maturity value is the value of money plus any accumulated interest.

In most discussions, the sum, S, is used for maturity value or the amount because it represents the sum of two terms, principal (P) and interest (I). To use the example of a loan, when you repay a loan you pay the principal plus the interest owing, which is the maturity value of the loan.

To calculate the sum or amount, the following formula is used:

$$S = P + I$$

Since $I = Prt$,

$$S = P + Prt$$

Factoring out the common term:

$$S = P(1 + rt)$$ **Formula 6.2**

Formula 6.2 can be used to determine, in one calculation, the amount or maturity value of a loan or a deposit.

EXAMPLE 6.6

A loan of \$1,800 is arranged at 18% for four months. Find (a) the interest and, (b) the amount or maturity value of the loan.

Solution (a) To find the interest we use $I = Prt$, where:

$$P = \$1{,}800$$
$$r = 0.18$$
$$t = \frac{4}{12}$$

Thus, the interest is:

$$I = \$1{,}800(0.18)\left(\frac{4}{12}\right)$$
$$I = \$108$$

(b) To find the amount, or maturity value, of the loan we use:

$$S = P + I$$
$$S = \$1{,}800 + \$108$$
$$S = \$1{,}908$$

or

$$S = P(1 + rt)$$
$$S = \$1{,}800\left[1 + (0.18)\ \frac{4}{12}\right]$$
$$S = \$1{,}908$$

B. Finding the Time

Suppose you need \$15,000 for a down payment on a house and you have only \$12,000. To determine how long it will take the \$12,000 to accumulate to the sum, \$15,000, we need to be able to calculate the time, t. Based on the formulas we have learned so far, the easiest way to find the time is to rearrange the interest formula $I = Prt$.

To find t:

Divide both sides of $I = Prt$ by Pr to obtain $\frac{I}{Pr} = t$

Rearrange the formula to put t on the left hand side of the equation:

$$t = \frac{I}{Pr}$$ **Formula 6.3**

EXAMPLE 6.7

John Adams wants to accumulate \$50 in interest and invests \$500 today. If the interest rate is 8%, how long will it take to accumulate \$50?

Solution In this example:

$$I = \$50$$
$$P = \$500$$
$$r = 0.08$$

The calculation for time is:

$$t = \frac{I}{Pr}$$

$$t = \frac{\$50}{(\$500)(0.08)}$$

$$t = 1.25 \text{ years}$$

EXAMPLE 6.8

Noel Stevens borrows \$5,000 to furnish her new apartment. If she wishes to pay a maximum of \$100 interest, when must she repay the loan if the interest rate is 10%?

Solution In this example:

$$I = \$100$$
$$P = \$5{,}000$$
$$r = 0.1$$

Now, applying Formula 6.3 and substituting:

$$t = \frac{I}{Pr}$$

$$t = \frac{\$100}{(\$5{,}000)(0.1)}$$

$$t = 0.2 \text{ years, or 73 days}$$

Noel must repay the loan in 73 days.

C. Finding the Interest Rate

The interest rate can be found by manipulating the original interest formula ($I = Prt$) in the same manner as we rearranged it to find the time.

To find r:

Divide both sides of $I = Prt$ by Pt to obtain $\frac{I}{Pt} = r$

Rearrange the formula to put r on the left hand side of the equation:

$$r = \frac{I}{Pt}$$ **Formula 6.4**

EXAMPLE 6.9

What interest rate is necessary to yield $150 on a $1,600 investment in eight months?

Solution In this example:

$$I = \$150$$

$$P = \$1{,}600$$

$$t = \frac{8}{12}$$

Thus, the calculation for the interest rate is:

$$r = \frac{I}{Pt}$$

$$r = \frac{\$150}{\left[(\$1{,}600)\ \frac{8}{12}\right]}$$

$$r = 0.1406, \text{ or } 14.06\% \text{ per year}$$

EXAMPLE 6.10

A friend offers to lend you $5,000 under the condition that you will repay $5,200 in two months. What is the interest rate being charged?

Solution To solve this problem we must first find the interest payment. This is done by subtracting $5,000 (money borrowed) from $5,200 (amount to be repaid), which yields $200. Substituting the known values into Formula 6.4 we have:

$$r = \frac{I}{Pt}$$

$$r = \frac{\$200}{\left[(\$5{,}000)\ \dfrac{2}{12}\right]}$$

$$r = 0.24, \text{ or } 24\% \text{ per year}$$

Some friend!

EXERCISE 6.2

1. Find the amount due on a loan of $3,500 after eight months if the interest rate is 16.5%.
2. A person borrowed $1,950 at 10% for three months. How much must be repaid?
3. On September 15, 1991, a person borrows $1,900 and agrees to repay the loan in 180 days with interest at 17%.
   a. What amount must be repaid?
   b. On what date will the loan be repaid? Use the exact interest.
4. Suppose Sam borrowed $3,400 at 14% and repaid $3,549.97. For how long did he borrow the money?
5. How many days are required for $500 to amount to $530 at 10%?
6. A person borrows $4,000 and agrees to pay $1,000 at the end of each six month period over two years. The loan must be repaid by the end of two years. If the interest rate is 4%, what must be the size of the last payment? Assume all interest is due with the final payment.
7. Suppose you deposit $500 in a savings account and at the end of one month you receive $4.50 in interest. What rate of interest are you being paid?
8. If $715 was paid to discharge (pay off) a loan of $675 on July 17, 1991, and the loan was taken out on May 3, 1991, what was the rate of interest being charged on the loan?
9. John bought a new television from a store that advertised no interest payments for three months. When he bought the television on May 5, 1991, the bill was $1,239.14. Three months later John sent the company a cheque for the full amount owing ($1,239.14). Shortly afterward, John received a statement from the company advising him that he still owed $49.30 since, although there were "no interest payments" for three months, he was still

obliged to pay the interest that had accumulated over the past three months. What interest rate has John been charged?

10. To encourage payment, we know that some firms offer a cash discount for early payment on the invoice (see Chapter 5). A firm has been sent an invoice for $1,245.30, with the terms 2/10, n/30. What rate of interest would a firm be prepared to pay on borrowed funds to take advantage of the cash discount?

6.3 Principal and Present Value

In this section we will examine the widely used concept of present value. Instead of beginning with the principal that is borrowed or invested it may be more appropriate to start from what you want to accumulate in the future, and then work backward to see what you must invest to reach the required amount. This is like someone deciding how much they will need to retire in so many years, then working in reverse to figure out what amount must be invested today to have the desired amount for the retirement in the future.

A. Principal

As you will recall from our earlier discussion, the principal refers to the initial amount of money borrowed or deposited. To find the value of the principal, we again use the formula $I = Prt$ and solve for P. Dividing both sides of the expression by rt yields:

$$P = \frac{I}{rt} \qquad \textbf{Formula 6.5}$$

Another way of expressing the principal is to use the expression

$$S = P + I$$

and substitute Prt for I. Remember that S is the maturity value or amount.

$$S = P + Prt$$

or

$$S = P(1 + rt)$$

Then rearrange the expression to solve for P.

$$P = \frac{S}{(1 + rt)} \qquad \textbf{Formula 6.6}$$

EXAMPLE 6.11

You are advised that you can receive \$100 interest in two months. If the interest rate is 8%, what principal must be invested to earn this interest?

Solution In this example:

$$I = \$100$$

$$t = \frac{2}{12}$$

$$r = 0.08$$

Thus, the calculation for principal is:

$$P = \frac{I}{rt}$$

$$P = \frac{\$100}{\left[(0.08)\,\frac{2}{12}\right]}$$

$$P = \$7{,}500$$

Therefore, the required principal to be invested is \$7,500.

EXAMPLE 6.12

Jerry and Anne need \$10,000 in three years for a down payment on a house. If the interest rate is 6%, how much would they have to deposit today (principal) to accumulate \$10,000 in three years?

Solution In this example:

$$S = \$10{,}000 \text{ (amount or maturity value)}$$

$$t = 3 \text{ years}$$

$$r = 0.06$$

The calculation for principal is:

$$P = \frac{S}{(1 + rt)}$$

$$P = \frac{\$10{,}000}{[1 + (0.06)3]}$$

$$P \doteq \$8{,}474.58$$

Therefore, if they deposit \$8,474.58 today at 6%, they will have \$10,000 in three years.

B. Present Value

One important concept used in business is present value. **Present value refers to today's value of a future amount.** For example, if a piece of land will have a value of $20,000 in three years and the interest rate is 10%, what is the price that should be paid for the land today? The answer to this question is called the present value (today's value) of the future amount of $20,000.

Using a time diagram, we can see the problem visually.

Figure 6.1 Bringing back a future value to find today's value (present value)

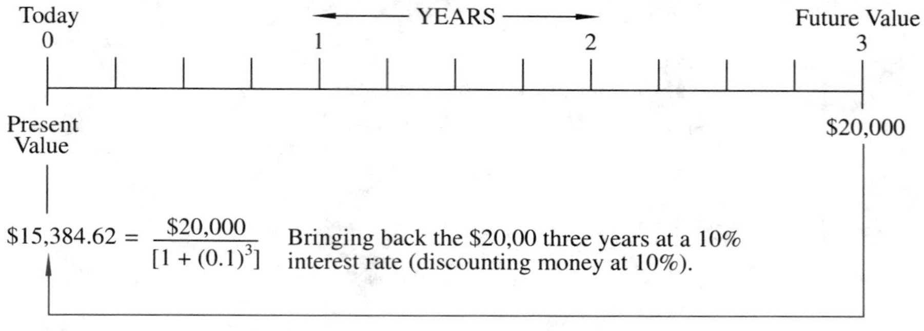

What we need to figure out is how to bring the $20,000, in three years, back in time to today. To perform this calculation, we simply find what principal, *P*, would have to be invested today to yield $20,000 in three years, when the interest rate is 10%. Therefore, we use:

$$P = \frac{S}{(1 + rt)}$$

$$P = \frac{\$20{,}000}{[1 + (0.1)3]}$$

$$P \doteq \$15{,}384.62$$

Figure 6.2 Moving the future value of $20,000 back in time (i.e., discounting) three years to find today's value

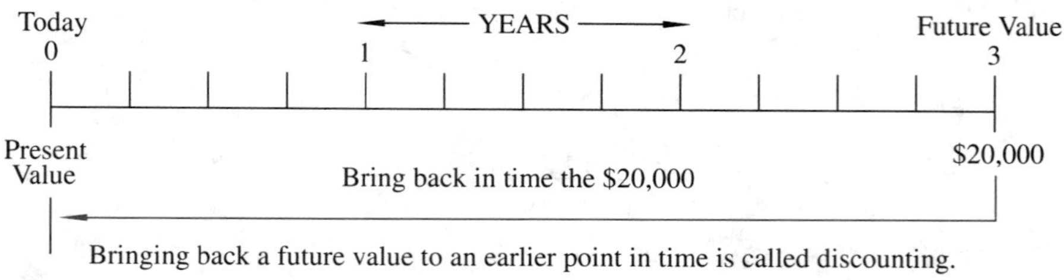

Thus, the present value of \$15,384.62 will yield the future value of \$20,000 in three years at an interest rate of 10%. Therefore, a fair price today for the land is \$15,384.62.

Note that the formula for present value is the same formula as used to find the principal, P (Formula 6.6), namely:

$$P = \frac{S}{(1 + rt)}$$

EXAMPLE 6.13

What is the maximum price that one should pay today (the present value) for a piece of land forecasted to have a value of \$35,000 in two years if the interest rate is 6%?

Solution Using the formula $P = \dfrac{S}{(1 + rt)}$ and substituting:

$S = \$35{,}000$ Future value.

$r = 0.06$

$t = 2$

$$P = \frac{\$35{,}000}{[1 + (0.06)2]}$$

$P = \$31{,}250$

Based on this calculation one would not want to pay any more than \$31,250, today, for land expected to be worth \$35,000 in two years, if the interest rate is 6%.

A time diagram for this problem would look as follows:

Figure 6.3

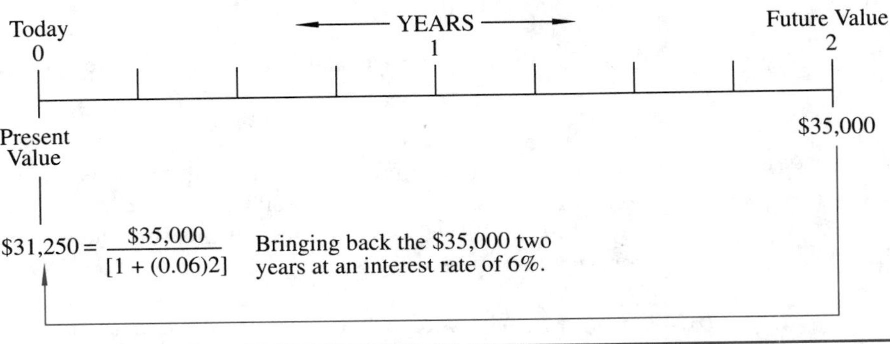

EXAMPLE 6.14

(*Note:* This real life example is fairly complicated. Work through each step of the solution slowly, making sure that you understand why each formula is used.)

A car rental agency has the cash available to buy five new cars for its fleet. After asking for quotes from different dealers, the best obtainable price per car is $15,000. One year from now, the price on the same car is expected to be $16,500 per car because of a factory price increase (inflation). The company can wait until next year to purchase the cars since the current fleet is in reasonably good shape. At present, the company has the cash in the bank and can collect simple interest at 12% per year.

(a) What is the most cost-effective decision (which is better, buy now or wait for a year)?
(b) Find the savings of the best decision.

Solution (a) The approach that most people would use to solve this problem would be to calculate the amount of money the company would have in one year by leaving the principal in the bank and compare this amount to the amount required to purchase the cars in one year's time.

STEP 1 Determine the principal:

$$P = \$15{,}000 \times 5$$

$$P = \$75{,}000 \qquad \text{5 cars @ \$15,000 each.}$$

STEP 2 Find the amount or future value of the principal in one year, assuming it is left in the bank at the 12% interest rate:

$$S = \$75{,}000[1 + (0.12)1]$$

$$S = \$84{,}000$$

STEP 3 Determine the cost of purchasing the cars in one year's time:

$$\$16{,}500 \times 5 = \$82{,}500$$

STEP 4 Comparing the two amounts, the best decision is to purchase the cars next year and save $1,500 ($84,000 minus $82,500). The conclusion is correct but the $1,500 savings does not measure the savings today. Rather, it measures a future savings.

(b) To find the savings <u>today</u>, we must use the concept of present value. That is, we must compare today's value of the future cost ($82,500) with the actual cost today ($75,000). The difference between these two values will give us <u>today's</u> savings.

STEP 1 To calculate today's value for the future amount of \$82,500 we use the present value formula:

$$P = \frac{S}{(1 + rt)}$$

Substituting: $S = \$82{,}500$; $r = 0.12$; $t = 1$ year

$$P = \frac{\$82{,}500}{[1 + (0.12)1]}$$

$$P \doteq \$73{,}660.71$$

STEP 2 Comparing the current price of \$75,000 with today's value of the future cost, \$73,660.71, the savings today of purchasing next year are:

$$\$75{,}000 - \$73{,}660.71, \text{ or } \$1{,}339.29$$

The savings generated in each case, \$1,500 one year from now and \$1,339.29 today, both express the equivalent savings but at different points in time. The relationship between the two values can be seen if we accumulate today's savings, \$1,339.29, for one year at 12% simple interest. Let's see what happens if we accumulate the savings for one year:

Using Formula 6.2, finding the amount or future value gives:

$$S = P(1 + rt)$$

Substituting: $P = \$1{,}339.29$; $r = 0.12$; $t = 1$ year:

$$S = \$1{,}339.29[1 + (0.12)1]$$

$$S \doteq \$1{,}500 \qquad \text{Any difference is due to rounding.}$$

EXERCISE 6.3

To make sure that you have a thorough understanding of present value, try the following practice exercises.

1. What is the present value of \$2,000 due in three years if the simple interest rate is 8% per annum?
2. A debt of \$2,400 is due in 1.5 years. If the debt is paid today and the interest rate today is $10\frac{3}{4}$%, find the required payment today that will satisfy the loan.
3. A debt of \$5,000 is due in six months. What is today's value of the debt if 15% simple interest is applied?
4. Sandra received three offers on a piece of property she owns. Offer 1 gave her \$42,000 in three years, offer 2 paid her \$35,000 in two years,

and offer 3 offered her \$28,000 cash today. Which offer is the best for Sandra if the interest rate is 11%, simple interest.

5. After 75 days John paid back a loan by making a payment of \$1,450. The payment included all interest and principal and was computed using an interest rate of 15% per annum. What was the original size of the loan?
6. Find the discounted value of \$2,300 due in five months if the interest rate is 11%.
7. Kathy repaid a loan on September 3, 1991, which was taken out on May 1, 1991. How much did Kathy borrow if \$5,750 was repaid as full payment to the loan (interest and principal)? Assume the interest rate charged on the loan was 16%.
8. A company is trying to decide whether to lease or buy a photocopier. The choices are to pay \$6,500 today to purchase the machine or to make three payments, \$2,500 today, \$3,000 in one year, and \$2,500 in three years. The company has more than \$6,500 in the bank and could pay cash for the copier. Which option is the least cost to the company, and how much will it save? Assume the company can invest money at 15% simple interest.

6.4 Equivalent Values

We already know that when money is put to work (for example, by being invested) its value grows to maturity. This process is continuous so that it is possible to calculate the value of the money at any point in time. In the case of an investment, we can find its accumulated value at any time. Each of the amounts calculated would be directly comparable and of equivalent value. For example, \$1,000 invested (or borrowed) at 12% has different values over time. The changing nature of money at a given interest rate can be seen in Figure 6.4. In particular, \$100 invested at 12% has a value of \$106 in six months and a value of \$112 in a year. Each of these three values is con-

Figure 6.4 Equivalent Values

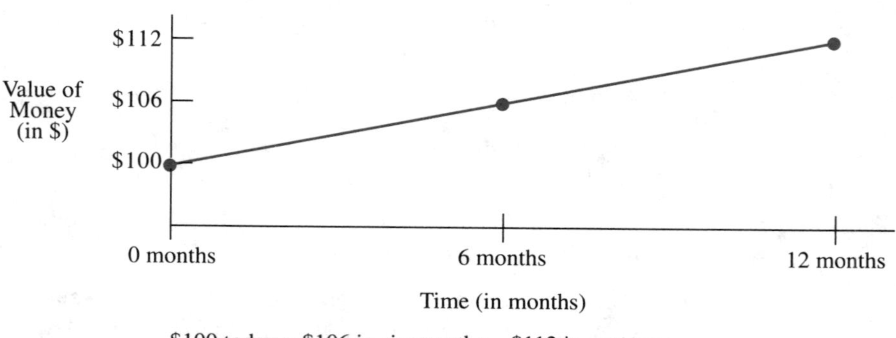

\$100 today = \$106 in six months = \$112 in one year if the interest rate is 12% per annum.

sidered **equivalent to each other** since each is based on the same principal and interest rate, but, evaluated at different points in time.

Sometimes there is a need to change the due date of a loan, for example, when one cannot meet a particular payment. When the due date is changed, the value of the debt is also changed. The value of the debt when changed is called an **equivalent value** — a new value that is equivalent to the old debt.

Suppose that a debt of $500 is due today and the payment cannot be paid as agreed. The credit manager of the institution from which the loan was taken permits an extension of the debt for two months, providing interest is paid at the simple rate of 12%. Therefore, in two months one would pay $500 plus interest at 12% for two months, yielding a final payment of $510.

The payment of $510 in two months is referred to as an equivalent value, since either $500 now or $510 in two months repays the debt.

EXAMPLE 6.15

A debt of $1,000 (principal and interest) is due today. Assume the debtor doesn't have enough money to repay the loan today, and the creditor agrees that the debt can be replaced by a new debt due in three months. If the money is worth 15%, what will be the value of the new debt?

Solution The new debt is found by solving for S, where:

$$S = P(1 + rt)$$

Substituting: $P = \$1{,}000$; $r = 0.15$; $t = \frac{3}{12}$

$$S = \$1{,}000\left[1 + (0.15)\ \frac{3}{12}\right]$$

$$S = \$1{,}037.50$$

Thus, $1,037.50 in three months is equivalent to $1,000 due today when the interest rate is 15%.

Unfortunately the calculation of equivalent payments becomes more complicated when more than one payment occurs. The problem is that a sum of money will have different values at different points in time. To resolve the problem we MUST select a focal point. **A focal point (also called a comparison point) is a common point in time when the new and old debt can be compared.** When using simple interest, different focal points will yield slightly different payments, so always be sure to use the focal date specified in the problem. The only time a focal point is understood, unless otherwise stated, is when only one payment is to be found in the future. That is, if there is only a single final payment and the focal date is not specified, use the last period as the focal point.

EXAMPLE 6.16

In Example 16.15 it was suggested that the loan of $1,000 would be repaid in three months with a single payment. Suppose it was decided to repay the debt in two equal payments — one at month three, the other at month six. Assume the focal date is agreed to be month three. (*Note:* That we could have selected any period to be the focal point; month three was simply for convenience.) What is the value of these two payments?

Solution

STEP 1 Let X be the value of each equal payment, one at month three and one at month six.

STEP 2 Move the old debt and the new debt to the focal date:

Old Debt: $\$1{,}000\left[1 + (0.15)\,\frac{3}{12}\right]$

New Debt: One payment at focal date $= X$

Second equal payment at month six brought back to

$$\text{focal date} = \frac{X}{\left[1 + (0.15)\,\frac{3}{12}\right]}$$

STEP 3 Set the old debt equal to the new debt and solve for X.

$$\underbrace{\$1{,}000\left[1 + (0.15)\,\frac{3}{12}\right]}_{\text{Old Debt}} = \underbrace{X + \frac{X}{\left[1 + (0.15)\,\frac{3}{12}\right]}}_{\text{New Debt}}$$

$$\$1{,}000(1.0375) = X + \frac{X}{(1 + 0.0375)}$$

$$\$1{,}037.50 = X\left[1 + \frac{1}{(1.0375)}\right]$$

$$\$1{,}037.50 \doteq X(1.963855)$$

$$X \doteq \frac{\$1{,}037.50}{1.963855}$$

$$X \doteq \$528.30$$

The required answer is two equal payments of \$528.30, one at month three and the other at month six.

The time diagram shows this graphically:

Figure 6.5

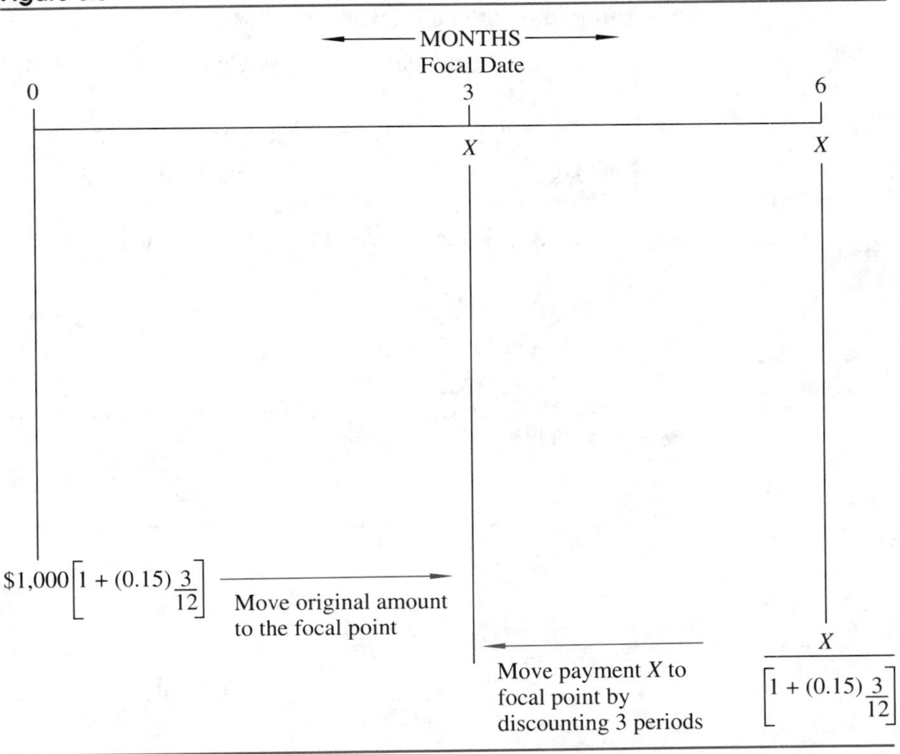

EXAMPLE 6.17

Bob Harris owes the Royal Bank \$800, due in five months, and \$1,000 plus 10% interest, due in eight months. If money is worth 12%, what single payment at month ten would be equivalent to the two original debts and satisfy the bank?

Solution Since there will only be one payment at month ten, the focal date becomes month ten. Let X be the value of the single payment. See Figure 6.6 below:

STEP 1 X is our value of the single payment at month ten.

STEP 2 Move the old debt and the new debt to the focal date.

$$\text{Old Debt} = \$800\left[1 + (0.12)\,\frac{5}{12}\right] + \$1{,}066.67\left[1 + (0.12)\,\frac{2}{12}\right]$$

(*Note:* \$1,066.67 resulted from the accumulation of \$1,000 at 10% from the beginning to month eight, when it is due.)

$$\text{New Debt} = X = \text{single payment at month ten}$$

STEP 3 Set the new debt equal to the old debt and solve for X.

$$\underline{\text{New Debt}} = \qquad\qquad \underline{\text{Old Debt}}$$

$$X = \$800\left[1 + (0.12)\,\frac{5}{12}\right] + \$1{,}066.67\left[1 + (0.12)\,\frac{2}{12}\right]$$

$$X = \$840 + \$1{,}088$$

$$X = \$1{,}928$$

Therefore, the single payment at month ten, which is equivalent to the old debt, is \$1,928.00. The time diagram is:

Figure 6.6

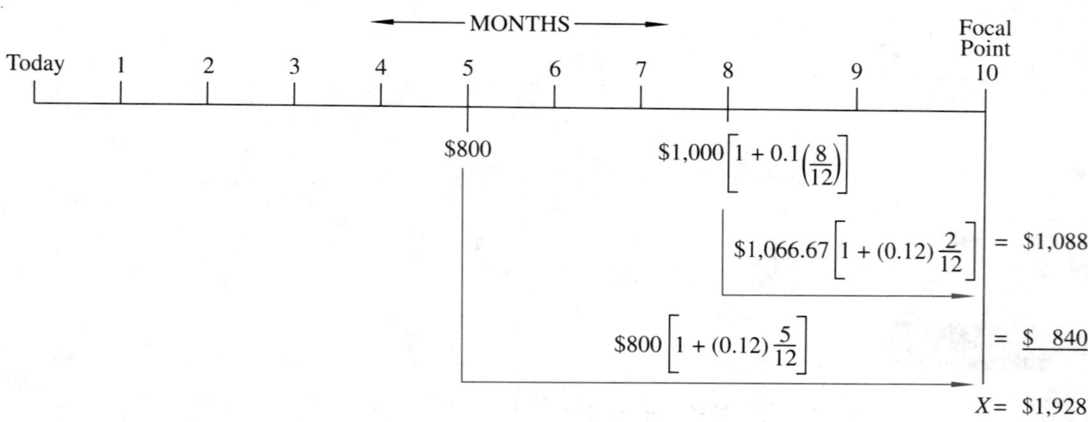

Equivalent payments are very important since they allow us to move debt to different points in time, while still satisfying the original debt.

EXERCISE 6.4

Since the concept of equivalent values can be a difficult one, it's particularly important to test your understanding of the topic by doing the following practice exercises.

1. A debt of $6,000 is due in eight months. If the interest rate is 15%, what is the required payment to discharge the debt if it is paid in (a) four months and (b) in six months?
2. A person owes a credit union $1,000 in two months and $500 in eight months. The credit manager has agreed to permit the person to repay the debt with one payment in six months. If the interest rate is 12%, what single payment in six months satisfies the debt?
3. Alex owes $1,200, due in three months, and $1,800, due in nine months. Due to financial problems he cannot meet the original obligation. The creditor has agreed to permit the settlement of the two debts by two equal payments in five months and eleven months. Assuming the focal date is five months from now, and the interest rate is 16%, what is the size of each new payment?
4. What would be the amount of a $4,000 debt after six months if money is worth 17%?
5. If money is currently worth 15%, calculate the two equal payments, one in eight months and the other in a year and a half from now that will satisfy two debts: $6,000 due two months ago with interest at 15%, and $4,500 with interest at 16%, due in one year. Use one year from now as the focal point.
6. Find the size of two equal payments, one due now and the other due in ten months, that are to replace four original debts of $400, $300, $500, and $200. The debts are due ten, eight, six, and four months ago, respectively. Assume money is worth 14.5%. Compute two sets of payments: one set using now as the focal point, and the other set using ten months as the focal point.

6.5 Partial Payments

Partial payments refer to the practice of repaying a debt in a series of payments rather than in a lump sum. When we have debt that is retired (that is, to be repaid) with partial payments, there must be an agreement between the creditor and debtor on how the partial payments will be credited to the debt. The most accepted method is the **Declining Balance method**.

The Declining Balance method requires the payment to be used to pay off the interest accumulated on the debt (called accrued interest). Any of the payment remaining after the interest is deducted is then used to reduce the principal. Therefore, each time a payment is made, a separate calculation for interest payment and principal reduction must occur.

EXAMPLE 6.18

Suppose you took out a \$2,000 loan at 15% to be repaid in one year. You decide to make payments of \$600 after four months and \$400 at the end of ten months. What is the outstanding balance of your loan at the end of the year? Use approximate time to solve the problem. (*Note:* The solution to this problem is fairly complex. Work through it slowly and methodically, making sure you understand exactly how each figure is calculated.)

Solution

Original Debt		\$2,000.00	
First payment, fourth month	\$600.00		
Deduct:			
Interest on \$2,000 for four months	\$100.00		← $(2{,}000)(0.15)\left(\frac{4}{12}\right)$
Amount to apply to principal	\$500.00	500.00	← (600 – 100)
Balance at end of the fourth month		\$1,500.00	
Second payment, ten months	\$400.00		
Deduct:			
Interest on \$1,500 for six months	\$112.50		← $(1{,}500)(0.15)\left(\frac{6}{12}\right)$
Amount to apply to principal	\$287.50	287.50	← (400 – 112.50)
Balance at end of the tenth month		\$1,212.50	
Add:			
Interest for remaining two months		30.31	← $(1{,}212.50)(0.15)\left(\frac{2}{12}\right)$
Balance at the end of the year		\$1,242.81	

EXERCISE 6.5

Find the unpaid balance at the specified date in the last column, incorporating all partial payments.

	Date of Loan	Amount Borrowed	Rate of Interest	1st Partial Payment		2nd Partial Payment		3rd Partial Payment		Date of Required
		P	*r*	Date	Amount	Date	Amount	Date	Amount	Balance
1.	May 1/90	$ 1,200	24%	July 1/90	$ 200	Sept. 5/90	$ 500	none	none	Oct. 31/90
2.	June 15/90	$15,000	15%	Aug. 5/90	$8,000	Sept. 4/90	$6,500	none	none	Oct. 15/90
3.	Jan. 20/90	$ 4,230	17%	Feb. 2/90	$3,500	Aug. 5/90	$ 500	none	none	Aug. 5/90
4.	May 20/90	$ 3,330	15%	Aug. 1/90	$1,500	Sept. 2/90	$ 750	Jan. 4/91	$500	April 30/91
5.	Mar. 9/90	$ 200	14%	July 7/90	$ 50	Aug. 5/90	$ 100	none	none	Sept. 30/90
6.	Feb. 10/90	$ 9,250	11%	Mar. 4/90	$4,500	June 6/90	$3,750	Jan. 4/91	$500	April 30/91
7.	June 9/91	$ 4,200	24%	Aug. 9/91	$ 200	Sept. 6/91	$3,500	none	none	Oct. 31/91

8. A $6,000 loan is negotiated September 1, 1991, at 18%. A requirement of the loan is that partial payments are to be made as follows: $500 on October 1; $1,500 on November 15; and, the balance on December 31, 1991. Find the balance due on December 31, 1991.

9. Allan borrowed $9,000 on September 1, 1991. He made partial payments of $1,000 on October 2, $3,500 on November 7, and $1,500 on November 29. If he wants to pay off the debt with a full payment on December 20, 1991, what is the size of the payment if the interest rate is 12% per annum?

10. On April 15, 1991, a loan is taken out to purchase a new car. The size of the loan is $24,000. If a payment of $5,000 is made on both May 3 and July 15, what is the outstanding balance on July 31, 1991? Assume the rate of interest is 15% per annum.

6.6 Demand Loans, Promissory Notes, and Discounting

Now that you are familiar with the terms associated with simple interest, such as principal, rate, time, maturity value, and equivalent values, it's time to examine two of the most common applications of simple interest: **demand loans** and **promissory notes**. If you have ever borrowed money from a bank or entered into an agreement with a merchant for the purchase of goods, you may have used one of these loan instruments yourself, perhaps without realizing it.

We also will examine the practice of **discounting**. One example of this common financial transaction occurs around income tax time, when firms offer immediate cash for your income tax refund, often demanding a hefty discount.

A. Demand Loans

A demand loan is a loan that is payable on demand. Demand loans are often taken out for consumer purchases such as a boat, an automobile, a holiday, and other expenditures for which we cannot afford the full payment at the time of purchase. Businesses often use demand loans as a method to acquire inventory or other necessities associated with running the business. This is especially true for small businesses.

When a demand loan is taken out, the borrower will need to sign a demand note that is a promise to pay the loan. In general, demand loans do not have regular payments, rather, interest is usually paid once a month with an understanding between the borrower and lender as to when the full amount of the loan is to be repaid. This type of agreement is made at the time the loan is taken out. However, the term demand loan means that it can be called at any time while the loan is outstanding, regardless of when the borrower agreed to repay the loan.

A demand loan is usually not a secured loan. To secure a loan means offering an asset to the bank or credit union as "protection" should one have problems in meeting the terms of the loan. The need for security is influenced by many factors. For example, if a person or business has been a reliable customer with an excellent financial record, a lending institution may not require any security, providing the loan is not too large.

The interest rate charged on a demand loan will reflect the risk involved. That is, the higher the risk perceived by the lender, the higher the rate charged on the loan. One feature about the interest rate on a demand loan is that the rate is generally based on an interest rate called the prime rate. **The prime rate is the rate of interest banks and credit unions charge their very best customers and is the lowest borrowing rate.** Often the interest rate on a demand loan is quoted at 2% or 3% above the prime rate. Thus, if the prime rate changes, the rate charged on a demand loan will also change.

The phenomenon of changing interest rates is common. Most people with loans listen to the news on Thursdays to find out if there has been a change in interest rates because the Bank of Canada sets the bank rate on that day. This action determines the interest rates at chartered banks, credit unions, and other financial institutions for the following week.

Remember, the name demand loan means exactly what it states — payable upon demand. Consequently, when one enters a loan agreement that is a demand loan, the institution has the right to "call" the loan (ask you to make the full payment) at any time, for any reason.

Consider the following example of a simple interest calculation for a demand loan:

EXAMPLE 6.19

The owners of Naylor's Garage took out a demand loan on June 1 for $1,500, at an interest rate of 15%, to purchase some badly needed equipment. On June 14, the prime rate increased and the rate on the demand loan was changed to 16%. If the loan is repaid on June 30, how much interest is due?

Solution Using the interest formula $I = Prt$ where:

$P = \$1{,}500$

$r = 0.15$ from June 1 to June 14 and 0.16 thereafter

$t = 13$ days from June 1 to June 14, and 16 days from June 14 to June 30

Calculation for June 1 to June 14:

$$I = \$1{,}500(0.15)\left(\frac{13}{365}\right)$$

$$\doteq \$8.01$$

Calculation for June 14 to June 30:

$$I = \$1{,}500(0.16)\left(\frac{16}{365}\right)$$

$$\doteq \$10.52$$

Thus, the total interest is $8.01 + $10.52, or $18.53.

B. Promissory Notes

Another type of loan transaction involves the use of a promissory note. **A promissory note is a written promise by the debtor, referred to as the maker of the note, to pay to the creditor, called the payee, a sum of money on the specified date with or without interest.** Promissory notes are sometimes used by banks and credit unions when the borrower wishes the loan to be outstanding for a definite period of time. It is similar to an I.O.U. you might write to a friend who has lent you a few dollars.

Promissory notes are legal promises to pay and have a very precise set of procedures for the borrower and the lender. An important feature of a promissory note is that it will have a **specific maturity date** and a **specific maturity value**. In Canada there is a requirement that, unless otherwise specified, the borrower be allowed three extra days, beyond the maturity date, to repay the promissory note. We call these **three days of grace**. The law that adds the three days of grace is the Bills of Exchange Act. Most financial institutions provide more than three days of grace — not by law — but simply as a matter of good business. That is, if someone cannot meet the obligation on the specified date, financial institutions often extend the period of repayment beyond three days. As a consequence, the notion of three days of grace is something that is not commonly discussed in financial circles — unless of course there is a legal issue with respect to its use.

A promissory note is negotiated for a particular time period. This time period is referred to as the **term** of the note. The term of a promissory note may be written in days, months, or years. In each case, there will be a maturity date. However, the legal repayment date will not actually be until three days after the maturity date. This is referred to as the **legal due date**. It may be helpful to visualize the three separate dates involved:

Figure 6.7 Promissory Note Dates

Legal Due Date

Date of Issue

Maturity Date

If the promissory note is marked "NO GRACE", three days of grace is not required and the maturity date and the legal due date will be the same.

The sample note, below, is one form of a promissory note:

Figure 6.8 Sample Promissory Note

PROMISSORY NOTE

$14,000 Victoria, July 2, 1992

Eighty days after date I promise to pay to the order of
John Murray Higginbottom

the sum of $ Fourteen thousand .00
for value received, with interest at 18 % per annum.

Signed John Doe

The following information can be determined from the sample promissory note:

Face value:	\$14,000
Date of note:	July 2, 1992
Term of the note:	80 days
Interest rate:	18%
Maturity date:	80 days after July 2, 1992, that is, September 20
Legal due date:	September 23, 1992 (maturity date plus three days of grace)
Maturity value:	$\$14{,}000 + \$14{,}000(0.18)\left(\frac{83}{365}\right)$, or \$14,573.04
Maker:	John Doe
Payee:	John Murray Higginbottom

In order to understand the terms, let's look at an example:

EXAMPLE 6.20

A promissory note is signed by Capital Drywall for \$2,500 (called the face value of the note) at an interest rate of 16%. The date of the note is October 15, 1991, and the term is 60 days. Find (a) the maturity date, (b) the legal due date, and (c) the maturity value of the note.

Solution

(a) Sixty days after October 15, 1991, is December 14, 1991 (see Table 6.1). The maturity date is therefore December 14, 1991.

(b) The legal due date is three days after the maturity date, or December 17, 1991. This accounts for the three days of grace.

(c) The maturity value includes principal (\$2,500) plus interest.

Using the interest formula $I = Prt$ where:

$$P = \$2{,}500$$

$$r = 0.16$$

$$t = \frac{63}{365}$$

Although the note is for 60 days, the period of grace is included in the interest calculation because one must pay for the use of the money for the full period it is used.

Substituting from above:

$$I = \$2{,}500(0.16)\left(\frac{63}{365}\right)$$

$$\doteq \$69.04$$

The maturity value is \$2,500 + \$69.04, or \$2,569.04.

C. Discounting

The term discounting was briefly defined earlier as the process that brings a maturity value back in time. This process is often used to allow for an early payment on a loan or provide for the resale of a note. Notes are resold when the holder of a note — the one who lent the money originally — needs cash before the note is due. An example of discounting a promissory note is when one wishes to repay a note earlier than the legal due date. However, because the note is a binding contract one must first find the maturity value, then discount the maturity value to find out the amount needed to repay the loan early.

For example, if a note for $1,500 is due in three months but is paid off one month early, what is the payment to satisfy the note? We must discount the maturity value of the note (the amount due in three months) to find the final payment. **The interest rate used to find the early payment is referred to as the discount rate.** When we discount there is often a need to calculate the dollar value of the discount; this is called the simple discount and is found by subtracting the discounted value of the note from the maturity value of the note.

It is important to understand that the rate of interest used in discounting a note **does not have to be the same as the interest rate on the note**. One reason that the discount rate and the interest rate on a note are different is that discounting takes place at a different point in time. Thus, the rate of interest that prevails in the market at the time of the discount will often be used for discounting. Another reason the discount rate may be different from the interest rate on the note is risk. For example, if the ability of the maker of a note is at all questionable, then the one who was purchasing the note would apply a very high discount rate to compensate for the risk.

The term "simple" is used to recognize that we are using simple interest procedures to perform the discount.

Promissory notes can be sold, for cash, if the maker of the note requires the money early. For example, suppose you loaned a friend $10,000 and shortly afterward discovered that you needed the money. The note cannot be called so you are forced to sell the note to someone. The price you get will depend on the discount rate used. Sometimes this can be very expensive if the purchaser of the note uses a very large discount rate. Next time you're reading the newspaper, look in the business classified section to see if you can find someone wanting to sell a promissory note. Other credit instruments besides notes are also negotiable.

When discounting, there will always be a **discount period**. In our example above, the note is being discounted one month early. This one month is called the discount period.

The discount rate refers to the rate used to discount notes and other credit instruments, or to an interest rate agreed upon to be used in determining the discount. When discounting a note, the monies received by the holder of the note (payee) at the date of the discount are referred to as the **proceeds.** The difference between the maturity value and the proceeds is the simple discount.

To calculate the simple discount and proceeds we must always determine the maturity value of the note. However, this step may be avoided in some circumstances since there are two types of promissory notes — **non-interest bearing** and **interest bearing.** Depending upon the type of note, the maturity value and thus our calculations to find the proceeds and simple discount will be different.

(i) Non-Interest Bearing Notes

A non-interest bearing note refers to a note whose maturity value is simply the face value on the note. For example, suppose we are advised that a debt is due in two years and will be retired by a note that specifies a payment of $2,500 (assume no grace period). In this example, the maturity value is $2,500 because we are advised that the note calls for the $2,500 payment in two years. Suppose we wish to settle the note today, what would be the proceeds and the simple discount? To answer this question we must know what the appropriate discount rate is; let's assume 15%. Now we must discount the maturity value of $2,500. Therefore, since we are bringing back a future value (we are bringing back the value two years before the due date) we use our formula to discount the future maturity value of $2,500. This yields:

$$P = \frac{S}{(1 + rt)}$$

$$P = \frac{\$2{,}500}{[1 + (0.15)2]}$$

$$\doteq \$1{,}923.08$$

Thus, the proceeds to the lender will be $1,923.08. The simple discount is found by subtracting the proceeds from the maturity value. Therefore:

$$\text{Simple Discount} = \$2{,}500 - \$1{,}923.08$$
$$= \$576.92$$

EXAMPLE 6.21

A note with a maturity value of $5,000 is due in $1\frac{1}{2}$ years. If the note is discounted today and the discount rate is 18%, what are (a) the proceeds and (b) the simple discount?

Solution (a) Using the formula $P = \dfrac{S}{(1 + rt)}$ and substituting:

$$S = \$5{,}000$$
$$r = 0.18$$
$$t = 1.5 \text{ years}$$
$$P = \text{Proceeds}$$
$$= \frac{\$5{,}000}{[1 + (0.18)1.5]}$$
$$\doteq \$3{,}937.01$$

(b) Simple discount $= \$5{,}000 - \$3{,}937.01$
$= \$1{,}062.99$

(ii) Interest Bearing Notes

An interest bearing note implies that the face value of the note must be repaid plus accumulated interest — at the specified rate.

To find the proceeds and simple discount for an interest bearing note one must first calculate the maturity value of the note. The maturity value is then discounted to obtain proceeds. The simple discount is found as above, by subtracting the proceeds from the maturity value. Consider the following example.

EXAMPLE 6.22

A person borrowed \$10,000 on February 15, 1991, and signed a promissory note, agreeing to repay the \$10,000 in six months plus 18% interest. Four months later, the loan is settled by discounting the note at an interest rate of 20% (discount rate). If the note has specified no grace, what are the proceeds?

Solution

STEP 1 Find the maturity value of the debt on August 15. Substituting:

$$P = \$10{,}000$$
$$r = 0.18$$
$$t = \frac{181}{365} \qquad \text{From Table 6.1 } (227 - 46 = 181)$$

Computing the maturity value using the amount formula:

$$S = P(1 + rt)$$
$$S = \$10{,}000\left[1 + (0.18)\frac{181}{365}\right]$$
$$= \$10{,}892.60$$

STEP 2 The second step is to find the proceeds, at month four (June 15), when the debt is settled.

Substituting:

$$S = \$10{,}892.60$$
$$r = 0.2$$
$$t = \frac{61}{365} \qquad \text{From Table 6.1 } (227 - 166 = 61)$$

The interest rate r is 0.2 since we are told the loan is discounted at 20%. The reason $t = \frac{61}{365}$ is that the discount period is two months (June 15 to August 15), that is, it is being paid off two months before the due date.

The proceeds, P, are:

$$P = \frac{S}{(1 + rt)}$$
$$P = \frac{\$10{,}892.60}{\left[1 + (0.2)\frac{61}{365}\right]}$$
$$\doteq \$10{,}540.30$$

Therefore, the proceeds are $10,540.30 when this loan is discounted two months early at an interest rate of 20%.

EXAMPLE 6.23

Donna Lee needs some money and all she has that is of any value is a promissory note payable to her in three years and four months. The face value of the note is $7,500 and requires interest to be paid at the rate of 13% annually. Donna placed an ad in the classified section of the Vancouver *Sun* and found a purchaser for the note. However, the purchaser demands that the note be discounted at 20%. How much would Donna receive as proceeds if she accepts the offer?

Solution

STEP 1 First we must calculate the maturity value of the note using the formula $S = P(1 + rt)$ where:

$$P = \$7{,}500$$
$$r = 0.13$$
$$t = \frac{40}{12} \qquad \text{The time is calculated based on three years and four months.}$$

$$S = \$7{,}500\left[1 + (0.13)\,\frac{40}{12}\right]$$
$$= \$10{,}750$$

STEP 2 Next we discount the maturity value at the discount rate of 20%. Using the formula:

$$P = \frac{S}{(1 + rt)}$$

Where:

$S = \$10{,}750$

$r = 0.20$ The discount rate

$t = 3\frac{4}{12}$, or $\frac{40}{12}$ years:

$$P = \frac{\$10{,}750}{\left[1 + (0.2)\frac{40}{12}\right]}$$

$$= \$6{,}450$$

Thus, the proceeds are $6,450. She must obviously need the money if she agrees to sell the note at the discounted price.

(iii) Use of the Present Value Formula

Before ending this section there is an important point that should be remembered. When a note is discounted and the proceeds are calculated, we use the present value formula, namely:

$$P = \frac{S}{(1 + rt)}$$ **Formula 6.6**

Remember, the procedure of discounting requires us to move a future value (maturity value) back in time to the date of discount.

EXERCISE 6.6

1. A company negotiates a demand loan for $50,000 on September 1, 1991. In the month of September, the rate of interest changed. Find the interest payable for the month of September (to end of month), given the following information.

September 1	16.25%
September 7	16.5%
September 14	17%
September 21	16.75%
September 28	17%

2. The District of Metchosin borrowed $100,000 by way of a demand loan on May 1. The rate of interest on May 1 was 8.75%. On May 11, the rate increased to 9%. If the loan was repaid on May 23, how much interest was due on the loan?

3. A four month promissory note for $630 was signed on April 12, 1991. If the note is discounted on July 2, 1991, find:
   a. the legal due date
   b. the maturity value
   c. the discount period

4. If the interest rate used for discounting the promissory note in problem 3 was 16%, find the simple discount and proceeds of the transaction.

5. If the interest rate had been 10% on the note in problem 4, would this have had any impact on the maturity value, proceeds, and simple discount? If there is a difference, recalculate the new values.

6. A debt of $2,400 is due in $1\frac{1}{2}$ years. If one wishes to pay the debt today, and the interest rate today is $10\frac{3}{4}$%, what is the expected simple discount?

7. A debt of $5,000 is due in six months. If the debt was satisfied today (paid off) and the rate of interest used to discount the debt is 15%, find the simple discount.

REVIEW EXERCISES

1. Find the exact time between March 16 and October 9.

2. What is the maturity date of a 90 day debt incurred on September 4?

3. What is the legal due date of a 120 day promissory note issued on April 16?

4. Calculate the simple interest due on a ten month loan of $60,000 if the interest rate is 16.5%.

5. Calculate the interest payable on a 60 day promissory note for $450 if the interest rate is 12% simple interest. The note was signed on July 2.

6. What principal will earn $940 in interest in seven months, if the interest rate is 14%?

7. How long will it take $1,200 to earn interest of $216, if the interest rate is 12%?

8. What rate of interest would produce $250 interest on a principal of $3,000 in 150 days?

9. What is the maturity value on the legal due date for a six month promissory note with a face value of $3,000, signed on August 22, at an interest rate of 13%?

10. Determine the cost of financing (the interest cost) on a demand note signed June 6, 1991, for $1,500 if the interest rate is 12.5%. The first part payment is $750 on September 14, 1991, after which the rate goes up to 13% until the note is paid in full on November 3, 1991.

11. Using the Declining Balance method, calculate the final payment needed on July 7 to pay off a debt of $5,500 incurred on March 20 with an interest rate of 14.5%. The following partial payments are made: $1,500 on May 4 and $2,000 on June 6.

12. What was the total cost of the loan described in problem 11?

13. A piece of land is expected to have a value of $25,000 in four years. If money is worth 12% simple interest, what is a fair price to pay for the land today? Ignore local land taxes and any other costs associated with acquisition of the land.

14. Suppose you purchase the property in problem 13 at the "fair price" you calculated. Two years after you purchase the property, you receive an offer of $20,000 for the property. Would you accept the offer? Assume that you have paid $500 at the end of each year for land taxes for each year you have held the property.

15. John lends a friend $500 at 15% and receives $50 in interest. How long does John's friend have use of the money?

16. Calculate the present value (the amount borrowed) of a debt that will amount to $518.33 in four months' time, if simple interest is charged at 11%.

17. If money is worth 15%, what is the value on June 14 of a non-interest bearing promissory note with a face value of $9,000 that matures on December 12?

18. What would be the equivalent value of a $4,000 debt after six months if money is worth 17%?

19. If money is worth 12%, calculate the single equivalent payment in nine months for two debts: $300 due two months ago and $500 due in one year. Use nine months from now as the focal date.

20. Find the size of two equal payments, one due now and one in eight months, that are to replace three original debts of $200 each, due six, four, and two months ago. Use a rate of interest of 12% and let the focal date be today.

21. Two debts, $500, due one month ago, and $700, due in three months, are to be replaced by three new payments, one of $200 due now, one of $400 due in four months, and the remainder due in eight months' time. Find the size of the final payment if money is worth 14%. Use now as the focal date.

22. Find (a) the proceeds and (b) the simple discount of a three month non-interest bearing promissory note signed on July 10 with a face value of $4,000, if discounting occurs at 13% (simple interest) on August 24.

23. Find the proceeds from discounting a promissory note of $2,000 that matures on March 5 if it is discounted on January 20 at 14%. Assume no grace period.

24. Calculate the simple discount on a 12%, three month, \$950 promissory note that was signed on September 6 and discounted at 13% simple interest on October 10.

25. If a 120 day, \$1,500 promissory note earning 14% simple interest is discounted at 17%, 60 days before its legal due date, what are the proceeds?

26. Suppose that you decide to discount a \$14,000 promissory note you are holding by selling it to a buyer on March 15, four months before it is due. If the discount rate is 17.5%, what will be the proceeds of the sale?

27. Metchosin Tractor company purchased a patent on a piece of equipment for \$1.5 million and agreed to pay the full amount plus interest at 6% in fifteen years. After eight years the company has been doing so well it wishes to repay the full patent cost. If money is worth 6% simple interest, how much should Metchosin Tractor offer the company it purchased the patent from to settle the outstanding debt? (Treat the agreement as a contract.)

28. You are thinking about buying a new car. The salesperson tells you that you can pay \$3,000 today and \$5,000 in two years, and drive away with the car today. If you know that the company charges 26% interest on outstanding balances, what should the cash price, today, be for the car?

29. The car salesperson in problem 28 says that there is a special on today. If you pay cash you can buy the car for \$6,500. Would you accept the offer? Give a reason for your answer.

30. A couple wants to set aside sufficient money for their daughter to attend college. The cost of college is expected to be \$6,000 a year. How much money would need to be placed, today, in an account that pays 12% simple interest, if the <u>interest</u> from the account is to be sufficient to pay the annual cost of attending college, regardless of how long the daughter goes to college?

SUMMARY OF FORMULAS

Formula 6.1	$I = Prt$	Finding simple interest, when principal, rate, and time are known.
Formula 6.2	$S = P(1 + rt)$	Finding the amount or future value using simple interest.
Formula 6.3	$t = \dfrac{I}{Pr}$	Finding the time period when interest, principal, and rate are known.
Formula 6.4	$r = \dfrac{I}{Pt}$	Finding the interest rate when principal, time, and interest are known.

Formula 6.5	$P = \dfrac{I}{rt}$	Finding the principal when interest, rate, and time are known.
Formula 6.6	$P = \dfrac{S}{(1 + rt)}$	Finding the principal when the amount, rate, and time are known.
"	$P = \dfrac{S}{(1 + rt)}$	This expression finds the present value of a future amount — it is the same as the expression to find the principal.
"	$P = \dfrac{S}{(1 + rt)}$	This expression is used to find the proceeds of a discounted note, where P = proceeds and S = maturity value.
Simple Discount	$= (S - P)$	S refers to the maturity value, P refers to the proceeds.

GLOSSARY OF TERMS

Amount the future value of money, which is found by adding principal plus interest.

Approximate Time when time is computed using 30 days per month and 360 days per year.

Declining Balance Method the process of subtracting accumulated interest from any partial payments on a loan. Any of the payment remaining is then subtracted from the outstanding principal.

Demand Loan a loan that is payable on demand and usually requires the signing of a demand note.

Discounting the process of bringing the value of money back in time.

Discount Rate the rate of interest used to discount future values.

Equivalent Value the value of money at different points in time.

Exact Time when time is computed using the exact number of days money has been outstanding. Each year has 365 days and each month the exact number of days.

Focal Point the point in time to which all values of money are brought. It refers to a reference point for calculating equivalent values.

Interest the "rent" paid for the use of money.

Interest Bearing Note the face value of the note accumulates interest until the maturity date.

Leap Years years when February has one additional day.

Legal Due Date the date a note or loan comes due. The legal due date for a promissory note is three days beyond the maturity date.

Maker the person who makes the promise to pay when using a promissory note.

Maturity Date the date a loan or investment matures.

Maturity Value the same as amount. It refers to the principal plus interest at some point in the future.

Non-Interest Bearing Note a note where the maturity value and the face value are the same and any interest to be paid has already been included in the face value of the note.

Partial payments payments made toward repaying a loan.

Present Value today's value of a future amount.

Principal the original value borrowed or invested.

Proceeds what one receives after discounting a note.

Promissory Note a written promise to pay a sum of money plus interest at a specific time (date) in the future.

Simple Discount the dollar value of the discount, which is found by subtracting the proceeds from discounting a note from the maturity value of the note.

Time Value of Money the fact that money has a different value at different points in time.

CHAPTER 7

Compound Interest

Chapter 7 introduces you to the concepts and calculations used with compound interest. Fortunately, many of the procedures for compound interest are similar to the topics discussed in Chapter 6. Topics such as finding the time, present value, equivalent values, and discounting interest and non-interest bearing notes will be examined using compound interest procedures. In addition, a more detailed discussion will be given to interest rates and, in particular, finding the "real" or **effective** rate of interest and its importance when comparing rates quoted or advertised by financial institutions.

Compound interest differs from simple interest in the procedure used to compute the interest. With simple interest we applied the annual interest rate and time to the principal to calculate the interest. The most important feature of simple interest was that the principal was always the original balance with which we started. That is, the principal did not change, regardless of the time involved.

Compound interest, on the other hand, requires the principal to change. The changing principal reflects the interest accumulated from previous periods. Two ways to think about compound interest are:

- a person who borrows is paying rent on the unpaid interest as well as a rent for the use of the initial (principal) amount borrowed;
- a depositor or a lender earns interest on unpaid interest as well as the principal.

Consequently, when compound interest is used it will yield more interest dollars than the same rate applied as simple interest.

The use of compound interest in business and government is most common where money is tied up for long periods of time. The best example is a residential mortgage. Other examples include some types of consumer loans, such as outstanding credit card balances.

Before proceeding with Chapter 7 you may wish to review:

- basic algebraic concepts (Chapters 3 and 4),
- the laws and rules of exponents (Chapter 3), and
- your calculator's special functions.

If you are using a different calculator than the one used in this text, you may find that some of your numbers are slightly different from those in the text because different chips are used in different calculators. These different chips produce slightly different results after five or six decimal places — this should not alarm you since these differences are only minor.

It's important that you thoroughly understand **the laws of exponents** before proceeding with this chapter. (See Chapter 3.)

OBJECTIVES

When you have completed this chapter you will be able to do the following:

1. explain the term compound interest;
2. find the compound amount;
3. find the present value using compound interest;
4. explain the concepts of nominal, effective, and equivalent rates of interest and be able to compute their values;
5. compute the time and interest rate for compound interest;
6. calculate equivalent payments using compound interest and use compound interest procedures on simple business finance problems.

7.1 Compound Interest

As explained in Chapter 6, interest refers to the cost of using money. **Compounding interest means that the interest cost will include interest calculated on interest, since the interest rate is applied to both the principal and interest for all previous periods.** For example, if a loan of \$1,000 is outstanding for two years and the interest rate is 12%, compounded yearly:

- at the end of the first year, the interest would be \$1,000 × 0.12, or \$120; and,
- in the second year the interest rate of 12% will be applied not just to the \$1,000, but also to the \$120 interest of the first year. Thus, in the second year the interest due would be 0.12 × \$1,120, or \$134.40.

If simple interest of 12% was used, the second year's interest would only be $120, since the simple interest rate always applies to the original principal and not to any accumulated interest. As you can see, the effects of compounding cause the interest cost to be $14.40 higher with compounding in the second year over a simple interest rate.

When compound interest is used we must **always** know how often the interest rate is calculated each year. That is, the interest rate, as with simple interest, is quoted annually, e.g., 10% per annum. However, with simple interest the calculation of interest was only once a year or fraction of a year, and only on the original principal. Compound interest, on the other hand, may involve calculations more than once a year, each using a new principal (interest plus principal).

The first term we must understand when dealing with compound interest is conversion period. The term **conversion period** refers to how often the interest is calculated over the term of the loan or deposit. The conversion period must be determined for each year or fraction of a year relevant to the problem at hand.

For example, if the interest rate is compounded semiannually (this means calculated twice a year), then the number of conversion periods per year would be two. If the loan or deposit was for two years then the total number of conversion periods would be four.

Another example would be where interest is compounded monthly. Here, the number of conversion periods would be twelve per year. The total number of conversion periods would depend upon how long the term was. **To figure out interest using compound interest, the total number of conversion periods must be determined before any computation of interest can occur.**

The method used to find the total number of conversion periods is simply to multiply the number of conversion periods per year by the number of years (or fractions of a year).

Examine Figure 7.1, which outlines some conversion periods:

Figure 7.1

Interest Period	Compound Period	Time	Total Number of Conversion Periods
18%	yearly	5 years	5 (5 × 1)
12%	semiannually	5 years	10 (5 × 2)
10%	quarterly	5 years	20 (5 × 4)
16%	monthly	5 years	60 (5 × 12)

From Table 7.1 you can see that as the number of compound periods per year changes the total number of conversion periods changes. Now let's turn to the formula used in compound interest to see how everything fits together.

7.2 Finding the Amount

A. Finding the Amount by Using the Compound Interest Formula

In Chapter 6, the **amount** referred to the principal plus interest and was defined as S. The same is true for compound interest calculations. Before we look at the formula, let's consider an example that will help us understand the compound method.

Suppose you visit your local credit union with a $10,000 inheritance and wish to invest the money in a term deposit for five years. To your surprise the credit union offers two options: the first option offers you 8% simple interest; the second option offers you 7.5% compounded quarterly. Which one would yield the most interest and how much interest could you expect to receive?

The best way to answer the question is to calculate the interest you will receive under each option. First let's consider the option offering simple interest.

Using $S = P(1 + rt)$, from Chapter 6 where:

$$P = 10{,}000$$
$$r = 0.08$$
$$t = 5$$

Thus, $S = \$10{,}000[1 + 0.08(5)]$

$$= \$14{,}000$$

The simple interest option would provide you with $4,000 in interest at the end of five years.

Now let's examine the second option offered by the credit union. To use compound interest we must first define some new terms:

n = the total number of conversion periods, that is, how often the interest is calculated over the entire time period;
i = the interest rate per conversion period;
P = the principal;
S = the amount.

Sometimes you will see the term compound period used in place of conversion period — both mean the same.

In our example, the value of n is found by multiplying the number of conversion periods per year by the number of years, or 4×5, which gives us a total of twenty conversion periods over the five year period.

The next step is to determine the interest rate per conversion period, i. **In all compound interest problems the interest per conversion period is found by dividing the annual rate by the number of conversion periods (compound periods) per year.** In our example, the annual rate is 7.5% compounded quarterly. The interest rate per conversion period is $\frac{(7.5\%)}{4}$, or 1.875%, per quarter.

We will use a decimal equivalent in the formulas to come, i.e., 0.01875.

In compound interest we must calculate the interest every conversion period and add it to the principal. The interest and principal become the basis on which to compute the interest for the next period. Consider the following:

Interest and principal in the first quarter is based on the calculation:

$$\$10{,}000\left[1 + \left(\frac{0.075}{4}\right)(1)\right] = \$10{,}187.50$$

Using the simple interest formula,

$$S = P(1 + rt) \text{where } r = 0.01875 \text{ and } t = 1 \text{ for one quarter.}$$

The $10,187.50 is the principal and interest after the first quarter.

In the second quarter the interest and principal calculations go as follows:

$$\$10{,}187.50\left[1 + \left(\frac{0.075}{4}\right)(1)\right] \doteq \$10{,}378.52$$

As you can see, the principal used each period to compute the amount (interest + principal) changes by the interest accumulated over the previous interest period. Consequently, the number of calculations will be repeated twenty times over to find the total of interest and principal using compound interest. To say the least, this involves a lot of calculations!

Fortunately, the compound interest formula makes the computation very easy and quick. The compound formula to find the **compound amount** is:

$$S = P(1 + i)^n$$ **Formula 7.1**

Where:

S = amount
P = principal
i = interest rate per conversion period
n = total number of conversion periods

In our problem we want to find S, where we know the following:

$P = \$10{,}000$

$i = \dfrac{0.075}{4}$, or 0.01875

$n = 4 \times 5$, or 20, conversion periods over the five years

Therefore, the amount, S, is:

$$S = \$10{,}000(1 + 0.01875)^{20}$$
$$\doteq \$14{,}499.48$$

As we can see, although the annual rate of 7.5% is less than the 8% simple interest, the effects of compounding certainly produce more interest. In particular, the compounding of interest in this problem produces $499.48 more interest and generates a total of $4,499.48 in interest over the five year period.

It should be clear that the compound interest formula saves a great deal of work, since it performs all the separate additions in one step. The mathematics involved in this formula are based on a topic called geometric progressions. If you are interested in this topic, take a look in Chapter 4, which explains the concepts of arithmetic and geometric series.

EXAMPLE 7.1

Fenstar Office Services has just invested $50,000 in computing equipment and software. Based on past performance, the company expects to have to replace the equipment in five years. If estimates of costs are correct, the company expects to pay $75,000 for the new equipment in five years. If the company has $50,000 cash, today, and can invest it at 10%, compounded semiannually, how much would be accumulated toward the equipment replacement in five years?

Solution To solve this problem, there are three steps:

STEP 1 Determine what is being sought. In this problem what is wanted is how much accumulates in five years, or S.

STEP 2 Identify the value of each term:

$S = \text{unknown}$

$P = \$50{,}000$

$n = 2 \times 5, \text{ or } 10$ — 2 times a year for five years.

$i = \dfrac{0.10}{2}, \text{ or } 0.05$ — Annual rate divided by number of compound periods.

STEP 3 Substitute the values into the compound interest formula (Formula 7.1) as follows:

$$S = P(1 + i)^n$$
$$S = \$50{,}000(1 + 0.05)^{10}$$
$$\doteq \$81{,}444.73$$

Therefore, Fenstar will accumulate more than it requires at the end of five years, namely, $81,444.73 – $75,000, or $6,444.73 more than required.

EXAMPLE 7.2

John Williams wants to invest $5,000 in a term deposit at a bank. If he is prepared to tie the money up for two years, the bank has two options available: either 12.5% compounded semiannually, or 12% compounded monthly. John doesn't know what to do, so he comes to you for advice. What would you recommend?

Solution Let's examine each option by determining the interest plus principal each will yield:

OPTION 1 At 12.5% compounded semiannually the amount would be found as follows:

$P = \$5{,}000$

$n = 2 \times 2 = 4$ Compounded semiannually for two years.

$$i = \frac{0.125}{2} = 0.0625$$

Using Formula 7.1, $S = P(1 + i)^n$

$$S = \$5{,}000(1 + 0.0625)^4$$
$$\doteq \$6{,}372.15$$

OPTION 2 Now considering 12% compounded monthly, the amount is:

$P = \$5{,}000$

$$i = \frac{0.12}{12} = 0.01$$

$n = 12 \times 2 = 24$ Compounded monthly.

Therefore:

$$S = \$5{,}000(1 + 0.01)^{24}$$

$$\doteq \$6{,}348.67$$

Based on the above calculations you would recommend that he select Option 1.

B. Finding the Compound Amount Using a Financial Calculator

A fast way to solve a question requiring a financial formula is with the pre-programmed financial calculator. Like home computers, there is a myriad of business calculators available. If you happen to own one that is different from the one used in this book, don't be concerned. In general, you will find that the steps in using the financial functions of your calculator will be similar to the steps presented for the Sharp calculator, the one used in this book.

The parts of the compound interest formula that will be computed using the financial calculator are: *S*, *P*, *n*, and *i*. To use the calculator used in this book, the Sharp Business/Financial EL-733 Calculator, there are six keys with which one must gain familiarity. These are the FV, PV, n, i, 2ndF, and COMP keys. Before using the calculator one must make sure the calculator is in **FINANCIAL MODE**. The way to determine if the Sharp EL-733 is in FINANCIAL MODE is to look at the display to see if FIN appears. If there are no "boxes" with FIN or STAT then the calculator is in regular mode (i.e., a standard calculator). To get to financial mode work through the following steps:

KEY

[2ndF] Depress

mode

[——→] Depress After depressing 2ndF, depress the key with the ——→ since this key changes the MODE of the calculator. The sequence to move from one MODE to the next is always 2ndF, MODE. Keep depressing the key sequence 2ndF, MODE until FIN appears in small print on the display. Once the FIN appears it means that the financial keys are activated.

CAUTION

If you should see BGN and FIN, together, you must look for the key with BGN and depress it. BGN is a special key that tells the calculator if payments or investments are made at the BEGINNING (BGN) of the period, rather than at the end of the period. The BGN function is not required at this point.

Now with FIN showing you are ready to start using the financial functions of your calculator. For problems involving compound interest, the most important keys are:

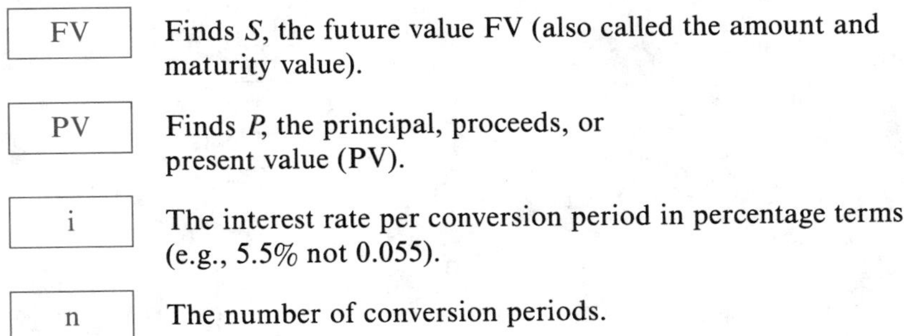

[FV] Finds *S*, the future value FV (also called the amount and maturity value).

[PV] Finds *P*, the principal, proceeds, or present value (PV).

[i] The interest rate per conversion period in percentage terms (e.g., 5.5% not 0.055).

[n] The number of conversion periods.

To see how to use the functions of the financial calculator Examples 7.1 and 7.2 are redone below using the Sharp EL-733 Financial Calculator.

Before trying a problem, check the decimal places shown on the display. If you find that your calculator's display shows no decimal places or only one decimal place you will want to increase the number of decimal places that are displayed. All calculations in this book use the maximum number of decimal places (9) the EL-733 will display. To set the decimal place depress the [2ndF] key, then depress the [BGN] key (*note:* the function being used is the TAB function, printed above the [BGN] key), depress 9 and then the [=] key.

Now your calculator is set to display nine decimal places. If you wish to reduce the number of decimal places repeat the steps and input the new number of decimal places you wish to have.

EXAMPLE 7.3 Using a Preprogrammed Financial Calculator (from 7.1)

Solution

1. Make sure your calculator is in financial mode with only FIN showing.
2. Determine the value of each term:

$S =$ unknown
$P = \$50{,}000$
$n = 2 \times 5 = 10$
$i = \frac{10\%}{2} = 5\%$ Annual rate **IN PERCENTAGE TERMS** divided by number of compound periods per year.

INPUT	DEPRESS	DISPLAY
50,000	[PV]	50,000
5	[i]	5
10	[n]	10
	[COMP]	10
	[FV]	–81,444.73

The future amount of $50,000 accumulated for ten semiannual periods at 5% per semiannual period is $81,444.73.

Note: The Sharp calculator gives a negative sign in front of future (FV) and present value (PV). This sign is to be ignored and taken as a positive value. (In the text examples, the negative sign from the calculator will not be shown.) Use of the negative sign for the Sharp is important in later calculations. If you are using a Texas Instruments Business Analyst calculator, the steps are identical with the exception of the COMP key. On the Texas Instruments calculator, the equivalent to the COMP key is the CPT (compute) key. Also, the answer on the Texas Instruments Business Analyst calculator (with the exception of the BA-II Plus and the Financial Investment Analyst) will be positive, so there is no sign to ignore.

Before proceeding with the next example, it is important to get into the habit of clearing the numbers from the calculator, before starting another problem. To clear the current numbers depress:

[2ndF] and [C · CE] ; this clears the current numbers from memory.

EXAMPLE 7.4 Using a Preprogrammed Financial Calculator (from 7.2)

Solution

1. Make sure your calculator is in financial mode with only FIN showing.

2. Make sure you have cleared the memory by using the key sequence:

   [2ndF] and [C · CE]

3. Identify the value of each term:

OPTION 1

At 12.5% compounded semiannually the amount would be found as follows:

$P = \$5{,}000$

$n = 2 \times 2 = 4$ Compounded semiannually for two years.

$$i = \frac{12.5\%}{2} = 6.25\%$$

Input the values for Option 1 into the calculator:

INPUT	DEPRESS	DISPLAY SHOWS
5,000	PV	5,000
6.25	i	6.25
4	n	4
	COMP	4
	FV	6,372.15 Negative sign has been dropped.

Using Formula 7.1 $S = P(1 + i)^n$

$$S = \$5{,}000(1 + 0.0625)^4$$
$$\doteq \$6{,}372.15$$

OPTION 2 Now considering 12% compounded monthly, the amount is:

$$P = \$5{,}000$$
$$i = \frac{12\%}{12} = 1\%$$
$$n = 12 \times 2 = 24 \qquad \text{Compounded monthly.}$$

Input the values for Option 2 into the calculator:

INPUT	DEPRESS	DISPLAY SHOWS
5,000	PV	5,000
1	i	1
24	n	24
	COMP	24
	FV	6,348.67

Using Formula 7.1 yields:

$$S = \$5{,}000(1 + 0.01)^{24}$$
$$\doteq \$6{,}348.67$$

Based on the above calculations you would recommend that John Williams select Option 1.

Before leaving this problem why don't you call a bank or credit union and tell them you want to invest $25,000 for five years. Ask them what the rates of interest will be if you wish the interest paid monthly or yearly. If the rates are different calculate the difference and see if they produce the same amount of interest.

For many examples that follow there will be a second solution using the functions of the Sharp EL-733 calculator.

EXERCISE 7.1

For problems 1 to 10 find the amount (future value).

	Length of Conversion Period	**Principal**	**Time Period (Years)**	**Interest Rate (%)**
1.	Annually	$ 450	2	15.0
2.	Quarterly	600	12	18.0
3.	Monthly	1,200	13	14.0
4.	Daily	2,500	5	17.7
5.	Semiannual	4,600	11	13.0
6.	Monthly	14,679	15	19.0
7.	Quarterly	12,670	7	14.8
8.	Yearly	15,000	6	10.0
9.	Quarterly	14,450	4	17.5
10.	Daily	56,467	8	12.4

11. Find the compound amount and the interest earned for each of the following:
  a. $12,000 for two and a half years at 15% compounded semiannually.
  b. $10,000 for four months at 11% compounded monthly.
  c. $1,000 for nine months at 12% compounded quarterly.

12. Compute the difference in accumulated interest for one year for two savings accounts. Each account has $1,000: one account pays 8% compounded quarterly and the other account pays 8% simple interest.

13. Flagstone, a company involved in surveying, receives an advance of $15,000 on a contract. If Flagstone invests the money in a savings account that pays interest at a rate of 5.75%, compounded semiannually, how much interest will accumulate in eighteen months?
14. What would $12,000 accumulate to in five years if the interest rate is 15% compounded daily?
15. Ann has just invested $10,000 in a five year GIC (guaranteed investment certificate). If she has been promised 12% compounded semiannually for the first three years and 11% compounded semiannually for the last two years, how much will she have at the end of five years?
16. John is wanting to retire in ten years. To make his retirement possible John plans to start depositing $10,000 in an RRSP every two years for ten years. If he can earn 12%, compounded monthly, how much will he have accumulated at the end of the ten years? Assume his first deposit is made in two years.
17. A loan of $5,000 is repaid with a payment of $1,000 at month six, $1,000 in one year, and a final payment at the end of two years. If the interest rate on the loan is 14.5%, compounded semiannually, what is the size of the final payment to repay the debt?
18. If the loan in problem 17 had been a demand loan with a variable interest rate of 12% compounded monthly for the first six months, 17% compounded monthly for the next six months, and 18% compounded monthly for the entire second year, what would the final payment be to discharge the loan?

7.3 Finding the Present Value and Compound Discount

A. Present Value

As discussed in Chapter 6, **present value refers to today's value of a future amount**. For example, suppose a friend offers you a deal that pays you $5,000 in five years, based on a certain payment being made today. If you know that the interest rate being offered at the bank is 10% compounded semiannually, can you determine the maximum price you should pay for the investment?

To answer this question we need to develop a formula for **present value** using the compound procedures. In Chapter 6 we used the term P for present value. The same applies to compound interest. The formula is simply a rearrangement of Formula 7.1 to find P. We begin with:

$$S = P(1 + i)^n \qquad \text{Formula 7.1}$$

Rearranging this formula to solve for P yields:

$$P = \frac{S}{(1 + i)^n}$$

Using negative exponents to represent division, the expression can be rewritten as:

$$P = S(1 + i)^{-n} \qquad \textbf{Formula 7.2}$$

Formula 7.2 is the method we use to compute present value using compound interest. (*Note:* If you are unclear about negative exponents please refer to Chapter 3, where there is a discussion of this topic.) Now let's apply this formula to our problem.

The first step requires us to identify all the values for the terms in our formula:

$S = \$5{,}000$ This is the future amount.

$n = 2 \times 5 = 10$ Compounded semiannually for five years.

$i = \frac{0.1}{2} = 0.05$

Using the formula $P = S(1 + i)^{-n}$, and making the appropriate substitutions we have:

$$P = \$5{,}000(1 + 0.05)^{-10}$$
$$\doteq \$3{,}069.57$$

Thus, if your friend wants you to pay any more than \$3,069.57, you would be better off to put your money in the bank, since you would earn more interest.

EXAMPLE 7.5

What is the present value of \$6,000 due in five years and four months if the value of money is 8% compounded monthly?

Solution To solve this problem there are two steps:

STEP 1 Identify the known terms:

$S = \$6{,}000$

$n = 64$ Twelve × five years and four months.

$i = \frac{0.08}{12}$, or 0.6666667%

STEP 2 Using the present value formula:

$P = S(1 + i)^{-n}$, and substituting from above:

$$P = \$6{,}000\left[1 + \frac{0.08}{12}\right]^{-64}$$

$$\doteq \$3{,}921.64$$

The present value of $6,000, due in five years and four months, at 8% compounded monthly is $3,921.64.

Calculator Solution Remember, the minus sign has not been shown in the final answer as displayed on the Sharp EL-733 calculator.

						Solution
Input	6,000	0.6666667	64			
Depress	FV	i	n	COMP	PV	3,921.64

B. Compound Discount

In Chapter 6 we introduced the concepts of discounting and simple discount. We used the term discounting to describe the process that moves a maturity value back in time to permit an early payment or to provide for the sale of a note. The dollar value of the discount, called the simple discount, was found by subtracting the discounted value from the maturity value. The monies received by the holder of the note at the date of discount were called the proceeds.

In financial transactions involving discounting and compound interest, **compound discount refers to the difference between the compound amount and the present value (or the discounted value).** For example, if a future amount is $5,000 and the present value of this future amount is $3,500 then the compound discount would be $1,500 ($5,000 – $3,500).

In terms of the symbols used in Chapter 6, the method is defined by:

$$\text{Compound Discount} = S - P$$

EXAMPLE 7.6

Find the present value and the compound discount of $2,000 due in four years, if the discount rate (interest rate used to discount) is 15% compounded quarterly.

Solution First we find the present value of the $2,000 due in four years using our present value formula:

$$P = S(1 + i)^{-n}$$

Where:

$$S = \$2{,}000$$

$$i = \frac{0.15}{4} = 0.0375 = 3.75\%$$

$$n = 4 \times 4 = 16$$

$$P = \$2{,}000(1 + 0.0375)^{-16}$$

$$\doteq \$1{,}109.74$$

Calculator Solution

						Solution
Input	2,000	3.75	16			
Depress	FV	i	n	COMP	PV	1,109.74

Now calculating the compound discount we have:

$$S - P = \$2{,}000 - \$1{,}109.74$$
$$= \$890.26$$

EXERCISE 7.2

For problems 1 to 10, find the present value.

	Length of Conversion Period	Amount	Time Period	Interest Rate
1.	Annually	$ 1,350	4 years	12.4
2.	Quarterly	2,600	16 years	13.0
3.	Monthly	2,200	15 years	15.0
4.	Daily	3,500	2 years	17.8
5.	Semiannually	5,600	18 years	14.0
6.	Monthly	16,679	10 years	17.0
7.	Quarterly	17,670	2 years	14.8
8.	Yearly	15,000	4 years	23.0
9.	Quarterly	11,450	7 years	15.5
10.	Daily	16,425	8 years	16.7

11. Find the proceeds and compound discount for a \$1,500 note if the note is discounted ten years before it is due. Assume money is worth 12% compounded monthly.

12. Eric Andrews borrowed a sum of money for four years. When the debt came due, Eric paid \$6,000 for the money borrowed, including interest. If the interest rate was 18% compounded semiannually, how much did Eric borrow?

13. Find the compound discount if \$2,800 is due five years from now and is discounted today at 18% compounded quarterly.

14. A piece of property is estimated to have a value in five years of \$120,000. The interest rate over the period is expected to be 10%, compounded monthly. What would be the maximum price one should offer, today, for the property? (Ignore any costs such as taxes and other acquisition costs.)

15. How much must be invested today at 15%, compounded annually, to ensure that a person would have \$200,000 in a retirement fund in twenty years?

7.4 Compound Discount for Interest Bearing and Non-Interest Bearing Notes

A. Interest Bearing Notes

When the topic of interest bearing notes was introduced in Chapter 6, it was emphasized that discounting of an interest bearing note would be based on the maturity value of the note. The maturity value of the note was found by adding principal and the accumulated interest.

For example, an interest bearing note for \$3,000 is signed and will be repaid in six months. If the interest rate is 24% compounded monthly, what is the maturity value of the note?

As can be seen, the concept of interest bearing implies that there is an interest rate attached to the note. To find the maturity value, we must first accumulate the \$3,000 at the specified interest rate. Therefore, the maturity value would be found by using the formula:

$S = P(1 + i)^n$, where S is the maturity value.

$$i = \frac{0.24}{12} = 0.02$$

$n = 6$ Interest is compounded monthly.

Now making the substitutions we have:

$$S = \$3{,}000(1 + 0.02)^6$$

$$S \doteq \$3{,}378.49$$

The value of the note, if held to maturity, would be \$3,378.49. However, suppose that the note is repaid early, three months before it is due, and the discount rate to be applied is 18%, compounded monthly. What is the value of the discount? The problem becomes a simple matter of discounting the **maturity value**, \$3,378.49, for three months, and subtracting this discounted value from the maturity value. That is:

$$P = S(1 + i)^{-n}$$

Now substituting:

$$P = \$3,378.49\left(1 + \frac{0.18}{12}\right)^{-3}$$

$$P \doteq \$3,230.91$$

Using a time diagram, the problem looks as follows:

Figure 7.2

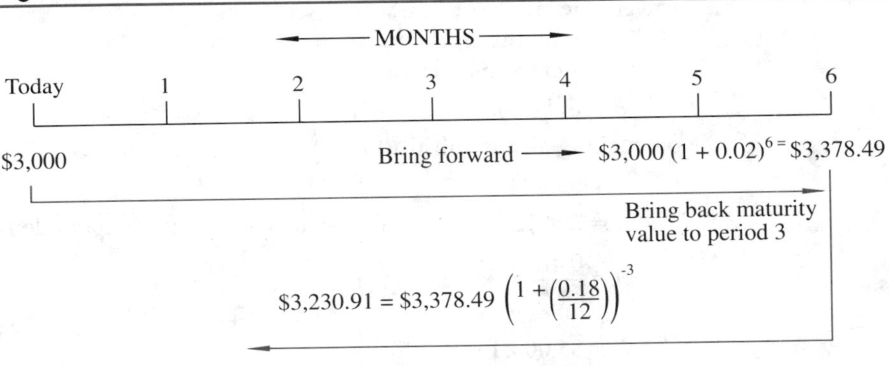

The compound discount is found by using the expression, developed above, namely, $S - P$. Again, substituting:

$$\$3,378.49 - \$3,230.91 = \$147.58$$

Please be sure that you understand the three steps involved in determining the compound discount.

1. Compute the maturity value. Remember this is a contracted amount and will be the amount to be discounted.
2. Discount the maturity value at the specified discount rate.
3. Compute the compound discount by subtracting the discounted value from the maturity value of the note.

Before leaving this section, recall that when we discount a note we are generally seeking to find one or both of the following:

- Compound Discount
- Proceeds, P, the dollars received after the discount.

B. Non-Interest Bearing Notes

In Chapter 6 we stated that a non-interest bearing note is a note where the maturity value of the note includes interest and principal. (Remember from our previous discussion that the interest is added to the principal to determine the value of the note.)

Suppose that a loan is repaid by signing a note that requires a \$5,000 payment in three years. In this case, all we know is that \$5,000 is the maturity value that includes interest and principal. Consequently, when we discount a non-interest bearing note we simply discount the face value of the note. For a non-interest bearing note, this is the maturity value of the note. It is important to realize that there is no need to accumulate interest, as was required with an interest bearing note.

Returning to the \$5,000 note, suppose that it is discounted at 18%, compounded monthly, two years before it is due. What are the proceeds? In this case, the discounted value of the note will give us the proceeds or the amount received after the note has been discounted.

To discount the non-interest bearing note two years early requires us to use our present value formula:

$$P = S(1 + i)^{-n}$$

Now making all the substitutions:

$$S = \$5{,}000$$

$$n = 2 \times 12 = 24 \qquad \text{Two years early, compounded monthly.}$$

$$i = \frac{0.18}{12} = 0.015$$

$$P = \$5{,}000(1 + 0.015)^{-24}$$

$$P \doteq \$3{,}497.72$$

Therefore, the proceeds are \$3,497.72 when the note is discounted two years before it is due.

EXAMPLE 7.7

Roberta Wade was given a note that would pay her \$4,500 on the due date of the note, which is in three and one-half years. Unfortunately, she needs money and places an ad in the paper to sell the note. After some negotiation, a local finance company offers to purchase the note at a discount rate of 15%, compounded monthly. What are the proceeds to Roberta and what is the value of the compound discount?

Solution The first thing we must identify is whether the note is an interest bearing note or non-interest bearing note. The question we should ask ourselves is, "Does the note have an interest rate?" that is, is there a statement that the value (face value) of the note is subject to an interest rate? Since the note will pay Roberta \$4,500 in three and a half years, we know that the value of the note includes any interest. There is no statement of an accumulation of interest so the note must be non-interest bearing. Therefore the calculations are as follows:

Discount the note using $P = S(1 + i)^{-n}$, where:

$S = \$4{,}500$

$i = \frac{0.15}{12}$, or 0.0125 $\quad$ i is the value of the discount rate.

$n = 3.5 \times 12 = 42$ conversion periods

$P = \$4{,}500(1 + 0.0125)^{-42}$

$\doteq \$2{,}670.68$

Calculator Solution

						Solution
Input	4,500	1.25	42			
Depress	FV	i	n	COMP	PV	2,670.68

EXAMPLE 7.8

Bonnie Wyerman signed a note agreeing to pay $10,000 in five years, plus interest at 16% compounded quarterly. After two and one-half years she unexpectedly received an inheritance and wanted to repay the note. She approached the bank that held the note and was advised that if she repaid the note early a discount rate of 8% compounded semiannually would be used. What would the early payment be to pay off the note?

Solution Again, as with the example above, we must first determine whether the note is interest or non-interest bearing. The statement that the amount must be repaid plus interest identifies the note as interest bearing. The steps to solve the problem are:

STEP 1 Because the note is an interest bearing note we must first calculate the maturity value of the note since this is a contracted amount. Using the amount formula:

$S = P(1 + i)^n$

Where:

$P = \$10{,}000$

$n = 5 \times 4 = 20$ $\quad$ Remember the note is for five years, compounded quarterly.

$i = \frac{0.16}{4}$, or 0.04

Therefore:

$S = \$10{,}000(1 + 0.04)^{20}$

$\doteq \$21{,}911.23$

STEP 2 Now we must discount the maturity value to find the amount she needs to pay, today, to pay off the note. However, please note that the discount rate is based on a different compounding period. This is something you must be looking for when interest bearing notes are discounted. Solving the problem we have:

$$P = S(1 + i)^{-n}$$

Where:

$S = \$21{,}911.23$

$n = 2.5 \times 2$ — Since the note is being discounted two and one-half years early.

$i = \frac{0.08}{2}$, or 0.04 — The interest rate used to discount is compounded semiannually.

Now substituting:

$$P = \$21{,}911.23(1 + 0.04)^{-5}$$
$$P \doteq \$18{,}009.43$$

It may seem that this is an extraordinary amount to pay, but recognize that **as the discount rate falls the value of the proceeds increase.** Conversely, **when the interest rate used to discount increases, the proceeds from the discount decrease.**

Calculator Solution

Step 1: Finding the Maturity Value						Maturity Value
Input	10,000	4	20			
Depress	PV	i	n	COMP	FV	21,911.23
Step 2: Finding the Discounted Value						**Discounted Value**
Input	21,911.23	4	5			
Depress	FV	i	n	COMP	PV	18,009.43

EXERCISE 7.3

Find the proceeds and the compound discount for the notes in problems 1 to 10.

	Length of Conversion Period	Interest Rate	Face Value of the Note	Term of the Note	Issue Date of the Note	Date of Discount	Discount Rate	Conversion Period for Discount
1.	—	—	$ 2,350	4 years	1989-01-15	1991-01-15	15.0	Annually
2.	Quarterly	13.0	4,600	16 years	1988-01-31	1994-03-31	12.0	Quarterly
3.	—	—	3,400	15 years	1990-03-31	1998-06-30	17.0	Monthly
4.	Daily	17.8	5,500	2 years	1991-11-30	1992-08-31	15.8	Monthly
5.	Semiannually	14.0	5,600	18 years	1988-12-30	1998-12-30	18.0	Yearly
6.	Monthly	17.0	7,500	10 years	1989-06-30	1995-09-30	19.0	Quarterly
7.	—	—	25,300	2 years	1989-07-31	1990-01-31	16.8	Semiannually
8.	Yearly	23.0	13,600	4 years	1988-08-31	1990-02-28	11.5	Semiannually
9.	Quarterly	15.5	13,450	7 years	1987-09-20	1992-06-20	12.6	Quarterly
10.	—	—	12,450	8 years	1988-10-31	1991-10-31	17.6	Yearly

11. Marlene was given a note that would pay her $2,100 on the due date. Since she needed some cash she discounted the note at 9% compounded monthly three months before the note was due. Find the proceeds and the compound discount.

12. A note has a face value of $5,000 and requires regular interest payments annually. If the interest rate is compounded quarterly at 14%, what is the interest payment due at the end of the first year?

13. Denise has a note that will pay her $4,000 plus 15% interest compounded semiannually in ten years. Denise needs the money and discounts the note to a friend at 15% compounded quarterly three years before it is due. Find the proceeds and the compound discount.

14. Find the proceeds and compound discount for a $3,000, five year note, with interest at 12% compounded quarterly, that is discounted ten months before maturity at 17% compounded monthly.

15. Compute the proceeds from the sale of a $1,700 two year note earning 12% compounded semiannually if it is discounted at 14% compounded quarterly, six months prior to the maturity date.

7.5 The Interest Rate

When using compound interest there are three terms used to describe the interest rate. It is important that you understand and are able to calculate each. These terms are:

- the **NOMINAL** rate of interest,
- the **EQUIVALENT** rate of interest, and
- the **EFFECTIVE** rate of interest.

A. The Nominal Rate of Interest

The nominal rate of interest refers to the rate quoted annually, regardless of the number of times the rate may be compounded. For example, if the rate is quoted as 12% compounded monthly then the nominal rate is 12%. If the rate is 16% compounded quarterly then the nominal rate is 16%.

An important point to note is that the nominal rate does not tell you what you are really being charged, since you now know that if you are quoted 12% compounded quarterly it would actually cost you more than, for example, 12% compounded annually. We will calculate this "real" rate when we examine the effective rate of interest later in this section.

EXAMPLE 7.9

Jennifer applied for a loan at the Bank of B.C. She was advised that the loan would be granted and the interest rate would be 18% compounded monthly. What is the nominal rate of interest on the loan?

Solution Based on the previous explanation, we would respond that the nominal rate of interest being charged on Jennifer's loan is 18%.

B. The Equivalent Rate of Interest

The equivalent rate of interest is a rate of interest that produces the same interest per year as a different interest rate, both being applied to the same principal. For example, the equivalent rate of interest can be used to find a rate of interest, compounded semiannually, which is equivalent to another rate, compounded monthly. This seems like a lot of double talk, so let's use an example to see what is meant.

Suppose a credit union currently charges 15% compounded monthly and now wishes to compound its rates semiannually, as currently done by local competing banks. However, the credit union wants the total interest calculated to be the same when the new compounding period is introduced, that is, they want the same amount of interest to be paid before and after the change in interest compounding periods. The question is, what would the rate of interest be, compounded semiannually, that is equivalent to the old rate of 15% compounded monthly? To answer this question, we turn to the equivalent rate of interest.

To compute equivalent rates of interest we must set up **equations of equivalence,** somewhat similar to those we used in equivalent payments in Chapter 6. In the compound interest formula, the term $(1 + i)^n$ is sometimes called the **accumulation factor**, since this term determines how large S is in the formula $S = P(1 + i)^n$.

To see how the accumulation factor is used in an equation of equivalence, let's consider the problem the credit union is trying to solve. What we need to figure out is how $(1 + i)^n$ can turn out to be the same, whether the rate is compounded monthly or semiannually — do you have any ideas?

First we must summarize what we know about the two accumulation factors.

- One of the factors is known to be based on 15% compounded monthly, or $\left[1 + \left(\frac{0.15}{12}\right)\right]^{12}$ each year.
- The other accumulation factor to be found will be compounded semiannually, $(1 + i)^2$.

Next, we must set the two accumulation factors equal to each other and determine what value of i yields the same as 15% compounded monthly. The reason that one year was selected was because this was the period over which the interest was quoted (15% per annum compounded monthly). Let's calculate the accumulation factor for one year based on the current practice of charging 15% compounded monthly.

Using the expression $(1 + i)^n$:

$n = 12$, the number of conversion periods for one year.

$$i = \frac{0.15}{12}, \text{ or } 0.0125$$

Substituting these into the expression we have:

$$(1 + 0.0125)^{12} = 1.160754518$$

The new interest rate must raise the same interest per year. Therefore, taking a similar position as above, we have:

$n = 2$ — This results from the semiannual compounding.

i = unknown — This is what we are trying to figure out. Remember, we are looking for an interest rate that, when compounded semiannually, will raise the same money as 15% compounded monthly.

Now, as above, we substitute and get:

$$(1 + i)^2$$

The only thing we know is that the value of i must give us 1.160754518, as calculated above. To find this value of i we set the two expressions equal to each other and solve for i. Therefore:

$$(1 + i)^2 = (1.160754518)$$

Using our knowledge of exponents we have:

$$(1 + i) = (1.160754518)^{\frac{1}{2}}$$

Next isolate i on the left hand side of the expression and solve for i.

$$i = (1.160754518)^{\frac{1}{2}} - 1$$
$$i = 0.077383181$$

This is the rate to be applied semiannually. The annual rate will be $(0.077383181 \times 2) = 0.154766361$, approximately 15.4766% per year. Therefore, an interest rate of 15.476,6% compounded semiannually, is **equivalent** to a rate of 15% compounded monthly.

If you are skeptical, let's look at a loan for $7,500 that has been outstanding at a credit union for one year. How much interest is due under the two situations? If everything goes according to plan, the amount of interest should be identical for both interest rates.

First, let's consider the current practice of charging 15% compounded monthly:

$P = \$7{,}500$

$i = \dfrac{0.15}{12}$, or 0.0125

$n = 12$ Since it's for one year.

Solving for S we have:

$$S = \$7{,}500(1 + 0.0125)^{12}$$
$$\doteq \$8{,}705.66$$

The second case involves calculating the interest for the same period at the equivalent rate of 15.4766% compounded semiannually. As above, let's make the appropriate substitutions:

$P = \$7{,}500$

$i = \dfrac{0.154766}{2}$, or 0.077383 The rate applied every six months.

$n = 2$ Two compounding periods per year.

Now solving for S, we have:

$$S = \$7{,}500(1 + 0.077383)^2$$
$$S \doteq \$8{,}705.66$$

Please note that it was necessary to use sufficient decimal places to ensure we have the same answer for the two calculations. Any rounding may have caused a slight difference in the final answer. In the real world, calculations would be done by computer to get an exact rate but the rate quoted to the public would be 15.48%. (The frequency of compounding would appear in the fine print.)

EXAMPLE 7.10

At what nominal rate, compounded quarterly, will a principal yield interest that is equivalent to a rate of 12% compounded semiannually?

Solution The most straight forward way of solving this problem is to do as we did above and set the two accumulation factors equal to each other. Therefore:

$(1 + i)^4$ This is the accumulation factor for one year at a rate of interest compounded quarterly.

$\left(1 + \frac{0.12}{2}\right)^2$ This represents the current accumulation factor for one year, where the interest is compounded semiannually.

Setting these two accumulation factors equal to each other we have:

$$(1 + i)^4 = \left[1 + \frac{0.12}{2}\right]^2$$

Rearranging both sides to isolate i:

$$(1 + i) = \left[1 + \frac{0.12}{2}\right]^{\frac{2}{4}}$$

$$i = \left[1 + \frac{0.12}{2}\right]^{\frac{2}{4}} - 1$$

$$i = (1 + 0.06)^{0.5} - 1$$

$$i = 0.029563014$$

The nominal rate is found by multiplying 0.029563014 by 4, which gives us 0.118252056 or approximately 11.83% compounded quarterly.

Based on our calculations we can conclude that 11.83% compounded quarterly is the equivalent of 12% compounded semiannually. Another way of looking at the solution is to realize that after one year the interest generated from 12% compounded semiannually is the same as the interest generated by 11.83% compounded quarterly.

The use of equivalent interest rates is of particular importance in Canada since every time money is borrowed, we are to be advised what the true rate of interest is by the lending institution. This rate must be expressed in terms of an annual rate, called the **effective rate of interest**. This requirement is part of the Interest Rate Act, which is a federal statute.

Now let's turn to the effective rate of interest and see how it is calculated using our knowledge of equivalent rate of interest calculations.

C. The Effective Annual Rate of Interest

As noted above, in Canada it is required by law that when we borrow money the effective rate of interest must be stated clearly in the loan agreement. In other words, borrowers must be told the true cost of borrowing.

For example, if you were taking out a loan at 14% compounded monthly or compounded semiannually, which one would you choose? With your current knowledge you would select 14% compounded semiannually since it will cost you less money.

Although you know which is the least costly, what is not stated is the actual interest cost per year. Rather, only the **nominal** rate is being quoted. In Canada, the requirement that every loan have a disclosure of the "real rate" of interest means that there must be a rate stated, which, if calculated only once a year, would yield the same interest as the loan agreement requires, regardless of how often the institution compounds the interest each year. This annual rate is called the **effective rate**. Let's consider the problem at hand:

To compute an effective rate of interest we must find i, which, if calculated once a year, yields exactly the same interest as the rate quoted, but compounded more than once a year. In our problem we have:

14% compounded monthly

This rate can be converted into an equivalent annual rate, compounded once a year. This converted annual rate is the effective rate. Using the procedure we learned in the previous section, set the two accumulation factors equal to each other:

$$(1 + i)^1 = \left[1 + \frac{0.14}{12}\right]^{12}$$

This expression states, in mathematical terms, "there is a rate i, calculated once a year, which is equivalent to 14% compounded monthly".

Solving for i we get:

$$\begin{aligned}(1 + i) &= (1 + 0.011666667)^{12} \\ i &= (1 + 0.011666667)^{12} - 1 \\ i &= 0.149342\end{aligned}$$

Therefore, 14.9342% calculated once a year gives you the same interest as the 14% compounded monthly.

The rate of 14.9342% is referred to as the effective rate since this is the annual cost of 14% compounded monthly. The same procedure can be used to compute the effective rate of 14% compounded semiannually. That is:

$$(1 + i)^1 = \left[1 + \frac{0.14}{2}\right]^2$$

$$i = \left[1 + \frac{0.14}{2}\right]^2 - 1$$

$$i = 0.1449, \text{ or } 14.49\% \text{ per annum}$$

EXAMPLE 7.11

Marilyn Anderson has been comparing the cost of a loan between two companies. One loan company has offered her a loan at 16% compounded monthly. The other company has offered her a loan at 16.5% compounded semiannually. If Marilyn were to ask you for advice, what would you recommend?

Solution This problem can be answered directly by calculating the effective rate of interest for each company. Let's do the first company:

OPTION 1

$$(1 + i)^1 = \left[1 + \frac{0.16}{12}\right]^{12}$$

$$i = (1 + 0.013333)^{12} - 1$$

$$i = 0.172270798, \text{ or } 17.23\% \text{ per year}$$

Now, turning to the second offer, we compute the effective rate as:

OPTION 2

$$(1 + i)^1 = \left[1 + \frac{0.165}{2}\right]^{2}$$

$$i = (1 + 0.0825)^2 - 1$$

$$i = 0.17180625, \text{ or } 17.18\% \text{ per year.}$$

Based on the above you would recommend that she take the 16.5% compounded semiannually since it is the loan that costs the least. Remember the effective rate tells you what rate, **calculated once a year**, is equivalent to the nominal rate compounded however many times the interest is compounded per year.

Often a formula is used to calculate the effective rate of interest. This formula is a simple way of transforming the quoted rate to an annual rate, equivalent to the old rate. The formula is:

Formula 7.3

$$\text{Effective Rate} = (1 + i)^m - 1$$

Where:

i = the interest rate per conversion period
m = the number of conversion periods per year

Reconsidering the example above, where Marilyn was having a problem, it becomes quite an easy matter to help her. Let's see how the formula would work for the first option, 16% compounded monthly:

OPTION 1

$i = \frac{0.16}{12}$, or 0.01333 This is the first interest rate quoted.

$m = 12$ The number of conversion periods per year.

Substituting for each of the terms:

$$\text{Effective Rate} = \left[1 + \left(\frac{0.16}{12}\right)\right]^{12} - 1$$

$$\doteq 0.172271$$

Now doing the same for the rate of 16.5% compounded semiannually:

OPTION 2

$i = \frac{0.165}{2}$, or 0.0825

$m = 2$ The interest is compounded only twice a year.

Substituting the information into Formula 7.3 yields:

$$\text{Effective Rate} = (1 + 0.0825)^2 - 1$$

$$\doteq 0.17181$$

Based on these calculations we arrive at the same conclusion as before. You may ask yourself, "which method do I use?" Either is acceptable, so use the method you understand best.

Next time you see a special ad for financing, for example, a car, which includes something about interest rates, look closely to see if the effective rate is quoted.

EXERCISE 7.4

1. Determine the appropriate rate of interest for each of the following.

a. Find the rate of interest compounded quarterly, equivalent to 15% compounded annually.

b. Find the rate of interest compounded monthly, equivalent to 18% compounded daily.

c. Find the rate of interest compounded annually, equivalent to 10% compounded monthly.

d. Find the rate of interest compounded semiannually, equivalent to 18% compounded daily.

e. Find the equivalent rate of interest compounded semiannually, to 15% compounded monthly.

2. Find the effective rate of interest for each of the following. Also, specify the nominal rate of interest.

a. 13.5% compounded monthly
b. 14.5% compounded quarterly
c. 18.0% compounded semiannually
d. 12% compounded quarterly
e. 10.5% compounded annually
f. 24.5% compounded daily
g. 15.5% compounded semiannually
h. 12% compounded daily

3. A loan is negotiated at 15% compounded monthly. What is the nominal rate?

4. George is contemplating the purchase of a new car that is going to cost him $14,500. He has arranged to finance the entire purchase price. The two banks with which he has been dealing have offered him the following terms. The Royal Bank has offered him a loan at a rate of 18% compounded monthly, while the Bank of Hong Kong has offered him a loan at 18.5% compounded semiannually. Help George by telling him which one is cheaper.

5. In problem 4, what rate of interest would the Royal Bank have to charge, compounded monthly, to make their interest rate the same as the Bank of Hong Kong?

6. What nominal rate compounded semiannually will yield interest that is equivalent to an effective rate of 15%?

7. A local bank is advertising saving certificates that pay 6.5% compounded quarterly. What is the real rate of interest being paid annually?

7.6 Fractional Periods

Up to now, all our time calculations have involved time periods that have been complete periods, that is, whole numbers for n. However, imagine a situation where a note is being discounted three and a half months before it is due, and assume the interest rate for discounting is compounded monthly. The solution to such a problem is to let $n = 3.5$ in our calculations. Moreover, it sometimes occurs that the period is something other than a half a period. For example, suppose a note is discounted twenty days before it is due. What would we do then?

A few years ago the answer would have been to calculate as many periods as one could with compound interest and then finish off the remaining period using an approximate method involving simple interest. Today, because of electronic calculators and computers, we can calculate the exact interest regardless of the fraction of a period involved.

For example, if there were only twenty days involved in the discount and the interest was compounded monthly for the discount, then the fraction used would be $\frac{20}{30}$ or .667. If the month is known, for example, March, then the time would be $\frac{20}{31}$. Remember, when there is no date specified and the interest rate is monthly we must treat the year as having 360 days and each month as having 30 days.

It will be of interest to note that financial institutions calculate the exact days in the month to determine the interest charge by computing a daily equivalent rate — for example, 12% compounded monthly can be converted to an equivalent rate, compounded daily. There are differences in each financial institution as to how the interest is calculated; the differences depend on company policy.

The use of exact fractional periods is common. One exception is calculations involving bond prices and bond interest. In the bond market an approximation method that uses simple interest has become the accepted procedure for calculations involving fractional periods. We shall examine this topic in a later chapter. Let's consider some examples of fractional periods and see how the calculations are done:

EXAMPLE 7.12

A note is discounted one month before it is due. The note is for a five year period. If the face value of the note is $6,500 and the interest rate on the note is 14% compounded semiannually, find the proceeds if the note is discounted at 12% compounded semiannually.

Solution

STEP 1 Since the note is an interest bearing note we must first find the maturity value. Use the formula:

$$S = P(1 + i)^n$$

Where:

$$P = \$6{,}500$$

$$i = \frac{0.14}{2}, \text{ or } 0.07$$

$$n = 2 \times 5, \text{ or } 10$$ Compounded semiannually for five years.

$$S = \$6{,}500(1 + 0.07)^{10}$$

$$S \doteq \$12{,}786.48$$

STEP 2 Next, we use the discount formula to discount the maturity value one month before it is due. In our example:

$n = \frac{1}{6}$ — The note is being discounted one month before it is due; the discount period is for one month. Since the discount rate is calculated every six months, the discount period is for only a fraction of the period, or $\frac{1}{6}$ months.

$i = \frac{0.12}{2}$, or 0.06 — Remember this is the discount rate.

$S = \$12{,}786.48$

Now using the discount formula:

$$P = S(1 + i)^{-n}$$

Substituting we have:

$$P = \$12{,}786.48(1 + 0.06)^{-\frac{1}{6}}$$

$$P \doteq \$12{,}662.91$$

Thus, if the note is discounted one month early the proceeds are $12,662.91.

Calculator Solution

Step 1: Finding the Maturity Value						Maturity Value
Input	6,500	7	10			
Depress	PV	i	n	COMP	FV	12,786.48
Step 2: Finding the Discounted Value						**Discounted Value**
Input	12,786.48	6	0.166667			
Depress	FV	i	n	COMP	PV	12,662.91

EXAMPLE 7.13

Find the amount of \$3,500 after four years and eight months if the interest rate is 12% compounded quarterly.

Solution This problem requires us to use the amount formula:

$$S = P(1 + i)^n$$

Substituting we have:

$$P = \$3{,}500$$

$$i = \frac{0.12}{4}, \text{ or } 0.03$$

$$n = 18.6667$$

Since there are three months in each quarter we find n by dividing the eight months by three months and adding this to the number of quarters in four years:

$$\frac{8}{3} = 2.66\dot{6} \text{ quarters}$$

$$4 \times 4 = 16 \text{ quarters}$$

Adding the two periods together we get the total number of quarters over which the accumulation will occur.

$$n = 18.6667 \qquad \text{Rounding}$$

Now making the substitutions into the amount formula:

$$S = \$3{,}500(1 + 0.03)^{18.6667}$$

$$S \doteq \$6{,}077.10$$

Therefore, the amount after 18.6667 quarters is \$6,077.10.

Calculator Solution

						Solution
Input	3,500	3	18.6667			
Depress	PV	i	n	COMP	FV	6,077.10

EXERCISE 7.5

For problems 1 to 10, find the accumulated value (future value) for each of the following.

	Length of Conversion Period	Amount	Time Period	Interest Rate
1.	Annually	$ 2,150	3.5 years	19.2
2.	Quarterly	3,500	16.2 years	17.0
3.	Monthly	12,300	1.6 years	16.0
4.	Annually	13,500	1.2 years	14.8
5.	Semiannually	5,600	6 years, 2 months	13.0
6.	Monthly	16,679	12 years, 2.5 months	11.0
7.	Quarterly	17,670	2 years, 5 months	17.8
8.	Yearly	15,000	4 years, 5 months	26.0
9.	Quarterly	11,450	7 years, 2 months	14.5
10.	Semiannually	16,425	8 years, 1 month	11.7

11. Fred Jones deposits $2,550 in a credit union that pays 12.2% compounded semiannually. What amount will accumulate in ten years and three months?

12. Find the present value of $4,000 due in six years and seven months if money is worth 8% compounded quarterly.

13. A non-interest bearing note is due in three years and has a maturity value of $6,730. If the note is discounted eighteen months early at 15% compounded annually, what are the proceeds and the compound discount?

7.7 Finding the Number of Periods, *n*

When we discussed simple interest we developed a method for finding how long it would take a principal to accumulate. We called this finding the time. The similar problem in compound interest involves finding the number of conversion periods it will take a principal to accumulate. From this, we can determine the length of time it will take to accumulate a sum in the future.

The formula we use is a little more complicated to develop since to find the value of n, an exponent, requires the use of logarithms. Please don't panic, you can review the subject of logarithms at your leisure (see Chapter 4 for a complete discussion). For now we'll show you how to perform the calculations.

Before we get too far along, look on your calculator for a key that has **ln** or **log** on it. Although you might have both, use only one; it does not matter which one. We will use **ln** in our examples only because this is the most common one programmed into business calculators.

To understand what we are about to do we must refer to the compound formula to find the amount, S:

$$S = P(1 + i)^n$$

Our objective is to isolate n so that if we know S, P, and i we can determine n. The first step is to rearrange the formula by dividing both sides by P:

$$\frac{S}{P} = (1 + i)^n$$

Rearranging this expression so that the term with n is on the left hand side of the expression gives:

$$(1 + i)^n = \frac{S}{P}$$

As can be seen, it is not possible to solve directly for n because it is an exponent. In order to get the value of n isolated, we must take the natural logarithm of both sides of the expression. This process yields:

$$n[\ln(1 + i)] = \ln\left[\frac{S}{P}\right]$$

Solving for n requires us to divide both sides of the expression by $\ln(1 + i)$ giving:

$$n = \frac{\ln\left(\frac{S}{P}\right)}{\ln(1 + i)}$$ **Formula 7.4**

In using this formula we must make sure we follow a precise set of steps to perform the computations. Study the steps in the following example:

EXAMPLE 7.14

How long will it take for \$1,500 to accumulate to \$2,146 if the interest rate is 12% compounded monthly?

Solution The first thing we must do is to identify the values for each term in our formula:

$S = \$2{,}146$

$P = \$1{,}500$

$i = \dfrac{0.12}{12}$, or 0.01 Since we know the interest rate is calculated each month.

Substituting the above into Formula 7.4 gives us the following:

$$n = \frac{\ln\left[\dfrac{\$2{,}146}{\$1{,}500}\right]}{\ln(1 + 0.01)}$$

$$n = \frac{\ln(1.43066666)}{\ln(1.01)}$$

To work out this last expression the following calculator steps are needed:

1. Enter 1.01 — before you depress the ln key (or the log key) check to see if the ln key operates as a second function key (this means you have to depress 2nd to operate the ln function).
2. After depressing the ln key you should get 0.009950331 — place this number in memory.
3. Now repeat Step 1 for 1.4306666. You should see 0.358140536 on the display.
4. Depress:
   - the division sign, followed by
   - recall memory, and finally,
   - the equals sign.
5. If all went according to plan you should see 35.99283 on your display, which represents the number of periods that the principal of \$1,500 would have to accumulate for to amount to \$2,146.

> *Note:* If you are using Log your solution will look as follows:
>
> $$\text{Log}(1.01) = 0.004321374$$
>
> $$\text{Log}\left(\frac{\$2{,}146}{\$1{,}500}\right) = 0.155538459$$
>
> $$n = 35.9928$$

In most cases we would round the answer to $n = 36$.

You may have wondered why the $\ln(1 + i)$ was entered first. This was simply because we needed this number to divide into $\ln\left(\frac{S}{P}\right)$. Starting with $\ln(1 + i)$ and using the memory saved us writing the numbers down and reentering them into the calculator.

For those who have a financial calculator you can find n directly as follows:

Financial Calculator Solution Using the Sharp EL-733 to find n requires an adjustment. Recall that PV and FV solutions with the Sharp produced a negative answer. To find n either the PV *or* the FV must have a minus sign placed in front of it when entered into the calculator. Failure to make this adjustment will produce an error message. One of the most direct ways to change the sign is to input the value (FV or PV) then depress the +/− key.

							Solution
Input	1,500	1	2,146				
Depress	PV	i	+/−	FV	COMP	n	35.9928269

EXAMPLE 7.15

How many years are needed for \$5,000 to generate \$1,500 in interest if the interest rate is 8% compounded semiannually?

Solution We know we are starting with a principal of \$5,000, but what may not be obvious is how we get the amount, S. If you'll recall from Chapter 6, $P + I$ gave us the value of S. Therefore, we have:

$$P = \$5{,}000$$

$$S = P + I$$

$$= \$5{,}000 + \$1{,}500$$

$$= \$6{,}500$$

$$i = \frac{0.08}{2}, \text{ or } 0.04$$

Substituting into Formula 7.4 gives us:

$$n = \frac{\ln\left[\frac{\$6{,}500}{\$5{,}000}\right]}{\ln(1 + 0.04)}$$

$$n \doteq \frac{0.2623643}{0.0392207}$$

$$n \doteq 6.68943$$

Therefore, the length of time **in years** will be $\frac{6.68943}{2}$, or 3.3447 years. The reason we divide by 2 is that the interest is compounded semiannually.

Calculator Solution

							Solution
Input	5,000	4	6,500				
Depress	PV	i	+/−	FV	COMP	n	6.68946

EXERCISE 7.6

For each of the following, find the number of periods required to accumulate the given principal to the corresponding amount at the specified interest rate.

	Length of Conversion Period	Amount	Principal	Interest Rate
1.	Annually	$ 5,150	$ 2,150	19.2
2.	Quarterly	6,300	3,500	17.0
3.	Monthly	32,300	12,300	16.0
4.	Annually	53,500	13,500	14.8
5.	Semiannually	35,900	5,600	13.0
6.	Monthly	66,779	16,679	11.0
7.	Quarterly	77,670	17,670	17.8
8.	Yearly	25,300	15,000	26.0
9.	Quarterly	31,350	11,450	14.5
10.	Semiannually	46,425	16,425	11.7

11. How long will it take for a couple to accumulate $10,000 for a down payment on a house if they can invest $6,000 today at 10.5% compounded quarterly?

12. How long, in years, will it take money to double in value if the interest rate is 13% compounded semiannually?

13. How long will it take money to triple its value if the interest rate is 8% compounded monthly?

14. How long will it take for $2,000 in a mutual fund to grow to $3,800 if the rate is guaranteed to be 8.5% compounded annually?

15. An advertisement for a local finance company reads "Save your money with us and double your investment in five short years". The fine print also states that the claim was based on the average rate of interest for the last five years, compounded monthly. If the current rate of interest is 7% compounded monthly, is the claim of the company true if the 7% rate prevails for the next five years?

7.8 Finding the Interest Rate

In some financial transactions, we know the amount we are going to invest or borrow and for how long. We also know how much we can expect to earn or pay. One example is being offered a chance to purchase an investment today knowing that you will receive a specified amount in the future. Although it may sound like a good deal, the interest rate is not specified, only the beginning and end values. What we need to do is to compute the interest rate, given this information. The procedure to find the interest rate simply requires us to manipulate the amount formula to solve for i. We, therefore, begin with Formula 7.1:

$$S = P(1 + i)^n$$

Then, we divide both sides of the formula by P:

$$\frac{S}{P} = (1 + i)^n$$

The next step requires us to take the nth root of both sides so that we can isolate i. Taking the nth root simply means we divide the exponent n by n and divide the exponent for $\left(\frac{S}{P}\right)$ by n. Remember the exponent for any number when not stated is 1. Let's see how this all comes together:

$$\left[\frac{S}{P}\right]^1 = (1 + i)^n$$

Dividing each exponent by n gives:

$$\left[\frac{S}{P}\right]^{\frac{1}{n}} = (1 + i)^{\frac{n}{n}}$$

Therefore:

$$\left[\frac{S}{P}\right]^{\frac{1}{n}} = (1 + i)$$

Finally we rearrange the expression so that i is on the left hand side:

$$(1 + i) = \left(\frac{S}{P}\right)^{\frac{1}{n}}$$

$$i = \left(\frac{S}{P}\right)^{\frac{1}{n}} - 1$$

Therefore, the formula to find i, the rate of interest, is:

$$i = \left(\frac{S}{P}\right)^{\frac{1}{n}} - 1$$ **Formula 7.5**

EXAMPLE 7.16

At what nominal interest rate, compounded monthly for 6.5 years, will $1,500 accumulate to an amount of $2,500?

Solution To solve the problem we must first determine the values for each term in Formula 7.5.

$S = \$2,500$

$P = \$1,500$

$n = 6.5 \times 12$, or 78

The value for n comes from the knowledge that the interest rate is compounded monthly. Now substituting into the formula:

$$i = \left(\frac{\$2,500}{\$1,500}\right)^{\frac{1}{78}} - 1$$

$$i \doteq (1.006571) - 1$$

$$i \doteq 0.006571$$

Therefore, the interest rate per month is 0.006571. To find the nominal rate per year we multiply this monthly rate by 12, which yields 0.078852, or 7.885% per year. To see if this is correct, let's find the value of S, using the amount formula:

$$S = P(1 + i)^n$$

$$S = \$1,500(1 + 0.006571)^{78}$$

$$S \doteq \$2,500$$

Calculator Solution (*Note:* the minus sign was placed in front of FV, necessary for the Sharp EL-733.)

							Solution
Input	1,500	78	2,500				
Depress	PV	n	+/−	FV	COMP	i	0.65705

EXAMPLE 7.17

Gayle is considering two investments with a local investment company. The first investment requires her to invest $4,000 for five years. In return, she receives $5,800 at the end of the five year period. The second investment requires Gayle to invest $4,300 for ten years and in return she will receive $8,000 at the end of the ten years. To determine the best investment Gayle asks you to find the interest rate being paid on each investment, based on annual compounding. From the information, provide her with some assistance in making the right decision.

Solution

OPTION 1

$S = \$5,800$

$P = \$4,000$

$n = 5 \times 1 = 5$

Substituting this information into our equation for i gives:

$$i = \left[\frac{\$5,800}{\$4,000}\right]^{\frac{1}{5}} - 1$$

$$i = (1.077144) - 1$$

$$i = 0.077144$$

Thus, the nominal interest rate for Option 1 is 7.7144% compounded annually.

OPTION 2

$S = \$8,000$

$P = \$4,300$

$n = 10 \times 1, \text{ or } 10$

Substituting this information into our equation for i gives:

$$i = \left[\frac{\$8,000}{\$4,300}\right]^{\frac{1}{10}} - 1$$

$$i = (1.064050) - 1$$

$$i = 0.064050$$

The nominal interest rate for Option 2 is 6.405% compounded annually. Based on the above, you would recommend Option 1, which offers the highest interest rate and the lower initial investment of $4,000.

Calculator Solution

			Option 1				Solution
Input	4,000	5	5,800				
Depress	PV	n	+/−	FV	COMP	i	7.7144
			Option 2				**Solution**
Input	4,300	10	8,000				
Depress	PV	n	+/−	FV	COMP	i	6.4050

EXERCISE 7.7

For Exercises 1 to 10, find the nominal interest rate.

	Length of Conversion Period	Amount	Principal	Time Period
1.	Annually	$ 4,300	$ 2,150	4 years
2.	Quarterly	5,600	3,500	5 years, 6 months
3.	Monthly	22,300	12,300	6 years, 6 months
4.	Annually	53,500	13,500	14 years
5.	Semiannually	10,900	5,600	5 years
6.	Monthly	29,800	16,679	6 years, 3 months
7.	Quarterly	25,670	17,670	3 years, 1 month
8.	Yearly	25,300	15,000	25 years, 3 months
9.	Quarterly	30,500	10,550	14 years
10.	Semiannually	23,425	8,425	11 years, 7 months

11. An investment grows from $750 to $1,000 in two years. What was the rate being paid if the interest is compounded annually? If the rate had been compounded monthly what would be the nominal rate?

12. The consumer price index rose from 120 in 1982 to 175 in 1987. What was the average annual inflation rate over this time?

13. At what rate of interest, compounded semiannually, will money double its value in three years?

7.9 Equivalent Payments Using Compound Interest

In Chapter 6 we introduced the concept of equivalent payments. The concept was used in problems requiring us to reschedule payments when loan or debt obligations couldn't be met. The methods used in compound interest are the same as for simple interest except we now move payments to different points in time using the compound formula.

It's interesting to note that our compound amount formula:

$$S = P(1 + i)^n$$

is an equation that expresses value at different points in time. In fact, S is the equivalent value of P after n periods at an interest rate i. Think about it this way. If we have \$50 today and the interest rate is 6% compounded annually, and the money is invested for two years, then:

$$\begin{aligned} S &= \$50(1 + 0.06)^2 \\ &= \$56.18 \end{aligned}$$

From the above we can say that \$50 today is equivalent to \$56.18 in two years at 6% compounded annually. A similar relation can be set up for our present value formula:

$$P = S(1 + i)^{-n}$$

Again, it will be necessary to have a focal point or comparison date. If no focal date is given select a focal date that falls on one of the dates of the new payments. If there is only one unknown payment, which is at the end of a future period, then use this future period as the focal point.

EXAMPLE 7.18

A debt of \$8,400 is due in seven years. If the value of money is 9.75% compounded monthly, what is the payment if the debt is paid off in five years?

Solution The following time diagram will help us visualize how we compute equivalent payments:

Figure 7.3

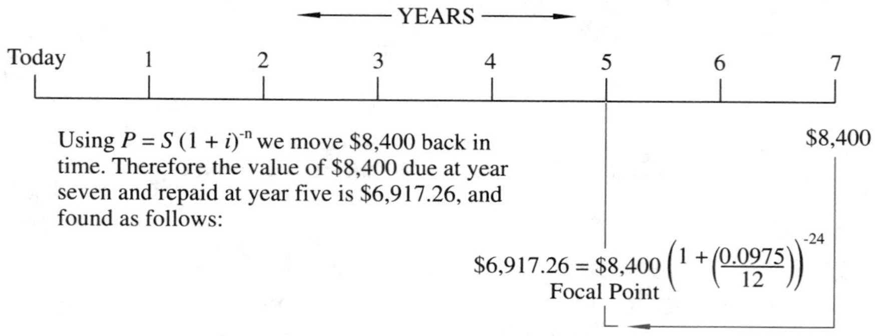
YEARS
Today
1
2
3
4
5
6
7
Using $P = S(1 + i)^{-n}$ we move \$8,400 back in time. Therefore the value of \$8,400 due at year seven and repaid at year five is \$6,917.26, and found as follows:
\$8,400
$\$6,917.26 = \$8,400\left(1 + \left(\frac{0.0975}{12}\right)\right)^{-24}$
Focal Point

Now setting up the equations:

$S = \$8{,}400$

$i = \dfrac{0.0975}{12}$, or 0.008125

$i = 0.008125$

$n = 12 \times 2$, or 24 — Since we are paying the loan off two years before the due date.

Using the present value formula to move the payment in year seven back to year five gives:

$P = S(1 + i)^{-n}$

$P = \$8{,}400(1 + 0.008125)^{-24}$

$P \doteq \$6{,}917.26$

Therefore, we can conclude that a \$6,917.26 payment at year five, two years early, will be equivalent to \$8,400 in year seven.

Calculator Solution

						Solution
Input	8,400	0.8125	24			
Depress	FV	i	n	COMP	PV	6,917.26

EXAMPLE 7.19

Brian Anderson owes \$1,400, due in three years, and \$40,000, due in eight years. Because he has had some financial problems he has asked to rearrange the payments to provide for a \$5,000 payment in four years and the balance in ten years. If money is worth 14% compounded semiannually, what is the final payment at year ten that would satisfy his creditor?

Solution The first step is to identify the focal point. Since there is only one payment at the end of year ten this will be the focal point. Drawing a time diagram for the problem:

Figure 7.4

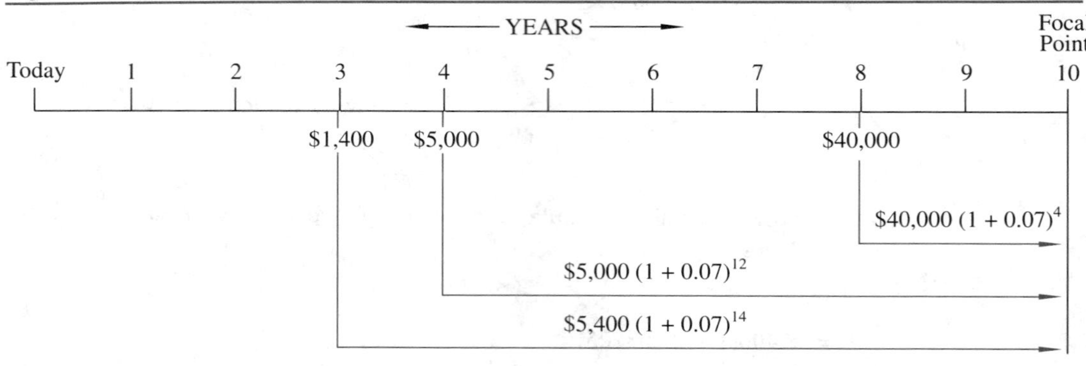

Now to set up the solution, let's move the old debt up to the focal point at year ten.

1. $\$1{,}400(1 + 0.07)^{14}$ — Moves the $1,400 from year three to year ten.

   $\$1{,}400(1 + 0.07)^{14} \doteq \$3{,}609.95$

2. $\$40{,}000(1 + 0.07)^{4}$ — Moves the $40,000 from year eight to year ten.

   $\$40{,}000(1 + 0.07)^{4} \doteq \$52{,}431.84$

Therefore, the value of the old debt at year ten is:

$$\$3{,}609.95 + \$52{,}431.84 = \$56{,}041.79$$

The new debt has a $5,000 payment at year four and a final payment of X dollars at year ten. We must move both payments to year ten as we did with the old debt. Therefore:

1. $\$5{,}000(1 + 0.07)^{12}$ — Moves the $5,000 payment from year four to year ten.

   $\$5{,}000(1 + 0.07)^{12} \doteq \$11{,}260.96$

2. X simply stays as X since it is the value of the final payment at year ten.

The value of the new debt at year ten is expressed as:

$$\$11{,}260.96 + X$$

Setting the old debt equal to the new debt and solving for X:

New Debt	=	Old Debt
$11,260.96 + X	=	$56,041.79
X	=	$56,041.79 – $11,260.96
X	=	$44,780.83

Therefore, the final payment in year ten that will satisfy the creditor is $44,780.83.

Calculator Solution

Old Debt

	Step 1: Move the $1,400 to the Focal Point					Value at Focal Point
Input	1,400	7	14			
Depress	PV	i	n	COMP	FV	3,609.95
	Step 2: Move the $40,000 to the Focal Point					
Input	40,000	7	4			
Depress	PV	i	n	COMP	FV	52,431.84
				Old debt at focal point		56,041.79

New Debt

	Step 1: Move the $5,000 to the Focal Point					Value at Focal Point
Input	5,000	7	12			
Depress	PV	i	n	COMP	FV	11,260.96
	Step 2: Set up the New Debt at the Focal Point					
				New debt at focal point		X + 11,260.96

New Debt	=	Old Debt
$11,260.96 + X	=	$56,041.79
X	=	$56,041.79 – $11,260.96
X	=	$44,780.83

You might wish to rework this problem using today as the focal point to see if you get the same answer.

One final example of equivalent payments is the situation where one has a series of equal payments over several years to repay a loan. Consider the following example:

EXAMPLE 7.20

What is the size of the annual payments, the first two being equal payments and the last two being equal but twice the size of the first two, made at the end of each year for the next four years. These payments will discharge a debt of $20,000 if money is worth 16% compounded semiannually. The focal point will be today.

Solution First we sketch a time diagram of the problem, using X to stand for the payments. X will be the value of each of the first two payments and $2X$ the value of the last two payments. Also, we know:

$$i = \frac{0.16}{2}, \text{ or } 0.08$$

Figure 7.5

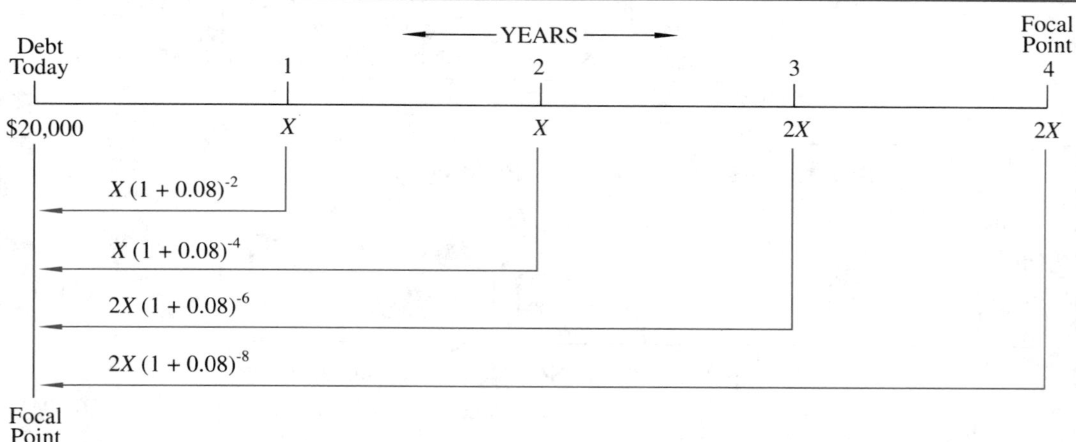

Debt — Setting the Payments Equal to the Debt

$$\$20{,}000 = X(1+0.08)^{-2} + X(1+0.08)^{-4} + 2X(1+0.08)^{-6} + 2X(1+0.08)^{-8}$$

Working out each of the expressions gives:

$\$20{,}000 \doteq X(0.857339) + X(0.7350299) + 2X(0.6301696) + 2X(0.5402689)$

Now working out the expression and reversing sides to solve for X gives:

$$(3.933246)X \doteq \$20{,}000$$

$$X \doteq \frac{\$20{,}000}{3.933246}$$

$$X \doteq \$5{,}084.86$$

Therefore, the payments will be $5,084.86 for the first two payments and 2 × $5,084.86, or $10,169.72, for the last two payments.

This problem could have been solved by taking everything up to year four. Try this alternative solution and see if you end up with the same size of payments.

EXERCISE 7.8

1. A payment of $6,000 will discharge a debt in exactly eleven months. If money is worth 12% compounded monthly, what is the equivalent payment for the debt if the payment is made:
a. seventeen months from now?
b. nine months from now?
c. 33 months from now?
d. four months from now?

2. Cecil has a small problem: he owes $3,800 in one and a half years, $5,000 in two years, and $4,500 in four years. Cecil knows he cannot make these payments. He will come into an inheritance in six years (currently it is held by a trustee). If money is worth 15% compounded monthly, what single payment in six years will satisfy these debts? If two equal payments were made, one at year six and one at year seven, what would be the size of these two payments? Assume money is worth 15% compounded monthly and that year six is the focal point.

3. Sally is going to purchase a car and is given two options by the car dealer. The first option is to pay $15,000 today or make three payments of $7,000 at the end of the next three years from the date of purchase. If the going rate of interest on car loans is 18% compounded monthly, what arrangement is the best deal for Sally?

4. A debt of $8,000 is due in four years. If the interest rate is 8% compounded quarterly, what is the value of the debt at:
a. the end of three years?
b. the end of one year?
c. the end of ten years?

5. Nigel owes the bank $3,000, due in one year, and $5,000, due in three years. After some negotiation the bank agrees to permit Nigel to make two equal payments to discharge the debt, one at the end of three years and the other at the end of six years. If the interest rate is 18% compounded monthly, what is the size of each payment? Use year three as the focal point.

6. In problem 5, suppose that three equal payments are arranged, one at year one, the second at year four, and the final payment at year six. What would be the size of each payment? Use year one as the focal point.

7. If Nigel agreed to make one payment at year three to discharge the original debt, outlined in problem five above, what would be the value of the payment?

REVIEW EXERCISES

1. What is the amount due today for a $5,200 debt incurred two years ago if money is worth 13.5% compounded semiannually?

2. $2,000 is invested at 17% compounded annually for four years. At the end of the four years, the monies are switched to a different investment plan that pays 16.5% compounded quarterly. How much will have accumulated altogether after a further two years have passed at the new rate?

3. A deposit of $2,500 has been accumulated at 12.75% compounded monthly for three and one-half years. After the three and a half years, an additional deposit of $500 is made, followed by another deposit of $700 a year after the $500 deposit. How much will have accumulated after six years?

4. How much has to be invested at 16.5% compounded quarterly to accumulate to $42,000 in fifteen years?

5. If a three year $5,500 note is discounted at 15%, compounded monthly, six months before maturity, what will be the compound discount?

6. Find the proceeds for a $3,000 five year note, bearing interest at 12%

compounded quarterly, discounted ten months before maturity, if the rate used to discount is 17% compounded monthly.

7. Calculate the compound discount on a $1,500 two year note discounted on September 10, 1995, at 13% compounded daily, if the note is signed on August 6, 1994, and bears interest at 12.5% compounded semiannually.
8. Calculate the proceeds of the sale of a $1,700 two year note earning 12% compounded semiannually if it is discounted at 14% compounded quarterly, six months before maturity.
9. If money is worth 14% compounded monthly, what single payment six months from now would satisfy an original debt of three $400 payments, one due four months ago, one due today, and one due in five months time? (Use now as the focal date.)
10. Two debts, one of $350, due a year ago, and the other of $400, due six months ago, are to be replaced by two new payments, one of $300, due now, and a final payment, due in six months. If money is worth 12% compounded semiannually, what will the final payment be?
11. What is the size of the four equal payments to be made at the end of each of the next four years to pay off a debt of $20,000 borrowed today, if the rate of interest is 16% compounded semiannually? Use today as the focal point.
12. A debt was arranged that required a payment of $1,200 in six months and $600 due in twelve months. Because the payment scheme cannot be met, the two payments are to be replaced by two equal payments, one due in nine months and the second due in eighteen months. What is the size of each payment if money is worth 13% compounded semiannually at the time of the change in the payment plan? (Use nine months from now as the focal date.)
13. What will a deposit of $650 amount to over three years and two months if interest is compounded monthly at 12.75%?
14. If money is worth 14% compounded semiannually, what is the discounted value of a $3,500 note due in three years if it is sold one and a half years before maturity?
15. If $5,000 accumulates to $6,250 in two and a half years, what is the annual nominal interest rate compounded semiannually?
16. Calculate the effective annual rate of interest on an investment with a nominal rate of interest of 15% compounded quarterly.
17. How many years will it take for a debt of $1,500 to accumulate to $2,055 at an interest rate of 12% compounded quarterly?
18. What will $622 accumulate to if interest is compounded daily at 15% for three years?
19. What deposit today will accumulate to $15,000 in six years if the interest rate is 12% compounded monthly?

SUMMARY OF FORMULAS

Formula 7.1 $S = P(1 + i)^n$

Used to find the amount S using compound interest. n refers to the number of conversion periods and i refers to the interest rate per conversion period.

Formula 7.2 $P = S(1 + i)^{-n}$

Used to find the present value using compound interest. The $-n$ is another way of expressing division of S by the term $(1 + i)^n$.

$S - P = \text{Compound Discount}$

Formula 7.3 $\text{Effective Rate} = (1 + i)^m - 1$

Used to find the effective rate of interest. m refers to the number of conversion periods per year and i refers to the rate per conversion period.

Formula 7.4

$$n = \frac{\ln\left(\frac{S}{P}\right)}{\ln(1 + i)}$$

Used to find the number of compound or conversion periods to accumulate to a sum, S, in the future.

Formula 7.5

$$i = \left[\frac{S}{P}\right]^{\frac{1}{n}} - 1$$

Used to find i, the interest rate per conversion period. If i is multiplied by the number of conversion periods per year, this produces the nominal interest rate per year.

GLOSSARY OF TERMS

Amount the sum of interest and principal. When compound interest is used, the amount includes accumulated interest on interest as well as interest on the original principal.

Compound Discount the difference between the maturity value of a note and the discounted value of the note when compound interest procedures apply to the interest calculations.

Compound Period the time between each successive interest calculation.

Conversion Period also called the compound period. It refers to the time between each interest calculation. (e.g., compounded monthly implies that the conversion period is each month.)

Effective Interest Rate a rate of interest compounded once a year that yields the same interest as another rate compounded *n* times a year. The effective rate is often called the real rate of interest.

Equivalent Rates the converting of an interest rate from one conversion period to another interest rate with a different conversion period, both yielding the same annual interest and both having the same effective rate.

Fractional Conversion Periods when the value of *n* is a mixed number or a number less than one. Fractional periods refer to partial conversion periods. For example, two months would be two-thirds of a conversion period if the interest rate is compounded quarterly.

Nominal Interest Rate the annual quotation of the interest rate, regardless of the number of times the interest is compounded. (e.g., for 12% compounded quarterly, the nominal rate is 12%.)

CHAPTER 8

Annuities

Most loans and some investments in business involve periodic payments, made at regular intervals, for a fixed number of periods. These financial arrangements are called **annuities**. One common example of an annuity is the mortgage used in the financing of a real estate purchase. A familiar example of an investment plan that meets the annuity criteria is a pension fund that makes regular payments.

Remember that in Chapter 7 we were only concerned with "fixed" values at different points in time. In this chapter, and in Chapters 9 and 10, attention is focused on business situations that involve a series of periodic payments made over time.

As you will learn, there are many kinds of annuities. The difference between each type is based on how or when the interest is calculated or when the payments occur. Consequently, you will need to examine each problem and situation to decide the annuity method that is appropriate for the problem at hand.

In this chapter, we will discuss in detail the ordinary simple annuity. In addition, an overview of some other annuities, the annuity due, the deferred annuity, and a general annuity, are briefly mentioned and will be discussed in detail in later chapters.

In this chapter, the common element for each annuity question is that the interest (compounding) period and the payment period will be the same.

We will begin with a brief discussion of ordinary simple annuities. We'll learn how to calculate the amount, present value, periodic payment, and the term. We'll also learn how to compute the value of a final payment when it's different from the regular payments. You'll be pleased to know that the calculations you'll be doing are extensions of the compound interest procedures you learned in Chapter 7.

OBJECTIVES

When you have completed Chapter 8, you should be able to perform all the calculations associated with an ordinary simple annuity. In particular, you should be able to:

1. explain the meaning of an annuity and distinguish between a simple annuity due, a deferred annuity, and an ordinary simple annuity;
2. calculate the amount, present value, periodic payment, and the term for an ordinary simple annuity;
3. calculate the outstanding balance of a loan at any point in the life of the loan, as well as determine the value of a final payment for a simple annuity when the final payment is different from the regular payment.

8.1 Annuities: The Basic Idea

A. Terminology of Annuities

An annuity refers to a financial transaction that involves a series of periodic payments made over time at regular intervals. The original meaning of annuity referred to payments over an annual period. The only annual reference that remains is that the interest rate is quoted annually.

To understand the topic of annuities there are two terms that you must become familiar with before proceeding. They are:

- **the payment interval**
- **the term of an annuity**

The payment interval refers to the period of time that separates two successive payments. For example, a mortgage with monthly payments would have a payment interval of one month. A mortgage with quarterly payments would have a payment interval of three months.

The term of an annuity refers to the time from the beginning of the first payment interval to the end of the final payment interval. For example, a mortgage taken out today and due to be repaid over sixty months at a constant interest rate is said to have a five year term.

Before we turn to the formulas associated with annuities, there is a need to understand the differences that may occur between annuities. The following two sections describe in detail more about the financial instrument of the annuity.

B. Different Types of Annuities

Annuities can be classified according to their term, the payment period, and the interest rate. The following descriptions will help explain the different ways to consider annuities.

(i) Classifying Annuities by the Term

Classifying annuities by their term provides the basis for three types of annuities. The first is called an **annuity certain**. An annuity certain is an annuity with a precise start date and end date. One example of an annuity certain is a loan agreement that requires 60 monthly payments starting at a specific time and ending five years later (60 payments). Here one would know the start and end date, thus making it an annuity certain.

Another way the term of an annuity may be structured is to have a specific start date but no ending. When this occurs the type of annuity is called a **perpetuity**. The name perpetuity refers to payments going on forever. A perpetuity requires that only interest be paid, leaving the principal untouched to allow it to continue to generate interest for the payments indefinitely.

An annuity also may be classified as a **contingent annuity**. To be a contingent annuity, the annuity will have a definite start date, but the ending point will be unknown. The typical type of contingent annuity is pension plans, which are designed to provide payments until the death of the recipient. This uncertainty over the ending of the payments makes the annuity a contingent annuity.

(ii) Classifying Annuities by Payments

In business it is common to consider annuities by when the payments are made in each payment period. On the one hand, there is the annuity that has payments at the end of each payment period, for example, at the end of each month or the end of each quarter. When an annuity has payments at the end of the payment period, the annuity is called an **ordinary annuity**. Consider a situation where a loan agreement is signed on August 1 and requires monthly payments at the end of each month. The first payment would be due on September 1 — the end of one month after August 1. Note that the date is not important, it is the time that must pass before the first payment is made that is important. Unless told otherwise, assume that the annuity you are working with is an ordinary annuity.

Some annuities require payments at the beginning of each period. The most common examples are rent and lease payments in real estate. When the payments come at the beginning of each period the annuity is called an **annuity due**. For example, if you rent an apartment today, September 1, and the owner requires payment today, and on the first of each month hereafter, the annuity is an annuity due because the payments start immediately and occur at the beginning of each payment period.

Another annuity, which can be either an ordinary annuity or an annuity due, is a **deferred annuity**. A deferred annuity is an annuity that does not commence payments until some point in the future. An example of a deferred annuity is when a retailer has a sale in the fall and advertises that there are no payments until spring. Since the payments are deferred until spring, the annuity is called a deferred annuity. Also, the payments could come at the end or the beginning of the period. Deferred simply refers to when the annuity commences the flow of payments.

(iii) Annuities Classified by the Interest Period

Annuities that have the interest conversion period and payment period coinciding are called **simple annuities**. For example, a loan that has monthly payments and an interest rate, compounded monthly, would be called a simple annuity. Thus an ordinary simple annuity would mean an annuity that has payments at the end of each payment period, with the interest conversion period and the payment period being the same. On the other hand, a simple annuity due means the payments come at the beginning of each period, and the interest rate and the payment period coincide. In business, and in this book, unless otherwise stated, when the word annuity is used in a problem it will mean ordinary annuity. An annuity due requires a clear statement in the financial contract before it occurs. Any problems requiring the application of an annuity due will make it clear that the payments are at the beginning of each period.

Another type of annuity is the **complex or general annuity**. Here the payment period and the interest period need not coincide. An example is a loan with monthly payments and the interest rate compounded semiannually. In this instance, since the payment period and interest period are different, the annuity is called a complex or general annuity. As well, the complex annuity may be an ordinary annuity, an annuity due, or a deferred annuity. In the real world, the most common example of a complex or general annuity is the standard home mortgage. If you call a bank and ask them how interest is calculated on mortgages you will be advised that the rate is compounded semiannually with payments being made monthly or biweekly.

8.2 Ordinary Simple Annuities

An ordinary simple annuity refers to an annuity that has the following characteristics:

- The payments are always made at the end of each payment interval.
- The interest rate will compound at the same interval as the payment interval.

A. The Amount of an Ordinary Simple Annuity

Let's consider an example. Suppose you want to save $15,000 and agree to make regular monthly deposits at the end of each month to accumulate the desired sum of $15,000 over a period of 48 months. The time, 48 months, is called the term of the annuity. Assume the interest rate you are being paid is 18%, compounded monthly. In this example we note that:

- There are regular payments (deposits) each month over 48 months. It is the regular payments that make this an annuity. The one month time period between payments is referred to as the payment interval.
- The payment (deposit) is made at the **end** of each month, which makes the annuity an ordinary annuity.
- The monthly payments (deposits) coincide with the interest period. Since the payment period and the interest period are the same, the annuity is a simple annuity.

When we combine the facts that the payments (deposits) are at the end of each period and that the interest compound period coincides with the payment (deposit) period you see why this type of annuity is called an ordinary simple annuity.

To see how an annuity works, let's consider another example. Suppose a couple decides to set aside $450 at the end of each month toward the purchase of a new home. If the interest rate is 8% compounded monthly, how much will they have after three months? How much will they have at the end of one year?

If we consider the first problem, how much is accumulated at the end of three months, we could use the amount formula for compound interest from Chapter 7

$$S = P(1 + i)^n$$

to calculate the value of S for each deposit as follows:

S_1 will be the first deposit at the end of month one, accumulated for two months (remember that the first payment does not occur until the end of the first month). Thus, the first payment will have two months to accumulate:

$$S_1 = \$450\left[1 + \frac{0.08}{12}\right]^2$$

$$= \$456.02$$

S_2 will be the accumulated second deposit made at the end of the second month. By the end of the third month only one month of interest will have accumulated, thus:

$$S_2 = \$450\left[1 + \frac{0.08}{12}\right]^1$$

$$= \$453.00$$

The time diagram shown below should help you visualize the process:

Figure 8.1

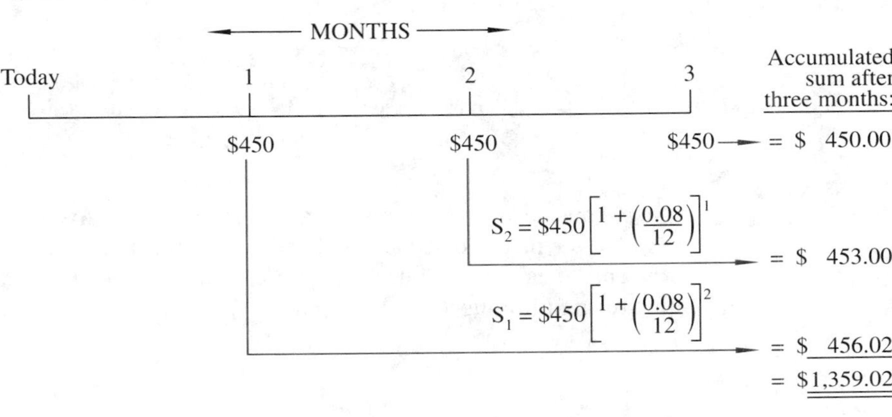

Now, since the third payment is made at the end of the third month, there will be no interest, thus S_3 is \$450.

Combining the three payments plus the interest tells us how much money would have accumulated at the end of three months, or:

$$\begin{aligned} S_1 + S_2 + S_3 &= \$456.02 + \$453 + \$450 \\ &= \$1{,}359.02 \end{aligned}$$

Therefore, if \$450 is deposited at the end of each month for three months, and interest is 8% compounded monthly, there will be \$1,359.02 in the account.

The second part of the problem requires us to compute how much would be accumulated at the end of one year. If we follow the method above we will have twelve separate calculations — one heck of a lot of calculations! Fortunately, the problem can be easily handled using annuities.

Before we get too far, we must define some new terms that are generally used in most finance books. The first is the **amount** of an ordinary simple annuity, S_n. The remaining terms can be defined in terms of our example:

R = the regular payment. In our example it is \$450.

i = the interest per payment period. In our problem it will be $\frac{0.08}{12}$.

n = the number of payments over which we wish to calculate the amount (sum) of the annuity; in this problem n would be 12.

S_n = the amount of an ordinary simple annuity.

Bringing these terms together, a formula can be stated that will calculate the sum of a series of regular payments. This sum will include accumulated interest and payments under the condition that each payment is made at the end of each payment period, and that interest is calculated coincidental with each payment period. The formula that computes this sum is:

$$S_n = \frac{R[(1+i)^n - 1]}{i} \qquad \textbf{Formula 8.1}$$

Now considering the problem at hand, we wish to calculate the amount of twelve payments of $450, made each month, when the payments are made at the end of each month and the interest rate is 8% compounded monthly. Substituting into our formula we have:

$R = \$450$

$i = \dfrac{0.08}{12}$

$n = 12$ Since we are interested in the amount at the end of twelve payments.

Using Formula 8.1:

$$S_n = \frac{R[(1+i)^n - 1]}{i}$$

$$S_n = \frac{\$450\left[\left(1+\frac{0.08}{12}\right)^{12} - 1\right]}{\frac{0.08}{12}}$$

$$S_n \doteq \$450(12.449926)$$

$$\doteq \$5{,}602.47$$

Thus, in twelve months there will be $5,602.47 in the account.

It is important to recognize that Formula 8.1 uses the method of geometric progressions referred to in Chapter 4. If you are interested in understanding how this procedure is used to compute the formula for S_n you may want to review the topic in geometric progression in Chapter 4.

If we recalculate the first part of the problem, where n was 3, using Formula 8.1, we should get the same answer that we found using the method of finding three values for S using compound interest. Substituting we have:

$R = \$450$

$i = \dfrac{0.08}{12}$

$n = 3$ Since we were interested in only the amount after three payments.

Now applying the formula:

$$S_n = \frac{\$450\left[\left(1 + \frac{0.08}{12}\right)^3 - 1\right]}{\frac{0.08}{12}}$$

$$S_n \doteq \$450(3.02004444)$$

$$S_n \doteq \$1{,}359.02$$ The same answer as first found using the compound interest method.

EXAMPLE 8.1

Maxwell Baker decides to set aside \$20 at the end of each month for his daughter Amanda's college education. If Amanda turns one year old today, how much will be available for her college education when she turns nineteen years old? Assume that the interest rate is 5% compounded monthly.

Solution First we assign all the terms:

$$R = \$20$$

$$i = \frac{0.05}{12}, \text{ or } 0.0041666\dot{6}$$

$$n = 18 \times 12, \text{ or } 216$$ This assumes the last payment falls on the girl's nineteenth birthday.

Now substituting into our Formula, 8.1, we have:

$$S_n = \frac{R[(1 + i)^n - 1]}{i}$$

$$S_n = \frac{\$20\left[\left(1 + \frac{0.05}{12}\right)^{216} - 1\right]}{\frac{0.05}{12}}$$

$$S_n = \$20(349.2020206)$$

$$S_n = \$6{,}984.04$$

Thus, if Mr. Baker makes these monthly deposits for 216 months he will have \$6,984.04 set aside for Amanda's education when she turns nineteen.

Calculator Solution Remember to clear the calculator by using the 2nd and C·CE key sequence.

						Solution
Input	20	0.416666	216			
Depress	PMT	i	n	COMP	FV	6,984.04

EXAMPLE 8.2

John is going to purchase a new home but he needs $10,000 for a down payment. He decides to save $250 each month (unless otherwise stated, remember, assume the annuity is an ordinary annuity) for the next three years at an interest rate of 6% compounded monthly. Will John have sufficient monies to make the down payment?

Solution First let's make the substitutions:

$R = \$250$

$i = \frac{0.06}{12}$, or 0.005

$n = 12 \times 3$, or 36   Three years of monthly payments.

Applying our formula for the amount of an annuity:

$$S_n = \frac{\$250[(1 + 0.005)^{36} - 1]}{(0.005)}$$

$$S_n \doteq \$9{,}834.03$$

Based on our calculations, John doesn't have quite enough money to make the down payment. He must wait until one smaller payment is made.

Calculator Solution

						Solution
Input	250	0.5	36			
Depress	PMT	i	n	COMP	FV	9,834.03

B. The Present Value of an Ordinary Simple Annuity

In Chapters 6 and 7 we used the concept of **present value** to determine today's value of a future amount. The same concept is often used with annuities. Remember that the process used to bring back a series of future payments to find the present value is called **discounting**. This value is often referred to as the **discounted value** or present value of an annuity. An example of when one would want to find the present or discounted value of an annuity is the purchase of a retirement annuity. A retirement annuity is designed to provide one with a monthly income, upon retirement, for a specified number of years.

Suppose your friend Barbara asks you to help her determine the appropriate price to pay for an annuity offering a retirement income of $1,000 a month for ten years. Assume the interest rate is 6% compounded monthly. To help in solving the problem, first identify the terms to be used:

R = the regular payments, in our problem this would be $1,000 per month.

i = the interest rate per payment period. In our example it would be $\left(\frac{0.06}{12}\right)$, or 0.005.

n = the number of payments. In this problem there are twelve payments per year for a period of ten years, or $10 \times 12 = 120$ payments.

A_n = the present value of an ordinary simple annuity.

Combining the terms, the present value of an annuity is found by the following formula:

$$A_n = \frac{R[1 - (1 + i)^{-n}]}{i} \qquad \textbf{Formula 8.2}$$

Note: Formula 8.2 uses a geometric progression outlined in Chapter 4.

If we make all the substitutions we have:

$$R = \$1{,}000$$

$$i = 0.005$$

$$n = 12 \times 10, \text{ or } 120$$

$$A_n = \frac{\$1{,}000[1 - (1 + 0.005)^{-120}]}{0.005}$$

$$A_n \doteq \$90{,}073.45$$

Calculator Solution

						Solution
Input	1,000	0.5	120			
Depress	PMT	i	n	COMP	PV	90,073.45

Therefore, if Barbara wants to have a monthly income of $1,000 for the next ten years, under the conditions of the problem, you would recommend that she pay no more than $90,073.45, at the interest rate of 6% compounded monthly.

EXAMPLE 8.3

Calculate the present value of an annuity that offers to pay you $1,000 every four months for one year using (a) the compound interest method and (b) the annuity formula. Assume the interest rate is 12% compounded every four months.

Solution (a) **Using the Compound Interest Method**

This method requires us to calculate the present value of each payment separately and add the present values to find the present value of the payments. Therefore:

$P = S(1 + i)^{-n}$ will be calculated for each payment.

Starting with the first payment:

$P_1 =$ The present value of the first payment of $1,000 made at the end of the first four months.

$$S_1 = \$1{,}000$$

$$i = \frac{0.12}{3}, \text{ or } 0.04$$

$$n = 1$$

$$P_1 = \$1{,}000(1 + 0.04)^{-1}$$
$$\doteq \$961.54$$

Calculating for the second payment:

$P_2 =$ The present value of the second payment made at the end of the second four months.

$$n = 2$$
$$S = \$1{,}000$$
$$P_2 = \$1{,}000(1 + 0.04)^{-2}$$
$$\doteq \$924.56$$

Now doing the same for the last payment in twelve months or three interest periods away:

$$P_3 = \$1{,}000(1 + 0.04)^{-3}$$
$$\doteq \$889$$

Adding the three present values we have:

$$\$961.54 + \$924.56 + \$889 = \$2{,}775.10$$

You may find it helpful to examine this example visually:

Figure 8.2

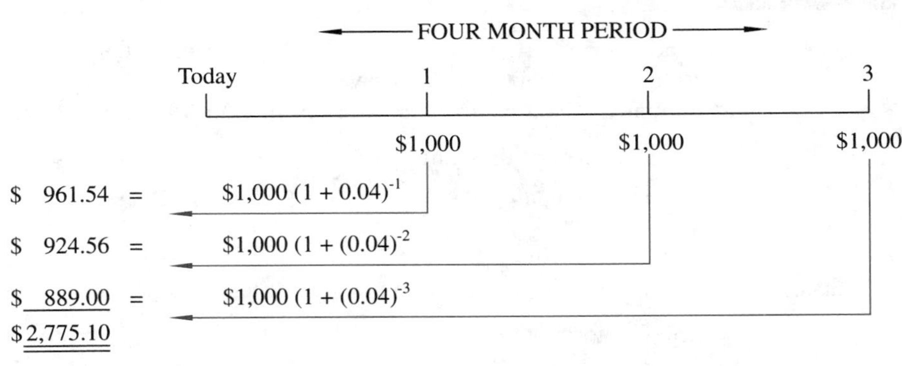

(b) Using the Annuity Method

As you will see, this method is much more direct in finding the present value of the payments. Assign values to the terms in Formula 8.2:

$$A_n = \frac{R[1 - (1 + i)^{-n}]}{i}$$

Where:

A_n = present value of the annuity (the unknown)

R = $1,000

$i = \frac{0.12}{3}$, or 0.04, every four months

n = 3 Since there are three payments for the year.

Substituting:

$$A_n = \frac{\$1{,}000[1 - (1 + 0.04)^{-3}]}{0.04}$$

$$A_n = \$2{,}775.09$$

This result is $0.01 different from the compound interest approach and occurs because of rounding differences. It is important to recognize the advantage of the annuity formula for finding the present value of an annuity, since it saves so many calculations when compared with the compound interest method.

Calculator Solution

						Solution
Input	1,000	4.0	3			
Depress	PMT	i	n	COMP	PV	2,775.09

EXAMPLE 8.4

Find the present value of a retirement annuity that will provide an annual payment of \$4,000, for four years, at an interest rate of 12% compounded annually. Also, identify the values of the following for this problem:

(a) The term of the annuity.
(b) The payment interval.

Solution The values for the term and payment interval are:

(a) The term is four years.
(b) The payment interval is twelve months, or one year.

The present value is found directly by using Formula 8.2:

$$A_n = \frac{R[1 - (1 + i)^{-n}]}{i}$$

Where:

$$R = \$4{,}000$$
$$i = 0.12$$
$$n = 4$$

Therefore:

$$A_n = \frac{\$4{,}000[1 - (1 + 0.12)^{-4}]}{0.12}$$

$$A_n \doteq \$12{,}149.40$$

Calculator Solution

						Solution
Input	4,000	12	4			
Depress	PMT	i	n	COMP	PV	12,149.40

EXERCISE 8.1

For each of the annuities in problems 1 to 10, find the amount and the present value.

	Payment Period	Payment	Term of the Annuity	Interest Rate and Conversion Period
1.	Annually	$ 1,350	4 years	12.4%, annually
2.	Quarterly	600	16 years	14.0%, quarterly
3.	Monthly	200	15 years	15.0%, monthly
4.	Daily	500	2 years	17.8%, daily
5.	Semiannually	450	18 years	14.0%, semiannually
6.	Monthly	879	10 years	17.0%, monthly
7.	Quarterly	670	2 years	14.8%, quarterly
8.	Yearly	900	4 years	23.0%, yearly
9.	Quarterly	1,450	7 years	15.5%, quarterly
10.	Daily	1,425	8 years	16.7%, daily

11. Susan has a Registered Retirement Savings Plan (RRSP) to which she makes monthly deposits of $100. She started the plan when she turned 50 years old. How much will be in her plan at age 60, assuming the interest rate is constant at 6% compounded monthly for the time she makes her deposits?
12. A friend loans you $10,000 and asks you to repay the loan in two years without interest. Assume you decide to set $400 aside each month to repay the loan. If you can get 4% interest on your money compounded monthly, how much would you have accumulated in your account at the end of the two years?
13. A housing co-op decides that it would be wise to have a reserve fund to cover unexpected maintenance costs. If the co-op decides to set aside $3,500 every six months in an account that pays 6% compounded semiannually, how much would be in its reserve fund at the end of four years?
14. Find the present value of an annuity that has regular semiannual payments of $2,500 for ten years. Assume the interest rate is 8% compounded semiannually.
15. An insurance company wants to sell you an annuity that will provide you with monthly payments of $500 for the next fifteen years. If you know you can get 8% on your money compounded monthly, what would be a fair price, today, for such an annuity?

8.3 Applications of Ordinary Simple Annuities

It is useful for you to see how annuities are used in everyday business and personal finance. The following examples are applications of the present value concept of an annuity. For the moment we will leave the application of the amount of an annuity, since most applications require just a little more background than we've covered to this point. But don't worry, we'll have many applications of amount in the future sections.

One of the most useful applications of the present value concept is with installment purchases. For example, suppose you are in the market to buy a new car. You visit a local dealer where you are advised that there are two ways you can buy the car you want:

a. You can purchase the car with a down payment of $1,000 and $400 a month for 48 months, with interest at a rate of 18% compounded monthly.

or:

b. For a limited time only, you can make an outright cash purchase for $10,500.

Which of these two options is best for you? To answer this we must compare the two options in today's dollars or present value. We know the cash price today in today's dollars, it's simply the $10,500. The first option is a little more difficult since we must calculate the present value of the down payment and the monthly payments of $400. The procedure we would adopt would be as follows.

The present value of the down payment is $1,000. Make sure you can explain to yourself why.

To calculate the present value of the monthly payments we would use Formula 8.2:

$$A_n = \frac{R[1 - (1 + i)^{-n}]}{i}$$

Where:

$R = \$400$

$i = \frac{0.18}{12}$, or 0.015

$n = 12 \times 4$, or 48, Remember there are monthly payments for four years.

Substituting the values into our annuity formula gives:

$$A_n = \frac{\$400[1 - (1 + 0.015)^{-48}]}{0.015}$$

$$A_n \doteq \$13{,}617.02$$

Adding the present value of the payments to the down payment gives us the value, today, of the installment plan, that is:

$$\$1{,}000 + \$13{,}617.02 = \$14{,}617.02$$

Comparing the two options, clearly, the cash purchase is substantially better, namely:

$$\$14{,}617.02 - \$10{,}500 = \$4{,}117.02$$

The thing to remember is that you would choose the option that has the lowest present value since you are making the payment (i.e., it's out of your pocket).

Calculator Solution

						Purchase Cost
	Option 1: $1,000 Down Plus Monthly Payments of $400					
Input	400	1.5	48			
Depress	PMT	i	n	COMP	PV	13,617.02
						+
					Down Payment	1,000.00
					Cash Value of Payment Plan	14,617.02
	Option 2: Cash Payment of $10,500					
					Cash Price Offered	10,500.00
					Savings by Paying Cash	4,117.02

EXAMPLE 8.5

What should be the cash price of a car that can be purchased for $500 down and 48 monthly payments of $350, if the interest rate is 24% compounded monthly? If you were to purchase the car under the installment plan how much does it cost you?

Solution To find the purchase price we must calculate the present value of the payments and add this to the down payment of $500. Therefore:

$$A_n = \frac{R[1 - (1 + i)^{-n}]}{i}$$

$$R = \$350$$

$$i = \frac{0.24}{12}, \text{ or } 0.02$$

$$n = 48$$

Substituting:

$$A_n = \frac{\$350[1 - (1 + 0.02)^{-48}]}{0.02}$$

$$A_n \doteq \$10{,}735.59$$

Therefore, the purchase price of the automobile today should be no more than:

$$\$500 + \$10{,}735.59 = \$11{,}235.59$$

To calculate the cost of the installment plan we must compare the cost of the installment payments, plus the down payment, with the present value price of $11,235.59. To undertake this calculation we must first calculate the cost of the payments over the 48 months, or:

$$48 \times \$350 = \$16{,}800$$

To compute the actual cost of the installment plan we would subtract the purchase price today, \$11,235.59, from the total cost of the car using payments, i.e.,

(Payments	+ Down Payment)	− (Cash Price)	=	Interest Cost
\$500	+ \$16,800	− \$11,235.59	=	\$6,064.41

You might be quite surprised at this difference but it is based on a real life example! This is one reason it is important that people be able to work out the cost of an installment plan, since many plans represent an enormous interest cost.

Calculator Solution

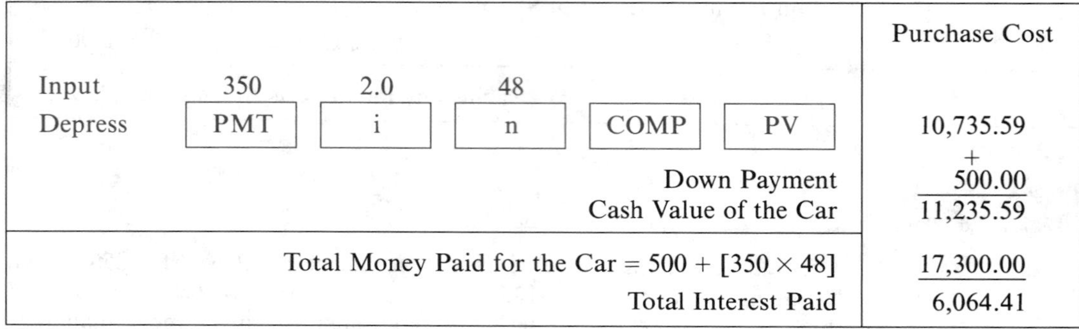

						Purchase Cost
Input	350	2.0	48			
Depress	PMT	i	n	COMP	PV	10,735.59
						+
					Down Payment	500.00
					Cash Value of the Car	11,235.59
					Total Money Paid for the Car = 500 + [350 × 48]	17,300.00
					Total Interest Paid	6,064.41

The time diagram for this example looks as follows:

Figure 8.3

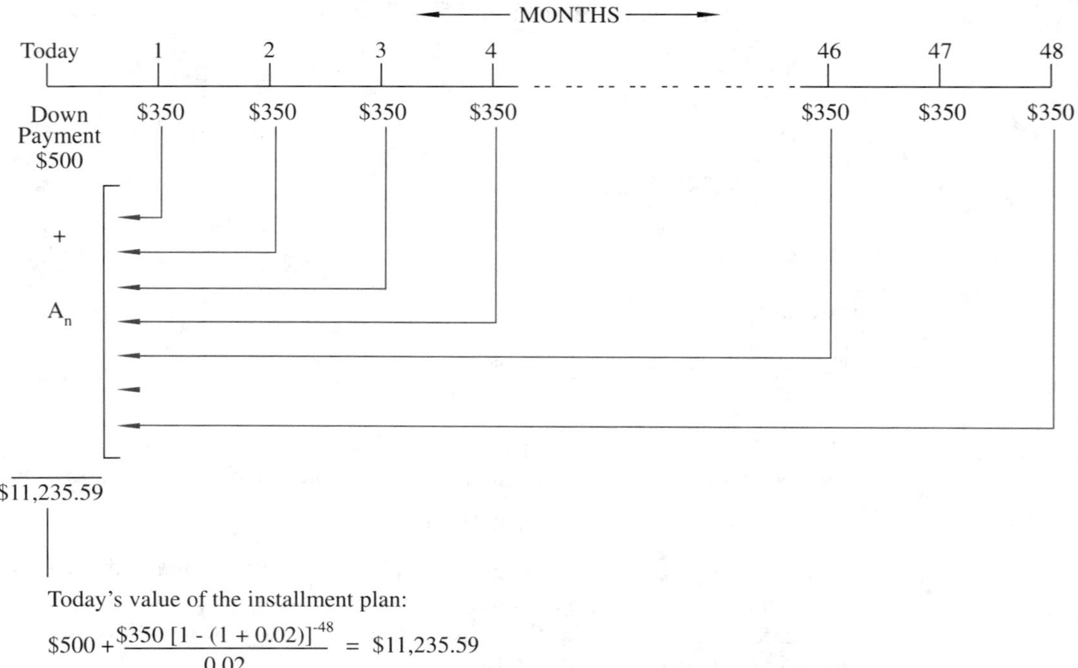

EXAMPLE 8.6

A house sells for \$15,000 cash plus monthly payments (excluding taxes) of \$750 for twenty-five years. If the interest rate being charged is 10% compounded monthly, what would have been the equivalent cash price for the house?

Solution To solve this problem, we must compute the present value of the monthly payments and add this to the down payment. Therefore:

$$A_n = \frac{R[1 - (1 + i)^{-n}]}{i}$$

Where:

$$R = \$750$$

$$i = \frac{0.1}{12}, \text{ or } 0.008333\dot{3}$$

$$n = 25 \times 12, \text{ or } 300$$

Therefore:

$$A_n = \frac{\$750\left[1 - \left(1 + \frac{0.1}{12}\right)^{-300}\right]}{\frac{0.1}{12}}$$

$$A_n \doteq \$82{,}535.42$$

Thus, the purchase price must have been:

\$15,000 + \$82,535.42 = \$97,535.42

Just before leaving this problem, can you calculate the financing cost of the house if you made all the 300 payments?

The solution requires us to compare the cash price with the total value of the payments. The value of the monthly payments is \$750 × 300 = \$225,000. Now subtract the actual amount financed, \$82,535.42, which gives \$142,464.58, the amount of interest paid! (Remember that there was a down payment of \$15,000, applied to the purchase price of \$97,535.42, which left an amount outstanding of \$82,535.42.)

Calculator Solution

						Purchase Cost
Input	750	0.83333	300			
Depress	PMT	i	n	COMP	PV	82,535.42
						+
					Down Payment	15,000.00
					Cash Value of Payment Plan	97,535.42
					Total Value of Payments = 750 × 300	225,000.00
					Subtract Amount Borrowed	82,535.42
					Total Interest Paid	142,464.58

EXAMPLE 8.7

Nexus Printing Ltd. is contemplating purchasing a new high speed photocopier. The company who is selling the equipment offers two options to Nexus. The first option is an outright purchase for \$250,000. There is an annual service contract that is necessary and costs \$2,500 at the end of every six months. The machine is expected to have a useful life to Nexus of five years and would then be sold for an estimated scrap value of \$24,500. The second option is to lease the equipment for \$32,000 every six months, plus pay a service contract of \$2,000, also every six months (the service cost is \$500 less per six months when leased). If money is worth 13% compounded semiannually, which is the best deal for the company? (Forget depreciation and the tax implications; as well, assume that the lease payments come at the end of each period.)

Solution First we compute the cost, in today's dollars, of the purchase decision. This is done by computing the present value of the purchase decision:

A. Present value of the purchase decision:

Present value of the machine = \$250,000

Present value of the service contract:

$$R = \$2{,}500$$

$$n = 2 \times 5 \text{ or } 10$$

$$i = \frac{0.13}{2}, \text{ or } 0.065$$

$$A_n = \frac{R[1 - (1 + i)^{-n}]}{i}$$

$$A_n = \frac{\$2{,}500[1 - (1 + 0.065)^{-10}]}{0.065}$$

$$A_n \doteq \$17{,}972.08$$

Present value of scrap value using $P = S(1 + i)^{-n}$:

$$\$24{,}500(1 + 0.065)^{-10} \doteq \$13{,}051.79$$

Bringing everything together, the present value of the purchase is:

Purchase Cost + Present Value of Service Contract − Present Value of Scrap Value

or:

$$\$250{,}000 + \$17{,}972.08 - \$13{,}051.79 = \$254{,}920.29$$

Thus, the cost in today's dollars of purchasing the equipment is $254,920.29. *Note:* The reason the scrap value is subtracted is that it has the effect of reducing the cost, since when sold for scrap the firm gets the proceeds of the sale.

Calculator Solution

Purchase Cost of the Machine Today						250,000.00
Present Value of the Service Contract						
Input	2,500	6.5	10			
Depress	PMT	i	n	COMP	PV	17,972.08
				Cost Without Scrap Value		267,972.08
Present Value of the Scrap Value						
Input	24,500	6.5	10			
Depress	FV	i	n	COMP	PV	13,051.79
				Cost of the Machine Less Scrap Value		254,920.29

Now turn to the lease cost.

B. Present value of the lease decision.

The present value of the lease contract is simply the present value of lease payments, where:

$R = \$32{,}000$

$n = 2 \times 5$, or 10

$i = \dfrac{0.13}{2}$, or 0.065

$$A_n = \frac{R[1 - (1 + i)^{-n}]}{i}$$

$$A_n = \frac{\$32{,}000[1 - (1 + 0.065)^{-10}]}{0.065}$$

$$A_n \doteq \$230{,}042.57$$

Present value of the service contract:

$R = \$2{,}000$

$n = 2 \times 5$, or 10

$i = \frac{0.13}{2}$, or 0.065

$$A_n = \frac{R[1 - (1 + i)^{-n}]}{i}$$

$$A_n = \frac{\$2{,}000[1 - (1 + 0.065)^{-10}]}{0.065}$$

$$A_n \doteq \$14{,}377.66$$

Therefore the present value (today's cost) of leasing is:

Present Value of Lease Payments	+	Present Value of the Service Contract

$230,042.57 + $14,377.66 = $244,420.23

Therefore, we can conclude that, based on our calculation, leasing at a present value of $244,420.23 is less than the present value of the purchase at $254,920.29. Thus leasing is the least costly with a saving of $10,500.06.

Calculator Solution

	Present Value of the Lease Payments					
Input	32,000	6.5	10			
Depress	PMT	i	n	COMP	PV	230,042.57
				Today's Value of the Lease Payments		230,042.57
	Present Value of the Service Contract					
Input	2,000	6.5	10			
Depress	PMT	i	n	COMP	PV	14,377.66
				Total Cost of the Lease Contract		244,420.23

EXERCISE 8.2

(Assume all annuities are ordinary annuities.)

1. Joanne is faced with two options in the purchase of a television. Al's Electronics offers the type of television she wants at \$100 down and twelve monthly payments of \$100. Ace Stereo is offering the same television at \$125 down and monthly payments of \$50 over two years. If both firms charge 18% compounded monthly, which is the best deal for Joanne?
2. What is the cash value of a piece of real estate that can be purchased for \$12,000 down and monthly payments of \$750 for five years? Assume money is worth 14% compounded monthly.
3. What is the interest (in dollars) collected from Al's and Ace's customers in problem 1 on the purchase of the television being considered by Joanne?
4. Remax Ltd. is going to purchase some new computer equipment. The new equipment is expected to save \$3,500 per month for the next six months because of increased efficiency. After the next six months there are no further savings. The computer has a useful life to Remax of two years. After two years the computer can be sold for \$2,500. If money is worth 15% compounded monthly to Remax, what is the maximum price that Remax should pay, today, for the computer system? (*Hint:* Find the present value of all future payments to Remax — don't forget, the sale of the computer is also a payment.)
5. A computer store offers a deal on a new micro computer. The store offers to sell the computer for \$200 down and monthly payments of \$100 for two years. If the bank charges 16% compounded monthly on loans, what should the cash price be for the computer?
6. A house is sold for \$40,000 cash and monthly payments of \$850 per month for twenty years. What is the cash price for the house if the interest rate on the loan is 10% compounded monthly?
7. In problem 6 calculate the interest cost of the mortgage if all the payments are made over the twenty year period.
8. John and Nancy are considering expanding their company with the purchase of some new equipment. The first type of equipment is expected to save \$1,000 per month for the next three years and can be sold for a scrap value of \$5,000 in three years. Another piece of equipment they are considering will save them \$1,500 per month for twelve months and has no expected scrap value. If money is worth 14.5% compounded monthly, and the cost of Machine 1 is \$32,000 and the cost of Machine 2 is \$14,500, which purchase is the least cost?

8.4 Finding the Size of the Payment (R) for an Ordinary Simple Annuity

A. Finding R When the Amount Is Known

Often we wish to find the value of each periodic payment when a future amount is already known. For example, suppose a young couple decides to set aside money each month to accumulate the down payment on a house. If they need $10,000 for the down payment, how much would they have to set aside each month for two years? If we know the interest rate it is possible to work backwards from our amount formula for an annuity to find the payment. Let's assume this young couple can earn 8% compounded monthly on their money.

To solve this problem we need to develop a new formula from Formula 8.1 to find R, the payment. Beginning with Formula 8.1,

$$S_n = \frac{R[(1+i)^n - 1]}{i}$$

we must rearrange this expression to isolate R. The easiest way is to divide both sides of the equation by

$$\frac{[(1+i)^n - 1]}{i}$$

which will leave R by itself on the right hand side of the equation. Thus:

$$\frac{S_n}{\frac{[(1+i)^n - 1]}{i}} = R$$

Switching the two sides gives:

$$R = \frac{S_n}{\frac{[(1+i)^n - 1]}{i}}$$ **Formula 8.3**

The most difficult part of the formula is sorting out the brackets.

Returning to the problem facing the young couple, let's see how this new formula makes our task simple. First we must identify the values of the known in our expression:

$R =$ Unknown monthly payment.

$i = \frac{0.08}{12}$

$n = 24$ The monthly payments for two years.

$S_n = \$10{,}000$ The amount they wish to have in two years.

Making the substitutions into Formula 8.3 we get:

$$R = \frac{\$10{,}000}{\dfrac{\left[\left(1 + \dfrac{0.08}{12}\right)^{24} - 1\right]}{\dfrac{0.08}{12}}}$$

$$R \doteq \frac{\$10{,}000}{25.93318973}$$

$$\doteq \$385.61$$

Thus, if this couple makes monthly deposits of \$385.61 into an account that earns 8% compounded monthly, they will have accumulated \$10,000 through interest and payments at the end of two years.

You may find that the payment will differ by a couple of cents depending on which calculator you use.

EXAMPLE 8.8

John Zilky is thinking about retiring in five years. He would like to have \$50,000 in an account upon retirement. If he decides to make monthly deposits in his local credit union where he can earn 8.5% compounded monthly, what would be the required monthly deposit to accumulate \$50,000 in five years?

Solution To solve this problem we need only apply Formula 8.3, after determining the values for each term in the formula. These are:

$R =$ unknown

$i = \dfrac{0.085}{12}$, or $0.0070833\dot{3}$

$n = 5 \times 12$, or 60 The number of payments over five years.

$S_n = \$50{,}000$

Substituting into our formula yields:

$$R = \frac{\$50{,}000}{\dfrac{\left[\left((1 + \dfrac{0.085}{12}\right)^{60} - 1\right]}{\dfrac{0.085}{12}}}$$

$$R \doteq \frac{\$50{,}000}{74.44243734}$$

$$R \doteq \$671.66$$

Therefore, if John makes regular payments of \$671.66 each month he will have \$50,000 in five years, providing the interest rate stays at 8.5% compounded monthly.

Calculator Solution

						Payment
Input	50,000	0.708333	60			
Depress	FV	i	n	COMP	PMT	671.66

EXAMPLE 8.9

A company plans to replace one of its automobiles at the end of four years. The trade-in value is estimated to be \$1,500 in four years and the replacement cost for the new car is expected to be \$16,500. How much would the company have to set aside, semiannually, to have sufficient funds to purchase the new car? Assume the company can earn 10% compounded semiannually.

Solution Based on the information, we know that if the new car will cost \$16,500 and the trade-in value of the old car is \$1,500, then the company will need to have \$16,500 – \$1,500 or \$15,000 in four years. Now we need to assign all the known values to our equation for determining the payment when the amount is known.

$$R = \text{unknown}$$

$$i = \frac{0.10}{2}, \text{ or } 0.05$$

$$n = 2 \times 4, \text{ or } 8$$

$$S_n = \$15{,}000$$

Now substituting into our formula:

$$R = \frac{\$15{,}000}{\frac{[(1 + 0.05)^8 - 1]}{0.05}}$$

$$R \doteq \frac{\$15{,}000}{9.5491089}$$

$$R \doteq \$1{,}570.83$$

Thus, if the company wishes to have sufficient funds to purchase the new automobile in four years it must set aside \$1,570.83 every six months.

Calculator Solution

						Payment
Input	15,000	5	8			
Depress	FV	i	n	COMP	PMT	1,570.83

B. Finding *R* when the Present Value Is Known

The formula for R when the present value is known relies on the initial formula for finding the present value of an ordinary simple annuity. As you may recall the formula was:

$$A_n = \frac{R[1 - (1 + i)^{-n}]}{i}$$

We must rearrange this formula to obtain an expression that will give R directly, given that we know A_n, i, and n. The first step is to divide both sides of the expression by

$$\frac{[1 - (1 + i)^{-n}]}{i}$$

which will leave R on the right hand side of the equation, that is:

$$\frac{A_n}{\frac{[1 - (1 + i)^{-n}]}{i}} = R$$

Rearranging so that R is on the left hand side of the expression gives:

$$R = \frac{A_n}{\frac{[1 - (1 + i)^{-n}]}{i}}$$

Formula 8.4

The best example of finding the payment when the present value is known is a personal loan. When someone borrows money they generally arrange to repay the loan with regular payments.

Two common types of personal loans are mortgages and loans for automobiles. In each case, when we borrow the money the present value of the money borrowed is the amount borrowed. Thus, if the present value, the interest rate, and the number of periods over which the loan will be repaid are known, it is a simple matter to work out the size of each payment. Let's see how it works with some specific examples:

EXAMPLE 8.10

Shirley buys a new car and has to borrow \$12,000 to complete the deal. Shirley's bank is happy to advance her the funds. If the interest rate is 18% compounded monthly and she makes monthly payments to repay the loan over 48 months, what would be the size of her monthly payments?

Solution The solution to the problem requires us to use our new Formula, 8.4, that is:

$$R = \frac{A_n}{\frac{[1 - (1 + i)^{-n}]}{i}}$$

First we must assign the values to each term in our expression, therefore:

$$R = \text{unknown}$$

$$i = \frac{0.18}{12}, \text{ or } 0.015$$

$$n = 12 \times 4, \text{ or } 48 \qquad \text{Four years.}$$

$$A_n = \$12{,}000$$

The last term, A_n, is the most important part. The reason the loan is treated as a present value is that the money borrowed today has a value of \$12,000, today, which is simply another way of looking at present value.

Now substituting into our formula:

$$R = \frac{\$12{,}000}{\frac{[1 - (1 + 0.015)^{-48}]}{0.015}}$$

$$R \doteq \frac{\$12{,}000}{34.04255365}$$

$$\doteq \$352.50$$

Thus, if monthly payments of \$352.50 are made at the end of each month the loan of \$12,000 will be paid off in 48 months.

Calculator Solution

						Payment
Input	12,000	1.5	48			
Depress	PV	i	n	COMP	PMT	352.50

EXAMPLE 8.11

Janice and Ed Franklin decide to purchase a house. They have found a three bedroom colonial that is going to cost $110,000, which they think is an excellent price. If the couple decides to put $25,000 down and mortgage the remainder at 10% compounded monthly over twenty-five years, what would be their monthly payment?

Solution If they put $25,000 down then the amount mortgaged would be $85,000. In terms of our formula we have:

$R =$ unknown monthly payment

$i = \frac{0.10}{12}$, or $0.008333\dot{3}$

$n = 12 \times 25$, or 300 — There will be 300 payments over the 25 year period.

$A_n = \$85{,}000$ — The present value of the loan.

Now substituting into the formula:

$$R = \frac{A_n}{\frac{[1 - (1+i)^{-n}]}{i}}$$

$$R = \frac{\$85{,}000}{\frac{\left[1 - \left(1 + \frac{0.10}{12}\right)^{-300}\right]}{\frac{0.10}{12}}}$$

$$R \doteq \frac{\$85{,}000}{110.0472301}$$

$$R \doteq \$772.40$$

Janice and Ed must make monthly payments of $772.39 over the twenty-five year period to repay the mortgage.

Calculator Solution

						Payment
Input	85,000	0.83333	300			
Depress	PV	i	n	COMP	PMT	772.40

EXERCISE 8.3

(Assume all annuities are ordinary annuities.)

For problems 1 to 10 find the required payments for the given amount and present value for each ordinary annuity.

	Payment Period	Present Value (A_n)	Amount (S_n)	Term of the Annuity	Interest Rate and Conversion Period
1.	Annually	$ 2,450	$ 3,345	4 years	11.4%, annually
2.	Quarterly	23,450	15,500	16 years	15.0%, quarterly
3.	Monthly	34,400	34,400	15 years	14.0%, monthly
4.	Annually	8,450	12,340	2 years	18.8%, annually
5.	Semiannually	89,500	90,000	18 years	13.0%, semiannually
6.	Monthly	85,000	89,000	10 years	18.0%, monthly
7.	Quarterly	4,500	10,000	2 years	13.8%, quarterly
8.	Yearly	12,500	15,000	4 years	21.0%, yearly
9.	Quarterly	1,450	3,450	7 years	16.5%, quarterly
10.	Monthly	31,425	25,500	8 years	15.7%, monthly

11. A couple wants to have sufficient money in an account to pay for their son's college education in fifteen years. If the couple can earn 9% compounded semiannually on their savings, what would be the semiannual payment to their savings account to have $20,000 available for the child's education?

12. Jerry signed a contract requiring a down payment of $2,000 and monthly payments of $250 for the next six years. If he missed the first ten payments, what payment at the end of month eleven would bring him up to date with his loan if the interest rate is 18% compounded monthly?

13. What is the value of the loan Jerry is repaying in problem 12?

14. A person has bought a car for $11,000 with $900 down and the balance financed over three years. If the interest rate charged is 18% compounded monthly, what would be the required monthly payment?

15. What will be the gross interest cost for the money financed in problem 14?

16. Joan has just bought a new house for $5,000 down and has arranged a $75,000 mortgage for the balance of the purchase price. The mortgage is to be repaid over 25 years with monthly payments and an interest rate of 11.5% compounded monthly. Find the size of the monthly payments. If she had decided on a 15 year mortgage instead of the 25 year mortgage, also with monthly payments and the same interest rate, what would be the necessary monthly payment over the 15 year period? How much interest would be saved by paying the mortgage off over the 15 year period rather than the 25 year period?

8.5 Finding the Term (Number of Payments), *n*, for an Ordinary Simple Annuity

Finding the term of an ordinary annuity is a little more awkward since, as with compound interest, the procedure to find the value of n requires us to use logarithms. The formulas for finding the amount and present value are:

$$S_n = \frac{R[(1+i)^n - 1]}{i} \quad \text{finding the amount}$$

and

$$A_n = \frac{R[1-(1+i)^{-n}]}{i} \quad \text{finding the present value.}$$

You will note that in each formula n is an exponent. Isolating an exponent requires us to use logarithms. It's not essential to understand how logarithms work — if you are interested, look in Chapter 4 for the explanation of logarithms. What you must understand is how to use the **log** or **ln** functions on your calculator.

The two sections following show you how to find n when you know all the other parts of the formula. The importance of this calculation can be seen when we discuss how a person can save a great deal of money by increasing a monthly mortgage payment by a few dollars.

A. Finding the Term, *n*, when the Amount Is Known

To find the value of n when the amounts R and i are known requires us to rearrange Formula 8.1 to isolate n. After a little algebra and the use of logarithms the expression to find n when Sn is known is:

$$n = \frac{\ln\left[1 + \frac{S_n i}{R}\right]}{\ln(1+i)} \qquad \textbf{Formula 8.5}$$

If you would like to examine the steps involved in deriving this formula please review Chapter 4's section on the rules of logarithms. (See Example 4.22.)

To see the use of this formula let's consider some examples:

EXAMPLE 8.12

If \$100 is deposited at the end of each month into an account that pays 5% compounded monthly, how long will it take to accumulate \$5,000?

Solution The first thing that should be recognized is whether we have knowledge of the future value (amount) or the present value of an annuity. In this problem we are aware of the future value since we are advised that we want to have an <u>accumulated value</u> of \$5,000, at some point in the future.

Turning to our formula, to find the value of n for a known amount we have:

$$n = \frac{\ln\left[1 + \frac{S_n i}{R}\right]}{\ln(1 + i)}$$

Now outlining the values we know from the problem:

$$R = \$100$$

$$i = \frac{0.05}{12}$$

$$S_n = \$5{,}000$$

Substituting into our formula gives:

$$n = \frac{\ln\left[1 + \frac{5{,}000\left(\frac{0.05}{12}\right)}{100}\right]}{\ln(1 + \frac{0.05}{12})}$$

$$n \doteq \frac{\ln[1 + 0.208333]}{\ln(1.00416666)}$$

$$n = 45.5126$$

Approximately 46 payments, where the 46th payment will be slightly less than the other payments.

Therefore, the length of time to accumulate the sum is:

$$\frac{45.5126}{12}\text{, or 3.79 years}$$

Approximately 3 years, 9 months, and 14 days, i.e., $0.79 \times 12 = 9.48$ months, $0.48 \times 30 = 14.4$ days.

Thus, if 46 payments are made with the first 45 at \$100 and the 46th being slightly less, there will be \$5,000 in the account. In a later section we will show you how to calculate the actual value of the 46th payment.

Calculator Solution Note the inclusion of the negative sign in front of the payment. If this is not done on EL-733 an error message will be given. Also, you will find that the answer does not appear on the display immediately since it takes about five seconds to do the calculations.

							Number of Payments
Input	5,000	0.41666	100				
Depress	FV	i	+/−	PMT	COMP	n	45.5126

EXAMPLE 8.13

If \$200 is deposited at the end of each quarter, how many years will it take to amount to \$12,000 if the interest rate is 16% compounded quarterly?

Solution As in the previous example we are looking to accumulate a specific amount. Thus, we would use the formula:

$$n = \frac{\ln\left[1 + \frac{S_n i}{R}\right]}{\ln(1 + i)}$$

Now, defining the known:

$$R = \$200$$

$$i = \frac{0.16}{4} = 0.04$$

$$S_n = \$12{,}000$$

Substituting into our formula yields:

$$n = \frac{\ln\left[1 + \frac{\$12{,}000(0.04)}{\$200}\right]}{\ln(1 + 0.04)}$$

$$n = \frac{\ln[3.4]}{\ln(1.04)}$$

$n = 31.20227$ quarters

Thus, to find the number of years divide by four (four quarters per year) to get 7.8 years.

Therefore, if the deposits are made every quarter for 31.20227 quarters or 7.8 years there will be \$12,000 in the account.

Calculator Solution

							Number of Payments
Input	12,000	4	200				
Depress	FV	i	+/−	PMT	COMP	n	31.20227

B. Finding the Term, *n*, when the Present Value Is Known

The procedure for finding n when the present value is known is very similar to finding n when the amount is known. The most significant difference is the use of a negative sign in the formula to follow. Unfortunately, solving for a negative exponent involves the use of negative signs, so please look carefully at the formula to see how these signs must be used to obtain the desired result. If you wish to study the algebra involved please review Chapter 4.

To find n when we know R, i, and A_n we will use the formula:

$$n = \frac{-\ln\left[1 - \frac{A_n i}{R}\right]}{\ln(1+i)}$$ **Formula 8.6**

Please note the negative signs. In particular, the negative sign in the front of the expression must be used since the remainder of the formula will give you a negative answer. The combination of the two negatives makes your final value for n a positive number.

EXAMPLE 8.14

Roger and Susan are negotiating a mortgage on a new home. They have decided that the maximum mortgage payment they can afford is \$850 a month. If the interest rate is 10% compounded monthly and the size of the mortgage is \$74,000, how many years will it take them to pay off the mortgage?

Solution To answer this question we are first going to find how many monthly payments of \$850 it will take to repay the mortgage. Once we have the number of monthly payments we will then convert this into years by dividing n by 12, since there are twelve months in each year.

The first step in our solution is to make sure we lay out what we know. Based on the information, we know:

$$R = \$850$$

$$i = \frac{0.10}{12}, \text{ or } 0.008333\dot{3}$$

$$A_n = \$74{,}000$$

Substituting into the Formula 8.6 gives:

$$n = \frac{-\ln\left[1 - \frac{\$74{,}000\left(\frac{0.10}{12}\right)}{\$850}\right]}{\ln\left(1 + \frac{0.10}{12}\right)}$$

$$n \doteq \frac{-[-1.2927672]}{(0.0082988)}$$

$$n \doteq -[-155.7776]$$

$$n \doteq 155.78 \text{ months, or } \left(\frac{155.78}{12}\right), \text{ or } 12.9815 \text{ years}$$

Therefore, the number of years required to repay a $74,000 mortgage is approximately thirteen years, and requires 156 payments. The first 155 payments will be $850 and the last payment will be a smaller payment, under the condition that the interest rate is 10% compounded monthly. A later section of the text explains how to find the value of the different last payment.

Calculator Solution

							Number of Payments
Input	74,000	0.83333	850				
Depress	PV	i	+/−	PMT	COMP	n	155.7776

EXAMPLE 8.15

A friend is contemplating buying a sailboat. He has been pricing a boat that will require him to finance $25,000 of the purchase price. Your friend can afford to spend $400 for monthly payments. If the interest rate is 18% compounded monthly, how long will it take to pay for the sailboat?

Solution As with the example above, the problem requires us to substitute values for the terms in Formula 8.6. The values are:

$$R = \$400$$

$$i = \frac{0.18}{12}, \text{ or } 0.015$$

$$A_n = \$25{,}000$$

Using Formula 8.6 and making the substitutions, we have:

$$n = \frac{-\ln\left[1 - \frac{\$25{,}000(0.015)}{\$400}\right]}{\ln(1 + 0.015)}$$

$$n \doteq \frac{-[-2.7725887]}{(0.01488861)}$$

$$n \doteq 186.222$$

Converting this to years gives:

$$n \doteq \frac{186.222}{12}$$

$$= 15.52 \text{ years}$$

Thus, there would be 187 payments, 186 of size $400 and a final, 187th smaller payment. A later section shows how to compute the value of the smaller last payment.

Calculator Solution

							Number of Payments
Input	25,000	1.5	400				
Depress	PV	i	+/−	PMT	COMP	n	186.2221

EXERCISE 8.4

(Assume all annuities are ordinary annuities.)

For each of the following ordinary annuities find the number of payments (the term) for the given amount and present value.

	Payment Period	Present Value (A_n)	Amount (S_n)	Payment per period R	Interest Rate and Conversion Period
1.	Annually	$ 2,450	$ 3,345	$ 500.00	11.4%, annually
2.	Quarterly	23,450	15,500	3,000.00	15.0%, quarterly
3.	Monthly	34,400	34,400	1,350.00	14.0%, monthly
4.	Annually	8,450	12,340	2,500.00	18.8%, annually
5.	Semiannually	45,500	90,000	4,500.00	13.0%, semiannually
6.	Monthly	85,000	89,000	1,950.00	18.0%, monthly
7.	Quarterly	4,500	10,000	200.00	13.8%, quarterly
8.	Yearly	2,800	15,000	650.00	21.0%, yearly
9.	Quarterly	550	3,450	50.00	16.5%, quarterly
10.	Monthly	31,425	25,500	450.00	15.7%, monthly

11. Bob is thinking about retiring and would like to do it at the earliest possible date. He has concluded that he must have an additional $60,000 in savings over what he currently has put aside. If Bob can set aside $1,000 a month, how long will it be before he retires? Assume he can earn 8% on his money compounded monthly.

12. The City of Colwood has determined that it must have $2,000,000 in reserve funds. Based on current tax revenue the city has calculated that it can set aside $125,000 every quarter. If the city can earn 6% compounded quarterly, how long will it take to accumulate the desired reserve funds?

13. A family has just purchased a new house and negotiated a mortgage for $85,000. They have been advised that the mortgage can be paid off over 25 years using monthly payments. To their surprise, the monthly payment necessary to repay the mortgage over the twenty-five year period is $100 a month less than they wish to pay. If the mortgage rate is 12% compounded monthly, how long will it take them to pay off the mortgage by making payments $100 higher than the payment necessary to repay the loan over a twenty-five year period? (*Hint:* First find R for the twenty-five year mortgage.)

14. Joan has just bought a new car and has arranged monthly payments of $500. If the loan is $15,000, at an interest rate of 13% compounded monthly, how many monthly payments will she need to make?

8.6 Finding the Outstanding Balance of a Loan, the Balance in a Fund, and the Value of the Last Payment

As we saw in the previous section, when we calculate the term of an annuity, or n, we often find that the number of payments does not work out to be an even number. In Example 8.15, we found that your friend needed to make 186.222 payments. In the real world the actual number of payments would be 187. When this occurs the value of the final payment will be different from the other payments. In this section we will show you how to compute the value of the last payment.

To find the value of the last payment we must know how to find the outstanding balance or the accumulated amount at any time during the term of an annuity. To get started, let's see how we can find out how much of the loan we've paid off or how much we've accumulated in an account before the end of the term of the annuity.

A. Finding the Outstanding Balance or the Accumulated Sum of an Annuity

How often have you heard someone talking about how much they have remaining to pay on a loan? Perhaps you have wanted to determine how much money you have in a retirement fund at a certain point in time. The method relies on a combination of the techniques you've learned up to this point in the text. Let's look first at finding the balance of a loan.

(i) Finding the Outstanding Balance on a Loan: Using Present Value

The method used to find the outstanding balance on a loan requires us to compute the present value of the remaining payments. For example, if you have a loan that must be paid off with 60 monthly payments and you have just made the 38th payment, to find out how much is still owing immediately upon paying the 38th payment, you would need to calculate the present value of the remaining 22 payments. This will work because the value of the remaining payments — present value — is today's value of the future payments. This "today's value" is the outstanding balance of the loan, that is, today's value of the loan.

Suppose you had been making monthly payments of \$133.47 on a loan of \$6,000 at an interest rate of 12% compounded monthly. On the 38th payment you want to determine the outstanding balance. Since there are 22 payments remaining you would find the present value of these payments using the present value formula for an ordinary simple annuity. That is, using Formula 8.1:

$$A_n = \frac{R[1 - (1 + i)^{-n}]}{i}$$

Where:

$R = \$133.47$

$i = \frac{0.12}{12}$, or 0.01

$n = 22$ The remaining payments.

Substituting into the formula yields:

$$A_n = \frac{\$133.47[1 - (1 + 0.01)^{-22}]}{0.01}$$

$$A_n \doteq \$2,624.07$$

Thus, the balance of a \$6,000 loan after making 38 monthly payments of size \$133.47 is \$2,624.07.

For all problems requiring us to find the outstanding balance of a loan that has regular payments, we will use the present value approach, although another approach is available and is shown in the next section.

EXAMPLE 8.16

Dianne bought a condominium for \$95,000. She made a down payment of \$10,000 and agreed to make equal payments at the end of each month for twenty years, with interest at 12% compounded monthly. (a) What is the size of each monthly payment? (b) What is the outstanding balance of the mortgage after the 36th payment?

Solution (a) To find the size of each monthly payment we use our formula to find R, namely:

$$R = \frac{A_n}{\frac{[1 - (1 + i)^{-n}]}{i}}$$

Determining the value of each term gives:

$A_n = \$85,000$

$i = \frac{0.12}{12}$, or 0.01

$n = 12 \times 20$, or 240

Substituting into the formula yields:

$$R = \frac{\$85,000}{\frac{[1 - (1 + 0.01)^{-240}]}{0.01}}$$

$$R \doteq \frac{\$85,000}{90.81941635}$$

$$R \doteq \$935.92$$

The regular monthly payments for the twenty year loan will be \$935.92.

(b) To find the outstanding balance after three years or 36 payments we must calculate the present value of the remaining payments. The remaining payments are found by subtracting the payments made from the total number of payments, that is, 240 – 36, or 204. Calculating the present value of the remaining 204 payments will give us the outstanding balance at the third year. Turning to our formula:

$$A_n = \frac{R[1 - (1 + i)^{-n}]}{i}$$

Where:

$R = \$935.92$
$i = 0.01$
$n = 204$

Substituting the values into the formula:

$$A_n = \frac{\$935.92[1 - (1 + 0.01)^{-204}]}{0.01}$$

$$A_n \doteq \$935.92[86.8647075]$$

$$A_n \doteq \$81{,}298.42$$

Believe it or not the balance on Dianne's mortgage is still $81,298.42 after three years of payments. This means that the principal has only been reduced by $85,000 – $81,298.42, or $3,701.58.

Calculator Solution

						Payment
Input	85,000	1	240			
Depress	PV	i	n	COMP	PMT	935.92
Computing the Outstanding Balance of the Loan						
						Loan Still Due
Input	935.92	1	204			
Depress	PMT	i	n	COMP	PV	81,298.42

(ii) Using Future Value to Find the Outstanding Balance for a Loan

A second approach to finding the outstanding balance on a loan uses information on what has occurred, rather than turning to the present value of payments to occur in the future. This second approach uses the accumulation formulas for S and S_n and focuses on the payments that have been made, in addition to the initial amount of the loan. To see how this method works consider Example 8.17:

EXAMPLE 8.17

A loan is to be repaid over 25 years with monthly payments. The size of the loan is \$160,000 and the interest rate is 14% compounded monthly. If monthly payments have been regularly made, how much is outstanding on the loan after three years of payments? Use the accumulation approach to find the outstanding balance.

Solution

STEP 1 First we must find R, the regular payment:

$$R = \frac{A_n}{\frac{[1-(1+i)^{-n}]}{i}}$$

Where:

$$A_n = \$160{,}000$$

$$i = \frac{0.14}{12}, \text{ or } 0.11666\dot{6}$$

$$n = 25 \times 12, \text{ or } 300$$

$$R = \frac{\$160{,}000}{\frac{\left[1-\left(1+\frac{0.14}{12}\right)^{-300}\right]}{\frac{0.14}{12}}}$$

$$R = \$1{,}926.02$$

STEP 2 Using the relation

Outstanding Balance = $S - S_n$

$S = P(1+i)^n$ The amount formula from Chapter 7.

Where:

$$R = \$1{,}926.02$$
$$P = \$160{,}000$$
$$S_n = \$160{,}000$$
$$i = \frac{0.14}{12}, \text{ or } 0.011666\dot{6}$$
$$n = 3 \times 12, \text{ or } 36$$

Note that n is 36, the number of payments that have been made. In the future value approach, n always refers to the number of payments that have been made when finding the outstanding balance.

Substituting everything:

$$\text{Outstanding Balance} = P(1+i)^n - \frac{R[(1+i)^n - 1]}{i}$$

$$\$160{,}000\left(1+\frac{0.14}{12}\right)^{36} - \frac{\$1{,}926.02\left[\left(1+\frac{0.14}{12}\right)^{36} - 1\right]}{\frac{0.14}{12}}$$

$$\text{Outstanding Balance} = \$242{,}922.56 - \$85{,}559.20$$
$$= \$157{,}363.36$$

Thus, the outstanding balance immediately after the 36th payment is \$157,363.36. If you compare this to the answer found by computing the present value of the remaining payments ($n = 264$), you will get the same answer. There may be a slight difference due to rounding.

To make sure you understand how this method works you should redo Example 8.16 using the amount formula.

Calculator Solution

						Payment
Input	160,000	1.16667	300			
Depress	PV	i	n	COMP	PMT	1,926.02
Computing the Outstanding Balance of the Loan						
Input	160,000	1.16667	36			
Depress	PV	i	n	COMP	FV	242,922.56
Input	1,926.02	1.16667	36			
Depress	PMT	i	n	COMP	FV	85,559.20
Subtracting to Find the Outstanding Balance						157,363.36

When you have need to find the outstanding balance, using either the present value or accumulation methods are acceptable. Each method has some advantage on certain types of problems. The choice by the writer to use the present value approach to find an outstanding balance is a personal preference.

(iii) Finding the Accumulated Amount at Any Point in Time

When we make regular payments to a retirement plan or some other fund, it may be necessary to figure out how much has accumulated in the fund at some point in time. The process is quite straight forward since we need only find the sum, S_n, for the number of periods for which payments have been made.

For example, suppose you have been making payments of $100 a month to an RRSP for the last eight years. If the interest rate is 8% compounded monthly, how much is in the fund at the end of eight years? To determine this we simply apply Formula 8.1, that is:

$$S_n = \frac{R[(1+i)^n - 1]}{i}$$

Where:

$$R = \$100$$

$$i = \frac{0.08}{12}$$

$$n = 12 \times 8, \text{ or } 96$$

Substituting into our formula gives:

$$S_n = \frac{\$100\left[\left(1 + \frac{0.08}{12}\right)^{96} - 1\right]}{\frac{0.08}{12}}$$

$$S_n \doteq \$100(133.868583)$$

$$S_n = \$13,386.86$$

Therefore, after eight years of payments you would have accumulated $13,386.86 in the retirement plan.

Calculator Solution

						Amount at Period 96
Input	100	0.66667	96			
Depress	PMT	i	n	COMP	FV	13,386.86

EXAMPLE 8.18

Susan entered into a pension plan requiring quarterly payments of $400 for the next fifteen years. If the fund guarantees her 6% compounded quarterly, how much will she have in the fund after ten years of payments?

Solution The solution to the problem requires us to accumulate the payments made over the ten year period. Our formula will be the amount formula for an annuity, namely:

$$S_n = \frac{R[(1+i)^n - 1]}{i}$$

Where:

$$R = \$400$$

$$i = \frac{0.06}{4}, \text{ or } 0.015$$

$$n = 4 \times 10, \text{ or } 40$$

Now substituting these values into our formula:

$$S_n = \frac{\$400[(1+0.015)^{40} - 1]}{0.015}$$

$$S_n = \$400(54.2678939)$$

$$S_n = \$21{,}707.16$$

After ten years, Susan will have $21,707.16 in her retirement fund.

Calculator Solution

						Amount at Period 40
Input	400	1.5	40			
Depress	PMT	i	n	COMP	FV	21,707.16

B. Finding the Value of the Last Payment

As you may remember, when we found out how to calculate the number of payments we found that the value of n was not an even number. When this occurs we must adjust the annuity payments, resulting in a smaller last payment. To see how this problem can be handled with the tools you've learned so far let's recall an example from Section 8.5:

EXAMPLE 8.19 (from 8.15)

Your friend was required to make 187 payments with the first 186 payments being \$400 and the last payment being different. Now let's see how we can find the exact value of the last payment.

The first step is to determine the outstanding balance at the end of period 186. Then we figure out how much interest will be due on the outstanding balance from period 186 to period 187. This interest plus the outstanding balance from period 186 will be the payment at period 187 that will pay off the debt.

To find the outstanding balance at the end of period 186 we must calculate the present value of the remaining payment. In this problem the remaining payment is a fractional period, or 0.222. Using our present value formula and making the substitutions we have:

$$A_n = \frac{R[1 - (1 + i)^{-n}]}{i}$$

Where:

$$R = \$400$$

$$i = \frac{0.18}{12}, \text{ or } 0.015$$

$$n = 0.222$$

Substituting we get:

$$A_n = \frac{\$400[1 - (1 + 0.015)^{-0.222}]}{0.015}$$

$$A_n \doteq \$400(0.219987705)$$

$$A_n \doteq \$88.00$$

Thus \$88.00 is outstanding at the end of the 186th period. If we figure out how much interest will be due on \$88.00 at the end of the 187th period we need only add this interest to the \$88.00 to find the value of the last payment.

To calculate the interest on the \$88.00 for one period we simply multiply the rate times the outstanding balance for one period.

$$\$88.00 \times 0.015 = \$1.32$$

Therefore, the value of the last payment is:

$$\$88.00 + \$1.32 = \$89.32$$

If your friend makes a payment of \$89.32 at the end of period 187 he will have paid off the entire debt.

Calculator Solution

						Balance
Input	400	1.5	0.222			
Depress	PMT	i	n	COMP	PV	88.00
Computing the Final Payment for the Loan						
					Interest for Last Period 88.00 (0.015)	1.32
					Final Payment at 187	89.32

EXAMPLE 8.20

Bonnie is going to purchase a small duplex. She wants to make monthly payments of $1,200. If the mortgage rate is 12% compounded monthly and the size of the mortgage is $105,000, what will be the value of the final (last) payment for the mortgage?

Solution

STEP 1 The first step in solving this problem is to determine the total number of payments. This can be done by applying our formula for finding n when the present value is known. The formula to find n is:

$$n = \frac{-\ln\left[1 - \frac{A_n i}{R}\right]}{\ln(1 + i)}$$

Where:

$$A_n = \$105{,}000$$

$$R = \$1{,}200$$

$$i = \frac{0.12}{12}, \text{ or } 0.01$$

Substituting into our formula:

$$n = \frac{-\ln\left[1 - \frac{105{,}000(0.01)}{1{,}200}\right]}{\ln(1 + 0.01)}$$

$$n = \frac{-\ln(0.125)}{\ln(1.01)}$$

$$n \doteq 208.98215$$

Since the final payment is very close to the 209th period we can surmise that the last payment will be very close in value to the first 208 payments ($1,200 per payment).

STEP 2 The next step is to find how much will be outstanding at the end of the 208th payment. This balance is found by using the present value method, where the present value is based on the fractional payment remaining of 0.98215. Using our formula:

$$A_n = \frac{R[1 - (1 + i)^{-n}]}{i}$$

Where:

$$R = \$1{,}200$$

$$i = \frac{0.12}{12}, \text{ or } 0.01$$

$$n = 0.98215$$

Substituting we get:

$$A_n = \frac{\$1{,}200[1 - (1 + 0.01)^{-0.98215}]}{0.01}$$

$$A_n = \$1{,}167.01$$

STEP 3 The final step is to compute the interest on the outstanding balance of $1,167.01 for the last period or period 209. Therefore, one period of interest would be:

$$(\$1{,}167.01) \times (0.01) = \$11.67$$

And the value of the final payment is:

$$\$1{,}167.01 + \$11.67 = \$1{,}178.68$$

As we expected, this payment is very close to the other payments made on the loan.

EXAMPLE 8.21

A loan of $6,000 is to be paid off with monthly payments of $1,000. If the interest rate is 12% compounded monthly, what is the value of the final payment?

Solution

STEP 1 The first step in solving this problem is to compute the total number of payments required to repay the debt. Using our formula:

$$n = \frac{-\ln\left[1 - \frac{A_n i}{R}\right]}{\ln(1 + i)}$$

Where:

$$R = \$1{,}000$$

$$i = \frac{0.12}{12}, \text{ or } 0.01$$

$$A_n = \$6{,}000$$

Substituting the values into our formula to find n gives:

$$n = \frac{-\ln\left[1 - \frac{6{,}000(0.01)}{1{,}000}\right]}{\ln(1 + 0.01)}$$

$$n \doteq 6.218427$$

STEP 2 To find the value of the last payment we must now compute the outstanding balance at the end of period six. Once the outstanding balance is computed for period six, this balance is accumulated for one period until the last payment is made in period seven, which is the outstanding balance from period six, plus one period of interest.

The outstanding balance at period six is found by using the formula:

$$A_n = \frac{R[1 - (1 + i)^{-n}]}{i}$$

Where:

$$R = \$1{,}000$$

$$i = 0.01$$

$$n = 0.218427$$

Now substituting into our formula:

$$A_n = \frac{\$1{,}000[1 - (1 + 0.01)^{-0.218427}]}{0.01}$$

$$A_n = \$217.11$$

STEP 3 Calculating the value of the last payment requires us to compute the interest for the last period on the balance outstanding, \$217.11, and add this to \$217.11.

$$\$217.11 \times 0.01 = \$2.17$$

Thus, the final payment is:

$$\$217.11 + \$2.17 = \$219.28$$

Calculator Solution

Finding the Number of Payments							
Input	1,000	1	6,000				
Depress	PMT	i	+/−	PV	COMP	n	6.218427
Computing the Outstanding Balance of the Loan							
Input	1,000	1	0.218427				
Depress	PMT	i	n	COMP	PV		217.11
Computing the Final Payment for the Loan							
						Interest for Last Period 217.11 (0.01)	2.17
						Final Payment	219.28

EXERCISE 8.5

For each of the following loans, find the outstanding balance at the time specified. Remember that the term of the loan refers to the time one may take to repay the loan. Also, assume that all payment periods and interest periods are the same.

	Payment Period	Original Amount of the Loan and Term: Amount	Term	Find the Outstanding Balance Immediately After the:	Interest Rate and Conversion Period
1.	Annually	$24,450	5 years	4th payment	12.0%, annually
2.	Quarterly	45,450	10 years	20th ”	13.5%, quarterly
3.	Monthly	60,400	20 years	150th ”	18.0%, monthly
4.	Annually	108,500	18 years	10th ”	24.0%, annually
5.	Semiannually	50,000	10 years	5th ”	15.6%, semiannually
6.	Monthly	175,000	4 years	36th ”	24.0%, monthly
7.	Quarterly	30,000	2 years	2nd ”	16.0%, quarterly
8.	Yearly	15,500	6 years	3rd ”	21.2%, yearly
9.	Quarterly	16,450	10 years	30th ”	16.8%, quarterly
10.	Monthly	275,000	25 years	180th ”	12.4%, monthly

11. Bill Semenchuk bought a small business for $100,000 and made a down payment of $25,000. The balance is to be repaid by quarterly payments over a ten year period. If the interest rate is 16% compounded quarterly, what would the balance of the loan be after six years?
12. A loan of $45,000 is to be amortized (paid off) over five years with monthly payments. If the interest rate is 10% compounded monthly, what is the outstanding principal at the end of 40 payments?
13. Denise decides that she will save $200 a month in a special savings account. If this account will pay her 8% compounded monthly, how much will she have in the account at the end of four and one-half years?
14. The District of Metchosin has a reserve fund to which it makes annual payments of $500,000 at the end of each year. How much will be in the fund at the end of five and one-half years, if the interest rate is 9.5% compounded annually?
15. Venture Research has just borrowed $75,000 for new computer equipment and has agreed to make monthly payments of $1,000 to repay the loan. What will be the value of the final payment to repay the debt if the interest rate is 13.5% compounded monthly?
16. Bonnie has purchased a piece of property for $70,000 and makes a down payment of $15,000. She has agreed to repay the required loan with semi-annual payments of $6,000. The interest rate on the loan is 12% compounded semiannually. What will be the value of her last payment?

8.7 Finding the Rate of Interest for an Annuity

Up to this point we have not explored finding the interest rate for an annuity. Unlike the annuity methods we have discussed so far, there is some "guessing" involved with calculating the interest rate.

Those of you with financial calculators will find the calculation of i very easy and precise. If you don't have a financial calculator, you must find a procedure that will approximate i for any of the annuities discussed.

To make the process clear we will choose two examples, one involving the amount of an ordinary simple annuity and the other dealing with the present value of an ordinary simple annuity. The important thing to understand is that we can use the identical method for any type of annuity, including those to be examined in the next two chapters.

A. The Approximate Method

To find the interest rate when the amount, payment, and n are known we would begin with the formula:

$$S_n = \frac{R[(1 + i)^n - 1]}{i}$$

Since our goal is to find i we must rearrange the formula to isolate i or:

$$\frac{S_n}{R} = \frac{[(1 + i)^n - 1]}{i}$$

As you can see, the value of i cannot be isolated since there is no way to get i by itself on one side of the expression.

To solve this problem we can closely approximate the value of i by using the procedure outlined in the next example.

EXAMPLE 8.22

The District of Gray River is setting up a reserve fund that will accumulate to $5,000,000 in three years. The payments that the District makes are $345,018 every quarter. If the interest rate compounds every quarter, what is the nominal rate? (Remember, the nominal rate of interest refers to the rate quoted annually, regardless of the number of times the rate may be compounded.)

Solution The first thing we do is to set the equation up with the known values. These are:

$$S_n = \$5{,}000{,}000$$

$$n = 4 \times 3, \text{ or } 12$$

$$R = \$345{,}018$$

Now substituting these into our formula for S_n we have:

$$S_n = \frac{R[(1 + i)^n - 1]}{i}$$

or:

$$\frac{S_n}{R} = \frac{[(1 + i)^n - 1]}{i}$$

$$\frac{\$5{,}000{,}000}{\$345{,}018} = \frac{[(1 + i)^{12} - 1]}{i}$$

$$14.491998 = \frac{[(1 + i)^{12} - 1]}{i}$$

The approach we now have to take is to "guess" at a value of i such that the value of $\frac{[(1 + i)^{12} - 1]}{i}$, from the right hand side of the equation above, comes out to be 14.492020, the value of the left hand side of the equation.

GUESS 1 One approach to guessing is to assume an annual rate of 12%. In this problem 12% would yield a rate of 3% each quarter. The reason 12% per year was selected was to provide a reference point. From the initial value, one knows whether to increase or decrease the rate in the second guess — it's not scientific, but rather, an arbitrary reference point. In this case, we let i be 3% $\left(\frac{12\%}{4}\right)$ to see whether the rate needs to be increased or decreased on the second guess.

Substituting the value of $i = 0.03$ into $\frac{[(1+i)^{12}-1]}{i}$ yields:

$$\frac{[(1+0.03)^{12}-1]}{0.03} \doteq 14.192030$$

Thus, 0.03 is too low so let's try another guess using the information from our last attempt. It would appear that if i increases then the expression $\frac{[(1+i)^{12}-1]}{i}$ will also rise.

Continuing our guessing, the next value we might choose is 3.5% since we need only increase the value of i slightly to reach 14.491998.

GUESS 2 Let i be 3.5%. Substituting we get:

$$\frac{[(1+0.035)^{12}-1]}{0.035} \doteq 14.601962$$

As you can see we are very close to the value we are seeking. Our third guess will be just slightly less than the 3.5% we've just tried.

GUESS 3 Let i be 3.25%. Substituting into our expression yields:

$$\frac{[(1+0.0325)^{12}-1]}{0.0325} \doteq 14.395285$$

FINAL SOLUTION We can see that we have gone a little bit too far with $i = 0.0325$. However, note that the value of $\left(\frac{S_n}{R}\right)$, 14.491998, is about half way between the two values for i, 3.5% and 3.25%. Since the value we want is approximately between the two we can try 3.375%, which is exactly half way. This gives:

$$\frac{[(1+0.03375)^{12}-1]}{0.03375} \doteq 14.498192$$

As we can see this value is still slightly too high, but it can be clearly concluded that the interest rate each quarter is somewhere between 3.25% and 3.375%.

If you have a financial calculator you will find that the exact interest rate is 3.367505% per quarter.

As a result, we would say that the final answer is in a range of values, namely:

$$3.25\% < i < 3.375\%$$

The nominal rate of interest is therefore somewhere between 13% and 13.5% compounded quarterly. The nominal rate was found by: 3.25% × 4 (quarters) and 3.375% × 4 (quarters). Based on our calculations, the interest rate is closer to 13.5% compounded quarterly.

Calculator Solution

Input	345,018	5,000,000		12			
Depress	PMT	+/−	FV	n	COMP	i	3.3675045%
The nominal rate (compounded quarterly) is 3.3675045 × 4							13.47%

You may be surprised that we're not as precise as we have been in the other sections on annuities. However, with the availability of financial calculators, it is only necessary to be within a range for interest rates since technology can help us be more precise.

Remember, i refers to the rate per conversion period. To find the annual or nominal rate we must multiply i by the number of conversion periods per year. Let's consider an example involving the present value of an annuity:

EXAMPLE 8.23

Bill and Eva have just bought a house from a vendor who offered to carry the financing (this means the current owner is owed money after the sale). The purchase price of the house was $125,000; they paid a $30,000 down payment and the vendor agreed to carry a mortgage with monthly payments of $947.21 for 25 years. What is the nominal rate of interest, compounded monthly, the vendor is charging?

Solution This problem deals with a known present value. The previous example dealt with a known future amount.

To solve the problem, set up an expression that allows us to substitute various values of i to approximate the correct value of i.

Remember that the formula for finding the present value of an ordinary simple annuity is:

$$A_n = \frac{R[(1-(1+i)^{-n}]}{i}$$

Rearranging this expression we have:

$$\frac{A_n}{R} = \frac{[1-(1+i)^{-n}]}{i}$$

Where:

$$A_n = \$95{,}000$$
$$R = \$947.21$$
$$n = 12 \times 25, \text{ or } 300$$

Now making the substitutions:

$$\frac{A_n}{R} = \frac{[1-(1+i)^{-n}]}{i}$$

$$\frac{\$95{,}000}{\$947.21} = \frac{[1-(1+i)^{-300}]}{i}$$

$$100.294549 = \frac{[1-(1+i)^{-300}]}{i}$$

GUESS 1 Use a guess of 12% compounded monthly. Therefore, substituting $i = \frac{0.12}{12}$, or 0.01 gives:

$$\frac{[1-(1+0.01)^{-300}]}{0.01} = 94.946551$$

This value is too low, so reduce the value of i. The negative exponent, $-n$, means that as $\boldsymbol{i}$ declines the value of $\frac{[1-(1+i)^{-n}]}{i}$ increases.

GUESS 2 Now we will drop to 11% compounded monthly, or:

$$i = \frac{0.11}{12}$$

which gives:

$$\frac{\left[1-\left(1+\frac{0.11}{12}\right)^{-300}\right]}{\frac{0.11}{12}} \doteq 102.029044$$

This guess provides a value that is slightly too high.

GUESS 3 Since the value of $\frac{[1-(1+i)^{-n}]}{i}$ decreases as i increases, try an i that is slightly higher than 11%. A possible next guess would be 11.25% ($i = \frac{0.1125}{12}$ or 0.009375), which gives:

$$\frac{[1-(1+0.009375)^{-300}]}{0.009375} \doteq 100.176356$$

FINAL SOLUTION Based on our guesses, the annual nominal rate of interest is somewhere between 11% and 11.25% compounded monthly, or

$$11\% < \text{nominal rate} < 11.25\%$$

Calculator Solution

Input	947.21	95,000		300			
Depress	PMT	+/−	PV	n	COMP	i	0.936151%
The nominal rate (compounded monthly) is 0.936151 × 12							= 11.234%

B. Finding the Interest Rate by Interpolation

There may be an occasion where one needs to compute a precise measure of the interest rate for an annuity, and no financial calculator is available. This can be accomplished by the method of interpolation, sometimes called the method of averages.

Interpolation requires some initial guessing to find a range within which the correct rate falls. Once a range is found, the method of interpolation provides an algebraic approach to determine a good estimate of the interest rate. The words "good estimate" are used because the method of interpolation assumes that the expressions we are using are linear. As you know, the annuity formulas are not linear because they have an exponent. However, as you will see, the error is extremely minor. The one thing you must do to keep the error small is to find two interest rates whose range is 1% or less, and within this range the rate we are seeking to find must fall. Example 8.23 demonstrates the interpolation method for a given present value of an annuity.

Remember the initial rates selected will be our best guesses until we find two rates that we can average out to find the interpolated value of i.

EXAMPLE 8.24 **Finding i for a Given Present Value**

An income retirement annuity has been designed to make regular payments of $600 every quarter. The annuity can be purchased for $9,000, today. The payments will last for five years and be made every quarter. What is the nominal rate, compounded quarterly, that is being paid on the annuity?

Solution To solve the problem, we first must substitute what we know into the formula:

$$A_n = \frac{R[1-(1+i)^{-n}]}{i}$$

$$A_n = \$9{,}000$$

$$R = \$600$$

$$n = 4 \times 5, \text{ or } 20$$

Rearranging the formula and substituting we get:

$$\frac{A_n}{R} = \frac{[1-(1+i)^{-n}]}{i}$$

$$\frac{\$9{,}000}{\$600} = \frac{[1-(1+i)^{-20}]}{i}$$

$$15 = \frac{[1-(1+i)^{-20}]}{i}$$

What must be done now is to guess different values of i to get a value of $\frac{A_n}{R}$ as close to 15 as possible.

Guessing, set $i = 0.02$ as a first try (8% per year, compounded quarterly). Substituting $i = 0.02$ gives:

$$\frac{[1-(1+i)^{-n}]}{i} = \frac{[1-(1+0.02)^{-20}]}{0.02}$$

$$= 16.35143334$$

Since the value of $\frac{A_n}{R}$ must be 15, the value of 16.35143334 is too high when $i = 0.02$. Thus, set $i = 0.03$ (12% per year, compounded quarterly) as a second guess and solve. This gives:

$$\frac{[1-(1+i)^{-n}]}{i} = \frac{[1-(1+0.03)^{-20}]}{0.03}$$

$$= 14.87747486$$

This second guess is far closer and we can see that the correct value of i falls between 2% and 3% per quarter.

Now we turn to interpolation to assist us in finding the value of i. This is done by using a table, as below:

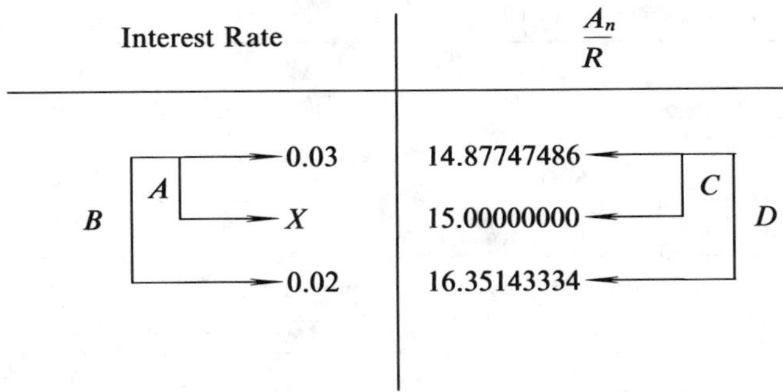

Interest Rate
$\frac{A_n}{R}$
0.03
X
0.02
A
B
14.87747486
15.00000000
16.35143334
C
D

What we now do is figure out what proportion of the 1% difference in the two rates we either subtract from 3% or add to 2%. To do this we simply solve for X using ratios. Note how the ratio is constructed, using the reference letters A, B, C, and D beside the vertical lines in the above table. These show how we set up a ratio to solve for X.

$$\frac{A}{B} = \frac{C}{D}$$

$$\frac{0.03 - X}{0.03 - 0.02} = \frac{14.87747486 - 15.00000000}{14.87747486 - 16.35143334}$$

$$\frac{0.03 - X}{0.01} = \frac{-0.12252514}{-1.47395848}$$ Now working through the steps to find X.

$$0.03 - X = 0.01\left(\frac{-0.12252514}{-1.47395848}\right)$$

$$-X = 0.01\left(\frac{-0.12252514}{-1.47395848}\right) - 0.03$$

$$-X = 0.01(0.083126588) - 0.03$$

$$-X = 0.00083126588 - 0.03$$

$$-X = -0.029168734$$ Multiply both sides by –1.

$$X = 0.029168734$$ The rate per quarter.

Thus, our interpolated value of i is 0.029168734, which is 0.116674936 per year compounded quarterly (4 times 0.029168734). If we had made the range narrower, say 2.5% to 3%, the value would have been 0.1165. The exact value using a financial calculator is 0.1164582637.

Calculator Solution

							Interest Rate
Input	9,000	600		20			
Depress	PV	+/−	PMT	n	COMP	i	2.91145659
				The nominal rate is 4 × 2.91145659			= 11.64583%

As you can see, the process is very tedious, but unless you have a financial calculator, this is the method you must use to find a good estimate of i for a given present value. The method to find i for an amount is identical, except we use $\frac{S_n}{R}$.

EXAMPLE 8.25 Finding *i* for a Given Amount or Future Value

An annuity will accumulate to $10,000 if regular monthly payments of $200 are made for three years. What is the nominal rate compounded monthly being paid on the annuity?

Solution To solve the problem we first must substitute what we know into the formula:

$$S_n = \frac{R[(1+i)^n - 1]}{i}$$

$$S_n = \$10{,}000$$

$$R = \$200$$

$$n = 12 \times 3, \text{ or } 36$$

Rearranging the formula and substituting we get:

$$\frac{S_n}{R} = \frac{[(1+i)^n - 1]}{i}$$

$$\frac{\$10{,}000}{\$200} = \frac{[(1+i)^{36} - 1]}{i}$$

$$50 = \frac{[(1+i)^{36} - 1]}{i}$$

What now must be done is to guess at values of i to get a value of $\frac{S_n}{R}$ as close to 50 as possible.

Guessing, set $i = 0.015$ as a first try (18% per year compounded monthly). Substituting $i = 0.015$ gives:

$$\frac{[(1+i)^n - 1]}{i} = \frac{[(1+0.015)^{36} - 1]}{0.015}$$

$$\doteq 47.27596920$$

Since the value of $\frac{S_n}{R}$ must be 50, the value of 47.27596920 is too low, when $i = 0.015$. Thus, set $i = 0.02$ (24% per year, compounded monthly) as our second guess and resolve. This gives:

$$\frac{[(1+i)^n - 1]}{i} = \frac{[(1+0.02)^{36} - 1]}{0.02}$$

$$\doteq 51.99436718$$

This second guess is far closer and we can see that the correct value of i falls between 1.5% and 2% per month. Now we turn to interpolation to assist us in finding the value of i. This is done by using a table, as below:

Interest Rate	$\frac{S_n}{R}$
0.015	47.27596920
X	50.00000000
0.02	51.99436718

(A: 0.015 to X; B: 0.015 to 0.02; C: 47.27596920 to 50.00000000; D: 47.27596920 to 51.99436718)

What we now do is figure out what proportion of the 0.5% difference in the two rates we either subtract from 2% or add to 1.5%. Setting up the ratio to solve for X.

$$\frac{A}{B} = \frac{C}{D}$$

$$\frac{0.015 - X}{0.015 - 0.02} = \frac{47.27596920 - 50.00000000}{47.27596920 - 51.99436718}$$

$$\frac{0.015 - X}{-0.005} = \frac{-2.724030800}{-4.718397980}$$ Now working through the steps to find X.

$$0.015 - X = 0.005\left(\frac{-2.724030800}{-4.718397980}\right)$$

$$-X = 0.005(0.577321118) - 0.015$$

$$-X = -0.017886606$$ Multiply both sides by −1.

$$X = 0.017886606$$ The rate per month.

Thus, our interpolated value of i is 0.017886606, which is 0.2146393 per year compounded monthly (12 times 0.017886606). The exact value using a financial calculator is 0.21549102.

Calculator Solution

							Interest Rate
Input	10,000	200		36			
Depress	FV	+/−	PMT	n	COMP	i	1.79575849
				The nominal rate is 12 × 1.79575849			21.549102%

EXERCISE 8.6

1. Using the approximate method, within $\frac{1}{2}\%$, at what nominal rate compounded quarterly will quarterly payments of \$1,500 accumulate to \$66,000 in eight years? What is the rate using the interpolation method?
2. Robert deposited \$750 each month in a RRSP. At the end of five years he has accumulated \$61,000. What is the approximate nominal rate of interest (within $\frac{1}{2}\%$) paid on the RRSP? Assume the rate is compounding monthly. What is the rate using the interpolation method?
3. John has an opportunity to buy a car for \$15,000 cash or pay \$5,000 down with monthly payments of \$913.76 for one year. If he knows the interest rate is compounded monthly, what is the approximate nominal rate of interest (within $\frac{1}{2}\%$) being charged on the financing? What is the rate using the method of interpolation?
4. The price of a retirement annuity is \$50,000 and will provide monthly payments of \$1,000 per month for five years. Find the interest rate being paid on the annuity using the method of interpolation.
5. The price of a home entertainment centre is \$8,500 and can be financed by equal monthly payments of \$275 for four years. Another option is to borrow the \$8,500 at a local credit union for 15%, compounded monthly. What would you recommend? What is the difference in the rate being charged by the credit union and the furniture store?

REVIEW EXERCISES

1. Calculate the amount of a fifteen year annuity where $750 deposits are made at the end of every month and the interest rate is 13% compounded monthly.
2. How much interest accumulates with a ten year annuity that has deposits of $200 at the end of every six months and interest compounded semi-annually at 14%?
3. If money is worth 14.5% compounded quarterly and deposits of $500 are made at the end of every three months for twelve years, what is the present value of this annuity?
4. If you wish to receive a $2,000 a month income for ten years, starting at the end of your first month of retirement twenty years from now, how much will be in the fund by the time you reach retirement age? Assume that money is worth 12% compounded monthly.
5. What would be the end of quarter deposits you would have to make for the next twenty years into an account paying 11.5% compounded quarterly, in order to set up the annuity described in problem 4?
6. How many years would it take you to accumulate $60,000 if you deposit $1,450 at the end of every six months and interest is paid at 12.75% compounded semiannually?
7. What is the cash value of a sixty month lease on property earning $2,750 at the end of each month, if money is worth 14% compounded monthly?
8. Dianne purchased a car for $13,500 on September 3, 1991. She made a down payment of $3,500 and agreed to repay the balance in twenty-four equal end of period payments on the third of each month. If the interest rate being charged on the loan is 18% compounded monthly, what is the total interest charge that she will pay for the loan?
9. Cheryl is going to purchase a computer priced at $10,500. She has saved $1,000 for a down payment and plans to repay the balance with equal monthly payments. The maximum amount she can afford to spend is $750 monthly and because she has a poor credit rating she must pay 24% compounded monthly.
   a. How long will it take her to get out of debt if the payments come at the end of each month?
   b. If the payments are to commence in two months and continue at the end of each month, how long will it take her to repay the debt?
   c. What is the interest cost for (a) and (b) as well as the dollar difference in interest cost between parts (a) and (b)?
10. Slycon Ltd. is contemplating the purchase of a new machine that will increase overall efficiency and save approximately $500 per month in labour costs. It is expected that the machine will last for eight years and

can then be sold for scrap, which will produce approximately $5,000. If the value of money is 15% compounded monthly, what is the maximum price that the company should pay for the machine?

11. Bill has just purchased an annuity that pays $350 per month for three years. Assume the end of month payments start at the end of one and a half years. If money is worth 12% compounded monthly, what should be the maximum price Bill should have paid for the annuity? If Bill invests the payments in a fund paying 12% compounded monthly, what will he have in the fund after the three year period?

12. Marlene decided to deposit $500 per month in a savings fund toward her goal of accumulating $100,000. How many deposits will be required to meet her goal if she can earn 15% compounded monthly? Unfortunately the interest rate dropped to 12% compounded monthly, after five years of payments. What new payments would Marlene need to make if she still wants to reach her goal in the time period first found when the interest rate was 15% compounded monthly?

13. A loan of $50,000 is to be repaid over four years with monthly payments. What is the size of each payment if the interest rate is 15% compounded monthly? How much interest was paid on the loan?

14. What is the cash price for a car that can be purchased for $5,000 down with end of month payments of $750 for four years? Assume the interest rate is 20% compounded monthly.

15. An appliance store advertises that a complete living room of furniture can be purchased for $500 down with end of month payments of $175 for five years. The furniture can be purchased for $5,000 cash. What is the nominal rate of interest compounded monthly that the store is charging? Use the interpolation method.

16. A loan of $45,000 is to be repaid with monthly payments of $1,000. The interest rate on the loan is 14% compounded monthly. What is the size of the last payment?

17. A company has been saving $350 per month towards the replacement of a piece of equipment used in their manufacturing process. The value of the equipment is $15,000. If the company can earn 12.5% compounded monthly, will the firm have sufficient funds to replace the equipment in three years? If not, how much would the firm need to make as a final payment at the end of three years to purchase the equipment?

18. An insurance company requires payments of $550 a month for four years to accumulate sufficient funds for a retirement annuity that will provide $500 monthly payments for ten years. All you know is that the monthly $500 payments are based on an interest rate of 12% compounded monthly. What was the rate of interest paid by the insurance company during the four years of payments of $550? Use the interpolation method.

SUMMARY OF FORMULAS

ORDINARY SIMPLE ANNUITIES

Formula 8.1 $$S_n = \frac{R[(1+i)^n - 1]}{i}$$ Used to find the amount of an ordinary simple annuity.

Formula 8.2 $$A_n = \frac{R[1 - (1+i)^{-n}]}{i}$$ Used to find the present value of an ordinary simple annuity.

Formula 8.3 $$R = \frac{S_n}{\dfrac{[(1+i)^n - 1]}{i}}$$ Used to find the payment R when the amount, i, and n are known.

Formula 8.4 $$R = \frac{A_n}{\dfrac{[1 - (1+i)^{-n}]}{i}}$$ Used to find the payment R when the present value, i, and n are known.

Formula 8.5 $$n = \frac{\ln\left[1 + \dfrac{S_n i}{R}\right]}{\ln(1+i)}$$ Used to find the number of payments when the amount, i, and R are known.

Formula 8.6 $$n = \frac{-\ln\left[1 - \dfrac{A_n i}{R}\right]}{\ln(1+i)}$$ Used to find the number of payments when the present value, i, and R are known.

GLOSSARY OF TERMS

Amortization Period the time period over which a debt is paid off or retired.

Amount of an Annuity the sum of the annuity payments plus accumulated interest.

Annuity a financial instrument that requires periodic payments. In general, the payments are made at the same period in time.

Annuity Certain annuities that have a definite start time and a definite end period.

Annuity Due annuities that have the payments at the beginning of each period.

Complex Annuity see General Annuity.

Contingent Annuity an annuity that has an unknown start date and/or an unknown end date. A pension plan is an example of a contingent annuity with a definite start date but an unknown end date.

Deferred Annuity when an annuity does not commence until some point in the future. Deferred annuities are only relevant when dealing with present values, e.g., a deferred loan.

General Annuity an annuity that allows for the payment period and the interest period to be different.

Interpolation the method used to find the interest rate for an annuity.

Lease Payment the payment for use of equipment, real estate, and other types of assets. In general, lease payments occur at the beginning of each period.

Ordinary Annuity an annuity where the regular payments come at the end of each payment period.

Payment Interval see Payment Period.

Payment Period the time between each regular payment of an annuity.

Perpetuity an annuity whose payments go on forever. The payments are always equal to the regular interest so that the original principal is never changed.

Simple Annuity an annuity that has the interest period (conversion period) and the payment period coinciding.

Term of an Annuity the time from the start to the finish of the annuity payments. However, sometimes in business the term of an annuity also refers to the time period that the interest rate is fixed for the annuity.

CHAPTER 9

Due and Deferred Annuities

Two annuities that were briefly described in Chapter 8 were the annuity due and the deferred annuity. Both of these annuities are commonly used in business.

An annuity due means that the regular payment comes at the beginning of the period — sometimes referred to as a payment in advance. One example of an annuity due is a rent payment. The second type of annuity that will be discussed in this chapter is the deferred annuity, which means that the annuity payments do not start immediately. That is, they commence at some point in the future. An example of a deferred annuity is purchasing a stereo on a payment plan in September, where payments don't commence until January of the following year (many variants of this type of scheme are found in the advertisements of your local paper).

OBJECTIVES

When you have completed Chapter 9, you should be able to perform all the calculations associated with an annuity due and a deferred annuity. In particular you should be able to:

1. explain the meaning of an annuity due and a deferred annuity;
2. recognize when the problem being considered requires the use of the methods for an annuity due or a deferred annuity as opposed to ordinary annuity procedures;
3. calculate the amount, present value, periodic payment, and the term for an annuity due;
4. calculate the present value, periodic payment, and the term for an annuity due.

9.1 Simple Annuity Due

Up to this point our discussion of annuities has focused on ordinary simple annuities. We learned that for simple annuities, the interest (compound) period and the payment period always coincide. Also, recall that an ordinary annuity has payments that always come at the end of the payment period.

In this section we will learn about another type of simple annuity. As with our discussion in Chapter 8, the interest period and the payment period will coincide, but this is where the similarity ends. Let's examine the special features of an **annuity due**.

An annuity due is an annuity that has payments that occur at the beginning of the payment period. Since the payment comes at the beginning of the period there will always be one extra interest period for each payment when finding the amount, and one less discount period when finding the present value of an annuity due. For example, if you are depositing money at the beginning of a period you would expect to earn interest for that period. The computations for an annuity due rely on our previous formulas for an ordinary simple annuity, with an adjustment to recognize the extra interest period associated with each payment.

(i) Amount of an Annuity Due

Finding the amount of an annuity due is very straight forward. All that must be done is account for the additional interest period. For example, think of a person making three payments of $1,000 at the beginning of each month to a savings account that pays 6% compounded monthly. If we examine the difference in the interest calculations that occur between an ordinary annuity and an annuity due, it will help us to understand how we arrive at the new formulas for an annuity due.

Using an ordinary simple annuity means that the three payments come at the end of each month. The amount at the end of the three months would be found by using Formula 8.1, or:

$$S_n = \frac{R[(1+i)^n - 1]}{i}$$

Where:

$$R = \$1{,}000$$

$$i = \frac{0.06}{12}, \text{ or } 0.005$$

$$n = 3$$

Substituting we have:

$$S_n = \frac{\$1{,}000[(1+0.005)^3 - 1]}{0.005}$$

$$S_n = \$3{,}015.03$$

Now look at the same problem when the payments are made at the beginning of each month.

With an annuity due the first payment is made at the start of the first month, the second at the beginning of the second month, and the third at the beginning of the third month. If we apply our compound interest formula from Chapter 7 we would find the amount of these three payments as follows:

$$\$1{,}000(1+0.005)^3 = \$1{,}015.08$$
$$\$1{,}000(1+0.005)^2 = \$1{,}010.03$$
$$\$1{,}000(1+0.005)^1 = \$1{,}005.00$$

If we total the payments and interest we see that the amount in the account at the end of three months is \$3,030.11, which is higher than the amount when the payments came at the end of each month. In this problem, the difference is \$3,030.11 – \$3,015.03, or \$15.08.

We can adjust our ordinary simple annuity formula to handle the change in the timing of the payments (to the beginning of each period) as follows:

$$S_n(\text{due}) = \frac{R(1+i)[(1+i)^n - 1]}{i}$$ **Formula 9.1**

Diagrammatically the additional interest can be seen as a result of the payments (R_1, R_2, R_3) coming at the beginning of the month.

Figure 9.1 A Comparison of Amount Calculations for an Annuity Due and an Ordinary Annuity

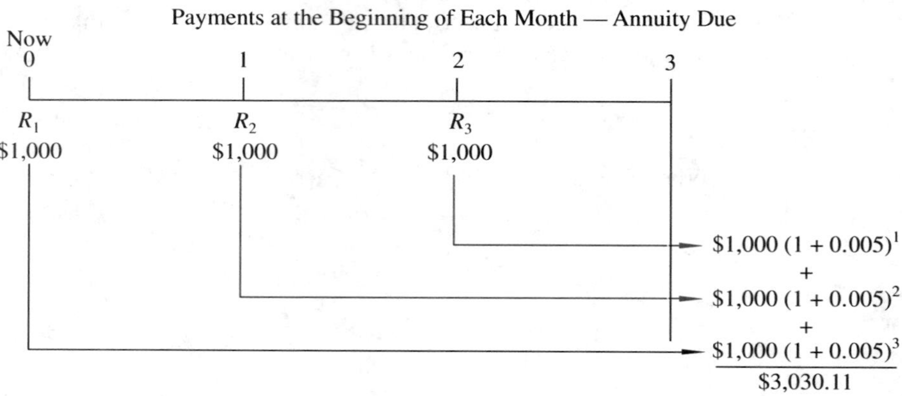

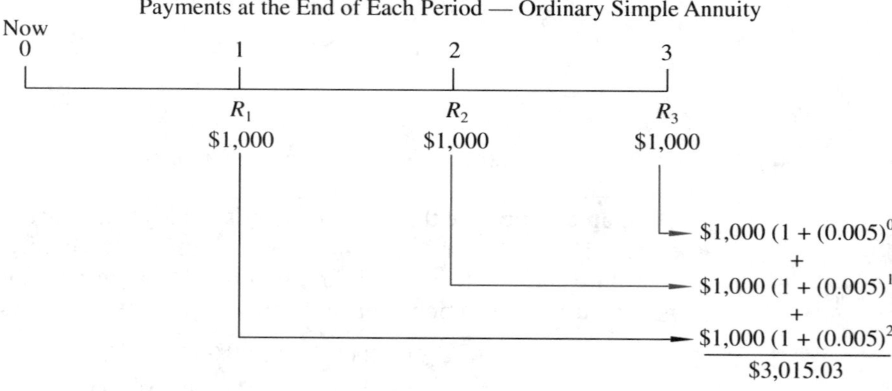

The first thing to note in Formula 9.1 is that we clearly show that we are looking at the amount of an annuity due by stating due after S_n.

The second thing you should notice is that there is an "extra" $(1 + i)$ on the right hand side of the equation to reflect the additional interest period associated with each payment in computing the amount. As well there will be one less interest period per payment for discounting.

Now applying this formula to the problem above:

$$S_n(\text{due}) = \frac{R(1 + i)[(1 + i)^n - 1]}{i}$$

Where:

$$R = \$1{,}000$$
$$i = 0.005$$
$$n = 3$$

Substituting into our formula we have:

$$S_n(\text{due}) = \frac{\$1{,}000(1 + 0.005)[(1 + 0.005)^3 - 1]}{0.005}$$

$$S_n(\text{due}) = \$1{,}000[3.030100]$$
$$S_n(\text{due}) = \$3{,}030.10$$

The $0.01 difference from the compound interest approach above is simply a rounding difference.

As you can see, the difference in this formula from our previous amount formula is the extra $(1 + i)$ portion.

It is important that you always read the problem looking for when the payment will occur — at the beginning or the end of the payment period. However, if it is not stated when the payments are made, assume an ordinary annuity. An annuity due requires a specific statement in the problem that the payments are in advance or at the beginning of the period.

EXAMPLE 9.1

Mark is starting an investment fund in which he plans to deposit $500 at the beginning of each month. If he can earn 10% compounded monthly, how much will be in the fund at the end of six years?

Solution The solution to this problem requires the recognition that the payments are made at the beginning of each period. Thus, we must apply our annuity due formula for finding the amount. Using Formula 9.1 gives:

$$S_n\,(\text{due}) = \frac{R(1 + i)[(1 + i)^n - 1]}{i}$$

Where:

$$R = \$500$$

$$i = \frac{0.10}{12}, \text{ or } 0.008333$$

$$n = 12 \times 6, \text{ or } 72$$

Substituting into our formula yields:

$$S_n\,(\text{due}) = \frac{\$500\left(1 + \frac{0.10}{12}\right)\left[\left(1 + \frac{0.10}{12}\right)^{72} - 1\right]}{\frac{0.10}{12}}$$

$$S_n\,(\text{due}) \doteq \$500(98.928908)$$

$$S_n\,(\text{due}) \doteq \$49{,}464.45$$

At the end of 72 periods, when all deposits of $500 have been made at the beginning of each period, and the interest rate is 10% compounded monthly, Mark will have $49,464.45 in his investment fund.

Calculator Solution Note the inclusion of the BGN key to recognize that the payments are at the beginning of the period.

Finding the Amount for an Annuity Due							
Input		$500	0.833333	72			
Depress	BGN	PMT	i	n	COMP	FV	49,464.45

(ii) Finding the Present Value of an Annuity Due

When we want to figure out the present value of an annuity due we must incorporate that each payment will be discounted one less interest period. The formula we will use to find A_n (due) is:

$$A_n \text{ (due)} = \frac{R(1+i)[1-(1+i)^{-n}]}{i} \qquad \textbf{Formula 9.2}$$

EXAMPLE 9.2

The monthly rent on an apartment is $750 per month, payable at the beginning of each month. If the current interest rate is 12% compounded monthly, what single payment twelve months in advance would be equivalent to a year's rent?

Solution In reading the problem we should note that a single payment, now, will be equivalent to twelve payments made at the beginning of each month. This single payment is simply the present value of the year's payments. Since the payments are made at the beginning of each period we must use Formula 9.2. Defining all the terms we have:

$$R = \$750$$

$$i = \frac{0.12}{12}, \text{ or } 0.01$$

$$n = 12$$

Substituting into Formula 9.2 gives:

$$A_n\text{ (due)} = \frac{\$750(1 + 0.01)[1 - (1 + 0.01)^{-12}]}{0.01}$$

$$A_n\text{ (due)} \doteq \$750(11.3676283)$$

$$A_n\text{ (due)} \doteq \$8{,}525.72$$

Therefore, a single payment of $8,525.72 is equivalent to twelve monthly payments of $750 made at the beginning of each month.

Calculator Solution

Finding the Present Value for an Annuity Due							
Input		$750	1	12			
Depress	BGN	PMT	i	n	COMP	PV	8,525.72

(iii) Finding the Payment, *R*, for Annuities Due

As with an ordinary simple annuity, often we need to find *R* when the interest rate, the number of periods, and either the amount or present value is known. The method we use rearranges the formula for S_n(due) to find *R*. If the amount, S_n(due), is known then we find *R* by the formula:

$$R = \frac{S_n\text{ (due)}}{\left[\frac{(1+i)[(1+i)^n - 1]}{i}\right]} \qquad \textbf{Formula 9.3}$$

If the present value is known then we simply rearrange Formula 9.2 to find *R*. That is:

$$R = \frac{A_n\text{ (due)}}{\left[\frac{(1+i)[1 - (1+i)^{-n}]}{i}\right]} \qquad \textbf{Formula 9.4}$$

EXAMPLE 9.3

Nick Krenshaw wants to accumulate $4,000 in eight months. If the first payment will be made today and the interest rate is 13% compounded monthly, what will be the required size of each monthly payment?

Solution This problem requires us to find R when the future amount is known. We can see that the problem tells us the values of i and n so all that is necessary is to determine which formula for R is appropriate. Since the payments are to start at the beginning we know we are working with an annuity due. Turning to Formula 9.3 and substituting would go as follows:

$$S_n \text{ (due)} = \$4{,}000$$

$$i = \frac{0.13}{12}, \text{ or } 0.0108333$$

$$n = 8$$

Applying Formula 9.3:

$$R = \frac{S_n \text{ (due)}}{\left[\frac{(1+i)[(1+i)^n - 1]}{i}\right]}$$

$$R = \frac{\$4{,}000}{\left[\frac{\left(1 + \frac{0.13}{12}\right)\left[\left(1 + \frac{0.13}{12}\right)^8 - 1\right]}{\frac{0.13}{12}}\right]}$$

$$R \doteq \frac{\$4{,}000}{8.40002}$$

$$R \doteq \$476.19$$

Payments of $476.19, made at the beginning of each period, for the next eight months, will accumulate to $4,000.

Calculator Solution

Input		4,000	1.08333	8			
Depress	BGN	FV	i	n	COMP	PMT	476.19

EXAMPLE 9.4

A loan of $6,000 is to be paid off over ten months, with payments commencing today. If the interest rate is 16% compounded monthly, what is the size of each payment?

Solution Our task is to find R given the present value, i, and n. To find R under these conditions, knowing that the payment comes at the beginning of each period, we would use Formula 9.4, or:

$$R = \frac{A_n\text{ (due)}}{\left[\dfrac{(1+i)[1-(1+i)^{-n}]}{i}\right]}$$

Where:

$A_n\text{(due)} = \$6{,}000$

$i = \dfrac{0.16}{12}$, or 0.01333

$n = 10$

Now substituting we have:

$$R = \frac{\$6{,}000}{\left[\dfrac{\left(1+\dfrac{0.16}{12}\right)\left[1-\left(1+\dfrac{0.16}{12}\right)^{-10}\right]}{\dfrac{0.16}{12}}\right]}$$

$$R \doteq \frac{\$6{,}000}{(9.4281994)}$$

$$R \doteq \$636.39$$

Thus, monthly payments of \$636.38 will pay off the debt if the ten payments begin today.

Calculator Solution

Input		6,000	1.3333	10			
Depress	BGN	PV	i	n	COMP	PMT	636.39

(iv) Finding the Term, *n*, for an Annuity Due

The value of n can be found, when we know either the amount or the present value as well as R and i, by rearranging Formulas 9.1 and 9.2, and then solving for n. Since the algebra is somewhat awkward, only the final expressions are provided. If you want to undertake the algebra please review the examples in the logarithm section of Chapter 4, especially parts (b) and (c) of Example 4.22.

$$n = \frac{\ln\left[1 + \frac{S_n\,(\text{due})i}{R(1+i)}\right]}{\ln(1+i)}$$ **Formula 9.5**

Formula 9.5 calculates the value of n when the amount, R and i are known for an annuity due.

To compute n when the present value, R, and i are known with an annuity due we use the following formula:

$$n = \frac{-\ln\left[1 - \frac{A_n\,(\text{due})i}{R(1+i)}\right]}{\ln(1-i)}$$ **Formula 9.6**

Use Formula 9.6 with special caution since people often forget the negative sign that precedes the first **ln**. The following two examples outline how to find n for a given present value or amount for an annuity due:

EXAMPLE 9.5

If \$200 is deposited at the beginning of each quarter, how many years will it take to accumulate \$12,000 if the interest rate is 16% compounded quarterly?

Solution This problem requires us to accumulate a specific amount, when the payments occur at the beginning of the period. Thus, we would use the formula:

$$n = \frac{\ln\left[1 + \frac{S_n\,(\text{due})i}{R(1+i)}\right]}{\ln(1+i)}$$

Now, defining the terms:

$$R = \$200$$

$$i = \frac{0.16}{4}, \text{ or } 0.04$$

$$S_n\,(\text{due}) = \$12{,}000$$

Substituting into our formula yields:

$$n = \frac{\ln\left[1 + \frac{\$12{,}000(0.04)}{\$200(1+0.04)}\right]}{\ln(1+0.04)}$$

$$n \doteq \frac{\ln[3.30769]}{\ln(1.04)}$$

$$n \doteq 30.50048 \text{ quarters, or dividing by four, } 7.63 \text{ years}$$

Therefore, if the deposits are made every quarter for 30.50048 quarters, or 7.63 years there will be $12,000 in the account. (The actual number of quarterly payments would be eight, with the first seven at $200, and the last payment being a smaller payment.)

Calculator Solution

Input		12,000	4	200				
Depress	BGN	FV	i	+/−	PMT	COMP	n	30.5048

EXAMPLE 9.6

You are negotiating a mortgage on a new home. Suppose you have decided that the maximum mortgage payment you can afford is $850, made at the beginning of each month. If the interest rate is 10% compounded monthly, and the size of the mortgage is $74,000, find how long, in years, it would take to repay the mortgage.

Solution To answer this question we are first going to find how many monthly payments it will take to repay the mortgage when the monthly payment is $850. Once we have the number of monthly payments, we will then convert this into years by dividing n by 12, since there are twelve months in each year.

The first step in our solution is to make sure we lay out what we know. Based on the information:

$$R = \$850$$

$$i = \frac{0.10}{12}$$

$$A_n\,(\text{due}) = \$74{,}000$$

Now substituting into Formula 9.6 gives:

$$n = \frac{-\ln\left[1 - \dfrac{\$74{,}000\left(\dfrac{0.10}{12}\right)}{\$850\left(1 + \dfrac{0.10}{12}\right)}\right]}{\ln(1 + \dfrac{0.10}{12})}$$

$$n \doteq \frac{-[-1.27116]}{(0.008299)}$$

$$n \doteq -[-153.17]$$

$$n \doteq 153.17$$

Consequently, it will take 154 payments to repay the mortgage. The value of the first 153 payments is $850 and the value of the 154th payment will be a smaller payment. The number of years to repay the mortgage is approximately thirteen years $\left[\frac{153.17}{12}\right]$.

Calculator Solution

Input		74,000	0.83333	850				
Depress	BGN	PV	i	+/−	PMT	COMP	n	153.174

Compare Examples 9.5 and 9.6 with Examples 8.12 and 8.13 that use the same numbers, but are ordinary annuities.

EXERCISE 9.1

For problems 1 to 5 find the amount and present value for the given annuities. Assume in each case that the payments come at the beginning of the period.

	Payment Period	Payment	Term of the Annuity	Interest Rate and Conversion Period
1.	Annually	$ 1,350	4 years	12.4%, annually
2.	Monthly	600	16 years	14.0%, monthly
3.	Monthly	200	15 years	15.0%, monthly
4.	Daily	500	2 years	17.8%, daily
5.	Semiannually	450	18 years	14.0%, semiannually

For problems 6 to 10 find the required payments for the given amount and present value.

	Payment Period	Present Value A_n(due)	Amount S_n(due)	Term of the Annuity	Interest Rate and Conversion Period
6.	Annually	$ 3,000	$45,000	6 years	12.4%, annually
7.	Quarterly	25,000	87,500	18 years	14.0%, quarterly
8.	Monthly	28,500	45,500	13 years	16.0%, monthly
9.	Annually	54,500	80,340	6 years	19.8%, annually
10.	Semiannually	41,500	75,000	20 years	15.0%, semiannually

For problems 11 to 20 find the number of payments (the term) for the given present value and amount for each annuity due.

	Payment Period	Present Value $A_n(due)$	Amount $S_n(due)$	Payment per Period R	Interest Rate and Conversion Period
11.	Annually	$ 6,450	$25,345	$ 4,500.00	10.8%, annually
12.	Quarterly	45,450	45,500	6,000.00	11.0%, quarterly
13.	Monthly	24,400	64,400	1,350.00	12.0%, monthly
14.	Annually	13,450	32,450	2,500.00	16.8%, annually
15.	Semiannually	67,500	150,000	9,500.00	16.0%, semiannually
16.	Monthly	34,000	189,000	3,950.00	21.0%, monthly
17.	Quarterly	134,500	100,000	18,200.00	23.8%, quarterly
18.	Yearly	123,500	145,000	23,500.00	21.0%, yearly
19.	Quarterly	1,250	24,450	50.00	14.5%, quarterly
20.	Monthly	21,425	56,500	450.00	25.7%, monthly

21. Mary is planning to take a year's leave of absence from her job to go travelling in two and one-half years. Her trip is expected to cost $28,000. Mary decides to deposit $800, starting today and continuing at the beginning of each month, in a special fund through her union. She plans to make the contributions for the next two and one-half years. If the fund pays 4% compounded monthly, will she have sufficient money to take the trip? How much will be in the fund?

22. Peter is given a choice between two investment funds. The first requires him to deposit, starting today, $275 each quarter. The second requires deposits of $285 at the end of each quarter. If the interest rate on each fund is 12% compounded each quarter, which fund would have the largest balance at the end of three years?

23. Rick and Terry McLean are going to rent an apartment. They find that the landlord is prepared to offer two methods of payment. Either they can pay $900 a month or they can pay $9,500 in a lump sum payment for the whole year. Both options require the payments to occur when they move into the apartment at the beginning of the month. If the couple can earn 8% on their money, compounded monthly, is the landlord offering them a good deal with the single annual payment?

24. Andrew wants to accumulate $65,000 in a retirement fund. If he can earn 8% on his money compounded annually, what annual payments, commencing today, will he need to make if he wants the $65,000 in twelve years?

25. Elizabeth has purchased a new house and has arranged a mortgage of $78,000. The mortgage company requires the payments to be made at the beginning of each month. What will be the monthly payments if the mortgage is to be paid off over a fifteen year period? Assume the interest rate is 10% compounded monthly.

26. In problem 25 if Elizabeth decides to increase her monthly payments by $150 per month, what will be the total number of payments required to repay the mortgage?

27. In problem 24, if Andrew were to increase the payments by $250 how long would it take him to reach his goal?

9.2 Deferred Annuities

Deferred annuities refer to annuities whose payments do not begin until some period in the future. A common example is where someone purchases a retirement fund today, but does not receive any payments until retirement at some point in the future. **The term deferred means exactly what it states: deferred until some point in the future.**

Our discussion of deferred annuities focuses on those annuities where the payments come at the **end** of each payment period. There are situations where a deferred annuity could have payments starting at the beginning of each period. However, these are left for you to consider using the procedures of the previous section.

The formulas we use are similar to those in the sections on ordinary simple annuities. The change we build into our old formulas must reflect the period of time for which the payments are deferred. **The deferral period refers to the length of time, in payment periods, that will pass before a payment occurs.** This period is generally represented by d.

Let's begin with the amount of a deferred annuity since it's very straight forward.

(i) Amount of a Deferred Annuity

The amount of a deferred annuity is the same as the amount of an ordinary simple annuity. That is, the deferral period has no influence on a future value.

Consider the situation where someone is making regular deposits to reach an amount of $5,000. If the payments do not commence for five years it simply means that the payments start five years from now. However, this deferral has no influence on the desired sum of $5,000. Thus, there is no need to concern ourselves with the situation of finding the amount of a deferred annuity since it would be dealt with by the formula for the amount of an ordinary annuity.

(ii) Present Value for a Deferred Annuity

The present value of a deferred annuity is found by using the following formula:

$$A_n\text{ (def)} = \frac{R(1+i)^{-d}[1-(1+i)^{-n}]}{i} \qquad \textbf{Formula 9.7}$$

In this formula, we see that the only difference between the ordinary annuity formula and the deferred annuity formula is the $(1 + i)^{-d}$ term. This term is used to discount the value of the annuity over the deferral period. The term d refers to deferral periods — that is, the number of deferral periods.

Also, note that Formula 9.7 is applicable to payments that are at the end of the payment period. If we want a deferred annuity due then we would need to turn to our formula for an annuity due and then add in the deferral factor $-(1 + i)^{-d}$. Let's look at an example to make things a little more clear:

EXAMPLE 9.7

Gordon Investments Ltd. is offering a retirement package that guarantees ten years of end of the month payments of \$650. The plan requires the investor to purchase the retirement plan today and not start receiving the payments for five years, with the first payment coming at the end of the first month following the five years. If the interest rate is 8% compounded monthly, what will be the purchase price of the retirement package?

Solution Since this plan does not provide payments for five years it is a deferred annuity. The most important thing we must do is find the number of payment periods in the deferral period, d. Since the payments are monthly, we must assume that the deferral period is based on five years of monthly payments. Therefore, the deferral period is 12×5, or 60, periods. First let's outline the information we have:

$R = \$650$

$i = \frac{0.08}{12}$, or 0.00666667

$n = 12 \times 10$, or 120 — Remember the payments are for ten years once they start.

$d = 12 \times 5$, or 60 — This is the number of payment periods that the annuity is deferred.

Turning to our present value formula for a deferred annuity we have:

$$A_n(\text{def}) = \frac{R(1+i)^{-d}[1-(1+i)^{-n}]}{i}$$

Making the appropriate substitutions yields:

$$A_n(\text{def}) = \frac{\$650\left(1+\frac{0.08}{12}\right)^{-60}\left[1-\left(1+\frac{0.08}{12}\right)^{-120}\right]}{\frac{0.08}{12}}$$

$$A_n\,(\text{def}) \doteq \$650\left(1+\frac{0.08}{12}\right)^{-60}[82.42148]$$

$$A_n\,(\text{def}) \doteq \$35{,}959.40$$

Thus, if you were thinking about purchasing this retirement package you would not want to pay any more than \$35,959.40 with a five year deferral, if the interest rate is 8% compounded monthly.

Calculator Solution The steps involved using the calculator for a deferred annuity are:
1. find the present value for an ordinary simple annuity;
2. discount the present value by the deferral factor – $(1 + i)^{-d}$.

Finding the Present Value for a Deferred Annuity						
Input	650	120	0.666667			
Depress	PMT	n	i	COMP	PV	53,573.95
Discounting PV for Deferral Period $(1 + 0.006667)^{-60}$ (53,573.95)						35,959.40

EXAMPLE 9.8

What is the present value of an annuity paying \$1,300 at the end of each semiannual period for four years if the first payment is to be made in 5.5 years? Assume the interest rate is 12% compounded semiannually and the payments are at the end of each period.

Solution The first thing we must do is find the number of deferral periods. Since the first payment is in 5.5 years there must be five years of deferral. Why only 5 and not 5.5? This is because the first payment occurs at the end of 5.5 years. Thus, since the payments come at the end of each period, only the first five years have no payments. If there were 5.5 years of deferral, then the first payment would occur at year six.

Defining the values for each term:

$R = \$1{,}300$

$i = \frac{0.12}{2}$, or 0.06

$n = 4 \times 2$, or 8 — The payments last for four years.

$d = 5 \times 2$, or 10 — Ten deferral periods.

Now substituting into our formula:

$$A_n(\text{def}) = \frac{R(1+i)^{-d}[1-(1+i)^{-n}]}{i}$$

$$A_n(\text{def}) = \frac{\$1{,}300(1+0.06)^{-10}[1-(1+0.06)^{-8}]}{0.06}$$

$$A_n(\text{def}) \doteq \$1{,}300(3.467516)$$

$$A_n(\text{def}) \doteq \$4{,}507.77$$

Therefore, the present value of a deferred annuity paying \$1,300 semiannually for four years is \$4,507.77.

Calculator Solution

Finding the Present Value for a Deferred Annuity						
Input	1,300	8	6			
Depress	PMT	n	i	COMP	PV	8,072.73
Discounting PV for Deferral Period $(1 + 0.06)^{-10}$ (8,072.73)						4,507.77

(iii) Finding *R* for a Deferred Annuity

As with the earlier annuities, finding R when the present value is known requires us to rearrange Formula 9.7, to solve for R. This rearrangement would result in:

$$R = \frac{A_n\,(\text{def})}{\dfrac{(1+i)^{-d}[1-(1+i)^{-n}]}{i}}$$

Formula 9.8

You will have an opportunity to use this formula in the practice exercises to follow:

EXAMPLE 9.9

Joan and Larry have just bought a new living room suite for $7,500 including taxes. The furniture was purchased at Moe's Low Cost Furniture Mart, which has a special offer of no payments for six months. If Moe's provide furniture loans at a rate of 28.5% compounded monthly, what would be the size of the regular monthly payments if the full amount must be repaid in 36 equal end of month payments? What would the size of the monthly payments be if they came at the beginning of each period?

Solution To find the end of month payments, the terms must be defined:

$$R = ?$$

$$A_n\,(\text{def}) = \$7{,}500$$

$$i = \frac{0.285}{12}\text{, or } 0.02375$$

$$n = 12 \times 3\text{, or 36 payments}$$

$$d = 6$$

There are six periods <u>without</u> payments, thus six deferral periods.

Applying Formula 9.8:

$$R = \frac{A_n\,(\text{def})}{\dfrac{(1+i)^{-d}[1-(1+i)^{-n}]}{i}}$$

Substituting the terms:

$$R = \frac{\$7{,}500}{\dfrac{(1+0.02375)^{-6}[1-(1+0.02375)^{-36}]}{0.02375}}$$

$$R \doteq \$359.48$$

Calculator Solution The steps involved using the calculator:

1. find the regular payment for an ordinary simple annuity;
2. divide the payment from 1 by the deferral factor, $(1+i)^{-d}$.

Finding the Payment for a Deferred Annuity						
Input	7,500	36	2.375			
Depress	PV	n	i	COMP	PMT	312.26
Accounting for the Deferral Period $\dfrac{(312.26)}{(1+0.02375)^{-6}}$						359.48

Beginning of Month Payments:

To find the payments at the beginning of each payment period, Formula 9.8 must be adjusted. As you will recall, the formulas for an annuity due had an extra (1 + i) term. Thus, Formula 9.8 would now look as follows:

$$R = \frac{A_n\,(\text{def})}{\dfrac{(1+i)(1+i)^{-d}[1-(1+i)^{-n}]}{i}}$$

The extra $(1 + i)$ has been added to account for the payment at the beginning of the period.

Substituting the terms:

$$R = \frac{\$7{,}500}{\dfrac{(1+0.02375)(1+0.02375)^{-6}[1-(1+0.02375)^{-36}]}{0.02375}}$$

$$R \doteq \$351.14$$

Therefore, the required end of the month payments are \$359.48, providing that they do not commence until seven months after the purchase. When the payments are at the beginning of each period, the size of the 36 regular payments is \$351.14.

Calculator Solution The steps involved using the calculator:

1. find the regular payment for an ordinary simple annuity due;
2. divide the payment from 1 by the deferral factor, $(1 + i)^{-d}$.

Finding the Payment for a Deferred Annuity Due							
Input		7,500	36	2.375			
Depress	BGN	PV	n	i	COMP	PMT	305.01
Accounting for the Deferral Period $\dfrac{(305.01)}{(1+0.02375)^{-6}}$							351.14

(iv) Finding *n* for a Deferred Annuity

To find the term or number of payments for a deferred annuity requires re-arranging Formula 9.7, using logarithms, and solving for n. As with the formula for n when we were dealing with ordinary simple annuities, there will be a negative sign at the beginning of the right side of the formula.

The other feature of this formula is that we must incorporate the value of d, reflecting the deferral periods. The formula is:

$$n = \frac{-\ln\left[1 - \frac{A_n(\text{def})i}{R(1+i)^{-d}}\right]}{\ln(1+i)}$$ **Formula 9.9**

EXAMPLE 9.10

Julio has \$50,000 in a retirement fund. If he plans to make no more contributions to the plan and plans to retire in four years, how long can he draw monthly payments of \$500 once he retires? Assume the interest rate on the fund is 6% compounded monthly.

Solution To solve the problem we must first find the value for each term:

$$R = \$500$$

$$i = \frac{0.06}{12}, \text{ or } 0.005$$

$$d = 12 \times 4, \text{ or } 48$$

We assume that four years pass and his first payment comes at four years and one month.

$$A_n(\text{def}) = \$50{,}000$$

Substituting into the formula gives:

$$n = \frac{-\ln\left[1 - \frac{A_n(\text{def})i}{R(1+i)^{-d}}\right]}{\ln(1+i)}$$

$$n = \frac{-\ln\left[1 - \frac{\$50{,}000(0.005)}{\$500(1+0.005)^{-48}}\right]}{\ln(1+0.005)}$$

$$n \doteq \frac{-\ln(0.364755)}{\ln(1.005)}$$

$$n \doteq 202.21$$

Therefore, if Julio makes no more payments to this retirement fund and retires in four years, he can draw \$500 a month for approximately 202 months, and a final smaller payment at month 203.

Calculator Solution The process to find n for an ordinary simple deferred annuity requires the payment to first be adjusted to account for the deferral period. This adjusted payment is then used for PMT in the calculator.

$$\text{Adjusted payment} = R\,(1 + i)^{-d}$$
$$\text{Adjusted payment} = \$500\,(1 + 0.005)^{-48}$$
$$= \$393.55^{**}$$

Input	(**) 393.55	0.5	50,000				
Depress	PMT	i	+/−	PV	COMP	n	202.21

EXERCISE 9.2

For each of the following find the required unknown (?) for the given deferred annuities.

	Payment Period	A_n *(def)*	Payments *R*	Term of the Payments	Payments Start at the End of	Interest Rate and Conversion Period
1.	Monthly	?	$2,500	20 years	13 months	11.0%, monthly
2.	Quarterly	150,500	?	14 years	2¼ years	10.8%, quarterly
3.	Yearly	80,500	17,500	?	4 years	14.0%, yearly
4.	Quarterly	75,450	?	10 years	3¼ years	12.5%, quarterly
5.	Quarterly	?	2,200	15 years	9 months	18.7%, quarterly

6. Richard is thinking about buying a retirement annuity that will not start regular end of month payments until after ten years have passed. The annuity he is currently contemplating offers him a monthly income of $400 for twenty years. If the interest rate is 9% compounded monthly, what should Richard expect to pay today for such an annuity?

7. To provide sufficient capital for a new road the District of Metchosin has arranged a loan through the provincial government. The loan is for $250,000 and the repayment does not start until after four years have passed. If the payments are to be made at the end of each semiannual period for eight years and the interest rate is 8% compounded semiannually, what will be the size of the regular payments?

8. Marie is going to retire in two years. She has a chance to invest $75,000 in an investment fund at 9% compounded annually. The fund is designed to commence payments at the end of two years. The payments will be at the end of each year. If each payment is $10,000, how many payments will Marie receive?

REVIEW EXERCISES

1. Calculate the future value for a fifteen year annuity where $150 deposits are made at the beginning of every month and the interest rate is 13% compounded monthly.
2. Find the amount and the total interest earned on a ten year annuity that requires deposits of $1,500 at the beginning of every six months. Assume the interest rate is 14% compounded semiannually.
3. A loan requires payments of $50 at the beginning of every three months for twelve years. If the interest rate is 14.5% compounded quarterly, what is the size of the loan? After three years of payments (immediately after the payment), how much is outstanding on the loan?
4. John wishes to receive $2,500 a month income, paid at the beginning of each month, for the first ten years of retirement. He plans to retire twenty years from now. How much must he set aside, starting today, and continuing at the beginning of each month for the next twenty years, in order to have the required monies to support his planned ten-year retirement income? Assume that money is worth 9% compounded monthly.
5. What would be the beginning of quarterly deposits one would have to make for the next twenty years into an account paying 12.5% quarterly, in order to support the retirement income required in problem 4?
6. How many years would it take you to build up $60,000 if you deposit $450 at the beginning of every six months and interest is paid at 12.75% compounded semiannually?
7. What is the cash value of a sixty month lease on property earning $1,750 at the beginning of each month, if money is worth 14% compounded monthly?
8. Brian purchased a car for $16,500. He made a down payment of $2,500 and agreed to repay the balance of the loan in twenty-four equal beginning of the month payments. However, the payments do not commence until the start of the fourth month after the purchase. If the interest rate being charged on the loan is 18% compounded monthly, what is the total interest charge that he will pay for the loan?
9. Computech Services Ltd. is going to purchase a computer priced at $210,000. The company has $10,000 cash for a down payment and plans to repay the balance of the loan with equal monthly payments. The maximum amount the company can afford to pay in monthly payments is $3,750. The interest rate charged by the company selling the computer is 18% compounded monthly, and they expect all payments to be made in advance each month.
   a. How long will it take Computech to get out of debt?

b. If the payments do not start for six months and continue at the beginning of each month thereafter, how long will it take to repay the debt?

c. Compare the difference in dollar cost of having the payments in (a) come at the beginning of each month to having the payments come at the end of each month. Which payment method has the highest interest cost? What is the dollar difference interest cost between the two payment methods?

10. Excon Ltd. is contemplating the purchase of a new machine that will increase overall efficiency and save approximately \$2,000 at the end of each month in labour costs. It is expected that the machine will last for eight years and can then be sold for scrap, which will produce approximately \$1,000. The savings are expected to start thirteen months after the installation of the new equipment. If money is worth 15% compounded monthly, what is the maximum price that the company should pay for the machine?

11. Anna has just leased some retail space in a shopping mall. The lease requires a full payment of the discounted value of the three-year lease payments in advance. It is computed based on beginning of the month payments of \$500, at an interest rate of 12% compounded monthly. In addition, Anna can cancel the lease at any time during the three-year period with one month notice. If she cancels the lease early she is entitled to a refund of the remaining payments, which are discounted at 12% compounded monthly, for early termination of the lease. However, if she cancels the lease, she is subject to a two month rent penalty that is subtracted from the refund of the discounted value of the remaining payments. What is the initial cost of the three year lease to Anna? If she gives notice that she wishes to cancel the lease on the first of the month, $1\frac{1}{2}$ years after commencing the lease, what is the size of the refund she should expect? Compute the total cost Anna paid for the mall space.

12. John is offered an investment opportunity that will pay him \$300 at the end of eleven months and regular \$150 end of the month payments thereafter. How many \$150 payments will he receive if the investment costs \$4,000 today? Assume that money is worth 15% compounded monthly.

13. A loan of \$10,000 is to be repaid over a four-year period with monthly payments that start at the end of the eighth month from the date of the loan. What is the size of each payment if the interest rate is 15% compounded monthly?

14. What is the cash price for a stereo television that can be purchased for \$500 down and monthly payments of \$50 for three years? Assume that the first payment is made today and that the interest rate is 20% compounded monthly.

SUMMARY OF FORMULAS

Simple Annuity Due

Formula 9.1 $$S_n(\text{due}) = \frac{R(1+i)[(1+i)^n - 1]}{i}$$ Used to find the amount for an annuity due.

Formula 9.2 $$A_n(\text{due}) = \frac{R(1+i)[1-(1+i)^{-n}]}{i}$$ Used to find the present value for an annuity due.

Formula 9.3 $$R = \frac{S_n(\text{due})}{\dfrac{(1+i)[(1+i)^n - 1]}{i}}$$ Used to find the payment for an annuity due, when the amount, i, and n are known.

Formula 9.4 $$R = \frac{A_n(\text{due})}{\dfrac{(1+i)[1-(1+i)^{-n}]}{i}}$$ Used to find the payment for an annuity due, when the present value, i, and n are known.

Formula 9.5 $$n = \frac{\ln\left[1 + \dfrac{S_n(\text{due})i}{R(1+i)}\right]}{\ln(1+i)}$$ Used to find the number of payments when the amount, i, and R are known.

Formula 9.6 $$n = \frac{-\ln\left[1 - \dfrac{A_n(\text{due})i}{R(1+i)}\right]}{\ln(1+i)}$$ Used to find the number of payments when the present value, i, and R are known for an annuity due.

Deferred Ordinary Simple Annuity

Formula 9.7 $$A_n(\text{def}) = \frac{R(1+i)^{-d}[1-(1+i)^{-n}]}{i}$$ Used to find the present value of a deferred annuity.

Formula 9.8 $$R = \frac{A_n(\text{def})}{\dfrac{(1+i)^{-d}[1-(1+i)^{-n}]}{i}}$$ Used to find the payment for a deferred annuity when the present value, i, and n are known.

Formula 9.9

$$n = \frac{-\ln\left[1 - \frac{A_n(\text{def})i}{R(1+i)^{-d}}\right]}{\ln(1+i)}$$

Used to find the number of payments when the present value, i, and R are known for a deferred annuity.

GLOSSARY OF TERMS

Amortization Period the time period over which a debt is paid off or retired.

Amount of an Annuity the sum of the annuity payments plus accumulated interest.

Annuity a financial instrument that requires periodic payments. In general, the payments are made at the same period in time.

Annuity Due annuities that have the payments at the beginning of each period.

Complex Annuity see General Annuity in Chapter 10.

Deferral Period the number of payment periods that pass without a payment. If a period has a payment, it is not part of the deferral period.

Deferred Annuity when an annuity does not commence until some point in the future. Deferred annuities are only relevant when dealing with present values, e.g., a deferred loan.

Lease Payment the payment for use of equipment, real estate, and other types of assets. In general, lease payments occur at the beginning of each period.

Simple Annuity an annuity that has the interest period (conversion period) and the payment period coinciding.

Term of an Annuity the term of an annuity refers to the time from the start to the finish of the annuity payments. However, sometimes in business the term of an annuity also refers to the time period that the interest rate is fixed for the annuity.

CHAPTER 10

General Annuities

The material in this chapter is an extension of Chapters 8 and 9. The major distinction among Chapters 8 and 9 and Chapter 10 is that the methods described in this chapter will be applicable to all annuity problems — regardless of whether the interest period and the payment period coincide. Since the methods in this chapter permit us to undertake annuity calculations, irrespective of whether the interest and payment period coincide, we call them **general annuity procedures**. In other texts you may see the name complex annuity methods. A complex annuity is simply another name for a general annuity.

Not only will we be studying annuities that have different interest and payment periods, but we also will learn about a very special type of annuity that has payments that go on forever, called a **perpetuity**.

Included in this chapter is an appendix that provides a brief discussion of the topics of Net Present Value and Discounted Cash Flow. These procedures are designed to provide a framework for using annuity procedures to evaluate business investment decisions.

OBJECTIVES

When you have completed this chapter you will be able to explain and do all the computations necessary to have a good working knowledge of general annuities and perpetuities. In particular, you will be able to:

1. explain the meaning of a general annuity;
2. calculate the amount and present value for an ordinary general annuity, a general annuity due, and a general deferred annuity;
3. calculate the periodic payment and the number of payments for general annuities — ordinary, due, and deferred;
4. explain the meaning of simple and general perpetuities, and be able to determine the present value for each;
5. evaluate investment decisions using net present value and discounted cash flow.

10.1 General Annuities and the Amount

With the annuities discussed so far, there has been the common feature that the interest period and the payment period coincided. As will be seen, this is not always the case in the real world. The topic of general annuities addresses the circumstance where payments and interest periods are different. Although general annuities allow for different interest and payment periods, the same methods are used to calculate general annuities as ordinary simple annuities, with one slight adjustment for interest rates. Equally important is that the formulas for general annuities can be used for both simple or general annuities. This is the reason for the title general annuities. (Remember that the terms general and complex mean the same.)

General annuities are common in government and corporate finance. Two applications are the retirement of long term debt, where a future sum is required, and a pension plan scheme that requires a future value for someone's retirement.

For example, suppose you are contributing to a pension plan that requires end of the month payments of $200. If the interest rate is 6% compounded semiannually, what is the amount after ten years? The first thing that should be noted is that the interest period and the payment period are different. There are two ways we can approach the problem.

One approach to the general annuity is to calculate an equivalent monthly rate, using the procedures outlined in Chapter 7, then replace $\boldsymbol{i}$ in the annuity formulas from Chapter 8 with the equivalent rate.

Another approach is to develop an annuity formula for an ordinary general annuity, which, as part of the calculations, transforms the interest rate to an equivalent rate. This second approach saves one step in the calculations over the first method. However, it can be confusing because of the number of terms in each annuity formula.

The approach taken in this book will be to show you both methods for finding the amount and present value for ordinary general annuities. In the later examples, you will find that the first method (finding the equivalent rate of interest and then substituting it into the annuity formula) is used — but please, use either method. Your choice of method is simply a personal preference. When our attention turns to a general annuity due and general deferred annuity only the first method, using the equivalent rate of interest, will be used.

A. Method 1: Using the Equivalent Rate of Interest

Turning to the problem at hand, we wish to compute the sum of $200 end of the month payments for ten years at an interest rate of 6% compounded semiannually. The formula we would use from Chapter 8 is:

$$S_n = \frac{R[(1 + i)^n - 1]}{i}$$

In this problem we know:

$$R = \$200$$

$$n = 120$$

$$i = \frac{0.06}{2}, \text{ or } 0.03 \text{ semiannually}$$

The difference in this problem is that the payments are monthly and the interest rate is calculated semiannually. Therefore, to use our S_n formula we must now convert the semiannual rate to a monthly equivalent rate of interest. Using the approach of Chapter 7, the calculation would be:

$$\left[1 + \frac{0.06}{2}\right]^2 = (1 + i)^{12}$$

The above expression states that there is a rate, i, that when compounded twelve times a year will yield interest the same as 6% compounded twice a year. Here the unknown value of i is the monthly rate of interest, equivalent to 6% compounded semiannually. Now solving for i yields:

$$i = (1.03)^{\frac{2}{12}} - 1$$

$$i = (1.03)^{\frac{1}{6}} - 1$$

$$i \doteq 0.0049386$$

Thus, 0.0049386 × 12, or 5.926% compounded monthly is equivalent to 6%

compounded semiannually. To solve our annuity problem, we now substitute the equivalent rate into our amount formula, that is:

$$S_n = \frac{R[(1+i)^n - 1]}{i} \quad \text{where } i \text{ will be } 0.0049386$$

Substituting the other values yields:

$$S_n \doteq \frac{\$200[(1+0.0049386)^{120} - 1]}{0.0049386}$$

$$S_n \doteq \$32{,}645.19$$

Thus, if we make payments of \$200 a month for ten years and the rate of interest is 6% compounded semiannually, the amount will be \$32,645.19.

From this last example, it is possible to develop a formula for finding the equivalent rate of interest derived from the $(1 + i)^n$ expression. This formula can be expressed as:

$$f = (1+i)^c - 1$$ **Formula 10.1**

Where:

f = the equivalent rate of interest
i = the rate of interest per conversion period

$$c = \frac{\text{(number of interest conversion periods per year)}}{\text{(number of payment periods per year)}}$$

In our example, f would have been found as follows:

$i = 0.03$ (compounded semiannually)

$$c = \frac{2}{12}, \text{ or } \frac{\text{2 semiannual conversions per year}}{\text{12 monthly payments per year}}$$

$$f = (1+0.03)^{\frac{2}{12}} - 1$$

$$f \doteq 1.0049386 - 1$$

$$f \doteq 0.0049386$$

Using the formula for the equivalent rate of interest, we can adjust the amount formula for an ordinary annuity to a general annuity formula as follows:

$$S_n = \frac{R[(1+f)^n - 1]}{f}$$ **Formula 10.2**

Calculator Solution

						Solution
Input	200	(f) 0.49386	120			
Depress	PMT	i	n	COMP	FV	32,645.19

B. Method 2: Using the General Annuity Formula

A second formula that could be used to find the amount of an ordinary general annuity would be to substitute the expression for f directly into our annuity formula. Therefore, everywhere f appears in Formula 10.2 substitute $(1 + i)^c - 1$, which yields the following:

$$S_{nc} = \frac{R([1 + (1 + i)^c - 1]^n - 1)}{[(1 + i)^c - 1]}$$

The reason S_{nc} was used instead of S_n was to make it clear that we are now using a general annuity formula that computes the equivalent rate in the process of finding the amount. Reducing the expression yields Formula 10.3, which calculates the amount of a general annuity, including the computation of the equivalent rate.

$$S_{nc} = \frac{R[(1 + i)^{nc} - 1]}{[(1 + i)^c - 1]} \qquad \textbf{Formula 10.3}$$

EXAMPLE 10.1

Find the amount of an annuity that requires payments of $1,000 at the end of each month for six years, if the interest rate is 18% compounded semiannually.

Solution If we apply Formula 10.3 directly we must first determine the value of each term in the expression:

$$R = \$1{,}000$$

$$i = \frac{0.18}{2}, \text{ or } 0.09$$

$$n = 12 \times 6, \text{ or } 72$$

$$c = \frac{2}{12}$$

$$S_{nc} = \frac{R[(1 + i)^{nc} - 1]}{[(1 + i)^c - 1]}$$

Now substituting:

$$S_{nc} = \frac{\$1{,}000[(1 + 0.09)^{(72)(\frac{2}{12})} - 1]}{[(1 + 0.09)^{\frac{2}{12}} - 1]}$$

$$S_{nc} \doteq \$1{,}000[125.3000545]$$

$$S_{nc} \doteq \$125{,}300.05$$

The amount of the annuity is $125,300.05.

Just to confirm that this result and the method using the equivalent rate of interest produce the same results, you should rework the problem using f and Formula 10.2.

10.2 General Annuities and Present Value

In our discussion above we noted that two methods can be used to compute the value of a general annuity. A similar approach will be used in this section on present value.

Before we get too far along, it is valuable to gain some idea of where one might use the general annuity method for present value in business and personal finance. The most common example that people experience is the standard residential mortgage. If you call your local bank or trust company and ask them how often they calculate the interest on a standard residential mortgage, you will normally find that the interest is compounded semiannually and the payments occur monthly. This is a good example of a general annuity. Other examples include certain consumer loans, credit card charges, and retirement plans.

A. Method 1: Using the Equivalent Rate of Interest

As you will recall, the present value of an ordinary simple annuity was found in Chapter 8 by using the formula:

$$A_n = \frac{R[1 - (1 + i)^{-n}]}{i}$$

Using our formula for finding the equivalent rate of interest we can adjust our ordinary simple annuity formula to provide for the difference in payment and interest period. As you will remember, the formula we used for the equivalent rate was:

$$f = (1 + i)^c - 1$$

Where c was defined as follows:

$$c = \frac{\text{The number of interest conversion periods per year}}{\text{The number of payment periods per year}}$$

Substituting f for i into our present value formula, we have the formula for finding the present value of a general annuity.

$$A_n = \frac{R[1 - (1 + f)^{-n}]}{f}$$ **Formula 10.4**

EXAMPLE 10.2

Ron and Susan have just purchased a house and arranged a mortgage with the Royal Bank. The mortgage is to have monthly payments of \$818.15 and will be paid off over 25 years. If the interest rate is 11% compounded semi-annually, what is the size of the mortgage?

Solution To find the size of the mortgage we must find the present value of the monthly payments over the 25 year period. We can see that the payment period and the interest period do not coincide, thus requiring the use of the general annuity formula. The first step is to find f, which is done as follows:

$$f = (1 + i)^c - 1$$

Where:

$$i = \frac{0.11}{2}, \text{ or } 0.055$$

$$c = \frac{2}{12}$$

This states that there are two interest periods per year divided by twelve payments per year.

Substituting these into our formula for f yields:

$$f = (1 + 0.055)^{\frac{2}{12}} - 1$$

$$\doteq 0.008963394$$

Now substituting the value of f into the annuity formula would go as follows:

$$A_n = \frac{R[1 - (1 + f)^{-n}]}{f}$$

$$R = \$818.15$$

$$n = 12 \times 25, \text{ or } 300$$ 12 payments per year for 25 years.

$$f = 0.00896339$$

$$A_n = \frac{\$818.15[1 - (1 + 0.00896339)^{-300}]}{0.00896339}$$

$$A_n = \$818.15[103.8929555]$$

$$A_n = \$85{,}000.02$$

Therefore, the size of the mortgage must be \$85,000, with the \$0.02 simply occurring through rounding.

Calculator Solution

						Solution
Input	818.15	(f) 0.896339	300			
Depress	PMT	i	n	COMP	PV	85,000.02

B. Method 2: Using the General Annuity Formula

Another method for finding the present value of a general annuity is to use a formula that converts the interest rate to an equivalent rate and computes the present value — all within one expression (A_{nc}). The way this formula is derived is to substitute the expression for f into the present value formula for an ordinary simple annuity. Let's see how it works:

$$A_n = \frac{R[1 - (1 + i)^{-n}]}{i} \qquad \text{From Chapter 8.}$$

Substitute f for i, where f is $(1 + i)^c - 1$ gives:

$$A_{nc} = \frac{R[1 - (1 + (1 + i)^c - 1)^{-n}]}{(1 + i)^c - 1}$$

If we bring all the terms together, we end up with:

$$A_{nc} = \frac{R[1 - (1 + i)^{-nc}]}{(1 + i)^c - 1}$$

The last expression is normally written as:

$$A_{nc} = \frac{R[1 - (1 + i)^{-nc}]}{(1 + i)^c - 1} \qquad \textbf{Formula 10.5}$$

Formula 10.5 permits us to do everything in one step so to speak. Consider Example 10.2, above, using this approach to present value:

$R = \$818.15$

$i = \frac{0.11}{2}$, or 0.055

$n = 12 \times 25$, or 300

$c = \frac{2}{12}$ $\qquad \frac{\text{interest conversion periods per year}}{\text{the number of payments per year}}$

Substituting into Formula 10.5 gives:

$$A_{nc} = \frac{\$818.15[1 - (1 + 0.055)^{-300(\frac{2}{12})}]}{(1 + 0.055)^{\frac{2}{12}} - 1}$$

$A_{nc} \doteq \$85,000.02$ The same as above.

The method you should use is the one you understand best, since both are equivalent. Let's look at another example before moving to the next section:

EXAMPLE 10.3

The Volke family purchased a small store including the inventory and agreed to pay the present owner $5,000 at the end of every three months for the next ten years. If the interest rate is 12% compounded semiannually, what would be the cash price of the store?

Solution The solution requires us to recognize that the payment period and the interest period do not coincide. Determining the value for each term gives:

$$i = \frac{0.12}{2}, \text{ or } 0.06$$

$$R = \$5,000$$

$$n = 4 \times 10, \text{ or } 40$$

$$c = \frac{2}{4}$$ Based on the interest being calculated twice a year with quarterly payments.

Substituting into our formula goes as follows:

$$A_{nc} = \frac{R[1 - (1 + i)^{-nc}]}{(1 + i)^c - 1}$$

$$A_{nc} = \frac{\$5,000[1 - (1 + 0.06)^{-40(\frac{2}{4})}]}{(1 + 0.06)^{\frac{2}{4}} - 1}$$

$$A_{nc} \doteq \$5,000[23.278928]$$

$$A_{nc} \doteq \$116,394.64$$

Thus, based on the information, we expect the purchase price was $116,395.64. (*Note:* the actual price was most likely $116,395; the difference occurs because of rounding error.)

EXERCISE 10.1

(Unless otherwise specified, assume all payments are at the end of each period.)

For problems 1 to 10 find the amount and present value for the given complex and simple annuities.

	Payment Period	Payment *R*	Term of the Annuity	Annual Interest Rate and Compound Period
1.	Monthly	$ 2,450	4 years	12.4%, annually
2.	Annually	650	16 years	14.0%, quarterly
3.	Quarterly	460	15 years	15.0%, monthly
4.	Semiannually	780	2 years	17.8%, daily
5.	Monthly	750	18 years	14.0%, semiannually
6.	Monthly	470	10 years	17.0%, annually
7.	Quarterly	800	2 years	14.8%, monthly
8.	Yearly	600	4 years	23.0%, monthly
9.	Quarterly	2,450	7 years	15.5%, quarterly
10.	Daily	3,500	8 years	16.7%, daily

11. Find the amount and present value of an annuity that has regular payments of $6,500 payable at the end of each six month interval for five years, if the interest rate is (a) 14% compounded annually, and (b) 14% compounded monthly.

12. A computer company has just purchased a building and agrees to pay a $40,000 down payment and make semiannual payments of $25,000 for the next five years. The interest rate is 18% compounded monthly. What is the price of the building?

13. If the company who sold the building in problem 12 decides to invest all the monies from the sale, including the semiannual payments, what will be the amount in their investment fund at the end of ten years? Assume the fund pays 12% compounded monthly.

14. Fred wishes to retire with a lump sum of $100,000 and then draw a monthly income for fifteen years of $945. Fred starts his pension savings with end of the month deposits of $250 for the next twenty years. If Fred expects the interest rate to be 6% compounded yearly, over the entire period of his plan, will everything work out the way he is planning?

15. A house can be purchased for $5,000 down with monthly payments of $750 per month for twenty years. If the interest rate is 10% compounded semiannually, what is the purchase price of the house?

10.3 Finding the Payment for an Ordinary General Annuity When the Amount and Present Value Are Known

Finding of the regular payment R, for an ordinary general annuity when the amount or present value is known, uses the methods used in Chapter 8 to find R for an ordinary annuity. The expressions we will use are a rearrangement of the earlier formulas introduced in this chapter. The derivation of the formulas below are shown for Formulas 10.2 and 10.4 — no expression is given for the method using "nc".

A. Finding *R* When the Amount Is Known

The expression for R, given the amount of an ordinary general annuity is found by rearranging

$$S_n = \frac{R[(1+f)^c - 1]}{f}$$

and solving for R. This gives:

$$R = \frac{S_n}{\frac{[(1+f)^n - 1]}{f}}$$

Formula 10.6

B. Finding *R* When the Present Value Is Known

As with finding R when the amount was known, we start with the expression for A_n and rearrange it to find R. Therefore:

$$A_n = \frac{R[(1-(1+f)^{-n}]}{f}$$

Rearranging for R gives:

$$R = \frac{A_n}{\frac{[(1-(1+f)^{-n}]}{f}}$$

Formula 10.7

These two formulas will find the payment R for an ordinary general annuity when the amount and present value are known.

EXAMPLE 10.4

Sally and Harry have just decided to invest in a fund to save \$20,000. They plan to use the money for their child's education and expect to contribute to the fund for fifteen years. What will be the required payment at the end of every two-month period if the interest rate paid by the fund is 10% compounded annually?

Solution Since the amount is known we use Formula 10.6. The value for each term is:

$$S_n = \$20{,}000$$

$$i = 0.10$$

$$n = 6 \times 15, \text{ or } 90$$

$$c = \frac{1}{6}$$ One interest period per year divided by six payments per year.

Substituting into our Formula 10.6 gives:

$$f = (1 + 0.1)^{\frac{1}{6}} - 1$$

$$\doteq 0.016012$$

$$R = \frac{S_n}{\frac{[(1+f)^n - 1]}{f}}$$

$$R \doteq \frac{\$20{,}000}{\frac{[(1 + 0.016012)^{90} - 1]}{0.016012}}$$

$$R \doteq \frac{\$20{,}000}{[198.4322444]}$$

$$R \doteq \$100.79$$

If payments of \$100.79 are made at the end of every two months for the next fifteen years there will be \$20,000 in the fund.

Calculator Solution

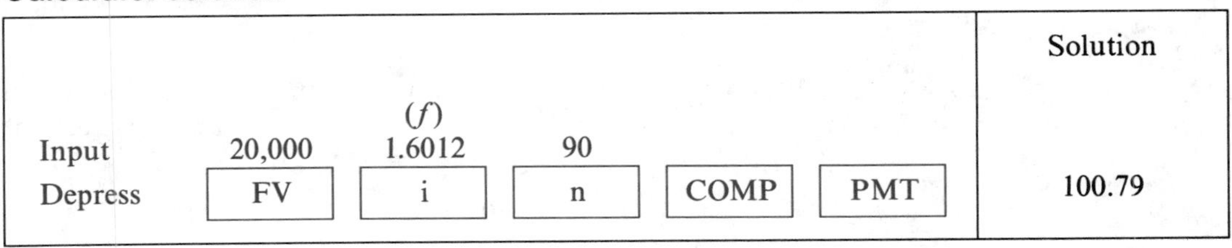

						Solution
Input	20,000	(f) 1.6012	90			
Depress	FV	i	n	COMP	PMT	100.79

EXAMPLE 10.5

Joan is thinking about purchasing a home in a small rural community. She has found a house that has an asking price of \$100,000. The Realtor advises her that the owner will accept \$95,000. She has \$10,000 to use as a down payment and she has a monthly "take home" income of \$2,100. Joan does not wish to have end of month payments more than 35% of her monthly income. The bank's current mortgage rate on a 25 year mortgage is 11.5% compounded semiannually. Can Joan afford to buy the house?

Solution The most direct way to solve this problem is to find the required payment on the mortgage, assuming she can purchase the house for \$95,000. Applying the \$10,000 down payment leaves a balance of \$85,000 to be financed over 25 years with monthly payments at 11.5% compounded semiannually. Using our formula we have:

$$R = \frac{A_n}{\left[\frac{[1-(1+f)^{-n}]}{f}\right]}$$

Where:

$$A_n = \$85{,}000$$

$$i = \frac{0.115}{2}, \text{ or } 0.0575$$

$$n = 12 \times 25, \text{ or } 300$$

$$c = \frac{2}{12}$$

$$f = (1 + 0.0575)^{\frac{1}{6}} - 1$$

$$\doteq 0.00936149$$

Substituting into our formula gives:

$$R = \frac{\$85{,}000}{\left[\frac{1-(1+0.00936149)^{-300}}{0.00936149}\right]}$$

$$R \doteq \frac{\$85{,}000}{[100.2948104]}$$

$$R \doteq \$847.50$$

Now we must determine whether the monthly payment of \$847.50 is greater or less than 35% of her monthly income. Therefore, 35% of her monthly income is:

$$0.35 \times \$2{,}100 = \$735$$

Thus, \$735 represents the maximum mortgage payment she is prepared to accept. Since the monthly mortgage payment is \$847.50, she will be unable to purchase the house. If Joan is prepared to increase the percentage to 41% of her monthly income she could just meet the payment.

Calculator Solution

						Solution
Input	85,000	(f) 0.936149	300			
Depress	PV	i	n	COMP	PMT	847.50

10.4 Finding the Term (Number of Payments) When the Amount or Present Value Is Known

A. Finding *n* When the Amount Is Known

The procedure for finding the number of payments, n, for a general annuity is again similar to the methods presented in Chapter 8. The major difference is that we must be able to accommodate situations where the interest period and the payment period are different. The change required is to modify the formulas from Chapter 8, replacing i with f, the equivalent rate of interest.

From Chapter 8, the formula for n when the amount was known was:

$$n = \frac{\ln\left[1 + \frac{S_n i}{R}\right]}{\ln(1 + i)}$$

Substituting f for i yields:

$$n = \frac{\ln\left[1 + \frac{S_n f}{R}\right]}{\ln(1 + f)}$$

Formula 10.8

EXAMPLE 10.6

Jill has started depositing money into a retirement fund. Once she has \$100,000 accumulated she plans to retire. Jill plans to deposit \$500 at the end of every three months to a RRSP that pays interest at 8% compounded annually. When can she retire?

Solution First, identify the values of the terms for Formula 10.8:

$$R = \$500$$

$$S_n = \$100{,}000$$

$$i = 0.08$$

$$c = \frac{1}{4}$$ One interest period per year divided by the number of payments per year.

$$f = (1 + 0.08)^{\frac{1}{4}} - 1$$ Finding the equivalent rate.

$$f \doteq 0.01942655$$

Substituting these into our formula:

$$n = \frac{\ln\left[1 + \frac{S_n f}{R}\right]}{\ln(1 + f)}$$

$$n \doteq \frac{\ln\left[1 + \frac{\$100{,}000(0.01942655)}{500}\right]}{\ln(1 + 0.01942655)}$$

$$n \doteq 82.4434$$

To find the number of years Jill has to wait, we divide the number of payments by four, yielding $\frac{82.4434}{4}$, or 20.611 years.

Calculator Solution

Input	500	1.942655	100,000				
Depress	PMT	i	+/−	FV	COMP	n	82.4464

B. Finding *n* When the Present Value Is Known

The procedure used to find the term or number of payments, when the present value is known, follows the method used for a given amount.

First, we identify the formula we used in Chapter 8 for finding n when the present value is known:

$$n = \frac{-\ln\left[1 - \frac{A_n i}{R}\right]}{\ln(1 + i)}$$

Next we modify the formula, replacing i with f:

$$n = \frac{-\ln\left[1 - \frac{A_n f}{R}\right]}{\ln(1+f)}$$ **Formula 10.9**

EXAMPLE 10.7

Don and Marion Patrick are considering buying a house. At a meeting with their bank manager they are advised that the monthly payment on a $100,000 mortgage is $962.53, based on payments over 25 years and an interest rate of 11% compounded semiannually. Instead, the Patricks decide to make monthly payments of $1,050. If the couple continues to make $1,050 payments over the life of the mortgage, how long will it take to repay it?

Solution The solution involves a direct application of Formula 10.9. Defining the terms gives us:

$$R = \$1{,}050$$

$$i = \frac{0.11}{2}, \text{ or } 0.055$$

$$c = \frac{2}{12}, \text{ or } \frac{1}{6}$$

$$f = (1 + 0.055)^{\frac{1}{6}} - 1, \text{ or } 0.00896339$$

$$A_n = \$100{,}000$$

Using Formula 10.9 and substituting terms we have:

$$n = \frac{-\ln\left[1 - \frac{A_n f}{R}\right]}{\ln(1+f)}$$

$$n \doteq \frac{-\ln\left[1 - \frac{\$100{,}000(0.00896339)}{\$1{,}050}\right]}{\ln(1 + 0.00896339)}$$

$$n \doteq \frac{-[-1.92179911]}{[0.00892346]}$$

$$n \doteq 215.36 \text{ payments, or } \frac{215.36}{12}, \text{ or } 17.95 \text{ years}$$

Therefore, if Don and Marion make monthly payments of $1,050 instead of $962.35, they will pay off their mortgage in 17.95 years, or 216 payments.

The first 215 payments will be $1,050. The final payment at period 216 will be a slightly smaller payment.

Calculator Solution

Input	1,050	0.896339	100,000				
Depress	PMT	i	+/−	PV	COMP	n	215.36

EXERCISE 10.2

For the ordinary annuities in problems 1 to 10, find the number of payments (the term) for the given present value and amount.

	Conversion Period	Present Value (A_n)	Amount (S_n)	Regular Payment and Payment Period R	Interest Rate
1.	Annually	$15,500	$85,000	$ 500.00, monthly	11.4%
2.	Quarterly	25,000	35,500	3,000.00, semiannually	12.8%
3.	Monthly	25,400	34,400	1,350.00, quarterly	18.6%
4.	Annually	10,450	95,500	2,500.00, monthly	11.4%
5.	Semiannually	89,500	45,000	4,500.00, monthly	19.2%
6.	Monthly	21,000	35,000	2,950.00, annually	13.0%
7.	Quarterly	4,500	10,000	200.00, monthly	18.1%
8.	Yearly	5,500	12,000	650.00, semiannually	22.5%
9.	Quarterly	2,450	15,450	50.00, monthly	16.3%
10.	Monthly	2,800	45,500	450.00, quarterly	19.1%

11. The City of Oakville wants to establish a fund of $20 million to act as a reserve against unforeseen emergencies. The City Council votes to deposit payments in a special trust fund that earns 9% compounded annually. What will be the necessary end of quarter payments if the City wants the fund in place at the end of eight years? If the City decides to set aside $800,000 every quarter, how long will it take to reach the $20 million goal?

12. Brian wants to have a retirement fund of $75,000 in place upon retirement. Brian decides to make monthly payments to a RRSP that pays 8.5% compounded quarterly. What are the necessary monthly payments if Brian wishes to retire in seven years? Also, upon retirement, Brian wants to have a monthly income of $1,000. For how long can he receive monthly payments of $1,000 if the interest rate remains at 8.5% compounded quarterly?

13. If $240 is deposited at the end of every three months, and money is worth 10% compounded semiannually, how long will it take to accumulate $5,000?

14. Eric and Kelly Crowley have arranged to buy a new house and will require a mortgage of $95,000. The interest rate is 10.5% compounded semiannually, and the mortgage will be based on a twenty-year amortization period. Find the size of the end of the month payments?

15. If the Crowleys in problem 14 decide to increase their monthly payment by $75, how long will it take to pay back the mortgage?

10.5 General Annuity Due

As you may recall, the main feature of an annuity due is that the payments come at the **beginning** of the period. As a result, when compared to an ordinary annuity, there is always one extra period of interest per payment when accumulating and one less discount period per payment.

In Chapter 9 we developed a series of formulas for an annuity due. In this chapter we'll modify our earlier annuity due method to allow for situations where the compound period and the payment period do not coincide. In the discussion that follows, all formula will be developed using the equivalent rate of interest, substituted for i.

A. Finding the Amount of a General Annuity Due

The formula used to find the amount of a simple annuity due in Chapter 9 was:

$$S_n(\text{due}) = \frac{R(1 + i)[(1 + i)^n - 1]}{i}$$

As before, replace i with the equivalent rate f. From our previous discussion of general annuities, f can be found by using the expression:

$f = (1 + i)^c - 1$ — Where c refers to the number of interest periods per year divided by the number of payments per year.

Now replacing i with f directly gives the amount formula for a general annuity due as:

$$S_n(\text{due}) = \frac{R(1 + f)[(1 + f)^n - 1]}{f} \qquad \textbf{Formula 10.10}$$

EXAMPLE 10.8

Gates West Electronics has established a fund to replace a piece of equipment. The expected cost of replacement in five years is $65,000. The company is going to set aside $800 a month, starting today (payments are at the beginning of the period). The firm can accumulate money at 7% compounded semi-annually. Will the company have enough money in five years to replace the machine?

Solution Since the payments start today we can see the appropriateness of the annuity due formula. Also, since the interest compounding period is different from the payment period, we use the general annuity method. Let's first identify the known values:

$$R = \$800$$

$$i = \frac{0.07}{2}, \text{ or } 0.035$$

$$n = 12 \times 5, \text{ or } 60$$

$$c = \frac{2}{12}$$

$$f = (1 + 0.035)^{\frac{2}{12}} - 1, \text{ or } 0.00575004$$

The formula we'll use is 10.10.

$$S_n(\text{due}) = \frac{R(1+f)[(1+f)^n - 1]}{f}$$

Substituting:

$$S_n(\text{due}) \doteq \frac{\$800(1 + 0.00575004)[(1 + 0.00575004)^{60} - 1]}{0.00575004}$$

$$S_n(\text{due}) \doteq \$800(71.818587)$$

$$S_n(\text{due}) \doteq \$57{,}454.87$$

Therefore, in five years Gates West won't have enough money in its fund to meet the $65,000 requirement.

Calculator Solution Note the inclusion of the BGN key to recognize that the payments are at the beginning of the period.

Finding the Amount for a General Annuity Due							
Input		$800	0.575004	60			
Depress	BGN	PMT	i	n	COMP	FV	57,454.87

B. Finding the Present Value of a General Annuity Due

To find the present value of a general annuity due, modify the simple annuity due formula to include f, the equivalent rate of interest. The f factor allows us to transform the interest rate in our formula to an equivalent rate. In turn, this allows us to compute directly the present value of a general annuity due.

The formula we developed for the present value of a simple annuity due was:

$$A_n(\text{due}) = \frac{R(1+i)[1-(1+i)^{-n}]}{i}$$

Replacing i with f yields:

$$A_n(\text{due}) = \frac{R(1+f)[1-(1+f)^{-n}]}{f}$$ **Formula 10.11**

EXAMPLE 10.9

What is the present value (buy out value) of a lease that has payments of $1,500 payable at the beginning of each month for five years? Assume the interest rate is 18% compounded semiannually. (Note that lease and rental payments are normally made at the beginning of a period.)

Solution As with the amount formula the first step is to find f:

$$i = \frac{0.18}{2}, \text{ or } 0.09$$

$$f = (1+i)^c - 1 \text{ where } c = \frac{2}{12}$$

Therefore:

$$f = (1+0.09)^{\frac{2}{12}} - 1$$

$$f \doteq 0.01446659$$

Next we list the known terms and substitute them into Formula 10.11:

$$R = \$1{,}500$$

$$f = 0.01446659$$

$$n = 12 \times 5, \text{ or } 60$$

$$A_n(\text{due}) \doteq \frac{\$1{,}500(1+0.01446659)[1-(1+0.01446659)^{-60}]}{0.01446659}$$

$$A_n(\text{due}) \doteq \$1{,}500(40.50332)$$

$$A_n(\text{due}) \doteq \$60{,}754.98$$

If someone wanted to buy out the lease today, it would be worth $60,754.98.

Calculator Solution

	Finding the Present Value for a General Annuity Due					
Input		$1,500	1.446659	60			
Depress	BGN	PMT	i	n	COMP	PV	60,754.98

C. Finding the Payment for a General Annuity Due

(i) Finding the Payment When the Amount Is Known

To find the payment for an amount of a general annuity due we must rearrange Formula 10.10 and solve for R. This yields:

$$R = \frac{S_n(\text{due})}{\frac{(1+f)[(1+f)^n - 1]}{f}}$$

Formula 10.12

EXAMPLE 10.10

A local government has a debt of $75,000 that comes due in five years. How much does the municipality need to set aside, at the beginning of each month, to have the required funds to repay the debt when it comes due? The municipality can earn 9% compounded annually.

Solution As with our previous examples, the first step is to find f, the equivalent rate of interest.

$$f = (1 + i)^c - 1$$

Where:

$$i = 0.09$$

$$c = \frac{1}{12}$$

Therefore, the value of f will be:

$$f = (1 + 0.09)^{\frac{1}{12}} - 1$$

$$f \doteq 0.007207323$$

Now defining the other values of the problem:

$S_n(\text{due}) = \$75{,}000$

$n = 12 \times 5$, or 60

Substituting all the knowns into Formula 10.12 yields:

$$R = \frac{S_n(\text{due})}{\dfrac{(1+f)[(1+f)^n - 1]}{f}}$$

$$R \doteq \frac{\$75{,}000}{\dfrac{(1+0.007207323)[(1+0.007207323)^{60} - 1]}{0.007207323}}$$

$$R \doteq \frac{\$75{,}000}{(75.27149373)}$$

$$R \doteq \$996.39$$

If the municipality sets aside $996.39 at the beginning of each month, it will have the required $75,000 in five years.

Calculator Solution

Input		$75,000	0.7207323	60			
Depress	BGN	FV	i	n	COMP	PMT	996.39

(ii) Finding the Payment When the Present Value Is Known

To find the payment of a general annuity due, we rearrange the present value formula for a general annuity due (Formula 10.11) and solve for R. The algebra is the same as that used to find R for an annuity due in Chapter 9. The expression for R is:

$$R = \frac{A_n(\text{due})}{\dfrac{(1+f)[1 - (1+f)^{-n}]}{f}}$$

Formula 10.13

EXAMPLE 10.11

Margaret Pearson has just arranged a mortgage that requires payments at the beginning of each month. The mortgage is $87,000 and the interest is compounded semiannually at 12%. What will be the size of the monthly payments if Margaret wants to repay the mortgage in ten years?

Solution Defining the value for each term:

$$A_n(\text{due}) = \$87{,}000$$

$$i = \frac{0.12}{2}, \text{ or } 0.06$$

$$c = \frac{2}{12}$$

$$n = 12 \times 10, \text{ or } 120$$

$$f = (1 + 0.06)^{\frac{2}{12}} - 1, \text{ or } 0.009758794$$

Substituting these into our formula we have:

$$R = \frac{A_n(\text{due})}{\frac{(1+f)[1-(1+f)^{-n}]}{f}}$$

$$R \doteq \frac{\$87{,}000}{\frac{(1+0.009758794)[1-(1+0.009758794)^{-120}]}{0.009758794}}$$

$$R \doteq \$1{,}221.76$$

Calculator Solution

Input		\$87,000	0.9758794	120			
Depress	BGN	PV	i	n	COMP	PMT	1,221.76

The value of each payment will be \$1,221.76, when the mortgage is repaid over 10 years with beginning of the month payments.

D. Finding the Number of Payments for a General Annuity Due

To find the number of payments for a general annuity due, we adjust our expressions for finding n for an ordinary annuity due to reflect a general annuity.

(i) Finding *n* for a Known Amount Given *R* and *i*

When S_n(due) is known, and the payments and compound period do not coincide, it is possible to find n by inserting f, the equivalent rate, into the formula for n given the amount of a simple annuity due (see Chapter 9). This would give:

$$n = \frac{\ln\left[1 + \frac{S_n(\text{due})f}{R(1+f)}\right]}{\ln(1+f)} \quad \text{(from Formula 9.5)} \qquad \textbf{Formula 10.14}$$

(ii) Finding *n* for a Known Present Value Given *R* and *i*

As with the amount, to find an expression for the number of payments for a general annuity due, we simply replace i with f in the ordinary annuity due formula for n. This yields:

$$n = \frac{-\ln\left[1 - \frac{A_n(\text{due})f}{R(1+f)}\right]}{\ln(1+f)} \quad \text{(from Formula 9.6)} \qquad \textbf{Formula 10.15}$$

EXERCISE 10.3

For problems 1 to 5 find the amount and present value for the given annuities. Assume in each case that the payments come at the beginning of the period.

	Payment Period	Payment	Term of the Annuity	Interest Rate and Conversion Period
1.	Annually	$ 2,500	6 years	15.0%, monthly
2.	Quarterly	1,600	14 years	12.0%, annually
3.	Monthly	1,250	17 years	17.0%, semiannually
4.	Quarterly	4,500	4 years	14.5%, monthly
5.	Semiannually	1,450	16 years	14.0%, annually

For problems 6 to 10 find the required payments for the given amount and present value for the following annuities.

	Payment Period	Present Value A_n(due)	Amount S_n(due)	Term of the Annuity	Interest Rate and Conversion Period
6.	Annually	$ 12,000	$ 45,000	6 years	16.5%, monthly
7.	Quarterly	35,000	65,500	18 years	12.0%, annually
8.	Monthly	14,500	21,500	13 years	18.5%, semiannually
9.	Annually	58,500	49,340	6 years	14.0%, quarterly
10.	Semiannually	85,500	74,000	20 years	13.0%, monthly

11. Find the amount of a retirement annuity that requires one to deposit $1,500 at the beginning of each quarter. The term of the annuity is ten years and the interest rate is 16% compounded annually.

12. What is the cash price for a lease that requires beginning of the month payments of $2,000 for seven years? The interest rate is 8% compounded semiannually.

13. An annuity offers monthly payments of $500 at the beginning of each month and has an interest rate of 9% compounded annually. If the annuity can be purchased today for $10,000, how long will the monthly payments continue?

14. How much money must be invested in a fund, at the beginning of each month, if a municipality requires $1,000,000 in fifteen years to repay a bond issue for local improvements? Assume the municipality can earn 10% compounded quarterly.

15. Ken has just arranged financing on a piece of property. The financing is for $250,000 and must be repaid by monthly payments over a ten year period. The payments are at the beginning of each month and the interest rate is 14% compounded semiannually. What is the size of each monthly payment?

10.6 General Deferred Annuity

A general deferred annuity can be handled by modifying the formulas developed in Chapter 9 for a deferred annuity. We just incorporate the equivalent rate of interest, f, for i.

Remember, deferring an annuity makes no difference to the amount of an annuity. That is, only present value is affected by a deferral period.

In addition, there will be a brief discussion of the situation where the payments come at the beginning of each payment period, making the annuity a general deferred annuity due.

A. Present Value of a Deferred General Annuity

The present value of a deferred general annuity can be found by substituting f for i in the formula:

$$A_n(\text{def}) = \frac{R(1+i)^{-d}[1-(1+i)^{-n}]}{i}$$ From Chapter 9.

Recalling that the formula for f is:

$$f = (1+i)^c - 1$$

Substituting yields:

$$A_n(\text{def}) = \frac{R(1+f)^{-d}[1-(1+f)^{-n}]}{f}$$ **Formula 10.16**

EXAMPLE 10.12

Julian is buying an income averaging annuity to defer income tax by averaging income over more than one year. The annuity will provide payments of \$400 at the end of each month for three years. The payments commence at the end of three years and the interest rate is 9% compounded semiannually. What should he pay today for the annuity?

Solution First we must find the value of each term for the formula. These are:

$R = \$400$

$i = \frac{0.09}{2}$, or 0.045

$c = \frac{2}{12}$, or $\frac{1}{6}$

$n = 12 \times 3$, or 36

$f = (1 + 0.045)^{\frac{1}{6}} - 1$, or 0.00736312

$d = 35$

This value results from the understanding that the first payment occurs at the end of the third year, or period 36, giving 35 deferral periods, i.e., there is a payment in period 36, therefore, this is not part of the deferral period.

Now substituting we have:

$$A_n(\text{def}) = \frac{R(1+f)^{-d}[1-(1+f)^{-n}]}{f}$$

$$A_n(\text{def}) \doteq \frac{\$400(1+0.00736312)^{-35}[1-(1+0.00736312)^{-36}]}{0.00736312}$$

$$A_n(\text{def}) \doteq \$400(24.38440)$$

$$A_n(\text{def}) \doteq \$9{,}753.70$$

A fair price to pay for the annuity, if it is to be deferred for 35 periods, is \$9,753.70.

Calculator Solution The steps involved using the calculator:

1. Find the present value for an ordinary general annuity;
2. Discount the present value by the deferral factor — $(1+f)^{-d}$.

Input	400	36	0.736312			
Depress	PMT	n	i	COMP	PV	12,609.01
Discount PV by the Deferral Factor $(1+0.00736312)^{-35}$ (12,609.01)						9,753.70

B. Finding the Payment for a General Deferred Annuity

The formula to find R for a general deferred annuity requires that i in the deferred formula of Chapter 9, be changed to f, the equivalent rate. Thus, rearranging Formula 10.16 and solving for R gives:

$$R = \frac{A_n(\text{def})}{\frac{(1+f)^{-d}[1-(1+f)^{-n}]}{f}}$$

Formula 10.17

EXAMPLE 10.13

Andrex Holdings has just borrowed \$300,000 to finance a new land development project. The repayment requires end of quarter payments to begin after three years have passed. The interest charged is 18% compounded monthly. If the loan must be repaid over five years, once the payments begin, what is the size of each quarterly payment?

Solution Defining the values for Formula 10.17:

$$A_n(\text{def}) = \$300{,}000$$

$$i = \frac{0.18}{12}, \text{ or } 0.015$$

$$c = \frac{12}{4}$$

$$n = 5 \times 4, \text{ or } 20$$

$$d = 3 \times 4, \text{ or } 12$$ Three years pass before payments commence.

$$f = (1 + 0.015)^{\frac{12}{4}} - 1$$

$$f \doteq 0.045678375$$

Now substituting these values yields:

$$R = \frac{A_n(\text{def})}{\dfrac{(1+f)^{-d}[1-(1+f)^{-n}]}{f}}$$

$$R \doteq \frac{\$300{,}000}{\dfrac{(1+0.045678375)^{-12}[1-(1+0.045678375)^{-20}]}{0.045678375}}$$

$$R \doteq \frac{\$300{,}000}{(7.5662689)}$$

$$R \doteq \$39{,}649.66$$

Thus, payments of $39,649.66 will be required every quarter for five years to repay the debt. These payments account for the three year deferral period.

Calculator Solution The steps involved using the calculator:

1. Find the regular payment for an ordinary general annuity;
2. Divide the payment from 1 by the deferral factor, $(1 + f)^{-d}$.

Finding the Payment for a Deferred Annuity Due						
Input	300,000	20	4.5678375			
Depress	PV	n	i	COMP	PMT	23,198.61
Accounting for the Deferral Period $\dfrac{(23{,}198.61)}{(1+0.045678375)^{-12}}$						39,649.66

C. Finding the Number of Payments for a General Deferred Annuity

Again, finding the term or number of payments, n, relies on an expression developed in Chapter 9. The formula for n with an ordinary deferred annuity was:

$$n = \frac{-\ln\left[1 - \frac{A_n(\text{def})i}{R(1+i)^{-d}}\right]}{\ln(1+i)}$$

Now replacing i with f, our formula for finding n with a deferred general annuity is:

$$n = \frac{-\ln\left[1 - \frac{A_n(\text{def})f}{R(1+f)^{-d}}\right]}{\ln(1+f)}$$

Formula 10.18

EXAMPLE 10.14

If Andrex Holdings in the previous example decides to increase the payments to \$50,000, how long will it take them to repay the debt?

Solution Taking the values from the example above gives us:

$A_n(\text{def}) = \$300{,}000$

$i = \frac{0.18}{12}$, or 0.015

$d = 3 \times 4$, or 12 From previous example.

$f = (1 + 0.015)^{\frac{12}{4}} - 1$, or 0.0456784

$R = \$50{,}000$

Now substituting these values into Formula 10.18 yields:

$$n = \frac{-\ln\left[1 - \frac{A_n(\text{def})f}{R(1+f)^{-d}}\right]}{\ln(1+f)}$$

Substituting:

$$n \doteq \frac{-\ln\left[1 - \frac{\$300{,}000(0.0456784)}{\$50{,}000(1+0.0456784)^{-12}}\right]}{\ln(1+0.0456784)}$$

$n \doteq 14.1475$, or approximately 3.54 years

If the owners of Andrex Holdings increase the size of each payment from \$39,649.68 to \$50,000 they will reduce the term of their loan by almost 1.5 years (i.e., from five years to 3.54 years).

Calculator Solution The process to find n for a deferred general annuity requires the payment to first be adjusted to account for the deferral period. This adjusted payment is then used for PMT in the calculator.

$$\text{Adjusted payment} = R(1+f)^{-d}$$
$$\text{Adjusted payment} = \$50{,}000(1+0.0456784)^{-12}$$
$$= 29{,}254.48^{**}$$

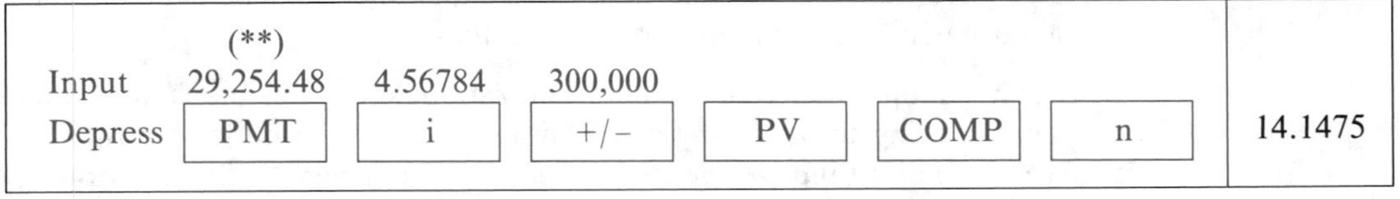

(**)
Input 29,254.48 4.56784 300,000
Depress PMT i +/− PV COMP n
14.1475

EXERCISE 10.4

For problems 1 to 5 find the unknown (?). Also, assume that all payments are end of period payments unless otherwise specified.

	Payment Period	A_n (def)	Payments R	Term of the Payments	Payments Start at the End of	Interest Rate and Conversion Period
1.	Monthly	\$?	\$3,500	15 years	10 months	11.0%, annually
2.	Quarterly	350,500	?	20 years	4 years	10.8%, monthly
3.	Yearly	25,500	5,500	?	2 years	15.5%, quarterly
4.	Quarterly	25,450	?	8 years	1 year	12.5%, monthly
5.	Monthly	?	2,200	15 years	8 months	18.7%, semiannually

6. Ryan Entertainment purchased an amusement park for \$1.5 million and agreed to pay \$250,000 now with the balance to be paid by monthly payments of \$25,000.80. The payments begin in twelve months. If the interest rate is 12% compounded semiannually, how many payments will be required to repay the entire debt? How many years will it take to repay the loan?

7. If Ryan's loan in problem 6 required repayment in fifteen years (monthly payments still begin in twelve months), what will be the size of the required monthly payment? Assume that the interest rate is 12% compounded semiannually.

8. A man is offered an annuity for retirement that will pay \$1,200 per month for ten years. The first payment is to be made in three years. The price of the annuity, today, is \$75,000. If the man can earn 8% compounded annually on his savings, is the annuity a good deal?

10.7 Perpetuities

The term "in perpetuity" means forever. In the area of business finance, **a perpetuity is an annuity that provides payments indefinitely — that is, never ending**. Since there is no end to this type of annuity, it's not possible to find its sum or future value.

Since you may be wondering where a perpetuity would be used, let's look at a few examples with which you may be familiar:

- A university or college sets up a bursary or scholarship fund that is designed to provide a flow of regular payments indefinitely for students.
- Local governments set aside monies so that funds will be available on a regular basis for cultural or heritage activities.

In each example, the goal of the organization setting up the flow of funds is to avoid having to make any contributions beyond the initial deposit. That is, once the initial fund has been established the payments will flow from the fund indefinitely.

You may have already guessed that these payments are nothing more than annual interest payments. Thus, providing the money paid out in awards each period does not exceed the interest income, the payments can continue indefinitely.

There are two types of perpetuities:

- simple perpetuities
- general perpetuities

A. Simple Perpetuities

When the continuous flow of payments come at the end of each period and the interest conversion period coincides with the payment period we have an ordinary simple perpetuity.

Thus, with perpetuities it is necessary to find a present value based on a series of payments that go on forever. Although this might sound complicated it is very easy to find. The expression we use for the present value looks slightly different in that there is no reference to n, the number of payments.

The term we use for the present value of a simple perpetuity is:

$$A_{\infty}$$

Since the payment each period is based on the interest collected, the expression used for an ordinary simple perpetuity is:

$$A_{\infty} = \frac{R}{i}$$

Formula 10.19

Where:

R = the interest payment each period

i = the interest rate per payment period

Formula 10.19 allows us to find what sum of money must be set aside at an interest rate of i to generate a payment of R dollars for an indefinite period.

For example, if you wanted to earn \$200 a year in interest from a savings account, how much would you need to place in the account if the interest rate is 8% compounded annually?

Since the payment is \$200, this must be the interest earned on the funds in the account. We need to find out what value in a savings account will pay \$200 in interest when 8% is applied annually.

First let's use our simple interest method from Chapter 6. That is, principal $(P) \times$ interest $(i) = \$200$. Solving for P gives us:

$$P = \frac{\$200}{i}$$

$$i = 0.08$$

$$P = \frac{\$200}{0.08}$$

$$P = \$2{,}500$$

Consequently, if you have \$2,500 in the bank and the interest rate is 8% compounded annually, you will generate \$200 in interest each year.

Now let's use our formula for finding the present value of a simple perpetuity:

$$A_\infty = \frac{R}{i}$$

Substituting we get:

$$A_\infty = \frac{\$200}{0.08}$$

$$A_\infty = \$2{,}500$$

As you can see, the result is the same as using our simple interest method.

EXAMPLE 10.15

Jeremy wants to retire and receive \$500 a month. When he dies he wants to pass the monthly payment on to his wife. Upon her death, Jeremy wants to pass it on to their only child, and then pass it on to future generations. Jeremy can earn 7.5% compounded monthly. How much will he need to set aside in a perpetuity to achieve his goal? How would it affect the answer if he wanted the payments to start today?

Solution This qualifies as a simple perpetuity since the payments are to go on forever and the payment and interest period coincide. Therefore, the terms of our annuity formula would be:

$$R = \$500$$

$$i = \frac{0.075}{12}, \text{ or } 0.00625$$

Substituting these into Formula 10.19 yields:

$$A_\infty = \frac{R}{i}$$

$$A_\infty = \frac{\$500}{0.00625}$$

$$A_\infty = \$80{,}000$$

Thus, if \$80,000 is placed in a fund earning 7.5% compounded monthly, it will produce \$500 a month in payments for his wife, child, and descendants. That is, the payments will continue forever since the fund is paying out money based on interest income only.

To have the payments begin immediately we must increase the size of the fund to handle the first payment. This is accomplished by depositing \$80,500, which provides the immediate payment of \$500 and leaves \$80,000 in the fund to provide the future \$500 payments.

Therefore, when the payments are to begin immediately the formula we use is:

$$A_\infty = R + \frac{R}{i}$$ **Formula 10.20**

B. General Perpetuities

The approach to general perpetuities follows the logic of our previous discussion on general annuities. That is, we need only adjust our simple perpetuity formula to incorporate the equivalent rate of interest by substituting f for i. Therefore, to find the present value of a general perpetuity with payments at the end of the period use:

$$A_\infty = \frac{R}{f}$$ **Formula 10.21**

Where:

R = the interest payment each period

$f = (1 + i)^c - 1$, the equivalent interest rate

When the payments are to begin immediately the formula for the general annuity is:

$$A_\infty = R + \frac{R}{f}$$ **Formula 10.22**

EXAMPLE 10.16

Find how much a Lottery Foundation must set aside to award a first prize of \$5,000 every six months for as long as the winner lives. (Assume the winner can will the payments to future generations.) Assume the interest rate is 12% compounded monthly. If the payments are to start immediately, how would this affect your answer?

Solution Defining the terms gives us:

$$R = \$5{,}000$$

$$i = \frac{0.12}{12}, \text{ or } 0.01$$

$$c = \frac{12}{2}, \text{ or } 6$$

$$f = (1 + 0.01)^6 - 1$$

$$f \doteq 0.0615202$$

Now substituting into Formula 10.21 we have:

$$A_\infty = \frac{\$5{,}000}{0.0615202}$$

$$A_\infty \doteq \$81{,}274.18$$

Thus, \$81,274.18 must be set aside.

If the annuity is to start immediately the present value would be:

$$A_\infty = R + \frac{R}{f}$$

$$A_\infty = \$5{,}000 + \frac{\$5{,}000}{0.0615202}$$

$$A_\infty = \$86{,}274.18$$

Therefore, the Lottery Foundation must set aside \$86,247.18.

Remember that the adjustment for payments to start immediately requires the addition of the first payment to the present value of the annuity.

EXERCISE 10.5

For the perpetuities in problems 1 to 5, find the present value.

	Payment Period	Payments R	Payments Start	Interest Rate and Conversion Period
1.	Monthly	$ 1,500	Immediately	12.0%, monthly
2.	Quarterly	3,500	In one year	13.8%, monthly
3.	Yearly	15,000	In two years	19.5%, quarterly
4.	Quarterly	2,000	Immediately	14.5%, quarterly
5.	Monthly	850	In one year	16.7%, semiannually

6. Find the present value of a perpetuity that has a payment of $10,000 at the end of each quarter and an interest rate of 8% compounded quarterly.

7. In problem 6, if the interest rate was 8% compounded annually, what would be the present value?

8. If the payment in problem 7 is to commence immediately, what would be the present value?

9. The Juan de Fuca College Foundation has established an annual scholarship of $4,000 for student awards. The best interest rate the college can receive is 9% compounded semiannually. How much must be deposited, today, to establish the scholarship? Assume that the first $4,000 will be awarded immediately.

10. A piece of farm land is leased for an annual payment of $15,000 — paid in advance. If the current interest rate is 15% compounded monthly, what would be a fair price to offer for the land? If there were annual land taxes of $2,000, paid at the end of each year, would this affect the price one would offer for the property? If yes, in what way would it affect the price?

REVIEW EXERCISES

1. If money is worth 13.5% compounded semiannually, what will have accumulated from end of the month deposits of $160 after fifteen years?

2. Jerry has made loan payments of $500 at the beginning of every three months for five years. He was charged 17% compounded semiannually on the loan. How much did he originally borrow?

3. Cheryl wishes to save $50,000 for a down payment on a house in eight years' time. How much must she save at the end of every month, for eight years, if the interest rate is 13% compounded quarterly?

4. A business valued at \$500,000 is bought for \$75,000 down and payments of \$30,000 at the end of every three months. How long will payments have to be made if money is worth 13.5% compounded monthly?

5. What is the size of the annual scholarships that can be paid indefinitely from a \$48,000 fund invested at 14.25% compounded semiannually? Assume the scholarship starts in one year.

6. A couple is saving for a sail boat, and in doing so deposits \$1,000 at the end of each quarter into a bank account that pays 8% compounded annually. Find the amount the couple will have saved after five years.

7. Hi Tech Electronics has set up a fund to replace equipment as it becomes obsolete. The fund requires end of the month payments of \$500. The fund pays 15% compounded semiannually. How much will be in the fund after ten years?

8. What was the purchase price for a piece of property that was purchased for \$5,000 down with monthly payments of \$600 over a twenty year period? Assume the mortgage has an interest rate of 10% compounded semiannually.

9. Terri and Greg bought a small cottage for \$45,000. They put \$5,000 down and negotiated a mortgage with the vendor for the balance of the purchase price. If the vendor charges 12.5% compounded semiannually and the mortgage is to be repaid over twenty years, find:

a. the required monthly payment;
b. the amount outstanding on the mortgage after two years of payments;
c. the interest paid by Terri and Greg after two years of payments;
d. the total interest cost for the mortgage over the twenty year period.

10. Jason purchased a \$15,000 car and financed the purchase with a personal loan from his credit union. If the interest rate is 18% compounded annually, how long will it take Jason to repay the loan with end of the month payments of \$450?

11. A couple has just purchased a house for \$89,000 by way of an \$83,000 mortgage and a \$6,000 down payment. If there are monthly payments of \$926.91 and the interest rate is 13% compounded semiannually, how long will it take the couple to repay the full amount of the mortgage?

12. If the couple in problem 11 decide to make payments of \$1,100 per month, instead of the \$926.91, how much would they save in interest?

13. Panco Holdings has purchased a piece of property for \$109,000 and agree to make monthly payments at the beginning of each month. If the interest rate is 12.6825% compounded annually, what would be the size of each monthly payment to repay the debt in ten years?

14. If Panco Holdings (from problem 13) made payments of \$1,200 at the beginning of each month, how long will it take to repay the loan?

15. Partex Ltd. is considering the purchase of new laser technology. The equipment can be purchased for \$500,000 and is expected to last five years.

After five years the machine can be sold for scrap parts and should generate \$50,000 in revenue. Partex has also been advised that the service contract on the new equipment will cost \$2,000 at the end of each month. If Partex decides not to undertake the service contract there will not be any warranty on the new equipment.

Another option is to lease the new equipment for \$12,500 paid at the end of each month; no other cost is incurred as the lease includes the service contract.

If Partex can earn 8% compounded annually, which option is better, to buy or to lease?

16. Renco International can purchase a piece of property for \$140,000. Renco has a plant located on the adjacent property and views this new parcel as a possible site for an expanded plant site in ten years. If the yearly land taxes are estimated to be 3% of the purchase price, and if Renco can earn 9% compounded semiannually, what must be the minimum value of the land in ten years to make the purchase worthwhile — regardless of whether Renco uses the site for their plant expansion? (Assume that taxes are paid at the end of each year.)

SUMMARY OF FORMULAS

Definition: $c = \dfrac{\text{number of conversion periods per year}}{\text{number of payment periods per year}}$

Formula 10.1 $f = (1 + i)^c - 1$ Used to find the equivalent rate of interest.

Ordinary General Annuities

Formula 10.2 $S_n = \dfrac{R[(1+f)^n - 1]}{f}$ Used to find the amount using the equivalent rate of interest, f.

Formula 10.3 $S_{nc} = \dfrac{R[(1+i)^{nc} - 1]}{[(1+i)^c - 1]}$ Used to find the amount. This formula calculates the effective rate as part of the total calculations.

Formula 10.4 $A_n = \dfrac{R[1 - (1+f)^{-n}]}{f}$ Used to calculate the present value using the equivalent rate of interest.

Formula 10.5 $A_{nc} = \dfrac{R[1-(1+i)^{-nc}]}{(1+i)^c - 1}$ Finds the present value by including the step of finding the equivalent rate as part of the calculations.

Formula 10.6 $R = \dfrac{S_n}{\dfrac{[(1+f)^n - 1]}{f}}$ Finds the payment when the amount is known, and uses f, the effective rate.

Formula 10.7 $R = \dfrac{A_n}{\dfrac{[1-(1+f)^{-n}]}{f}}$ Finds the payment when the present value is known, using f, the effective rate.

Formula 10.8 $n = \dfrac{\ln\left[1 + \dfrac{S_n f}{R}\right]}{\ln(1+f)}$ Finds n, the number of payments, when the amount, R and f, are known.

Formula 10.9 $n = \dfrac{-\ln\left[1 - \dfrac{A_n f}{R}\right]}{\ln(1+f)}$ Finds n when the present value, R and f, are known.

General Annuity Due

Formula 10.10 $S_n(\text{due}) = \dfrac{R(1+f)[(1+f)^n - 1]}{f}$ Finds the amount for a complex annuity due.

Formula 10.11 $A_n(\text{due}) = \dfrac{R(1+f)[1-(1+f)^{-n}]}{f}$ Finds the present value of an annuity due.

Formula 10.12 $R = \dfrac{S_n(\text{due})}{\dfrac{(1+f)[(1+f)^n - 1]}{f}}$ Finds the payment for a given amount for a complex annuity due.

Formula 10.13 $R = \dfrac{A_n(\text{due})}{\dfrac{(1+f)[1-(1+f)^{-n}]}{f}}$ Finds the payment for a given present value for a complex annuity due.

Formula 10.14 $n = \dfrac{\ln\left[1 + \dfrac{S_n(\text{due})f}{R(1+f)}\right]}{\ln(1+f)}$ Finds n for a complex annuity due, given R, i, and $S_n(\text{due})$.

Formula 10.15

$$n = \frac{-\ln\left[1 - \dfrac{A_n(\text{due})f}{R(1+f)}\right]}{\ln(1+f)}$$

Finds n for a complex annuity due, given R, i, and A_n(due).

General Deferred Annuity

Formula 10.16

$$A_n(\text{def}) = \frac{R(1+f)^{-d}[1-(1+f)^{-n}]}{f}$$

Used to calculate the present value using the equivalent rate of interest for a complex deferred annuity.

Formula 10.17

$$R = \frac{A_n(\text{def})}{\dfrac{(1+f)^{-d}[1-(1+f)^{-n}]}{f}}$$

Finds the payment when the present value of a complex deferred annuity is known, using f, the equivalent rate.

Formula 10.18

$$n = \frac{-\ln\left[1 - \dfrac{A_n(\text{def})(f)}{R(1+f)^{-d}}\right]}{\ln(1+f)}$$

Finds n for complex deferred annuity, given R, i, and A_n(def).

Simple and General Perpetuities

Formula 10.19 $A_\infty = \dfrac{R}{i}$

Finds the present value for a simple ordinary perpetuity.

Formula 10.20 $A_\infty = R + \dfrac{R}{i}$

Finds the present value for a simple perpetuity due.

Formula 10.21 $A_\infty = \dfrac{R}{f}$

Finds the present value for a complex perpetuity.

Formula 10.22 $A_\infty = R + \dfrac{R}{f}$

Finds the present value for a complex perpetuity due.

GLOSSARY OF TERMS

General Annuity an annuity that may have different payment and interest periods. General annuities are also called complex annuities.

c the conversion factor used in computing the equivalent rate of interest, *f*. It is found by dividing the number of interest conversion periods per year by the number of payment periods per year.

General Annuity Due an annuity that has payments at the beginning of each period, as well as the possibility that the interest period and the payment period may be different.

General Deferred Annuity an annuity that has payments that start at some point in the future. In addition, the interest period and the payment period may be different.

Perpetuities an annuity that provides payments indefinitely. Perpetuities may be simple or general (complex); simple means the payment period and the interest period coincide and a complex perpetuity provides for the payment period and the interest period to be different.

APPENDIX

Investment Applications of Annuities

10.A.1 Net Present Value

Although not specifically referred to in our earlier discussions, when an investment or an expenditure by a company is being contemplated, often those making the decision will use the **net present value (NPV)** approach. This approach simply requires one to compare the future cash flows to the future cash outlays. The difference between the two is called the net present value.

For example, assume a firm is contemplating the purchase of two types of equipment. The first piece of equipment costs \$50,000 and will last five years. The expected savings to the company in terms of its operation costs is estimated to be \$1,600 per month. Further, the equipment is expected to last five years, at which time its value is assumed to be zero. Another piece of equipment cost \$75,000 and is expected to save \$1,750 per month for six years, at which time it would be sold for an estimated scrap value of \$1,500. If the firm expects to earn 10% compounded monthly on its money, which piece of equipment is the best investment for the company? Another way this question could have been asked is, which piece of equipment has the highest net present value to the firm?

To compute the net present value of the options facing the firm, the following relation is used:

Net Present Value	=	Present Value of Cash Inflows	–	Present Value of Cash Outflows

For the problem at hand, the choice of equipment would be made based on the equipment with the highest net present value (NPV).

The rule is to choose the option with the highest net present value, all other factors being equal. These other factors would include risk and tax considerations as well as a variety of other factors. If a single option is being evaluated, then, providing it has a positive net present value, it is worth undertaking. If the net present value is zero the firm would be indifferent, and if it is negative, it would suggest the venture is not worthwhile.

Using the NPV approach to the two types of equipment, we compute the NPV for each piece of equipment:

Equipment A

Cost = \$50,000 — Outlay today.

Scrap Value = 0

$R = \$1{,}600$ — Monthly inflow of savings.

$n = 12 \times 5$, or 60

$$i = \left(\frac{0.10}{12}\right)$$

$$\text{Present value of inflows} = \$1{,}600\left[\frac{1-\left[1+\dfrac{0.10}{12}\right]^{-60}}{\dfrac{0.10}{12}}\right]$$

$$\doteq \$75{,}304.59$$

Present value of outflows = \$50,000

$$\text{Net Present Value} \doteq \$75{,}304.59 - \$50{,}000$$

$$\doteq \$25{,}304.59$$

Equipment B

Cost = \$75,000 — Outlay today.

Scrap Value = \$1,500 — In six years.

$R = \$1{,}750$ — Monthly inflow of savings.

$n = 12 \times 6$, or 72

$$i = \left(\frac{0.10}{12}\right)$$

$$\text{Present value of inflows} = \$1{,}750\left[\frac{1-\left[1+\dfrac{0.10}{12}\right]^{-72}}{\dfrac{0.10}{12}}\right] + \$1{,}500\left(1+\frac{0.10}{12}\right)^{-72}$$

$$\doteq \$95{,}287.93$$

Present value of outflows = \$75,000

$$\text{Net Present Value} \doteq \$95{,}287.93 - \$75{,}000$$

$$\doteq \$20{,}287.93$$

Since the NPV of Equipment A is higher than Equipment B, A would be selected.

EXAMPLE 10.A.1

West Coast Research Ltd. has developed a robotic underwater submarine for exploring the sea bottom at very deep depths. The development is on paper only and to make a prototype requires \$150,000, \$200,000, and \$300,000 over the next three years. If all tests go well, West Coast expects to be able to sell the submarines for a net profit (after all costs) of \$50,000 per unit. West Coast estimates it will be able to sell six units per year for the three years following the development of the prototype. All cash needs are assumed to occur at the end of each fiscal year. As well, sales are expected to occur at the end of each year. If the owners of West Coast require a return on investment of 16% compounded annually, is this project viable?

Solution

Cost = \$150,000, \$200,000, \$300,000 Outlays — each outlay will need to be evaluated separately.

R = \$50,000 × 6, or \$300,000 Inflow of net profit.

$n = 3$

$d = 3$

$i = 0.16$

Since the company does not receive the estimated net profit until after the development of the prototype, this delayed income is treated as an annuity deferred; deferred for the three years until the income commences.

$$\text{Present value of inflows} = \$300{,}000(1 + 0.16)^{-3}\left[\frac{[1 - (1 + 0.16)^{-3}]}{0.16}\right]$$

$$\doteq \$431{,}653.91$$

$$\text{Present value of outflows} = \$150{,}000(1 + 0.16)^{-1} + 200{,}000(1 + 0.16)^{-2} + 300{,}000(1 + 0.16)^{-3}$$

$$\doteq \$470{,}140.23$$

$$\text{Net Present Value} \doteq \$431{,}653.91 - \$470{,}140.23$$

$$\doteq -\$38{,}486.32$$

Calculator Solution

Finding the Present Value of the Inflows						
Input	300,000	3	16			
Depress	PMT	n	i	COMP	PV	673,766.86
Discounting PV by the Deferral Period $673{,}766.86(1 + 0.16)^{-3}$						431,653.91

Input	150,000	16	1			
Depress	FV	i	n	COMP	PV	129,310.34
Input	200,000	16	2			
Depress	FV	i	n	COMP	PV	148,632.58
Input	300,000	16	3			
Depress	FV	i	n	COMP	PV	192,197.30
					Present Value of Outflows	470,140.23

Since the NPV is negative the project should not be undertaken and therefore it is not viable.

10.A.2 Discounted Cash Flow

If the discounting involves future flows of payments or future fixed sums, the resulting value is sometimes called the **discounted cash flow** (DCF) of future payments. In this case, note that DCF is simply today's value of a future series of payments. A firm using this method of evaluating investment options will select the option that has the highest DCF for those cases where money is flowing to the firm, and the lowest DCF if the firm is making cash outlays. Consider Examples 10.A.2. and 10.A.3., which use DCF as the basis between two options. Example 10.A.2. deals with cash flow to the firm and requires the firm to select the highest DCF, while 10.A.3. is a problem that uses DCF when payments are made by the firm, requiring the firm to choose the option with the lowest DCF.

EXAMPLE 10.A.2

Bayles Holdings is considering two rental investments. The first investment is a building that generates a monthly income of \$10,000, paid at the beginning of each month. The building is expected to have a remaining useful life of five years, at which time the building would be demolished and the land sold. The estimated value of the land in five years is \$250,000. The second investment is a building that generates a monthly income of \$7,000, paid at the beginning of each month. The estimated life of the second building is ten years; at this time the building would be demolished and the land sold. The estimated value of the land in ten years is \$150,000. Both buildings are being offered for sale at the same price. Using DCF, which option would be best for Bayles Holdings? Assume that money is worth 12% compounded monthly.

Solution Each option generates a cash flow, thus the choice will be based on the option that has the highest DCF.

OPTION 1 **Building 1**

$R = \$10,000$

Note that the payments are at the beginning of the period, thus, use an annuity due.

$n = 12 \times 5, \text{ or } 60$

$i = \dfrac{0.12}{12}, \text{ or } 0.01$

Present Value of the Cash Flow (DCF):

$$DCF = \$10,000(1 + 0.01)\left[\frac{[1 - (1 + 0.01)^{-60}]}{0.01}\right] + \$250,000(1 + 0.01)^{-60}$$

$$DCF \doteq \$591,658.29$$

OPTION 2 **Building 2**

$R = \$7,000$

Payments are at the beginning of the period.

$n = 12 \times 10, \text{ or } 120$

$i = \dfrac{0.12}{12}, \text{ or } 0.01$

Present Value of the Cash Flow (DCF):

$$DCF = \$7,000(1 + 0.01)\left[\frac{[1 - (1 + 0.01)^{-120}]}{0.01}\right] + \$150,000(1 + 0.01)^{-120}$$

$$DCF \doteq \$538,231.91$$

Calculator Solution

Finding the Discounted Cash Flow of Building 1							
Input		10,000	60	1			
Depress	BGN	PMT	n	i	COMP	PV	454,045.89
Discount the Future Cash Flow From the Sale of the Land							
Input	250,000	1	60				
Depress	FV	i	n	COMP	PV		137,612.40
				Discounted Cash Flow (DCF)			591,658.29

Finding the Discounted Cash Flow of Building 2							
Input		7,000	120	1			
Depress	BGN	PMT	n	i	COMP	PV	492,782.69
Discount the Future Cash Flow From the Sale of the Land							
Input	150,000	1	120				
Depress	FV	i	n	COMP	PV		45,449.22
				Discounted Cash Flow (DCF)			538,231.91

Using DCF as the decision rule, the choice would be Building 1, which has the highest DCF for Bayles.

EXAMPLE 10.A.3

Horizon Technology manufactures special computer equipment. The company has had such an increase in demand for its products that it must increase its production capabilities. One option being considered is to purchase the required equipment for $100,000. If the equipment is purchased it is expected that the maintenance and repair costs will be $10,000 per year for five years — maintenance is assumed to occur at the end of each year. After five years, the equipment will have no salvage value and will need to be replaced. Another option is to lease the equipment for five years for $3,000 per month, paid at the beginning of each month. If money is worth 15% compounded annually, which option is best for the company?

Solution Since each option requires cash outlays, the choice will be based on the option that has the lowest DCF.

OPTION 1 Purchasing the equipment

Present Value of the Purchase option (i.e., DCF):

$$= \$10{,}000\left[\frac{[1-(1+0.15)^{-5}]}{0.15}\right] + \$100{,}000$$

$$\text{DCF} \doteq \$133{,}521.55$$

OPTION 2 Leasing the equipment

Present Value of the Lease option (DCF):

$R = \$3{,}000$ At the beginning of each month.

$$c = \frac{1}{12}$$

$$f = (1+0.15)^{\frac{1}{12}} - 1, \text{ or } 0.01171492$$

$$n = 12 \times 5, \text{ or } 60$$

Since the payments are at the beginning of each month an annuity due will be required. Therefore the DCF of the lease option is:

$$DCF \doteq \$3{,}000(1+0.01171492)\left[\frac{[1-(1+0.01171492)^{-60}]}{(0.01171492)}\right]$$

$$DCF \doteq \$130{,}273.34$$

Calculator Solution

Finding the Discounted Cash Flow of Purchasing

Input	10,000	5	15			
Depress	PMT	n	i	COMP	PV	33,521.55
				Add the Purchase Cost Today		100,000.00
				Discounted Cash Flow (DCF)		133,521.55

Finding the Discounted Cash Flow of Leasing

Input		3,000	60	1.171492			
Depress	BGN	PMT	n	i	COMP	PV	130,273.34
					Discounted Cash Flow (DCF)		130,273.34

Based on the DCF, the lease option represents the lowest discounted cash outlay to the firm. Thus, using DCF, the recommendation would be to lease the equipment.

EXERCISE 10.A.1

For each of the following problems, use the NPV or DCF approach as appropriate to determine the best investment option.

1. A company is considering replacing some old equipment. The cost of new equipment is $150,000 immediately. In addition, the new equipment requires the purchase of a service contract to maintain the warranty that comes with the new equipment. The cost of the service contract is $3,000 every six months, payable at the beginning of each six month period. The new equipment is expected to save the company $2,000 per month for five years. If the rate of return required by the company is 10% compounded monthly, should the equipment be purchased?
2. Venture Developments expects 15% compounded monthly on its investments. Currently, two properties are being considered for investment. The first property is expected to produce an income of $300,000 per year for five years and can then be sold for $250,000, when the building will be demolished. The cost of the property is $1,000,000. The second property is expected to produce an annual income of $425,000 and is expected to have a resale value of $400,000 in six years, when the building is demolished. The cost of the second property is 2.1 million dollars. Which purchase would be best for Venture?
3. Metchosin Processing is considering a project that requires outlays of $20,000 per year for eight years. At the end of the project there is an expectation that the equipment acquired over the period can be sold for a scrap value of $50,000. The payoff from the project is estimated to be $45,000 per year for the last five years. No income is expected until after year three. Metchosin Processing uses 12% compounded quarterly as its required return on investments. Should the project be undertaken?
4. ASA Computers currently sells 10,000 units of the 486-type per year. Based on its projections it expects a 10% increase in demand for each of the next four years. The cost per computer is $1,400 and the selling price per unit is $2,000. A new assembly process is being considered that will require an outlay of $500,000, which is expected to reduce the unit cost to $1,000. After four years it is estimated that the assembly process can be sold for $100,000 to a smaller company. If ASA expects 12% compounded monthly on its money, should the new assembly process be installed?

5. Sinetics Research Ltd. has developed a robotic assembly unit for automobiles. The development is preliminary. Sinetics is considering making a prototype that would require $200,000, $450,000, and $500,000 over the next three years. If all tests go well, Sinetics expects to be able to sell the robotic units for a net profit of $250,000 per unit. Sinetics estimates it can sell two units per year, for each of the three years following the development of the prototype. All cash needs are assumed to be required at the end of each fiscal year. Sales are expected to occur at the end of each year. If the owners of Sinetics require a return on investment of 19% compounded semiannually, is this project viable?
6. A piece of equipment can be leased or purchased. If it is purchased, the price is $100,000 and is expected to last five years. The lease cost is $2,200 at the beginning of each month for five years. The machine has no residual value after five years. If money is worth 18% compounded monthly, should the equipment be purchased or leased? If the machine had a residual value of $30,000 would this change the decision?
7. John is selling a piece of property and has received three offers. The first offer is $50,000 today, $120,000 in a year, and $200,000 in three years. The second offer is $20,000 today, $80,000 in a year, and $350,000 in five years. The third offer is $250,000 cash. If the market rate of interest is 12% compounded annually, which offer has the highest DCF?
8. Westport Transport is considering leasing five new trucks at a quarterly cost of $3,500 per truck, paid in advance every quarter. A second option is to purchase the trucks at a cost of $100,000 per truck. If the trucks are purchased, they can be sold at the end of three years for 30% of the initial purchase price. In either case, Westport must provide the maintenance of the trucks. Also, if the trucks are leased, Westport has the option of purchasing the trucks for $50,000 each at the end of the lease. The length of the lease is three years. If money is worth 16% compounded semiannually, which option is best for the company?

CHAPTER 11

Annuity Applications to Business Problems

This chapter is designed to provide a perspective on some of the applications of annuities in business finance. In the first section, we'll discuss the topic of debt and how repayment of debt with the use of annuities occurs. In particular, we will explore the use of **amortization schedules** and **sinking fund schedules**, two common tools in debt analysis.

The second section of the chapter will focus on the concept of **capitalized cost**. Capitalized cost is a way of accounting for assets such as equipment and buildings that wear out over time and require periodic replacement. What must be understood is how businesses can ensure that there are sufficient funds to permit the replacement of assets as they wear out.

You also will learn how to use capitalized cost as a method for decision making to determine the least cost alternative. For example, a company may need to decide between different types of equipment, all providing the same service, but each having some unique feature — taking all things into consideration, which piece of equipment is the most cost effective?

In the final section of the chapter we will turn our attention to **depletion allowances**, which provide a means of dealing with **wasting assets**. Here we will show you how to handle resources that can't be replaced in the short run and, in many cases such as mines or gravel pits, simply can't be replaced.

OBJECTIVES

When you have completed this chapter you will have gained an understanding of some of the more useful applications of annuities in business. In particular, you will be able to:

1. set up an Amortization Schedule for the amortization of debt for both simple and general annuities;
2. set up a Sinking Fund Schedule for simple and general annuities as well as understand some applications of sinking funds;
3. explain the concept of capitalized cost and be able to use it in making decisions involving assets that have a limited life;
4. use capitalized cost in evaluating various options involving the acquisition of assets;
5. explain the meaning of a depletion allowance, compute the value of an investment, compute the yield rate of an investment, and account for depleting resources when evaluating investments.

11.1 Debt Reduction and Extinction

A. Amortization of Debt with an Amortization Schedule

Amortizing debt means paying off debt by using regular or irregular payments; whether the payments are equal payments or unequal makes no difference. An amortization schedule is developed to show the retiring of the debt over time.

Amortization tables are used to provide a listing — in table form — of interest, principal, and the running balance of a loan (outstanding balance) for each period a payment has been made. Whether we are dealing with a simple annuity or a general annuity, the procedures are the same. The goal in building an amortization schedule is to be able to see exactly what the status of the loan is today, and in addition, what the status will be at some point in the future.

To get a better understanding of the idea, let's consider a simple problem that involves constructing an amortization schedule for both an ordinary simple annuity and a general annuity.

EXAMPLE 11.1

Janice and Phil Grantham have taken out a mortgage of $61,818.44 to cover legal expenses and the purchase of a piece of property. The mortgage is to be amortized over six months with end of the month payments and an annual interest rate of 12%. Set up an amortization schedule for each of the following circumstances:

(a) Assume the interest rate is compounded monthly;
(b) Assume the interest rate is compounded semiannually.

Solution (a) 12% compounded monthly:

To set up the amortization of the loan we must first determine the payments required. Since the interest is compounded monthly, with end of the month payments, we use an ordinary simple annuity:

$$A_n = \$61{,}818.44$$

$$i = \frac{0.12}{12}, \text{ or } 0.01$$

$$n = 6$$

Now to find R we use Formula 8.4 from Chapter 8:

$$R = \frac{A_n}{\frac{[(1 - (1 + i)^{-n}]}{i}}$$

Substituting we have:

$$R = \frac{\$61{,}818.44}{\frac{[(1 - (1 + 0.01)^{-6}]}{0.01}}$$

$$R \doteq \$10{,}666.67$$

Calculator Solution

						Payment
Input	61,818.44	1	6			
Depress	PV	i	n	COMP	PMT	10,666.67

Next we set up an amortization schedule that looks as follows:

Table 11.1 Amortization of a Loan

A	B	C	D	E
Payment Period	**Regular Payment**	**Payment to Interest**	**Payment to Principal**	**Outstanding Balance**
0				$61,818.44
1	$10,666.67	$618.18	$10,048.49	$51,769.95
2	$10,666.67	$517.70	$10,148.97	$41,620.98
3	$10,666.67	$416.21	$10,250.46	$31,370.52
4	$10,666.67	$313.71	$10,352.96	$21,017.56
5	$10,666.67	$210.18	$10,456.49	$10,561.06
6	$10,666.67	$105.61	$10,561.06	$0
Totals	$64,000.02	$2,181.59	$61,818.43	N/A

The calculations involved in the above schedule are based on the payments being made at the end of the period and the interest rate per period corresponding to the payment period. The actual table entries are based on the following calculations:

1. **Regular Payments** =

   Column B: Period 1: $10,666.67
   Period 2: $10,666.67
   . . .
   Period 6: $10,666.67

2. **Payment to Interest** = the outstanding balance of the previous period multiplied by the interest rate per period

   Column C: Period 1: $61,818.44(0.01) = $618.18
   This is the method used to calculate the interest on the outstanding balance each period. Multiply the interest rate per period by the outstanding balance of the previous period as follows:

   Period 1: $61,818.44(0.01) = $618.18
   Period 2: $51,769.95(0.01) = $517.70
   . . .
   Period 6: $10,561.06(0.01) = $105.61

3. **Payment to Principal** = payment − interest per period

   Column D: Period 1: $10,666.67 − $618.18 = $10,048.49
   Period 2: $10,666.67 − $517.70 = $10,148.97
   . . .
   Period 6: $10,666.67 − $105.61 = $10,561.06

4. **Outstanding Balance** = the previous period's outstanding balance minus payment to principal in the current period

Column E: Period 1: \$61,818.44 – \$10,048.49 = \$51,769.95
Period 2: \$51,769.95 – \$10,148.97 = \$41,620.98
. . .
Period 6: \$10,561.06 – \$10,561.06 = \$0

(b) 12% compounded semiannually:
This problem is identical to the previous problem with the one exception that the interest rate and the conversion period are different. As done in Chapter 10, take the ordinary simple annuity formula and substitute the equivalent rate of interest, f, for i. This is the best method because we need an interest rate per period to compute the interest portion of the payment. As above, the interest paid each period is found by multiplying the outstanding balance of the previous period by the **interest rate per period — in this case** f.

Anyone with a home mortgage would use this as the procedure to set up an amortization schedule for their mortgage.

As in (a) above, our first step is to find R using our annuity formula, but replacing i with f, where:

$$f = [(1 + i)^c - 1]$$

Therefore:

$$R = \frac{A_n}{\frac{[1 - (1 + f)^{-n}]}{f}}$$

Defining the terms of the expression for R yields:

$$c = \frac{2}{12}, \text{ or } \frac{1}{6}$$

$$i = \frac{0.12}{2}, \text{ or } 0.06$$

Therefore, f is:

$$f = (1 + 0.06)^{\frac{1}{6}} - 1$$

$$f \doteq 0.009758794$$

And R is:

$$R = \frac{\$61{,}818.44}{\frac{[1 - (1 + 0.009758794)^{-6}]}{0.009758794}}$$

$$R \doteq \$10{,}657.83$$

Calculator Solution

						Payment
Input	61,818.44	(f) 0.9758794	6			
Depress	PV	i	n	COMP	PMT	10,657.83

Now the steps are the same as in part (a) with the value of f being used to determine the interest payment each period. The amortization schedule will look as follows:

Table 11.2 Amortization of a Loan for a GENERAL Annuity

A	B	C	D	E
Payment Period	**Regular Payment**	**Payment to Interest**	**Payment to Principal**	**Outstanding Balance**
0				$61,818.44
1	$10,657.83	$ 603.27	$10,054.56	$51,763.88
2	$10,657.83	$ 505.15	$10,152.68	$41,611.20
3	$10,657.83	$ 406.08	$10,251.75	$31,359.45
4	$10,657.83	$ 306.03	$10,351.80	$21,007.65
5	$10,657.83	$ 205.01	$10,452.82	$10,554.83
6	$10,657.83	$ 103.00	$10,554.83	$0
Totals	$63,946.98	$2,128.54	$61,818.44	N/A

The calculations required for Table 11.2 are based on the payments being made at the end of the period and the interest rate per period corresponding to the payment period (for this problem it is an equivalent rate).

1. **Regular Payment** =

   Column B: Period 1: $10,657.83
   Period 2: $10,657.83
   . . .
   Period 6: $10,657.83

2. **Payment to Interest** = the outstanding balance of the previous period multiplied by the interest rate per period

   Column C: Period 1: $61,818.44(0.009758794) ≐ $603.27
   Period 2: $51,763.88(0.009758794) ≐ $505.15
   . . .
   Period 6: $10,554.83(0.009758794) ≐ $103.00

3. **Payment to Principal** = payment – interest per period

Column D: Period 1: $10,657.83 – $603.27 = $10,054.56
Period 2: $10,657.83 – $505.15 = $10,152.68
. . .
Period 6: $10,657.83 – $103.00 = $10,554.83

4. **Outstanding Balance** = the previous period's outstanding balance minus payment to principal in the current period

Column E: Period 1: $61,818.44 – $10,054.56 = $51,763.88
Period 2: $51,763.88 – $10,152.68 = $41,611.20
. . .
Period 6: $10,554.83 – $10,554.83 = $0

This example has demonstrated how we can construct an amortization schedule for either ordinary simple annuities or general annuities. It is important to recognize that, in this example, the payments were all the same.

To handle problems where the last payment is different from the others, simply compute the interest payable for the last period and add this interest to the outstanding balance. The sum of these will give us the entry for the value of the last payment. Consider the following example involving a general annuity:

EXAMPLE 11.2

A contractor has a debt of $6,000 that must be discharged by payments of $2,000 every quarter. The interest rate being charged is 12% compounded monthly. Set up an amortization schedule to show how the debt will be discharged.

Solution In this example, we don't know the number of payments that will be required. Using a little common sense, we can quickly surmise that there will most likely be four payments. Each $2,000 payment will include both principal and interest. Therefore, we will need more than three payments. To confirm our suspicion, we can determine n by using the formula developed in Chapter 8 to find n for an ordinary simple annuity, namely:

$$n = \frac{-\ln\left[1 - \frac{A_n i}{R}\right]}{\ln(1 + i)}$$

However, since we are dealing with a general annuity, it will be necessary to replace i with f, the equivalent rate. Replacing i with f, where $f = [(1 + i)^c - 1]$ gives:

$$n = \frac{-\ln\left[1 - \frac{A_n f}{R}\right]}{\ln(1 + f)}$$

$$c = \frac{12}{4}, \text{ or } 3$$

$$i = \frac{12}{12}, \text{ or } 0.01$$

Therefore, f is:

$$f = (1 + 0.01)^3 - 1$$

$$f = 0.030301$$

Solving for n yields:

$$A_n = \$6{,}000$$

$$R = \$2{,}000$$

$$n = \frac{-\ln\left[1 - \frac{\$6{,}000(0.030301)}{\$2{,}000}\right]}{\ln(1 + 0.030301)}$$

$$n \doteq 3.192640$$

We can see that three payments of \$2,000 will be made with a smaller fourth payment.

Calculator Solution

							Number of Payments
Input	6,000	3.0301	2,000				
Depress	PV	i	+/−	PMT	COMP	n	3.192640

To find the value of the last payment we can either solve for it directly or work through the amortization schedule. Using the direct method outlined in Section 8.6 of Chapter 8, the value of the last payment can be found by taking the discounted value of the remaining payments — after the 3rd payment, that is, $n = 0.192640$.

Therefore, the outstanding balance immediately after the 3rd payment is the discounted value of the remaining payments ($n = 0.192640$). Finding the discounted value:

$$A_n = \frac{R[1 - (1 + f)^{-n}]}{f}$$

$$A_n \doteq \frac{\$2{,}000[1 - (1 + 0.030301)^{-0.192640}]}{0.030301}$$

$A_n \doteq \$378.47$ The outstanding balance after the third payment of \$2,000 is made.

Now add one more period of interest, for the period the balance of \$378.47 will be outstanding:

interest for last period	+	balance at period 3	=	last smaller payment
\$378.47(0.030301)	+	\$378.47	≐	\$389.94

Calculator Solution

The Outstanding Balance of the Loan After the 3rd Payment						Balance Due
Input	2,000	3.0301	0.192640			
Depress	PMT	i	n	COMP	PV	378.47
Smaller Final Payment = 378.47 (1 + 0.030301)						389.94

Setting up the amortization schedule results in:

Table 11.3 Amortization of a Loan

A	B	C	D	E
Quarter	**Regular Payment**	**Payment to Interest**	**Payment to Principal**	**Outstanding Balance**
0				\$6,000.00
1	\$2,000.00	\$181.81	\$1,818.19	\$4,181.81
2	\$2,000.00	\$126.71	\$1,873.29	\$2,308.52
3	\$2,000.00	\$ 69.95	\$1,930.05	\$ 378.47
4	\$ 389.94	\$ 11.47	\$ 378.47	\$0
Totals	\$6,389.94	\$389.94	\$6,000.00	N/A

Table 11.3 uses the same procedures as the two previous amortization schedules. The entries in Columns C and B use the following procedures:

1. **Payment to Interest** = the outstanding balance of the previous period multiplied by the interest rate per period

   Column C: Period 1: \$6,000(0.030301) ≐ \$181.81
   Period 2: \$4,181.81(0.030301) ≐ \$126.71
   . . .
   Period 4: \$378.47(0.030301) ≐ \$11.47

2. **Payment to Principal** = payment – interest per period

   Column D: Period 1: \$2,000 – \$181.81 = \$1,818.19
   Period 2: \$2,000 – \$126.71 = \$1,873.29
   . . .
   Period 4: \$389.94 – \$11.47 = \$378.47

3. **Outstanding Balance** = the previous period's outstanding balance minus payment to principal in the current period

   Column E: Period 1: \$6,000 – \$1,818.19 = \$4,181.81
   Period 2: \$4,181.81 – \$1,873.29 = \$2,308.52
   . . .
   Period 4: \$378.47 – \$378.47 = \$0

B. Partial Amortization Tables

It's worth noting that you can start at any point in an amortization schedule by using the present value approach to find the outstanding balance, and then construct the desired table entries. Finding the present value of the remaining payments will give you the outstanding balance of the period just completed, from which you can compute interest and payment to principal for the next period. Just to make sure you understand how to find the table entries for an amortization table at any point in time, consider Example 11.3:

EXAMPLE 11.3

Omega Holdings has arranged a \$200,000 mortgage on a piece of property. The arrangements are that the mortgage will be amortized over twenty years with monthly payments based on an interest rate of 10% compounded monthly. Show the amortization schedule entries for the 36th and 37th payments.

Solution The first step is to find R. Since this is an ordinary simple annuity, the method to find R uses the formula:

$$R = \frac{A_n}{\dfrac{[1 - (1 + i)^{-n}]}{i}}$$

Where:

$$A_n = \$200{,}000$$
$$n = 12 \times 20, \text{ or } 240$$
$$i = \frac{0.10}{12}, \text{ or } 0.00833333$$

Substituting these into the formula yields:

$$R = \frac{\$200{,}000}{\dfrac{\left[1 - \left(1 + \dfrac{0.10}{12}\right)^{-240}\right]}{\dfrac{0.10}{12}}}$$

$$R \doteq \$1{,}930.04$$

Calculator Solution

						Payment
Input	200,000	0.833333	240			
Depress	PV	i	n	COMP	PMT	1,930.04

Now to find the entries for periods 36 and 37 we need to know the outstanding balance for period 35 from which we can determine the appropriate schedule entries. To compute the outstanding balance for period 35 we use the method outlined in Chapter 8, where we calculated the present value of the outstanding (remaining) payments, in this case 240 – 35), or 205. Using our present value formula for an ordinary simple annuity, we have:

$$A_n = \frac{R[1 - (1 + i)^{-n}]}{i}$$

Where:

$$R = \$1{,}930.04$$
$$i = \frac{0.10}{12}, \text{ or } 0.00833333$$
$$n = 205$$

Substituting into our annuity formula gives:

$$A_n = \frac{\$1{,}930.04\left[1 - \left(1 + \dfrac{0.10}{12}\right)^{-205}\right]}{\dfrac{0.10}{12}}$$

$$A_n \doteq \$189{,}347.47$$

Calculator Solution

The Outstanding Balance of the Loan After the 205th Payment						Balance Due
Input	1,930.04	0.833333	205			
Depress	PMT	i	n	COMP	PV	189,347.47

The value of $189,347.47 is the amount outstanding at period 35. It forms the basis of our calculations to find the entries for our amortization for periods 36 and 37. Setting up Table 11.4 gives us the following:

Table 11.4 Amortization Table for Periods 36 and 37

A	B	C	D	E
Month	**Regular Payment**	**Payment to Interest**	**Payment to Principal**	**Outstanding Balance**
35				$189,347.47
36	$1,930.04	$1,577.90	$352.14	$188,995.32
37	$1,930.04	$1,574.96	$355.08	$188,640.24

This procedure can be used for any amortization table and will apply to both general and ordinary simple annuities.

C. Amortization Schedule for an Annuity Due

When we have an annuity due, the payment will be subtracted from the outstanding balance at the start of the first period, immediately reducing the outstanding balance by the **full** amount of the payment. In the second period, the payment will now need to cover interest and principal as required in the examples for an ordinary annuity. Just to make sure you understand this concept, consider Example 11.4, which is Example 11.1, part (a), redone, but now with the payments at the beginning of each period:

EXAMPLE 11.4

Janice and Phil Grantham have taken out a mortgage of $61,818.44 to cover legal expenses and the purchase of a piece of property. The mortgage is to be amortized over six months with an annual interest rate of 12% compounded monthly. Set up an amortization schedule with payments at the beginning of each month.

Solution To set up the amortization for the loan we must first determine the payments required. Since the interest is compounded monthly, with beginning of the month payments, we use the method for a simple annuity due, which was introduced in Chapter 9:

$$A_n(\text{due}) = \$61{,}818.44$$

$$i = \frac{0.12}{12}, \text{ or } 0.01$$

$$n = 6$$

Now, to find R we use Formula 9.4 from Chapter 9:

$$R = \frac{A_n(\text{due})}{\dfrac{(1+i)[1-(1+i)^{-n}]}{i}}$$

Substituting we have:

$$R = \frac{\$61{,}818.44}{\dfrac{(1+0.01)[1-(1+0.01)^{-6}]}{0.01}}$$

$$R \doteq \$10{,}561.06$$

Calculator Solution

Input		61,818.44	1	6			
Depress	BGN	PV	i	n	COMP	PMT	10,561.06

Next we set up an amortization schedule that looks as follows:

Table 11.5 Amortization of a Loan, with Beginning of Period Payments

A	B	C	D	E
Payment Period	**Regular Payment at Beginning of Period**	**Payment to Interest**	**Payment to Principal**	**Outstanding Balance Beginning of Period**
0				$61,818.44
1	$10,561.06	$0	$10,561.06	$51,257.38
2	$10,561.06	$ 512.57	$10,048.49	$41,208.89
3	$10,561.06	$ 412.09	$10,148.97	$31,059.92
4	$10,561.06	$ 310.60	$10,250.46	$20,809.46
5	$10,561.06	$ 208.09	$10,352.97	$10,456.49
6	$10,561.06	$ 104.56	$10,456.50	($0.01)
Totals	$63,366.36	$1,547.91	$61,818.45	N/A

The calculations involved in the above schedule are based on the payments being made at the beginning of the period. The interest rate per period corresponds to the payment period. The actual table entries are based on the following calculations:

1. **Regular Payments** =

   Column B: Period 1: \$10,561.06
   Period 2: \$10,561.06
   . . .
   Period 6: \$10,561.06

2. **Payment to Interest** = the outstanding balance at the beginning of the previous period multiplied by the interest rate per period

   Column C This is the method used to calculate the interest on the outstanding balance at the beginning of the previous period. Multiply the interest rate per period by the outstanding balance at the beginning of the previous period as follows:

   Period 1: **There is no interest since the payment is made at the beginning of each period, and therefore the entire payment goes towards the principal.**
   Period 2: $\$51{,}257.38(0.01) \doteq \$512.57$
   . . .
   Period 6: $\$10{,}456.49(0.01) \doteq \$104.56$

3. **Payment to Principal** = payment − interest per period

   Column D: Period 1: \$10,561.06 − \$0 = \$10,561.06
   Period 2: \$10,561.06 − \$512.57 = \$10,048.49
   . . .
   Period 6: \$10,561.06 − \$104.56 = \$10,456.50

4. **Outstanding Balance** = the previous period's outstanding balance at the beginning of the period, minus the payment to principal in the current period

   Column E: Period 1: \$61,818.44 − \$10,561.06 = \$51,257.38
   Period 2: \$51,257.38 − \$10,048.49 = \$41,208.89
   . . .
   Period 6: \$10,456.49 − \$10,456.50 = \$0.01
   Differences due to rounding error.

EXERCISE 11.1

For each of the debts in the following table, assuming all the payments occur at the end of the period, find; (a) the size of each regular payment; (b) the outstanding balance of the debt at the specified time; and (c) the total interest paid on the loan up to the date of finding the outstanding balance on each debt.

	Size of the Loan	**Payment Period**	**Amortization Period**	**Interest Rate and Conversion Period**	**Find the Outstanding Balance after**
1.	$13,500	Monthly	3 years	12.4%, monthly	15th payment
2.	5,000	Yearly	15 years	14.0%, yearly	14th payment
3.	12,000	Quarterly	16 years	15.0%, quarterly	3rd payment
4.	7,900	Monthly	4 years	17.8%, semiannually	11th payment
5.	211,000	Monthly	20 years	14.0%, semiannually	185th payment
6.	192,000	Semiannually	25 years	17.0%, monthly	20th payment
7.	8,500	Yearly	2 years	14.8%, quarterly	2nd payment
8.	15,500	Semiannually	6 years	23.0%, yearly	8th payment
9.	35,600	Quarterly	9 years	15.5%, quarterly	12th payment
10.	4,500	Monthly	10 years	16.7%, monthly	48th payment

11. For problems 3 and 5 above, assume the loan payment you found is increased by 25%. Find the new amortization period for each of the loans with the larger payments. Also, how much interest is saved with the new, larger payment?

12. A debt of $80,000 is to be amortized with end of the month payments of $2,500. The interest rate on the debt is 11% compounded monthly. Construct an amortization schedule showing the last three table entries that would complete the repayment of the debt. (*Note:* the last payment will be a smaller payment.)

13. The Andrex company has a mortgage of $65,000 on a property and has been making regular payments of $3,500 at the end of each quarter. If the interest rate is 8% compounded quarterly, what would be the first three entries in the amortization schedule showing repayment of this loan? Also, find the value of the last payment.

14. A note is signed for a loan for which there is a repayment plan that must be met to adhere to the conditions of the note. The value of the note is $10,000 and requires four equal payments made every three months, with interest charged at 18% compounded annually. Construct an amortization schedule to show the entire repayment of the note.

11.2 Sinking Funds and Sinking Fund Schedules

Sinking funds refer to the accumulation of regular deposits in order to reach a sum of money in the future to repay an outstanding debt when it comes due.

Sinking funds are used frequently by governments and corporations for the repayment of debt. There are a number of situations where sinking funds are used.

One example is where an entire debt comes due at one point in time, in the future, rather than being due over time. For example, when a government or a company sells a bond, the only thing they must pay each year is the interest on the bond, with the repayment of the full amount of the bond at some point in the future. (Bonds will be discussed in more detail in Chapter 12.) This situation involves a long term debt that requires regular interest installments, with the principal being paid at a point in time in the future called the maturity date. Since the full principal comes due at once, there will be a need to have the accumulated amount to repay the debt. The method used to accumulate the required principal is a sinking fund.

Sinking funds are also used in situations where the government or business can earn a higher interest rate on an investment than the interest rate expected for debt or borrowed money. The sinking fund in this situation can be used to reduce the cost of borrowing.

You may ask how such a circumstance might arise. Suppose company management expects the interest rate in the market to rise in the next year. They would use a sinking fund system, borrowing now at a fixed rate of interest and then investing the repayment of the loan in a sinking fund at a higher interest rate in the future. This action would reduce the cost of borrowing to the company.

A common use of a sinking fund is when a school board or municipality borrows money from the provincial government. In most provinces, the provincial government will expect the interest, called the **interest expense**, on the debt to be repaid each year, with the full amount of the principal to be repaid at one point in time in the future. To ensure there is sufficient money to repay the full principal when the loan is due, the provincial government will expect money to be set aside annually (usually each year) in a fund that will accumulate to the required principal to repay the loan when it comes due. This fund, which accumulates to the required principal, is called a sinking fund.

For example, suppose a school board needs $3 million to build a new high school. The province would first need to approve the capital expenditure, that is, money spent on buildings and equipment rather than on day-to-day operations. Then arrangements would be made for the school board to borrow the money through a financing authority of the government. In general, the borrowed money would require annual interest payments (the interest expense) and a payment to a sinking fund that accumulates to $3 million at a date specified by the province.

In the private sector, corporations use sinking funds to repay long term debt such as bonds. Again, as with the school board, the purpose of the fund is to allow the corporation to put the money to work while insuring that the required money will be available when the bond issue matures (when the money must be repaid to the people who purchased the bonds).

When a sinking fund is established there are two expenses each year, one being a payment to the sinking fund and the other a payment of interest to the creditor(s). The payments for either or both may occur more than once a year, but the expenses for both are considered as annual expenditures in the yearly budget of a company or government organization. This distinction will become clear in the following examples.

The methods used for sinking funds, like the pension plans examined earlier, use the annuity amount formula.

Consider the example where the borrower, a small fire district, must (a condition of getting the loan) use a sinking fund to repay a debt:

EXAMPLE 11.5

The View Royal Fire District needs a new fire truck that will cost $300,000. The province will lend the necessary money provided a sinking fund is established to provide for repayment of the debt. The loan must be repaid in four years. Monies for repayment will come from a tax increase on the land owners who are part of the fire district. The interest expense on the loan must be paid every six months as per the loan agreement with the province. The fire district will earn 8% compounded annually on the sinking fund. The interest rate on the loan is 12% compounded semiannually. The sinking fund payment must be made annually at the end of each year.

(a) Set up a sinking fund schedule to show the accumulation of the fund and the book value of the debt for each year.

(b) Show the total annual interest expense associated with the loan and the total annual payments that must be made to service the loan.

Solution (a) Sinking Fund Schedule

There is a new term used in this example that you should make sure you understand — **book value**. Book value refers to the difference between the original amount of the loan and the accumulated amount of the sinking fund, calculated each time a payment is made to the sinking fund. In general, the book value is shown after each payment is made to the fund.

What we must find in this problem is R, since we know that we must have $300,000 after four years. That is, what must the payment be to the sinking fund each year to accumulate to $300,000 in four years?

Using our formula for R from Chapter 8, we have:

$$R = \frac{S_n}{\frac{[(1+i)^n - 1]}{i}}$$

Substituting we have:

$$S_n = \$300{,}000$$

$$i = 0.08$$

$$n = 4$$

$$R = \frac{\$300{,}000}{\frac{[(1+0.08)^4 - 1]}{0.08}}$$

$$R = \$66{,}576.24$$

Calculator Solution

						Payment
Input	300,000	8	4			
Depress	FV	i	n	COMP	PMT	66,576.24

Thus, annual payments of $66,576.24 to a fund that pays 8% compounded annually, will accumulate to $300,000. The sinking fund schedule would look as follows:

Table 11.6 Sinking Fund Schedule for the View Royal Fire District

A	B	C	D	E	F
Year	**Regular Payment**	**Payment of Interest**	**Increase in Fund**	**Accumulated Balance in the Fund**	**Accumulated Book Value of the Debt**
					$300,000.00
1	$ 66,576.24	$0	$ 66,576.24	$ 66,576.24	$233,423.76
2	$ 66,576.24	$ 5,326.10	$ 71,902.34	$138,478.58	$161,521.42
3	$ 66,576.24	$11,078.29	$ 77,654.53	$216,133.11	$ 83,866.89
4	$ 66,576.24	$17,290.65	$ 83,866.89	$300,000.00	$0
Totals	$266,304.96	$33,695.04	$300,000.00	N/A	N/A

The values in Table 11.6 are based on the following calculations:

Column C: Column E (of the previous period) $\times i$
Period 2: $66,576.24 $\times$ 0.08 ≐ $5,326.10
. . .
Period 4: $216,133.11 $\times$ 0.08 ≐ $17,290.65

Column D: Column B + Column C
Period 2: $66,576.24 + $5,326.10 = $71,902.34
. . .
Period 4: $66,576.24 + $17,290.65 = $83,866.89

Column E: Column D + Column E (of the previous period)
Period 2: $71,902.34 + $66,576.24 = $138,478.58
. . .
Period 4: $83,866.89 + $216,133.11 = $300,000

Column F: Loan – Column E = Book value
Period 1: $300,000 – $66,576.24 = $233,423.76
. . .
Period 4: $300,000 – $300,000 = 0

(b) **Interest Expense and Annual Payments to Service the Loan**
Note that there are two costs associated with this loan. The first is the interest expense associated with the actual loan — 12% compounded semi-annually. Since the interest must be paid every six months, the cost of the loan each year will be:

$$\text{Interest cost on loan} = \$300{,}000 \times \frac{0.12}{2}$$
$$= \$18{,}000 \text{ every six months}$$

The interest is paid every six months making the annual expenditure to service the interest on the loan $36,000 ($18,000 $\times$ 2). Also, note that compounding has no effect. Remember, compounding implies interest upon interest. Since the interest is paid every six months, there is no interest upon which to pay interest. It would become relevant only if the regular interest payment was missed; then interest on interest would be due.

The second part of the annual cost to the fire district is the annual sinking fund payment of $66,576.24.

Therefore, the total annual expenditure this fire district must make in the repayment of this debt is:

$$\$36{,}000 + \$66{,}576.24 = \$102{,}576.24$$

Each year the fire district would show two expenditures in its budget associated with the debt — interest payments and the payment to the sinking fund, totalling $102,576.24.

Sinking fund schedules can be set up for general annuities. As with our discussion of amortization tables, you will find it easier to use f for i in the sum formula (S_n). The reason for preferring the equivalent rate formula is that the column to compute interest requires the interest rate per payment period. This is exactly what the equivalent rate provides.

The use of sinking funds generally involves long term debt, and the length of a sinking fund schedule varies, depending on the length of time until repayment is required. If you wanted a complete sinking fund schedule, you would have the schedule computer generated. However, it may be necessary to find the schedule entries for selected periods. This may be done more quickly by hand. **A schedule that shows only selected periods is called a partial sinking fund schedule.**

To set up a partial sinking fund schedule, we use our formula for S_n, find S_n for the necessary period, and determine the schedule values. Consider the following example:

EXAMPLE 11.6

A small municipality is setting up a sinking fund with annual payments to repay a debt of \$520,000. The sinking fund will earn 12.55088% compounded annually. If the fund is to accumulate the desired sum of \$520,000 over 28 years, construct a partial sinking fund schedule that shows the fund at periods 3, 27, and 28.

Solution As with our previous example we must determine the annual payment required to accumulate the sum of \$520,000. We begin with our formula:

$$R = \frac{S_n}{\frac{[(1+i)^n - 1]}{i}}$$

Substituting we have:

$$S_n = \$520{,}000$$
$$n = 28$$
$$i = 0.1255088$$

$$R = \frac{\$520{,}000}{\frac{[(1+0.1255088)^{28} - 1]}{0.1255088}}$$

$$R \doteq \$2{,}472.03$$

Calculator Solution

						Payment
Input	520,000	12.55088	28			
Depress	FV	i	n	COMP	PMT	2,472.03

Inserting everything into a sinking fund schedule requires the same calculations as in our previous example. The one difference is that we find the accumulated balance directly by using S_n for the previous period. In this problem, we need the sums for period 2 and 26 to compute the table entries, as requested, upon which we can base the calculations for the following period's schedule entries.

Table 11.7 A Partial Sinking Fund Schedule

A	B	C	D	E	F
Year	**Regular Payment**	**Payment of Interest**	**Increase in Fund**	**Accumulated Balance in the Fund**	**Accumulated Book Value of the Debt**
0					$520,000.00
2	$ 2,472.03			$ 5,254.32	$514,745.68
3	$ 2,472.03	$ 659.46	$ 3,131.49	$ 8,385.81	$511,614.19
26				$406,344.37	
27	$ 2,472.03	$50,999.79	$53,471.82	$459,816.19	$ 60,183.80
28	$ 2,472.03	$57,710.98	$60,183.01	$519,999.21	$0.79
Totals	$ 69,216.84	N/A	N/A	N/A	N/A

The calculations for Table 11.7 are undertaken as follows:

Column E:

$$\textbf{Period 2: } S_2 = \$2{,}472.03\,\frac{[(1+0.1255088)^2-1]}{0.1255088}$$

$$\doteq \$5{,}254.32$$

$$\textbf{Period 3: } S_3 = \$2{,}472.03\,\frac{[(1+0.1255088)^3-1]}{0.1255088}$$

$$\doteq \$8{,}385.82$$

$$\textbf{Period 26: } S_{26} = \$2{,}472.03\,\frac{[(1+0.1255088)^{26}-1]}{0.1255088}$$

$$\doteq \$406{,}344.37$$

$$\textbf{Period 27: } S_{27} = \$2{,}472.03\,\frac{[(1+0.1255088)^{27}-1]}{0.1255088}$$

$$\doteq \$459{,}816.20$$

$$\textbf{Period 28: } S_{28} = \$2{,}472.03\,\frac{[(1+0.1255088)^{28}-1]}{0.1255088}$$

$$\doteq \$519{,}999.21$$

Calculator Solution

	End of Period 2					Amount
Input	2,472.03	12.55088	2			
Depress	PMT	i	n	COMP	FV	5,254.32

	End of Period 3					Amount
Input	2,472.03	12.55088	3			
Depress	PMT	i	n	COMP	FV	8,385.82

	End of Period 26					Amount
Input	2,472.03	12.55088	26			
Depress	PMT	i	n	COMP	FV	406,344.37

	End of Period 27					Amount
Input	2,472.03	12.55088	27			
Depress	PMT	i	n	COMP	FV	459,816.20

	End of Period 28					Amount
Input	2,472.03	12.55088	28			
Depress	PMT	i	n	COMP	FV	519,999.21

Column C:

Period 3: Interest = \$5,254.32(0.1255088) ≐ \$659.46
Period 27: Interest = \$406,344.37(0.1255088) ≐ \$50,999.79
Period 28: Interest = \$459,816.20(0.1255088) ≐ \$57,710.88

Column D:

Period 3: Interest + Payment = \$659.46 + \$2,472.03
= \$3,131.49
Period 27: Interest + Payment = \$50,999.79 + \$2,472.03
= \$53,471.82
Period 28: Interest + Payment = \$57,710.98 + \$2,472.03
= \$60,183.01

The remaining columns are completed using the same methods as used in constructing Table 11.6.

EXERCISE 11.2

For each of the sinking funds in the following table, find (a) the size of each regular payment; (b) the amount in the fund at the specified time; (c) how much interest has accumulated in the sinking fund as of the date of finding the amount in the fund; and (d) assuming the interest on the debt is paid annually, find the annual interest expense on the debt.

	Amount to Accumulate in Sinking	Payment Period	Accumulation Period	Interest Rate and Conversion Period for the Fund	Interest Rate and Conversion Period on the Loan	Find Balance in Fund after Payment . . .
1.	$ 16,500	Monthly	3 years	15.4%, monthly	16.4%, yearly	12
2.	15,000	Yearly	15 years	11.0%, yearly	10.0%, quarterly	14
3.	22,000	Quarterly	16 years	18.0%, quarterly	19.0%, quarterly	3
4.	15,900	Monthly	4 years	14.8%, semiannually	23.8%, semiannually	19
5.	150,000	Monthly	20 years	17.0%, semiannually	21.0%, semiannually	150
6.	126,000	Semiannually	25 years	14.0%, monthly	22.0%, monthly	18
7.	54,500	Yearly	6 years	17.8%, quarterly	19.8%, monthly	4
8.	63,500	Semiannually	18 years	20.0%, yearly	18.0%, yearly	16
9.	45,600	Quarterly	9 years	18.5%, quarterly	14.5%, quarterly	10
10.	23,500	Monthly	10 years	13.7%, monthly	14.7%, semiannually	24

11. A debt of $180,000 is to be amortized by using a sinking fund. The payments are to be made at the end of each month for the next five years. The interest rate is 12% compounded monthly. Construct a sinking fund schedule showing the first and last two entries. Show the book value for each of the four periods.

12. The City of Winnipeg has just borrowed $7.5 million for twenty years through the sale of bonds. The money is to assist in undertaking major sewer reconstruction. The city has started a sinking fund to handle repayment of the bond issue when it becomes due. The fund is to accumulate money at 8% compounded annually. The interest rate on the bond is 10% annually, payable every six months. Rounding all calculations to the nearest dollar, find:

- **a.** the annual payment to the sinking fund. Construct a partial schedule for periods 3, 17, and 18.
- **b.** the annual budget expenditure to service the interest expense for the debt as well as the sinking fund.
- **c.** the book value of the debt after fifteen years.
- **d.** the entries for the schedule in part (a) if the interest rate on the sinking fund had been 8% compounded semiannually.

11.3 Capitalization and Capitalized Cost

A. Capitalization

Capitalization refers to assigning a value to an asset that will go on producing wealth or income indefinitely. For example, leasing a piece of land will produce income indefinitely. The method of determining the value of the land, based on the lease income, is called capitalization.

The process of capitalization involves converting an unlimited number of payments to a single value today. This is what we called the present value of a perpetuity. (See Chapter 10 if you've forgotten how to apply the concept.) Such a process is useful for evaluating assets and, in some cases, liabilities. In the field of real estate, the procedures of capitalized costs are often used to assist in estimating the value of income producing properties.

B. Asset and Liability Valuations

Consider the example of a piece of land that can be leased for $5,000 per year for farming purposes. What is the value of the land? What may come to mind are the alternative uses of the land and how the use will influence its value. If we find that the land is in an ALR (ALR land refers to an Agricultural Land Reserve, which imposes major restrictions on the use of farm land) then the only use will be agricultural. Therefore, the value will be largely determined by its farm income potential, which in this case is $5,000 per year. (For our purposes, we assume that the market value of the land is determined by its income potential.) If we know the current market rate of interest, we can estimate the value of the land using the capitalized cost approach for evaluating an asset.

EXAMPLE 11.7

A piece of land in an agricultural reserve can be leased for $5,000 per year. Because the land is in the reserve its only approved use is farming. If the taxes on the land are $200 per year, what would an investor be prepared to pay for the land if its use must continue to be agricultural and the current income is considered to be maximum for agricultural purposes? Assume the net return expected by the investor is 8% per year.

Solution The first thing we note is that the investor expects a net return of 8%. This means that after taxes and any other expenses associated with the land are paid, the investor expects to receive 8%. Since we have information only on taxes, we must assume that any other expenses are the responsibility of the person who is leasing the land.

The net annual income is therefore:

$$\$5{,}000 - \$200 = \$4{,}800$$

Based on this net income, we can determine the estimated value of the asset by using the formula for finding the present value of a simple perpetuity.

$$A_\infty = \frac{R}{i}$$

The values for the two terms are:

$$R = \$4{,}800$$

$$i = 0.08$$

$$A_\infty = \frac{\$4{,}800}{0.08}$$

$$A_\infty = \$60{,}000$$

Thus, if the investor expects a return of 8% net on this property, the investor would be willing to spend up to $60,000 to purchase the property. This answer assumes that the only costs associated with the land are the land taxes.

EXAMPLE 11.8

B.C. Hydro has been leasing an easement to access its power lines. An easement refers to having the right to use part of the land for access, placing of power lines, etc. Usually, easements are purchased. The current value of the lease is $250 per year. In order to ensure continual access, B.C. Hydro has decided to expropriate (force the property to be sold to B.C. Hydro) the land over which it has the easement. The land has a limited alternative use and other factors are not important in determining the value. If the interest rate is estimated to be approximately 10% compounded semiannually, what should be the expropriation price?

Solution Again we turn to our perpetuity formula, but note that the interest period and the payment period are not the same. Consequently, we must use the general perpetuity method.

$$A_\infty = \frac{R}{f}$$

Where f was found by the expression:

$$f = (1 + i)^c - 1$$

The values of the terms are:

$$R = \$250$$

$c = \frac{2}{1}$ Number of interest periods per year divided by the number of payments per year.

$$i = \frac{0.10}{2}, \text{ or } 0.05$$

$$f = (1 + 0.05)^2 - 1$$

$$f = 0.1025$$

$$A_\infty = \frac{\$250}{0.1025}$$

$$A_\infty \doteq \$2{,}439.02$$

Therefore, the approximate value of the land is $2,440, rounded to the nearest convenient number, for an offer to purchase.

C. Capitalized Cost

In the previous section we learned how to determine the capitalized value of a piece of land. In fact, the method used holds true for any asset that has an indefinite life.

A slightly different situation involves assets that have only a limited life, requiring the assets to be refurbished or replaced. Two common examples of such assets are buildings and pieces of equipment. In each case the owners must plan for the replacement of the asset if they are to protect their investment. **The process used to account for the replacement of an asset with a limited life is called capitalizing the cost of the asset.**

The capitalized cost of an asset is the original cost of the asset plus the monies needed for renewal of the asset. In the case of renewals, we need to calculate the present value of future renewals. Again, since we are talking about an indefinite number of renewals, we will be using the methods of a perpetuity.

The procedure for computing the capitalized cost uses the terms below. Take special care to study f, which is a single equivalent rate over the replacement period for the asset:

$K =$ capitalized cost

$F =$ original cost or initial cost of the asset

$i =$ interest rate per compound period

$f = (1 + i)^c - 1$, the single, equivalent rate of interest over the replacement period

$$c = \frac{\text{number of conversion periods per year}}{\text{number of replacement periods per year}}$$

OR

$c =$ number of compounding periods per replacement period

Please note how the term c is being used. Even when we are computing the value of f, the single equivalent rate of interest over the replacement period, we must make sure that c is properly defined. This value is dependent upon how many interest conversions (compound periods) are included in the replacement period. For example, if an asset is to be replaced every ten years and the interest rate is compounded quarterly, then the value of c would be 4×10, or 40.

Bringing the terms together, the expression for the capitalized cost of an asset, K, is:

$$K = F + \frac{\text{(Periodic Replacement Cost)}}{f}$$ **Formula 11.1**

Let's put the formula to work with an example involving the purchase of a warehouse. Make sure you work through each step carefully.

EXAMPLE 11.9

Canim Holdings Ltd. has just bought a newly constructed warehouse for \$300,000. The life of the warehouse is expected to be 25 years, based on an engineer's report. If Canim can invest its money at 10% compounded semiannually, what is the capitalized cost of the warehouse? The expected replacement cost of the warehouse is \$200,000, based on current construction costs.

Solution First, we must define the terms for this problem. Based on our definitions we have:

$$F = \$300{,}000$$

$$i = \frac{0.10}{2}, \text{ or } 0.05$$

$c = 2 \times 25$, or 50, Two conversion periods per year times the replacement period, which is 25 years.

Periodic replacement cost = \$200,000

Therefore, the capitalized cost of the warehouse is:

$$K = \$300{,}000 + \frac{\$200{,}000}{f}$$

$$f = (1 + 0.05)^{50} - 1$$

$$f \doteq 10.4673998$$

$$K \doteq \$300{,}000 + \frac{200{,}000}{10.4673998}$$

$$K \doteq \$300{,}000 + \$19{,}106.94$$

$$K \doteq \$319{,}106.94$$

This means that the present cost of the warehouse plus its future replacement cost is \$319,106.94. If we consider the difference between the capitalized cost, \$319,106.94, and the original cost, \$300,000, we have the present value of the replacement cost, \$19,106.94. If you invested the present value of the replacement cost today, at 10% compounded semiannually, you would find that the company has exactly enough money to rebuild the warehouse. That is,

$$\$19{,}106.94(1 + 0.05)^{50} = \$219{,}106.94$$

Subtracting the money required to replace the warehouse (\$200,000) we have \$19,106.94 which, if invested for another 25 years at 10% compounded semiannually, will accumulate, again, to the value of the replacement cost of the warehouse and continue to do so indefinitely. Therefore, Canim will always have sufficient money to replace the warehouse once the initial \$19,106.94 has been invested.

If you're wondering about inflation, can you figure out how this could be included in the calculations? Canim would need to either increase the expected replacement cost by an estimated amount to cover inflation or reduce the interest rate by the expected inflation rate to reflect the real increase in money. Either approach would ensure that the amount in their fund would always be sufficient to provide for replacement at current prices.

EXAMPLE 11.10

The Municipality of Granisle has just acquired a piece of land, with buildings, for its road maintenance yard. The land is valued at $50,000. The buildings are valued at $75,000 and have an expected life of ten years, with an estimated salvage value on materials of $10,000. The current value of the municipality's road equipment is $400,000 with an expected life of three years and an estimated salvage value of $200,000. If the municipality can earn 8% compounded semiannually on its money, what is the capitalized cost of the road maintenance yard, the buildings, and equipment? (Don't worry about the impact of inflation.)

Solution The cost of the land is its capitalized cost, or:

$50,000. (This is because the land will never require replacement as other types of assets do.)

The original cost of the buildings is $75,000 and their replacement value is: $75,000 – $10,000, or $65,000 (subtract out expected salvage or residual value). The original cost of the equipment is $400,000 and the replacement value is:

$400,000 – $200,000, or $200,000

Defining the terms we have:

$$i = \frac{0.08}{2}, \text{ or } 0.04$$

The value of c will be different for each asset:

$C_{\text{buildings}} = 2 \times 10$, or 20	Twenty compounding periods per replacement cycle for the buildings.
$C_{\text{equipment}} = 2 \times 3$, or 6	Six compounding periods per replacement cycle for the equipment.

Now calculating the capitalized cost of each we have:

Capitalized cost of the land = \$50,000

Capitalized cost of the buildings:

$$K = \$75{,}000 + \frac{\$65{,}000}{f}$$

Where f is:

$$f = (1 + 0.04)^{20} - 1, \text{ or } 1.191123143$$

$$K \doteq \$75{,}000 + \frac{\$65{,}000}{1.191123143}$$

$$K \doteq \$75{,}000 + \$54{,}570.34$$

$$K \doteq \$129{,}570.34$$

Capitalized cost of the equipment:

$$K = \$400{,}000 + \frac{\$200{,}000}{f}$$

Where f is:

$$f = (1 + 0.04)^{6} - 1, \text{ or } 0.26531902$$

$$K \doteq \$400{,}000 + \frac{\$200{,}000}{0.26531902}$$

$$K \doteq \$400{,}000 + \$753{,}809.51$$

$$K \doteq \$1{,}153{,}809.51$$

Therefore, the capitalized cost of the road maintenance yard, the buildings, and the equipment is:

$$K = \$50{,}000 + \$129{,}570.34 + \$1{,}153{,}809.51$$

$$K = \$1{,}333{,}379.85$$

Another approach can be used to find the capitalized cost of an asset. This second approach examines the case where a firm would make annual payments to a sinking fund that would provide for future replacement of the asset. Once these payments are determined, then their present value would give the capitalized cost of the assets. Consider Example 11.10 and assume Granisle uses a sinking fund to save the funds required for the periodic replacement of the buildings and equipment.

Since each asset has a different life, there is a need to compute both payments. Assuming the payments are annual and made at the end of each year, the payments would be computed as follows:

$$R = \frac{S_n}{\frac{(1+f)^n - 1}{f}}$$

$c = 2 \quad \dfrac{\text{two interest periods per year}}{\text{one payment per year}}$

$f = (1 + 0.04)^2 - 1$

$f \doteq 0.0816$ for both buildings and road equipment

$n = 3$ for road equipment

$S_n = \$400{,}000 - \$200{,}000$ for road equipment

$n = 10$ for buildings

$S_n = \$75{,}000 - \$10{,}000$ for buildings

It is important to note that c is computed based on the definitions used in Chapter 10 since we are dealing with payments for a complex annuity. This was done to show that there are now annual payments to a fund, which will accumulate to the required amounts for replacement. In the original Example 11.10, the capitalized cost is based on investing a sum today, which will accumulate to the desired replacement amount. Now, substituting into the formula for R, the payments for the two sinking funds are:

$$R_{\text{buildings}} = \frac{\$75{,}000 - \$10{,}000}{\left[\frac{(1 + 0.0816)^{10} - 1}{0.0816}\right]}$$

$$\doteq \$4{,}452.94$$

Calculator Solution

						Payment
Input	65,000	8.16	10			
Depress	FV	i	n	COMP	PMT	4,452.94

$$R_{equipment} = \frac{\$400{,}000 - \$200{,}000}{\left[\frac{(1 + 0.0816)^3 - 1}{0.0816}\right]}$$

$$\doteq \$61{,}510.86$$

Calculator Solution

						Payment
Input	200,000	8.16	3			
Depress	FV	i	n	COMP	PMT	61,510.86

Therefore, the annual payment that must be made to a sinking fund to have sufficient funds to replace equipment every three years and buildings every ten years would be:

$$\$4{,}452.94 + \$61{,}510.86 = \$65{,}963.80$$

What is implicit with these payments is that we assume that they will be made indefinitely to allow for the replacement of the asset every ten years. Thus, every ten years we have sufficient funds to replace the asset. Since these payments will need to occur indefinitely, we can compute their present value by using the perpetuity formula. Thus, the present value of these payments is:

$$A_\infty = \frac{R}{f}$$

$$= \frac{\$65{,}963.80}{0.0816}$$

$$\doteq \$808{,}379.90$$

Now, adding the present values to determine the capitalized cost of the yard and equipment gives:

Equipment +	Buildings +	Land +	Present Value of future payments	
\$400,000 +	\$75,000 +	\$50,000 +	\$808,379.90	= \$1,333,379.90

As can be seen, the results are the same as in the original example. (There is a \$0.05 rounding difference.)

The important feature of this second approach is that it recognizes the more realistic situation of business and government needing to accumulate the required replacement funds.

EXAMPLE 11.11

The District of Metchosin has just purchased a new fire truck for \$195,000. Based on requirements from the insurance underwriters, the truck must be replaced every twenty years. The District can accumulate funds at 9.5% compounded annually. Use the sinking fund approach to determine the capitalized cost of the asset. The scrap value of the truck is estimated to be \$7,800.

Solution

STEP 1 The estimated replacement cost, incorporating the scrap value:

Replacement Cost = \$195,000 – \$7,800

Annual Payment to fund:

$$R = \frac{S_n}{\dfrac{(1+f)^n - 1}{f}}$$

$$c = 1 \; \frac{\text{one interest period per year}}{\text{one payment per year}}$$

Note: in this problem, since $c = 1$, i could have been used.

$$f = (1 + 0.095)^1 - 1$$

$$f = 0.095$$

$$n = 20$$

$$S_n = \$195{,}000 - \$7{,}800$$

$$R = \frac{\$195{,}000 - \$7{,}800}{\left[\dfrac{(1+0.095)^{20} - 1}{0.095}\right]}$$

$$\doteq \$3{,}458.84$$

Calculator Solution

						Payment
Input	187,200	9.5	20			
Depress	FV	i	n	COMP	PMT	3,458.84

STEP 2 Determine the capitalized cost using the information above. Therefore, the capitalized cost of the new fire truck, based on the estimates, will be found by finding the present value of the annual payments of \$3,458.84. Assuming the truck will be replaced indefinitely — every twenty years — we use the perpetuity formula to find the present value of the payments:

$$A_\infty = \frac{R}{f}$$

$$= \frac{\$3{,}458.84}{0.095}$$

$$\doteq \$36{,}408.84$$

Capitalized Cost = Initial Truck Cost + Present Value of the annual payments to the sinking fund

$$K = \$195{,}000 + \$36{,}408.84$$

$$K = \$231{,}408.84$$

Thus, the capitalized cost of the new fire truck is \$231,408.84. The annual payments to the fund are \$3,458.84. If these payments are continued for twenty years, there will be sufficient funds to replace the fire truck — assuming costs are constant.

D. Investment Costs and Capitalized Values

As seen in the previous examples, the capitalized cost of an investment represents the present cost of the investment plus future replacement costs.

An investor or business also should consider the interest that could have been earned on the money set aside to capitalize the cost of the asset, as well as the interest on the money used for the initial purchase. Often in finance, consideration of the interest forgone is included as part of the cost of the asset. This interest forgone (an opportunity cost in economics) is called the **periodic investment cost (PIC)** and is based on the capitalized cost of the asset.

If we review the capitalized cost of \$1,333,379.85 from Example 11.10, the periodic investment cost (PIC) can be determined as follows:

$$PIC = \$1{,}333{,}379.85 \times (\text{annual effective rate})$$

$$\text{Annual effective rate, } f = (1 + i)^c - 1$$

$$\text{Annual effective rate, } f = (1 + 0.04)^2 - 1$$

$$\text{Annual effective rate, } f = 0.0816$$

$$PIC = \$1{,}333{,}379.85(0.0816)$$

$$PIC \doteq \$108{,}803.80$$

Thus, if the municipality in Example 11.10 can earn 8% compounded semi-annually on its money, then the annual investment cost is $108,803.80. This is the interest forgone as a result of purchasing the road equipment yard and setting up a fund to replace the depreciating assets as required over time.

E. Comparison of Buying Costs

When businesses and governments are faced with decisions involving the purchase of one make or brand of equipment over another, there must be a consistent decision-making process. Consideration must be given to the expected life of the equipment, residual or salvage value, price, flexibility of the equipment (flexibility refers to possible alternative uses), and, in the case of private companies, potential tax implications. Tax considerations will be excluded from current consideration, however, it is vital to appreciate that the tax savings must be considered in the decision making process of business. Because of the complexity of tax considerations, discussion of this topic is left to be explained by a good tax accountant.

A systematic approach for evaluating different options involves setting up a decision rule that uses the techniques of capitalized cost and periodic investment cost.

(i) Decision Rule Using Capitalized Cost

When the capitalized cost method is used, the alternatives are evaluated by computing the capitalized cost of each, and then comparing the values. The decision rule is to select the option that has the lowest capitalized cost. Can you explain why? To see how this procedure works consider the following example:

EXAMPLE 11.12

Westcom Electronics is evaluating two pieces of equipment used to manufacture mother-boards for the computers it produces. Equipment A has an expected life of five years, after which it is felt that it can be sold for about 10% of its original cost of $350,000. Equipment B has an expected life of eight years and is expected to have no scrap value. Its cost is $425,000. If the company can earn 8% compounded annually, which piece of equipment is the most cost effective?

Solution Identifying the terms:

EQUIPMENT A

$$F = \$350{,}000$$
$$i = 0.08$$
$$c = 5$$
$$f = (1 + 0.08)^5 - 1$$
$$f \doteq 0.4693281$$

Therefore, the capitalized cost of Equipment A is:

$$K = F + \frac{\text{(Periodic Replacement Cost)}}{f}, \text{ or:}$$

$$K \doteq \$350{,}000 + \frac{\$350{,}000 - \$35{,}000}{0.4693281}$$

$$K \doteq \$1{,}021{,}172.26$$

EQUIPMENT B

$$F = \$425{,}000$$
$$i = 0.08$$
$$c = 8$$
$$f = (1 + 0.08)^8 - 1$$
$$f \doteq 0.8509302$$

Therefore, the capitalized cost of Equipment B is:

$$K = F + \frac{\text{(Periodic Replacement Cost)}}{f}, \text{ or:}$$

$$K \doteq \$425{,}000 + \frac{\$425{,}000}{0.8509302}$$

$$K \doteq \$924{,}453.42$$

Based on the above, the equipment that has the lowest capitalized cost is Equipment B, and, consequently, using capitalized cost as the criterion, we would select it as the most cost effective to purchase.

(ii) Decision Rule Using the Periodic Annual Investment Cost Method

In Example 11.12, the decision could also have been made using the periodic annual investment cost method. Before we can use this method, the capitalized cost of the assets must be determined. From the capitalized cost, the annual investment cost is determined. For Example 11.12, the periodic annual investment costs (PIC) of the two pieces of equipment are:

<u>PIC for Equipment A</u>:

Capitalized Cost $\times\ i$, or
$\$1{,}021{,}172.26 \times 0.08 \doteq \$81{,}693.78$

<u>PIC for Equipment B</u>:

Capitalized Cost $\times\ i$, or
$\$924{,}453.42 \times 0.08 \doteq \$73{,}956.27$

Using a decision rule that selects the equipment with the lowest annual investment cost again leads us to select Equipment B. It should also be noted that if the rate had been, for example, compounded semiannually, then the periodic investment cost would be determined by an annual equivalent rate using the f formula, where f would be the annual equivalent rate.

F. Refurbishing an Asset and Capitalized Cost: A Decision Tool

One use of capitalized cost is in the evaluation of whether a business or government should undertake a refurbishing (rebuilding) of a piece of equipment. It's somewhat like trying to decide whether it's worth spending a great deal of money to fix up an old car. If the "fixing" will keep the car running for another year, then you must compare this with the cost to replace the car and the subsequent savings on maintenance costs.

Consider Example 11.13, which shows how one would use the capitalized cost concept to evaluate what should be paid for an upgrade that extends the life of the equipment:

EXAMPLE 11.13

Volk Transport purchased a large tractor trailer unit for $150,000. The expected life of the tractor trailer is five years. After three years, the mechanics at Volk Transport said it would be possible to overhaul this tractor trailer unit and get four more years use out of the truck (extending its useful life to seven years instead of five years). The trade-in value of the truck at five years — assuming a major overhaul does not occur — is $15,000. If Volk can invest money at 10% compounded annually, what is the maximum price Volk should pay for the overhaul?

Solution First we find the capitalized cost of the truck with the known information that it will be replaced every five years. Defining what we know:

$$i = 0.10$$

$$c = \frac{5}{1}, \text{ or } 5$$

$$f = (1 + 0.1)^5 - 1, \text{ or } 0.61051$$

Scrap value = $15,000   Trade-in value.

The capitalized cost is therefore:

$$K = \$150{,}000 + \frac{(\$150{,}000 - \$15{,}000)}{0.61051}$$

$$K \doteq \$150{,}000 + 221{,}126.60$$

$$K \doteq \$371{,}126.60$$

From this capitalized cost we can see that the amount of $221,126.60 is that portion that is left to accumulate after the expenditure of $150,000 is made.

Consequently, after three years (the time the overhaul on the truck is to occur) the amount that would have accumulated would be:

$$\$221{,}126.60(1+0.1)^3 \doteq \$294{,}319.50$$

If the truck is overhauled with money from the fund at year three, then there must be sufficient monies left over to accumulate to $371,126.60. This is the amount that would be required to replace the truck at the end of year seven and leave sufficient funds to accumulate for the next replacement. Thus, we discount $371,126.60 back to year three to see how much we would require, at year three, that would accumulate to $371,126.60 by year seven.

Discounting from year seven to year three is four periods, therefore:

$$\$371{,}126.60(1+0.1)^{-4} \doteq \$253{,}484.46$$

Consequently, if there is $253,484.46 in the fund at the end of three years it will accumulate to $371,126.60 in seven years. Since we know that there will be $294,319.50 in the fund at year three, the amount that can be spent on the overhaul will be:

$$\$294{,}319.50 - \$253{,}484.46 = \$40{,}835.04$$

Volk could spend $40,835.04 and still have the necessary money available to replace the truck at year seven. So, providing the overhaul costs are less than $40,835.04, it is worth doing. The $40,835.04 is the maximum price Volk should be prepared to spend to extend the life to seven years.

One last point: if the trade-in value was to be reduced by extending the life of the truck, then the capitalized cost would rise, since the difference between the replacement cost ($150,000) and the trade-in value (currently $15,000) would decrease. For example, if the trade-in value was zero at year seven, then the fund would need to raise the entire $150,000 rather than $135,000 as is currently required.

EXERCISE 11.3

For each of the following, find the capitalized cost of the asset.

	Initial Asset Cost	Scrap or Residual Value	Replacement Period in Years	Interest Rate and Conversion Period
1.	$66,500	$ 4,000	20 years	10.0%, annually
2.	75,000	8,500	16 years	11.0%, annually
3.	82,000	12,000	6 years	12.0%, quarterly
4.	55,900	14,000	4 years	10.8%, semiannually
5.	70,000	nil	10 years	12.4%, semiannually
6.	26,000	nil	5 years	14.0%, annually

7. A trucking company has just bought four new trucks at a cost of $48,000 per truck. The trucks can be traded in every five years and will have a trade-in value of $12,000 per truck. If money is worth 8% compounded annually, what is the capitalized cost of the truck purchase?

8. Suppose the trucks in problem 7 can be used for seven years but the trade-in value drops to $7,000 per truck. If the cost of money remains at 8%, which option — trading the truck in at five years or at seven years — is best for the company? Make sure you show the calculations to support your reasoning.

9. A sailboat costs $124,000 and must be overhauled every four years at a cost of $12,500. What is the capitalized cost of the boat if money is worth 14% compounded quarterly? (What assumption must be made in answering this problem?)

10. A small printing company is considering going into the desktop publishing business. After researching the market, it must decide between two pieces of equipment. Equipment A has a cost of $40,000 and an expected life of eight years. In addition, this equipment is expected to have a residual value of 10% of the purchase price at the end of its expected life. Equipment B has a price tag of $30,000, an expected life of five years, and a residual value of 8% of its initial cost. If the company can earn 7% compounded semiannually, which piece of equipment should be purchased? Also, show the periodic investment cost of the two pieces of equipment.

11. A computer costs $3,500 and has an expected life of five years. The equipment can be upgraded at a cost of $200, which will extend its useful life to seven years — providing the upgrade is done at the point of purchase. If the trade-in value of the computer is zero and money is worth 9% annually, is the price for the upgrade a good investment?

12. The District of Metchosin has a fire hall that requires replacement every twenty-five years. The current hall was built for $75,000. The replacement cost is expected to be the initial cost plus increased construction costs over the period. Available data suggest that construction costs have risen at a rate of 5% annually (assume compounded annually). If some major renovation work is done at year twenty, the useful life of the hall can be extended to 32 years (the initial 25 plus 7 years extended life). If the District can invest money at 9.25% compounded semiannually, find the maximum amount the District can afford to spend to extend the life of the fire hall. (Assume there is no residual or scrap value in the old fire hall. Also, assume that the extension of useful life must occur at year twenty.)

13. What would be the capitalized cost of a window cleaning business that had an initial cost of $3,500 and replacement costs of $950 every year? Assume that money is worth 17% compounded annually.

14. How much could a company spend to overhaul equipment that has to be replaced every twenty years at a fixed cost of $75,000? The overhaul being considered would take place four years before replacement is due.

The overhaul will extend the life of the equipment by three years. Assume money is worth 10.5% compounded annually.

11.4 Depletion of Resources and Wasting Assets

A. Finding the Value of an Investment

Many investments require the purchase of an asset whose value declines over time until it is worthless. These assets are called **wasting assets** and the decline in their value over time is referred to as **depletion**. Examples include natural resources such as oil, natural gas, gravel pits, and mines; in each case their value declines over time as we "use the natural resource".

Before undertaking an investment, an investor must consider the fact that wasting resources may be used up, leaving little or no resale value. Moreover, in some cases, such as a mine, there is an additional liability to undertake proper restoration of the area mined (usually part of the environmental regulations of the mining permit). As a consequence, investors will expect a return on their investment that is sufficient to recover their initial investment in the asset, which now has no value or very little value. They also expect a rate of return for undertaking the investment and any expenditures associated with any applicable government regulations, such as site restorations for mining or tree replanting in the logging industry. The method used to restore or recover the initial investment is called a **depletion reserve**. Other needs, such as site restoration, are handled as part of another reserve the company establishes or includes in the depletion reserve, since these are costs that must be recovered by the firm from the income of the operation.

A depletion reserve is a fund that accumulates to the value of the original investment. This fund is built from the income flow of the depleting asset. The income must provide for both a return on the investment plus a payment to the depletion reserve fund. The size of the depletion reserve depends upon whether there is any residual value for the wasting asset upon completion of the undertaking and any other costs that may be warranted at the project's end. If there is a residual value in the land, then the size of the depletion reserve fund will be less than if there was no residual value.

Setting up a depletion reserve should be undertaken as part of the calculations that determine the annual net income expected from an investment. That is, out of each dollar of income received from an investment (which will be based on an expected yield rate) a portion must go to a return on the investment. The other portion must go to a fund that will recover the initial investment (a depletion reserve fund) and other costs that occur at the end of the project. Putting all this into a formula would give an expression such as:

Formula 11.2: Finding the Annual Net Income

annual net income = annual investment income + annual payment to depletion reserve + annual contribution to a reserve for other requirements

A problem requiring payment to a fund, such as an environment fund, can be handled by increasing the payment to the depletion reserve fund by the required additional payment. This would give us a shorter version of Formula 11.2:

Formula 11.2A: Finding the Annual Net Income

annual net income = annual investment income + annual payments to depletion reserve and other requirements

As can be seen, this expression requires us to know what investment return an investor expects as well as the rate of interest that will be received on funds invested in the reserve fund. Consider the following example, and make sure you follow how each component of the **annual net income** expression is determined and, in particular, the annual investment income:

EXAMPLE 11.14

Amco Investments is considering the purchase of a mine that will generate an expected net annual income of $100,000. This income is based on the current market price of copper and the annual ore that will be mined from the property. The ore has an estimated supply of ten years. After the end of the project, the property will have no market value (this results from the remote location of the property). Amco can earn 9% compounded annually on its invested money. Investments occur at the end of each fiscal year. Given that Amco requires a 15% return on investments, what should Amco offer as a purchase price to acquire the property?

Solution The unknown value is the purchase price. Based on our knowledge of the net income from the property, we must decide how this income should be divided between return on investment and the necessary payment to the reserve fund to recover the investment. The return on the investment portion of the $100,000 will determine the purchase price for the property.

Since we are interested in finding the purchase price, let us call this unknown X, which, in addition to being the purchase price, is also the value of the investment.

First, let's consider how much Amco must get from the investment in terms of investment income.

$$X = \text{purchase price or value of the investment}$$
$$0.15X = \text{required return on the investment}$$

Second, we must find the annual payment to a depletion reserve fund that will be sufficient, at the rate of 9% compounded annually, to recover the investment (purchase price of the land), once the ore is used up. We use the S_n formula that accumulates payments of R dollars each period. In our example, this will be R dollars per year for ten years, the remaining time the supply of ore is expected to last.

To reach a future value, S_n, with regular payments, R, we use the formula:

$$R = \frac{S_n}{\frac{[(1+i)^n - 1]}{i}}$$

Now since the future value is the original investment or purchase price, we can replace S_n with X, the term we defined as the unknown purchase price.

$$R = \frac{X}{\frac{[(1+i)^n - 1]}{i}}$$

From the problem we can determine the values for i and n necessary to find R. These are:

$$n = 10$$
$$i = 0.09$$

Therefore:

$$R = \frac{X}{\frac{[(1+0.09)^{10} - 1]}{0.09}}$$

$$R \doteq \frac{X}{15.192929718}$$

The purchase price of the land can now be set out as the sum of the required investment income and the annual payment to the depletion reserve fund.

$$\$100{,}000 = 0.15X + R$$

Substituting the expression for the payment to the depletion reserve from above yields:

$$\$100{,}000 \doteq 0.15X + \frac{X}{15.192929718}$$

$$\$100{,}000 \doteq X(0.15 + 0.06582009)$$

$$\$100{,}000 \doteq (0.21582009)X$$

$$X \doteq \$463{,}348.89$$

Therefore, Amco should be prepared to pay up to $463,348.89 for the property. This price will ensure that from the expected income of $100,000 the return on the investment will be 15% and, in addition, that sufficient money remains after the 15% return on investment to make a payment to a depletion reserve fund that will recover the purchase price of the mine, once the ore has been completely removed.

A question that may have come to mind from Example 11.14 is, "what would happen if the land had some potential value?"

If there is some resale worth in the land, the value of the investment should rise. That is, the company should be willing to pay more for the investment since the land can be sold once the mining has been completed. This additional value must be reflected in the offer to purchase the mine. To understand how to incorporate a residual value for the land, study Example 11.15:

EXAMPLE 11.15

Suppose Amco knows that the property has potential, since a lake is included as part of the mine site. Further, suppose Amco determines that there is recreation potential in the lake and, if the mining operation uses care in extracting the resource, it could sell lots around the lake. Based on this information, Amco estimates the value of the land after the mining operation will be $150,000. How would this change the purchase price determined above in Example 11.14?

Solution The only item that will change is the payment to the reserve fund that should now decrease since there is some residual value in the land. This change will represent a decline in the required value of S_n, since the residual value of $150,000 will now be subtracted from the previous value of the reserve requirement. That is, if the land has a value of $150,000 when the ore has been removed, it means that some of the original investment can be recovered in the sale of the land.

Therefore, the required size of the reserve fund payment will now be determined by the expression:

$$R = \frac{[X - \$150{,}000]}{\frac{[(1 + i)^n - 1]}{i}}$$

Note that the payment to the depletion reserve will be reduced by the residual value of the land. And, X represents the purchase price of the land from Example 11.14.

From the original problem, we know:

$$n = 10$$

$$i = 0.09$$

Therefore:

$$R = \frac{[X - \$150{,}000]}{\frac{[(1 + 0.09)^{10} - 1]}{0.09}}$$

$$R \doteq \frac{[X - \$150{,}000]}{15.192929718}$$

Now substituting this into our original expression to determine the purchase price, we have:

$$\$100{,}000 \doteq 0.15X + \frac{[X - \$150{,}000]}{15.192929718}$$

$$\$100{,}000 \doteq 0.15X + \frac{X}{15.192929718} - \frac{\$150{,}000}{15.192929718}$$

$$\$100{,}000 \doteq 0.21582009X - \$9{,}873.01$$

$$X \doteq \$509{,}095.38$$

Therefore, if the land has a residual value of \$150,000, Amco should be prepared to pay \$509,095.38 for the mine. This price will ensure a return of 15% and a depletion reserve payment that will be sufficient to recover the initial investment after the mining operation and the sale of the land.

B. Finding the Return on an Investment

Finding the yield rate or rate of return on an investment is important prior to undertaking a major expenditure. In Examples 11.14 and 11.15 Amco knew the investment should yield a return of 15%. Sometimes this return must be calculated. What we want to do in this section is determine how to estimate the return, based on the expected costs, the investment required, and the life of the income flow from the venture. Consider the following example:

EXAMPLE 11.16

Tregen Mine company is contemplating the purchase of a new mining property. Based on their geologists' reports, Tregen estimates that the income potential of the new site is $550,000 per year. The supply of ore is expected to last ten years. Major site work is required at the mine and is expected to cost $750,000. The mine is being offered for sale at a price of $1,000,000. If the company can invest its money in a fund that accumulates at 8% compounded annually, and assuming the land has no resale value, what would be the estimated rate of return if Tregen purchases the mine?

Solution To solve this problem, first define a term for the rate of return, the unknown. Let the rate of return be defined as r. Now based on the information:

Annual Income = $550,000
Price = $1,000,000
Site Work = $750,000
Total Investment = $1,000,000 + $750,000
= $1,750,000
r = Annual Rate of Return
Annual Income on Investment = $1,750,000$r$
$i = 0.08$ The rate at which the money accumulates.
$n = 10$ The number of years the ore is expected to last.

To calculate the annual deposit into the reserve fund the company must cover all the "up front money", which is the purchase price and the site work. To recover the investment the company must set aside R dollars each year for the ten years. R can be found by using our accumulation formula as follows:

$$R = \frac{S_n}{\dfrac{[(1+i)^n - 1]}{i}}$$

$S_n = \$1,750,000$ That includes the initial purchase price plus the investment in the site of $750,000. Remember, both must be recovered when all the ore has been removed.

$$R = \frac{\$1,750,000}{\dfrac{[(1+0.08)^{10} - 1]}{0.08}}$$

$$R \doteq \frac{\$1,750,000}{14.4865625}$$

$$R \doteq \$120,801.61$$

Now, turning to Formula 11.2A, we have:

$$\text{Annual Net Income} = \text{Annual Investment Income} + \text{Annual Payments to Depletion Reserve and Other Requirements}$$

Substituting the values into 11.2A:

$$\$550{,}000 \doteq \$1{,}750{,}000r + \$120{,}801.61$$

$$\$1{,}750{,}000r \doteq \$550{,}000 - \$120{,}801.61$$

$$r \doteq \frac{\$429{,}198.39}{\$1{,}750{,}000}$$

$$r \doteq 0.24526$$

Consequently, this purchase for Tregen, based on preliminary estimates of costs and revenues, should generate an approximate rate of return (the yield rate) of 24.53%.

C. Determining a Single Period Increase in the Depletion Fund

The increase in the depletion fund (interest and payment) in any particular year or period may be found by using the sinking fund procedure outlined earlier in this chapter. That is, all a depletion reserve represents is a sinking fund accumulating to recover the monies necessary to recover the initial investment and any other payments (such as clean up, site preparation, etc.). Computing the change in the value of the depletion reserve for any period can be found as shown in Example 11.17 below:

EXAMPLE 11.17

An orchard was purchased to yield 18%. The current income from the orchard is $100,000 per year. The trees are expected to have a productive life for another ten years. If the land is estimated to have a value of $75,000 when the trees become unproductive, and a depletion fund earning 6% annually is established, what is the increase in the depletion reserve in year six?

Solution First find the purchase price of the orchard. As before, let X represent the purchase price. Therefore:

X = Purchase Price
Annual Income = $100,000
Annual Investment Income = $0.18X$

The annual deposit to the fund is found by:

$$\text{Annual depletion deposit} = \frac{S_n}{\dfrac{[(1+i)^n - 1]}{i}}$$

Where:

$(X - \$75{,}000) = S_n$ The purchase price of the orchard less the residual value of the land.

$i = 0.06$

$n = 10$

$$\text{Annual depletion deposit} = \frac{(X - \$75{,}000)}{\dfrac{[(1 + 0.06)^{10} - 1]}{0.06}}$$

$$\text{Annual depletion deposit} \doteq \frac{(X - \$75{,}000)}{13.18079494}$$

Now using Formula 11.2A to find the purchase price we have:

$$\$100{,}000 \doteq 0.18X + \frac{(X - \$75{,}000)}{13.18079494}$$

$$0.25586796X \doteq \$105{,}690.10$$

$$X \doteq \$413{,}065.01$$

To find the payment to the depletion fund, substitute the value of X into the expression for the **annual depletion deposit**, which gives:

$$\text{Annual depletion deposit} \doteq \frac{(X - \$75{,}000)}{(13.18079494)}$$

Substituting the value of \$413,065.01 for X gives:

$$\text{Annual depletion deposit} \doteq \frac{\$413{,}065.01 - \$75{,}000}{(13.18079494)}$$

$$\text{Annual depletion deposit} \doteq \$25{,}648.30$$

The final step is to use the depletion payment to find the amount in the fund when $n = 5$. Using the amount formula gives:

$$S_n = \frac{R[(1 + i)^n - 1]}{i}$$

$$S_n = \frac{\$25{,}648.30[(1 + 0.06)^5 - 1]}{0.06}$$

$$S_n \doteq \$144{,}581.85$$

Therefore, the increase in the fund in the sixth year will be the sum of the interest earned on the balance at the end of year five plus the periodic increase for period six. That is:

$$\$144{,}581.85(0.06) + \$25{,}648.30 = \$34{,}323.21$$

The periodic increase in the fund in the sixth year is \$34,323.21.

EXERCISE 11.4

1. An oil well has been placed on the market for sale. The oil reserves in the well are expected to last four years and the residual value of the land around the well is estimated at $20,000. The income from the well is currently $19,000 per year, before depletion allowances. If funds can be accumulated at 12% compounded annually, find the annual depletion allowance to recover the investment over the four year period. Assume the expected rate of return is 16%.
2. A mine can be purchased for $180,000. Based on the geologist's report the mine is expected to generate an annual income of $31,000. The estimated supply of ore at the current utilization rate is estimated at ten years. The property is expected to have a value of $25,000 once the mining is completed. If the depletion fund earns 10% compounded quarterly, what would be the annual yield rate to a company that purchases the mine at the asking price of $180,000? (Assume payments to the depletion fund are made annually.)
3. A gold mine is available for sale. Telco Investments has reviewed the mine and sends its geologists to the site to determine the potential of the mine. Based on the most current world prices, Telco estimates that the mine will generate an annual income of $25,000 for eight years. The salvage value of the land is expected to net $10,000 after the gold has been extracted. If Telco can earn 12% compounded annually on any money put into a depletion fund, what should the company be prepared to pay for the property to earn a yield rate of 14.25% on its investment?
4. If the gold mine in problem 3 was expected to have a residual value of $25,000, how would this impact the purchase price of the mine?
5. West Isle Logging has been offered a timber lease on crown land that is expected to yield an annual income of $40,000 for the next five years. Once the timber is removed, the site must be replanted and the land returned to the province. The expected cost to replant the site is $5,000. What should West Isle be prepared to pay for the rights to log the land if it wishes to recover the cost of the lease and the replanting cost through a depletion reserve? West Isle has established a policy that requires all investments to yield a minimum return of 15%. Currently West Isle can invest money in a depletion fund that pays 13% annually.
6. A sawmill has just acquired the rights for a piece of property for $200,000. The estimated annual income for the timber is $50,000 for the next eight years. The company can earn 10% on funds that it accumulates. Determine the yield on the investment if the company knows it will need to reforest the site upon completion of the logging and sawmill operations. The expected cost to reforest the site is $38,000.

REVIEW EXERCISES

1. A loan of \$7,520 is to be repaid over seven years with monthly payments and an effective interest rate of 19.0827%. Set up an amortization schedule for the first two payments and the last two payments for this loan.

2. Greg and Terri have just purchased a home for \$105,000. Upon the purchase they put up a \$15,000 down payment, with the balance made by a first mortgage of \$90,000 that is amortized over twenty years with end of the month payments. If the mortgage has an interest rate of 23.21% compounded annually, find:
   a. the monthly payments;
   b. the amount outstanding after the 24th payment; and
   c. set up a partial amortization schedule to show the first two payments and the last two payments of the loan.

3. Harold signs a note for \$5,000 and agrees to repay the note by one payment in fifteen months. He also agrees to pay interest on the note every three months at the rate of 10.125% compounded semiannually. If Harold uses a sinking fund paying 18% compounded quarterly to accumulate the money to repay the face value of the note, answer the following questions. (Assume the payments to the sinking fund are quarterly.)
   a. Find the total interest expense of the debt to Harold.
   b. Construct a sinking fund schedule for the debt.

4. A local Recreation Commission is considering whether to build a new arena that is expected to cost \$1.5 million. The members of the Commission need to decide whether to borrow the money and levy a tax on the local property owners to pay for the repayment of the debt. The cost of borrowing the money is 12% compounded semiannually with the interest being payable every six months. The money will be borrowed from the province and will require full payment in five years. If the Commission decides to go ahead with the project, there will be a need to set up a sinking fund to provide for the repayment of the debt. The sinking fund pays 10.25% compounded annually. A friend of yours is a member of the Commission and is complaining that he can't get the actual cost per year and the overall cost of the arena from the administration. Help him out by constructing the appropriate sinking fund schedule. Compute the annual and total cost of this project to the local taxpayers. Total cost means the borrowing cost and the sinking fund expenditures for the arena over the five year period.

5. A company wishes to set up a fund to replace equipment that will cost \$70,000 five years from now, making equal sized payments at the beginning of each of the next five years. If money is worth 12% compounded annually, what is the size of the annual payment?

6. Calculate the interest and increase into the fund described in problem 5 during the fourth payment period.

7. Construct a partial sinking fund schedule to show the last two payments of a sinking fund that requires $80,000 to be accumulated in ten years. The interest rate on the fund is 13% compounded semiannually. The regular deposits will be made at the end of every six months.

8. Calculate the purchase price for a mine that is expected to provide a net annual income of $125,000 for ten years. The site has no residual value. This investment is undertaken under the expectation of yielding 12% compounded annually. The company can invest money in a depletion reserve fund that earns 9.5% compounded annually.

9. If the land around the mine described in problem 8 could be sold for $6,000 when the ore is exhausted, what impact would this have on the purchase price? Calculate the change in the price that will occur with this new information.

10. How much should be paid for land containing an oil well that is estimated to produce for fifteen years and have an annual income of $86,000? Assume the prospective buyers wish to earn 15% on their investment and that a reserve fund earning 10.5% compounded annually can be established.

11. Compute the yield rate (return on investment) for an investor who purchases an orchard for $300,000. The orchard is expected to be productive for twenty years, after which time the property will be worth about $65,000. The expected annual net income is $35,000 and a depletion reserve can be established that earns 9.5% compounded annually.

12. A pulp company purchases land and timber rights on property that is expected to be productive for twelve years. The company expects to earn 15% on all investments. The purchase of the timber rights and the land is based on an assumption that the land will have resale value of $85,000 after logging. A reserve fund to cover the initial cost of the timber rights is set up at 12% compounded annually. If the annual net income from the timber is estimated to be $125,000, find:

a. The purchase of the land and timber rights;

b. The increase in the depletion reserve in the eighth year.

13. Calculate the capitalized cost of land leased for $250,000 per year, if money is worth 6.50% compounded semiannually.

14. Calculate the capitalized cost of a video store that has $34,500 in equipment and annual replacement costs of $15,000 for new videos and VCR's. Assume that money is worth 14% compounded monthly.

15. Determine if it would be economically feasible to spend $95,000 on the overhaul of equipment that has to be replaced every ten years. The overhaul being considered must take place two years before replacement is due.

It would extend the life of the equipment by three years. Assume money is worth 8.5%.

16. Calculate the annual investment cost of an asset that originally costs $12,000 and will need replacement parts worth $250 every quarter. Assume money is worth 12.5% compounded semiannually.

17. Decide which of the two investments listed below is best if money is worth 10.5% compounded annually. Also, find the dollar difference in capital costs.

Choice A: Initial cost of $12,000 with an expected life of ten years and scrap value of $450.

Choice B: Initial cost of $11,600 with an expected life of seven years and scrap value of $600.

18. Calculate the annual investment cost advantage of the best choice in problem 17.

19. A company must buy new safety equipment every eight years at a cost of $6,000. The salvage value of the equipment is $850. A new type of equipment is coming on the market that will last ten years and have a salvage value of 12% of the original cost. Money is worth 14.5% compounded annually. Compare the two choices and identify the highest price the company should pay for the new type of equipment.

SUMMARY OF FORMULAS

Formula 11.1 $K = F + \frac{\text{(Periodic Replacement Cost)}}{f}$

This formula is used to find the capitalized cost based on the original cost and the periodic replacement cost. f is the factor based on the number of interest conversion periods in a replacement period.

The formula for f was:
$f = (1 + i)^c - 1$, where c = the number of conversion periods in a replacement period.

Formula 11.2

annual net income = annual investment income + annual payment to depletion reserve and other funds

Where:

Annual net income: Income per year from the project.

Annual investment income: Income based on the purchase or investment cost. It is found by multiplying the yield rate expected times the investment.

Annual payment to depletion reserve and other funds: This is based on the accumulation formula S_n, and determines the payment out of annual income that must be made to recover the cost of a wasting asset and other costs such as an environmental fund.

Formula 11.2A Finding the annual net income:

annual net income = annual investment income + annual payments to depletion reserve and other requirements

GLOSSARY OF TERMS

Amortization of a Debt to retire (pay off) a debt over time with regular payments.

Amortization Schedule a schedule that shows the regular payments made on a debt, depicting the portion of interest and principal associated with each payment as well as the outstanding balance on the debt at each period the loan payment is made.

Book Value the net amount of a debt outstanding that is found by subtracting the accumulated balance in a sinking fund from the original amount of the debt.

Capitalization the process of computing the present value of an unlimited number of future payments.

Capitalized Cost the present value of the initial cost of an asset plus the unlimited future replacement costs (also called renewal cost) of an asset.

Depletion the use of wasting asset over time. The term depletion, in the context of finance, means to use up an asset.

Depletion Allowance the amount of money set away each period to recover the cost of the initial purchase of a depleting asset (wasting asset).

Interest Expense the interest that is paid on a debt. This interest expense is normally determined at a different rate than that paid on a sinking fund.

Partial Sinking Fund Schedule a sinking fund schedule that shows only selected periods, not the entire sinking fund.

Periodic Investment Cost the interest on the capitalized cost of an asset. It should be thought of as the opportunity cost of the investment, that is, the interest income forgone.

Periodic Replacement Cost the cost to replace an asset when it is worn out. The periodic replacement cost may change over time to reflect increased costs associated with inflation.

Refurbishing an Asset the process of repairing an asset to increase its useful life beyond its normal life expectancy.

Residual Value also referred to as scrap value or salvage value. It is the cash value of an asset at the point in time it is to be replaced.

Scrap Value see Residual Value.

Sinking Fund a fund established to accumulate sufficient funds to repay a debt.

Sinking Fund Schedule a schedule of payments that shows the accumulated amount in the sinking fund, interest paid to the fund each period, and, sometimes, the accumulated Book Value of a debt.

Wasting Assets assets that are used up over time. The most common example is natural resources.

Yield Rate a term used to describe the rate of return to an investor from an investment.

CHAPTER 12

Stocks and Bonds

The topic of "stocks and bonds" is of interest to many people. During the 1980's and early 1990's much attention was focused on the stock market. First, there was the severe decline in October 1987, and then, in 1990, the high interest rates and the Persian Gulf crisis. Since then the market has had its share of ups and downs. After the stock market "crash" of 1987, there was an increase in investor interest in bonds because they offer an alternative to buying shares or stocks in companies as an investment. By late 1990, interest in bonds began to dissipate with the expectation of changing interest rates.

One source of money for businesses is internal, involving the earnings retained after all the "bills" have been paid. In addition, there are two major sources of external corporate financing:

- Equity financing
- Debt financing

Equity financing refers to raising money through the sale of shares or stock. The word equity means ownership. When you hold a share in a company you own a part of that company. In return, the company gets an inward flow of money that can be used to finance operations or assist with a major capital project, such as building a new plant. It's important to note that governments cannot sell equity; they raise money through debt financing or taxes.

Debt financing, on the other hand, implies the borrowing of money. When large sums of money need to be borrowed for long periods of time, corporations and governments often sell bonds or debentures to raise the money. This is called a **bond issue or a debenture issue. A bond refers to a written promise to repay a sum of money at a fixed time in the future. In return, the purchaser**

of the bond or debenture is paid interest for the use of the money at a rate specified.

A bond is secured by a pledge of assets, whereas a debenture is similar to a bond except that it's not secured by assets. Since there is more risk with a debenture, there is generally a higher rate of return on this form of investment.

The major emphasis in this chapter will be on the method used to determine bond and debenture prices. We'll examine the relevance of the **yield rate** (the rate of return expected by an investor) in determining the price of both types of instruments. Since this text is an introductory course in the Mathematics of Finance there won't be a full discussion of the many types of bonds available in the marketplace.

You'll be pleased to know that the technical calculations in this chapter are based on the techniques you've learned in the previous five chapters.

OBJECTIVES

When you have completed this chapter you will be able to:

1. explain the meaning of equity and debt financing and, in particular, the terms common shares, preferred shares, debentures, and bonds;
2. calculate the purchase price of a bond;
3. calculate bond premiums and bond discounts;
4. explain the meaning of the terms face value, redemption value, par value, yield rate, and bond rate;
5. calculate the approximate yield rate on a bond;
6. read and understand published bond tables;
7. amortize a bond premium and accumulate a bond discount.

12.1 Equity Financing

As noted in the introduction, equity financing refers to raising money through the sale of shares, a method used by private businesses. Equity financing has two forms, which are the issuing of:

- **common shares**
- **preferred shares**

Common shares give the holder the right to vote on policy decisions of the company when a general meeting of shareholders is called. This participatory right of common shareholders is a fundamental principle of being a part owner of a company. The ability to influence any decisions is dependent on the number of common shares one owns. In many large companies, individuals holding common shares have only a tiny percentage of all the stock of the company. Therefore, the influence of any single shareholder on policy is minimal. An investor looks for two sources of return when purchasing a common share. The first is the dividend payment. Dividends are paid to common shareholders based on the profits of the company. Since profits go up and down over the business cycle, dividends tend to fluctuate as well. As a consequence, investors interested in dividends look at the long term performance of the company and, in particular, the dividends paid over a number of years. The second component of return on common shares is the expected increase in the share price on the market. When combined, the dividend and the change in the market value of the share determine the return to the investor.

The second type of share or equity in a company is the preferred share. This is a share that guarantees a specific annual return from the company. The holder of a preferred share gets a fixed payment each year as specified at the time of issuing the share by the company. However, preferred shareholders do not normally have any voting privileges on company policy, as do common shareholders, nor do they normally share in profits, as do the common shareholders.

To understand a preferred share, consider the example of a company issuing preferred shares for sale at an issue price (or **par value**) of $50 per share. Assume the company offers a rate of return on the preferred shares of 8% per year. Regardless of what one pays for the stock, whether the shares are purchased at a price per share that is higher or lower than par value, one will still receive a guaranteed return of $4 per year per share ($50 × 0.08).

While preferred shareholders are guaranteed an annual return on their shares, common shareholders only get a return on their investment if the company "declares" a dividend. If the preferred shareholder doesn't enjoy the same voting rights as the common shareholder why would an investor buy a preferred share? The answer is that the rate of return offered to a preferred shareholder is sometimes higher than that offered on bonds or debentures. Even if the rate of interest is lower, there are often very special tax incentives on the income from a preferred share that increase the effective rate of return to the investor. Also, because there is a guaranteed annual return based on the issue price rather than on market price, the investment is considered less risky than buying common shares.

12.2 Reading and Understanding Stock Market Quotations

Common and preferred shares are traded (bought and sold) on stock exchanges in Vancouver, Toronto, Montreal, and other Canadian cities, in addition to exchanges around the world. The stocks traded can be one of two types:

- **Listed** stocks: the stocks are traded on a recognized exchange.

- **Unlisted** stocks: the stocks are traded on an unlisted market. If you turn to the financial section of your local paper, you will find a section that has a heading "Over the Counter" which refers to unlisted stocks.

Every daily newspaper has some type of summary page of stock market activity. The most common format is that used by *The Globe and Mail* and *The Financial Post*. To help you understand how to read the stock section, shown below is a listing of each column for the Industrial Stocks section of *The Financial Post*. The values were taken from one trading day. The stock examined is MacMillan Bloedel, a B.C. company in the wood industry.

Table 12.1 A Market Quotation of a Stock from the Toronto Stock Exchange: Quotation for April 1, 1991, as it appeared in *The Financial Post*, April 2, 1991. Reprinted with permission of *The Financial Post*.

52 Week						Close				
High	Low	Company	Div. Rate	High	Low	Close or Latest	Net Chg	Vol 100's	Yield %	P/E Ratio
$20	14¼	MacMillan Bloedel	0.60	$19.875	$19.625	$19.75	–¼	8,796	3.0	53.4

The interpretation of the headings and values are:

High $20: the highest price the stock has traded for in the past 52 weeks;

Low 14¼: the lowest price the stock has traded at in the past 52 weeks;

52 Week: the time period for which the high and low price is quoted (week 1 to week 52 **inclusive**);

Company: identifies the company;

Div Rate: $0.60 is the dividend rate on the stock over the latest 12-month trading period and represents $0.60 per share;

High: for this trading day, this was the highest price the stock traded;

Low: the lowest the stock traded this day;

Close or Latest: the closing price for this trading day;

Net Chg.: the change recorded from the closing price on the previous trading day;

Vol 100's: the number of shares that traded this day, in 100's;

Yield %: the annual yield of the stock;

P/E Ratio: the market price of the stock divided by the earnings per share (earnings per share is not given in the quotation).

When stocks are first brought to the market by a company they are offered at a **par value**, which is the issue price. The issue price is the value per share that the company sets for the stock when it is offered for sale for the first time.

Rarely do stocks ever trade at their par value or issue price. The first day of trading determines the interest in a stock. If there are many buyers the value will rise above the issue price. The opposite trend is generally the case, that is, stock prices tend to fall below their issue price, at least until investors have had a chance to view the potential of the stock.

It's very important to remember that the market price of a stock is the result of the actions of buyers and sellers. If there are more sellers, then the price will fall. If there are more buyers, then the price will rise. The price will only stabilize when the number of buyers and sellers are the same.

The most common calculation that you need to be able to do is determine yield rate for a particular stock. Remember that the yield rate is the rate of return expected by the investor. The following examples are intended to provide you with a simple procedure to compute an approximate return, excluding any commissions that one might pay to a broker. A broker is someone who acts on your behalf in the purchase and sale of your shares.

EXAMPLE 12.1

An investor is trying to decide between two investments. Rolex Inc. common shares are trading at $80½ while Triac Electronic's common shares are trading at $74¼. Rolex has been consistent in paying an annual dividend of $3.50 per common share to shareholders, while Triac has been averaging $2.25 per share. If both investments are over one year, which stock has the best rate of return?

Solution To answer this question we simply need to compare the expected dividend for each company to the current share price:

$$\text{Rolex's rate of return} = \frac{\$\ 3.5}{\$80.5}$$

$$\doteq 0.043478$$

$$\text{Triac's rate of return} = \frac{\$\ 2.25}{\$74.25}$$

$$\doteq 0.030303$$

Based on this simple analysis, the investor would buy Rolex stock.

EXAMPLE 12.2

Suppose you are thinking about buying a MacMillan Bloedel preferred share that is trading at \$36¼ (\$36.25). If the share pays 7½% annually on a par value of \$50, what would be your rate of return each year?

Solution The preferred dividend is based on the rate quoted for dividends on the original issue price. Remember that, even though you may buy the share at less than the par value, you still receive the dividend (7½%) on the basis of the share's issue price. Therefore:

First, figure out the actual amount of interest paid annually on the share:

$$0.075 \times \$50 = \$3.75$$

Next, we divide the interest paid by the purchase price of the stock:

$$\frac{\$3.75}{\$36\frac{1}{4}} = 0.10345$$

If you buy the preferred share for $\$36\frac{1}{4}$, you will earn 10.345% per annum on your investment.

12.3 Debt Financing

As we noted in the introduction, businesses and governments who need to borrow money for a long period of time often prepare and sell a bond issue. A bond is a written promise to pay to the purchaser a specific sum of money at a specific point in the future. In addition, the issuer promises to pay interest, generally semiannually, for the use of the money.

It was noted earlier that a similar type of instrument to a bond is a debenture. Bonds are secured by a pledge of assets while debentures are simply a legal commitment by the borrower to repay the amount borrowed.

Debt financing can take a variety of forms including bonds, debentures, mortgages, and a range of loans that are available to companies. This type of financing is not limited to corporations. Most newspapers on any given day carry at least one story dealing with government debt. Perhaps more than any other topic, the level of debt for school boards, municipalities, and federal and provincial governments poses concern to many business and government leaders. In order to raise the money to pay for government deficits, bond and debenture issues are common.

Government bonds and debentures are often considered to be a good long term investment. For example, the non-market Canada Savings Bonds issued in October 1987 (shortly after the severe stock market decline) were a great investment compared to other types of bank and credit union investments.

The term **non-market bond** is used to describe Canada Savings Bonds since they are not bought and sold on the bond market. Instead, they are bought and sold through local financial institutions at the value specified on the bond. The seller receives the face value amount even if the bonds are cashed in before the **maturity date** (the time the bond holders are paid back the principal).

Government of Canada bonds, on the other hand, are subject to market conditions. When they are sold before maturity, they must be sold through a broker at whatever the market says the bond is worth.

Bonds and debentures are sold on two markets:

- the primary securities market
- the secondary securities market

Primary markets are where bonds are sold when they are first issued by a company or government agency. A dealer or brokerage house sells the bonds on behalf of the issuing company or government agency.

The **secondary security market** is where bonds are resold after being initially purchased. *The Financial Post* bond quotation is an example of the secondary market. It is this secondary market that provides the means to transfer ownership and set the value of bonds and debentures over time.

There are several terms you need to understand in our discussion of bonds and debentures (note that from here on the term bond will be used since the terms and calculations that apply to bonds in general apply to debentures):

Face Value or Par Value
This is the value stated on the bond or the issue price. In general, the face value is stated in a denomination of $1,000 or higher. However, when the sale is also to appeal to small investors, denominations of $100 sometimes occur.

Maturity Date
This is the date when the bondholder can expect to have the full value of the bond repaid. An equivalent term that is sometimes used is **redemption date**. This refers to the date when the bond is redeemed, that is, when the money is paid back to the bondholder by the company or government agency that issued the bond.

Redemption Value
The value the company or government pays to the bondholder when the bond is redeemed. If a bond is redeemed at face value, then we say the bond is redeemed at **par value**, sometimes referred to as par. It is possible to have a bond redeemed at more than par value to make the bond more attractive to the investor when first offered for sale.

Bond Rate
This is the rate of interest used to determine the interest the bond pays to the bond holder. It is also called the **coupon rate** and the **contract rate**. Those of you who have had a Canada Savings Bond have probably "cut" the coupon off to collect the interest. (This may date some of us, since coupons have not been used on recent issues.)

Yield Rate
When bonds are sold on the open market the purchaser will want a particular rate of return on their investment. This return is called yield rate and will change over time depending on the current rates of interest being paid when the bond is purchased. The yield rate is the factor that determines the purchase price of the bond when it is sold on the open market.

Interest Dates
This refers to the time periods when interest is paid to the bondholder. Most bonds pay interest semiannually. Often abbreviations are used, such as J-J, for bonds that have interest payable on January 1 and July 1.

Accrued Interest
The interest that has accumulated on a bond since the interest was last paid.

Purchase Price
This is the price of a bond based upon the yield rate, the rate of return expected by an investor, which in turn is based on the prevailing interest rates at the time the bond is purchased. It is important to understand that the purchase price of a bond is not necessarily the price that you read in the paper. The value in the paper is the quoted price and, if there is any accrued interest on the bond, then this interest must be added to the quoted price to get the purchase price.

The discussion that follows uses the following symbols to stand for each of the terms above:

F — face value of the bond
RD — the redemption value of the bond
PP — the purchase price of the bond
r — the bond or coupon rate of the bond
i — the yield rate expected by the purchaser
n — the number of remaining interest periods until the redemption or maturity date
R — the interest payment each period, based on the bond rate ($R = F \times r$)

With these definitions in place, we can now examine how the price of a bond is determined to yield a given return.

12.4 Determining the Purchase Price of a Bond on an Interest Date

Bonds can be purchased at any time. However, the procedures differ depending on whether the bond is purchased on the date interest is regularly paid (interest date) or whether it is purchased "between interest dates". Our discussion in the first section focuses on the purchasing of bonds on an interest date.

At the outset, it is important to understand that when someone purchases a bond there are two payments the buyer will receive:

- the regular interest payments, usually paid every six months;
- the redemption value of the bond when it matures or is redeemed.

Therefore, the price that an investor will be prepared to pay for a bond depends on:

R: the regular interest payment ($F \times r$);

RD: the redemption or maturity value.

What must be done is to compute the present value of the remaining interest payments using the yield rate as the interest rate, then, add this present value of interest payments to the present value of the redemption value, also based on the yield rate. By adding these two present values, one can determine the price an investor would be prepared to pay for a bond to generate the required return. The price paid by an investor will ensure the investor obtains the required yield on the investment, since the basis for the computations was the yield rate expected by the investor.

The sum of these two present values can more clearly be expressed in a formula:

STEP 1 Set up an expression for calculating the present value of the remaining interest periods:

$$\frac{R[1 - (1 + i)^{-n}]}{i}$$

Where:

$R = F \times r$

F = face value

r = bond rate

i = yield rate

n = number of remaining interest periods

STEP 2 Next, develop an expression that will find the present value of the redemption value:

$$RD(1+i)^{-n}$$

Where:

RD = redemption value
i = yield rate
n = number of interest periods remaining

STEP 3 Adding these two present values together gives a formula for the **purchase price of a bond** on an interest date (remember, an interest date is the date on which the interest is paid):

$$PP = \frac{R[1-(1+i)^{-n}]}{i} + RD(1+i)^{-n}$$ **Formula 12.1**

In the following examples you will find two terms being used depending upon whether the purchase price is greater than the face value or less than the face value.

If the purchase price is greater than the redemption value, then the bond is said to be purchased at a **premium**. Conversely, when a bond is purchased at a price that is less than the redemption value, the bond is said to be purchased at a **discount**.

What determines whether there is a discount or a premium is the relationship between the yield rate and the bond rate. If the yield rate is higher than the bond rate, then the bond is generally purchased at a discount. If the bond rate is greater than the yield rate, then the bond is generally purchased at a premium.

One exception may arise if the bond is redeemed (RD) at a higher value than the face value. This sometimes occurs to make the bonds more attractive to investors. It also occurs if the bonds may be redeemed before the maturity date by the issuing company — if this is possible, the bond is called a **callable bond**. When the redemption value is greater than the face value, it normally results in a statement that the bond will be redeemed at a value in excess of 100% of the face value. For example, a bond with a face value of $1,000 that is to be redeemed at $1,100 is said to be redeemable at 110 (i.e., 110% of the face value). When this occurs, it complicates the problem sufficiently so that it cannot be said in advance whether a premium or discount will apply.

This special case will be examined in Example 12.4.

EXAMPLE 12.3

A $5,000 Government of Canada bond pays the holder an interest rate of 9.5% payable semiannually. The bond will be redeemed at par in ten years. An investor wants to purchase the bond on the bond market to yield a return of 12% payable semiannually. What would be the purchase price of the bond?

Solution Since the bond pays 9.5% on $5,000 semiannually, the regular interest payment will be:

$$R = F \times r$$

$$= \$5{,}000\left[\frac{0.095}{2}\right]$$

$$= \$237.50$$

From the information given, the remaining number of interest periods is:

$$n = 10 \times 2, \text{ or } 20$$

The redemption value of the bond in ten years is the par value or the face value of the bond:

$$RD = \$5{,}000$$

Now to compute the purchase price, we must calculate the present values of the payments and the redemption value. Since the yield rate is the rate the investor wants to receive, it is the rate we must use to find the present values in determining the purchase price. Substituting the values into our formula, we have:

$$PP = \frac{\$237.50[1 - (1 + i)^{-n}]}{i} + \$5{,}000(1 + i)^{-n}$$

Substituting the remaining values gives:

$$i = \frac{0.12}{2}, \text{ or } 0.06 \qquad \text{The yield rate.}$$

$$n = 20$$

$$PP = \frac{\$237.50[1 - (1 + 0.06)^{-20}]}{0.06} + \$5{,}000(1 + 0.06)^{-20}$$

$$PP \doteq \$2{,}724.11 + \$1{,}559.02$$

$$PP \doteq \$4{,}283.13$$

Therefore, if the investor pays $4,283.13 for the bond the guaranteed return is 12% compounded semiannually. Since the bond is purchased at a price less than the redemption, it is said to have been bought at a **discount**. The value of the discount is:

$$\$5{,}000 - \$4{,}283.13 = \$716.87$$

The most important thing to note about this example is that the yield rate is the rate that must be used to determine the present values, and thus the purchase price. The bond rate is used only to find the regular income payments. The reason for this is that the price must be based on the return the investor wants to receive, in this case, 12% compounded semiannually. Only the yield rate will generate a price that guarantees this return.

Calculator Solution

Step 1: Find the Discounted Value of the Future Interest Payments at the Yield Rate						
Input	237.50	6	20			
Depress	PMT	i	n	COMP	PV	2,724.11
Step 2: Find the Discounted Value of the Redemption Value at the Yield Rate						
Input	5,000	6	20			
Depress	FV	i	n	COMP	PV	1,559.02
					Purchase Price	4,283.13

EXAMPLE 12.4

A large gas and oil company needs to raise $10,000,000 for capital expansion of its plant. The company issues fifteen year bonds to raise the money. The bonds are redeemable at 102. The rate of interest on the bond is 9% payable semiannually. If at the time of the bond issue interest rates are 8% compounded semiannually, what amount of money will the company receive from the bond issue?

Solution We should start by noting an important piece of information in this problem. **We are told that the bonds will be redeemed at 102; this means that for every dollar of face value, $1.02 will be paid upon redemption.** The reason a company may offer such an arrangement is to encourage people to buy their bond and hold it until it is redeemed. To the investor this represents a slight increase in the return, since upon redemption the bondholder will get an additional \$0.02 per \$1.

Now turning to the problem at hand, the information given is:

$r = \frac{(0.09)}{2}$ The bond rate.

$i = \frac{(0.08)}{2}$ The yield rate.

$R = 0.045 \times \$10,000,000$

$\doteq \$450,000$ Remember that interest payments are based on the bond rate.

$RD = \$10,000,000 \times (1.02)$

$= \$10,200,000$ Redemption value for the entire bond issue.

$n = 15 \times 2, \text{ or } 30$

Substituting into Formula 12.1 gives:

$$PP = \frac{R[1 - (1 + i)^{-n}]}{i} + RD(1 + i)^{-n}$$

$$PP = \frac{\$450,000[1 - (1 + 0.04)^{-30}]}{0.04} + \$10,200,000(1 + 0.04)^{-30}$$

$$PP = \$7,781,414.99 + \$3,144,850.41$$

$$PP = \$10,926,265.40$$

Thus, the company will raise \$10,926,265.40 from the bond issue, \$926,265.40 more than the initial issue, that is:

$$\$10,926,265.40 - \$10,000,000 = \$926,265.40$$

If the bonds were in denominations of \$1,000 an investor would pay \$1,092.63 for each \$1,000 bond, resulting in the payment of a \$92.63 premium. It is important to note that the premium is paid by the purchaser to the seller. That is why the company receives more than the face value of the bonds issued: the total premium is paid to the company as part of the purchase price.

Calculator Solution

	Step 1: Find the Discounted Value of the Future Interest Payments at the Yield Rate					
Input	450,000	4	30			
Depress	PMT	i	n	COMP	PV	7,781,414.99
	Step 2: Find the Discounted Value of the Redemption Value at the Yield Rate					
Input	10,200,000	4	30			
Depress	FV	i	n	COMP	PV	3,144,850.41
					Purchase Price	10,926,265.40

One other situation must be considered before moving to other bond calculations. Suppose an investor wants to earn a yield rate that is not only different from the bond rate, but is also compounded at a different interval than the current bond rate. This type of problem can be handled very easily by using the equivalent rate formula we discussed in earlier chapters. All we need to do is to find f, the equivalent rate. The value of f will need to be converted to the interest period on the bond.

EXAMPLE 12.5

Hi-Tech Electronics is a new company in the compact disk industry. In order to implement some major changes in its production methods, the company decides to build a new factory. To raise the required $2,000,000, a bond issue is undertaken. Interest on the bonds is set at 10%, compounded semiannually, and the bonds are for fifteen years. If we assume that the bonds are redeemed at par value (i.e., 100), how much money will Hi-Tech raise with this bond issue if investors expect a yield of 8% compounded monthly? What would investors pay for a $1,000 bond if they expect 8% compounded monthly?

Solution The first thing we note in this example is that the yield rate is at a different interval than the interest paid on the bond. To address this problem, we must first find an equivalent rate of interest for the yield rate, such that the yield rate corresponds to the payment period of the bond interest. Therefore, to find the purchase price we proceed as follows:

STEP 1 First we find f

Where:

$$f = (1 + i)^c - 1$$

$$i = \frac{0.08}{12}$$

$$c = \frac{12}{2}, \text{ or } \frac{6}{1}$$

Note: the yield rate is compounded monthly and the interest payment on the bond is semiannually, thus c is found as outlined in Chapter 10.

$$c = \frac{\text{(number of interest conversion periods per year)}}{\text{(number of payment periods per year)}}$$

$$f = \left(1 + \frac{0.08}{12}\right)^{\frac{6}{1}} - 1$$

$$f = 0.040672622$$

STEP 2 Now identify all the components we require for our purchase price formula:

$$RD = \$2{,}000{,}000$$

$$r = \frac{0.10}{2}, \text{ or } 0.05$$

$$n = 2 \times 15, \text{ or } 30$$

$i = 0.040672622$ Substituted from f above.

$$R = \$2{,}000{,}000 \times (0.05), \text{ or } \$100{,}000$$

Substituting into our purchase price formula gives:

$$PP = \frac{\$100{,}000[1 - (1 + 0.040672622)^{-30}]}{0.040672622} + \$2{,}000{,}000(1 + 0.040672622)^{-30}$$

$$PP \doteq \$1{,}715{,}168.36 + \$604{,}792.11$$
$$PP \doteq \$2{,}319{,}960.47$$

As can be seen, the bond issue will generate a premium for Hi-Tech, since it raises $319,960.47 more than the issue price.

The price an investor would pay for a $1,000 bond is found by first computing the premium per $1,000,000 of bonds, or:

$$\frac{\$2,319,960.47}{2} = \$1,159,980.23$$

Therefore, every $1,000 bond must be worth:

$$\frac{\$1,159,980.23}{1,000} = \$1,159.98$$

A premium of $159.98 will be paid by the purchaser of a $1,000 bond.

Calculator Solution

Step 1: Find the Discounted Value of the Future Interest Payments at the Yield Rate						
Input	100,000	4.067262	30			
Depress	PMT	i	n	COMP	PV	1,715,168.36
Step 2: Find the Discounted Value of the Redemption Value at the Yield Rate						
Input	2,000,000	4.067262	30			
Depress	FV	i	n	COMP	PV	604,792.11
					Purchase Price	2,319,960.47

This problem demonstrates an important concept, namely, how to handle situations where the yield rate is compounded at a different time period than when the bond rate is applied. As can be seen, it is easily handled by finding the equivalent rate of interest, f.

EXERCISE 12.1

1. A $1,000 bond will be redeemed on July 1, 2007, at par value. The coupon rate on the bond is 8% annually, paid semiannually, and is payable on July 1 and January 1 of each year. If the bond is purchased on July 1, 1991, and is expected to yield 10% compounded semiannually, what is the purchase price? What is the value of the premium or discount? If the bond is redeemed at 105, what will be the discount or premium?

2. Find the purchase price of a $5,000 bond with a bond rate of 10% annually, interest paid semiannually, if the market rate of interest is 12% paid semiannually. Assume the bond is redeemed at par value and it has twelve interest periods remaining.
3. Kristen Williams buys a $10,000 Government of Canada Bond that pays 14% annually, interest paid semiannually, and is redeemable at 102 in ten years. If Kristen wants to receive 15% compounded semiannually, what would she pay for this bond? Suppose she holds the bond for two years until market rates of interest fall to 8% compounded semiannually. At what price would Kristen be able to sell the bond? What will be the discount or premium?
4. $200,000 worth of bonds pay interest semiannually at an annual rate of 9%. The bonds are sold ten years before they will be redeemed at par value. If the bonds are purchased to yield 11% compounded monthly, what is the purchase price for the bonds? What will be the discount or premium paid on this purchase?
5. An investor purchases $80,000 worth of bonds with an annual bond rate of 7%, with interest paid semiannually on April 1 and October 1. The bonds will be redeemed on April 1, 1997. Find the purchase price and size of premium or discount, on April 1, 1991, under the following conditions:
   a. The bonds are purchased to yield 9% semiannually (redeemed at 105).
   b. The bonds are purchased to yield 12% compounded quarterly (redeemed at 100).

12.5 Purchase Price of Bonds Between Interest Periods

Often bonds are not purchased on the convenient dates when interest is paid. In fact, most bond sales occur at points in time other than the interest date. The method used to compute bond prices between interest periods relies on an approximation using both compound and simple interest procedures.

The first step requires us to compute the purchase price of the bond at the interest date immediately preceding the actual purchase date. Then we accumulate this purchase price to the date when the purchase occurs. The procedure we use to bring the price forward, from the immediately preceding interest period, to the actual date of purchase, uses the simple interest method of Chapter 6. The easiest way to understand the process is to look at an example:

EXAMPLE 12.6

A bond with a face value of $100,000 is purchased on September 4, 1991. The interest is payable on April 1 and October 1 at 11% compounded semiannually. If the bond is redeemable at 102 on October 1, 1993, find the purchase price on September 4, 1991, for an investor who wants to earn 14% compounded semiannually.

Solution From the information in this problem we can see that the interest date that **precedes** the purchase date is April 1, 1991. The time that has elapsed between the interest date and the purchase date is (247 – 91), or 156 days. This was found using the Table of Days of the Year in Chapter 6. We must also determine the number of days between interest dates, that is, between April 1 and October 1. Again using the Table of Days we calculate (274 – 91), or 183 days. Time Diagram 12.1 shows the steps involved.

Let's work through each part of the solution in steps:

STEP 1 Find the purchase price at the interest period immediately preceding the purchase date. Use Formula 12.1:

$$PP = \frac{R[1 - (1 + i)^{-n}]}{i} + RD(1 + i)^{-n}$$

Where:

$$r = \frac{0.11}{2}, \text{ or } 0.055$$

$$F = \$100{,}000$$

$$R = (0.055) \times \$100{,}000, \text{ or } \$5{,}500$$

$$i = \frac{0.14}{2}, \text{ or } 0.07$$

$$RD = \$100{,}000 \times 1.02, \text{ or } \$102{,}000$$

$n = 5$ This takes us back to April 1, 1991.

Now substituting into our equation:

$$PP = \frac{\$5{,}500[1 - (1 + 0.07)^{-5}]}{0.07} + \$102{,}000(1 + 0.07)^{-5}$$

$$PP \doteq \$22{,}551.09 + \$72{,}724.59$$

$$PP \doteq \$95{,}275.68$$

If the bond was purchased on April 1, 1991, the purchase price would be $95,275.68.

STEP 2 The next step is to bring the purchase price from April 1 forward to the actual purchase date of September 4, 1991. We do this by accumulating the purchase price on April 1 to September 4 using simple interest for the number of days that have elapsed. Remember that the time between these two days is 156 days with 183 days being the total days in the interest period from April 1 to October 1, 1991.

$$PP \doteq \$95{,}275.68\left[1 + 0.07\left(\frac{156}{183}\right)\right]$$

$$PP \doteq \$100{,}960.98$$

Therefore, the purchase price of the bond on September 4, 1991, is $100,960.98.
Diagrammatically the problem looks as follows:

Figure 12.1 Time diagram of a bond purchase *between* interest dates

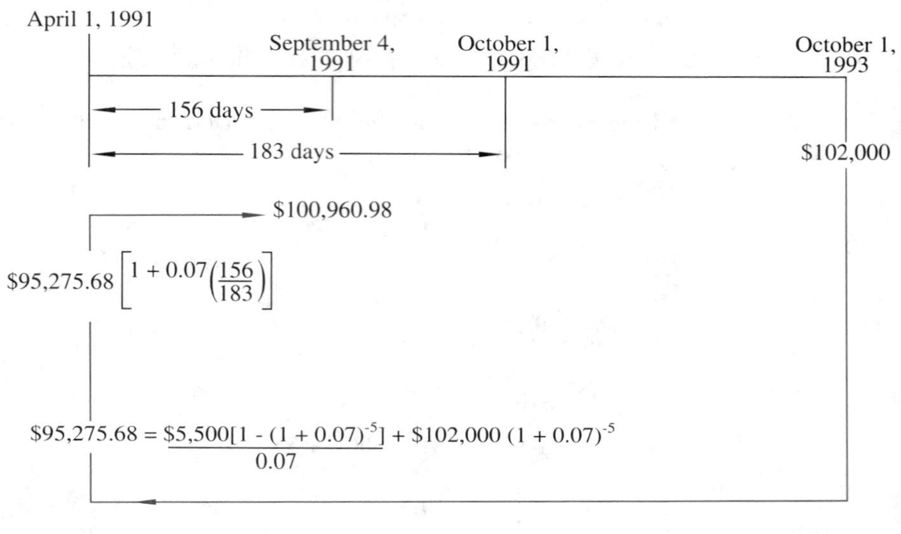

Calculator Solution

	Step 1: Find the Discounted Value of the Future Interest Payments at the Yield Rate					
Input	5,500	7	5			
Depress	PMT	i	n	COMP	PV	22,551.09
	Step 2: Find the Discounted Value of the Redemption Value at the Yield Rate					
Input	102,000	7	5			
Depress	FV	i	n	COMP	PV	72,724.59
			Purchase Price on Preceding Interest Period			95,275.68
	Moving the Price to the Purchase Date					
			95,275.68 $\left[1 + (0.07)\frac{156}{183}\right]$			100,960.98

12.6 Flat Price, Quoted Price, and Accrued Interest

In Example 12.6 the purchase price of \$100,960.98 is called the **flat price**. What this means is that the price on September 4 includes the **accrued interest** from the last interest period, April 1,1991. More precisely, the accrued interest from April 1 to September 4 is:

$$\$100{,}000\left[0.055\left(\frac{156}{183}\right)\right] \doteq \$4{,}688.52$$

The bond seller expects to receive the interest upon the sale of the bond. Therefore, when the bond is sold, the price the bondholder considers to be the selling price is:

$$\$100{,}960.98 - \$4{,}688.52 = \$96{,}272.46$$

This price is called the **quoted price**. The relationship between the flat price, quoted price, and accrued interest can be seen in the following expressions:

Quoted Price = Flat Price − Accrued Interest
Flat Price = Quoted Price + Accrued Interest

It is important to note that the accrued interest is accruing at the bond rate, not the yield rate. When you consider what is actually occurring, the bond was accumulating interest to the bondholder from the preceding interest date, April 1 (from Example 12.6) to the purchase date of September 4. Now the price must be adjusted to reflect this interest since the seller of the bond needs to be compensated for the time the bond has been held since the last interest payment.

To get everything straight, let's consider an example:

EXAMPLE 12.7

A \$100,000 bond has a bond rate of 12% and will be redeemed on September 1, 1995. Interest is payable semiannually on September 1 and March 1. Find the quoted price, flat price, and accrued interest if the bond is purchased on April 30, 1991. Assume the investor expects to receive 10% payable semiannually.

Solution To find the purchase price, we must first calculate a price on the interest date preceding the purchase date, March 1. Then this price is accumulated to the point where the purchase occurs on April 30. Following the previous example:

$$r = \frac{0.12}{2}, \text{ or } 0.06$$

$$F = \$100{,}000$$

$$R = \$100{,}000 \times 0.06, \text{ or } \$6{,}000$$

$$i = \frac{0.10}{2}, \text{ or } 0.05$$

$n = 9$ These are the remaining interest periods from March 1, 1991, to September 1, 1995.

Substituting the information in Formula 12.1 gives:

$$PP = \frac{\$6{,}000[1 - (1 + 0.05)^{-9}]}{0.05} + \$100{,}000(1 + 0.05)^{-9}$$

$$PP \doteq \$42{,}646.93 + \$64{,}460.89$$

$$PP \doteq \$107{,}107.82$$

Next, accumulate the purchase price on the interest date of March 1, 1991, to the purchase date of April 30, 1991. However, remember that since the computation of the purchase price is based on the yield rate, this is the rate that will be used to move the price on March 1 ($107,107.82) to the purchase date of April 30. To accumulate to April 30, the number of days between the purchase date and the interest payment date must be found. Turning to the Table of Days of the Year.

Purchase date April 30,	120 days
Interest date March 1,	60 days
Total number of days	60 days

The number of days in the interest period between March 1 and September 1 is 184 (244 – 60).

Now, accumulating the interest from the interest date to the purchase date we have the flat price:

$$\text{Flat Price} = \$107{,}107.82\left[1 + (0.05)\frac{60}{184}\right] \text{ Remember to use the yield rate.}$$

$$\doteq \$108{,}854.14 \quad \text{The purchase on April 30, 1991.}$$

To calculate the quoted price we must subtract the accrued interest **that accrues to the owner of the bond up to the time the bond is sold**. In this problem the interest that belongs to the holder is from March 1 to April 30, and will be paid based on the bond rate. Thus the quoted price will be:

$$\text{Accrued Interest} = \$100{,}000\left[(0.06)\frac{60}{184}\right], \text{ or } \$1{,}956.52$$

$$\text{Quoted Price} \doteq \$108{,}854.14 - \$1{,}956.52$$

$$\doteq \$106{,}897.62$$

The purchase price on the interest date is shown below in the time diagram.

Figure 12.2 Time Diagram of the Purchase *between* Interest Dates for Example 12.7

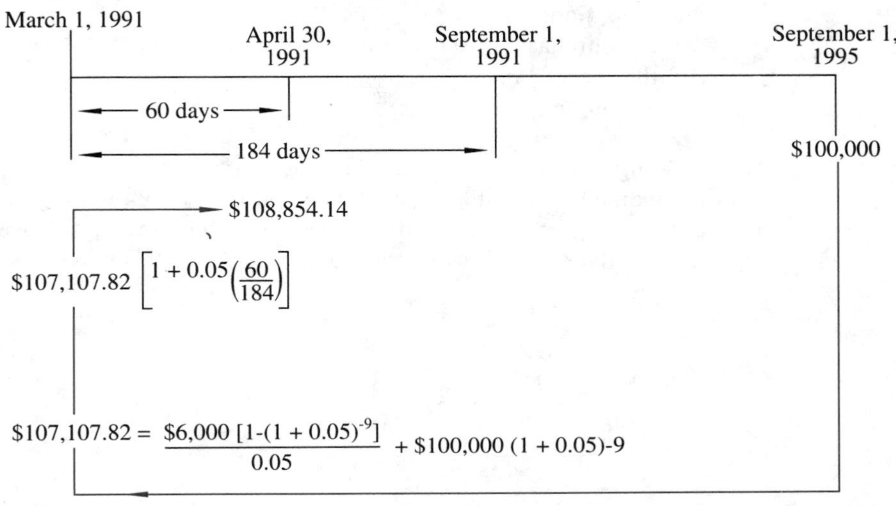

Calculator Solution

	Step 1: Find the Discounted Value of the Future Interest Payments at the Yield Rate					
Input	6,000	5	9			
Depress	PMT	i	n	COMP	PV	42,646.93
	Step 2: Find the Discounted Value of the Redemption Value at the Yield Rate					
Input	100,000	5	9			
Depress	FV	i	n	COMP	PV	64,460.89
	Purchase Price on Preceding Interest Period					107,107.82
	Moving the Price to the Purchase Date					
	$107{,}107.82\left[1 + (0.05)\dfrac{60}{184}\right]$					108,854.14
	Accrued Interest = $\$100{,}000\left[(0.06)\dfrac{60}{184}\right]$					1,956.52
	Quoted Price = \$108,854.14 – \$1,956.52					106,897.62

EXAMPLE 12.8

A $5,000 bond pays 9% semiannually and is redeemable at par on May 1, 2001. If the bond is purchased on March 20, 1991, to yield 10% payable semiannually, find:
(a) the purchase price (flat price);
(b) the accrued interest;
(c) the quoted price.

Solution Finding the purchase price (flat price) first requires finding the price on the immediately preceding interest date and then accumulating up to the purchase date. Also, since the bond is redeemable on May 1, this will be one of the interest dates, and six months later would be November 1.

First defining the terms:

$$RD = \$5{,}000$$

$$F = \$5{,}000$$

$$r = \frac{0.09}{2}, \text{ or } 0.045$$

$$i = \frac{0.10}{2}, \text{ or } 0.05$$

$n = 21$ This value takes us back to the interest date prior to the purchase date, November 1, 1990. If you lay out the interest periods to 2001 you will find that there are 21. (Remember the time from November 1, 1990, to May 1, 2001, is 10.5 years. Therefore, 10.5×2 is 21 periods.)

$$R = \$5{,}000 \times 0.045, \text{ or } \$225$$

Days = 139 The time from November 1, 1990, to the purchase date of March 20.

Total Days = 181 The number of days in the interest period from November 1, 1990, to May 1, 1991.

Now turning to Formula 12.1, substitute the information as follows:

(a) Purchase or Flat Price:

$$PP = \frac{R[1 - (1 + i)^{-n}]}{i} + RD(1 + i)^{-n}$$

$$PP = \frac{\$225[1 - (1 + 0.05)^{-21}]}{0.05} + \$5{,}000(1 + 0.05)^{-21}$$

$$PP \doteq \$2{,}884.76 + \$1{,}794.71$$

$$PP \doteq \$4{,}679.47$$

The price of \$4,679.47 is the purchase price on the preceding interest period (November 1, 1990). Next, this price is moved to the actual purchase date, March 20, 1991, by adjusting for the number of days between November 1 and March 20 as follows:

$$\text{Purchase Price (Flat Price)} = \$4{,}679.47\left[1 + (0.05)\frac{139}{181}\right]$$

$$\doteq \$4{,}859.15$$

Thus, the purchase price on March 20 is \$4,859.15.

(b) Accrued Interest:

The accrued interest is also found by using simple interest procedures:

$$\text{Accrued Interest} = \$5{,}000\left[(0.045)\frac{139}{181}\right]$$

$$\doteq \$172.79$$

(c) Quoted Price:

The quoted price, also referred to as the market price, is found by subtracting the accrued interest (at the bond rate) from the purchase price:

$$\text{Quoted Price} = \$4{,}859.15 - \$172.79$$

$$= \$4{,}686.36$$

Calculator Solution

	Step 1: Find the Discounted Value of the Future Interest Payments at the Yield Rate					
Input	225	5	21			
Depress	PMT	i	n	COMP	PV	2,884.76
	Step 2: Find the Discounted Value of the Redemption Value at the Yield Rate					
Input	5,000	5	21			
Depress	FV	i	n	COMP	PV	1,794.72
	Purchase Price on Preceding Interest Period					4,679.47
	Moving the Price to the Purchase Date					
	$4{,}679.47\left[1 + (0.05)\frac{139}{181}\right]$					4,859.15
	Accrued Interest $= 5{,}000\left[(0.045)\frac{139}{181}\right]$					172.79
	Quoted Price = \$4,859.15 – \$172.79					4,686.36

EXERCISE 12.2

For each of the following, find (a) the purchase price; (b) the premium or discount; (c) the accrued interest; and (d) the quoted price.

	Face Value of Bonds	Redemption at	Time Before Redemption Years	Months	Yield Rate and Conversion Period	Bond Rate Payable Semiannually
1.	$ 16,500	100	20	0	12.0%, semiannually	10.0%
2.	5,000	100	16	0	8.0%, semiannually	11.0%
3.	4,000	105	6	3	11.5%, annually	12.0%
4.	5,900	103	4	2	9.5%, semiannually	10.8%
5.	120,000	95	10	5	11.4%, semiannually	12.4%
6.	50,000	100	5	2	12.0%, monthly	14.0%
7.	18,000	89	4	1	12.5%, annually	10.5%
8.	15,000	110	7	0	10.5%, quarterly	13.0%
9.	20,000	92	9	0	15.0%, semiannually	12.0%
10.	25,000	101.5	6	1	14.0%, annually	11.0%

11. A $10,000 bond will be redeemed at par on May 1, 1999. Interest on the bond is currently at 10% payable semiannually on November 1 and May 1. Find the purchase price if the bond is purchased on June 20, 1991, to yield 9% paid semiannually.

12. A $15,000 bond that has a coupon rate of 12% payable semiannually will be redeemed at 104 on March 1, 1994. If the bond is purchased on September 20, 1991 to yield 10% payable semiannually, what is the purchase price and the value of the premium or discount?

13. On May 30, 1991, Jennifer Watson bought a bond with a face value of $1,000, redeemable at par on October 1, 1998. The interest rate on the bond is 8% payable semiannually on April 1 and October 1. What was the purchase price if she purchased the bond to yield 14% paid semiannually?

14. On May 31, 1991, a $10,000 bond was purchased. The bond had a coupon rate of 9% payable semiannually. It is to be redeemed at par on March 1, 1995, and pays interest on March 1 and September 1. If the bond is purchased to yield 10% to the buyer, payable semiannually, find:

a. the flat price;
b. the accrued interest;
c. the quoted price.

15. A $5,000 bond, redeemable at par on September 1, 1995, is paying a coupon rate of 12% paid semiannually. Find the flat price and the quoted price if the bond is purchased on June 15, 1991, to yield 8% payable semiannually.

16. If the bond in problem 15 had been redeemed at 110, what would have been the quoted price and the flat price?

17. A \$100,000 bond paying 10% per annum with semiannual interest payments is redeemable at par on December 1, 1999. If the bond is purchased on November 1, 1991, to yield 11% compounded monthly, with interest paid semiannually, find the purchase price and the quoted price.

12.7 Finding the Premium and Discount Directly from the Bond Rate and the Yield Rates

If we know the redemption value and the face value of a bond, it is possible to find the value of the premium or discount directly. The process we use requires us to compare the bond and yield rates. In particular, **if the bond is redeemed at par**, we can generalize about whether the bond sale will result in a premium or a discount.

For every investment, an investor has an expectation of a certain rate of return. This expected rate is used to determine the purchase price of an investment such as a bond. Over time, the expected rate varies depending on general market rates of interest, rates of inflation, and other factors. On the following pages, three different cases are presented. The first two cases assume the face value, par value, and redemption value are the same. For the third case, the redemption value is different from the face value. Review each one carefully.

CASE I: Premium (Bond rate > Yield rate)

If the bond rate is greater than the yield rate, and the bond is redeemed at par, then the purchase price will result in a **premium**.

Perhaps the easiest way to think about this situation is to consider a \$100 bond that pays 10% interest semiannually. This means that every six months the holder of the bond receives \$5 in interest. Now, if interest rates in general fall, say to 8% payable semiannually, then a purchaser of the bond, at that time, can only expect \$4 every interest period. Since the \$100 bond will continue to pay \$5 interest until the bond is redeemed, the price of the bond must rise on the market sufficiently to ensure that \$5 is, on the average, only 4% of the purchase price in each semiannual interest period. (Note that these figures only apply to this case; sometimes there is only an annual interest period.) This increase in purchase price to compensate for a bond rate that is higher than the current market rate is what we have been referring to as a premium.

Knowing something about interest rates helps investors to make capital gains in the bond market. That is, if you buy bonds when interest rates are very high and then sell those bonds at a future point in time when interest rates have fallen, you will definitely sell the bonds at a premium and this premium is referred to as a capital gain from the bond sale.

The relationship between the bond rate and the yield rate can best be seen in the following expression:

$$\text{Premium} = F(r - i)\,\frac{[1 - (1 + i)^{-n}]}{i}$$ **Formula 12.2**

It is important to note that the redemption value is assumed to be par value. To see how this formula is useful, consider the following example:

EXAMPLE 12.9

A $10,000 bond is paying a bond rate of 10.5% payable semiannually. If the bond is redeemable in ten years at par, and an investor purchases the bond today to yield a rate of 9% payable semiannually, what is the value of the premium?

Solution Define the known terms:

$$F = \$10{,}000$$

$$r = \frac{0.105}{2}, \text{ or } 0.0525$$

$$i = \frac{0.09}{2}, \text{ or } 0.045$$

$$n = 10 \times 2, \text{ or } 20$$

Since $r > i$, Formula 12.2 will be used. Substituting the value of the premium is found as follows:

$$\text{Premium} = F(r - i)\,\frac{[1 - (1 + i)^{-n}]}{i}$$

$$\text{Premium} = \$10{,}000(0.0525 - 0.045)\,\frac{[1 - (1 + 0.045)^{-20}]}{0.045}$$

$$\text{Premium} \doteq \$10{,}000(0.097559523)$$

$$\text{Premium} \doteq \$975.60$$

If you want to check this result, simply calculate the purchase price using Formula 12.1 and subtract the redemption value from this price. The results should be the same.

Calculator Solution

Note that PMT is: [10,000 (0.0525 – 0.045) = 75]

Input	75	4.5	20			
Depress	PMT	i	n	COMP	PV	975.60

CASE II: Discount (Yield rate > Bond rate)
When an investor purchases bonds at a discount it ensures that the interest income is equivalent to the current market rate of interest.

Let's rethink the example of the \$100 bond paying 10% with semiannual interest of \$5. It should be clear that if the interest rate rises, say, to 12% payable semiannually, then the bond price must change to ensure that the \$5 is 6% of the purchase price to the investor. Again, assuming that the bond is redeemed at par, we can calculate the discount directly by using the formula:

$$\text{Discount} = F(i - r)\frac{[1 - (1 + i)^{-n}]}{i}$$ **Formula 12.3**

EXAMPLE 12.10

A \$1,000 bond redeemable in eight years has a coupon (bond) rate of 8% payable semiannually. If the bond is purchased to yield 10% compounded semiannually, what is the discount?

Solution Identify the known terms:

$F = \$1{,}000$

$r = \dfrac{0.08}{2}$, or 0.04

$i = \dfrac{0.10}{2}$, or 0.05

$n = 8 \times 2$, or 16

Since $i > r$, Formula 12.3 will be used. Substituting and solving:

$$\text{Discount} = \$1{,}000(0.05 - 0.04)\frac{[1 - (1 + 0.05)^{-16}]}{0.05}$$

$$\doteq \$1{,}000(0.108377695)$$

$$\text{Discount} \doteq \$108.38$$

Thus, to ensure a yield rate of 10% the purchaser would pay $108.38 less than $1,000, or $891.62.

Calculator Solution

	Note that PMT is: [1,000 (0.05 – 0.04) = 10]					
Input	10	5	16			
Depress	PMT	i	n	COMP	PV	108.38

CASE III (Redemption value ≠ Face value)
If the redemption value does not equal the face value, all that needs to be done is to substitute redemption value into our expressions where appropriate. That is, a purchaser who will receive a payment (over the face value) at the maturity date, must take this "extra" value into consideration when determining the purchase price. To account for this "extra" payment we adjust our formula from above as follows:

$$\text{Premium} = (Fr - RDi)\frac{[1-(1+i)^{-n}]}{i} \qquad \textbf{Formula 12.4}$$

It is important to note that we have replaced the face value expression, F, associated with the yield rate, with the redemption value, RD. This accounts for the payment at the end that is above the face value of the bond.

Also, remember that it is possible for the redemption value to be less than the face value of the bond; this also must be accounted for in determining the purchase price.

In Formula 12.4, if the result is a negative number, this means a discount must be appropriate and will be subtracted from the redemption value. We can summarize our discussions of this special case in which the redemption value is different from the face value as follows:

Purchase Price = Redemption Value + Premium

If the premium is negative, then this is a discount. Thus, if a negative value occurs make sure that it is included in the addition to find the purchase price:

Purchase Price = Redemption Value + (Premium)

Remember the Negative Premium Is Simply a Discount, that Is Subtracted from the Redemption Value

To see how these formulas can be directly applied, consider Example 12.11:

EXAMPLE 12.11

A $10,000 bond will be redeemed on March 1, 1995. The bond interest is 12% payable semiannually on March 1 and September 1. Find the purchase price if the date of the purchase is March 1, 1991, at a yield rate of 10% knowing that the bond has a redemption value of 105.

Solution Again, let's define the information from the problem:

$$F = \$10{,}000$$

$$r = \frac{0.12}{2}, \text{ or } 0.06$$

$$i = \frac{0.10}{2}, \text{ or } 0.05$$

$$RD = \$10{,}000 \times (1.05), \text{ or } \$10{,}500$$

$$n = 2 \times 4, \text{ or } 8$$

Now, turning to Formula 12.4, we have:

$$\text{Premium} = (Fr - RDi)\,\frac{[1 - (1 + i)^{-n}]}{i}$$

Where:

$$\text{Premium} = [\$10{,}000(0.06) - \$10{,}500(0.05)]\,\frac{[1 - (1 + 0.05)^{-8}]}{0.05}$$

$$\text{Premium} \doteq \$484.74$$

Thus, the purchase price will be:

Purchase Price = Redemption Value + Premium
Purchase Price = $10,500 + $484.74
Purchase Price = $10,984.74

Checking this answer using Formula 12.1:

$$PP = \frac{R[1 - (1 + i)^{-n}]}{i} + RD(1 + i)^{-n}$$

Where:

$$R = \$10{,}000(0.06), \text{ or } \$600$$

$$i = 0.05$$

$$r = 0.06$$

$$RD = \$10{,}500$$

$$n = 8$$

Substituting:

$$PP = \$600\,\frac{[1-(1+0.05)^{-8}]}{0.05} + \$10{,}500(1+0.05)^{-8}$$

$$PP \doteq \$3{,}877.93 + \$7{,}106.81$$

$$PP \doteq \$10{,}984.74$$

Purchase Price = $10,984.74

As can be seen, the purchase price is the same as the method that finds the purchase price directly by calculating the discount directly.

Calculator Solution

Note that PMT is: [10,000 (0.06) –10,500 (0.05) = 75]

						Premium
Input	75	5	8			
Depress	PMT	i	n	COMP	PV	484.74

EXAMPLE 12.12

In Example 12.11 suppose the bond rate had been 10% paid semiannually, and the desired yield rate was 12%. What would the purchase price be? Again, use the method described in this section.

Solution Again, setting up the problem with the information:

$$F = \$10{,}000$$

$$r = \frac{0.10}{2},\ \text{or } 0.05$$

$$i = \frac{0.12}{2},\ \text{or } 0.06$$

$$RD = \$10{,}000 \times (1.05),\ \text{or } \$10{,}500$$

$$n = 2 \times 4,\ \text{or } 8$$

Now, turning to Formula 12.4, we have:

$$\text{Premium} = (Fr - RDi)\,\frac{[1-(1+i)^{-n}]}{i}$$

$$= [\$10{,}000(0.05) - \$10{,}500(0.06)]\,\frac{[1-(1+0.06)^{-8}]}{0.06}$$

$$\text{Premium} \doteq -\$807.27$$

Note: since it is a negative premium, it is a discount.

Thus the purchase price will be:

Purchase Price = Redemption Value + Premium
Purchase Price = $10,500 + (–$807.27)
Purchase Price = $9,692.73

Calculator Solution (The negative sign in front of the payment tells us that there will be a discount.)

Note that PMT is: [10,000 (0.05) – 10.500 (0.06) = –130]						Discount
Input	–130	6	8			
Depress	PMT	i	n	COMP	PV	–807.27

In this example, it can be seen that a negative premium is simply a discount.

EXERCISE 12.3

For each of the following, find the purchase price and the premium or discount directly by using the methods of Section 12.7.

	Face Value of Bonds	Redemption at	Time Before Redemption Years	Yield Rate and Conversion Period	Bond Rate Payable Semiannually
1.	$14,500	101	10	11.0%, semiannually	11.0%
2.	6,000	102	15	9.0%, semiannually	12.0%
3.	3,000	106	5	10.5%, annually	12.0%
4.	8,000	102	6	10.5%, semiannually	10.8%
5.	25,000	101	10	10.4%, semiannually	10.4%
6.	45,000	100	8	11.0%, monthly	12.0%
7.	20,000	70	5	11.5%, annually	11.5%
8.	10,000	105	9	11.5%, quarterly	12.0%
9.	15,000	100	10	12.0%, semiannually	13.0%
10.	30,000	110	11	12.0%, annually	11.0%

11. Bonds totalling $30,000 have a bond rate of 8% with interest payable semiannually. The bonds have just been sold to an investor who expects to make 10% payable semiannually. If the bonds are redeemable in five years, what is the total premium or discount, and what is the purchase price for all the bonds? (Use the direct method.)

12. If the yield rate in problem 11 had been 7% payable semiannually, what would have been the purchase price and the premium or discount?

12.8 Determining the Approximate Yield Rate on a Bond Investment

As mentioned earlier, after bonds have been issued they may be purchased and sold on the secondary bond market. Let's examine a page out of *The Financial Post* on bond quotations:

Figure 12.3 Bond Quotations. Bond prices supplied by *The Financial Post* Information Services for April 1, 1991, as it appeared in *The Financial Post* April 2, 1991. Reprinted with the permission of *The Financial Post*.

Provincial Bonds

	Int. Rate %	Maturity Date	Bid %	Yield %
Alta Govt Tel	9½	Jul 8/97	97.55	10.03
Alberta	10¼	Nov 1/93	101.30	9.66
Br Columbia	10¼	Nov 25/97	100.90	10.06
Manitoba	9⅝	Sep 3/02	99.15	0.00
Ontario Hydro	9	Dec 15/91	99.40	9.89
Ontario Hydro	10	Dec 8/94	100.55	9.81
Ontario Hydro	10¼	Jul 12/98	100.95	10.06
Ontario Hydro	9¼	Jan 6/04	92.90	10.26
Ontario Hydro	10½	Jan 15/10	99.40	10.57
Quebec	10¼	Apr 7/98	99.13	10.43
Quebec	10¾	Feb 1/99	101.13	10.53
Quebec	11	Apr 1/09	101.38	10.82
Quebec Hydro	10¼	Jul 16/12	95.25	10.82
Saskatchewan	9⅞	Jul 6/99	97.45	10.34

Canada Bonds

Supplied by: FP DataGroup
Closing rates for Monday

	Int. Rate %	Maturity Date	Bid %	Yield %
Canada	9	Sep 1/91	99.58	9.88
Canada	9¼	Jul 1/92	99.69	9.50
Canada	10¾	May 1/93	102.38	9.45
Canada	9½	Jun 15/94	100.29	9.38
Canada	10	Mar 1/95	101.85	9.42
Canada	9¼	May 1/96	99.50	9.37
Canada	9¾	Oct 1/97	101.40	9.45
Canada	10½	Jul 1/00	105.30	9.62
Canada	9½	Oct 1/01	99.60	9.56
Canada	10	May 1/02	102.30	9.65
Canada	10¼	Feb 1/04	104.10	9.68
Canada	10	Jun 1/08	101.75	9.78
Canada	9	Mar 1/11	94.40	9.64
Canada	10¼	Mar 15/14	104.25	9.78
Canada	10½	Mar 15/21	106.25	9.85

Corporate Bonds

	Int. Rate %	Maturity Date	Bid %	Yield %
Alta Energy	10½	Jun 30/96	99.88	10.52
Avco	11	May 17/94	100.00	10.99
Bell	10	Jun 15/14	98.75	10.21
Bell	10.55	Feb 15/15	98.88	10.68
Bc Tel	10½	Jun 12/00	100.38	10.43
Bc Tel	12	May 31/10	110.25	10.73
Cons. Gas	13¼	Mar 15/93	105.00	10.32
C.i.b.c	10⅜	Jan 31/00	98.75	10.59
Domtar	10.85	Aug 5/17	84.25	12.96
Gaz Metro	11½	Nov 15/05	101.75	11.25
Imperial Oil	12	Mar 31/93	103.63	9.93
Int Provl Pipe	10.80	Apr 15/08	99.88	10.81
Labatt J	10⅜	Apr 21/98	99.63	10.45
Loblaw	10	Apr 15/07	92.38	11.02
Noranda Mines	10½	Jul 29/99	96.00	11.25
Nova	12⅛	Jul 15/93	102.75	10.71
Nova	11.20	Jun 1/14	93.75	12.00
Royal Bank	10.90	Jan 15/99	102.00	10.51
Transalta	12	Apr 19/93	103.63	9.98
Transalta	10⅛	Jun 22/99	99.00	10.30
Tor Dom Ctr	10.70	May 12/98	101.38	10.42
Tr Cda Pipe	10.55	Mar 20/98	99.63	10.63
Tr Cda Pipe	10½	Aug 20/10	96.50	10.94
Trizac	10¼	Jun 22/09	90.50	12.10
Union Gas	10⅜	Jul 11/11	95.25	11.22
Union Gas	11½	Aug 20/15	104.00	11.02

As you can see, there are columns headed "Int. rate", "Maturity Date", etc. These have a precise meaning to the skilled reader of bond market statistics. The first column gives the bond by name. The second column tells the bond rate or coupon rate being paid on the face value of the bond. The next column gives the maturity date of the bond. The Bid column refers to the current price a bond buyer is prepared to pay for the bond.

Although the bond table from *The Financial Post* includes the yield rate there may be occasions where one does not have immediate access to such information. If so, then one may need to know how to approximate the yield rate on a bond, given the current market price. The easiest method is to compare the **average investment** and **average income**, and from these two measures determine the **approximate yield rate**.

The **average annual investment** refers to the amount that is invested, on the average, from the purchase date to the maturity date.

The **average annual income** is computed based on the yearly interest income and is adjusted up or down depending on whether a discount or premium was paid at the time of purchase. As with the average annual investment, the average income is averaged from the purchase date to the maturity date.

The best way to understand these concepts is to work through how the **average annual investment** and a **average income** are computed. Consider the following information about the annual investment in a bond.

A. Measuring Average Investment

Consider a bond with a face value of \$10,000 and a bond rate of 12% payable semiannually, which is purchased at 104. The bond will be redeemed in five years. Therefore, if the bond is purchased on an interest date, its quoted price will be \$10,400. The average annual investment is a function of the redemption value and the quoted price. (*Note:* the redemption value and the quoted price will be the same if the bond is redeemed at par value.) The measure of average investment, which will be defined as I, can be found using the following formula:

$$I = \frac{(\text{Quoted Price} + \text{Redemption Value})}{2} \qquad \textbf{Formula 12.5}$$

In our example, we have a quoted price of \$10,400, or (\$10,000 × 1.04). The face value is simply the \$10,000 value of the bond. Thus, the average annual investment is:

$$I = \frac{(\$10{,}400 + \$10{,}000)}{2}$$

$$I = \$10{,}200$$

Thus, \$10,200 is the average value of the investment, which is an average of the purchase price and the redemption value.

B. Measuring Average Annual Income

To determine the value of the income on a bond investment consideration must first be given to whether a premium or discount was paid when the bond was acquired. A premium on a bond has the net effect of reducing the investor's annual income, since paying a premium, in effect, reduces the total interest income over the remaining interest periods by the amount of the premium. A discount, on the other hand, has the effect of increasing the income over time, since the investor gets a larger sum than the purchase price upon redemption of the bond. To account for a premium or discount in the determination of average income, the following simple formula is provided. Note that the average income per year is represented by *AI*.

$$AI = \left[\frac{\text{Sum of Remaining Interest Payments} - \text{Premium}}{\text{Number of Remaining Interest Periods}}\right] \times \left[\begin{matrix}\text{Number of interest}\\ \text{periods per year}\end{matrix}\right]$$

Formula 12.6

or if there is a discount then,

$$AI = \left[\frac{\text{Sum of Remaining Interest Payments} + \text{Discount}}{\text{Number of Remaining Interest Periods}}\right] \times \left[\begin{matrix}\text{Number of interest}\\ \text{periods per year}\end{matrix}\right]$$

In the problem we started above, the total value of interest payments is found by finding the number of payments and then multiplying by the interest paid per period. That is:

$n = 5 \times 2$, or 10. Remaining interest periods.

$$\text{Sum of the Interest Payments} = 10 \times \$10{,}000\left(\frac{0.12}{2}\right)$$

$$\text{Total Interest Payments} = \$6{,}000$$

The value of the premium is \$400, and, thus, the calculation of average income, *AI*, would be:

$$AI = \frac{[\$6{,}000 - \$400]}{10} \text{ per interest period} \times \left[\begin{matrix}\text{2 interest periods}\\ \text{per year}\end{matrix}\right]$$

$$AI = \$1{,}120 \text{ per year}$$

C. The Approximate Yield Rate

Now bringing the Average Investment (I) and the Average Income (AI) together, the approximate yield rate can be calculated as:

$$\text{Approximate Yield Rate} = \frac{AI}{I} \qquad \textbf{Formula 12.7}$$

Continuing with the example and substituting from above, we have:

$$I = \$10{,}200$$
$$AI = \$1{,}120$$

Therefore, the approximate yield rate is:

$$\text{Approximate Yield Rate} = \frac{AI}{I}$$

$$\text{Approximate Yield Rate} = \frac{\$1{,}120}{\$10{,}200}$$

$$\text{Approximate Yield Rate} \doteq 0.1098, \text{ or } 10.98\%, \text{ per year}$$

To make sure everything is clear, consider the following example. Since this section involves three new concepts, please make sure you work through each step slowly and carefully.

EXAMPLE 12.13

A $5,000 bond that has a bond rate of 10% payable semiannually is purchased at 97.375. If the bond is redeemable at 105, find the approximate yield rate. Assume the bond will be redeemed in fifteen years.

Solution First, we find the quoted price of the bond:

$$\text{Quoted price} = \$5{,}000(0.97375)$$
$$\text{Quoted price} = \$4{,}868.75$$

To determine the redemption value we have:

$$RD = \$5{,}000(1.05), \text{ or } \$5{,}250$$

The average investment (I) is:

$$I = \frac{(\$5{,}250 + \$4{,}868.75)}{2}$$

$$I = \$5{,}059.38$$

Computing average income, AI:

$$R = F \times r$$

$$= \$5{,}000(0.05), \text{ or } \$250$$

$n = 2 \times 15$, or 30 Remaining interest payments.

Discount = (\$5,250 − \$4,868.75), or \$381.25

Value of the Remaining Payments = \$250 × 30

= \$7,500

$$AI = \frac{(\$7{,}500 + \$381.25)}{30} \times (2 \text{ interest periods per year})$$

$$AI = \$525.42$$

Bringing the average investment and the average income per interest period together to find the approximate yield rate using Formula 12.7, gives:

$$\text{Approximate Yield Rate} = \frac{AI}{I}$$

$$\text{Approximate Yield Rate} = \frac{\$525.42}{\$5{,}059.38}$$

$$\text{Approximate Yield Rate} \doteq 0.1039$$

Therefore, the approximate annual yield rate is:

$$i = 10.39\% \text{ per year}$$

EXERCISE 12.4

Find the approximate yield rate for problems 1 to 7.

	Face Value of Bonds	Quoted Price	Time Before Redemption in Years	Bond Rate Payable Semiannually
1.	\$ 14,500	15,000	10	17.0%
2.	6,000	6,200	15	14.0%
3.	3,000	2,850	5	11.0%
4.	8,000	7,500	6	13.8%
5.	25,000	26,500	10	12.4%
6.	45,000	48,500	8	14.0%
7.	20,000	18,500	5	10.5%

8. Calculate the approximate yield rate on a $5,000 bond that pays 10.5% in semiannual payments. The bond is redeemable at 105 in five years and is purchased at 98.75.

9. A $10,000, 12% bond with interest paid semiannually is redeemable on March 1, 1997. The bond is bought at the quoted price of 92 on March 1, 1991. What is the approximate yield rate?

10. A $4,000 bond pays 7% per annum with semiannual payments. The bond is to be redeemed on September 1, 2000. If interest is payable on March 1 and September 1, and the bond is quoted at 96 on March 1, 1991, what would be the yield rate to someone who purchased it on this date?

11. If the bond in problem 10 is redeemable at 95, what is the approximate yield rate?

12.9 Amortization of a Premium and the Accumulation of a Discount

When a bond is purchased at a premium or discount, there must be a way to account for the discount or the premium in the interest payments. That is, if one has purchased a bond at a premium, there is a clear expectation that the premium will be accounted for over the remaining interest periods. The two methods used to account for premiums are:

- amortizing a premium
- accumulating a discount

Both rely on the procedures outlined in the amortization and accumulation sections of Chapter 11.

A. Amortization of a Premium

Purchasing a bond at a premium results in a payment that will not be "redeemable" upon the maturity of the bond. The process that recovers a premium is the payment of regular interest. This can be seen with an amortization table, which shows how the book value of a bond declines until the book value is the same as the redemption value.

The best way to explain the process is with an example. Consider the following:

EXAMPLE 12.14

A $100,000, 12% bond pays interest semiannually and is redeemable in three and one-half years. Find the purchase price and set up an amortization table to amortize the bond premium if the bond is purchased to yield 10% paid semiannually.

Solution Defining the known terms we have:

$$F = \$100{,}000$$

$$r = \frac{0.12}{2}, \text{ or } 0.06$$

$$i = \frac{0.10}{2}, \text{ or } 0.05$$

$$R = \$100{,}000(0.06), \text{ or } \$6{,}000$$

$$n = 2 \times (3.5), \text{ or } 7$$

$$RD = \$100{,}000$$

Now turning to the purchase price Formula, 12.1, we have:

$$PP = \frac{R[1 - (1 + i)^{-n}]}{i} + RD(1 + i)^{-n}$$

Substituting:

$$PP = \frac{\$6{,}000[1 - (1 + 0.05)^{-7}]}{0.05} + \$100{,}000(1 + 0.05)^{-7}$$

$$PP \doteq \$105{,}786.37 \qquad \text{A premium of } \$5{,}786.37.$$

Calculator Solution

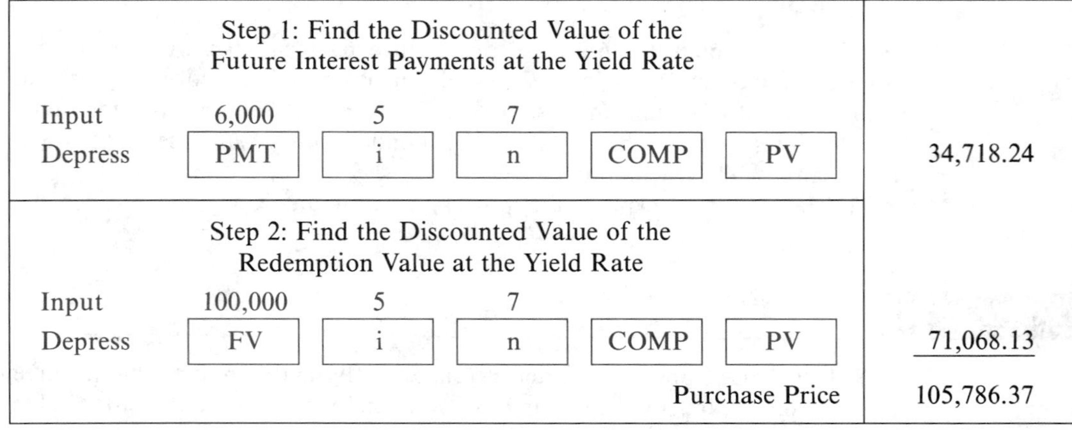

Step 1: Find the Discounted Value of the Future Interest Payments at the Yield Rate						
Input	6,000	5	7			
Depress	PMT	i	n	COMP	PV	34,718.24
Step 2: Find the Discounted Value of the Redemption Value at the Yield Rate						
Input	100,000	5	7			
Depress	FV	i	n	COMP	PV	71,068.13
					Purchase Price	105,786.37

Constructing an amortization table follows the procedure we used in Chapter 11. Now, setting up five columns, we have:

Table 12.2 Amortization of a Premium

A	B	C	D	E
Interest Period	**Interest on Bond**	**Yield Interest**	**Premium Amortization**	**Book Value (*PP*) $105,786.37**
1	$ 6,000	$ 5,289.32	$ 710.68	$105,075.69
2	$ 6,000	$ 5,253.78	$ 746.22	$104,329.47
3	$ 6,000	$ 5,216.47	$ 783.53	$103,545.94
4	$ 6,000	$ 5,177.30	$ 822.70	$102,723.24
5	$ 6,000	$ 5,136.16	$ 863.84	$101,859.40
6	$ 6,000	$ 5,092.97	$ 907.03	$100,952.37
7	$ 6,000	$ 5,047.62	$ 952.38	$100,000.00
Totals	$42,000	$36,213.62	$5,786.38	N/A

The calculations involved in the above table are based on the following logic:

Column B: 100,000(0.06) = $6,000 This is constant for all periods since the coupon is based on the bond rate.

Column C reflects payment of interest, at the yield rate, times the book value of the bond. This is done as:

Column C:	Period 1:	$105,786.37(0.05)	= $5,289.32
	Period 2:	$105,075.69(0.05)	= $5,253.78
	Period 3:	$104,329.47(0.05)	= $5,216.47
	. . .		
	Period 7:	$100,952.37(0.05)	= $5,047.62
Column D:	Period 1:	$6,000 – $5,289.32	= $710.68
	Period 2:	$6,000 – $5,253.78	= $746.22
	Period 3:	$6,000 – $5,216.47	= $783.53
	. . .		
	Period 7:	$6,000 – $5,047.62	= $952.38
Column E:	Period 1:	$105,786.37 – $710.68	= $105,075.69
	Period 2:	$105,075.69 – $746.22	= $104,329.47
	Period 3:	$104,329.47 – $783.53	= $103,545.94
	. . .		
	Period 7:	$100,952.37 – $952.38	= $100,000.00

The above bond amortization schedule shows that the premium can be recovered by the investor through the periodic interest payments. In particular, since the investor is being paid a higher rate (the bond rate) than expected (yield rate), this difference will generate the monies to recover the premium paid for the bond.

The one computation that you must make sure that you understand is the calculation involving the Book Value of the bond. The Book Value is the basis of the calculation for the yield interest and the premium amortization. The underlying premise of the table values is that an investor will receive the yield rate on the initial purchase price, while the actual interest payments are those paid at the bond rate — in this problem, the bond rate payments are $6,000.

Finally, if you look at the totals in the above bond amortization schedule, you will note that the difference between the total interest paid at the bond rate and the interest at the yield rate exactly equals the value of the premium. This tells us that the premium has been entirely recovered in interest payments.

B. Accumulation of a Discount

When a bond is purchased at a discount we know that the price is less than the face value of the bond. However, the entire face value will be paid when the bond is redeemed on the maturity date. Also we know that the interest that is paid on the bond is less than the market rate of interest (yield rate) applied to the face value of the bond. As a result, each period will result in an "interest deficit" that will be recovered once the bond is redeemed at the full redemption value. This can be seen by adjusting the Book Value each year up to the time the bond is redeemed. We must increase the Book Value each period by adding the periodic "deficits" in interest.

To understand how this accumulation occurs, consider the following example:

EXAMPLE 12.15

A $10,000 Government of Canada bond was bought by an investor and had a coupon rate of 14% payable every six months. The bond is redeemable in two years. If the bond is purchased to yield 15%, find the purchase price and construct an Accumulation Table to show how the discount will accumulate to the redemption value.

Solution The first step is to find the purchase price of the bond. Using Formula 12.1, we have:

$$r = \frac{0.14}{2}, \text{ or } 0.07$$

$$i = \frac{0.15}{2}, \text{ or } 0.075$$

$$F = \$10{,}000$$

$$RD = \$10{,}000$$

$$R = Fr$$

$$= \$10{,}000(0.07)$$

$$= \$700$$

Now, substituting into our formula for *PP*:

$$PP = \frac{\$700[1 - (1 + 0.075)^{-4}]}{0.075} + \$10{,}000(1 + 0.075)^{-4}$$

$$PP \doteq \$9{,}832.53$$

Calculator Solution

	Step 1: Find the Discounted Value of the Future Interest Payments at the Yield Rate					
Input	700	7.5	4			
Depress	PMT	i	n	COMP	PV	2,344.53
	Step 2: Find the Discounted Value of the Redemption Value at the Yield Rate					
Input	10,000	7.5	4			
Depress	FV	i	n	COMP	PV	7,488.01
					Purchase Price	9,832.53

As we can see, the bond is purchased at a discount of \$167.47. To accumulate the discount we will set up a table similar to Table 11.6, used for a sinking fund in Chapter 11.

Table 12.3 Accumulation of a Discount

A	B	C	D	E
Interest Period	**Interest on Bond**	**Yield Interest**	**Discount Accumulation**	**Book Value (*PP*) \$9,832.53**
1	\$ 700	\$ 737.44	\$ 37.44	\$ 9,869.97
2	\$ 700	\$ 740.25	\$ 40.25	\$ 9,910.22
3	\$ 700	\$ 743.27	\$ 43.27	\$ 9,953.49
4	\$ 700	\$ 746.51	\$ 46.51	\$10,000.00
Totals	\$2,800	\$2,967.47	\$167.47	N/A

The calculations involved in the above table are based on the following logic:

Column B: \$10,000(0.07) = \$700 — This is constant for all periods since the coupon is based on the bond rate.

Column C:	Period 1:	\$9,832.53(0.075)	= \$737.44
	Period 2:	\$9,869.97(0.075)	= \$740.25
	Period 3:	\$9,910.22(0.075)	= \$743.27
	Period 4:	\$9,953.49(0.075)	= \$746.51
Column D:	Period 1:	\$737.44 – \$700	= \$37.44
	Period 2:	\$740.25 – \$700	= \$40.25
	Period 3:	\$743.27 – \$700	= \$43.27
	Period 4:	\$746.51 – \$700	= \$46.51
Column E:	Period 1:	\$9,832.53 + \$37.44	= \$9,869.97
	Period 2:	\$9,869.97 + \$40.25	= \$9,910.22
	Period 3:	\$9,910.22 + \$43.27	= \$9,953.49
	Period 4:	\$9,953.49 + \$46.51	= \$10,000.00

Based on the above table, you can see the interest **earned** by the purchaser and how this is adjusted using the yield rate for each period the bond is held. Moreover, it can be seen that the total of Column D is exactly the value of the discount. That is, we have accounted for the discount received over the remaining interest periods of the bond.

EXERCISE 12.5

For problems 1 to 7, find the purchase price and accumulate the discount or amortize the premium, whichever is appropriate.

	Face Value of Bonds	Time Before Redemption in Years	Bond Rate Payable Semiannually	Purchased to Yield Semiannually
1.	\$ 3,500	2.5	17.0%	16.0%
2.	4,000	2	14.0%	17.0%
3.	1,500	3	11.0%	12.0%
4.	2,400	3.5	13.8%	16.8%
5.	1,300	4	12.4%	11.4%
6.	5,000	1.5	14.0%	15.0%
7.	1,000	2	10.5%	13.5%

8. A $4,000 corporate bond has a coupon rate of 11% payable semiannually, and is redeemable in two and a half years. If the bond is purchased to pay an investor a yield rate of 15% compounded semiannually, find the purchase price and construct an amortization or accumulation, whichever is appropriate.
9. If the bond in problem 8 was purchased by an investor who wanted to earn 10% compounded semiannually, construct the appropriate accumulation or amortization table.

12.10 Other Types of Bonds

There are many types of bonds sold on the market. Two of these special types of bonds are serial bonds and annuity bonds. Both of these bonds use the procedures outlined earlier in the calculation of purchase price. In each case, a detailed discussion can be found in texts on finance: only a brief summary of how each operates is provided below.

An **annuity bond** is where the issuer promises to pay both the principal and the interest over time. When an annuity bond is purchased, the amount paid for the bond (the face value when the bond is first purchased) is paid back over time, rather than by a single payment at the redemption date. Although annuity bonds are not commonly used any more, understanding the difference between these and the bonds we have discussed so far is of value. The purchase price of an annuity bond is determined by finding the present value of the regular bond payments, using the yield rate as the rate to discount the payments.

Serial bonds, on the other hand, are more commonly used in the marketplace. This type of bond is issued in a series with the bonds' redemption dates spread over time rather than all bonds being redeemed on the same date. You should think about a serial bond as a group of bonds purchased under the same "umbrella" or indenture. For example, a company might issue $20 million worth of bonds with $10 million being redeemed at five years in the future, $5 million being redeemed at ten years in the future, and the remaining $5 million being redeemed at twenty years in the future. The problem is bringing all this information together to find the purchase price.

To fully explore these and other types of bonds refer to an investment that focuses on Canadian securities, and, in particular, the myriad of bond types that exist in the marketplace.

REVIEW EXERCISES

1. An investor bought 5,000 shares of B.C. Resources at $0.755 and received a dividend of $0.05 one year later when the shares were sold at $0.80. What was the investor's gain for all transactions in this problem?

2. What was the over all percentage gain in problem 1?
3. If money is worth 14% compounded semiannually, what is the value of a $150 bond bearing interest at 10.5% paid semiannually if it is bought today and matures in five years?
4. What should be the purchase price of a $1,000 bond redeemable at 105 and bearing semiannual coupons at 9.75% if it is sold two years before maturity and money is worth 11% compounded annually?
5. A $2,500 bond, redeemable at par on September 1, 1995, bearing interest at 9.5% payable semiannually, is bought to yield 13% semiannually on June 6, 1990. What was the price?
6. What price should one pay for a $500 bond, purchased on December 11, 1990, if the desired yield rate is 13% compounded quarterly? Assume the bond matures on April 1, 1994, and bears 11.5% coupons payable on April 1 and October 1.
7. Calculate the premium or discount on the sale of a $1,000 bond carrying semiannual coupons at 9.5% and redeemable at 102 in three years if it is bought to yield 11% compounded semiannually.
8. What is the purchase price of the bond sold in problem 7?
9. Compute the premium or discount on the sale of a $2,000 bond redeemable at 101.5 in four years' time if it is bought to yield 12% compounded quarterly and the coupon rate is 10.75% semiannually.
10. What is the purchase price of the bond sold in problem 9?
11. Calculate the premium or discount on the sale of a $1,000 bond that is redeemable at 103 on June 1, 1994, if it is sold to yield 10.5% annually. The coupons are payable semiannually at a rate of 13% and the date of the sale is December 1, 1991.
12. What is the purchase price of the bond sold in problem 11?
13. Construct a bond schedule for a $1,000 bond with interest payable at 10% semiannually, redeemable at par, and bought to yield 12% semiannually 1.5 years before maturity.
14. What is the gain or loss on a $2,000 bond sold at 99.5 to yield 13% compounded semiannually, with 14% semiannual coupons redeemable at 103 in three years?
15. If a $500 bond bearing 9.5% semiannual coupons is purchased at 97.5 and is redeemable at 102 in four years' time, what is the approximate yield rate?

SUMMARY OF FORMULAS

Formula 12.1 $$PP = \frac{R[1 - (1 + i)^{-n}]}{i} + RD(1 + i)^{-n}$$ Finding the purchase price of a bond on an interest date.

Formula 12.2 $$\text{Premium} = F(r - i)\,\frac{[1 - (1 + i)^{-n}]}{i}$$ Finding the premium directly.

Formula 12.3 $$\text{Discount} = F(i - r)\,\frac{[1 - (1 + i)^{-n}]}{i}$$ Finding the discount directly.

Formula 12.4 $$\text{Premium} = (Fr - RDi)\,\frac{[1 - (1 + i)^{-n}]}{i}$$ Finding the premium or discount when the redemption value is not equal to the face value.

Formula 12.5 $$I = \frac{(\text{Quoted Price} + \text{Redemption Value})}{2}$$ Average annual investment.

Formula 12.6 Average annual income, *AI*: Purchased with a Premium.

$$AI = \left[\frac{\text{Sum of Remaining Interest Payments} - \text{Premium}}{\text{Number of Remaining Interest Periods}}\right] \times \left[\begin{matrix}\text{Number of interest} \\ \text{periods per year}\end{matrix}\right]$$

Formula 12.6 Average annual income, *AI*: Purchased with a Discount.

$$AI = \left[\frac{\text{Sum of Remaining Interest Payments} + \text{Discount}}{\text{Number of Remaining Interest Periods}}\right] \times \left[\begin{matrix}\text{Number of interest} \\ \text{periods per year}\end{matrix}\right]$$

Formula 12.7 $$\text{Approximate Yield Rate} = \frac{AI}{I}$$ The approximate annual yield rate.

GLOSSARY OF TERMS

Accumulation of a Discount the process of adjusting the book value of a bond by accumulating the bond discount over the remaining interest periods on the bond.

Amortization of a Premium the process of adjusting the book value of a bond by amortizing the bond premium over the remaining interest periods on the bond.

Approximate Yield Rate an average yield rate based on a comparison of the annual average income and the average investment.

Bond a debt that is promised to be repaid at a specific point in time called the maturity date. Bonds are secured by a pledge of specific assets of the issuing organization.

Bond Rate the rate of interest paid on a bond. The bond rate determines the regular interest income from the bond. The bond rate is sometimes called the contract rate or the coupon rate on a bond.

Common Stock the manner in which one holds ownership in a company. People who purchase common stock are called common shareholders and receive compensation for the purchase of stock by being paid dividends.

Contract Rate see Bond Rate.

Coupon Rate see Bond Rate.

Debenture a debt that is promised to be repaid at a specific time, called the maturity date. A debenture is not secured by the assets of the company or government who issued the debentures.

Debt Financing the process of raising money with debt that includes loans, bonds, and debentures. There is no sale of ownership in using debt financing to raise money.

Discount when a bond is purchased at a price less than the redemption value the bond is said to be purchased at a discount. The discount is the difference between the redemption value and the purchase price.

Equity Financing raising money for a company by selling some of the ownership. This is accomplished by the sale of stock to investors.

Face Value the dollar value specified on the bond. Generally, bonds are in denominations (face value) of $1,000, $5,000, and $10,000. When bonds are to be sold to many investors, including very small investors, other denominations may be used — some may be less than $1,000.

Flat Price the purchase price of a bond that includes any accrued interest on the bond.

Preferred Stock preferred stock or shares are stocks that have a predefined rate of return based on their par value. Preferred shareholders are paid their income before common shareholders receive any dividends. There are many different types of preferred shares sold in the market.

Premium when a bond is purchased at a price that is greater than the redemption value the bond is said to be purchased at a premium. The premium is the difference between the purchased price and the redemption value.

Quoted Price the price of a bond excluding the accrued interest.

Redeemable at > 100 or < 100 when a bond is said to be redeemable at 103, for example, this means that the bond will be redeemed at a rate of $103 for every $100 of the bond's face value, i.e., redeemable at a **premium**. Conversely, if a bond is redeemable at 95, for example, this means that for every $100 of face value only $95 will be paid, i.e., redeemable at a **discount**.

Redeemable at 100 when a bond is said to be redeemable at 100 it is said to be redeemable at par value.

Redeemable Bond when a bond is said to be redeemable it means that, with proper notice, the bond may be redeemed before the maturity date on the bond.

Redemption Value the amount paid by the issuer of a bond to the bondholder on or before the maturity date on the bond.

Yield Rate the rate of interest or return expected by investors when purchasing a bond. The yield rate is determined by the market rate of interest and the degree of risk associated with the investment.

Student Solutions

EXERCISE 1.1

A. 1. 718
3. 4,186
5. 51,197

B. 7. 123,111
9. 37,079

C. 11. 210
13. 31,611
15. 2,604

D. 17. 12, remainder: 10
19. 68, remainder: 103

E. 21. $2,517.00
23. $\$5 \times 24 \times 4 = \$480.00$
25. $3.00 per tape

EXERCISE 1.2

1. 0
3. 258,570
5. –3,360
7. 54
9. –2

EXERCISE 1.3

A. 1. $\frac{1}{6}$ 3. $\frac{1}{3}$ 5. $\frac{4}{5}$ 7. $\frac{1}{4}$

B. 9. $1\frac{1}{4}$ 11. $3\frac{1}{2}$ 13. $4\frac{1}{2}$

C. 15. $11\frac{1}{8}$ 17. $\frac{5}{24}$ 19. $1\frac{1}{34}$ 21. $\frac{19}{40}$

23. $\frac{1}{3}$ 25. $\frac{2}{3}$ 27. $-\frac{21}{200}$ 29. $\frac{6}{19}$

EXERCISE 2.1

1. 2:3
3. Tax Ratio: 200:750 = 4:15
   Other Deduction Ratio: 100:750 = 2:15
5. Fed. Gov't.: 300:525 = 1:1.75
   Prov. Gov't.: 150:525 = 1:3.5
   Local Gov't.: 75:525 = 1:7

EXERCISE 2.2

A. 1. 15.3 3. 0.23 5. 0.1

B. 7. –21.69 9. 60.57 11. 0 13. $27.65 15. 0.17

C. 17.

$$\begin{array}{r} 24.4 \\ 41\overline{)1{,}000.4} \\ \underline{82} \\ 180 \\ \underline{164} \\ 164 \\ \underline{164} \\ 0 \end{array}$$

You travelled 24.4 kilometres per litre.

19. $\frac{\$55}{16} = \$3.44$ per hour

21. a. $\frac{3}{4} = 0.75$ b. $0.4 = \frac{2}{5}$ c. $\frac{5}{4} = 1.25$

d. $0.45 = \frac{9}{20}$ e. $\frac{7}{3} = 2.3333$, repeating f. $0.34 = \frac{17}{50}$

EXERCISE 2.3

1. $0.15 \times 45 = 6.75$
3. 34.5%
5. $\left[\frac{27}{25{,}500}\right] \times 100\% = 0.1058824\%$
7. $115 \div 0.3 = 383.33$, or 383
9. Part 1: $\$6 \div \$15 = 0.4 = 40\%$
   Part 2: $\$15 \times 0.75 = \$11.25$; $\$11.25 + \$15.00 = \$26.25$
   (or: $\$15 \times 1.75 = \$26.25$)
11. Since the part is 45% of the total price, the part must cost:

$$0.45 \times \$240{,}000 = \$108{,}000$$

The increase in the part cost of 10% is:

$$0.1 \times \$108{,}000 = \$10{,}800$$

Therefore the new price of the telephone system will be:

$$\$10{,}800 + \$240{,}000 = \$250{,}800$$

An alternative approach is:

$$\$240{,}000 \times (0.45) \times (0.1) + \$240{,}000 = \$250{,}800$$

EXERCISE 3.1

A. **1.** 3 **3.** 23, 43 **5.** 546, –23 **7.** 2.31, 0.26, 121

B. **9.** s, r **11.** t, s, s **13.** dx, sx **15.** jk, am

C. **17.** $34x + 3x$
$= 37x$
$= 37(1)$
$= 37$

19. $132x + 3xy + (-4x) + 15xy$
$= 128x + 18xy$
$= 128(1) + 18(1)(3)$
$= 128 + 54$
$= 182$

21. $14axy - (-23axy) - 56axy - (-24axy)$
$= 14axy + 23axy - 56axy + 24axy$
$= 5axy$
$= 5(1)(3)(4)$
$= 60$

23. $(3y + 13x + 12u) - (-12y + 2x - 13u)$
$= 3y + 13x + 12u + 12y - 2x + 13u$
$= 15y + 11x + 25u$
$= 15(3) + 11(1) + 25(u)$
$= 45 + 11 + 25u$
$= 56 + 25u$

25. $4s + 5r + 5.5s - 11.5r$
$= 9.5s - 6.5r$
$= 9.5(9) - 6.5r$
$= 85.5 - 6.5r$

27. $2t + 3s + (-5t) - 5s$
$= -3t - 2s$
$= -3(7) - 2(9)$
$= -21 - 18$
$= -39$

29. $2.4x - (-0.13x)$
$= 2.4x + 0.13x$
$= 2.53x$
$= 2.53(1)$
$= 2.53$

31. $(1.4a + 1.43x) - (-1.2a - 0.25x)$
$= 1.4a + 1.43x + 1.2a + 0.25x$
$= 2.6a + 1.68x$
$= 2.6(4) + 1.68(1)$
$= 10.4 + 1.68$
$= 12.08$

D.

33. a. A = Number of Acres
L = Number of Lots
P = Price for the Acreage

Revenue = \$145,000(L)

$L = 4A$

Per Lot for Development = \$65,000($4A$)

Profit per Development = \$145,000($4A$) – \$65,000($4A$) – P

b. $A = 40$
P = \$1,000,000
From "a" above we substitute into the profit expression:
Therefore = \$145,000(4)(40) – \$65,000(4)(40) – \$10,000,000
= \$2,800,000

c. $A = 0.5$
$P = \$100,000$
From "a" above we substitute into the profit expression:
Profit = \$145,000(4)(0.5) – \$65,000(4)(0.5) – \$100,000
= \$290,000 – \$230,000
= \$60,000

d. $A = 2.5$
$P = \$400,000$
From "a" above we substitute into the profit expression:
Profit = \$145,000(4)(2.5) – \$65,000(4)(2.5) – \$400,000
= \$400,000

EXERCISE 3.2

A.

1. $3^3 \times 3^2 = 3^{3+2} = 3^5 = 243$
3. $4^2 \times 5^2 = 16 \times 25 = 400$
5. $7^0 \times 2^5 = 1 \times 2^5 = 32$
7. $(1.4)^1 \times (1.8)^0 = 1.4 \times 1 = 1.4$
9. $x^2 \times x^3 = x^{2+3} = x^5$
11. $(r^2 \times r)^2 = (r^3)^2 = r^6$
(alternatively, $(r^2)^2(r)^2 = r^4 \times r^2 = r^6$)
13. $(1 + 0.08)^2 = (1.08)^2 = 1.1664$ (NOT $1^2 + (0.08)^2$!)
15. $(1 + 0.005)^4 = 1.020$
17. $(x^2 \times y^3)x = x^{2+1} \times y^3 = x^3 \times y^3 = (xy)^3$
19. $(y^2y^3y^2)^2 = (y^{2+3+2})^2 = (y^7)^2 = y^{7\times 2} = y^{14}$

B.

21. $3\sqrt{12} = 12^{\frac{1}{3}} = 12^{0.333} = 2.289$
23. $({}^4\sqrt{5^2}\ )^2 = (5^{\frac{2}{4}})^2 = (5^{\frac{1}{2}})^2 = 5^{\frac{1}{2}\times 2} = 5^1 = 5$
25. ${}^2\sqrt{1.5} = (1.5)^{\frac{1}{2}} = 1.225$

C.

27. ${}^2\sqrt{4^3} = 4^{\frac{3}{2}} = 4^{1.5} = 8$
29. ${}^5\sqrt{a^2} = a^{\frac{2}{5}} = a^{0.4}$
31. $\dfrac{1}{{}^2\sqrt{2^4}} = \dfrac{1}{2^{\frac{4}{2}}} = 2^{-\frac{4}{2}} = 2^{-2} = 0.25$

EXERCISE 3.3

1. Polynomial, Binomial (as written; added together, it becomes a Monomial)
3. Polynomial, Binomial
5. Polynomial, Trinomial
7. Monomial
9. Monomial

EXERCISE 3.4

1. $6x + (-3x) = (6 - 3)x = 3x$
3. $(3x + 2x - 3) + (x + 15)$
   $= (5x - 3) + (x + 15)$
   $= 5x - 3 + x + 15$
   $= 6x + 12$
5. $40x - 6x = (40 - 6)x = 34x$
7. $(-45xy) - (5xy) = (-45 - 5)xy = -50xy$
9. $(3xy + 5b - 7s) + (0xy + 5b - 7s)$
   $$\begin{array}{r} (3xy + \ \ 5b - \ \ 7s) \\ \underline{+(0xy + \ \ 5b - \ \ 7s)} \\ = 3xy + 10b - 14s \end{array}$$
11. $16x - (-4x) + (2x) = 16x + 4x + 2x = (16 + 4 + 2)x = 22x$
13. $(2ax + 4ax) - (-3ax + 5ax) = 6ax - 2ax = 4ax$
15. $(13x + 3x) - (2x - 3x) = 16x - (-x) = 17x$
17. $(-12cs) - 9cs = -21cs$
19. $34x + (-15x) + a = 19x + a$

EXERCISE 3.5

1. $4x(-3x) = -12x^{1+1} = -12x^2$
3. $(3a + 4x - 20x)(x + 4)$
   $= (3a - 16x)(x + 4)$
   $= 3a \times x - 16x \times x + 3a \times 4 - 16x \times 4$
   $= 3ax - 16x^2 + 12a - 64x$
5. $\dfrac{36x}{6x} = 6x^{1-1} = 6x^0 = 6$
7. $\dfrac{(-90xy + 15x^2y^{-1})}{(5xy)} = \dfrac{-90xy}{5xy} + \dfrac{15x^2y^{-1}}{5xy}$
   $= -18 + 3xy^{-2}$ (that is, $\dfrac{y^{-1}}{y} = y^{-1+(-1)}$)

9. $(15vx - 3xv^2)(xv + v^2)$
$= 15vx \times xv - 3xv^2 \times xv + 15vx \times v^2 - 3v^2x \times v^2$
$= 15v^2x^2 - 3v^3x^2 + 15v^3x - 3v^4x$

11. $(-16x)(-4x) = 64x^2$

13. $(2ax + 4ax)(-3ax) = -6a^2x^2 - 12a^2x^2 = -18a^2x^2$

15. $\dfrac{x^2y^2(3x)}{(xy)} = \dfrac{3x^3y^2}{xy} = 3x^{3-1}y^{2-1} = 3x^2y$

17. $\dfrac{(-18x^4y^2)}{2x^{-2}y} = -9x^{4-(-2)}y^{2-1} = -9x^6y$

19. $34x^2(-15x)12ax = (34)(-15)(12)x^{2+2}a = -6{,}120ax^4$

EXERCISE 3.6

1. $4x + 16 = 4(x + 4)$

3. $36 + 6x^2 = 6(6 + x^2)$

5. $3y^3 + y^2 + y - y^3$
$= y(3y^2 + y + 1 - y^2)$
$= y(2y^2 + y + 1)$

7. $P + Prt = P(1 + rt)$

9. $S - Sdt = S(1 - dt)$

11. $12x^3 - 4x = 4x(3x^2 - 1)$

13. $400ws - 100sx - sw + 12wx$
$= 100s(4w - x) - w(s - 12x)$

EXERCISE 3.7

A.

1.
$$2t - 14 = 0$$
$$2t - 14 + 14 = 0 + 14$$
$$2t = 14$$
$$t = 7$$

3. $5x - 15 = 10$
$$5x = 10 + 15$$
$$x = \frac{10 + 15}{5} = \frac{25}{5} = 5$$

5.
$$x(1.01) = 500$$
$$x = \frac{500}{1.01} = 495.0495$$

7.
$$3x + 15 = 2x + 45$$
$$3x + 15 - 2x - 15 = 2x + 45 - 2x - 15$$
$$x = 30$$

B.

9. $3x + 4r = 10$

$$3x = 10 - 4r$$

$$x = \frac{10 - 4r}{3}$$

11. $x(1 + i) + x(1 + i) + x(1 + i) = 500$

$$3x(1 + i) = 500$$

$$\frac{3x(1 + i)}{3(1 + i)} = \frac{500}{3(1 + i)}$$

$$x = \frac{500}{3(1 + i)} = \frac{166.67}{(1 + i)}$$

13. $24x + 12y = 44y$

$$24x = 44y - 12y$$

$$24x = 32y$$

$$x = \frac{32y}{24} = \frac{4y}{3} = 1.33y$$

15. $15y + 15 = 15y + 15x$

$$15y - 15y + 15 = 15x$$

$$15 = 15x$$

$$x = 1$$

17. $x - 20{,}000 = \frac{[1 + (1 + 0.11)]}{0.11}$

$$x = 20{,}000 + \frac{[1 + (1.11)]}{0.11}$$

$$x = 20{,}000 + \frac{2.11}{0.11}$$

$x = 20{,}000 + 19.18 = 20{,}019.18$ Rounded.

EXERCISE 3.8

1. $\frac{1}{2}x + 5x = 165$

$$2\left(\frac{1}{2}x\right) + 2(5x) = 2(165) \quad \text{or} \quad 0.5x + 5x = 165$$

$$x + 10x = 330 \qquad 5.5x = 165$$

$$11x = 330 \qquad x = \frac{165}{5.5}$$

$$x = \frac{330}{11} = 30 \qquad x = 30$$

3. $\frac{2}{7} + 3x = 0.55,$

$$7 \times \frac{2}{7} + 7 \times (3x) = 7(0.55)$$
$$2 + 21x = 3.85$$
$$21x = 1.85$$
$$x = \frac{1.85}{21}$$
$$x = 0.0881$$

or

$$0.2857 + 3x = 0.55$$
$$3x = 0.55 - 0.2857$$
$$3x = 0.2643$$
$$x = 0.0881$$

5. $\frac{3}{8}(1 + 4x) - 10 = 2x + \frac{1x}{8},$

$$8[\frac{3}{8}(1 + 4x)] - 8(10) = 8(2x) + 8[\frac{1x}{8}]$$
$$3(1 + 4x) - 80 = 16x + x$$
$$3 + 12x - 80 = 17x$$
$$-77 = 17x - 12x$$
$$-77 = 5x$$
$$x = \frac{-77}{5} = -15.4$$

or

$$0.3750(1 + 4x) - 10 = 2x + 0.1250x$$
$$0.3750 + 1.5x - 10 = 2x + 0.1250x$$
$$1.5x - 9.625 = 2.1250x$$
$$-9.625 = 0.6250x$$
$$= -15.4$$

7. $\frac{3}{4}(16 + 4x) + 100 = 150 + \frac{1x}{4},$

$$4[\frac{3}{4}(16 + 4x)] + 4(100) = 4(150) + 4(\frac{1x}{4})$$

$$3(16 + 4x) + 400 = 600 + x$$
$$48 + 12x + 400 = 600 + x$$
$$12x - x = 600 - 400 - 48$$
$$11x = 152$$
$$x = 13.8182$$

or

$$0.7500(16 + 4x) + 100 = 150 + 0.2500x$$
$$12 + 3x + 100 = 150 + 0.2500x$$
$$3x - 0.2500x = 150 - 112$$
$$2.7500x = 38$$
$$x = 13.8182$$

9.

$$1{,}680 = 1{,}500(1 + 0.12t)$$
$$\frac{1{,}680}{1{,}500} = 1 + 0.12t$$
$$0.12t = \frac{1{,}680}{1{,}500} - 1$$
$$t = \frac{0.12}{0.12} = 1$$

EXERCISE 3.9

A.

1. Cost: \$45,000 + \$15x
   Revenue: \$20x

   Break-even point:

$$\begin{aligned} \text{Revenue} &= \text{Cost} \\ \$20x &= \$45{,}000 + \$15x \\ \$20x - \$15x &= \$45{,}000 \\ \$5x &= \$45{,}000 \\ x &= \frac{\$45{,}000}{\$5} \\ x &= 9{,}000 \text{ units} \end{aligned}$$

3. Cost = \$140,000 + \$1,500x
   Revenue = \$2,450x

   Break-even point:

$$\begin{aligned} \$2{,}450x &= \$140{,}000 + \$1{,}500x \\ \$950x &= \$140{,}000 \\ x &= 147.37, \text{ or } 148 \text{ units} \end{aligned}$$

5. Cost = \$250,000 + \$500x
   Revenue = \$1,750x

   Break-even point:

$$\begin{aligned} \$1{,}750x &= \$250{,}000 + \$500x \\ \$1{,}250x &= \$250{,}000 \\ x &= 200 \text{ units} \end{aligned}$$

B.

7. Cost = \$150x + \$250,000
   Revenue = \$450x

   Break-even point:

$$\begin{aligned} \$450x &= \$150x + \$250{,}000 \\ 300x &= 250{,}000 \\ x &= 833.33, \text{ or } 834 \text{ units} \end{aligned}$$

9. Fixed Cost = \$6,000 + \$12,500 = \$18,500
   Variable Cost = \$125x
   Total Cost = \$18,500 + \$125x
   Revenue = \$175x

   Break-even point:

$$\begin{aligned} \$175x &= \$18{,}500 + \$125x \\ \$50x &= \$18{,}500 \\ x &= 370 \text{ units} \end{aligned}$$

Profit:

$$\begin{aligned} \text{Revenue} &= \text{Costs} + \text{Profit} \\ \$175x &= \$18{,}500 + \$125x + \$15{,}000 \\ \$50x &= \$33{,}500 \\ x &= 670 \text{ units} \end{aligned}$$

11. Current cost per converter = $\$1{,}250x$
New cost per converter = $\$900x + \$50{,}000$

Break-even point:

$$\begin{aligned} \$1{,}250x &= \$50{,}000 + \$900x \\ \$350x &= \$50{,}000 \\ x &= 142.86, \text{ or } 143 \text{ installations} \end{aligned}$$

EXERCISE 4.1

A.

1. Equation ①: $4x - 3y = -3$
Equation ②: $5x - y = 10$

Multiply Equation ② by 3:

$$\begin{aligned} 3(5x - y) &= 3(10) \\ 15x - 3y &= 30 \end{aligned}$$

Subtract Equation ① from new Equation ②:

$$\begin{array}{rl} 15x - 3y = 30 & ② \\ \underline{-(4x - 3y = -3)} & ① \\ 11x + 0y = 33 & \\ x = 3 & \end{array}$$

Substitute $x = 3$ into Equation ②:

$$\begin{aligned} 5(3) - y &= 10 \\ 15 - y &= 10 \\ 15 - 10 &= y \\ y &= 5 \end{aligned}$$

Therefore, the solution is $x = 3$, $y = 5$.

Checking:
Equation ①: $4(3) - 3(5) = 12 - 15 = -3$
Equation ②: $5(3) - (5) = 15 - 5 = 10$

3. Equation ①: $2x + 7y = 5$

   Equation ②: $3x + 2y = 6$

   It is easiest to eliminate the x's.

   Multiply Equation ① by 3 and ② by 2:

$$3(2x + 7y) = 3(5)$$
$$6x + 21y = 15$$

$$2(3x + 2y) = 2(6)$$
$$6x + 4y = 12$$

   Subtract ② from ①:

$$\begin{array}{r} 6x + 21y = 15 \\ \underline{-(6x + 4y = 12)} \\ 0 + 17y = 3 \\ y = \frac{3}{17} \end{array}$$

   Substitute $y = \frac{3}{17}$ in ②:

$$3x + 2\left(\frac{3}{17}\right) = 6$$
$$3x + \frac{6}{17} = 6$$
$$3x = 6 - \frac{6}{17}$$
$$3x = \frac{102}{17} - \frac{6}{17}$$
$$3x = \frac{96}{17}$$
$$x = \frac{32}{17}$$

   Therefore, the solution is $x = \frac{32}{17}$, $y = \frac{3}{17}$.

   Checking by substituting into equations:

   Equation ①: $2\left(\frac{32}{17}\right) + 7\left(\frac{3}{17}\right) = \frac{64}{17} + \frac{21}{17} = \frac{85}{17} = 5$

   Equation ②: $3\left(\frac{32}{17}\right) + 2\left(\frac{3}{17}\right) = \frac{96}{17} + \frac{6}{17} = \frac{102}{17} = 6$

5. Equation ①: $x + y = 25$

   Equation ②: $\underline{x - y = 1}$ Eliminate y's by adding ① and ②.

$$2x + 0 = 26$$
$$x = 13.$$

Substitute into ①:

$$(13) + y = 25$$
$$y = 25 - 13$$
$$y = 12$$

Therefore, the solution is $x = 13$, $y = 12$.

Checking:

Equation ①: $(13) + (12) = 25$

②: $(13) - (12) = 1$

B.

7. Equation ①: $x - y = 3$

Equation ②: $5x - y = 10$

Solve ① for x: $x = y - 3$

Substitute for x in ②:

$$5(y - 3) - y = 10$$
$$5y - 15 - y = 10$$
$$4y = 25$$
$$y = \frac{25}{4}$$

Substitute for y into ①:

$$x - \frac{25}{4} = -3$$
$$x = \frac{25}{4} - 3$$
$$x = \frac{25}{4} - \frac{12}{4}$$
$$x = \frac{13}{4}$$

Therefore, the solution is $x = \frac{13}{4}$, $y = \frac{25}{4}$.

Checking:

Equation ①: $\frac{13}{4} - \frac{25}{4} = \frac{-12}{4} = -3$

Equation ②: $5\left(\frac{13}{4}\right) - \frac{25}{4} = \frac{65}{4} - \frac{25}{4} = \frac{40}{4} = 10$

9. Equation ①: $x + 2y = 5$
Equation ②: $-x + y = 6$

Solve ② for y:

$$y = 6 + x$$

Substitute into ①:

$$\begin{aligned} x + 2(6 + x) &= 5 \\ x + 12 + 2x &= 5 \\ 3x &= -7 \\ x &= \frac{-7}{3} \end{aligned}$$

Substitute $x = \frac{-7}{3}$ into ②

$$\begin{aligned} -\left(\frac{-7}{3}\right) + y &= 6 \\ y &= 6 - \frac{7}{3} \\ y &= \frac{18}{3} - \frac{7}{3} \\ y &= \frac{18 - 7}{3} \\ y &= \frac{11}{3} \end{aligned}$$

Therefore, the solution is $x = \frac{-7}{3}, y = \frac{11}{3}$.

Checking:

Equation ①: $\left(\frac{-7}{3}\right) + 2\left(\frac{11}{3}\right) = \frac{-7}{3} + \frac{22}{3} = \frac{15}{3} = 5$

Equation ②: $-\left(\frac{-7}{3}\right) + \left(\frac{11}{3}\right) = \frac{18}{3} = 6$

11. Equation ①: $x + y = 25$
Equation ②: $x - y = 1$

Solve ② for x: $x = y + 1$

Substitute ② into ①:

$$\begin{aligned} (y + 1) + y &= 25 \\ 2y + 1 &= 25 \\ 2y &= 25 - 1 \\ 2y &= 24 \\ y &= 12 \end{aligned}$$

Substitute $y = 12$ into ①:

$$\begin{aligned} x + (12) &= 25 \\ x &= 25 - 12 \\ x &= 13 \end{aligned}$$

Therefore, the solution is $x = 13$, $y = 12$.

Checking:

Equation ①: $x + y = 13 + 12 = 25$
Equation ②: $x - y = 13 - 12 = 1$

EXERCISE 4.2

A.

1. $2x + y = 10$ | *Point*

	Point
When $x = 0$: $2(0) + y = 10$; $y = 10$	$(0, 10)$ y-intercept
When $y = 0$: $2x + (0) = 10$; $2x = 10$; $x = 5$	$(5, 0)$ x-intercept

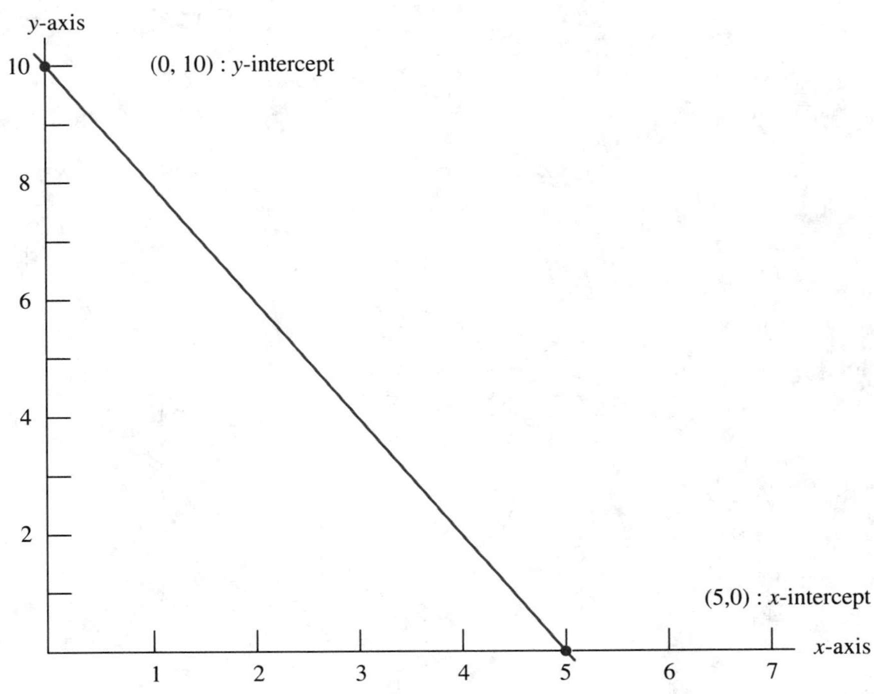

3. $x = 5$
   When $y = 0$, $x = 5$; x can never equal 0 (Point is (5, 0): x-intercept), thus the line is parallel to the Y axis.

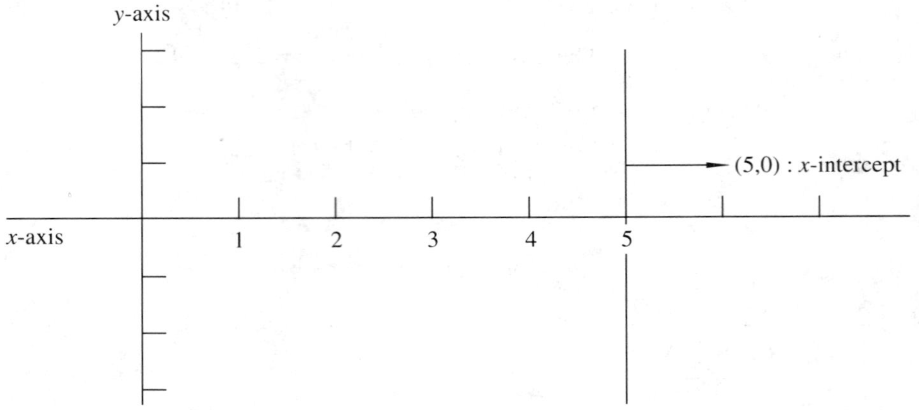

5. $4y = 3x + 5$ — *Point*

   When $x = 0$: $4y = 5$, $y = \dfrac{5}{4}$ — $\left(0, \dfrac{5}{4}\right)$ y-intercept

   When $y = 0$: $4(0) = 3x + 5$, $3x = -5$, $x = -\dfrac{5}{3}$ — $\left(-\dfrac{5}{3}, 0\right)$ x-intercept

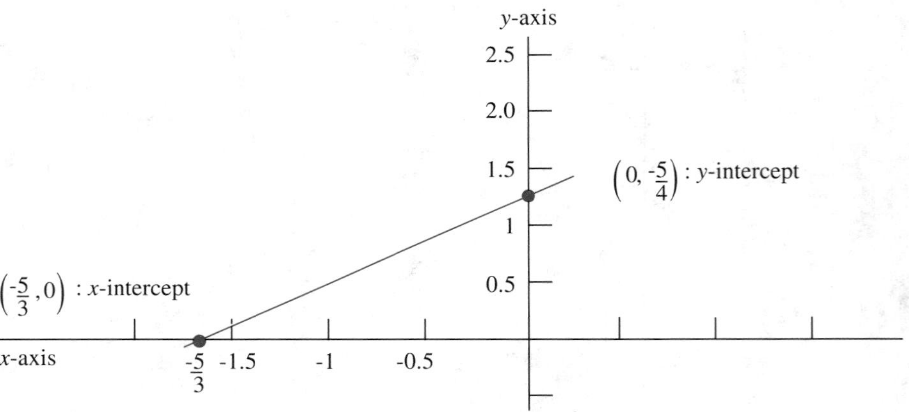

7. $0.5x - 0.4y = 1$ — *Point*

   When $x = 0$: $-0.4y = 1$; $y = -\dfrac{1}{0.4} = -2.5$ — (0, –2.5) y-intercept

   When $y = 0$: $0.5x = 1$; $x = \dfrac{1}{0.5} = 2$ — (2, 0) x-intercept

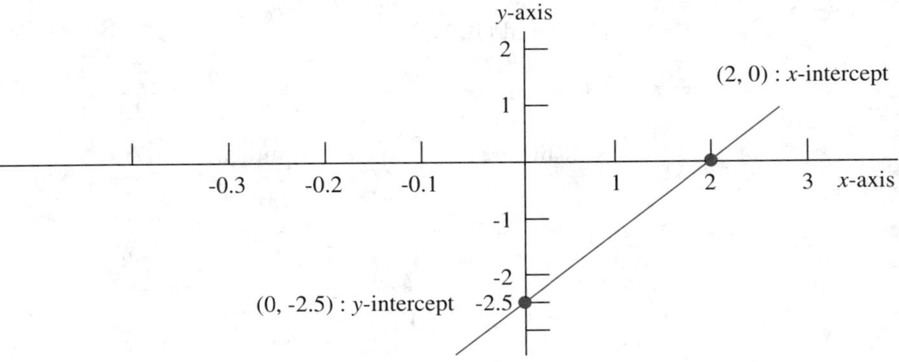

B.

9. (0, 4) and (5,0)

Slope: $m = \dfrac{\text{change in } y}{\text{change in } x} = \dfrac{y_2 - y_1}{x_2 - x_1} = \dfrac{0-4}{5-0} = \dfrac{-4}{5}$

or, $\dfrac{4-0}{0-5} = \dfrac{4}{-5} = \dfrac{-4}{5}$

Substituting into $y = b + mx$

$$y = b + \left(\frac{-4}{5}\right)x$$

$$y = b - \left(\frac{4}{5}\right)x$$

Any point on this line satisfies this equation, so we can substitute either of our points for x and y, and find b.

Substituting (0, 4) into $y = b - \left(\frac{4}{5}\right)x$, we get:

$$4 = b - \left(\frac{4}{5}\right)(0)$$

$$4 = b$$

(This makes sense, since (0, 4) is the y-intercept, i.e., the point at $x = 0$!)

Substituting our slope, $m = \dfrac{-4}{5}$, and y-intercept, $b = 4$, into $y = b + mx$, we get:

$$y = 4 - \left(\frac{4}{5}\right)x$$

11. (3, 4) and $(1, 2\frac{1}{2})$

Slope: $m = \dfrac{y_2 - y_1}{x_2 - x_1} = \dfrac{4 - 2\frac{1}{2}}{3 - 1} = \dfrac{1\frac{1}{2}}{2} = \dfrac{\frac{3}{2}}{2} = \dfrac{3}{4}$

Substitute $m = \dfrac{3}{4}$ and (3, 4) into $y = b + mx$:

$$4 = b + \left(\frac{3}{4}\right)(3)$$

$$4 = b + \left(\frac{9}{4}\right)$$

$$4 - \left(\frac{9}{4}\right) = b$$

$$b = \frac{16 - 9}{4} = \frac{7}{4}$$

Substitute slope, $m = \dfrac{3}{4}$, and y-intercept, $b = \dfrac{7}{4}$, into $y = b + mx$

$$y = \frac{7}{4} + \frac{3x}{4} \quad \text{Equation of line.}$$

13. (3, 5) and (4, 5)

$$m = \frac{y_2 - y_1}{x_2 - x_1} = \frac{5 - 5}{4 - 3} = \frac{0}{1} = 0$$

$m = 0$, therefore the graph is a horizontal line — we can note that $y = 5$ regardless of x, therefore the equation of line is $y = 5$ (and $b = 5$ as well).

Substitute $m = 0$ and (3, 5) into $y = b + mx$:

$$5 = b + (0)(3)$$
$$b = 5$$

Substituting $m = 0$ and $b = 5$ into $y = b + mx$:

$$y = 5 + (0)x$$
$$y = 5 \text{ (horizontal line)}$$

EXERCISE 4.3

1. $4x - 3y = -3$ ①
$5x - y = 10$ ②

For equation ①: $4x - 3y = -3$

When $x = 0$, $4(0) - 3y = -3$, $y = 1$ (0, 1)

When $y = 0$, $4x - 3(0) = -3$, $4x = -3$, $x = -\dfrac{3}{4}$ $\left(-\dfrac{3}{4}, 0\right)$

For equation ②: $5x - y = 10$

When $x = 0$, $5(0) - y = 10$, $y = -10$ (0, –10)

When $y = 0$, $5x - 0 = 10$, $5x = 10$, $x = 2$ (2, 0)

Algebraic approach:

Solve ② for y:

$$y = 5x - 10$$

Substitute into ①:

$$\begin{aligned} 4x - 3(5x - 10) &= -3 \\ 4x - 15x + 30 &= -3 \\ -11x &= -33 \\ x &= 3 \end{aligned}$$

Substitute into ②:

$$\begin{aligned} 5(3) - y &= 10 \\ 15 - y &= 10 \\ y &= 5 \end{aligned}$$

Graphic approach:

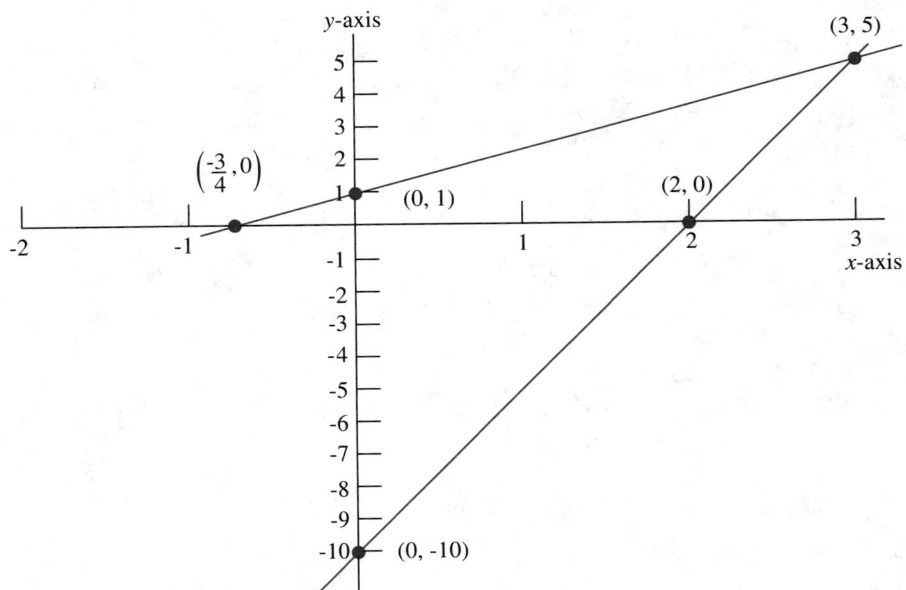

3. $2x + y = 5$ ①
$3x + 2y = 2$ ②

For equation ①: $2x + y = 5$

When $x = 0$, $2(0) + y = 5$, $y = 5$ $(0,5)$

When $y = 0$, $2x + 0 = 5$, $2x = 5$, $x = \frac{5}{2}$ $\left(\frac{5}{2}, 0\right)$

For equation ②: $3x + 2y = 2$

When $x = 0$, $3(0) + 2y = 2$, $2y = 2$, $y = 1$ $(0, 1)$

When $y = 0$, $3x + 2(0) = 2$, $3x = 2$, $x = \frac{2}{3}$ $\left(\frac{2}{3}, 0\right)$

Graphic approach:

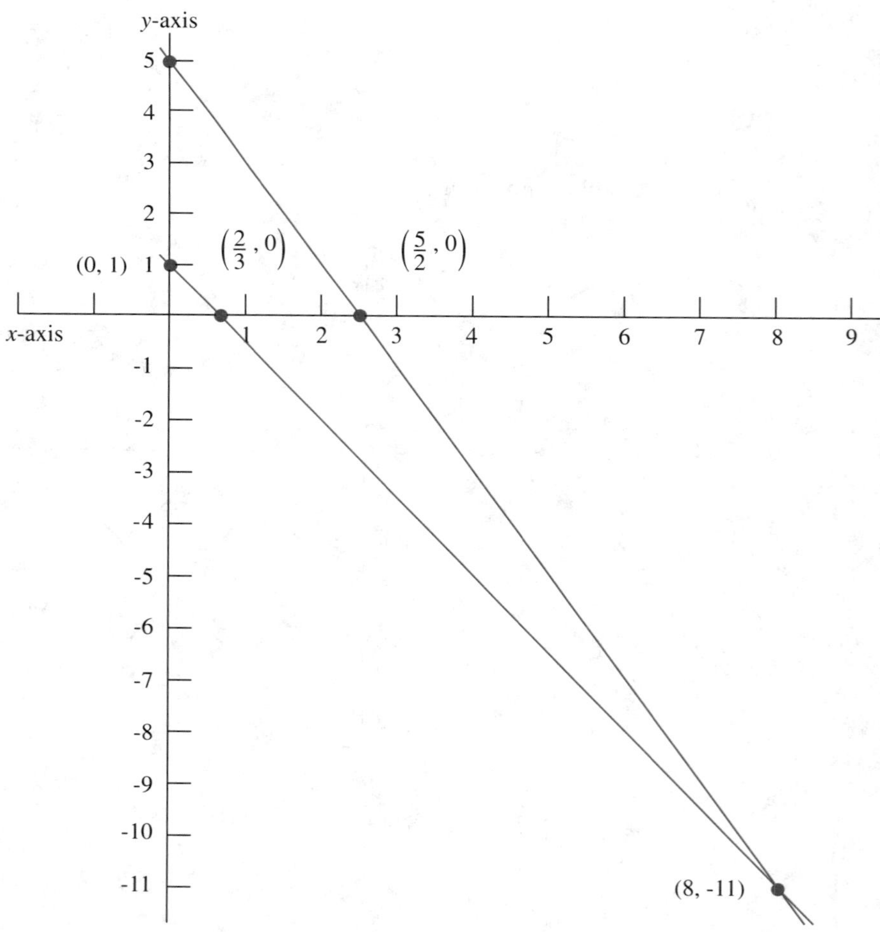

Algebraically: Substitute ①: $x = 5 - 2x$ into ②

$$3x + 2(5 - 2x) = 2$$
$$3x + 10 - 4x = 2$$
$$-x = -8$$
$$x = 8$$

$$2(8) + y = 5$$
$$16 + y = 5$$
$$y = -11$$

5. $x + y = 9$ ①
$x - y = 1$ ②

For equation ①: $x + y = 9$
When $x = 0$, $0 + y = 9$, $y = 9$ (0, 9)
When $y = 0$, $x + 0 = 9$, $x = 9$ (9, 0)

For equation ②: $x - y = 1$
When $x = 0$, $0 - y = 1$, $y = -1$ (0, –1)
When $y = 0$, $x - 0 = 1$, $x = 1$ (1, 0)

Graphic approach:

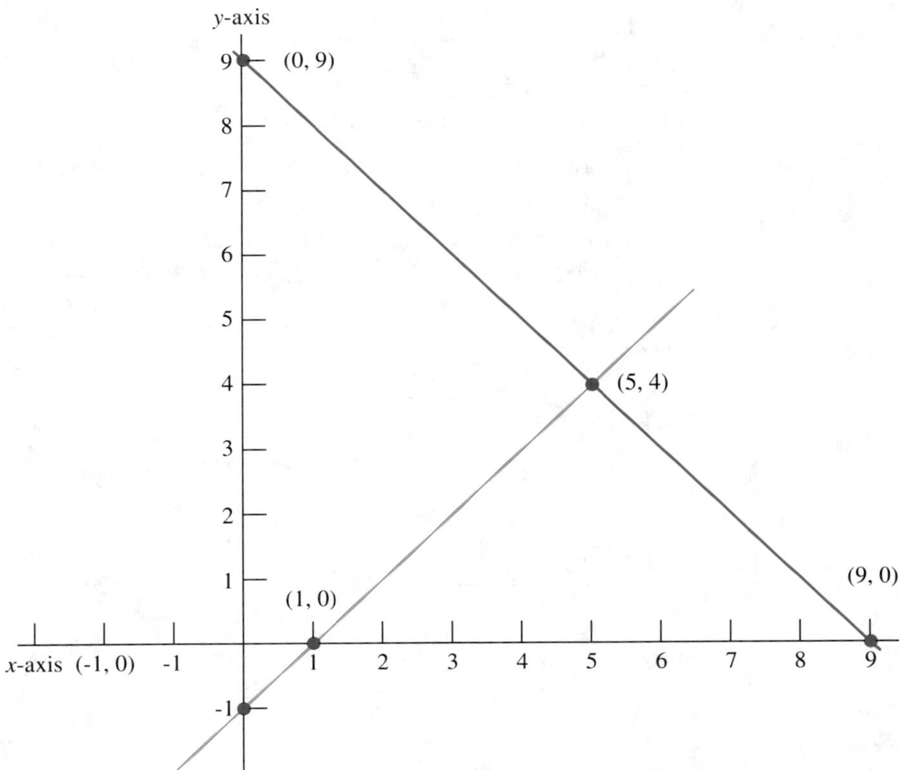

Algebraically: Add ① and ②:

$$\begin{aligned} x + y &= 9 \\ \underline{x - y} &\underline{= 1} \\ 2x + 0 &= 10 \\ x &= 5 \end{aligned}$$

Solving for y substitute $x = 5$ into ①:

$$\begin{aligned} 5 + y &= 9 \\ y &= 4 \end{aligned}$$

EXERCISE 4.4

1. From question:
   $x =$ units
   Fixed costs: \$30,000

   Variable cost per unit is: $\dfrac{\$50{,}000}{10{,}000 \text{ units}} = \$5$ (i.e., \$5 per unit)

   Total costs: = Fixed cost + Variable costs = \$30,000 + \$5x
   Total revenue: = \$10x

   Algebraically:
   $$\begin{aligned} \$10x &= \$30{,}000 + \$5x \\ \$5x &= \$30{,}000 \\ x &= 6{,}000 \text{ units is the break-even point} \end{aligned}$$

   Total revenue at break-even point is \$10(6,000) = \$60,000.

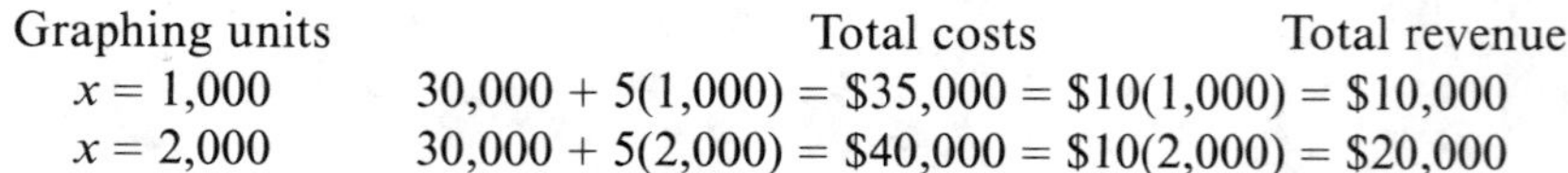

Graphing units	Total costs	Total revenue
$x = 1{,}000$	30,000 + 5(1,000) = \$35,000 =	\$10(1,000) = \$10,000
$x = 2{,}000$	30,000 + 5(2,000) = \$40,000 =	\$10(2,000) = \$20,000

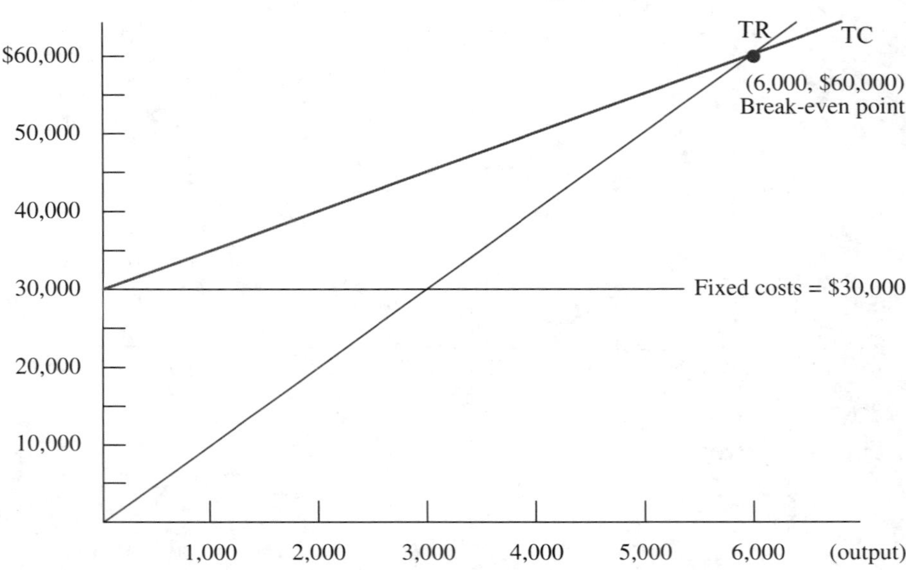

3. x = units
Revenue = \$50x
Old total cost = \$150,000 + \$30x
New total cost = \$220,000 + \$30x

Notice that the slope remains the same; the line is moved up vertically by the amount of the advertising costs, \$70,000.

Find costs:

Units	*Old cost*	*New cost*	*Revenue*
5,000	\$150,000 + \$30(5,000) = \$300,000	\$220,000 + \$30(5,000) = \$370,000	\$50(5,000) = \$250,000
10,000	\$150,000 + \$30(10,000) = \$450,000	\$220,000 + \$30(10,000) = \$520,000	\$50(10,000) = \$500,000

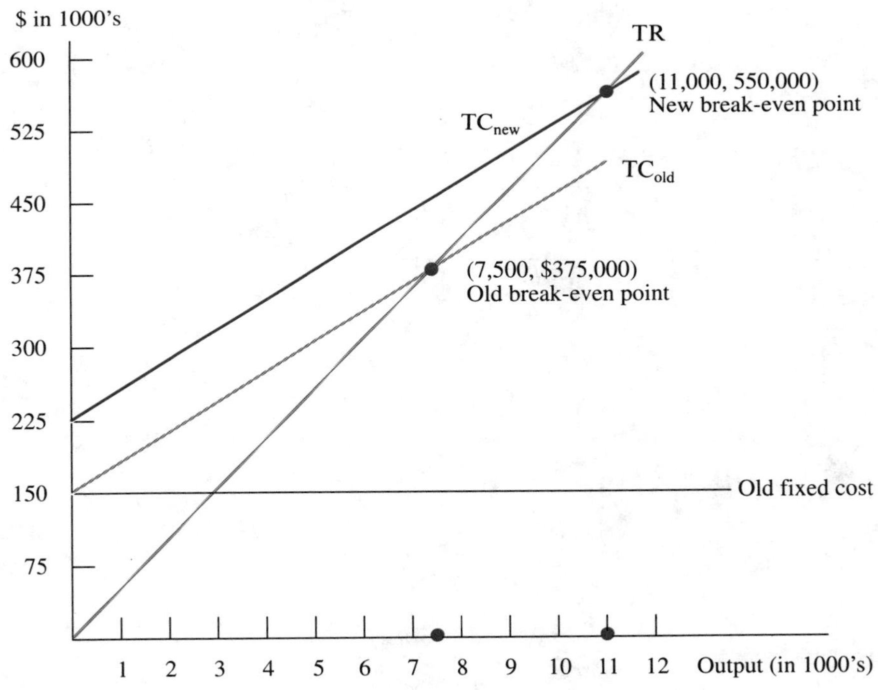

Algebraically:

Old break-even point:

$$\begin{aligned} \$50x &= \$150{,}000 + \$30x \\ \$20x &= \$150{,}000 \\ x &= 7{,}500 \text{ units} \end{aligned}$$

New break-even point:

$$\begin{aligned} \$50x &= \$220{,}000 + 30x \\ \$20x &= \$220{,}000 \\ x &= 11{,}000 \text{ units} \end{aligned}$$

EXERCISE 4.5

A.

1. 2, 5, 8, . . . to 6 terms

$a = 2$ First term
$d = 5 - 2 = 3$ Difference
$n = 6$ Number of terms

Last term:
$$t_n = a + (n - 1)d$$
$$t_n = 2 + (6 - 1)3$$
$$t_n = 17$$

Sum:
$$S_n = \frac{n}{2}(a + t_n)$$
$$S_n = \frac{6}{2}(2 + 17)$$
$$S_n = 57$$

3. 0.1, 0.5, 0.9, . . . to 6 terms

$a = 0.1$
$d = 0.5 - 0.1 = 0.4$
$n = 6$

Last term:
$$t_n = a + (n - 1)d$$
$$t_n = 0.1 + (6 - 1)(0.4)$$
$$t_n = 2.1$$

Sum:
$$S_n = \frac{n}{2}(a + t_n)$$
$$S_n = \frac{6}{2}(0.1 + 2.1)$$
$$S_n = 6.6$$

5. 0.1, 0.9, 1.7, . . . to 6 terms

$a = 0.1$
$d = 0.9 - 0.1 = 0.8$
$n = 6$

Last term:
$$t_n = a + (n - 1)d$$
$$t_n = 0.1 + (6 - 1)(0.8)$$
$$t_n = 4.1$$

Sum:
$$S_n = \frac{n}{2}(a + t_n)$$
$$S_n = \frac{6}{2}(0.1 + 4.1)$$
$$S_n = 12.6$$

7. 9, 6, 3, . . . to 10 terms

$a = 9$
$d = 6 - 9 = -3$
$n = 10$

Last term:
$$t_n = a + (n - 1)d$$
$$t_n = 9 + (10 - 1)(-3)$$
$$t_n = -18$$

Sum:
$$S_n = \frac{n}{2}(a + t_n)$$
$$S_n = \frac{10}{2}(9 - 18)$$
$$S_n = -45$$

9. −2, −6, −10, . . . to 12 terms

$a = -2$
$d = -6 - (-2) = -4$
$n = 12$

Last term:
$$t_n = a + (n - 1)d$$
$$t_n = -2 + (12 - 1)(-4)$$
$$t_n = -46$$

Sum:
$$S_n = \frac{n}{2}(a + t_n)$$
$$S_n = \frac{12}{2}(-2 + (-46))$$
$$S_n = -288$$

11. 2, 16, 30, . . . to 6 terms

$a = 2$
$d = 16 - 2 = 14$
$n = 6$

Last term:
$$t_n = a + (n - 1)d$$
$$t_n = 2 + (6 - 1)(14)$$
$$t_n = 72$$

Sum:
$$S_n = \frac{n}{2}(a + t_n)$$
$$S_n = \frac{6}{2}(2 + 72)$$
$$S_n = 222$$

B.

13. $t_n = 10$
$d = 2$
$n = 5$

Find a and S_n.

$$t_n = a + (n - 1)d$$
$$10 = a + (5 - 1)2$$
$$10 = a + 8$$
$$a = 2$$
$$S_n = \frac{n}{2}(a + t_n)$$
$$S_n = \frac{5}{2}(2 + 10)$$
$$S_n = 30$$

15. $S_n = 48$
$a = 3$
$n = 6$

Find t_n and d.

$$S_n = \frac{n}{2}(a + t_n)$$
$$48 = \frac{6}{2}(3 + t_n)$$
$$48 = 3(3 + t_n)$$
$$48 = 9 + 3t_n$$
$$48 - 9 = 3t_n$$
$$39 = 3t_n$$
$$t_n = 13$$

$$t_n = a + (n - 1)d$$
$$13 = 3 + (6 - 1)d$$
$$13 - 3 = 5d$$
$$10 = 5d$$
$$d = 2$$

17. $a = 3$
$n = 4$
$S_n = 30$

Find t_n and d.

$$S_n = \frac{n}{2}(a + t_n)$$

$$30 = \frac{4}{2}(3 + t_n)$$

$$30 = 2(3 + t_n)$$

$$15 = 3 + t_n$$

$$t_n = 12$$

$$t_n = a + (n - 1)d$$

$$12 = 3 + (4 - 1)d$$

$$9 = 3d$$

$$d = 3$$

19. $a = -16$
$n = 10$
$S_n = 20$

Find t_n and d.

$$S_n = \frac{n}{2}(a + t_n)$$

$$20 = \frac{10}{2}(-16 + t_n)$$

$$20 = 5(-16 + t_n)$$

$$4 = -16 + t_n$$

$$t_n = 20$$

$$t_n = a + (n - 1)d$$

$$20 = -16 + (10 - 1)d$$

$$36 = 9d$$

$$d = 4$$

EXERCISE 4.6

A.

1. 2, 6, 18, . . . to 6 terms

$a = 2$

$n = 6$

$r = \frac{6}{2} = 3$

Last term: $t_n = ar^{n-1}$

$t_n = (2)(3)^{6-1}$

$t_n = 486$

Sum: $S_n = \frac{a(1 - r^n)}{1 - r} = \frac{(2)(1 - 3^6)}{1 - 3} = \frac{2(1 - 729)}{-2} = 728$

3. 0.1, 0.3, 0.9, . . . to 6 terms

$a = 0.1$

$n = 6$

$r = \frac{0.3}{0.1} = 3$

Last term: $t_n = ar^{n-1}$

$t_n = (0.1)(3)^{6-1}$

$t_n = 24.3$

Sum: $S_n = \frac{a(1 - r^n)}{1 - r} = \frac{(0.1)(1 - 3^6)}{1 - 3} = \frac{0.1(1 - 729)}{-2} = 36.4$

5. 1, 0.5, 0.25, . . . to 9 terms

$a = 1$

$n = 9$

$r = \frac{0.5}{1} = 0.5$

Last term: $t_n = ar^{n-1}$

$t_n = (1)(0.5)^{9-1}$

$t_n = 0.00390625$

Sum: $S_n = \frac{a(1 - r^n)}{1 - r} = \frac{(1)(1 - 0.5^9)}{1 - 0.5}$

$S_n = \frac{(1 - 0.001953125)}{0.5} = 1.99609375$

7. 3, 9, 27, . . . to 12 terms

$a = 3$

$n = 12$

$r = \frac{9}{3} = 3$

Last term: $t_n = ar^{n-1}$

$t_n = (3)(3)^{12-1}$

$t_n = 531{,}441$

Sum: $S_n = \dfrac{a(1-r^n)}{1-r} = \dfrac{(3)(1-3^{12})}{1-3}$

$S_n = \dfrac{(3)(1-531{,}441)}{-2} = 797{,}160$

9. –2, 6, –18, . . . to 12 terms

$a = -2$

$n = 12$

$r = \dfrac{6}{-2} = -3$

Last term: $t_n = ar^{n-1}$

$t_n = (-2)(-3)^{12-1}$

$t_n = (-2)(-177{,}147)$

$t_n = 354{,}294$

Sum: $S_n = \dfrac{a(1-r^n)}{1-r} = \dfrac{(-2)(1-(-3)^{12})}{1-(-3)}$

$S_n = \dfrac{(-2)(1-531{,}441)}{4} = 265{,}720$

11. –1, 8, –64, . . . to 12 terms

$a = -1$

$n = 12$

$r = \dfrac{8}{-1} = -8$

Last term: $t_n = ar^{n-1}$

$t_n = (-1)(-8)^{12-1}$

$t_n = 8{,}589{,}934{,}592$

Sum: $S_n = \dfrac{a(1-r^n)}{1-r} = \dfrac{(-1)(1-(-8)^{12})}{1-(-8)}$

$S_n = \dfrac{(-1)(1-(6.871947673 \times 10^{10})}{9} = 7{,}635{,}497{,}415.21$

B.

13. $t_n = 10$

$r = 2$

$n = 2$

Find a and S_n.

$t_n = ar^{n-1}$

$a = \dfrac{t_n}{r^{n-1}} = \dfrac{10}{2^{2-1}} = \dfrac{10}{2^1} = 5$

$S_n = \dfrac{a(1-r^n)}{1-r} = \dfrac{(5)(1-2^2)}{1-2} = \dfrac{(5)(1-4)}{1-2} = \dfrac{(5)(-3)}{-1} = 15$

15. $t_n = 32$
$a = 2$
$n = 5$

Find r and S_n.

$$t_n = ar^{n-1}$$
$$32 = (2)r^{5-1}$$
$$\frac{32}{2} = r^4$$
$$16 = r^4$$
$$r = \sqrt[4]{16} = 16^{\frac{1}{4}} = 2$$

$$S_n = \frac{a(1-r^n)}{1-r} = \frac{(2)(1-2^5)}{1-2} = \frac{(2)(1-32)}{-1}$$
$$= \frac{(2)(-31)}{-1} = 62$$

17. $t_n = 512$
$a = 1$
$n = 10$

Find r and S_n.

$$t_n = ar^{n-1}$$
$$\frac{t_n}{a} = r^{n-1}$$
$$\frac{512}{1} = r^{10-1}$$
$$512 = r^9$$
$$(512)^{\frac{1}{9}} = r$$
$$r = 2$$

$$S_n = \frac{a(1-r^n)}{1-r} = \frac{(1)(1-2^{10})}{1-2} = \frac{(1)(-1{,}023)}{-1} = 1{,}023$$

19. $a = 12$
$n = 5$
$r = 4$

Find t_n and S_n.

$t_n = ar^{n-1} = (12)(4)^{5-1} = 3{,}072$

$$S_n = \frac{a(1-r^n)}{1-r} = \frac{(12)(1-4^5)}{1-4} = \frac{(12)(-1{,}023)}{-3} = 4{,}092$$

EXERCISE 4.7

A.

1. $2^7 = 128$: $\log_2 128 = 7$
3. $144^{0.5} = 12$: $\log_{144} 12 = 0.5$
5. $9^{\frac{1}{3}} = 2.080084$: $\log_9 2.080084 = \frac{1}{3}$

B.

7. $\log_3 243 = 5$: $3^5 = 243$
9. $\log_5 625 = 4$: $5^4 = 625$
11. $\log_9 6{,}561 = 4$: $9^4 = 6{,}561$

EXERCISE 4.8

A.

1. $3^5 = 243$: $\log_3 243 = 5$
3. $6^7 = 279{,}936$: $\log_6 279{,}936 = 7$
5. $2^{-9} = 0.001953125$: $\log_2 0.001953125 = -9$
7. $144^{-2} = 0.000048225$: $\log_{144} 0.000048225 = -2$
9. $3^x = 27$: $\log_3 27 = x$

B.

11. $\ln 15 = 2.708050201$

13. $4^{2x} = 65{,}536$, taking the logarithm

$$2x \times \ln 4 = \ln 65{,}536$$

$$x = \frac{\ln 65{,}536}{\ln 4}$$

$$x = 8$$

15.
$$5^x = 15{,}625$$
$$x\ln 5 = \ln 15{,}625$$
$$x = \frac{\ln 15{,}625}{\ln 5} = 6$$

17. $\ln 65 = 4.17438727$

EXERCISE 5.1

1. Extension Column Total: $21 \times \$3,500 = \$73,500$
   Dollar Value of the Trade Discount: $\$73,500 \times 0.25 = \$18,375$
3. a. $6 \times \$27.50 = \$165$
   b. $10 \times \$456.95 = \$4,569.50$
   c. $4 \times \$350.65 = \$1,402.60$
   d. $\$165.00 + \$4,569.50 + \$1,402.60 = \$6,137.10$
   e. $\$6,137.10 \times 0.33 = \$2,025.24$
   f. $\$6,137.10 - \$2,025.24 = \$4,111.86$
   g. $\$4,111.86 + \$150.00 = \$4,261.86$
5. Net Price: $0.85 \times \$450 = \$382.50$
   NCF: 0.85
7. Trade Discount: $1 - \left(\dfrac{\$850}{\$1,200}\right) = 0.29166$, or 29.2%
   NCF: $1 - 0.291660 = 0.7083$
9. Net Price: $\$4,600 \times 0.711392 = \$3,272.40$: NCF: 0.711392
11. List Price: $\left(\dfrac{\$6,860}{0.7038}\right) = \$9,747.09$: NCF: 0.7038
13. Discount: 0.25: List Price: $\left(\dfrac{\$3,230}{0.75}\right) = \$4,306.67$
15. $(\$6,500 \times 4)(0.40) = \$10,400$

EXERCISE 5.2

1. $\$5,230 \times 0.01 = \$52.30$
   $\$5,230 - \$52.30 = \$5,177.70$
3. \$1,200.00
5. \$3,900.00
7. Value of Payment: $\left(\dfrac{\$1,345}{0.97}\right) = \$1,386.60$
   Balance Due: $\$3,509.12 - \$1,386.60 = \$2,122.52$
9. Amount of Payment: $\$3,000 \times 0.98 = \$2,940$
   Balance Due: $\$3,546 - \$3,000 = \$546$
11. The amount owing is: $\$1,237.76 + (\$3,567 - \$3,567(0.01)) = \$4,769.09$

EXERCISE 5.3

1. Markup: $\$1,795 - \$1,200 = \$595$
   R_{mp}: $\dfrac{\$595}{\$1,795} = 0.3314763$
3. Product Cost: $\$1,250 - 0.3(\$1,250) = \$875$
   Markup: $\$1,250 - \$875 = \$375$

5. Product Cost: \$1,200 – \$850 = \$350

   R_{mp}: $\dfrac{\$850}{\$1{,}200} = 0.7083$, or 70.83%

7. Price: \$575

   R_{mp}: $\left(\dfrac{\$75}{\$575}\right) = 0.1304348$, or 13%

9. Product Selling Price: $\dfrac{\$1{,}200}{0.4} = \$3{,}000$

   Cost: \$3,000 – \$1,200 = \$1,800

11. Markup: \$395 – \$200 = \$195

    R_{mc}: $\dfrac{\$195}{\$200} = 0.975$

13. $R_{mc} = \dfrac{M}{C}$ but $SP = C + M$, therefore, $M = SP - C$.

    $R_{mc} = \dfrac{SP - C}{C}$; $R_{mc} = 0.3$; $SP = \$250$

    Therefore, $0.3 = \dfrac{\$250 - C}{C}$ and $C = \dfrac{\$250}{1.3} = \$192.31$

    $M = SP - C = \$250 - \$192.31 = \$57.69$

15. Product Cost: \$3,200 – \$850 = \$2,350

    R_{mc}: $\left(\dfrac{\$850}{\$2{,}350}\right) = 0.361702127$

17. Markup: \$400 × 0.41 = \$164

    Price: \$400 + \$164 = \$564

19. Product Cost: $\left(\dfrac{\$7{,}200}{0.4}\right) = \$18{,}000$

    Price: \$18,000 + \$7,200 = \$25,200

21. Cost $= \left(\dfrac{\$120}{0.3}\right) = \$400$

    $R_{mp} = \dfrac{\$120}{\$520} = 0.2307692$

EXERCISE 5.4

1. R_{mp}: $\dfrac{\$1{,}795.00 - \$1{,}200.00}{\$1{,}795.00} = 0.331476$

   Markdown Price: (\$1,795)(0.75) = \$1,346.25

3. $C = \$1{,}250 - \$500 = \$750$

   Markdown Price: \$1,250(0.88) = \$1,100

5. Product Cost: \$1,100 – \$875 = \$225

   Markdown Price: \$1,100 × 0.9 = \$990

7. $SP = \dfrac{\text{Markdown Price}}{1 - \text{Markdown }\%} = \dfrac{\$1{,}000}{0.75} = \$1{,}333.33$

$R_{mp} = \dfrac{\$833.33}{\$1{,}333.33} = 0.6249991$

9. Cost: $700(0.9)(0.85) = $535.50
$SP = 1.3 \times \$535.50 = \$696.15$

Sale Price = $696.15 × 0.85 = $591.73
Tom makes: $591.73 – $535.50 = $56.23

11. Markup Rate: $1 - \dfrac{\$2{,}349.25}{\$3{,}195.95} = 0.264897761$, or $\dfrac{\$3{,}195.95 - \$2{,}349.25}{\$3{,}195.95} = 0.2649$

Markdown Rate: $\dfrac{\$250}{\$3{,}195.95} = 0.078224002$

EXERCISE 6.1

1. a. $I = Prt$; $P = \$1{,}000$; $r = 0.1$; $t = 1$
$I = (\$1{,}000)(0.1)(1) = \$100$

b. $I = Prt$; $P = \$1{,}000$; $r = 0.1$; $t = \dfrac{6}{12}$

$I = (\$1{,}000)(0.1)\left(\dfrac{6}{12}\right) = \$50$

c. $I = Prt$; $P = \$1{,}500$; $r = 0.115$; $t = \dfrac{5}{12}$

$I = (\$1{,}500)(0.115)\left(\dfrac{5}{12}\right) = \$71.88$

d. $I = Prt$; $P = \$725$; $r = 0.185$; $t = \dfrac{8}{12}$

$I = (\$725)(0.185)\left(\dfrac{8}{12}\right) = \$89.42$

3. a. May 20 + 30 days = June 20
b. Aug. 10 + 90 days = Nov. 10
c. Aug. 30 + 90 days = Nov. 30

5. Exact Interest and Exact Time: $I = Prt = (\$730)(0.18)\left(\dfrac{92}{365}\right) = \$33.12$

Exact Interest and Approximate Time: $I = Prt = (\$730)(0.18)\left(\dfrac{90}{365}\right) = \$32.40$

Ordinary Interest and Exact Time: $I = Prt = (\$730)(0.18)\left(\dfrac{92}{360}\right) = \$33.58$

Ordinary Interest and Approximate Time: $I = Prt = (\$730)(0.18)\left(\dfrac{90}{360}\right)$
$= \$32.85$

EXERCISE 6.2

1. $S = P(1 + rt)$; $P = \$3{,}500$; $r = 0.165$; $t = \dfrac{8}{12}$

$$S = \$3{,}500\left[1 + (0.165)\left(\frac{8}{12}\right)\right] = \$3{,}885$$

3. a. $S = P(1 + rt)$; $P = \$1{,}900$; $r = 0.17$; $t = \dfrac{180}{365}$

$$S = \$1{,}900\left[1 + (0.17)\left(\frac{180}{365}\right)\right] = \$2{,}059.29$$

b. $258 + 180 - (1 \text{ for leap year}) = 437 - 365 = 72$

The 72nd day from the Day of the Year Table is March 13, 1991.

5. $t = \dfrac{I}{(Pr)}$; $I = 30$; $P = \$500$; $r = 0.1$

$$t = \frac{\$30}{(\$500 \times 0.1)} = 0.6 = 0.6 \times 365 = 219 \text{ days}$$

7. $r = \dfrac{I}{(Pt)}$; $I = \$4.50$; $P = \$500$; $t = \dfrac{1}{12}$

$$r = \frac{\$4.50}{\left[\$500\left(\frac{1}{12}\right)\right]} = 0.108, \text{ or } 10.8\%$$

9. $r = \dfrac{I}{(Pt)}$; $I = \$49.30$; $P = \$1{,}239.14$; $t = \dfrac{92}{365}$

$$r = \frac{\$49.30}{\$1{,}239.14\left(\frac{92}{365}\right)} = 0.1578, \text{ or } 15.78\%, \text{ is the interest rate charged.}$$

EXERCISE 6.3

1. $P = \dfrac{S}{(1 + rt)}$; $S = \$2{,}000$; $r = 0.08$; $t = 3$

$$P = \frac{\$2{,}000}{[1 + (0.08)(3)]} = \$1{,}612.90$$

3. $P = \dfrac{S}{(1 + rt)}$; $S = \$5{,}000$; $r = 0.15$; $t = \dfrac{6}{12} = 0.5$

$$P = \frac{\$5{,}000}{[1 + (0.15)(0.5)]} = \$4{,}651.16$$

5. Find P (the original principal) where $P = S(1 + rt)^{-1}$

$$\text{Loan} = \$1{,}450\left[1 + (0.15)\left(\frac{75}{365}\right)\right]^{-1} = \$1{,}406.64$$

7. $P = \dfrac{S}{[1 + rt]}$

$S = \$5{,}750$

$r = 0.16$

$t = \dfrac{125}{365}$

$$P = \frac{\$5{,}750}{\left[1 + (0.16)\left(\frac{125}{365}\right)\right]} = \$5{,}451.30$$

EXERCISE 6.4

1. a. Old Debt = \$6,000
Discount = 4 months, i.e., four months early

X = required payment, where $X = \dfrac{S}{(1 + rt)}$

$S = \$6{,}000$

$r = 0.15$

$t = \dfrac{4}{12}$

$$X = \frac{\$6{,}000}{\left[1 + (0.15)\left(\frac{4}{12}\right)\right]} = \$5{,}714.29$$

b. Old Debt = \$6,000
Discount = 2 months, i.e., two months early

X = required payment, where $X = \dfrac{S}{(1 + rt)}$

$S = \$6{,}000$

$r = 0.15$

$t = \dfrac{2}{12}$

$$X = \frac{\$6{,}000}{\left[1 + (0.15)\left(\frac{2}{12}\right)\right]} = \$5{,}853.66$$

3. New Debt at the focal point — Old Debt at the focal point

$$X + \frac{X}{\left[1 + (0.16)\left(\frac{6}{12}\right)\right]} = \$1{,}200\left[1 + (0.16)\left(\frac{2}{12}\right)\right] + \frac{\$1{,}800}{\left[1 + (0.16)\left(\frac{4}{12}\right)\right]}$$

$$X + 0.9259259X = \$1{,}232 + \$1{,}708.86$$
$$1.9259259X = \$2{,}940.86$$
$$X = \$1{,}526.99$$

5. New Debt at the focal point (one year from now)

$$\frac{X}{\left[1 + (0.15)\left(\frac{6}{12}\right)\right]} + X\left[1 + (0.15)\left(\frac{4}{12}\right)\right] = 0.9302326X + 1.05X$$

Old Debt at the focal point (one year from now)

$$\$6{,}000\left[1 + (0.15)\left(\frac{14}{12}\right)\right] + \$4{,}500\left[1 + (0.16)\left(\frac{12}{12}\right)\right] = \$7{,}050 + \$5{,}220$$

Set new debt equal to old debt at the focal point.

New Debt — Old Debt

$$0.9302326X + 1.05X = \$7{,}050 + \$5{,}220$$
$$1.9802326X = \$12{,}270$$
$$X = \$6{,}196.24$$

The size of the two equal payments will be \$6,196.24

EXERCISE 6.5

1.

	$	$ 1,200.00
Original Debt		
1st Payment	200.00	
Interest (May 1–July 1, 61 days @ 0.24)	48.13	
Amount to Principal	151.87	
Balance		1,048.13
2nd Payment	500.00	
Interest (July 1–Sept 5, 66 days @ 0.24)	45.49	
Amount to Principal	454.51	
Balance		593.62
Interest (Sept 5–Oct 31, 56 days @ 0.24)	21.86	
Balance 10/31/90		$ 615.48

3.

Original Debt	$	$ 4,230.00
1st Payment	3,500.00	
Interest (Jan 20–Feb 2, 13 days @ 0.17)	25.61	
Amount to Principal	3,474.39	
Balance		755.61
2nd Payment	500.00	
Interest (Feb 2–Aug 5, 184 days @ 0.17)	64.75	
Amount to Principal	435.25	
Balance on August 5		320.36

5.

Original Debt	$	200.00
1st Payment	50.00	
Interest (Mar. 9–July 7,120 days @ 0.14)	9.21	
Amount to Principal	40.79	
Balance after Payment		159.21
2nd Payment	100.00	
Interest (July 7–Aug. 5, 29 days @ 0.14)	1.77	
Amount to Principal	98.23	
Balance After 2nd Payment		60.98
Interest (Aug 5–Sept 30, 56 days)		1.31
Balance on April 4		$ 62.29

7.

Original Debt	$	$ 4,200.00
1st Payment	200.00	
Interest (June 9–Aug. 9, 61 days @ 0.24)	168.46	
Amount to Principal	31.54	
Balance after Payment		4,168.46
2nd Payment	3,500.00	
Interest (Aug 9–Sept 6, 28 days @ 0.24)	76.75	
Amount to Principal	3,423.25	
Balance after 2nd Payment		745.21
Interest (Sept 6–Oct 31, 55 days)		26.95
Balance on April 4		$ 772.16

9.

Original Debt	$	$ 9,000.00
1st Payment, Oct. 2 (31 days)	1,000.00	
Deduct: Interest on $9,000 for 31 days	91.73	
Amount to Principal	908.27	
Balance after Payment		8,091.73
2nd Payment, Nov. 7 (36 days)	3,500.00	
Deduct: Interest	95.77	
Amount to Principal	3,404.23	
Balance after 2nd Payment		4,687.50
3rd Payment, Nov. 29 (22 days)	1,500.00	
Deduct: Interest	33.90	
Amount to Principal	1,466.10	
Balance after 3rd Payment		3,221.40
Add: Interest (21 days), Nov. 29 to Dec. 20		22.24
Final Payment must be:		$ 3,243.64

EXERCISE 6.6

1.

Sept. 1 to Sept. 7 (6 days):	$I = \$50{,}000(0.1625)\left(\frac{6}{365}\right)$	= $133.56
Sept. 7 to Sept. 14 (7 days):	$I = 50{,}000(0.165)\left(\frac{7}{365}\right)$	= $158.22
Sept. 14 to Sept. 21 (7 days):	$I = 50{,}000(0.17)\left(\frac{7}{365}\right)$	= $163.01
Sept. 21 to Sept. 28 (7 days):	$I = 50{,}000(0.1675)\left(\frac{7}{365}\right)$	= $160.62
Sept. 28 to Sept. 30 (2 days):	$I = 50{,}000(0.17)\left(\frac{2}{365}\right)$	= $ 46.58
Interest Due on September 30 is:		$661.99

3. a. August 15, 1991
b. $630
c. 44 days — August 15 to July 2 (3 days of grace to get August 15.)

5. $S = \$630 + \$630(0.1)\left(\frac{125}{365}\right) = \$651.58$ (Time includes 3 days of grace.)

$$\text{Proceeds} = \frac{\$651.58}{\left[1 + (0.16)\left(\frac{44}{365}\right)\right]} = \$639.25$$

Simple Discount = $651.58 – $639.25 = $12.33

7. $S = \$5{,}000$
$i = 0.15$
$t = \dfrac{6}{12}$

$$P = \frac{\$5{,}000}{\left[1 + (0.15)\dfrac{6}{12}\right]} = \$4{,}651.16$$

Simple Discount = \$5,000.00 – \$4,651.16 = \$348.84

EXERCISE 7.1

For problems 1 to 10, use formula $S = P(1 + i)^n$.

1. $P = \$450$
$i = 0.15$
$n = 2$

$$S = \$450(1 + 0.15)^2 = \$595.13$$

3. $P = \$1{,}200$
$i = \dfrac{0.14}{12} = 0.0116666667$
$n = 156$

$$S = \$1{,}200(1.0116666667)^{156} = \$7{,}328.62$$

5. $P = \$4{,}600$
$i = \dfrac{0.13}{2} = 0.065$
$n = 22$

$$S = \$4{,}600(1.065)^{22} = \$18{,}384.39$$

7. $P = \$12{,}670$
$i = \dfrac{0.148}{4} = 0.037$
$n = 28$

$$S = \$12{,}670(1.037)^{28} = \$35{,}041.43$$

9. $P = \$14{,}450$

$i = \dfrac{0.175}{4} = 0.04375$

$n = 16$

$S = \$14{,}450(1.04375)^{16} = \$28{,}668.94$

11. a. $P = \$12{,}000$

$i = \dfrac{0.15}{2} = 0.075$

$n = 5$

$S = \$12{,}000(1.075)^5 = \$17{,}227.55$

$S - P = \$5{,}227.55$

b. $P = \$10{,}000$

$i = \dfrac{0.11}{12} = 0.0091666$

$n = 4$

$S = \$10{,}000(0.009166)^4 = \$10{,}371.74$

$S - P = \$371.74$

c. $P = \$1{,}000$

$i = \dfrac{0.12}{4} = 0.03$

$n = 3$

$S = \$1{,}000(1.03)^3 = \$1{,}092.73$

$S - P = \$92.73$

13. $P = \$15{,}000$

$i = \dfrac{0.0575}{2} = 0.02875$

$n = 3$

$S = \$15{,}000(1.02875)^3 = \$16{,}331.30$

$S - P = \$1{,}331.31$

15. $i = \dfrac{0.12}{2}$; $S = \$10{,}000(1 + 0.06)^6 = \$14{,}185.19$

$i = \dfrac{0.11}{2}$; $S = \$14{,}185.19(1 + 0.055)^4 = \$17{,}572.96$

17. STEP 1: Calculate amount outstanding at month six.

$P = \$5{,}000$

$i = \dfrac{0.145}{2} = 0.0725$

$n = 1$

$S = \$5{,}000(1.0725) = \$5{,}362.50$

$S - \text{Payment} = \$5{,}362.50 - \$1{,}000.00 = \$4{,}362.50$

STEP 2: Calculate amount outstanding at one year.

$P = \$4{,}362.50$

$i = 0.0725$

$n = 1$

$S = \$4{,}362.50(1.0725) = \$4{,}678.78$

$S - \text{Payment} = \$4{,}678.78 - \$1{,}000.00 = \$3{,}678.78$

STEP 3: Calculate final payment.

$P = \$3{,}678.78$

$i = 0.0725$

$n = 2$

$S = \$3{,}678.78(1.0725)^2 = \$4{,}231.54$

The final payment must be: \$4,231.54.

EXERCISE 7.2

For problems 1 to 10, use formula $P = S(1 + i)^{-n}$.

1. $S = \$1{,}350$
$i = 0.124$
$n = 4$

$P = \$1{,}350(1.124)^{-4} = \$845.80$

3. $S = \$2{,}200$

$i = \dfrac{0.15}{12} = 0.0125$

$n = 180$

$P = \$2{,}200(1.0125)^{-180} = \$235.13$

5. $S = \$5{,}600$

$i = \dfrac{0.14}{2} = 0.07$

$n = 36$

$P = \$5{,}600(1.07)^{-36} = \$490.20$

7. $S = \$17{,}670$

$i = \dfrac{0.148}{4} = 0.037$

$n = 8$

$P = \$17{,}670(1.037)^{-8} = \$13{,}213.15$

9. $S = \$11{,}450$

$i = \dfrac{0.155}{4} = 0.03875$

$n = 28$

$P = \$11{,}450(1.03875)^{-28} = \$3{,}949.08$

11. $S = \$1{,}500$

$i = \dfrac{0.12}{12} = 0.01$

$n = 120$

$P = \$1{,}500(1.01)^{-120} = \$454.49$

$S - P = \$1{,}045.51$ compound discount

13. $S = \$2{,}800$

$i = \dfrac{0.18}{4} = 0.045$

$n = 20$

$P = \$2{,}800(1.045)^{-20} = \$1{,}161.00$

$S - P = \$1{,}639.00$ compound discount

15. $S = \$200{,}000$

$i = 0.15$

$n = 20$

$P = \$200{,}000(1.15)^{-20} = \$12{,}220.06$

EXERCISE 7.3

1. Non-Interest Bearing

$S = \$2{,}350$
$i = 0.15$
$n = 2$

$P = \$2{,}350(1.15)^{-2} = \$1{,}776.94$

$S - P = \$573.06$

3. Non-Interest Bearing

$S = \$3{,}400$
$i = \dfrac{0.17}{12} = 0.01416$
$n = 81$

$P = \$3{,}400(1.01416)^{-81} = \$1{,}087.99$

$S - P = \$2{,}312.01$

5. Maturity Value:

$P = \$5{,}600$
$i = \dfrac{0.14}{2} = 0.07$
$n = 36$

$S = \$5{,}600(1.07)^{36} = \$63{,}974.08$

Discount:

$S = \$63{,}974.08$
$i = 0.18$
$n = 8$

$P = \$63{,}974.08(1.18)^{-8} = \$17{,}019.55$

$S - P = \$46{,}954.53$

7. Non-Interest Bearing: Find the Discount:

$S = \$25{,}300$
$i = \dfrac{0.168}{2} = 0.084$
$n = 3$

$P = \$25{,}300(1.084)^{-3} = \$19{,}862.44$

$S - P = \$5{,}437.56$

9. Maturity Value:

$P = \$13{,}450$

$i = \dfrac{0.155}{4} = 0.03875$

$n = 28$

$S = \$13{,}450(1.03875)^{28} = \$38{,}997.01$

Discount:

$S = \$38{,}997.01$

$i = \dfrac{0.126}{4} = 0.0315$

$n = 9$

$P = \$38{,}997.01(1.0315)^{-9} = \$29{,}499.06$

$S - P = \$9{,}497.95$

11. Discount (Non-Interest Bearing):

$S = \$2{,}100$

$i = \dfrac{0.09}{12} = 0.0075$

$n = 3$

$P = \$2{,}100(1.0075)^{-3} = \$2{,}053.45$

$S - P = \$46.55$

13. STEP 1: Maturity Value.

$P = \$4{,}000$

$i = \dfrac{0.15}{2} = 0.075$

$n = 4$

$$S = \$4{,}000\left[1 + \left(\frac{0.15}{2}\right)\right]^{20} = \$16{,}991.40$$

STEP 2: Find the proceeds.

$P = \$16{,}991.40$

$i = \dfrac{0.15}{4} = 0.0375$

$n = 4$

$$P = \$16{,}991.40\left[1 + \left(\frac{0.15}{4}\right)\right]^{-12} = \$10{,}923.76$$

Compound Discount = \$16,991.40 – \$10,923.76 = \$6,067.64

15. Maturity Value:

$P = 1{,}700$

$i = \dfrac{0.12}{2} = 0.06$

$n = 4$

$S = \$1{,}700(1.06)^4 = \$2{,}146.21$

Discount:

$S = \$2{,}146.21$

$i = \dfrac{0.14}{4} = 0.035$

$n = 2$

$P = \$2{,}146.21(1.035)^{-2} = \$2{,}003.51$

Compound Discount = \$2,146.21 – \$2,003.51 = \$142.70

EXERCISE 7.4

1. a.

$$(1 + i)^4 = 1.15$$
$$1 + i = (1.15)^{0.25}$$
$$1 + i = 1.03558076$$
$$i = 0.03558076$$

Annual Rate = 0.03558076(4) = 0.142232305

b.

$$(1 + i)^{12} = \left[1 + \left(\frac{0.18}{365}\right)\right]^{365}$$
$$1 + i = \left[1 + \left(\frac{0.18}{365}\right)\right]^{\frac{365}{12}}$$
$$1 + i = 1.015109311$$
$$i = 0.015109311$$

Annual Rate = 0.015109311(12) = 0.181311733

c.

$$(1 + i) = \left[1 + \left(\frac{0.10}{12}\right)\right]^{12} = 1.104713067$$

$i = 0.104713067$, the annual rate.

d.

$$(1 + i)^2 = \left[1 + \left(\frac{0.18}{365}\right)\right]^{365}$$
$$1 + i = \left[1 + \left(\frac{0.18}{365}\right)\right]^{\frac{365}{2}} = 1.094150009$$
$$i = 0.094150009$$

Annual Rate = 0.094150009(2) = 0.188300018

e. $$(1+i)^2 = \left[1+\left(\frac{0.15}{12}\right)\right]^{12}$$

$$1+i = \left[1+\left(\frac{0.15}{12}\right)\right]^{\frac{12}{2}} = 1.077383181$$

$$i = 0.077383181$$

$$\text{Annual Rate} = (0.077383181)2 = 0.154766361$$

3. Nominal Rate = 15%

5. To find the rate that makes the two equivalent:

$$(1+i)^{12} = \left[1+\left(\frac{0.185}{2}\right)\right]^2$$

$$i = 0.0148540,$$

or 0.178248 (0.0148540 × 12), or 17.8248%, which compounded monthly is the same as 18.5% compounded semiannually.

7. Effective or Real Rate $= \left[1+\left(\frac{0.065}{4}\right)\right]^{m=4} - 1 = 0.066601608$

EXERCISE 7.5

1. $P = \$2,150$
   $i = 0.192$
   $n = 3.5$

   $S = \$2,150(1+0.192)^{3.5} = \$3,975.62$

3. $P = \$12,300$
   $i = \frac{0.16}{12} = 0.01333$
   $n = 19.2$

   $S = \$12,300(1.01333)^{19.2} = \$15,861.70$

5. $P = \$5,600$
   $i = \frac{0.13}{2} = 0.065$
   $n = 12.33$

   $S = \$5,600(1.065)^{12.3\dot{3}} = \$12,175.87$

7. $P = \$17,670$
   $i = \frac{0.178}{4} = 0.0445$
   $n = 9.6667$

   $S = \$17,670(1.0445)^{9.6667} = \$26,916.47$

9. $P = \$11{,}450$

$i = \dfrac{0.145}{4} = 0.03625$

$n = 28.6667$

$S = \$11{,}450(1.03625)^{28.6667} = \$31{,}777.70$

11. $\$2{,}550[1 + (\dfrac{0.122}{2})]^{20.5} = \$8{,}584.31$

13. $\$6{,}730(1 + 0.15)^{-1.5} = \$5{,}457.18$
Compound Discount = \$6,730 – \$5,457.18 = \$1,272.82

EXERCISE 7.6

For problems 1 to 10, use formula $n = \dfrac{\ln\left[\dfrac{S}{P}\right]}{\ln(1+i)}$.

1.

$$n = \frac{\ln\left[\dfrac{5{,}150}{2{,}150}\right]}{\ln(1.192)},\ i = 0.192$$

$n = 4.974721005$ years

3.

$$n = \frac{\ln\left[\dfrac{32{,}300}{12{,}300}\right]}{\ln(1.0133)},\ i = \frac{0.16}{12}$$

n = 72.89176594, or 6.074 years

5.

$$n = \frac{\ln\left[\dfrac{35{,}900}{13{,}500}\right]}{\ln(1.065)},\ i = \frac{0.13}{2}$$

$n = 29.50340013$, or 14.752 years

7.

$$n = \frac{\ln\left[\dfrac{77{,}670}{17{,}670}\right]}{\ln(1.0445)},\ i = \frac{0.178}{4}$$

$n = 34.00685667$, or 8.502 years

9.

$$n = \frac{\ln\left[\dfrac{31{,}350}{11{,}450}\right]}{\ln(1.03625)},\ i = \frac{0.145}{4}$$

$n = 28.286128$, or 7.072 years

11.

$$n = \frac{\ln\left[\dfrac{10{,}000}{6{,}000}\right]}{\ln\left[1 + \left(\dfrac{0.105}{4}\right)\right]}$$

$n = 19.714$, or 4.929 years

13.

$$n = \frac{\ln\left[\dfrac{3}{1}\right]}{\ln\left[1 + \left(\dfrac{0.08}{12}\right)\right]}$$

$n = 165.34$ periods, or 13.778 years

15.

$$n = \frac{\ln[2]}{\ln\left[1 + \left(\dfrac{0.07}{12}\right)\right]}$$

$n = 119.17$ or 9.931 years, therefore the claim is incorrect.

EXERCISE 7.7

For problems 1 to 10, use formula $i = \left(\dfrac{S}{P}\right)^{\frac{1}{n}} - 1$

1. $S = \$4{,}300$
$P = \$2{,}150$
$n = 4$

$$i = \left(\frac{\$4{,}300}{\$2{,}150}\right)^{\frac{1}{4}} - 1$$

$i = 0.189207115$

Nominal Rate $= 0.189207115$

3. $S = \$22{,}300$
$P = \$12{,}300$
$n = 78$

$$i = \left(\frac{\$22{,}300}{\$12{,}300}\right)^{\frac{1}{78}} - 1$$

$i = 0.007657211$

Nominal Rate $= 0.007657211(12) = 0.091886537$

5. $S = \$10{,}900$
$P = \$5{,}600$
$n = 10$

$$i = \left(\frac{\$10{,}900}{\$5{,}600}\right)^{\frac{1}{10}} - 1$$

$i = 0.068867438$
Nominal Rate $= 0.068867438(2) = 0.137734876$

7. $S = \$25{,}670$
$P = \$417{,}670$
$n = 12.3333$
$i = \left(\dfrac{\$25{,}670}{\$17{,}670}\right)^{\frac{1}{12.3333}} - 1$
$i = 0.030743216$
Nominal Rate = 0.030743216(4) = 0.122972866

9. $S = \$30{,}500$
$P = \$10{,}550$
$n = 56$
$i = \left(\dfrac{\$30{,}500}{\$10{,}550}\right)^{\frac{1}{56}} - 1$
$i = 0.019137985$
Nominal Rate = 0.019137985(4) = 0.076551941

11. $S = \$1{,}000$
$P = \$750$
$n = 2$ (annually)
$n = 24$ (monthly)
$i = \left(\dfrac{\$1{,}000}{\$750}\right)^{\frac{1}{2}} - 1 = 0.1547$ (annually)
$i = \left(\dfrac{\$1{,}000}{\$750}\right)^{\frac{1}{24}} - 1 = 0.01205882$ (monthly)
Nominal Rate = 0.01547 (annually)
Nominal Rate = 0.01205882(12) = 0.14471 (monthly)

13. $S = 2$
$P = 1$
$n = \dfrac{1}{6}$
$i = \left(\dfrac{2}{1}\right)^{\frac{1}{6}} - 1 = 0.122462048$ semiannually, or 24.49% annually

EXERCISE 7.8

1. **a.** $\$6{,}000(1.01)^{6} = \$6{,}369.12$
b. $\$6{,}000(1.01)^{-2} = \$5{,}881.78$
c. $\$6{,}000(1.01)^{22} = \$7{,}468.30$
d. $\$6{,}000(1.01)^{-7} = \$5{,}596.31$

3. Option 1:
$15,000 is today's cash payment.

Option 2:

$$\$7{,}000(1.015)^{-12} + \$7{,}000(1.015)^{-24} + \$7{,}000(1.015)^{-36}$$
$$= \$5{,}854.71 + \$4{,}896.81 + \$4{,}095.63$$
$$= \$14{,}847.15$$

Option 2 is better by \$152.85.

5. Old Debt to Focal Date

$$\$3{,}000\left[1 + \left(\frac{0.18}{12}\right)\right]^{24} + \$5{,}000 = \$9{,}288.51$$

New Debt to Focal Date

$$X + X\left[1 + \left(\frac{0.18}{12}\right)\right]^{-36} = 1.585088X$$

Set New Debt Equal to Old Debt

$$1.585088X = \$9{,}288.51$$
$$X = \frac{\$9{,}288.51}{1.585088}$$
$$X = \$5{,}859.93$$

7. $$\$3{,}000\left[1 + \left(\frac{0.18}{12}\right)\right]^{24} + \$5{,}000 = \$9{,}288.51$$

EXERCISE 8.1

For problems 1 to 10, use formulas:

Amount:

$$S_n = \frac{R[(1+i)^n - 1]}{i}$$

Present Value:

$$A_n = \frac{R[1 - (1+i)^{-n}]}{i}$$

1. $R = \$1{,}350$
   $i = 0.124$
   $n = 4$

$$S_n = \frac{\$1{,}350[(1.124)^4 - 1]}{0.124}$$

$$S_n = \$6{,}490.00$$

$$A_n = \frac{\$1{,}350[1 - (1.124)^{-4}]}{0.124}$$

$$A_n = \$4{,}066.12$$

3. $R = \$200$

$i = \dfrac{0.15}{12} = 0.0125$

$n = 180$

$$S_n = \frac{\$200[1.0125)^{180} - 1]}{0.0125}$$

$S_n = \$133{,}701.35$

$$A_n = \frac{\$200[1 - (1.0125)^{-180}]}{0.0125}$$

$A_n = \$14{,}289.93$

5. $R = \$450$

$i = \dfrac{0.14}{2} = 0.07$

$n = 36$

$$S_n = \frac{\$450[(1.07)^{36} - 1]}{0.07}$$

$S_n = \$67{,}011.06$

$$A_n = \frac{\$450[1 - (1.07)^{-36}]}{0.07}$$

$A_n = \$5{,}865.84$

7. $R = \$670$

$i = \dfrac{0.148}{4} = 0.037$

$n = 8$

$$S_n = \frac{\$670[(1.037)^{8} - 1]}{0.037}$$

$S_n = \$6{,}107.93$

$$A_n = \frac{\$670[1 - (1.037)^{-8}]}{0.037}$$

$A_n = \$4{,}567.35$

9. $R = \$1{,}450$

$i = \dfrac{0.155}{4} = 0.03875$

$n = 28$

$$S_n = \frac{\$1{,}450[(1.03875)^{28} - 1]}{0.03875}$$

$S_n = \$71{,}074.55$

$$A_n = \frac{\$1{,}450[1 - (1.03875)^{-28}]}{0.03875}$$

$$A_n = \$24{,}513.49$$

11. $R = \$100$

$i = \dfrac{0.06}{12} = 0.005$

$n = 120$

$$S_n = \frac{\$100[(1 + 0.005)^{120} - 1]}{0.005}$$

$$S_n = \$16{,}387.93$$

13. $R = \$3{,}500$

$i = \dfrac{0.06}{2} = 0.03$

$n = 8$

$$S_n = \frac{\$3{,}500[(1.03)^{8} - 1]}{0.03}$$

$$S_n = \$31{,}123.18$$

15. $R = \$500$

$i = \dfrac{0.08}{12} = 0.04$

$n = 180$

$$A_n = \frac{\$500[1 - (1 + 0.00667)^{-180}]}{0.00667}$$

$$A_n = \$52{,}320.30$$

EXERCISE 8.2

1. Option 1

$R = \$100$

$i = \dfrac{0.18}{12} = 0.015$

$n = 12$

$$A_n = \frac{\$100[1 - (1.015)^{-12}]}{0.015}$$

$$A_n = \$1{,}090.75$$

$\$100 + \$1{,}090.75 = \$1{,}190.75$

Option 2

$R = \$50$

$i = \dfrac{0.18}{12} = 0.015$

$n = 24$

$$A_n = \frac{\$50[1 - (1.015)^{-24}]}{0.015}$$

$A_n = \$1{,}001.52$

$\$125 + \$1{,}001.52 = \$1{,}126.52$

Option 2 is a better deal and is $64.23 less.

3. Al's: $100 × 12 = $1,200 – $1,090.75 = $109.25
Ace's: $50 × 24 = $1,200 – $1,001.52 = $198.48

5. $$\text{Cash Price} = \frac{\$100[1 - (1 + 0.0133)^{-24}]}{0.0133} + \$200$$

Cash Price = $2,242.35

7. ($850 × 240) – $88,080.93 = $115,919.07

EXERCISE 8.3

Finding R given Present Value

$$R = \frac{A_n}{\dfrac{[1 - (1 + i)^{-n}]}{i}}$$

or

Finding R given Amount

$$R = \frac{S_n}{\dfrac{[(1 + i)^n - 1]}{i}}$$

1. R = unknown
$A_n = \$2{,}450$
$S_n = \$3{,}345$
$n = 4$
$i = 0.114$

$$A_n : R = \frac{\$2{,}450}{\dfrac{[1 - (1.114)^{-4}]}{0.114}}$$

$R = \$796.45$

$$S_n : R = \frac{\$3{,}345}{\dfrac{[(1.114)^{4} - 1]}{0.114}}$$

$R = \$706.07$

3. $R =$ unknown
$A_n = \$34{,}400$
$S_n = \$34{,}400$
$n = 180$
$i = \dfrac{0.14}{12} = 0.0116667$

$$A_n : R = \frac{\$34{,}400}{\dfrac{[1 - (1.0116667)^{-180}]}{0.0116667}}$$

$R = \$458.12$

$$S_n : R = \frac{\$34{,}400}{\dfrac{[(1.0116667)^{180} - 1]}{0.0116667}}$$

$R = \$56.79$

5. $R =$ unknown
$A_n = \$89{,}500$
$S_n = \$90{,}000$
$n = 36$
$i = \dfrac{0.13}{2} = 0.065$

$$A_n : R = \frac{\$89{,}500}{\dfrac{[1 - (1.065)^{-36}]}{0.065}}$$

$R = \$6{,}489.94$

$$S_n : R = \frac{\$90{,}000}{\dfrac{[(1.065)^{36} - 1]}{0.065}}$$

$R = \$676.20$

7. R = unknown
A_n = \$4,500
S_n = \$10,000
$n = 8$

$$i = \frac{0.138}{4} = 0.0345$$

$$A_n : R = \frac{\$4{,}500}{\dfrac{[1 - (1.0345)^{-8}]}{0.0345}}$$

R = \$653.28

$$S_n : R = \frac{\$10{,}000}{\dfrac{[(1.0345)^{8} - 1]}{0.0345}}$$

R = \$1,106.73

9. R = unknown
A_n = \$1,450
S_n = \$3,450
$n = 28$

$$i = \frac{0.165}{12} = 0.04125$$

$$A_n : R = \frac{\$1{,}450}{\dfrac{[1 - (1.04125)^{-28}]}{0.04125}}$$

R = \$88.28

$$S_n : R = \frac{\$3{,}450}{\dfrac{[(1.04125)^{28} - 1]}{0.04125}}$$

R = \$67.73

11. S_n = \$20,000
$n = 30$

$$i = \frac{0.09}{2} = 0.045$$

$$R = \frac{\$20{,}000}{\dfrac{[(1.045)^{30} - 1]}{0.045}}$$

R = \$327.83

13. $R = \$250$

$$i = \frac{0.18}{12} = 0.015$$

$n = 72$

$$A_n = \frac{\$250[1 - (1.015)^{-72}]}{0.015} = \$10{,}961.17$$

15. Total Payments – Loan = (\$365.14 × 36) – \$10,100 = \$3,045.04

EXERCISE 8.4

For problems 1 to 10, use formulas:

$$n = \frac{\ln\left[1 + \frac{S_n}{R}(i)\right]}{\ln(1 + i)}$$

$$n = \frac{-\ln\left[1 - \frac{A_n}{R}(i)\right]}{\ln(1 + i)}$$

1. $S_n = \$3{,}345$

$A_n = \$2{,}450$

$R = \$500$

$i = 0.114$

$n = ?$

$$n = \frac{\ln\left[1 + \frac{\$3{,}345}{\$500}(0.114)\right]}{\ln(1.114)}$$

$n = 5.25$ years

$$n = \frac{-\ln\left[1 - \frac{\$2{,}450}{\$500}(0.114)\right]}{\ln(1.114)}$$

$n = 7.58$ years

3. $S_n = \$34{,}400$

$A_n = \$34{,}400$

$R = \$1{,}350$

$$i = \frac{0.14}{12} = 0.011667$$

$n = ?$

$$n = \frac{\ln\left[1 + \frac{\$34{,}400}{\$1{,}350}(0.011667)\right]}{\ln(1.011667)}$$

$n = 22.439$ months, or 1.87 years

$$n = \frac{-\ln\left[1 - \frac{\$34{,}400}{\$1{,}350}(0.011667)\right]}{\ln(1.011667)}$$

$n = 30.42$ months, or 2.535 years

5. $S_n = \$90{,}000$
   $A_n = \$89{,}500$
   $R = \$4{,}500$
   $i = \frac{0.13}{2} = 0.065$
   $n = ?$

$$n = \frac{\ln\left[1 + \frac{\$90{,}000}{\$4{,}500}(0.065)\right]}{\ln(1.065)}$$

$n = 13.226$ semiannual periods, or 6.613 years

$$n = \frac{-\ln\left[1 - \frac{\$45{,}000}{\$4{,}500}(0.065)\right]}{\ln(1.065)}$$

$n = 17.0016$ semiannual periods, or 8.501 years

7. $S_n = \$10{,}000$
   $A_n = \$4{,}500$
   $R = \$200$
   $i = \frac{0.138}{4} = 0.0345$
   $n = ?$

$$n = \frac{\ln\left[1 + \frac{\$10{,}000}{\$200}(0.0345)\right]}{\ln(1.0345)}$$

$n = 29.556$ quarters, or 7.389 years

$$n = \frac{-\ln\left[1 - \frac{\$4{,}500}{\$200}(0.0345)\right]}{\ln(1.0345)}$$

$n = 44.142$ quarters, or 11.036 years

9. $S_n = \$3{,}450$
$A_n = \$550$
$R = \$50$
$i = \dfrac{0.165}{4} = 0.04125$
$n = ?$

$$n = \frac{\ln\left[1 + \dfrac{\$3{,}450}{\$50}(0.04125)\right]}{\ln(1.04125)}$$

$n = 33.326$ quarters, or 8.3315 years

$$n = \frac{-\ln\left[1 - \dfrac{\$550}{\$50}(0.04125)\right]}{\ln(1.04125)}$$

n = 14.959 quarters, or 3.740 years

11. $R = \$1{,}000$
$i = \dfrac{0.08}{12} = 0.00\dot{6}$
$S_n = \$60{,}000$

$$n = \frac{\ln\left[1 + \dfrac{\$60{,}000}{\$1{,}000}(0.00\dot{6})\right]}{\ln(1.0066)}$$

$n = 50.639$ months, or 4.22 years

13. Part 1: Find R.

$A_n = \$85{,}000$
$R = ?$
$i = \dfrac{0.12}{12} = 0.01$
$n = 300$

$$R = \frac{A_n}{\dfrac{[1 - (1 + i)^{-n}]}{i}}$$

$$R = \frac{\$85{,}000}{\dfrac{[1 - (1.01)^{-300}]}{0.01}}$$

$R = \$895.24$

Part 2: Find n using the new R.

$A_n = \$85{,}000$

$i = \frac{0.12}{12} = 0.01$

$R = \$895.24 + \$100.00 = \$995.24$

$n = ?$

$$n = \frac{-\ln\left[1 - \frac{\$85{,}000}{\$995.24}(0.01)\right]}{\ln(1.01)}$$

$n = 193.42$, or 16.118 years

EXERCISE 8.5

$$\text{STEP 1: } R = \frac{A_n}{\frac{[1-(1+i)^{-n}]}{i}}$$

Find the present value of the remaining payments using:

$$\text{STEP 2: } A_n = \frac{R[1-(1+i)^{-n}]}{i}$$

1. $A_n = \$24{,}450$
   $i = 0.12$
   $n = 5$
   $R = ?$

   $$\text{STEP 1: } R = \frac{\$24{,}450}{\frac{[1-(1.12)^{-5}]}{0.12}} = \$6{,}782.67$$

   The outstanding balance is found by finding the P.V. of the remaining payments. In this problem the number of remaining payments are $(5 - 4 = 1)$; therefore the outstanding balance is:

   $$\text{STEP 2: } A_n = \frac{\$6{,}782.67[1-(1.12)^{-1}]}{0.12} = \$6{,}055.96$$

3. $A_n = \$60{,}400$
   $i = \frac{0.18}{12} = 0.015$
   $n = 240$

   $R = ?$

$$\text{STEP 1: } R = \frac{\$60{,}400}{\frac{[1-(1.015)^{-240}]}{0.015}} = \$932.16$$

The outstanding balance is found by finding the P.V. of the remaining payments. In this problem the number of remaining payments are (240 – 150 = 90); therefore the outstanding balance is:

$$\text{STEP 2: } A_n = \frac{\$932.16[1-(1.015)^{-90}]}{0.015} = \$45{,}871.47$$

5. $A_n = \$50{,}000$

   $i = \dfrac{0.156}{2} = 0.078$

   $n = 20$

   $R = ?$

$$\text{STEP 1: } R = \frac{\$50{,}000}{\frac{[1-(1.078)^{-20}]}{0.078}} = \$5{,}017.05$$

The outstanding balance is found by finding the P.V. of the remaining payments. In this problem the number of remaining payments are (20 – 5 = 15); therefore the outstanding balance is:

$$\text{STEP 2: } A_n = \frac{\$5{,}017.05[1-(1.078)^{-15}]}{0.078} = \$43{,}472.79$$

7. $A_n = \$30{,}000$

   $i = \dfrac{0.16}{4} = 0.04$

   $n = 8$

   $R = ?$

$$\text{STEP 1: } R = \frac{\$30{,}000}{\frac{[1-(1.04)^{-8}]}{0.04}} = \$4{,}455.83$$

The outstanding balance is found by finding the P.V. of the remaining payments. In this problem the number of remaining payments are (8 – 2 = 6); therefore the outstanding balance is:

$$\text{STEP 2: } A_n = \frac{\$4{,}455.83[1-(1.04)^{-6}]}{0.04} = \$23{,}358.10$$

9. $A_n = \$16{,}450$

$i = \dfrac{0.168}{4} = 0.042$

$n = 40$

$R = ?$

STEP 1: $R = \dfrac{\$16{,}450}{\dfrac{[1 - (1.042)^{-40}]}{0.042}} = \$856.01$

The outstanding balance is found by finding the P.V. of the remaining payments. In this problem the number of remaining payments are (40 – 30 = 10); therefore the outstanding balance is:

STEP 2: $A_n = \dfrac{\$856.01[1 - (1.042)^{-10}]}{0.042} = \$6{,}874.38$

11. $A_n = \$75{,}000$

$i = \dfrac{0.16}{4} = 0.04$

$n = 40$

$R = ?$

STEP 1: $R = \dfrac{\$75{,}000}{\dfrac{[1 - (1.04)^{-40}]}{0.04}} = \$3{,}789.26$

The outstanding balance is found by finding the P.V. of the remaining payments, that is, (40 – 24 = 16); therefore the outstanding balance is:

STEP 2: $A_n = \dfrac{\$3{,}789.26[1 - (1.04)^{-16}]}{0.04} = \$44{,}153.60$

13. $S_n = ?$

$i = \dfrac{0.08}{12} = 0.00666667$

$n = 54$

$R = \$200$

$S_n = \dfrac{\$200[(1.00666667)^{54} - 1]}{0.00666667} = \$12{,}948.54$

15. Find n:

$$n = \frac{-\ln\left[1 - \frac{A_n}{R}(i)\right]}{\ln(1+i)}$$

$$n = \frac{-\ln\left[1 - \frac{\$75{,}000}{1{,}000}(0.01125)\right]}{\ln(1.01125)}$$

$n = 165.9306842$

In this problem, 165 payments of size $1,000 will be made plus one smaller payment at period 166. Thus we must find the outstanding balance immediately after the 165th payment. The outstanding balance is found by finding the P.V. of the remaining payments; that is, (165.930684260 – 165 = 0.93068426020); therefore the outstanding balance after the 165th payment is:

$$= \frac{\$1{,}000[1 - (1.01125)^{-0.9306842}]}{0.01125} = \$920.69$$

Now accumulate the outstanding balance for one period (this is to the end of period 166):

$$\$920.69 \times (1 + 0.01125) = \$931.04$$

The final smaller payment is $931.04 at period 166.

EXERCISE 8.6

1. $S_n = \$66{,}000$
$i = ?$
$R = \$1{,}500$
$n = 32$

$$S_n = \frac{R[(1+i)^n - 1]}{i}$$

Now substituting:

$$\$66{,}000 = \frac{\$1{,}500[(1+i)^{32} - 1]}{i}$$

Rearranging gives:

$$\frac{\$66{,}000}{\$1{,}500} = \frac{[(1+i)^{32} - 1]}{i}$$

$$44 = \frac{[(1+i)^{32} - 1]}{i}$$

Now we must substitute values of i that yield 44 for our S_n formula.

GUESS 1: Let the nominal rate be 8% or $i = \dfrac{0.08}{4} = 0.02$.

Substitute $i = 0.02$

$$44.2270296 = \frac{[(1 + 0.02)^{32} - 1]}{0.02} \quad \text{This is too high, i.e., } > 44.$$

Since this is too high we must decrease the value of i.

GUESS 2: Let the nominal rate be:

$$7\frac{2}{3}\%, \text{ or } i = \frac{0.0766\dot{6}}{4} = 0.019166667$$

Substitute:
$i = 0.019166667$

$$43.6116762 = \frac{[(1 + 0.019166667)^{32} - 1]}{0.019166667} \quad \text{This is too low, i.e., } < 44.$$

From these two guesses it can be seen that the nominal rate is between $7\frac{2}{3}\%$ and 8% compounded monthly. Going between to $7.833\dot{3}\%$ to determine the rate within $\frac{1}{2}\%$ gives:

Final GUESS: Let the nominal rate be:

$$7.833\dot{3}\%, \text{ or } i = \frac{0.07833\dot{3}}{4} = 0.019583333$$

$$43.9180298 = \frac{[(1 + 0.019583333)^{32} - 1]}{0.019583333}$$

Therefore the nominal rate must fall between 8% and $7.833\dot{3}\%$ compounded quarterly.

Using interpolation gives:

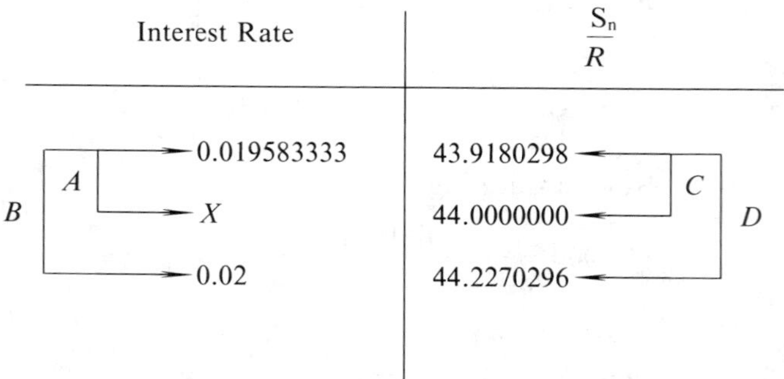

Interest Rate
$\frac{S_n}{R}$
0.019583333
A
B
X
0.02
43.9180298
C
44.0000000
D
44.2270296

What we now do is figure out what proportion of the 0.000416667 difference in the two rates we either subtract from 2% or add to 1.958333%. Setting up the ratio to solve for X.

$$\frac{A}{B} = \frac{C}{D}$$

$$\frac{0.019583333 - X}{-0.019583333 - 0.02} = \frac{43.9180298 - 44.0000000}{43.9180298 - 44.2270296}$$

$$\frac{0.019583333 - X}{-0.000416667} = \frac{-0.08019702}{-0.3089998}$$ Now working through the steps to find X.

$$0.019583333 - X = -0.000416667 \left[\frac{-0.08019702}{-0.3089998}\right]$$

$$-X = -0.000416667 \left[\frac{-0.08019702}{-0.3089998}\right] -0.019583333$$

$$-X = -0.019693865$$ Multiply both sides by -1.

$$X = 0.019693865$$

Therefore the nominal rate using interpolation is 1.9693865% per month, or: 1.9693865% × 4 = 7.87755% per year, compounded quarterly.

3. $A_n = \$10,000$
   $i = ?$
   $R = \$913.76$
   $n = 12$

   $$A_n = \frac{R[1 - (1 + i)^{-n}]}{i}$$

   Now substituting:

   $$\$10,000 = \frac{\$913.76[1 - (1 + i)^{-12}]}{i}$$

   Rearranging gives:

   $$\frac{\$10,000}{\$913.76} = \frac{[1 - (1 + i)^{-12}]}{i}$$

   $$10.9437927 = \frac{[1 - (1 + i)^{-12}]}{i}$$

   Now we must substitute values of i that yield 10.94379268 for our A_n formula.

   GUESS 1: Let the nominal rate be:

   $$17.5\%, \text{ or } i = \frac{0.175}{12} = 0.014583333$$

   Substitute $i = 0.0145833333$

   $$10.9358694 = \frac{[1 - (1 + 0.014583333)^{-12}]}{0.014583333}$$ Too high, i.e., < 10.9437927.

   Since this is too high we must decrease the value of i.

GUESS 2: Let the nominal rate be:

$$17\%, \text{ or } i = \frac{0.17}{12} = 0.01416667$$

Substitute $i = 0.01416667$

$$10.96434097 = \frac{[1 - (1 + 0.01416667)^{-12}]}{0.01416667} \quad \text{Too low, i.e.,} > 10.9437927.$$

From these two guesses it can be seen that the nominal rate is between 17% and 17.5% compounded monthly, which is within $\frac{1}{2}\%$.

Using interpolation gives:

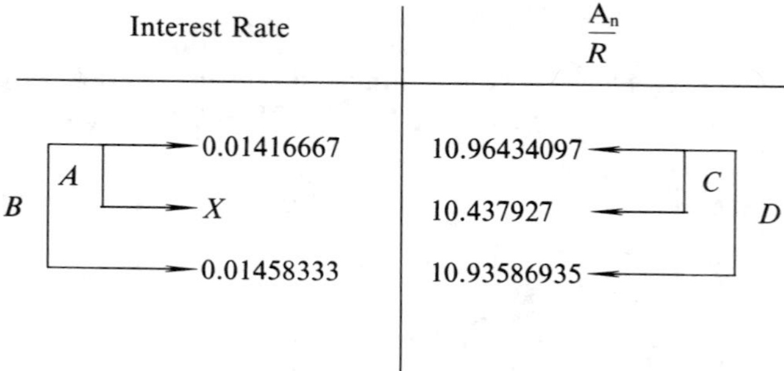

Interest Rate
$\frac{A_n}{R}$
0.01416667
X
0.01458333
A
B
10.96434097
10.437927
10.93586935
C
D

Now figure out what proportion of the 0.5% difference in the two rates we either subtract from 1.416667% or add to 1.458333%. These show how we set up a ratio to solve for X.

$$\frac{A}{B} = \frac{C}{D}$$

$$\frac{0.01416667 - X}{0.01416667 - 0.01458333} = \frac{10.96434097 - 10.94379268}{10.96434097 - 10.93586935}$$

$$-X = -0.000416667\left[\frac{-0.020548286}{-0.02847136}\right] - 0.01416667$$

$$-X = -0.000416660[0.72171768] - 0.01416667$$

$$-X = -0.014467385$$

$$X = 0.014467385, \text{ or } 17.361\% \text{ compounded monthly}$$

5. $A_n = \$8{,}500$
   $i = ?$
   $R = \$275$
   $n = 48$

$$A_n = \frac{R[1 - (1 + i)^{-n}]}{i}$$

Now substituting:

$$\$8{,}500 = \frac{\$275[1 - (1 + i)^{-48} - 1]}{i}$$

Rearranging gives:

$$\frac{\$8{,}500}{\$275} = \frac{\$275[1-(1+i)^{-48}-1]}{i}$$

$$30.90909091 = \frac{\$275[1-(1+i)^{-48}]}{i}$$

Now select two rates: Let $i = 0.02$ at 24% compounded monthly and
$i = 0.019166667$ at 23% compounded monthly:

$i = 0.02$:

$$30.67311957 = \frac{[1-(1+0.02)^{-48}]}{0.02}$$

$i = 0.019166667$:

$$31.19981554 = \frac{[1-(1+0.019166667)^{-48}]}{0.019166667}$$

Using interpolation gives:

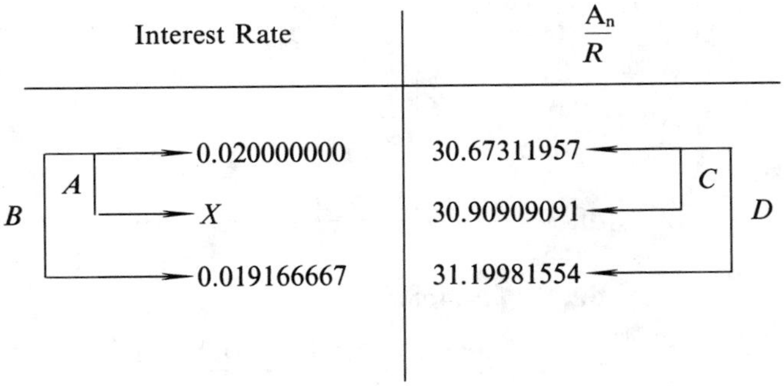

	Interest Rate	$\frac{A_n}{R}$	
B (A: 0.020000000 to X)	0.020000000	30.67311957	D (C: 30.67311957 to 30.90909091)
	X	30.90909091	
	0.019166667	31.19981554	

Now interpolating to find i, we set up a ratio to solve for X.

$$\frac{A}{B} = \frac{C}{D}$$

$$\frac{0.02 - X}{0.02 - 0.019166667} = \frac{30.67311957 - 30.90909091}{30.67311957 - 31.19981554}$$

$$-X = 0.000833333\left[\frac{-0.23597134}{-0.52669597}\right] - 0.02$$

$$-X = -0.019626648$$

$X = 0.019626648$, or 23.552% per year compounded monthly

Therefore the difference between the store and the credit union is 23.552% – 15%, or 8.552% per year.

EXERCISE 9.1

For problems 1 to 5, use formulas:

$$A_n(\text{due}) = \frac{R(1+i)[1-(1+i)^{-n}]}{i}$$

$$S_n(\text{due}) = \frac{R(1+i)[(1+i)^n-1]}{i}$$

1. $R = \$1{,}350$
$n = 4$
$i = 0.124$

$$A_n(\text{due}) = \frac{\$1{,}350(1.124)[1-(1.124)^{-4}]}{0.124}$$

$A_n(\text{due}) = \$4{,}570.31$

$$S_n(\text{due}) = \frac{\$1{,}350(1.124)[(1.124)^4-1]}{0.124}$$

$S_n(\text{due}) = \$7{,}294.76$

3. $R = \$200$
$n = 180$
$i = 0.0125$

$$A_n(\text{due}) = \frac{\$200(1.0125)[1-(1.0125)^{-180}]}{0.0125}$$

$A_n(\text{due}) = \$14{,}468.55$

$$S_n(\text{due}) = \frac{\$200(1.0125)[(1.0125)^{180}-1]}{0.0125}$$

$S_n(\text{due}) = \$135{,}372.62$

5. $R = \$450$
$n = 36$
$i = 0.07$

$$A_n(\text{due}) = \frac{\$450(1.07)[1-(1.07)^{-36}]}{0.07}$$

$A_n(\text{due}) = \$6{,}276.45$

$$S_n(\text{due}) = \frac{\$450(1.07)[(1.07)^{36}-1]}{0.07}$$

$S_n(\text{due}) = \$71{,}701.83$

For problems 6 to 10, use formulas:

$$R = \frac{A_n(\text{due})}{\dfrac{(1+i)[1-(1+i)^{-n}]}{i}}$$

$$R = \frac{S_n(\text{due})}{\dfrac{(1+i)[(1+i)^{n}-1]}{i}}$$

7. $A_n(\text{due}) = \$25{,}000$

$S_n(\text{due}) = \$87{,}500$

$n = 72$

$i = 0.035$

$$R = \frac{\$25{,}000}{\dfrac{(1.035)[1-(1.035)^{-72}]}{0.035}}$$

$R = \$922.94$

$$R = \frac{\$87{,}500}{\dfrac{(1.035)[(1.035)^{72}-1]}{0.035}}$$

$R = \$271.35$

9. $A_n(\text{due}) = \$54{,}500$

$S_n(\text{due}) = \$80{,}340$

$n = 6$

$i = 0.198$

$$R = \frac{\$54{,}500}{\dfrac{(1.198)[1-(1.198)^{-6}]}{0.198}}$$

$R = \$13{,}612.00$

$$R = \frac{\$80{,}340}{\dfrac{(1.198)[(1.198)^{6}-1]}{0.198}}$$

$R = \$6{,}787.60$

For problems 11 to 20, use formulas:

$$n = \frac{-\ln\left[1 - \frac{A_n(\text{due})}{R(1+i)}(i)\right]}{\ln(1+i)} \quad \text{or } n = \frac{\ln\left[1 + \frac{S_n(\text{due})}{R(1+i)}(i)\right]}{\ln(1+i)}$$

11. $A_n(\text{due}) = \$6{,}450$
$S_n(\text{due}) = \$25{,}345$
$R = \$4{,}500$
$i = 0.108$

$$n = \frac{-\ln\left[1 - \frac{\$6{,}450}{\$4{,}500(1.108)}(0.108)\right]}{\ln(1.108)}$$

$n = 1.467356944$

$$n = \frac{\ln\left[1 + \frac{\$25{,}345}{\$4{,}500(1.108)}(0.108)\right]}{\ln(1.108)}$$

$n = 4.267$

13. $A_n(\text{due}) = \$24{,}400$
$S_n(\text{due}) = \$64{,}400$
$R = \$1{,}350$
$i = 0.01$

$$n = \frac{-\ln\left[1 - \frac{\$24{,}400}{\$1{,}350(1.01)}(0.01)\right]}{\ln(1.01)}$$

$n = 19.8157$

$$n = \frac{\ln\left[1 + \frac{\$64{,}400}{\$1{,}350(1.01)}(0.01)\right]}{\ln(1.01)}$$

$n = 38.8766$

15. $A_n(\text{due}) = \$67{,}500$
$S_n(\text{due}) = \$150{,}000$
$R = \$9{,}500$
$i = 0.08$

$$n = \frac{-\ln\left[1 - \dfrac{\$67{,}500}{\$9{,}500(1.08)}(0.08)\right]}{\ln(1.08)}$$

$n = 9.709$

$$n = \frac{\ln\left[1 + \dfrac{\$150{,}000}{\$9{,}500(1.08)}(0.08)\right]}{\ln(1.08)}$$

$n = 10.064$

17. $A_n(\text{due}) = \$134{,}500$
$S_n(\text{due}) = \$100{,}000$
$R = \$18{,}200$
$i = 0.0595$

$$n = \frac{-\ln\left[1 - \dfrac{\$134{,}500}{\$18{,}200(1.0595)}(0.0595)\right]}{\ln(1.0595)}$$

$n = 9.2768$

$$n = \frac{\ln\left[1 + \dfrac{\$100{,}000}{\$18{,}200(1.0595)}(0.0595)\right]}{\ln(1.0595)}$$

$n = 4.653$

19. $A_n(\text{due}) = \$1{,}250$
$S_n(\text{due}) = \$24{,}450$
$R = \$50$
$i = 0.03625$

$$n = \frac{-\ln\left[1 - \dfrac{\$1{,}250}{\$50(1.03625)}(0.03625)\right]}{\ln(1.03625)}$$

$n = 58.296010$

$$n = \frac{\ln\left[1 + \dfrac{\$24{,}450}{\$50(1.03625)}(0.03625)\right]}{\ln(1.03625)}$$

$n = 81.336$

21. $R = \$800$
$n = 30$
$i = 0.0033$

$$S_n(\text{due}) = \frac{\$800(1.0033)[(1.0033)^{30} - 1]}{0.0033}$$

$S_n(\text{due}) = \$25{,}280.90$

No, she won't have sufficient money to take the trip.

23. $R = \$900$
$n = 12$
$i = \dfrac{0.08}{12}$

$$A_n(\text{due}) = \frac{\$900\left(1 + \left(\frac{0.08}{12}\right)\right)\left[1 - \left(1 + \left(\frac{0.08}{12}\right)\right)^{-12}\right]}{\left(\frac{0.08}{12}\right)}$$

$A_n(\text{due}) = \$10{,}415.18$

Yes, it is a good deal.

25.
$$R = \frac{A_n(\text{due})}{\dfrac{(1+i)[1-(1+i)^{-n}]}{i}}$$

$$R = \frac{\$78{,}000}{\dfrac{(1 + (\frac{0.1}{12}))[1 - (1 + (\frac{0.1}{12}))^{-180}]}{(\frac{0.1}{12})}}$$

$R = \$831.26$

27.
$$n = \frac{\ln\left[1 + \dfrac{S_n(\text{due})\ (i)}{R(1+i)}\right]}{\ln(1+i)}$$

$$n = \frac{\ln\left[1 + \dfrac{\$65{,}000}{\$3{,}421.46(1.08)}(0.08)\right]}{\ln(1.08)}$$

$n = 11.41461827$

EXERCISE 9.2

1. $$A_n(\text{def}) = \frac{R(1+i)^{-d}[1-(1+i)^{-n}]}{i}$$

$$A_n(\text{def}) = \frac{\$2{,}500(1.00916\dot{6})^{-12}[1-(1.00916\dot{6})^{-240}]}{0.00916\dot{6}}$$

$$A_n(\text{def}) = \$217{,}083.23$$

3. $$n = \frac{-\ln\left[1 - \dfrac{A_n(\text{def})}{R(1+i)^{-d}}(i)\right]}{\ln(1+i)}$$

$$n = \frac{-\ln\left[1 - \dfrac{\$80{,}500}{\$17{,}500(1.14)^{-3}}(0.14)\right]}{\ln(1.14)}$$

$$n = 23.5186$$

5. $$A_n(\text{def}) = \frac{\$2{,}200(1.04675)^{-2}[1-(1.04675)^{-60}]}{0.04675}$$

$$A_n(\text{def}) = \$40{,}179.86$$

7. $$R = \frac{\$250{,}000}{\dfrac{(1.04)^{-8}[1-(1.04)^{-16}]}{0.04}}$$

$$R = \$29{,}362.65$$

EXERCISE 10.1

For problems 1 to 10, use the following formulas:

$$S_{nc} = \frac{R[(1+i)^{nc}-1]}{[(1+i)^c-1]}$$

$$A_{nc} = \frac{R[1-(1+i)^{-nc}]}{[(1+i)^c-1]}$$

$$c = \frac{\text{\# of conversion periods}}{\text{\# of payment periods}}$$

$$S_n = \frac{R[(1+f)^n - 1]}{f}$$

$$A_n = \frac{R[1-(1+f)^{-n}]}{f}$$

1. $R = \$2{,}450$
$i = 0.124$
$n = 48$
$c = \dfrac{1}{12}$

$$nc = \frac{48}{12} = 4$$

$$f = [(1.124)^{\frac{1}{12}} - 1] = 0.00978875$$

$$S_{nc} = \frac{\$2{,}450[(1.124)^{\frac{48}{12}} - 1]}{[(1.124)^{\frac{1}{12}} - 1]}$$

$S_{nc} = \$149{,}201.08$

$$A_{nc} = \frac{\$2{,}450[1-(1.124)^{-\frac{48}{12}}]}{[(1.124)^{\frac{1}{12}} - 1]}$$

$A_{nc} = \$93{,}477.42$

3. $R = \$460$
$i = 0.0125$
$n = 60$
$c = 3$
$nc = 180$
$f = [(1.0125)^3 - 1]$

$$S_{nc} = \frac{\$460[(1.0125)^{180} - 1]}{[(1.0125)^3 - 1]}$$

$S_{nc} = \$101{,}233.68$

$$A_{nc} = \frac{\$460[1-(1.0125)^{-180}]}{[(1.0125)^3 - 1]}$$

$A_{nc} = \$10{,}819.80$

5. $R = \$750$
$i = 0.07$
$n = 216$
$c = \dfrac{2}{12} = \dfrac{1}{6}$
$nc = 36$
$f = [(1.07)^{\frac{1}{6}} - 1]$

$$S_{nc} = \frac{\$750[(1.07)^{36} - 1]}{[(1.07)^{\frac{1}{6}} - 1]}$$

$S_{nc} = \$689{,}398.35$

$$A_{nc} = \frac{\$750[1 - (1.07)^{-36}]}{[(1.07)^{\frac{1}{6}} - 1]}$$

$A_{nc} = \$60{,}346.80$

7. $R = \$800$
$i = \dfrac{0.148}{12}$
$n = 8$
$c = \dfrac{12}{4} = 3$
$nc = 24$

$$f = \left[\left(1 + \left(\frac{0.148}{12}\right)\right)^3 - 1\right]$$

$$S_{nc} = \frac{\$800\left[\left(1 + \left(\frac{0.148}{12}\right)\right)^{24} - 1\right]}{\left[\left(1 + \left(\frac{0.148}{12}\right)\right)^3 - 1\right]}$$

$S_{nc} = \$7{,}304.96$

$$A_{nc} = \frac{\$800\left[1 - \left(1 + \left(\frac{0.148}{12}\right)\right)^{-24}\right]}{\left[\left(1 + \left(\frac{0.148}{12}\right)\right)^3 - 1\right]}$$

$A_{nc} = \$5{,}443.18$

9. $R = \$2{,}450$

$$i = \frac{0.155}{4} = 0.03875$$

$n = 28$

$c = 1$

$nc = 28$

$$S_n = \frac{\$2{,}450[(1.03875)^{28} - 1]}{(0.03875)}$$

$S_n = \$120{,}091.47$

$$A_n = \frac{\$2{,}450[1 - (1.03875)^{-28}]}{(0.03875)}$$

$A_n = \$41{,}419.34$

For problems 11 to 15, the formulas will be using f.

11. $R = \$6{,}500$
$n = 10$

a. $f = (1 + 0.14)^{\frac{1}{2}} - 1 = 0.0677078$

$$S_n = \frac{\$6{,}500[(1.0677078)^{10} - 1]}{0.0677078}$$

$S_n = \$88{,}840.47$

$$A_n = \frac{\$6{,}500[1 - (0.0677078)^{-10}]}{0.0677078}$$

$A_n = \$46{,}140.95$

b. $f = \left[1 + \left(\frac{0.14}{12}\right)^{\frac{12}{2}} - 1\right] = 0.0720737$

$$S_n = \frac{\$6{,}500[(1.0720737)^{10} - 1]}{0.0720737}$$

$S_n = \$90{,}691.38$

$$A_n = \frac{\$6{,}500[1 - (1.0720737)^{-10}]}{0.0720737}$$

$A_n = \$45{,}218.85$

13. $R = \$25{,}000$ for 5 years

The down payment will accumulate for the full 10 years at 12% compounded monthly.

$$\$40{,}000(1.01)^{120} = \$132{,}015.48$$

The cash payments will occur for five years and then accumulate for five years.

$$f = \left[1 + \left(\frac{0.12}{12}\right)\right]^{\frac{12}{2}} - 1$$

$$= 0.0615202$$

$$S_n = \frac{\$25{,}000[(1.0615202)^{10} - 1]}{0.0615202}$$

$$S_n = \$331{,}881.79$$

Accumulating for sixty periods: $\$331{,}881.79(1.01)^{60} = \$602{,}928.55$

$$\$602{,}928.55 + \$132{,}015.48 = \$734{,}944.03$$

15. $R = \$750$

$n = 240$

$$f = \left[1 + \left(\frac{0.10}{2}\right)\right]^{\frac{2}{12}} - 1 = 0.0081648$$

$$\text{Purchase Price} = \$5{,}000 + \frac{\$750[1 - (1.0081648)^{-240}]}{0.0081648}$$

$$\text{Purchase Price} = \$83{,}809.29$$

EXERCISE 10.2

For problems 1 to 10, use formulas:

$$n = \frac{\ln\left[1 + \frac{S_n}{R}(f)\right]}{\ln(1 + f)} \quad \text{or} \quad n = \frac{-\ln\left[1 - \frac{A_n}{R}(f)\right]}{\ln(1 + f)}$$

1. $R = \$500$

$f = (1 + 0.114)^{\frac{1}{12}} - 1 = 0.009037017$

$A_n = \$15{,}500$

$S_n = \$85{,}000$

A_n:

$$n = \frac{-\ln\left[1 - \frac{\$15{,}500}{\$500}(0.009037017)\right]}{\ln(1 + 0.009037017)}$$

$n = 36.53772482$

S_n:

$$n = \frac{\ln\left[1 + \frac{\$85{,}000}{\$500}(0.009037017)\right]}{\ln(1.009037017)}$$

$n = 103.4525635$

3. $R = \$1{,}350$

$f = \left(1 + \frac{0.186}{12}\right)^3 - 1 = 0.047224474$

$A_n = \$25{,}400$

$S_n = \$34{,}400$

A_n:

$$n = \frac{-\ln\left[1 - \frac{\$25{,}400}{\$1{,}350}(0.047224474)\right]}{\ln(1.047224474)}$$

$n = 47.5452377$

S_n:

$$n = \frac{\ln\left[1 + \frac{\$34{,}400}{\$1{,}350}(0.047224474)\right]}{\ln(1.047224474)}$$

$n = 17.12011546$

5. $R = \$4{,}500$

$f = \left(1 + \frac{0.192}{2}\right)^{\frac{1}{6}} - 1 = 0.0153952$

$A_n = \$89{,}500$

$S_n = \$45{,}000$

A_n:

$$n = \frac{-\ln\left[1 - \frac{\$89{,}500}{\$4{,}500}(0.0153952)\right]}{\ln(1.0153952)}$$

$n = 23.9275024$

S_n:

$$n = \frac{\ln\left[1 + \frac{\$45{,}000}{\$4{,}500}(0.0153952)\right]}{\ln(1.0153952)}$$

$n = 9.3725319$

7. $R = \$200$

$$f = \left(1 + \frac{0.181}{4}\right)^{\frac{4}{12}} - 1 = 0.01486137865$$

$A_n = \$4{,}500$

$S_n = \$10{,}000$

A_n:

$$n = \frac{-\ln\left[1 - \frac{\$4{,}500}{\$200}(0.0146137865)\right]}{\ln(1.014867865)}$$

$n = 27.59198988$

S_n:

$$n = \frac{\ln\left[1 + \frac{\$10{,}000}{\$200}(0.01486137865)\right]}{\ln(1.014867865)}$$

$n = 37.66581945$

9. $R = \$50$

$$f = \left(1 + \frac{0.163}{4}\right)^{\frac{4}{12}} - 1 = 0.013402893$$

$A_n = \$2{,}450$

$S_n = \$15{,}450$

A_n:

$$n = \frac{-\ln\left[1 - \frac{\$2{,}450}{\$50}(0.013402893)\right]}{\ln(1.013402893)}$$

$n = 80.31266118$

S_n:

$$n = \frac{\ln\left[1 + \frac{\$15{,}450}{\$50}(0.013402893)\right]}{\ln(1.013402893)}$$

$n = 122.980307025$

11. $S_n = \$20{,}000{,}000$

$f = (1 + 0.09)^{\frac{1}{4}} - 1 = 0.021778181$

$n = 32$

a.

$$R = \frac{\$20{,}000{,}000}{\dfrac{[(1.021778181)^{32} - 1]}{0.021778181}}$$

$R = \$438{,}827.33$

b.

$$n = \frac{\ln\left[1 + \dfrac{\$20{,}000{,}000}{\$800{,}000}(0.021778181)\right]}{\ln(1.021778181)}$$

$n = 20.17555848$

13. $S_n = \$5{,}000$

$f = (1 + 0.05)^{\frac{1}{2}} - 1 = 0.024695077$

$$n = \frac{\ln\left[1 + \dfrac{\$5{,}000}{\$240}(0.02469077)\right]}{\ln(1.02469077)}$$

$n = 17.0146037$, or 4.25 years (approximately)

15. $A_n = \$95{,}000$

$$f = \left[1 + \left(\frac{0.105}{2}\right)\right]^{\frac{1}{6}} - 1 = 0.008564515$$

$$n = \frac{-\ln\left[1 - \dfrac{\$95{,}000}{\$1{,}009.30}(0.008564515)\right]}{\ln(1.008564515)}$$

$n = 192.37$ months

EXERCISE 10.3

For problems 1 to 5, use formulas:

$$S_n(\text{due}) = \frac{R(1+f)[(1+f)^n - 1]}{f} \quad \text{and} \quad A_n(\text{due}) = \frac{R(1+f)[1 - (1+f)^{-n}]}{f}$$

1. $R = \$2{,}500$
$n = 6$
$$f = \left[1 + \left(\frac{0.15}{12}\right)\right]^{12} - 1 = 0.1607545177$$
$$A_n(\text{due}) = \frac{\$2{,}500(1.1607545177)[1 - (1.1607545177)^{-6}]}{0.1607545177}$$
$$A_n(\text{due}) = \$10{,}671.35$$
$$S_n(\text{due}) = \frac{\$2{,}500(1.1607545177)[(1.607545177)^{6} - 1]}{0.1607545177}$$
$$S_n(\text{due}) = \$26{,}101.26$$

3. $R = \$1{,}250$
$n = 204$
$$f = (1.085)^{\frac{1}{6}} - 1 = 0.013689519$$
$$A_n(\text{due}) = \frac{\$1{,}250(1.013689519)[1 - (1.013689519)^{-204}]}{0.013689519}$$
$$A_n(\text{due}) = \$86{,}782.22$$
$$S_n(\text{due}) = \frac{\$1{,}250(1.013689519)[(1.013689519)^{204} - 1]}{0.013689519}$$
$$S_n(\text{due}) = \$1{,}390{,}086.60$$

5. $R = \$1{,}450$
$n = 32$
$$f = (1.14)^{\frac{1}{2}} - 1 = 0.06770782518$$
$$A_n(\text{due}) = \frac{\$1{,}450(1.06770782518)[1 - (1.0677078518)^{-32}]}{0.0677078518}$$
$$A_n(\text{due}) = \$20{,}055.56$$
$$S_n(\text{due}) = \frac{\$1{,}450(1.06770782518)[1.0677078518)^{32} - 1]}{0.0677078518}$$
$$S_n(\text{due}) = \$163{,}197.10$$

For problems 6 to 10, use formulas:

$$R = \frac{A_n(\text{due})}{\dfrac{(1+f)[1-(1+f)^{-n}]}{f}} \quad \text{or} \quad R = \frac{A_n(\text{due})}{\dfrac{(1+f)[(1+f)^{n}-1]}{f}}$$

7. $A_n(\text{due}) = \$35{,}000$
$S_n(\text{due}) = \$65{,}500$
$n = 72$

$f = (1.12)^{\frac{1}{4}} - 1 = 0.028737345$

$A_n(\text{due})$:

$$R = \frac{\$35{,}000}{\dfrac{(1.028737345)[1 - (1.028737345)^{-72}]}{0.028737345}}$$

$R = \$1{,}123.86$

$S_n(\text{due})$:

$$R = \frac{\$65{,}500}{\dfrac{(1.028737345)[(1.028737345)^{72} - 1]}{0.028737345}}$$

$R = \$273.50$

9. $A_n(\text{due}) = \$58{,}500$
$S_n(\text{due}) = \$49{,}340$
$n = 6$
$f = (1.035)^4 - 1 = 0.147523$

$A_n(\text{due})$:

$$R = \frac{\$58{,}500}{\dfrac{(1.147523)[1 - (1.147523)^{-6}]}{0.147523}}$$

$R = \$13{,}380.88$

$S_n(\text{due})$:

$$R = \frac{\$49{,}340}{\dfrac{(1.147523)[(1.147523)^{6} - 1]}{0.147523}}$$

$R = \$4{,}942.65$

11. $R = \$1{,}500$
$n = 40$

$f = (1.16)^{\frac{3}{12}} - 1 = 0.037801986$

$$S_n(\text{due}) = \frac{\$1{,}500(1.037801986)[(1.037801986)^{40} - 1]}{0.037801986}$$

$S_n(\text{due}) = \$140{,}484.45$

13. $R = \$500$

$A_n(\text{due}) = \$10{,}000$

$f = 0.007207323$

$$n = \frac{-\ln\left[1 - \dfrac{\$10{,}000}{\$500(1 + 0.007207323)}(0.007207323)\right]}{\ln(1.007207323)}$$

$n = 21.50694$

15. $A_n(\text{due}) = \$250{,}000$

$n = 120$

$f = 0.01134026$

$$R = \frac{\$250{,}000}{\dfrac{(1.01134026)[1 - (1.01134026)^{-120}]}{0.01134026}}$$

$R = \$3{,}780.13$

EXERCISE 10.4

1. $f = (1.11)^{\frac{1}{12}} - 1 = 0.008734593$

$R = \$3{,}500$

$n = 180$

$d = 9$

$$A_n(\text{def}) = \frac{\$3{,}500(1.008734593)^{-9}[1 - (1.008734593)^{-180}]}{0.008734593}$$

$A_n(\text{def}) = \$293{,}094.18$

3. $f = \left[1 + \left(\dfrac{0.155}{4}\right)\right]^4 - 1 = 0.164244371$

$A_n(\text{def}) = \$25{,}500$

$R = \$5{,}500$

$d = 1$

$$n = \frac{-\ln\left[1 - \dfrac{\$25{,}500}{\$5{,}500(1.164244371)^{-1}}(0.164244371)\right]}{\ln(1.164244371)}$$

$n = 14.3126242$

5. $f = \left[1 + \left(\frac{0.187}{12}\right)\right]^{\frac{1}{6}} - 1 = 0.015008777$

$R = \$2{,}200$

$n = 180$

$d = 7$

$$A_n(\text{def}) = \frac{\$2{,}200(1.015008777)^{-7}[1 - (1.015008777)^{-180}]}{0.015008777}$$

$A_n(\text{def}) = \$123{,}024.14$

7. $n = 180$

$d = 11$

$f = (1 + 0.06)^{\frac{1}{6}} - 1 = 0.009758794$

$A_n(\text{def}) = 1{,}250{,}000$

$$R = \frac{\$1{,}250{,}000}{\frac{(1.009758794)^{-11}[1 - (1.009758794)^{-180}]}{0.009758794}}$$

$R = \$16{,}435.32$

EXERCISE 10.5

1. $R = \$1{,}500$
$i = 0.01$
$A_\infty = \frac{\$1{,}500}{0.01} + \$1{,}500 = \$151{,}500$

3. $R = \$15{,}000$
$f = \left[1 + \left(\frac{0.195}{4}\right)\right]^4 - 1 = 0.209728452$
$A_\infty = \frac{\$15{,}000}{0.209728452} = \$71{,}521.05$

Payments start at the end of two years, thus, 1 deferral period:

$\$71{,}521.05(1.209728452)^{-1} = \$59{,}121.58$

5. $R = \$850$

$f = (1.0835)^{\frac{1}{6}} - 1 = 0.013455816$

$A_\infty = \frac{\$850}{0.013455816} = \$63{,}169.71$

$\$63{,}169.71(1.013455816)^{-11} = \$54{,}532.56$

7. $R = \$10{,}000$

$f = (1.08)^{\frac{1}{4}} - 1 = 0.019426546$

$$A_\infty = \frac{\$10{,}000}{0.019426546} = \$514{,}759.52$$

9. $R = \$4{,}000$

$f = (1.045)^2 - 1 = 0.092025$

$$A_\infty = \frac{\$4{,}000}{0.092025} + \$4{,}000 = \$47{,}466.45$$

EXERCISE 10.A.1

1. Use NPV:

$$f = \left(1 + \frac{0.1}{12}\right)^{\frac{12}{2}} - 1 = 0.0510533$$

Outflows:

$$\$150{,}000 + \$3{,}000(1 + 0.0510533)\left[\frac{1 - (1 + 0.0510533)^{-10}}{(0.0510533)}\right] = \$174{,}233.80$$

Inflows: Savings

$$i = \frac{0.10}{12} = 0.00833333$$

$$\$2{,}000\ \frac{[1 - (1 + 0.00833333)^{-60}]}{(0.00833333)} = \$94{,}130.74$$

NPV = Inflows – Outflows If this is + then the expenditure should occur.

NPV = \$94,130.74 – \$174,233.80 = –\$80,103.06

Since the NPV is negative the expenditure should not be undertaken.

3. $f = \left(1 + \frac{0.12}{4}\right)^4 - 1 = 0.1255088$

Outflows:

$$\$20{,}000\ \frac{[1 - (1 + 0.1255088)^{-8}]}{(0.1255088)} = \$97{,}469.33$$

Inflows: Note that the income is deferred for 3 years.

$$\$45{,}000(1 + 0.1255088)^{-3}\ \frac{[1 - (1 + 0.1255088)^{-5}]}{(0.1255088)} + \$50{,}000(1 + 0.1255088)^{-8}$$

= \$112,238.56 + \$19,416.85 = \$131,655.41

NPV = \$131,655.41 – \$97,469.33 = \$34,186.08

Since the NPV is positive the project should be undertaken.

5. $f = \left(1 + \frac{0.19}{2}\right)^2 - 1 = 0.199025$

Outflows:

$\$200{,}000(1 + 0.199025)^{-1} =$	\$ 166,802.19
$\$450{,}000(1 + 0.199025)^{-2} =$	\$ 313,008.43
$\$500{,}000(1 + 0.199025)^{-3} =$	\$ 290,058.29
Total Outflows:	\$ 769,868.92

Inflows:

$$\frac{\$500{,}000(1 + 0.199025)^{-3}[1 - (1 + 0.199025)^{-3}]}{(0.199025)} = \$611{,}936.52$$

NPV = Inflows – Outflows = \$611,936.52 – \$769,868.92 = –\$157,932.40

Since the NPV is negative don't undertake to make the robotic unit.

7. This problem requires one to select the option with the highest DCF:

OPTION 1:
$\$50{,}000 + \$120{,}000(1 + 0.12)^{-1} + \$200{,}000(1 + 0.12)^{-3} = \$299{,}498.91$

OPTION 2:
$\$20{,}000 + \$80{,}000(1 + 0.12)^{-1} + \$350{,}000(1 + 0.12)^{-5} = \$290{,}027.97$

OPTION 3:
\$250,000 today

The best decision is Option 1.

EXERCISE 11.1

For problems 1 to 10, use formulas:

a. $$R = \frac{A_n}{\frac{[1 - (1 + i)^{-n}]}{i}}$$

b. $$\text{P.V.} = A_n = \frac{R[1 - (1 + i)^{-n}]}{\text{i}}$$

c. (number of payments)(R) – (A_n – Balance) = Total Interest Payments

1. Loan = \$13,500

$i = \frac{0.124}{12} = 0.01033$

$n = 3 \times 12 = 36$

$$R = \frac{\$13{,}500}{\frac{[1 - (1.01033)^{-36}]}{0.01033}}$$

$R = \$450.98$

b. $n = (3 \times 12) - 15 = 21$

$$\text{P.V.} = A_n = \frac{\$450.98[1 - (1.01033)^{-21}]}{0.01033}$$

$A_n = \$8{,}474.35$

c. (15)($450.98) – ($13,500.00 – $8,474.35) = $1,739.05
Total interest paid at 15th payment is $1,739.05.

3. Loan = $12,000

$i = \dfrac{0.15}{4} = 0.0375$

$n = 64$

a.

$$R = \frac{\$12{,}000}{\frac{[1 - (1.0375)^{-64}]}{0.0375}}$$

$R = \$497.12$

b. $n = 64 - 3 = 61$

$$\text{P.V.} = A_n = \frac{\$497.12[1 - (1.0375)^{-61}]}{0.0375}$$

$A_n = \$11{,}853.22$

c. (3)($497.12) – ($12,000.00 – $11,853.22) = $1,344.68

5. Loan = $211,000

$f = (1.07)^{\frac{1}{6}} - 1 = 0.01134026$

$n = 240$

a.

$$R = \frac{\$211{,}000}{\frac{[1 - (1.01134026)^{-240}]}{0.01134026}}$$

$R = \$2{,}564.02$

b. $n = 240 - 185 = 55$

$$\text{P.V.} = A_n = \frac{\$2{,}564.02[1 - (1.01134026)^{-55}]}{0.01134026}$$

$A_n = \$104{,}495.08$

c. (185)($2,564.02) – ($211,000.00 – $104,485.08) = $367,838.78

7. Loan = \$8,500

$f = (1 + \left(\frac{0.148}{4}\right))^4 - 1 = 0.156418486$

$n = 2$

a. $R = \dfrac{\$8{,}500}{\dfrac{[1 - (1.156418486)^{-2}]}{0.156418486}}$

$R = \$5{,}271.28$

b. $n = 0$

$\text{P.V.} = A_n = \dfrac{\$5{,}271.28[1 - (1.156418486)^{-0}]}{0.156418486}$

$A_n = 0$ There is no outstanding balance after two payments.

c. (2)(\$5,271.28) – (\$8,500 – 0) = \$2,042.56

9. Loan = \$35,600

$i = \dfrac{0.155}{4} = 0.03875$

$n = 36$

a. $R = \dfrac{\$35{,}600}{\dfrac{[1 - (1.03875)^{-36}]}{0.03875}}$

$R = \$1{,}850.31$

b. $n = 24$

$\text{P.V.} = A_n = \dfrac{\$1{,}850.31[1 - (1.03875)^{-24}]}{0.03875}$

$A_n = \$28{,}576.15$

c. (12)(\$1,850.31) – (\$35,600 – \$28,576.15) = \$15,179.96

11. a. Loan = \$12,000 from number 3

$i = \dfrac{0.15}{4} = 0.0375$

$R = (\$497.12)(1.25) = \$621.40$ (i.e., a 25% increase in the payment)

$$n = \frac{-\ln\left[1 - \dfrac{\$12{,}000(0.0375)}{\$621.40}\right]}{\ln(1.0375)}$$

$n = 34.99$,or 35 payments

Savings = Value of old payments – Value of new payments

[(64)(\$497.12) – (35)(\$621.40)] = \$10,066.68

b. Loan = \$211,000 from number 5

$f = (1.07)^{\frac{1}{6}} - 1 = 0.01134026$

$R = (\$2,564.02)(1.25) = \$3,205.03$ (i.e., a 25% increase in the payment)

$$n = \frac{-\ln\left[1 - \frac{\$211,000(0.01134026)}{\$3,205.03}\right]}{\ln(1.01134026)}$$

$n = 121.7305013$

Savings = Value of old payments – Value of new payments

240(\$2,564.02) – 121.7305013(\$3,205.03) = \$225,214.89

Alternative solution: If one assumes that there will be 121 regular payments of \$3,205.03 and a smaller final payment at period 122 then:

(121)(3,205.03) = \$387,808.63 Value of first 121 payments.

Smaller last payment:

Find outstanding balance at the end of period 121.

$$\frac{\$3,205.03[1 - (1.01134026)^{-0.730513}]}{0.01134026} = \$2,318.50$$

Accumulate outstanding balance to the end of period 122.

(\$2,318.50)(1.01134026) = \$2,344.83

Therefore the total value of payments under the new scheme is:

\$387,808.63 + \$2,344.83 = \$390,153.46

Savings = Value of old payments – Value of new payments
240(\$2,564.02) – \$390,153.46 = \$225,211.34

13.

Quarter	Regular Payment	Payment to Interest	Payment to Principal	Outstanding Balance
0	–	–	–	\$65,000.00
1	\$3,500.00	\$1,300.00	\$2,200.00	\$62,800.00
2	\$3,500.00	\$1,256.00	\$2,244.00	\$60,556.00
3	\$3,500.00	\$1,211.12	\$2,288.88	\$58,267.12

The value of the last payment is:

Compute n, where $i = \frac{0.08}{4}$

$$n = \frac{-\ln\left[1 - \frac{\$65,000(0.02)}{\$3,500}\right]}{\ln(1.02)}$$

$n = 23.44667$

Find the outstanding balance at period 23, immediately after the 23rd payment.

$$\frac{\$3,500.00[1 - (1.02)^{-0.44667}]}{0.02}$$

$= \$1,541.08$

Final Payment $= \$1,541.08(1.02) = \$1,571.90$

EXERCISE 11.2

For problems 1 to 10, use formulas:

a. $R = \dfrac{S_n}{\dfrac{[(1 + i)^n - 1]}{i}}$

b. $S_n = \dfrac{R[(1 + i)^n - 1]}{i}$

c. $S_n - [(R) \times (n)]$, where $n =$ period when the balance is desired.

d. (Debt) × (Interest Rate on Debt per interest period): This solution assumes no compounding since all the interest is paid when due.

1. a. $S_n = \$16,500$

$i = \dfrac{0.154}{12} = 0.0128333$

$n = 36$

$$R = \frac{\$16,500}{\dfrac{[(1.01283)^{36} - 1]}{0.01283}}$$

$R = \$363.47$

b. $S_n = \dfrac{\$363.46[(1.01283)^{12} - 1]}{0.01283}$

$S_n = \$4,683.06$

c. $\$4,683.06 - (\$363.47 \times 12) = \$321.42$

d. $\$16,500 \times 0.164 = \$2,706.00$

3. a. $S_n = \$22,000$

$i = \dfrac{0.18}{4} = 0.045$

$n = 64$

$$R = \frac{\$22{,}000}{\frac{[(1.045)^{64} - 1]}{0.045}}$$

$R = \$62.95$

b. $S_n = \dfrac{\$62.95[(1.045)^3 - 1]}{0.045}$

$S_n = \$197.48$

c. $\$197.48 - (62.95 \times 3) = \$8.63$

d. $f = \left[1 + \left(\dfrac{0.19}{4}\right)\right]^4 - 1 = 0.2039713$

$\$22{,}000 \times 0.2039713 = \$4{,}487.37$

5. a. $S_n = \$150{,}000$

$f = \left[1 + \left(\dfrac{0.17}{2}\right)\right]^{\frac{2}{12}} - 1 = 0.01368951948$

$n = 240$

$$R = \frac{\$150{,}000}{\frac{[(1.0136895)^{240} - 1]}{0.0136895}}$$

$R = \$81.70$

b. $S_n = \dfrac{\$81.70[(1.0136895)^{150} - 1]}{0.0136895}$

$S_n = \$39{,}908.24$

c. $\$39{,}908.24 - (\$81.70 \times 150) = \$27{,}653.24$

d. $f = \left[1 + \left(\dfrac{0.21}{2}\right)\right]^{\frac{2}{1}} - 1 = 0.221025$

$\$150{,}000 \times 0.221025 = \$33{,}153.75$

7. a. $S_n = \$54{,}500$

$f = \left[1 + \left(\dfrac{0.178}{4}\right)\right]^4 - 1 = 0.1902379$

$n = 6$

$$R = \frac{\$54{,}500}{\frac{[(1.1902379)^6 - 1]}{0.1902379}}$$

$R = \$5{,}625.08$

b. $S_n = \dfrac{5{,}625.08[(1.1902379)^4 - 1]}{0.1902379}$

$S_n = \$29{,}773.97$

c. $29,773.97 – ($5,625.08 × 4) = $7,273.65

d. $f = \left[1 + \left(\dfrac{0.198}{12}\right)\right]^{12} - 1 = 0.21699444$

$54,500 × 0.216994440 = $11,826.20

9. a. $S_n = \$45{,}600$

$i = \dfrac{0.185}{4} = 0.04625$

$n = 36$

$$R = \frac{\$45{,}600}{\dfrac{[(1.04625)^{36} - 1]}{0.04625}} = \$515.41$$

b. $S_n = \dfrac{\$515.41[(1.04625)^{10} - 1]}{0.04625}$

$S_n = \$6{,}370.42$

c. $6,370.42 – ($515.41 × 10) = $1,216.32

d. $f = \left[1 + \left(\dfrac{0.145}{4}\right)\right]^{\frac{4}{1}} - 1 = 0.1530766$

$45,600 × 0.1530766 = $6,980.29

11. $S_n = \$180{,}000$

$i = \dfrac{0.12}{12} = 0.01$

$n = 60$

$$R = \frac{\$180{,}000}{\dfrac{(1.01)^{60} - 1}{0.1}} = \$2{,}204$$

Period	Regular Payment	Payment to Interest	Increase in Fund	Accumulated Balance in Fund	Book Value of Debt
0	–	–	–	–	$180,000.00
1	$2,204	$ 0	$2,204	$ 2,204.00	$177,796.00
2	$2,204	$ 22.04	$2,226.04	$ 4,430.04	$175,569.96
•					
58	$2,204			$172,110.49	
59	$2,204	$1,721.10	$3,925.10	$176,035.59	$ 3,964.41
60	$2,204	$1,760.36	$3,964.36	$179,999.95	0.00

EXERCISE 11.3

1. $K = \$66{,}500 + \dfrac{\$66{,}500 - \$4{,}000}{(1.10)^{20} - 1} = \$77{,}412{,}27$

3. $K = \$82{,}000 + \dfrac{\$82{,}000 - \$12{,}000}{(1.03)^{24} - 1} = \$149{,}777.30$

5. $K = \$70{,}000 + \dfrac{\$70{,}000}{(1.062)^{20} - 1} = \$100{,}038.36$

7. $K = \$192{,}000 + \dfrac{\$192{,}000 - \$48{,}000}{(1.08)^{5} - 1} = \$498{,}821.62$

9. $K = \$124{,}000 + \dfrac{\$12{,}500}{\left[1 + \dfrac{0.14}{4}\right]^{16} - 1} = \$141{,}030.30$

   This answer assumes that $12,500 spent on an overhaul every four years will keep the boat indefinitely, and that the cost of an overhaul is constant at $12,500.

11. OPTION 1:

$$K = \$3{,}500 + \frac{\$3{,}500}{(1.09)^{5} - 1} = \$9{,}998.04$$

   OPTION 2:

$$K = \$3{,}700 + \frac{\$3{,}700}{(1.09)^{7} - 1} = \$8{,}168.39$$

   This answer assumes that the upgrade is done at the next replacement. Clearly, the upgrade at $200.00 is a good deal.

13. $K = \$3{,}500 + \dfrac{\$950}{(1.17)^{1} - 1} = \$9{,}088.24$

EXERCISE 11.4

1. Find the expected cost of the oil well: let cost be x.

$$\$19{,}000 = x(0.16) + \frac{\dfrac{(x - \$20{,}000)}{(1.12)^{4} - 1}}{0.12}$$

   $x = \$62{,}791.24$

   Therefore, if the cost is $62,791.24, the amount that must be recovered is: $62,791.24 – $20,000 = $42,791.24

Annual depletion allowance is:

$$\frac{\$42{,}791.24}{\dfrac{(1.12)^4 - 1}{0.12}} = \$8{,}953.40$$

3. Let x = price to be paid:

$$\$25{,}000 = x(0.1425) + \frac{(x - \$10{,}000)}{\dfrac{(1.12)^8 - 1}{0.12}}$$

$x = \$115{,}338.27$

5. Let x = price to be paid:

$$\$40{,}000 = x(0.15) + \frac{(x + \$5{,}000)}{\dfrac{(1.13)^5 - 1}{0.13}}$$

$x = \$128{,}907.50$

EXERCISE 12.1

1.

$$\text{PP} = \frac{R[1 - (1 + i)^{-n}]}{i} + \text{RD}(1 + i)^{-n}$$

$\text{RD} = \$1{,}000$

$i = \dfrac{0.10}{2} = 0.05$

$n = (2003 - 1987) \times 2 = 16 \times 2 = 32$

$r = \dfrac{0.08}{2} = 0.04$

$R = \dfrac{\$1{,}000 \times 0.08}{2} = \$40$

a.

$$\text{PP} = \frac{\$40[1 - (1.05)^{-32}]}{0.05} + \$1{,}000(1.05)^{-32}$$

$\text{PP} = \$841.97$

Discount = \$1,000 – \$841.97 = \$158.03

b. $\text{RD} = \$1{,}000(1.05) = \$1{,}050$

$$\text{PP} = \frac{\$40[1 - (1.05)^{-32}]}{0.05} + \$1{,}050(1.05)^{-32}$$

$\text{PP} = \$852.47$

Discount = \$1,050 – \$852.47 = \$197.53

3. a. RD $= \$10{,}000(1.02) = \$10{,}200$

$$i = \frac{0.15}{2} = 0.075$$

$$n = 20$$

$$r = \frac{0.14}{2} = 0.07$$

$$R = \frac{\$10{,}000 \times 0.14}{2} = \$700$$

$$\text{PP} = \frac{\$700[1 - (1.075)^{-20}]}{0.075} + \$10{,}200(1.075)^{-20}$$

PP = \$9,537.36

b. RD $= \$10{,}000(1.02) = \$10{,}200$

$$i = \frac{0.08}{2} = 0.04$$

$$n = 16$$

$$r = \frac{0.14}{2} = 0.07$$

$$R = \frac{\$10{,}000 \times 0.14}{2} = \$700$$

$$\text{PP} = \frac{\$700[1 - (1.04)^{-16}]}{0.04} + \$10{,}200(1.04)^{-16}$$

PP = \$13,602.47

Premium: \$13,602.37 – \$10,200 = \$3,402.47

5. a. RD $= \$80{,}000(1.05) = \$84{,}000$

$$i = \frac{0.09}{2} = 0.045$$

$$n = 12$$

$$r = \frac{0.07}{2} = 0.035$$

$$R = \frac{\$80{,}000 \times 0.07}{2} = \$2{,}800$$

$$\text{PP} = \frac{\$2{,}800[1 - (1.045)^{-12}]}{0.045} + \$84{,}000(1.045)^{-12}$$

PP = \$75,063.79

Discount: \$84,000 – \$75,063.79 = \$8,936.21

b. RD $= \$80{,}000$

$$f = \left[1 + \left(\frac{0.12}{4}\right)\right]^{\frac{4}{2}} - 1 = 0.0609$$

$$n = 12$$

$$r = \frac{0.07}{2} = 0.035$$

$$R = \frac{\$80{,}000 \times 0.07}{2} = \$2{,}800$$

$$\text{PP} = \frac{\$2{,}800[1 - (1.0609)^{-12}]}{0.0609} + \$80{,}000(1.0609)^{-12}$$

PP $= \$62{,}714.07$

Discount: $\$80{,}000 - \$62{,}714.07 = \$17{,}285.93$

EXERCISE 12.2

1. RD $= \$16{,}500$
   $F = \$16{,}500$
   $r = 0.05$
   $i = 0.06$
   $n = 40$
   $R = 0.05 \times 16{,}500 = \$825$

   a. $$\text{PP} = \frac{\$825[1 - (1.06)^{-40}]}{0.06} + \$16{,}500(1.06)^{-40}$$

   PP $= \$14{,}017.36$

   b. Discount: $\$16{,}500 - \$14{,}017.36 = \$2{,}482.64$

   c. No interest, therefore, Quoted Price = Flat or Purchase Price.

   d. No accrued interest.

3. RD $= \$4{,}200$
   $F = \$4{,}000$
   $r = 0.06$
   $i = 0.055935604$ $[f = (1 + 0.115)^{\frac{1}{2}} - 1)]$

   $n = 13$

   $R = 240$

   a. $$\text{PP} = \frac{\$240[1 - (1.055935604)^{-13}]}{0.055935604} + \$4{,}200(1.055935604)^{-13}$$

   $$\text{PP} = \$4{,}245.97\ [1 + (0.055935604)(\tfrac{1}{2})] = \$4{,}364.72$$

b. Premium: \$4,364.72 – \$4,200 = \$164.72

c. Quoted Price = \$4,364.72 – \$120 = \$4,244.72

d. Accrued Interest = $\$4{,}000\left[\left(0.06\right)\left(\frac{1}{2}\right)\right] = \$120$

5. RD = \$114,000
$F = \$120{,}000$
$r = 0.062$
$i = 0.057$
$n = 21$
$R = \$120{,}000 \times 0.062 = \$7{,}440$

a. $$PP = \frac{\$7{,}440[1-(1.057)^{-21}]}{0.057} + \$114{,}000(1.057)^{-21}$$

$$PP = \$125{,}366.89[1 + (0.057)(\frac{1}{6})] = \$126{,}557.88$$

b. Premium: \$126,557.88 – \$114,000 = \$12,557.88

c. Quoted Price = \$126,557.88 – \$1,240 = \$125,317.88

d. Accrued Interest = $\$120{,}000\ [(0.062)(\frac{1}{6})] = \$1{,}240$

7. RD = \$16,020
$F = \$18{,}000$
$r = 0.0525$
$i = 0.060660172\ [f = (1 + 0.125)^{½} - 1]$
$n = 9$
$R = \$18{,}000 \times 0.0525 = \$945$

a. $$PP = \frac{\$945[1-(1.060660172)^{-9}]}{0.060660172} + \$16{,}020(1.060660172)^{-9}$$

$$PP = \$15{,}838.40\left[1 + \left(0.060066172\right)\left(\frac{5}{6}\right)\right] = \$16{,}639.03$$

b. Premium: \$16,639.03 – \$16,020 = \$619.03

c. Quoted Price = \$16,639.03 – \$787.50 = \$15,851.53

d. Accrued Interest = $\$18{,}000\left[\left(0.0525\right)\left(\frac{5}{6}\right)\right] = \$787.50$

9. RD = \$18,400
$F = \$20{,}000$
$r = 0.06$
$i = 0.075$
$n = 18$
$R = \$1{,}200$

a. $$PP = \frac{\$1{,}200[1-(1.075)^{-18}]}{0.075} + \$18{,}400(1.075)^{-18}$$

$$PP = \$16{,}652.92$$

b. Discount: \$18,400 – \$16,652.92 = \$1,747.08

c. Quoted Price = \$16,652.92

d. No accrued interest.

11. $F = \text{RD} = \$10{,}000$
$r = 0.05$
$i = 0.045$
$n = 16$ and $\frac{50}{184}$ periods
$R = \$500$

$$\text{PP} = \frac{\$500[1-(1.045)^{-16}]}{0.045} + \$10{,}000(1.045)^{-16}$$

Move forward to purchase date, 50 days later:

$$\text{PP} = \$10{,}561.70\left[1+(0.045)\left(\frac{50}{184}\right)\right] = \$10{,}690.85$$

13. $F = \text{RD} = \$1{,}000$
$r = 0.04$
$i = 0.07$
$n = 15$ and $\frac{59}{183}$ periods
$R = \$40$

$$\text{PP} = \frac{\$40[1-(1.07)^{-15}]}{0.07} + \$1{,}000(1.07)^{-15}$$

Move forward to purchase date, 59 days later:

$$\text{PP} = \$726.76\left[1+(0.07)\left(\frac{59}{183}\right)\right] = \$743.16$$

15. $F = \text{RD} = \$5{,}000$
$r = 0.06$
$i = 0.04$
$n = 9$ and $\frac{106}{184}$ periods

$R = \$300$

a. $$\text{PP} = \frac{\$300[1-(1.04)^{-9}]}{0.04} + \$5{,}000(1.04)^{-9}$$

$$\text{PP} = \$5{,}743.53\left[1+(0.04)\left(\frac{106}{184}\right)\right] = \$5{,}875.88$$

b. Accrued Interest = $\$5{,}000(0.06)(\frac{106}{184}) = \$172.83$

Quoted Price = $\$5{,}875.88 - \$172.82 = \$5{,}703.05$

17. $F = \text{RD} = \$100{,}000$
$r = 0.05$
$i = 0.056275928 \; \left(f = \left(1 + \frac{0.11}{12}\right)^6 - 1\right)$
$n = 17$ and $\frac{153}{183}$ periods

$R = \$5{,}000$

a. $$\text{PP} = \frac{\$5{,}000[1 - (1.056275928)^{-17}]}{0.056275928} + \$100{,}000(1.056275928)^{-17}$$

$$\text{PP} = \$93{,}244.77\left[1 + \left(0.056275928\right)\left(\frac{153}{183}\right)\right] = \$97{,}631.97$$

b. Quoted Price = $\$97{,}631.97 - \left[\left(\$5{,}000\right)\left(\frac{153}{183}\right)\right] = \$93{,}451.64$

EXERCISE 12.3

1. RD = $14,645
$F = \$14{,}500$
$r = 0.055$
$i = 0.055$
$n = 20$
$R = \$797.50$

$$\text{Discount} = [(\$14{,}500)(0.055) - (\$14{,}645)(0.055)]\,\frac{[1 - (1.055)^{-20}]}{0.055}$$

Discount = $95.30

PP = $14,645 – $95.30 = $14,549.70

3. RD = $3,180
$F = \$3{,}000$
$r = 0.06$
$i = 0.0511898 \; (f = (1 + 0.105)^{\frac{1}{2}} - 1)$

$n = 10$

$$\text{Premium} = [(\$3{,}000)(0.06) - (\$3{,}180)(0.0511898)]\,\frac{[1 - (1.0511898)^{-10}]}{0.0511898}$$

Premium = $132.18

PP = $3,180 + $132.18 = $3,312.18

5. RD = \$25,250
F = \$25,000
r = 0.052
i = 0.052
n = 20

$$\text{Premium} = [(\$25{,}000)(0.052) - (\$25{,}250)(0.052)]\ \frac{[1 - (1.052)^{-20}]}{0.052}$$

Discount = \$159.30

PP = \$25,250 – \$159.30 = \$25,090.70

7. RD = \$20,000
F = \$14,000
r = 0.0575
$i = 0.0559356\ (f = (1 + 0.115)^{\frac{1}{2}} - 1)$
n = 10

$$\text{Premium} = [(\$20{,}000)(0.0575) - (\$14{,}000)(0.0559356)]\ \frac{[1 - (1.0559356)^{-10}]}{0.0559356}$$

Premium = \$2,753.20

PP = \$14,000 + \$2,753.20 = \$16,753.20

9. RD = \$15,000
F = \$15,000
r = 0.065
i = 0.06
n = 20

$$\text{Premium} = [(\$15{,}000)(0.065) - (\$15{,}000)(0.06)]\ \frac{[1 - (1.06)^{-20}]}{0.06}$$

Premium = \$860.24

PP = \$15,000 + \$860.24 = \$15,860.24

11. F = \$30,000
r = 0.04
i = 0.05
n = 10

$$\text{Discount} = \$30{,}000[0.05 - 0.04]\ \frac{[1 - (1.05)^{-10}]}{0.05} = \$2{,}316.52$$

Discount = –\$2,316.52

PP = \$30,000 – \$2,316.52 = \$27,683.48

EXERCISE 12.4

1. $$I = \frac{\$14{,}500 + \$15{,}000}{2} = \$14{,}750$$

$$AI = \frac{\$24{,}650 - \$500}{20} \times 2 = \$2{,}415$$

Therefore, the approximate yield rate = $\left(\frac{\$2{,}415}{\$14{,}750}\right) = 0.1637$

3. $$I = \frac{\$3{,}000 + \$2{,}850}{2} = \$2{,}925$$

$$AI = \frac{\$1{,}650 + \$150}{5} = \$360$$

Therefore, the approximate yield rate = $\left[\frac{\$360}{\$2{,}925}\right] = 0.123076923$

5. $$I = \frac{\$25{,}000 + \$26{,}500}{2} = \$25{,}750$$

$$AI = \frac{\$31{,}000 - \$1{,}500}{10} = \$2{,}950$$

Therefore, the approximate yield rate = $\left[\frac{\$2{,}950}{\$25{,}750}\right] = 0.114563106$

7. $$I = \frac{\$20{,}000 + \$18{,}500}{2} = \$19{,}250$$

$$AI = \frac{\$10{,}500 + \$1{,}500}{5} = \$2{,}400$$

Therefore, the approximate yield rate = $\left[\frac{\$2{,}400}{\$19{,}250}\right] = 0.124675324$

9. $$I = \frac{\$9{,}200 + \$10{,}000}{2} = \$9{,}600$$

$$AI = \frac{\$7{,}200 + \$800}{6} = \$1{,}333.33$$

Therefore, the approximate yield rate = $\left[\frac{\$1{,}333.33}{\$9{,}600}\right] = 0.1388885$

11. $$I = \frac{\$3{,}840 + \$3{,}800}{2} = \$3{,}820$$

$$AI = \frac{\$2{,}660 - \$40}{19} \times 2 = \$275.79$$

Therefore, the approximate yield rate = $\left[\frac{\$275.79}{\$3{,}820}\right] = 0.072196$

EXERCISE 12.5

1. Since $i > r$, and the bond is redeemed at par, there is a premium.

$$\text{Premium} = [\$3{,}500(0.085) - \$3{,}500(0.08)]\,\frac{[1 - (1 + 0.08)^{-5}]}{0.08} = \$69.87$$

PP = \$3,500 + \$69.87 = \$3,569.87

A	B	C	D	E
Interest Period	**Interest on Bond**	**Yield Interest (0.08) × E**	**Premium Amortization**	**Book Value (PP) \$3,569.87**
1	\$ 297.50	\$ 285.59	\$11.91	\$3,557.96
2	\$ 297.50	\$ 284.64	\$12.86	\$3,545.10
3	\$ 297.50	\$ 283.61	\$13.89	\$3,531.21
4	\$ 297.50	\$ 282.50	\$15.00	\$3,516.21
5	\$ 297.50	\$ 281.30	\$16.20	\$3,500.00
Totals	\$1,487.50	\$1,417.64	\$69.86	N/A

3. Since $r < i$, and the bond is redeemed at par, there is a discount.

$$\text{Discount} = [\$82.50 - \$90.00]\,\frac{[1 - (1 + 0.06)^{-6}]}{0.06} = -\$36.88$$

PP = \$1,500 − \$36.88 = \$1,463.12

A	B	C	D	E
Interest Period	**Interest on Bond**	**Yield Interest (0.06) × E**	**Discount Accumulation**	**Book Value (PP) \$1,463.12**
1	\$ 82.50	\$ 87.79	\$ 5.29	\$1,468.41
2	\$ 82.50	\$ 88.10	\$ 5.60	\$1,474.01
3	\$ 82.50	\$ 88.44	\$ 5.94	\$1,479.95
4	\$ 82.50	\$ 88.79	\$ 6.30	\$1,486.25
5	\$ 82.50	\$ 88.17	\$ 6.67	\$1,492.92
6	\$ 82.50	\$ 89.58	\$ 7.08	\$1,500.00
Totals	\$495.00	\$531.87	\$ 36.88	N/A

5. Since $i > r$, and the bond is redeemed at par, there is a premium.

$$\text{Premium} = [\$1{,}300(0.057) - \$1{,}300(0.062)]\frac{[1 - (1 + 0.057)^{-8}]}{0.057} = \$40.85$$

$$PP = \$1{,}300 + \$40.85 = \$1{,}340.85$$

A	B	C	D	E
Interest Period	**Interest on Bond**	**Yield Interest (0.057) × E**	**Premium Amortization**	**Book Value (PP) $1,340.85**
1	$ 80.60	$ 76.43	$ 4.17	$1,336.68
2	$ 80.60	$ 76.19	$ 4.41	$1,332.27
3	$ 80.60	$ 75.94	$ 4.66	$1,327.61
4	$ 80.60	$ 75.67	$ 4.93	$1,322.68
5	$ 80.60	$ 75.39	$ 5.21	$1,317.47
6	$ 80.60	$ 75.10	$ 5.50	$1,311.97
7	$ 80.60	$ 74.78	$ 5.82	$1,306.15
8	$ 80.60	$ 74.45	$ 6.15	$1,300.00
Totals	$644.80	$603.95	$40.85	N/A

7. Since $r < i$, and the bond is redeemed at par, there is a discount.

$$\text{Discount} = [\$1{,}000(0.07) - \$1{,}000(0.0675)]\frac{[1 - (1 + 0.0675)^{-4}]}{0.0675} = -\$51.10$$

$$PP = \$1{,}000 - \$51.10 = \$948.90$$

A	B	C	D	E
Interest Period	**Interest on Bond**	**Yield Interest (0.0675) × E**	**Discount Accumulation**	**Book Value (PP) $948.90**
1	$ 52.50	$ 64.05	$11.55	$ 960.45
2	$ 52.50	$ 64.83	$12.33	$ 972.78
3	$ 52.50	$ 65.66	$13.16	$ 985.94
4	$ 52.50	$ 66.55	$14.05	$1,000.00
Totals	$210.00	$261.09	$51.09	N/A

9. Since $i > r$, and the bond is redeemed at par, there is a premium.

$$\text{Premium} = [\$4{,}000(0.055) - \$4{,}000(0.05)]\,\frac{[1 - (1 + 0.05)^{-5}]}{0.05} = \$86.59$$

PP = \$4,000 + \$86.59 = \$4,086.59

A	B	C	D	E
Interest Period	**Interest on Bond**	**Yield Interest (.075) × E**	**Premium Amortization**	**Book Value (PP) \$4,086.59**
1	\$ 220.00	\$ 204.33	\$15.67	\$4,070.92
2	\$ 220.00	\$ 203.55	\$16.45	\$4,054.47
3	\$ 220.00	\$ 202.72	\$17.28	\$4,037.19
4	\$ 220.00	\$ 201.86	\$18.14	\$4,019.05
5	\$ 220.00	\$ 200.95	\$19.05	\$4,000.00
Totals	\$1,100.00	\$1,013.41	\$86.59	N/A

Index

To The Owner of this Book

We are interested in your reaction to *Mathematics for Business* by Brian Killip. With your comments, we can improve this book in future editions. Please help us by completing this questionnaire.

1. What was your reason for using this book?
   ____________university course
   ____________college course
   ____________continuing education course
   ____________personal interest
   ____________other (specify)
2. If you used this text for a program, what was the name of that program?
3. Which school do you attend?
4. Approximately how much of the book did you use?
   ________¼ ________½ ________¾ ________all
5. Which chapters or sections were omitted from your course?
6. What is the best aspect of this book?
7. Is there anything that should be added?
8. Please add any comments or suggestions.

Fold here

Business
Reply Mail
No Postage Stamp
Necessary if Mailed
in Canada

POSTAGE WILL BE PAID BY

Scott Duncan
Editorial Director
DRYDEN, CANADA
55 Horner Avenue
Toronto, Ontario
M8Z 9Z9

Tape shut